OBSERV

HANDBOOK

2007

EDITOR
PATRICK KELLY

NINETY-NINTH YEAR OF PUBLICATION

136 DUPONT STREET, TORONTO ON M5R 1V2
2006

ISSN 0080-4193
ISBN 0-9738109-3-9

PRINTED IN CANADA
BY UNIVERSITY OF TORONTO PRESS

TABLE OF CONTENTS

Key to Marginal Chapter Symbols

Basic Data
Time
Optics and Observing
The Sky Month by Month
Eclipses and Transits
The Moon
The Sun
Planets and Satellites
Asteroids
Meteors, Comets, and Dust
Stars
Nebulae and Galaxies

THE *OBSERVER'S HANDBOOK*

The *Observer's Handbook* is one of Canada's oldest scientific publications. Created by C.A. Chant, Professor of Astronomy at the University of Toronto, it first appeared nearly a century ago as *The Canadian Astronomical Handbook for 1907,* a small (13 × 17 cm), 108-page publication. A second edition covered the year 1908, but for the following two years most of the information that would have appeared was published instead in installments in the *Journal of the RASC*. The Council of the Society decided to return to a separate publication for 1911 with a new name—the *Observer's Handbook*—and it has been published annually ever since.

Each year some 12 000 copies of the Handbook are distributed to many countries throughout the world, to amateur and professional astronomers, to educators at school and university levels, and to many observatories, planetaria, and libraries. The Handbook is the main source of income for the Royal Astronomical Society of Canada. Since the first edition in 1907, the various editors, assistant editors, editorial assistants (see p. 6), and contributors (see the inside front cover) have voluntarily contributed their time and expertise to produce this unique book.

EDITORS OF THE *OBSERVER'S HANDBOOK*

		Position	**Editions**	**RASC President**
C.A. Chant	(1865–1956)	Editor	1907–1957	1903–1907
Frank Hogg	(1904–1951)	Assistant Editor	1939–1951	1940–1942
Ruth Northcott	(1913–1969)	Assistant Editor	1952–1957	1962–1964
		Editor	1958–1970	
John Percy	(1941–	Editor	1971–1981	1978–1980
Roy Bishop	(1939–	Editor	1982–2000	1984–1986
Rajiv Gupta	(1958–	Editor	2001–2006	2002–2004
Patrick Kelly	(1958–	Editor	2007–	

The *Observer's Handbook* is intended to be "a companion which the observer would wish always to have in his pocket or on the table before him."

C.A. Chant, Toronto, 1906

"We believe that the *Observer's Handbook* is a truly significant contribution that Canadian astronomy in general and our Society in particular has been making to the dissemination of astronomical knowledge for half a century. I trust that it will still occupy the same position of respect after the first hundred years."

Ruth Northcott, Ottawa, 1964

"The more one knows, the more one can benefit from the Handbook. It inspires all who leaf through its pages to learn and question what the tables, graphs and data mean, perhaps to speculate on the mysteries of the Universe, and above all, to get out and look beyond our world. You have in your hands a key to the Universe—a key which will fit many doors. Please use it well and treasure it."

Peter Broughton, Toronto, 1992
Author of *Looking Up, A History of the RASC*

"The *Observer's Handbook* is the single most useful publication for the observational astronomer. Its combination of authoritative data, informative diagrams, and concise text is unique. Anyone interested in astronomy, beginner or expert, amateur or professional, student or teacher, will find the *Observer's Handbook* indispensable. Its international reputation for quality is a credit both to its many contributors and to Canadian astronomy."

Roy Bishop, Halifax, 2000

HOW TO USE THIS HANDBOOK

This Handbook is a concise, high-density compilation of information that is of interest to observers. By reading the following points, you will allow yourself to reap maximum benefit from it.

(1) The Handbook is composed of various *sections*. Related sections are grouped into chapters, as listed in the CONTENTS. Chapter titles are given in large dark-grey boxes and section titles against light background shades, both of which extend to the edge of the page. The section title and chapter title are given in headers at the top of the pages. In addition, staggered marginal symbols (see p. iii for a key) mark the edges of the pages in each chapter. These various identifiers are meant to facilitate the quick location of desired material.

(2) References to other sections are given in SMALL CAPITAL TYPE, and this type is generally reserved for this purpose. Internet email addresses and Web sites are also given in a distinctive font.

(3) The INDEX at the back contains a listing of keywords.

(4) Alternate blocks of rows are shaded in most tables, in order to make the location of entries easier. Every table has a shaded header with the titles of the various columns given in bold type. Detailed explanation of the meaning of the columns is usually given in accompanying text.

(5) SI symbols and abbreviations are used throughout. See pp. 29 and 32 in the section SOME ASTRONOMICAL AND PHYSICAL DATA for the most common abbreviations. The letter "m" is used to denote both minutes of right ascension and metres; the meaning will be clear from the context. Minutes of time are usually abbreviated "min".

(6) The time scale Universal Time is generally used. Times of day are usually given in the 24-hour clock, using numerals separated by colons. The section TIME AND TIME SCALES on pp. 35–40 explains the various time scales used in astronomy.

(7) The section TERMINOLOGY AND SYMBOLS on p. 16 lists Greek letters (and other symbols) and defines some basic terms.

(8) The section TEACHING AND THE *OBSERVER'S HANDBOOK* on pp. 13–15 gives an overview of the contents of this Handbook.

(9) The Web site of the Handbook is www.rasc.ca/handbook. Resources related to the Handbook, including a page of links to all web sites cited in the Handbook, are given at this site, and any updates and corrections will also be posted there.

Cover photos

The image on the front cover was produced by Jack Newton, who is known world-wide for his astroimaging. He used a Borg 101-mm f/4 refractor and a Canon 20Da SLR camera to capture the California Nebula. The image is a composite of 15 six-minute exposures stacked in MaxImDL and processed in Adobe Photoshop. The Califonia Nebula (NGC 1499) is the tenth item in the DEEP-SKY CHALLENGE OBJECTS *section, found on page 262.*

Dan Falk took the photo on the back cover on the evening of 2004 Jun. 8 (the day of the transit of Venus) from Cape Sounion, at the southeastern tip of Greece's Attica peninsula. In this five-minute south-facing exposure, the stars of Lupus, Libra, Hydra, and Centaurus are seen trailing above the Temple of Poseidon (c. 600 BC; re-built c. 440 BC). The bright star at right-centre is Theta Centauri. The photo was taken using a Minolta XD-11 and a 35–135-mm zoom lens, set near the 35-mm end. The film was Ektachrome 400.

EDITOR'S COMMENTS

Shortly after I joined the RASC, the Handbook acquired a new editor, Roy Bishop of the Halifax Centre. It quickly became obvious that working on the Handbook had become a labour of love for him as new sections were added and existing sections expanded. It was soon referred to by many Halifax Centre members as "the Bible according to Bishop." To this day, when questions arise after Centre meetings, Roy can often be heard piping in with "The answer is in the Handbook!"

Rajiv Gupta of the Vancouver Centre continued the tradition of adding more information to the Handbook, as well as making improvements to its appearance. He automated a lot of the tasks and put together an editorial team to assist in the production. Both changes have been of great assistance during my transition as the new editor and I thank Rajiv for the assistance that he has provided. He is also staying on as contributor of five sections (see inside front cover).

There has been one change in authorship. John Spray and Jason Hines, both of the University of New Brunswick in Fredericton, and Richard Grieve of National Resources Canada are now working with James Whitehead on the METEORITE IMPACT CRATERS OF NORTH AMERICA section. I welcome these new contributors to the Handbook.

Now the editorship is back in Nova Scotia, and I am writing this only a 15-minute drive from Roy's Maktomkus Observatory. I never would have predicted that 20 years ago. I was not sure what to expect when I took on this job, but I certainly was not anticipating having so much fun. I have had wonderful conversations with many of the contributors. The editorial team has also been a pleasure to work with. Both groups deserve most of the credit for the book you are holding. (Thanks also to the solar system for ensuring that there were no transits or total solar eclipses during my first year!)

Next year will mark the 100th edition of the Handbook. There are already plans for expanded sections and new features, but suggestions are always welcome.

Clear skies, or, as we say in Klingon, chalmey Huv.

Patrick Kelly
handbookeditor@rasc.ca
Falmouth, 2006 Sep. 3

THE *OBSERVER'S HANDBOOK*

EDITOR
Patrick Kelly

COPY EDITOR
Betty Robinson

EDITOR'S ASSISTANT AND PROOFREADER
James Edgar

PROOFREADER
Bruce McCurdy

In addition to the 50 contributors listed on the inside front cover, several other individuals and organizations played a role in the production of this Handbook.

Some of the data contained herein comes from the publications *Astronomical Phenomena for the Year 2007* and *The Astronomical Almanac 2007*, both prepared jointly by the U.S. Naval Observatory's Nautical Almanac Office and Her Majesty's Nautical Almanac Office.

Corrections or suggestions for improvement that were incorporated in this edition were provided by Jeff Baldwin, Roy Bishop, Anne Cowley, Donna Giesler, Anton Jopko, Ken Kingdon, and Alan Whitman.

THE ROYAL ASTRONOMICAL SOCIETY OF CANADA

The beginnings of the Royal Astronomical Society of Canada go back to the mid-1800s. Then, in 1890, the Society was incorporated within the province of Ontario, received its Royal Charter from King Edward VII in 1903, and was federally incorporated in 1968. The National Office of the Society (containing the business office and library) is located at 136 Dupont St, Toronto ON M5R 1V2; telephone: (416) 924-7973 or (888) 924-7272 from within Canada; email: nationaloffice@rasc.ca; Web site: www.rasc.ca.

The RASC has more than 4500 members, who are from many countries and all walks of life. Members receive the *Observer's Handbook* (published in September for the next calendar year) and electronic access to the bimonthly *Journal of the RASC,* which contains review articles, research papers on historical and contemporary topics, education notes, general notes of astronomical interest, book reviews, news items concerning the Society and its Centres, informal articles, and letters. (A print version of the *Journal of the RASC* is available at an extra cost.) Also included in membership is *SkyNews,* Canada's popular bimonthly astronomy magazine.

Membership fees are $55 per year, with a reduced rate for persons under 21 years of age. Life membership is $2100. (For members outside of Canada, these figures are to be read as U.S. dollars, to cover higher mailing costs.) An applicant may affiliate with one of the Centres of the Society across Canada or join the Society directly as an unattached member (some Centres levy a surcharge above the regular membership fee).

The Society currently has 28 Centres located throughout Canada, in every province and in most major Canadian cities. Most Centres hold monthly meetings at which prospective members are welcome. Details on each Centre's activities as well as contact information for the Centre are available at its Web site; for links to the Centres' Web sites, visit www.rasc.ca.

REPORTING OF ASTRONOMICAL DISCOVERIES

To report a possible significant discovery (e.g. a new comet, nova, or supernova), a message should be sent to the International Astronomical Union's Central Bureau for Astronomical Telegrams. Send electronic mail to cbat@cfa.harvard.edu. Messages are monitored at all times. If this preferred method of communication is unavailable, a telephone call may be made to (617) 495-7244 or -7440 or -7444, but telephone calls are discouraged and these numbers will not be answered at all times. Also, a follow-up letter should be sent to the Central Bureau at 60 Garden St, Cambridge MA 02138, USA. Inexperienced observers should have their observation checked before contacting the Central Bureau.

For any new object, specify the date and time of observation, RA and Dec (with equinox), magnitude, and some physical description. For photographic and CCD discoveries, confirmation with a second image is highly desirable. In the case of a new comet, the rate of motion in RA and Dec should also be indicated.

Reports may instead be filled out at cfa-www.harvard.edu/iau/cbat.html. Recent IAU circulars and subscription information are also available at this URL.

SELECTED OBSERVATORIES AND PLANETARIA

By James Edgar

Some observatories and selected *star parties* with URL, latitude and longitude to nearest minute, and elevation in metres and feet are given below, ordered by longitude from east to west.

Location	Lat.	Long.	Alt. (m/ft.)
Anglo-Australian Observatory—Siding Spring, Australia www.aao.gov.au	31°17′S	149°04′E	1164/3819
Mount Stromlo Observatory—Canberra, Australia www.mso.anu.edu.au/home.php	35°19′S	149°00′E	767/2516
Perth Observatory—Bickley, Australia www.wa.gov.au/perthobs	32°00′S	116°08′E	391/1283
Nova East—Smileys Provincial Park, Nova Scotia halifax.rasc.ca/ne/home.html	45°01′N	63°58′W	150/492
St. Croix Observatory—Windsor, Nova Scotia halifax.rasc.ca/sco.html	44°57′N	64°02′W	65/213
Gemini South Observatory—Cerro Tololo, Chile www.gemini.edu	30°14′S	70°43′W	2725/8940
Las Campanas Observatory—Cerro Las Campanas, Chile www.lco.cl	29°00′S	70°42′W	2282/7486
European Southern Observatory—La Silla, Chile www.ls.eso.org/index.html	29°15′S	70°44′W	2400/7980
Paranal Observatory—Antofagasto, Chile www.eso.org/paranal/site/paranal.html	24°40′S	70°25′W	2635/8645
Mont Mégantic Observatory—Mont Mégantic, Québec www.astro.uMontréal.ca/omm	45°27′N	71°09′W	1114/3654
Stellafane—Springfield, Vermont www.stellafane.com	48°16′N	72°31′W	387/1270
Van Vleck Observatory—Middletown, Connecticut www.astro.wesleyan.edu	41°33′N	72°40′W	65/213
I.K. Williamson Observatory—Montréal, Québec www.rascMontréal.org	45°31′N	73°35′W	80/262
Helen Sawyer Hogg Observatory—Ottawa, Ontario www.sciencetech.technomuses.ca	45°24′N	75°53′W	58/190
SmartScope—Ottawa, Ontario ottawa.rasc.ca/smartscope/smartscope.html	45°21′N	75°53′W	58/190
David Dunlap Observatory—Toronto, Ontario www.astro.utoronto.ca/DDO	43°52′N	79°25′W	244/800
Hamilton Centre Observatory—Waterdown, Ontario www.hamiltonrasc.ca/observatory.htm	43°23′N	79°55′W	104/341
Allegheny Observatory—Pittsburgh, Pennsylvania www.pitt.edu/~aobsvtry	40°29′N	80°01′W	380/1247
Carr Astronomical Observatory—Collingwood, Ontario toronto.rasc.ca/content/CAO.shtml	44°30′N	80°23′W	176/577
Starfest—Mount Forest, Ontario www.nyaa-starfest.com	44°04′N	80°50′W	400/1312
Winter Star Party—Camp Wesumkee, Florida www.scas.org/wsp.htm	24°39′N	81°19′W	1/4
Sudbury Neutrino Observatory—Creighton, Ontario www.sno.phy.queensu.ca/sno	46°46′N	81°20′W	−2073/−6800

Location	Lat.	Long.	Alt. (m/ft.)
Hallam Observatory—Comber, Ontario www.mnsi.net/~rasc/observatory/wcpo.html	42°14′N	82°31′W	181/594
Yerkes Observatory—Williams Bay, Wisconsin astro.uchicago.edu/yerkes	42°34′N	88°33′W	334/1050
Texas Star Party—Fort Davis, Texas www.texasstarparty.org	30°36′N	103°57′W	1500/4921
McDonald Observatory—Fort Davis, Texas www.as.utexas.edu/mcdonald/mcdonald.html	30°40′N	104°01′W	2075/6808
Kalium Observatory—Regina, Saskatchewan telescope.ras.sk.ca	50°26′N	104°37′W	577/1894
Sleaford Observatory—Saskatoon, Saskatchewan www.usask.ca/psychology/sarty/rasc/sleaford.html	52°06′N	105°57′W	526/1728
Saskatchewan Summer Star Party—Cypress Hills Park, Sask. www.usask.ca/psychology/sarty/rasc/starparty.html	49°39′N	109°31′W	1272/4174
Steward Observatory—Tucson, Arizona james.as.arizona.edu/~psmith/61inch	32°25′N	110°44′W	2510/8230
Kitt Peak National Observatory—Tucson, Arizona www.noao.edu/kpno	31°57′N	111°36′W	2120/7049
Lowell Observatory—Flagstaff, Arizona www.lowell.edu	35°11′N	111°39′W	2212/7260
Telus World of Science—Edmonton, Alberta www.odyssium.com/observatory.html	53°34′N	113°34′W	677/2221
Wilson Coulee Observatory—Okotoks, Alberta calgary.rasc.ca/tourrequest.htm	50°46′N	114°02′W	1127/3697
Alberta Star Party—Caroline, Alberta calgary.rasc.ca/asp2007.htm	52°08′N	114°43′W	1072/3517
Riverside Telescope Makers Conference—Camp Oakes, Calif. www.rtmcastronomyexpo.org	34°14′N	116°45′W	2316/7600
Palomar Observatory—San Diego, California www.astro.caltech.edu/palomar	33°21′N	116°52′W	1706/5597
Mt. Wilson Observatory—Pasadena, California www.mtwilson.edu	34°13′N	118°03′W	1740/5700
Dominion Radio Astrophysical Observatory—Penticton, B.C. www.drao-ofr.hia-iha.nrc-cnrc.gc.ca	49°19′N	119°37′W	545/1788
Mount Kobau Star Party—Osoyoos, British Columbia www.mksp.ca	49°07′N	119°44′W	1860/6102
Goldendale Observatory—Goldendale, Washington www.perr.com/gosp.html	45°51′N	120°47′W	640/2100
Pine Mountain Observatory—Pine Mountain, Oregon pmo-sun.uoregon.edu	43°47′N	120°57′W	1905/6250
Lick Observatory—San Jose, California mthamilton.ucolick.org	37°21′N	121°38′W	1290/4232
Prince George Centre Observatory—Prince George, B.C. www.vts.bc.ca/pgrasc/tour.html	53°45′N	122°51′W	691/2296
Gordon Southam Observatory—Vancouver, B.C. www.hrmacmillanspacecentre.com/observatory.htm	49°16′N	123°09′W	6/21
Dominion Astrophysical Observatory—Victoria, B.C. www.hia-iha.nrc-cnrc.gc.ca/dao/index_e.html	48°31′N	123°25′W	238/780
James Clerk Maxwell Telescope—Mauna Kea, Hawaii www.jach.hawaii.edu/JCMT	19°50′N	155°28′W	4092/13 426
Canada-France-Hawaii Telescope—Mauna Kea, Hawaii www.cfht.hawaii.edu	19°50′N	155°28′W	4204/13 793

A selection of North American planetaria with URL, phone number, and related information, ordered alphabetically by city, is given below.

Planetarium	Notes
Lodestar Astronomy Center—Albuquerque www.unm.edu/~cygnus (505) 841-5955	Part of University of New Mexico outreach; Infinity Express multimedia program; astronomy store; astrophoto contests
Fiske Planetarium—Boulder fiske.colorado.edu (303) 492-5001	Evening shows and weekend matinees; observatory available following shows for stargazing; school groups welcome
Telus World of Science—Calgary www.calgaryscience.ca (403) 268-8300	Join "Seymour Sky" at the Planetarium dome; several programs, multimedia shows, and kits available for kids of all ages
Adler Planetarium—Chicago www.adlerplanetarium.org/visitors-guide/index.shtml (312) 922-7827	Historic, first in Western Hemisphere; large collection of historic instruments; Doane Observatory on-site
Christa McAuliffe Planetarium—Concord www.starhop.com/home.htm (603) 271-7827	Dedicated to first "Teacher In Space" who tragically died in shuttle *Challenger* disaster 1986 Jan. 28
Margaret Zeidler Star Theatre—Edmonton www.odyssium.com/mzt.htm (780) 452-9100	Gift shop; IMAX theatre; café; laser shows; numerous science programs and computer lab at Telus World of Science
ASTROLab du Mont Mégantic—Mont Mégantic, www.astrolab-parc-national-mont-megantic.org (819) 888-2941	Cosmic Rhythms multimedia show; dark skies; astronomy evenings; on-site lodging; open house for teachers; school programs
Planétarium de Montréal—Montréal www.planetarium.Montréal.qc.ca (514) 872-4530	Programs for all ages and groups; activity sheets; classroom kits; advanced workshop for teachers and educators
Hayden Planetarium—New York www.amnh.org/rose (212) 769-5200	At American Museum of Natural History; programs, courses, and lectures; Zeiss Mark IX Universarium Star Projector
Harry C. Kendall Planetarium—Portland www.omsi.edu/visit/planetarium (503) 797-4000	Fifty-two-foot domed theatre with Digistar 3 projection; presentations on astronomy, space science, and lasers; school programs
Doran Planetarium—Sudbury laurentian.ca/physics/planetarium/planetarium.html (705) 675-1151	Programs include Lecture, School, and Specialty series; largest planetarium in northern Ontario
Ontario Science Centre—Toronto www.ontariosciencecentre.ca (416) 696-1000	In central Toronto; OMNIMax theatre; kids' sleepovers; summer day camps; home of the RASC Toronto Centre
MacMillan Planetarium—Vancouver www.hrmacmillanspacecentre.com (604) 738-7827	Close to downtown Vancouver; special laser shows in summer; numerous programs for school groups of all ages; teacher packages
Centre of the Universe—Victoria www.hia-iha.nrc-cnrc.gc.ca/cu/main_e.html (250) 363-8262	Interactive exhibits; Starlab planetarium; multimedia shows; family-friendly weekend events; Plaskett (1.8 m) Telescope
Albert Einstein Planetarium—Washington www.nasm.si.edu/visit/planetarium (877) 932-4629	At National Air and Space Museum; café; IMAX theatre; special exhibits commemorate 100th year of powered flight
Northern Lights—Watson Lake, Yukon www.northernlightscentre.ca (867) 536-7827	Canada's only all-dome video planetarium; daily shows; programs concentrate on aurora borealis and northern experience
Aldrin Planetarium—West Palm Beach www.sfsm.org/planetarium.html (561) 832-1988	Laser shows; telescopes; exhibits; science camps; Larry the Cat In Space; teachers' programs; birthday party programs
Manitoba Planetarium—Winnipeg www.manitobamuseum.mb.ca (204) 956-2830	In central Winnipeg; science centre, museum, and planetarium in one site; school programs; Guide/Scout badge program

RECOMMENDED READING AND ATLASES

Astronomy, a nontechnical monthly magazine for amateur astronomers (Canada and U.S.: (800) 533-6644; www.astronomy.com).

The Backyard Astronomer's Guide (2nd. ed.), by Terence Dickinson and Alan Dyer. Firefly Books (Canada: (800) 387-6192, United States: (800) 387-5085), 2002. The best guide to equipment and techniques for amateur astronomers, by two experienced observers.

Catalogue of the Astronomical Society of the Pacific ((415) 337-1100; www.astrosociety.org), an excellent source of astronomical educational resources such as books, slides, videos, globes, posters, software, teachers' classroom activity guides, and more.

Catalogue of Sky Publishing Corporation, a good source of books, atlases, globes, slide sets, software, and posters ((800) 253-0245; skytonight.com).

Exploring the Night Sky, by Terence Dickinson. Firefly Books (see above), 1987. A guide to stargazing, recommended for children.

A Field Guide to the Stars and Planets, by Jay M. Pasachoff. Houghton Mifflin Company, New York, 2000. In the Petersen Field Guides series, this classic work (currently in its 4th edition) is packed with star maps and accessible information.

Nightwatch (3rd ed.), by Terence Dickinson. Firefly Books (see above), 1998. An excellent introductory observing guide.

Sky & Telescope, a monthly magazine widely read by both amateur and professional astronomers ((800) 253-0245; skytonight.com).

SkyNews, the Canadian magazine of astronomy and stargazing, published bimonthly ((866) 759-0005; www.skynewsmagazine.com).

Starlight Nights, by Leslie Peltier (1900–1980), 1965. Sky Publishing Corporation. Anyone who enjoys the night sky should read this book.

Atlas of the Moon, by Antonín Rükl. Sky Publishing Corp. 2004. A first-rate lunar atlas for amateur astronomers.

Bright Star Atlas 2000.0, by Wil Tirion. Introductory atlas containing 9000 stars to magnitude 6.5 and 600 clusters, nebulae, and galaxies on 10 charts.

Millennium Star Atlas, by Roger Sinnott and Michael Perryman. A comprehensive atlas based on data from the HIPPARCOS satellite. Three volumes, each covering 8 hours in RA. Contains more than 1 000 000 stars to magnitude 11 and more than 10 000 clusters, nebulae, and galaxies on 1548 charts.

Sky Atlas 2000.0 (2nd ed.), by Wil Tirion and Roger Sinnott, 1998. Large format and well done. Contains 81 000 stars to magnitude 8.5 and 2700 clusters, nebulae, and galaxies on 26 charts; laminated version available.

Uranometria 2000.0 Deep Sky Atlas, by Wil Tirion, Barry Rappaport, and Will Remaklus. A second edition of the popular atlas, with stellar data from the HIPPARCOS satellite. Contains more than 280 000 stars to magnitude 9.75 and 30 000 clusters, nebulae, and galaxies on 220 double-page charts.

Computer-based Planetarium Programs: Several are available, for example, *ECU (Earth Centered Universe), MegaStar, RedShift 5, Starry Night, TheSky,* and *Voyager 4,* For more information, see the catalogues listed above or do an Internet search at, for example, www.google.com.

Many of these items are available from Sky Publishing Corp, 49 Bay State Rd, Cambridge MA 02138-1200, USA; (800) 253-0245, skytonight.com.

SELECTED INTERNET RESOURCES

The World Wide Web is an important source of astronomical information. A selection of Web sites together with a reference to a page number in this Handbook (if any) is given below. A listing of all Web sites mentioned in this Handbook, with URL links to the various sites, is available at:

www.rasc.ca/handbook/websites.html

URL	Description
www.aavso.org	American Association of Variable Star Observers (p. 239)
www.lpl.arizona.edu/alpo	Association of Lunar and Planetary Observers
www.astrosociety.org	Astronomical Society of the Pacific (p. 15)
www.astronomy.com	*Astronomy* magazine (p. 11)
www.cascaeducation.ca	Canadian Astronomical Society's education Web site (p. 13)
www.space.gc.ca	Canadian Space Agency
www.cleardarksky.com/csk	Clear Sky Clock, by Attila Danko (p. 71)
www.mreclipse.com	Eclipse photography and safety (p. 117)
heritage.stsci.edu	Hubble Heritage Site, access to HST images
cfa-www.harvard.edu/iau/cbat.html	International Astronomical Union Central Bureau (p. 7); see also www.iau.org
www.darksky.org	International Dark-Sky Association (p. 74)
www.imo.net	International Meteor Organization (p. 203)
www.lunar-occultations.com/iota	International Occultation Timing Association (p. 136)
www.jpl.nasa.gov	Jet Propulsion Laboratory, activities for adults and kids
miac.uqac.uquebec.ca	Meteorites and Impacts Advisory Committee, Canadian Space Agency (p. 205)
cdsads.u-strasbg.fr	NASA Astrophysics Data System (ADS); bibliographic database, access to millions of articles
sunearth.gsfc.nasa.gov/eclipse	NASA eclipse site (p. 117)
nedwww.ipac.caltech.edu	NASA/IPAC Extragalactic Database (p. 269)
spaceflight.nasa.gov	NASA space flight site giving current information on Space Shuttle missions and ISS activities
www.rasc.ca/handbook	*Observer's Handbook* Web site (p. 5)
planetary.org	Planetary Society—contains over 2000 pages of information about space exploration
www.rasc.ca	Royal Astronomical Society of Canada (p. 7)
www.saguaroastro.org	Saguaro Astronomy Club, includes observing list database (p. 77)
www.heavens-above.com	Satellite tracking information, including International Space Station and Space Shuttle
simbad.u-strasbg.fr/simbad	SIMBAD astronomical database
skytonight.com	*Sky & Telescope* and Sky Publishing (p. 11)
www.skynews.ca	*SkyNews*—Canada's astronomy magazine (p. 11)
www.stsci.edu	Space Telescope Science Institute; access to Digitized Sky Survey
www.seds.org	Students for the Exploration and Development of Space
vizier.hia.nrc.ca/viz-bin/VizieR	VizieR service; access to most astronomical catalogues

TEACHING AND THE *OBSERVER'S HANDBOOK*

BY JOHN R. PERCY

You are holding in your hand a valuable resource for teaching astronomy. Every user of this Handbook, whether amateur or professional astronomer or teacher in any setting, at any level, can contribute to education in astronomy; see *JRASC, 96* (October 2002), p. 196, for information on how you can too.

As a result of curriculum renewal in Canada, the United States, and other countries, astronomy is now taught in many elementary and secondary schools; see *JRASC, 96* (June 2002), p. 114. The Canadian Astronomical Society, in partnership with the RASC and other organizations, has now embarked on a major education and public outreach initiative and has created a Canadian astronomy education Web site: www.cascaeducation.ca. The RASC has published *Skyways,* by Mary Lou Whitehorne, an excellent astronomy guide for teachers; a French version, *Explorons l'astronomie,* is now available.

The Night Sky

Teachers should make sure that their students are aware of what can be seen in the night sky, even though "the stars come out at night, but the students don't." THE SKY MONTH BY MONTH section of this Handbook (pp. 78–105) provides an excellent guide. Star charts can be found in many books and magazines (see p. 11) as well as in MAPS OF THE NIGHT SKY (pp. 274–281). (Study the first page of this section to get the most out of these maps.) Make sketches, including the horizon and compass points, to record the appearance and changes of the sky. Observational activities, with good record-keeping procedures (p. 76), can enable students to "learn science by doing science" and may be especially suitable for students in "applied" streams. Students can use sky-simulation software to predict what they might see in the sky, or to explain what they have previously observed and recorded. Even the study of light pollution (pp. 72–74) can be an educational experience; see *JRASC, 96* (February 2002), p. 24, and www.astrosociety.org/education/publications/tnl/44/lightpoll.html.

Seasons, Scale of the Solar System, and the Phases of the Moon

Surveys show that these basic astronomical concepts are misunderstood by most people. One common misconception is that it is hottest in the summer because of the shape of Earth's orbit—many people assume we are closest to the Sun in the summer. Then why are the seasons reversed in the Southern Hemisphere? Even those who know that the seasons are due to the tilt of Earth's axis may think that, because of the tilt, the hemispheres are closer to the Sun during their respective summers.

Other misconceptions relate to a lack of understanding of the scale of the solar system. Assuming a high speed that we are familiar with, say that of a commercial jet plane, how long would it take to travel to the Moon? To the Sun? If a beach ball represents the Sun, the solar system fits in your town, but the next nearest star is another beach ball on the opposite side of Earth! The sections PRINCIPAL ELEMENTS OF THE SOLAR SYSTEM (pp. 18–19), THE BRIGHTEST STARS (pp. 221–230), and THE NEAREST STARS (pp. 231–235) are useful references for constructing such models.

Here is a useful hands-on activity to illustrate phases of the Moon: Choose a day when the Sun and Moon are both visible in the sky (in the afternoon when the Moon is near first quarter or in the morning when the Moon is near last quarter; see THE SKY MONTH BY MONTH (pp.78–105). Hold a ball in your hand so that the Sun shines on it, and extend it toward the Moon. You will see the ball and the Moon illuminated by the Sun in the *same* way—a clear demonstration that the Moon is a spherical, nonluminous body floating in space.

These concepts are so basic that it is worth teaching them correctly, that is, monitoring the students' preconceptions through interviews and discussions, and being absolutely sure that they understand the concepts and can explain them from their understanding—not just from memorization. See also www.learner.org/teacherslab/pup.

The Sun

(1) Track the path of the Sun in the sky during one day and over successive days and weeks. This may be done safely and simply by using the shadow of a pole. Sunrise/sunset data and the changing position of the Sun in the heavens are given on pp. 165–166 and p. 158, respectively. This connects effectively with archaeoastronomy and multicultural astronomy; see 128.241.173.3/education/publications/tnl/53/multicultural.html.

(2) Using binoculars or a small telescope, project an image of the Sun on a sheet of white cardboard. Observe sunspots, and watch the Sun rotate from day to day. Practise setting up such a demonstration ahead of time, then it can be set up very quickly. These observations can be supplemented with daily images of the Sun available on the Internet (see, e.g. sohowww.nascom.nasa.gov). **Warning:** Never observe the Sun directly, especially by looking through binoculars or a telescope. Permanent eye damage could result. When projecting a solar image, use a barrier to prevent anyone from looking directly into the light beam. See the sections FILTERS (pp. 58–61) and VIEWING A SOLAR ECLIPSE—A WARNING (p. 125) in this Handbook.

The Moon

(1) Keep a "Moon journal" as a class project: Observe and record where the Moon is, what shape it is, and when it rises and sets. Note how these variables change over several days and weeks. (Don't forget that the Moon can be visible in the daytime.)

(2) Draw the general appearance of the Moon's surface as seen with your naked eye. Many features, including the regions of the Apollo landing sites, can be identified using the MAP OF MOON on pp. 126–127. A video of one of the Apollo missions is worth showing to a class.

(3) Eclipses: a three-dimensional model, to the correct scale, is a great aid in explaining eclipses and why there is not an eclipse every two weeks. See the ECLIPSES IN 2007 section in this Handbook (pp. 110–124) for information on eclipses that may be visible from your locality this year.

(4) If ocean tides occur in your area, correlate the times and the range of the tide with the Moon's position in your sky, its phases, and distances. Lunar phases, perigees, and apogees are tabulated in THE SKY MONTH BY MONTH (pp.78–105), and an overview of tides appears in the TIDES AND THE EARTH–MOON SYSTEM article in this Handbook (pp. 152–156).

The Planets

(1) Nothing can stimulate student interest like direct experience, so observe the planets when they are visible. See THE SKY MONTH BY MONTH and THE PLANETS FOR 2007 sections (pp. 170–182 for the latter) for the visibility of the planets during the year.

(2) Develop an awareness of Earth as a planet. Study photographs of Earth from space. For a hands-on experience, place an Earth globe in sunlight with its north pole oriented northward. Then rotate and tilt the globe so your locality is at the "top" of the globe (the globe will then be oriented the same way in space as planet Earth). The regions on Earth where the Sun is rising or setting at that moment will be apparent. Note which pole is experiencing 24 hours of daylight. Slowly turn the globe eastward about its axis (counterclockwise when viewed from the north) to show a sped-up day/night progression.

(3) Use Web sites, videos, and posters to capture the excitement of planetary exploration (see the catalogues in RECOMMENDED READING AND ATLASES on p. 11).

(4) See www.thursdaysclassroom.com/10feb00/teach10.html for an excellent cratering activity that enables students to study the cratering process in the classroom.

Comets and Asteroids

These are interesting topics, especially as it now appears that collisions between these objects and Earth may explain the extinctions of species such as the dinosaurs. Use the section METEORITE IMPACT CRATERS OF NORTH AMERICA (pp. 207–211) to have students locate nearby impact craters on geographical maps. See THE BRIGHTEST ASTEROIDS (p. 194) for a finder chart to locate a bright asteroid in the night sky (only binoculars are needed). There is a classic demonstration of "Creating a Comet" (out of dry ice and sand) described at www.noao.edu/education/crecipe.html.

Is a Telescope Necessary?

Binoculars and telescopes can be useful but are not essential; much interesting astronomy can be done with the unaided eye. However, binoculars are often available and should be used when helpful. See the section BINOCULARS (pp. 54–57) for a guide to their selection and use. The inexpensive, make-it-yourself *Project STAR* telescopes are highly recommended. See TELESCOPE PARAMETERS (p. 45) and TELESCOPE EXIT PUPILS (pp. 46–49) for a summary of some quantitative aspects of telescopes.

Resources

In addition to the list of reading material below, you may be able to make use of the following:

(1) See the SELECTED OBSERVATORIES AND PLANETARIA section in this Handbook (pp. 8–10). Take your students to visit one of these.

(2) The Royal Astronomical Society of Canada is the largest organization of amateur astronomers in Canada. Their 28 Centres across Canada (see the section THE ROYAL ASTRONOMICAL SOCIETY OF CANADA on p. 7) offer a wide variety of activities that might be interesting to you and your students. For example, a member of the RASC might be willing to visit your class and demonstrate a telescope. The Astronomical Society of the Pacific's *Project ASTRO How-To Manual* can facilitate such visits. See www.astrosociety.org/education/astro/project_astro.html.

Astronomical Society of the Pacific, 390 Ashton Ave, San Francisco CA 94112, USA. In addition to their excellent astronomical slides and other material (send for their catalogue), the ASP publishes a free quarterly teachers' newsletter; download current and back issues from www.astrosociety.org/education/publications/tnl/tnl.html.

Project STAR Hands-on Science Materials, Learning Technologies Inc, 40 Cameron Ave, Somerville MA 02144, USA; (617) 628-1459; www.starlab.com. Unique, high-quality, low-cost materials for introducing students (and teachers) to astronomy.

SkyNews, Box 10, Yarker ON K0K 3N0; (866) 759-0005; www.skynewsmagazine.com. Bimonthly. General astronomy from a Canadian perspective. Included with RASC membership.

The Universe at Your Fingertips, and *More Universe at Your Fingertips,* edited by Andrew Fraknoi et al. Astronomical Society of the Pacific, 390 Ashton Ave, San Francisco CA 94112, USA. Another excellent collection of teaching activities and resources for grades 3–12. See also www.astrosociety.org/education/activities/astroacts.html.

BASIC DATA

TERMINOLOGY AND SYMBOLS

COORDINATE SYSTEMS

Astronomical positions are usually measured in a system based on the *celestial poles* and *celestial equator,* the intersections of Earth's rotation axis and equatorial plane, respectively, and the infinite sphere of the sky. *Right ascension* (RA or α) is measured in hours (h), minutes (m), and seconds (s) of time, eastward along the celestial equator from the vernal equinox (see below). *Declination* (Dec or δ) is measured in degrees (°), minutes (′), and seconds (″) of arc, northward (N or +) or southward (S or –) from the celestial equator toward the north or south celestial pole.

Positions can also be measured in a system based on the *ecliptic,* the intersection of Earth's orbital plane and the infinite sphere of the sky. The Sun appears to move eastward along the ecliptic during the year. *Longitude* is measured eastward along the ecliptic from the vernal equinox; *latitude* is measured at right angles to the ecliptic, northward or southward toward the north or south ecliptic pole. The *vernal equinox* is one of the two intersections of the ecliptic and the celestial equator; it is the one at which the Sun crosses the celestial equator moving from south to north.

An object is *in conjunction with the Sun* if it has the same longitude as the Sun and *at opposition* if its longitude differs from that of the Sun by 180°. Mercury and Venus are in *superior* conjunction when they are more distant than the Sun and in *inferior* conjunction when they are nearer than the Sun (see the diagram at the right). An object is *stationary* when its reaches an extreme longitude.

Two *nonsolar* objects are in conjunction if they have the same RA. Generally, but not always, close mutual approaches correspond to conjunctions; following Jean Meeus, we use the term *quasi-conjunction* to denote close (< 5°) nonconjunctional approaches.

If an object crosses the ecliptic moving northward, it is at the *ascending node* of its orbit; if it crosses the ecliptic moving southward, it is at the *descending node.*

Elongation is the geocentric angle between an object and the Sun, or between a satellite and its primary, measured in the plane formed by Earth and the other two bodies.

SYMBOLS

Sun, Moon, and Planets

☉ Sun	☾ Last Quarter	⊕ Earth	♅ Uranus
🌑 New Moon	☾ Moon generally	♂ Mars	♆ Neptune
🌕 Full Moon	☿ Mercury	♃ Jupiter	♇ Pluto
☽ First Quarter	♀ Venus	♄ Saturn	

Signs of the Zodiac

♈ Aries.................... 0°	♌ Leo.................. 120°	♐ Sagittarius....... 240°
♉ Taurus................ 30°	♍ Virgo............... 150°	♑ Capricornus..... 270°
♊ Gemini.............. 60°	♎ Libra................ 180°	♒ Aquarius.......... 300°
♋ Cancer............... 90°	♏ Scorpius.......... 210°	♓ Pisces.............. 330°

The Greek Alphabet

Α, α........alpha	Η, η.......eta	Ν, ν.......nu	Τ, τ........tau
Β, β.......beta	Θ, θ, ϑ...theta	Ξ, ξ.......xi	Υ, υ.......upsilon
Γ, γ........gamma	Ι, ι.........iota	Ο, ο.......omicron	Φ, φ.......phi
Δ, δ.......delta	Κ, κ.......kappa	Π, π.......pi	Χ, χ.......chi
Ε, ε........epsilon	Λ, λ.......lambda	Ρ, ρ........rho	Ψ, ψ......psi
Ζ, ζ........zeta	Μ, μ......mu	Σ, σ.......sigma	Ω, ω......omega

SOLAR-SYSTEM GEOMETRY

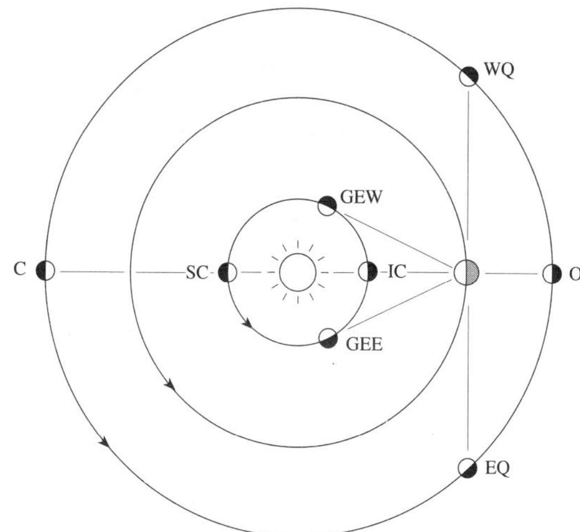

The diagram is a simplified view of our solar system, from the north side. Earth is shown (middle orbit) together with an inferior planet (i.e. Mercury or Venus) and a superior planet (e.g. Mars). Four special geometrical configurations of the inferior planet relative to Earth are shown; in counterclockwise chronological sequence they are inferior conjunction (IC), greatest elongation west (GEW), superior conjunction (SC), and greatest elongation east (GEE). Four special configurations of the superior planet relative to Earth are also shown; in clockwise chronological sequence they are opposition (O), eastern quadrature (EQ), conjunction with the Sun (C), and western quadrature (WQ).

PLANETARY HELIOCENTRIC LONGITUDES FOR 2007

The heliocentric longitude of a planet is the angle between the vernal equinox and the planet, as seen from the Sun. It is measured in the ecliptic plane, in the direction of the orbital motion of the planet (counterclockwise as viewed from the north side of the ecliptic plane). Knowing these heliocentric longitudes and the distances of the planets from the Sun (see p. 19), one can construct a diagram or model showing the relative orientations of the Sun and planets on any date.

UT	Me °	V °	E °	Ma °	J °	S °	U °	N °	P °
Jan. 1.0	269	318	100	245	243	140	344	319	267
Feb. 1.0	24	7	132	261	245	141	344	319	267
Mar. 1.0	180	52	160	277	247	142	345	320	267
Apr. 1.0	274	102	191	296	250	143	345	320	267
May 1.0	30	150	220	314	252	144	345	320	267
Jun. 1.0	195	201	250	334	255	146	346	320	268
Jul. 1.0	283	249	279	353	257	147	346	320	268
Aug. 1.0	54	298	308	12	259	148	346	321	268
Sep. 1.0	209	347	338	31	262	149	347	321	268
Oct. 1.0	295	35	7	48	264	150	347	321	268
Nov. 1.0	79	84	38	65	267	151	347	321	268
Dec. 1.0	218	133	68	81	269	152	348	321	269
Jan. 1.0	308	183	100	96	272	153	348	321	269

PRINCIPAL ELEMENTS OF THE SOLAR SYSTEM

PHYSICAL ELEMENTS

Object (Pronun.)	**Equatorial Diameter** km	**Oblate-ness**	**Mass** Earth=1	**Den-sity** t/m³	**Grav-ity*** Earth=1	**Escape Speed*** km/s	**Rotation Period** d	**Inclina-tion†** °	**Albedo**
Sun	1 392 530	0	332 946.0	1.41	27.9	617.5	25–35‡	— —	
Mercury (mûr′kū-rē)	4 879	0	0.055 274	5.43	0.38	4.2	58.646	0.0	0.11
Venus (vē′nŭs)	12 104	0	0.815 005	5.24	0.90	10.4	243.019	2.6	0.65
Earth (ûrth)	12 756	1/298	1.000 000	5.52	1.00	11.2	0.9973	23.4	0.37
Moon	3 475	0	0.012 300	3.35	0.17	2.4	27.3217	6.7	0.12
Mars (märz)	6 792	1/148	0.107 447	3.94	0.38	5.0	1.0260	25.2	0.15
Jupiter (jo͞o′pĭ-tẽr)	142 980 ††	1/15.4	317.833	1.33	2.53	59.5	0.4101‡‡	3.1	0.52
Saturn (săt′ûrn)	120 540 ††	1/10.2	95.163	0.69	1.06	35.5	0.4440	26.7	0.47
Uranus[A] (yûr′ȧ-nŭs)	51 120 ††	1/43.6	14.536	1.27	0.90	21.3	0.7183	82.2	0.51
Neptune[B] (nĕp′tyo͞on)	49 530 ††	1/58.5	17.149	1.64	1.14	23.5	0.6712	28.3	0.41
Pluto[C] (plo͞o′tō)	2 306	0	0.002 2	2.03	0.08	1.3	6.3872	57.5	0.3

*At the equator †Inclination of equator to orbital plane ‡Depending on latitude ††At 1 atmosphere (101.325 kPa)
‡‡For the most rapidly rotating part, the equatorial region
[A]Discovered by Sir William Herschel, 1781 Mar. 13 [B]Discovered by Johann G. Galle, 1846 Sep. 23
[C]Discovered by Clyde Tombaugh, 1930 Feb. 18 As the Handbook goes to press, the IAU has made a definition of a planet that reclassifies Pluto as a dwarf planet. More on this in the 2008 edition.
Pronunciation guide: ȧ gȧgȧ; ē wē; ĕ mĕt; ẽ makẽr; ĭ bĭt; ō gō; o͞o mo͞on; ū ūnite; ŭ sŭn; û ûrn

OSCULATING ORBITAL ELEMENTS FOR 2007

The tables at the right give the orbital elements of the planets and 30 largest main-belt asteroids, the latter provided by Dr. Brian Marsden. At any given time or "epoch," six basic quantities determine each body's elliptical orbit, for example:

(1) the mean distance from the Sun, a, equal to the semimajor axis of the ellipse;
(2) the eccentricity e of the ellipse;
(3) the inclination i of the orbital plane to the ecliptic;
(4) the longitude Ω of the ascending node of the orbital plane on the ecliptic;
(5) the longitude $\tilde{\omega}$ of perihelion;
(6) the body's mean longitude L at the given epoch.

The date of the ecliptic and equinox used to measure the last four quantities must also be specified, and may be different from the given epoch. Other, equivalent parameters may be substituted: the distance q of perihelion in place of a; the argument of perihelion, $\omega = \tilde{\omega} - \Omega$, in place of $\tilde{\omega}$; or the mean anomaly, $M = L - \tilde{\omega}$, or time T of perihelion in place of L. Once six fundamental quantities are known, all other attributes of the orbit of the body, such as the sidereal period P and synodic period S, can be derived.

If the body followed a perfectly elliptical orbit as predicted by classical orbital mechanics, then for a fixed ecliptic and equinox the first five quantities above would be constant over time. However, because of perturbations caused by the gravitational influence of other bodies, the orbits are not perfectly elliptical; hence the orbital elements depend on the epoch. The given *osculating* elements can be used to determine an elliptical orbit that is a close approximation to the actual path of the body for times near the given epoch. Two epochs, corresponding to Jan. 20 and Aug. 8, are provided for the planets; the elements for these epochs can be linearly interpolated to other epochs in 2007 for precision of a few arcseconds (typically 1″ or 2″). For the asteroids one epoch, corresponding to Oct. 27, is given, with resulting precision of about 1′.

HELIOCENTRIC OSCULATING ORBITAL ELEMENTS FOR 2007
REFERRED TO THE MEAN ECLIPTIC AND EQUINOX OF J2000.0

Planet	Epoch Julian Date 245	Mean Distance *a* au	Eccen-tricity *e*	Incli-nation *i* °	Long. of Asc. Node Ω °	Long. of Perihelion ϖ °	Long. at Epoch *L* °	Sidereal Period *P* a	Synodic Period* *S* d
Elements are for epochs 2007 Jan. 20 and 2007 Aug. 8 respectively.									
Mercury	4120.5	0.387 099	0.205 638	7.0046	48.3224	77.4664	352.0688	0.2409	115.88
	4320.5	0.387 098	0.205 646	7.0045	48.3218	77.4703	90.5347	0.2409	115.88
Venus	4120.5	0.723 328	0.006 778	3.3946	76.6620	131.222	348.2675	0.6152	583.92
	4320.5	0.723 340	0.006 764	3.3946	76.6613	131.458	308.6941	0.6152	583.96
Earth†	4120.5	0.999 992	0.016 701	0.0009	175.6	102.9488	118.9008	1.0000	—
	4320.5	0.999 994	0.016 724	0.0009	175.1	103.0659	316.0217	1.0000	—
Mars	4120.5	1.523 738	0.093 358	1.8492	49.5386	336.0816	265.0874	1.8810	779.88
	4320.5	1.523 677	0.093 320	1.8491	49.5368	336.1200	9.8958	1.8809	779.93
Jupiter	4120.5	5.202 082	0.048 932	1.3038	100.5097	14.6813	248.3654	11.8598	398.89
	4320.5	5.202 360	0.048 917	1.3038	100.5097	14.6219	264.9881	11.8607	398.88
Saturn	4120.5	9.557533	0.054 242	2.4874	113.6315	93.4102	136.3280	29.4980	378.07
	4320.5	9.551089	0.053 850	2.4877	113.6357	92.8568	143.0010	29.4681	378.08
Uranus	4120.5	19.18639	0.047 561	0.7719	73.9787	172.6784	343.2677	84.4023	369.65
	4320.5	19.20451	0.046 592	0.7719	74.0039	172.9147	345.6046	84.1614	369.64
Neptune	4120.5	30.121 00	0.007 150	1.7707	131.7829	30.420	320.0651	165.3143	367.47
	4320.5	30.15862	0.007 825	1.7712	131.7804	22.300	321.2779	165.6241	367.47
Pluto	4120.5	39.79836	0.254 371	17.1235	110.3212	224.6501	249.0622	251.0818	366.71
	4320.5	39.81345	0.254 306	17.1173	110.3306	224.8346	249.9178	250.2246	366.71

* Synodic period = (product of *P*s of two planets) ÷ (difference of the *P*s). Tabular values are relative to Earth.
† Values are actually for the Earth-Moon barycentre.

Asteroid	Diameter km	Mean Distance *a* au	Eccen-tricity *e*	Incli-nation *i* °	Long. of Asc. Node Ω °	Long. of Perihelion ϖ °	Long. at Epoch *L* °	Sidereal Period *P* a	Synodic Period* *S* d
Elements are for epoch Julian Date 245 4400.5 (2007 Oct. 27)									
(1) Ceres	957	2.766 527	0.079 610	10.5866	80.4068	153.4492	52.2001	4.6015	466.67
(2) Pallas	524	2.771 869	0.230 766	34.8408	173.1365	123.4492	5.9391	4.6149	466.30
(4) Vesta	512	2.361 687	0.089 307	7.1351	103.9143	253.8929	289.9666	3.6294	504.17
(10) Hygiea	444	3.137 354	0.117 757	3.8422	283.4529	236.5712	3.6903	5.5571	445.41
(704) Interamnia	329	3.062 614	0.150 109	17.2917	280.3888	16.1726	62.5688	5.3597	449.04
(511) Davida	326	3.167 131	0.185 757	15.9376	107.6668	86.0845	43.8898	5.6364	444.04
(15) Eunomia	320	2.644 032	0.187 418	11.7382	293.2677	31.1646	71.9371	4.2993	475.96
(52) Europa	302	3.096 591	0.105 189	7.4800	128.7513	112.7164	309.4564	5.4491	447.35
(3) Juno	274	2.668 733	0.257 611	12.9667	170.1021	57.9823	224.4255	4.3597	473.97
(87) Sylvia	261	3.487 951	0.080 280	10.8567	73.3230	339.1102	153.6707	6.5141	431.50
(31) Euphrosyne	256	3.148 640	0.225 657	26.3174	31.2334	93.1969	160.6519	5.5871	444.88
(16) Psyche	239	2.919 090	0.139 594	3.0960	150.3455	18.0937	199.0527	4.9874	456.86
(88) Thisbe	232	2.766 849	0.165 052	5.2189	276.7641	313.3858	183.0408	4.6023	466.65
(65) Cybele	230	3.434 187	0.105 357	3.5482	155.8023	261.5040	227.7443	6.3641	433.35
(324) Bamberga	228	2.683 146	0.337 957	11.1048	328.0365	12.0197	241.0413	4.3951	472.84
(451) Patientia	225	3.060 932	0.077 212	15.2219	89.3945	69.7459	116.6277	5.3553	449.12
(19) Fortuna	225	2.441 739	0.159 050	1.5734	211.3695	33.2763	226.0509	3.8155	494.99
(107) Camilla	223	3.475 648	0.078 131	10.0492	173.1281	122.9053	170.3756	6.4797	431.91
(48) Doris	222	3.110 021	0.074 788	6.5538	183.7432	81.2105	111.4193	5.4846	446.70
(45) Eugenia	215	2.721 219	0.081 819	6.6089	147.9267	233.3670	72.0737	4.4890	469.95
(29) Amphitrite	212	2.554 720	0.072 796	6.0957	356.4965	59.8191	50.3274	4.0833	483.72
(7) Iris	211	2.385 087	0.231 447	5.5274	259.7204	45.0793	141.9660	3.6835	501.37
(121) Hermione	209	3.449 300	0.136 257	7.6012	73.1995	10.4139	303.3702	6.4061	432.82
(423) Diotima	209	3.069 544	0.040 908	11.2369	69.5475	273.8631	279.9024	5.3779	448.69
(9) Metis	209	2.386 688	0.121 715	5.5751	68.9672	75.1486	309.2929	3.6872	501.18
(13) Egeria	208	2.575 883	0.085 864	16.5438	43.2905	124.2339	30.5061	4.1342	481.80
(532) Herculina	207	2.770 310	0.178 458	16.3141	107.6012	184.3053	351.2798	4.6110	466.41
(94) Aurora	204	3.158 679	0.087 572	7.9664	2.7044	62.5853	354.9097	5.6138	444.42
(702) Alauda	195	3.191 447	0.021 944	20.6135	289.9686	282.3648	329.1925	5.7014	442.95
(6) Hebe	190	2.425 547	0.201 912	14.7522	138.7372	18.2867	88.8556	3.7776	496.76

NATURAL SATELLITES OF THE PLANETS

By Philip D. Nicholson

Of the 155 natural satellites listed in the table, all but 6 orbit the giant planets Jupiter (62), Saturn (47), Uranus (27), and Neptune (13). With a few exceptions, these moons may be divided into three groups, which presumably reflect their different origins. Closest to the planets are small ring moons, 20 km to 200 km in diameter and with strong evolutionary and dynamical connections to the planetary ring systems. Most of these objects were discovered during the *Voyager* flybys of 1979–1989, and all are very difficult to observe from Earth. These include the shepherd satellites Prometheus, Pandora, Cordelia, Ophelia, and Galatea; the co-orbital satellites Janus and Epimetheus; and Pan, which orbits within the Encke gap in Saturn's A-ring.

Next come the larger "regular" satellites in near-circular orbits in or near the planets' equatorial planes, thought to have been formed in situ via accretion in circumplanetary disks at the dawn of the solar system. The dividing line between the first two groups is fuzzy, but the regular satellites may be considered to start beyond about three planetary radii, that is, at Amalthea, Mimas, Puck, and Proteus. This group extends out to Callisto, Iapetus, Oberon, and Proteus but probably does not include Triton, which is now thought to have been captured. There are numerous orbital resonances among the regular satellites, for example, Io:Europa:Ganymede (1:2:4), Mimas:Tethys (1:2), Enceladus:Dione (1:2), and Titan:Hyperion (3:4); the origin of the orbital resonance is generally ascribed to orbital expansion driven by tidal interaction with Jupiter or Saturn. Temporary capture in similar resonances in the past may have been responsible for the anomalously large inclinations of Miranda and (perhaps) Naiad. Tidal energy dissipation within Io is responsible for this moon's spectacular volcanic activity, and similar heating at a lower level may still occur within Europa and Enceladus.

The third and outermost group—and the group whose numbers have increased so much in recent years—comprises the "irregular" satellites. These generally small bodies (2 km to 200 km in diameter, except for 340-km Nereid) move in quite eccentric orbits at large inclinations to the planets' orbital planes. Their orbits are not random; rather, they fall into several more-or-less tight clusters in semimajor axis and inclination: three or four at Jupiter (all but one retrograde) centred on Himalia, Ananke, Pasiphae, and Carme and three at Saturn (one retrograde) centred on Albiorix, Siarnaq, and Phoebe. These clusters are believed to be due to collisional disruptions of a smaller number of original objects captured from heliocentric orbits. The situation at Uranus and Neptune remains unclear, although there are now nine Uranian irregulars (all but one retrograde) and six Neptunians (three retrograde). The orbits of the irregular satellites, along with that of the Earth's Moon, are subject to strong solar gravitational perturbations and thus maintain approximately fixed inclinations to their respective planet's orbital planes rather than to their equators.

In 2005, two new satellites of Pluto were discovered in HST images, orbiting in the same plane as the Pluto–Charon system. It appears that all three satellites are quite close to a unique orbital resonance with periods in the ratio 1:4:6.

Eight satellites have received official names from the International Astronomical Union. Their designation in previous editions follows in parentheses.

Saturn: Daphnis (2005 S1).
Uranus: Cupid (2003 U2), Ferdinand (2001 U2), Francisco (2001 U3), Mab (2003 U1), Margaret (2003 U3), Perdita (1986 U10)
Neptune: Psamathe (2003 U1).

TABLE OF NATURAL SATELLITES OF THE PLANETS

Name (Pronunciation)	Diameter km	Mass[A] Pt	Density t/m³	Visual Mag.[B]	Albedo	Mean Dist. from Planet 10³ km	Orbital Period d	Eccen-tricity	Orbit Incl.[C] °	Discovery
Satellite of Earth										
Moon* (mo͞on)	3475.	73 490. (10)	3.34	−12.7	0.11	384.4	27.322	0.0554	5.16	—
Satellites of Mars										
I Phobos* (fō′bŏs)	22.	0.0107 (0.00002)	1.87	11.4	0.07	9.38	0.319	0.0151	1.1	A. Hall, 1877
II Deimos* (dī′mŏs)	12.	0.0022 (0.0002)	2.3	12.5	0.07	23.46	1.262	0.0002	1.8v	A. Hall, 1877
Satellites of Jupiter										
XVI Metis (mē′tĭs)	43.	—	—	17.5	0.06	128.0	0.295	0.0012	0.02	S. Synnott, *Voyager 2,* 1979
XV Adrastea (ȧ-drăs′tē-ȧ)	16.	—	—	18.7	≈0.05	129.0	0.298	0.0018	0.39	D. Jewitt et al., *Voyager 1,* 1979
V Amalthea* (ăm′′l-thē′ȧ)	167.	—	—	14.1	0.09	181.4	0.498	0.0031	0.39	E. Barnard, 1892
XIV Thebe** (thē′be)	99.	—	—	16.0	0.05	221.9	0.675	0.0177	1.07	S. Synnott, *Voyager 1,* 1979
I Io*[D] (ī′ō)	3643.	89 330. (10)	3.53	5.0	0.62	421.8	1.769	0.0041	0.04	Galileo, 1610
II Europa*[D] (ū-rō′pȧ)	3122.	48 000. (10)	3.01	5.3	0.68	671.1	3.551	0.0094	0.47	Galileo, 1610
III Ganymede*[D] (găn′ĕ-mēd′)	5262.	148 200. (10)	1.94	4.6	0.44	1 070.	7.155	0.0011	0.17	Galileo, 1610
IV Callisto* (kȧ-lĭs′tō)	4820.	107 600. (10)	1.83	5.6	0.19	1 883.	16.689	0.0074	0.19	Galileo, 1610
XVIII Themisto (thē-mĭs′tō)	4.[E]	—	—	21.0	—	7 284.	130.	0.24	43.	C. Kowal, 1975[F]
XIII Leda (lē′dȧ)	≈20.	—	—	19.5	—	11 165.	241.	0.16	27.	C. Kowal, 1974
VI Himalia*** (hĭm′ȧ-lĭ-ȧ)	185.	—	—	14.6	0.03	11 461.	251.	0.16	27.	C. Perrine, 1904
X Lysithea*** (lĭs′ĭ-thē′ȧ)	≈35.	—	—	18.3	—	11 717.	259.	0.11	28.	S. Nicholson, 1938
VII Elara (ē′lȧr-ȧ)	85.	—	—	16.3	0.03	11 741.	260.	0.22	26.	C. Perrine, 1905
XLVI Carpo (kȧr′po)	3.[G]	—	—	23.0	—	16 989.	456.	0.43	51.	S. Sheppard et al., 2003
2003 J12	1.[G]	—	—	23.9	—	17 582.	490.	0.51	151.	S. Sheppard et al., 2003

Pronunciation guide: ă tăp; â câre; ā dāte; ȧ gȧgȧ; ē wē; ĕ mĕt; ī īce; ĭ bĭt; ō gō; ŏ hŏt; ô ôrb; oo book; o͞o mo͞on; ŭ ŭp; ū cūte; û ûrn

For some background on the satellites' names, visit planetarynames.wr.usgs.gov/append7.html.

Visual magnitudes are at mean opposition distance.

* synchronous rotation; ** probably synchronous; *** asynchronous; **** chaotic rotation; (no asterisk) rotation unknown

[A] The numbers in parentheses are possible errors.

[B] Jovian, Saturnian, and Uranian irregular satellites discovered in 1997–2001 are CCD-R magnitudes (675 nm); the solar V–R is 0.53.

[C] Inclinations of inner satellites (those closer than 100 planetary radii) are relative to the planet's *equator.* As customary, inclinations for outer satellites (those beyond Jupiter IV, Saturn VIII, Uranus IV, and Neptune I) are relative to the planet's *orbital plane.* Iapetus is an intermediate case. For our Moon, the inclination relative to Earth's orbital plane is 5°; relative to Earth's equator it varies between 18° and 29° in an 18.61-year cycle. A value >90° indicates retrograde motion.

[D] Laplace resonance; longitudes satisfy L(Io) − 3L(Europa) + 2L(Ganymede) ≈ 180°. Also, the mean motions are such that the three periods are nearly 1:2:4.

[E] Diameters assume an albedo of 0.06.

[F] Initially detected in 1975 and then lost; recovered in 2000 by S. Sheppard and D. Jewitt.

[G] Diameters assume an albedo of 0.04.

TABLE OF NATURAL SATELLITES OF THE PLANETS (continued)

Name (Pronunciation)	Diameter km	Mass[A] Pt	Density t/m³	Visual Mag.[B]	Albedo	Mean Dist. from Planet 10^3 km	Orbital Period d	Eccen-tricity	Orbit Incl.[C] °	Discovery
Satellites of Jupiter (continued)										
XXXIV Euporie (ū-pôr′ĭ-ē)	2.[E]	—	—	23.1	—	19 304.	551.	0.14	146.	S. Sheppard et al., 2001
2003 J3	2.[G]	—	—	23.4	—	20 221.	584	0.20	148.	S. Sheppard et al., 2003
2003 J18	2.[G]	—	—	23.4	—	20 514.	597.	0.02	146.	B. Gladman et al., 2003
XXXV Orthosie (ôr-thō-sĭ′ē)	2.[E]	—	—	23.1	—	20 720.	623.	0.28	146.	S. Sheppard et al., 2001
XXXIII Euanthe (ū-ǎn′thē)	3.[E]	—	—	22.8	—	20 797.	620.	0.23	149.	S. Sheppard et al., 2001
XXII Harpalyke (hȧr-pă-lĕ′kē)	3.[E]	—	—	22.2	—	20 858.	623.	0.23	149.	S. Sheppard et al., 2000
XXVII Praxidike (prăk-sĭ′dī-kē)	5.[E]	—	—	21.2	—	20 907.	625.	0.23	149.	S. Sheppard et al., 2000
XXIX Thyone (thī′ō-nē)	3.[E]	—	—	22.3	—	20 939.	627.	0.23	149.	S. Sheppard et al., 2001
2003 J16	2.[G]	—	—	23.3	—	20 957.	616.	0.22	149.	B. Gladman et al., 2003
XXIV Iocaste (ī-ō-kăs′tē)	4.[E]	—	—	21.8	—	21 061.	632.	0.22	149.	S. Sheppard et al., 2000
XL Mneme (nē′mē)	2.[G]	—	—	23.3	—	21 069.	620.	0.23	149.	B. Gladman, S. Sheppard, 2003
XXX Hermippe (hĕr-mĭ′pē)	4.[E]	—	—	22.1	—	21 131.	634.	0.21	151.	S. Sheppard et al., 2001
XLII Thelxinoe (thĕl-kĭ′nō-ē)	2.[G]	—	—	23.4	—	21 162.	628.	0.22	151.	S. Sheppard et al., 2004
XLV Helike (hĕl′ĭ-kē)	4.[G]	—	—	22.6	—	21 263.	635.	0.16	155.	S. Sheppard et al., 2003
XII Ananke*** (ȧ′năn-kē)	≈30.	—	—	18.8	—	21 276.	630.	0.24	149.	S. Nicholson, 1951
2003 J15	2.[G]	—	—	23.5	—	22 627.	690.	0.19	147.	S. Sheppard et al., 2003
XXXII Eurydome (ū-rĭd′ō-mē)	3.[E]	—	—	22.7	—	22 865.	717.	0.28	150.	S. Sheppard et al., 2001
2003 J17	2.[G]	—	—	23.4	—	22 922.	714.	0.24	165.	B. Gladman et al., 2003
XLIII Arche (ȧr′kē)	3.[G]	—	—	22.8	—	22 931.	724.	0.26	165.	S. Sheppard et al., 2002
XXXVIII Pasithee (pȧ-sĭ′thē)	2.[E]	—	—	23.2	—	23 004.	719.	0.27	165.	S. Sheppard et al., 2001
2003 J10	2.[G]	—	—	23.6	—	23 041.	716.	0.43	165.	S. Sheppard et al., 2003
XXI Chaldene (kăl′dĕ-nē)	3.[E]	—	—	22.5	—	23 100.	724.	0.25	165.	S. Sheppard et al., 2000
XXVI Isonoe (ī-sō′nō-ē)	3.[E]	—	—	22.5	—	23 155.	726.	0.25	165.	S. Sheppard et al., 2000
XXV Erinome (ē-rĭn′ō-mē)	3.[E]	—	—	22.8	—	23 196.	729.	0.27	165.	S. Sheppard et al., 2000
XXXVII Kale (kȧ′lē)	2.[E]	—	—	23.0	—	23 217.	729.	0.26	165.	S. Sheppard et al., 2001
XXXI Aitne (ă-ĭt′nē)	3.[E]	—	—	22.7	—	23 229.	730.	0.26	165.	S. Sheppard et al., 2001
XX Taygete (tā-ĭj′ĕ-tē)	4.[E]	—	—	21.9	—	23 280.	732.	0.25	165.	S. Sheppard et al., 2000
2003 J9	1.[G]	—	—	23.7	—	23 384.	733.	0.26	165.	S. Sheppard et al., 2003
XI Carme (kȧr′mē)	≈45.	—	—	17.6	—	23 404.	734.	0.25	165.	S. Nicholson, 1938
XXXVI Sponde (spŏn′dē)	2.[E]	—	—	23.0	—	23 487.	748.	0.31	151.	S. Sheppard et al., 2001
XIX Megaclite (mĕg-ă-klī′tē)	4.[E]	—	—	21.7	—	23 493.	753.	0.42	153.	S. Sheppard et al., 2000
2003 J5	4.[G]	—	—	22.4	—	23 495.	739.	0.25	165.	S. Sheppard et al., 2003
2003 J19	2.[G]	—	—	23.7	—	23 533.	740.	0.26	165.	B. Gladman et al., 2003
2003 J23	2.[G]	—	—	23.5	—	23 563.	732.	0.27	146.	S. Sheppard et al., 2004

TABLE OF NATURAL SATELLITES OF THE PLANETS (continued)

Name (Pronunciation)	Diameter km	Mass[A] Pt	Density t/m³	Visual Mag.[B]	Albedo	Mean Dist. from Planet 10³ km	Orbital Period d	Eccen- tricity	Orbit Incl.[C] °	Discovery
Satellites of Jupiter (continued)										
XXIII Kalyke (kȧ-lē′kē)	4.[E]	—	—	21.8	—	23 566.	742.	0.25	165.	S. Sheppard et al., 2000
VIII Pasiphae (pȧ-sĭf′ȧ-ē′)	≈60.	—	—	17.0	—	23 624.	744.	0.41	151.	P. Melotte, 1908
XLVII Eukelade ((ū-kĕ-lā′dē)	4.[G]	—	—	22.6	—	23 661.	746.	0.27	165.	S. Sheppard et al., 2003
2003 J4	2.[G]	—	—	23.0	—	23 930.	755.	0.36	150.	S. Sheppard et al., 2003
XXXIX Hegemone (hē-jĕ′mō-nē)	3.[G]	—	—	22.8	—	23 947.	740.	0.33	155.	S. Sheppard et al., 2003
XLVIII Cyllene (sĭ-lē′nē)	2.[G]	—	—	23.2	—	23 951.	752.	0.41	150.	S. Sheppard et al., 2003
XLI Aoede (ā-ō′dē)	4.[G]	—	—	22.5	—	23 981.	762.	0.43	158.	S. Sheppard et al., 2003
IX Sinope*** (sĭ-nō′pē)	≈38.	—	—	18.1	—	23 939.	759.	0.25	158.	S. Nicholson, 1914
2003 J14	2.[G]	—	—	23.6	—	24 011.	779.	0.34	145.	S. Sheppard et al., 2003
XLIV Kallichore (kă-lĭ-kō′rē)	2.[G]	—	—	23.7	—	24 043.	765.	0.26	166.	S. Sheppard et al., 2003
XXVIII Autonoe (ô-tŏn′ō-ē)	3.[E]	—	—	22.0	—	24 046.	761.	0.32	152.	S. Sheppard et al., 2001
XVII Callirrhoe (kă-lĭr′ō-ē)	7.[E]	—	—	20.7	—	24 103.	759.	0.28	147.	J. Scotti, T. Spahr, 1999
2003 J2	2.[G]	—	—	23.2	—	29 541.	980.	0.23	161.	S. Sheppard et al., 2003
Satellites of Saturn										
XVIII Pan[H] (păn)	26.	—	—	19.4	≈0.5	133.6	0.575	0.0002	0.007	M. Showalter, 1990
XXXV Daphnis (dăf-nĭs)	7.	—	—	23.4[I]	—	136.5	0.594	≈0.	≈0.	Cassini ISS team, 2005
XV Atlas (ăt′lăs)	20.	—	—	19.0	0.4	137.7	0.602	0.0012	0.01	R. Terrile, *Voyager 1,* 1980
XVI Prometheus** [J] (prō-mē′thē-ŭs)	100.	—	—	15.8	0.6	139.4	0.613	0.002	0.006	S. Collins, D. Carlson, *Voyager 1,* 1980
XVII Pandora** [J] (păn-dôr′ȧ)	85.	—	—	16.4	0.5	141.7	0.629	0.004	0.052	S. Collins, D. Carlson, *Voyager 1,* 1980
XI Epimetheus* [K] (ĕp′ȧ-mē′thē-ŭs)	120.	0.5 (0.1)	0.61	15.6	0.5	151.4	0.694	0.010	0.35	J. Fountain, S. Larson, 1978
X Janus* [K] (jā′nŭs)	180.	1.9 (0.1)	0.66	14.4	0.6	151.5	0.695	0.007	0.17	A. Dollfus, 1966
I Mimas* (mī′măs)	397.	38. (1)	1.16	12.8	0.6	185.6	0.942	0.0206	1.57	W. Herschel, 1789
XXXII Methone (mĕth-ō′nē)	3.	—	—	25.1[I]	—	194.3	1.010	0.001	0.02	Cassini ISS team, 2004
XXXIII Pallane (pă-lă′nē)	4.	—	—	24.5[I]	—	212.3	1.154	0.004	0.18	Cassini ISS team, 2004
II Enceladus* (ĕn-sĕl′ȧ-dŭs)	499.	65. (2)	1.61	11.8	1.0	238.1	1.370	0.0001	0.01	W. Herschel, 1789
III Tethys* (tē′thĭs)	1060.	627. (5)	0.96	10.3	0.8	294.7	1.888	0.0001	0.168	G. Cassini, 1684
XIII Telesto (tȧ-lĕs′tō)	25.	—	—	18.5	0.7	294.7	1.888[L]	≈0.	1.16	B. Smith et al., 1980
XIV Calypso** (kȧ-lĭp′sō)	19.	—	—	18.7	1.0	294.7	1.888[M]	≈0.	1.47	D. Pascu et al., 1980

[H]Orbits within the Encke gap. Discovered in *Voyager* images (1980–81).
[I]Magnitudes are estimated from published diameters, which is the reverse of the practice for irregular satellites.
[J]Prometheus and Pandora are shepherds of the F-ring.
[K]Co-orbital satellites
[L]Telesto librates about the trailing (#5) Lagrangian point of Tethys's orbit.
[M]Calypso librates about the leading (#4) Lagrangian point of Tethys's orbit.

TABLE OF NATURAL SATELLITES OF THE PLANETS (continued)

Name (Pronunciation)	Diameter km	Mass[A] Pt	Density t/m³	Visual Mag.[B]	Albedo	Mean Dist. from Planet 10³ km	Orbital Period d	Eccen-tricity	Orbit Incl.[C] °	Discovery
Satellites of Saturn (continued)										
IV Dione* (dī-ō′nē)	1120.	1 097. (2)	1.46	10.4	0.6	377.4	2.737	0.0002	0.002	G. Cassini, 1684
XII Helene (hȧ-lēn′)	30.	—	—	18.4	0.6	377.4	2.737[N]	≈0.	0.21	P. Laques, J. Lecacheux, 1980
XXXIV Polydeuces (pŏl-i-dū′sēz)	3.5	—	—	24.8[I]	—	377.4	2.737[O]	0.018	0.17	Cassini ISS team, 2004
V Rhea* (rē′ȧ)	1530.	2 308. (60)	1.23	9.7	0.6	527.1	4.518	0.0009	0.327	G. Cassini, 1672
VI Titan** (tī′t′n)	5550.[P]	134 570. (20)	1.88	8.4	0.2	1 221.9	15.945	0.0288	0.33	C. Huygens, 1655
VII Hyperion**** (hī-pēr′ī-ŏn)	283.	—	—	14.4	0.3	1 464.1	21.276	0.0175	0.57	W. Bond, G. Bond, W. Lassell, 1848
VIII Iapetus* (ī-ăp′ĕ-tŭs)	1436.	1 590. (150)	1.09	11.0v	0.08–0.4	3 560.8	79.331	0.0284	7.57	G. Cassini, 1671
XXIV Kiviuq (kē-vyook′)	14.[E]	—	—	21.9	—	11 365.	449.	0.33	46.	B. Gladman et al., 2000
XXII Ijiraq (ē-jē-rȧk′)	10.[E]	—	—	22.5	—	11 442.	451.	0.32	47.	J. Kavelaars et al., 2000
IX Phoebe*** (fē′bē)	220.	—	—	16.5	0.08	12 944.3	548.	0.1644	175.	W. Pickering, 1898
XX Paaliaq (pȧ-lyȧk′)	19.[E]	—	—	21.2	—	15 198.	687.	0.36	45.	B. Gladman et al., 2000
XXVII Skadi (skȧ′dē)	6.[E]	—	—	23.5	—	15 641.	728.	0.27	153.	J. Kavelaars et al., 2000
XXVI Albiorix (ăl′bē-ôr-ĭks)	26.[E]	—	—	20.4	—	16 394.	783.	0.48	34.	M. Holman, T. Spahr, 2000
2004 S11	6.[E]	—	—	24.1	—	16 899.	820.	0.33	41.	S. Sheppard, D. Jewitt, 2005
XXVIII Erriapo (ĕr-rē-ăp′ō)	8.[E]	—	—	22.9	—	17 604.	871.	0.47	34.	J. Kavelaars et al., 2000
2004 S13	6.[E]	—	—	24.5	—	18 057.	906.	0.26	167.	S. Sheppard, D. Jewitt, 2005
XXIX Siarnaq (syȧr-nȧk′)	32.[E]	—	—	20.0	—	18 195.	896.	0.30	46.	B. Gladman et al., 2000
XXI Tarvos (tȧr′vŏs)	13.[E]	—	—	22.0	—	18 239.	926.	0.54	33.	J. Kavelaars et al., 2000
XXXI Narvi (nȧr′vē)	5.[E]	—	—	24.1	—	18 719.	956.	0.35	135.	S. Sheppard et al., 2003
XXV Mundilfari (mŭnd′ĭl-fȧr-ē)	6.[E]	—	—	23.7	—	18 722.	952.	0.21	167.	B. Gladman et al., 2000
2004 S17	4.[E]	—	—	25.2	—	19 099.	985.	0.23	167.	S. Sheppard, D. Jewitt, 2005
2004 S15	6.[E]	—	—	24.2	—	19 372.	1007.	0.15	158.	S. Sheppard, D. Jewitt, 2005
XXIII Suttung (sŭt′tŭng)	6.[E]	—	—	23.8	—	19 465.	1017.	0.11	176.	B. Gladman et al., 2000
2004 S10	6.[E]	—	—	24.4	—	19 614.	1026.	0.24	167.	S. Sheppard, D. Jewitt, 2005
2004 S12	5.[E]	—	—	24.8	—	19 906.	1049.	0.40	164.	S. Sheppard, D. Jewitt, 2005
2004 S18	7.[E]	—	—	23.8	—	19 959.	1053.	0.77	148.	S. Sheppard, D. Jewitt, 2005
XXX Thrym (thrĭm)	6.[E]	—	—	23.8	—	20 219.	1092.	0.49	176.	B. Gladman et al., 2000
2004 S9	5.[E]	—	—	24.7	—	20 291.	1079.	0.21	158.	S. Sheppard, D. Jewitt, 2005
2004 S14	6.[E]	—	—	24.4	—	20 304.	1080.	0.29	163.	S. Sheppard, D. Jewitt, 2005
2004 S7	6.[E]	—	—	24.5	—	20 577.	1102.	0.55	166.	S. Sheppard, D. Jewitt, 2005
2004 S16	4.[E]	—	—	25.0	—	22 611.	1269.	0.13	163.	S. Sheppard, D. Jewitt, 2005

[N]Helene librates about the leading (#4) Lagrangian point of Dione's orbit with a period of 769 d.
[O]Polydeuces librates about the trailing (#5) Lagrangian point of Dione's orbit with a period of 792 d.
[P]Titan's cloud-top diameter; solid-body diameter equals 5150 km.

TABLE OF NATURAL SATELLITES OF THE PLANETS (continued)

Name (Pronunciation)	Diameter km	Mass[A] Pt	Density t/m³	Visual Mag.[B]	Albedo	Mean Dist. from Planet 10³ km	Orbital Period d	Eccen-tricity	Orbit Incl.[C] °	Discovery
Satellites of Saturn (continued)										
XIX Ymir (ē′mĕr)	16.[E]	—	—	21.6	—	23 130.	1315.	0.33	173.	B. Gladman et al., 2000
2004 S8	6.[E]	—	—	24.6	—	23 609.	1354.	0.19	168.	S. Sheppard, D. Jewitt, 2005
Satellites of Uranus										
VI Cordelia[Q] (kôr-dēl′yȧ)	25.[R]	—	—	24.2	—	49.8	0.335	≈0.	0.08	*Voyager 2*, 1986
VII Ophelia[Q] (ō-fēl′yȧ)	30.[R]	—	—	23.9	—	53.8	0.376	0.01	0.10	*Voyager 2*, 1986
VIII Bianca (bē-äng′kȧ)	45.[R]	—	—	23.1	—	59.2	0.435	0.001	0.19	*Voyager 2*, 1986
IX Cressida (krĕs′ĭ-dȧ)	65.[R]	—	—	22.3	—	61.8	0.464	≈0.	0.01	*Voyager 2*, 1986
X Desdemona (dĕz′dȧ-mō′nȧ)	60.[R]	—	—	22.5	—	62.7	0.474	≈0.	0.11	*Voyager 2*, 1986
XI Juliet (jo͞o′lē-ĕt)	85.[R]	—	—	21.7	—	64.4	0.493	0.001	0.06	*Voyager 2*, 1986
XII Portia (pôr′shȧ)	110.[R]	—	—	21.1	—	66.1	0.513	≈0.	0.06	*Voyager 2*, 1986
XIII Rosalind (rŏz′ȧ-lĭnd)	60.[R]	—	—	22.5	—	69.9	0.558	≈0.	0.28	*Voyager 2*, 1986
XXVII Cupid (cū′pĭd)	18.	—	—	25.9	—	74.4	0.613	≈0.	≈0.	M. Showalter, J. Lissauer, 2003
XIV Belinda (bȧ-lĭn′dȧ)	68.[R]	—	—	22.1	—	75.3	0.624	≈0.	0.03	*Voyager 2*, 1986
XXV Perdita (pûr′dī-tȧ)	26.	—	—	23.6	—	76.4	0.638	0.003	0.07	E. Karkoschka, 1999[S]
XV Puck (pŭk)	155.	—	—	20.4	0.07	86.0	0.762	≈0.	0.32	*Voyager 2*, 1985
XXVI Mab (măb)	24.[R]	—	—	25.4	—	97.7	0.923	0.003	0.13	M. Showalter, J. Lissauer, 2003
V Miranda*[T] (mĭ-răn′dȧ)	472.	66. (8)	1.2	15.8	0.32	129.9	1.413	0.0013	4.34	G. Kuiper, 1948
I Ariel*[T] (âr′ē-ĕl)	1158.	1 350. (120)	1.7	13.7	0.39	190.9	2.520	0.0012	0.04	W. Lassell, 1851
II Umbriel*[T] (ŭm′brē-ĕl′)	1169.	1 170. (140)	1.4	14.5	0.21	266.0	4.144	0.0040	0.13	W. Lassell, 1851
III Titania* (tĭ′tā′nē-ȧ)	1578.	3 520. (90)	1.7	13.5	0.27	436.3	8.706	0.0011	0.079	W. Herschel, 1787
IV Oberon* (ō′bȧ-rŏn)	1523.	3 010. (80)	1.6	13.7	0.23	583.5	13.463	0.0014	0.068	W. Herschel, 1787
XXII Francisco (frăn′cĭs-cō)	14.[E]	—	—	25.3	—	4 276.	267.	0.15	145.	M. Holman, J. Kavelaars, 2001
XVI Caliban (kăl′ĭ-băn)	60.[R]	—	—	22.4	—	7 231.	580.	0.16	141.	B. Gladman et al., 1997
XX Stephano (stĕf′ă-nō)	20.[R]	—	—	24.1	—	8 004.	677.	0.23	144.	B. Gladman et al., 1999
XXI Trinculo (trĭn′cū-lō)	14.[E]	—	—	25.3	—	8 504.	749.	0.22	167.	M. Holman, J. Kavelaars, 2002
XVII Sycorax (sĭk′ō-răks)	120.[R]	—	—	20.8	—	12 179.	1288.	0.52	159.	P. Nicholson et al., 1997
XXIII Margaret (mȧr′gȧr-ĕt)	15.[E]	—	—	25.2	—	14 345.	1687.	0.66	57.	D. Jewitt, S. Sheppard, 2003
XVIII Prospero (prŏs′pĕr-ō)	30.[R]	—	—	23.2	—	16 256.	1978.	0.44	152.	M. Holman et al., 1999
XIX Setebos (sĕt′ē-bōs)	35.[R]	—	—	23.3	—	17 418.	2225.	0.59	158.	J. Kavelaars et al., 1999
XXIV Ferdinand (fûr′dĭn-nănd)	16.[E]	—	—	25.0	—	20 901.	2887.	0.37	170.	M. Holman, J. Kavelaars, 2001

[Q]Cordelia and Ophelia are shepherds of the ε-ring.
[R]Diameter assumes the same albedo (0.07) as Puck.
[S]In *Voyager 2* (January 1986) images
[T]Near resonance(?); L(Miranda) – 3L(Ariel) + 2L(Umbriel) drifts slowly (period ≈ 12.5 years).

TABLE OF NATURAL SATELLITES OF THE PLANETS (continued)

Name (Pronunciation)	Diameter km	Mass[A] Pt	Density t/m³	Visual Mag.[B]	Albedo	Mean Dist. from Planet 10³ km	Orbital Period d	Eccen-tricity	Orbit Incl.[C] °	Discovery
Satellites of Neptune										
III Naiad (nī′ăd)	60.	—	—	24.6	≈0.06	48.2	0.294	≈0.	4.74	*Voyager 2*, 1989
IV Thalassa (thȧ-lăs′ȧ)	80.	—	—	23.9	≈0.06	50.1	0.311	≈0.	0.21	*Voyager 2*, 1989
V Despina (dĭs-pĭn′ȧ)	150.	—	—	22.5	0.06	52.5	0.335	≈0.	0.07	*Voyager 2*, 1989
VI Galatea (găl′ȧ-tē′ȧ)	160.	—	—	22.4	≈0.06	62.0	0.429	≈0.	0.05	*Voyager 2*, 1989
VII Larissa** (lȧ-rĭs′ȧ)	190.	—	—	22.0	0.06	73.5	0.555	0.001	0.20	*Voyager 2*, 1989
VIII Proteus** (prō′tē-ŭs)	420.	—	—	20.3	0.06	117.6	1.122	≈0.	0.039	*Voyager 2*, 1989
I Triton* (trī′t′n)	2706.	21 400. (50)	2.06	13.5	0.76	354.8	5.877	≈0.	157.	W. Lassell, 1846
II Nereid*** (nēr′ē-ĭd)	340.	—	—	19.7	0.16	5 513.4	360.	0.75	7.23	G. Kuiper, 1949
2002 N1	50.[E]	—	—	24.4	—	15 686.	1875.	0.57	134.	M. Holman, J. Kavelaars, 2002
2002 N2	27.[E]	—	—	25.7	—	22 452.	2919.	0.30	48.	M. Holman, J. Kavelaars, 2002
2002 N3	33.[E]	—	—	25.3	—	22 580.	2982.	0.48	35.	M. Holman, J. Kavelaars, 2002
2002 N4	43.[E]	—	—	24.7	—	46 570.	8863.	0.53	132.	M. Holman, J. Kavelaars, 2002
X Psamathe (săm′ă-thē)	36.[E]	—	—	25.1	—	46 738.	9136.	0.45	137.	D. Jewitt et al., 2003
Satellites of Pluto										
I Charon* (kâr′ĕn)	1208.	1 620. (90)	1.65	17.3	0.37	19.57	6.387	0.00	0.0[U]	J. Christy, 1978
II Nix (nĭx)	36.[G]	—	—	23.4	—	48.68	24.856	0.02	0.0[U]	H. Weaver, S. Stern, 2005
III Hydra (hī′drȧ)	36.[G]	—	—	23.3	—	64.78	38.207	0.05	0.2[U]	H. Weaver, S. Stern, 2005

[U]Nix and Hydra orbit in the same plane as the Pluto–Charon binary. Their orbital periods are in the ratio 1:4:6 (Charon:Nix:Hydra). The inclinations are with respect to Pluto's assumed equatorial plane. Most other references give these inclinations with respect to the ecliptic, which are about 96°.

ORBITAL MOTION
BY ROY BISHOP

Whether you are observing a distant galaxy, the stars in a globular cluster, the waltz of Jupiter's Galilean satellites, or the drift of the Moon during an occultation or merely uttering an expletive as an artificial satellite passes through the field of your camera, an understanding of orbital motion is central to an appreciation of the heavens.

Among early cosmologies were those of **Aristotle** (340 BC) and **Ptolemy** (published as the *Almagest,* c. 150 AD), and the superior heliocentric model proposed by **Copernicus** (*De revolutionibus,* 1543). These attempts at modelling the heavens used complex systems of circles upon circles, of eccentric deferents and epicycles. John Milton, a contemporary of Galileo, wrote the following lines in his epic poem "Paradise Lost" (1674), possibly expressing his discontent with the Ptolemaic and Copernican systems of compounded circles:

From Man or Angel the great Architect
Did wisely to conceal, and not divulge
His secrets to be scann'd by them who ought
Rather admire; or if they list to try
Conjecture, he his Fabric of the Heav'ns
Hath left to thir disputes, perhaps to move
His laughter at thir quaint Opinions wide
Hereafter, when they come to model Heav'n
And calculate the Stars, how they will wield
The mighty frame, how build, unbuild, contrive
To save appearances, how gird the Sphere
With Centric and Eccentric scribbl'd o'er,
Cycle and Epicycle, Orb in Orb.

Kepler, using observations accumulated by Tycho Brahe, broke with the 2000-year preoccupation with circles when he discovered that the planets move in an elegantly simple way along elliptical paths (*Astronomia nova,* 1609). Although he had discovered *how* the planets move, Kepler was unable to explain quantitatively *why* they move in this way.

Galileo strongly supported the Copernican heliocentric universe (*Dialogue on the Two Chief World Systems,* 1632) and achieved brilliant insights concerning the motion of objects (*Two New Sciences,* 1638); however, he ignored Kepler's ellipses and did not apply his mechanics to the sky.

Newton united the heavens and Earth by showing that the laws governing motions on Earth also apply to the heavens. In his *Principia* (1687), the greatest book in the physical sciences, Newton presented his three laws of motion and the first ever physical force law, his law of gravitation. He used these to explain the motions not only of bodies on Earth, but also of the planets, comets, stars, equinoxes, tides, etc. Newton was the first to realize that the Moon is falling toward Earth just as freely as does an apple, and that the elliptical orbit of the centre of mass of the Earth–Moon system is the path that results (as he described it) as these two bodies free-fall under the action of the Sun's gravitational force.

In popular-level explanations of phenomena involving rotary motion, such as spinning wheels, automobiles on corners, tides, and orbital motion, "centrifugal force" is usually invoked. This is unfortunate because centrifugal force is a fiction, and its use in a popular description of motion obscures understanding.[(1)]

In the case of orbits, the common misconception is that the inward gravitational force is balanced by an outward "centrifugal force." Newton's view is simpler: There is only one force, the inward pull of gravity. There is *no physical agent* to cause an outward force. (Note that forces cause accelerations, not vice versa.) Also, if there *were* an outward supporting force, the two forces would cancel and, as Galileo realized, the body would then move along a straight line. If you choose a rotating reference frame and then ignore the rotation (mistake no. 1), you have to pretend there is a "centrifugal force" (mistake no. 2) in order to make sense of motions occurring within this frame. The two mistakes effectively cancel, but the description has been made needlessly complicated, and if you do not realize what you have done, you do not understand the motion.

Einstein's general theory of relativity (GTR) of 1915 superseded Newton's description of gravity. The arbiter of which is a good theory and which theory is wrong is nature. Newton's laws are accurate enough for most of NASA's calculations, but they do not work exactly. For example, if the computer programs used in the Global Positioning System (GPS) were based on Newton's gravitation, the system would be a multibillion-dollar boondoggle. Einstein's conception of gravitation is essential to the operation of this satellite-based navigation system. In the case of strong gravitation and/or speeds approaching the speed of light, Newton's laws fail dramatically. The GTR may be wrong too, but so far it has passed all experimental tests. Science does not hie after ultimate explanations or "truth"; its goal is a rational, coherent description of the measurable physical world, a description that has beauty in its simplicity, a description that makes sense. In the courtroom of nature, any aspect of science is falsifiable. Modern technology is making possible increasingly precise tests of general relativity (for instance, see *Sky & Telescope,* July 2004, p. 22).

According to Einstein's GTR, gravitation is not a mysterious force that one mass exerts upon a distant mass; gravitation is the geometry (non-Euclidean) of the 4-dimensional spacetime within which we and the stars exist. Golf balls (if air friction is ignored), satellites, planets, stars, and light follow *geodesics,* the straightest possible, force-free paths through a spacetime whose geometry is shaped by mass–energy. The difficulty in intellectually grasping a non-Euclidean spacetime originates with us. Common sense is inadequate. This is not surprising, given that our common sense is based on the Euclidean, 3-dimensional geometry of straight lines, rectangles, and spheres we learned in the crib by age 2. The underlying cause of our delusion is that our senses and thought processes are constrained by the speed of neuron signals. Compared to light, neuron signals ooze along at a very slow rate, about one ten-millionth the speed of light. Consequently, to us a second of time is brief, light looks instantaneous, relativistic effects seem foreign, and time appears to be independent of space.

Gravitation is geometry. That is why no one has ever felt a force of gravity. Like the centrifugal force, it never did exist. A force of gravity was the glue Newton invented to make his naïve, Euclidean, space-plus-time model of the universe approximate reality. Newton himself was well aware of the unsatisfactory nature of several of his assumptions, far more so than most people who came after him.

When you release a coin from your hand, you see the coin "fall" because the contact force of the ground on your feet (the *only* force you feel) accelerates you the other way. An orbiting astronaut experiences no such force, so he remains beside a released coin. Orbital motion could not be simpler—*no* forces are involved.

What would Milton have written had he been familiar with the conjectures of Newton and Einstein?

(1) Brief descriptions of tides in the Newtonian context (without invoking the obfuscating centrifugal force!) and in the context of the general theory of relativity appear on pp. 152 and 156, respectively.

SOME ASTRONOMICAL AND PHYSICAL DATA

BY ROY BISHOP

Many of the numbers listed below are based on measurement. Exceptions include defined quantities (indicated by ≡), quantities calculated from defined quantities (e.g. m/ly, au/pc), and numbers of mathematical origin such as π and conversion factors in angular measure. Of those based on measurement, some are known to only approximate precision and the equal sign is reduced to ≈. Many others are known to quite high precision (the uncertainties occur after the last digit given), and several are from "the 2002 CODATA recommended values of the fundamental physical constants" (see physics.nist.gov/cuu/constants). The units (Système International (SI) where possible), symbols, and nomenclature are based on recommendations of the International Astronomical Union and the International Union of Pure and Applied Physics.

LENGTH

1 metre (m) = the distance travelled by light in a vacuum in $(299\,792\,458)^{-1}$ s

1 astronomical unit (au)	= 1.495 978 706 9 × 10^{11} m = 499.004 783 8 light-s	
1 light-year (ly)	= 9.460 536 × 10^{15} m (based on average Gregorian year)	
	= 63 239.8 au	
1 parsec (pc)	= 3.085 678 × 10^{16} m = 206 264.8 au = 3.261 631 ly	
1 mile*	≡ 1.609 344 km	
1 micron*	≡ 1 μm	*Indicates deprecated unit;
1 angstrom*	≡ 0.1 nm	unit on right is preferred

TIME

1 second (s) ≡ 9 192 631 770 periods of the radiation involved in the transition between the two hyperfine levels of the ground state of the ^{133}Cs atom at mean sea level

Day:	Mean sidereal (equinox to equinox)	= 86 164.0909 s
	Mean rotation (fixed star to fixed star)	= 86 164.0993 s
	Day (d)	≡ 86 400. s
	Mean solar	= 86 400.0004 s
Month:	Draconic (node to node)	= 27.212 221 d
	Tropical (equinox to equinox)	= 27.321 582 d
	Sidereal (fixed star to fixed star)	= 27.321 662 d
	Anomalistic (perigee to perigee)	= 27.554 550 d
	Synodic (new Moon to new Moon)	= 29.530 589 d
Year:	Eclipse (lunar node to lunar node)	= 346.620 075 d
	Tropical (equinox to equinox) (a)	= 365.242 190 d
	Average Gregorian	≡ 365.242 5 d
	Average Julian	≡ 365.25 d
	Sidereal (fixed star to fixed star)	= 365.256 363 d
	Anomalistic (perihelion to perihelion)	= 365.259 635 d

EARTH

Mass, M_E = 5.9742 × 10^{24} kg Age ≈ 4.6 Ga Central T ≈ 5000 K to 6000 K

Geocentric gravitational constant, GM_E = 3.986 004 42 × 10^{14} m^3/s^2

Radius: Equatorial, a = 6378.14 km Polar, b = 6356.75 km

Mean = $(a^2b)^{1/3}$ = 6371.00 km Of metallic core = 3475 km

Solar parallax = 8.794 15″ (Earth equatorial radius ÷ 1 au)

1° of latitude = 111.132 95 – 0.559 82 cos 2φ + 0.001 17 cos 4φ km (at latitude φ)

1° of longitude = 111.412 88 cos φ – 0.093 50 cos 3φ + 0.000 12 cos 5φ km

1 knot = 1 nautical mile ($\approx$ 1′ of latitude) per hour $\equiv$ 1.852 km/h = 0.51444 m/s
Distance of sea horizon for eye h metres above sea level
(allowing for refraction) $\approx 3.9h^{1/2}$ km $\approx 2.1h^{1/2}$ nautical miles
Atmospheric pressure: 1 atm $\equiv$ 101.325 kPa (There is $\approx$1 kg of air above 1 cm^2.)
Density of air at sea level (1 atm, 20 °C) = 1.2 kg/m^3
Values of atmospheric refraction for various elevations (assuming 1 atm, 10 °C):
90°: 0′; 44°: 1′; 26°: 2′; 18°: 3′; 11°: 5′; 6°: 8′; 4°: 12′; 2°: 18′; 0°: 34′
Speed of sound in standard atmosphere = 331 m/s $\approx$ 1 km/3 s $\approx 10^{-6}\,c$
Magnetic field at surface $\approx 5 \times 10^{-5}$ T (**B** field comes out of a N-seeking pole)
Magnetic poles: 83°N, 115°W; 65°S, 139°E
Standard acceleration of gravity $\equiv$ 9.806 65 m/s^2
Meteoritic flux $\approx 1 \times 10^{-15}$ kg/(m^{2}s) $\approx 10^4$ t/a over entire Earth
Obliquity of ecliptic = 23.4393° (2000.0)   Constant of aberration = 20.495 52″
Annual general precession = −50.29″ (2000.0); Precession period $\approx$ 25 800 a
Escape speed from Earth = 11.2 km/s   Mean orbital speed = 29.786 km/s
Escape speed at 1 au from Sun = 42.1 km/s (= $\sqrt{2}$ × orbital speed)

SUN

Mass = 1.9891×10^{30} kg   Radius = 696 265 km   Eff. Temp. $\approx$ 5780 K
Output: Power = 3.85×10^{26} W, $M_{\mathrm{bol}} = 4.79$
Luminous intensity = 2.84×10^{27} cd, $M_{\mathrm{v}} = 4.82$
At 1 au outside Earth's atmosphere:
Energy flux = 1.37 kW/m^2, $m_{\mathrm{bol}} = -26.78$
Illuminance = 1.27×10^5 lx, $m_{\mathrm{v}} = -26.75$
Inclination of the solar equator on the ecliptic of date = 7.25°
Longitude of ascending node of the solar equator on the ecliptic of date = 76°
Period of rotation at equator $\equiv$ 25.38 d (sidereal), 27.2753 d (mean synodic)
Solar wind speed near Earth $\approx$ 450 km/s (travel time, Sun to Earth $\approx$ 4 d)
Solar velocity = 19.4 km/s toward α = 18.07h, δ = +30° (solar apex)
Location in Milky Way Galaxy: $\approx$ 25 kly from centre, $\approx$ 50 ly N of galactic plane, on the inner edge of the Orion arm

MILKY WAY GALAXY

Mass $\approx 10^{12}$ solar masses   Diameter $\approx$ 300 kly (including the galactic halo)
Centre: α = 17h 45.7m, δ = −29°00′; N pole: α = 12h 51m, δ = 27°08′ (2000.0)
Rotation speed at Sun $\approx$ 230 km/s, period $\approx$ 200 Ma
Velocity relative to 3 K background radiation $\approx$ 600 km/s toward $\alpha \approx$ 10h, $\delta \approx$ −20°

CONSTANTS

Speed of light, $c \equiv$ 299 792 458 m/s (This, in effect, defines the metre.)
Planck's constant, $h = 6.626\,07 \times 10^{-34}$ J·s = $4.135\,667 \times 10^{-15}$ eV·s
Gravitational constant, $G = 6.672 \times 10^{-11}$ N·m^2/kg^2
Elementary charge, $e = 1.602\,176 \times 10^{-19}$ C
Constant in Coulomb's law $\equiv 10^{-7}\,c^2$ (SI units) (This defines the coulomb.)
Avogadro constant, $N_A = 6.022\,142 \times 10^{26}$ kmol^{-1}
Boltzmann constant, $k = 1.380\,65 \times 10^{-23}$ J/K = 8.617×10^{-5} eV/K $\approx$ 1 eV/10^{4}K
Stefan-Boltzmann constant, $\sigma = 5.6704 \times 10^{-8}$ W/(m^{2}K^4)
Wien's Law: $\lambda_m T = 2.8978 \times 10^{-3}$ m·K (per dλ)
Hubble constant, $H = 71 \pm 4$ km/(s·Mpc)   Age of universe = 13.7 ± 0.2 Ga
−273.15 °C (degree Celsius) = 0 K (kelvin) (lowest thermodynamic temperature)
Volume of ideal gas at 0 °C, 101.325 kPa = 22.4140 m^3/kmol
Water: fusion at 0 °C: 0.333 MJ/kg   vapourization at 100 °C: 2.26 MJ/kg
specific heat and density (near 20 °C): 4.18 kJ/(kg·C°) and 1.00 t/m^3

MASS AND ENERGY

Mass is a measure of sluggishness of response to a net force. (SI unit: kg)
Weight (≠ mass) is the force required to support a body. (SI unit: N)
(1 pound-mass* = 0.453 59 kg) (1 pound-force* = 4.4482 N)

1 kilogram (kg) ≡ mass of a platinum-iridium cylinder stored in Paris, France
1 atomic mass unit (u) ≡ 1/12 of the mass of an atom of ^{12}C
= $1.660\,539 \times 10^{-27}$ kg = N_A^{-1} = 931.4940 MeV
1 joule (J) ≡ work done by a force of 1 N acting through a distance of 1 m
≈ the kinetic energy gained by this Handbook in falling freely 0.4 m
1 electron-volt (eV) ≡ the kinetic energy gained by a particle carrying one unit of elementary electrical charge *(e)* in falling through an electrical potential difference of one volt (V)
= $1.602\,176 \times 10^{-19}$ J

Electron mass = $9.109\,38 \times 10^{-31}$ kg = 548.579 91 μu = 0.510 998 9 MeV
Proton mass = $1.672\,622 \times 10^{-27}$ kg = 1.007 276 467 u = 938.2720 MeV
Neutron mass = $1.674\,927 \times 10^{-27}$ kg = 1.008 664 92 u = 939.565 MeV

Some atomic masses: ^{1}H (1.007 825 u) ^{2}H (2.014 102 u) ^{4}He (4.002 603 u)

Thermochemical calorie* (cal) = 4.184 J
1 erg*/s = 10^{-7} J/s = 10^{-7} W
1 BTU*/h = 1054.35 J/h = 0.292 88 W
1 horsepower* = 745.7 W
1 eV per event = 23 060 cal/mol
$C + O_2 \rightarrow CO_2$ + 4.1 eV   4 ^{1}H → ^{4}He + 26.73 MeV

*Indicates deprecated unit; unit on right is preferred.

Highest cosmic-ray energy (carried by protons) ≈ 10^{20} eV
Power output (average) of an adult human ≈ 100 W
1 kg of TNT or milkshake releases 4.2 MJ ≈ 1000 kcal ≈ 1 kWh
Fuel oil: 6.36 GJ/barrel (1 barrel ≡ 42 U.S. gallons = 35.0 Imp. gallons = 159 L)

Relation between rest mass *(m)*, linear momentum *(p)*, total energy *(E)*, kinetic energy *(KE)*, and $\gamma \equiv (1 - v^2/c^2)^{-0.5}$, where *c* is the speed of light and *v* is the speed of the object: $E = \gamma mc^2 = mc^2 + KE = [(mc^2)^2 + (pc)^2]^{0.5}$

MAGNITUDE RELATIONS (See also p. 50.)

Log of light intensity ratio ≡ 0.4 times magnitude difference
Distance modulus *(D)* ≡ apparent magnitude *(m)* – absolute magnitude *(M)*
Log of distance in ly = 0.2*D* + 1.513 435 (neglecting absorption)
Magnitude of sum of magnitudes m_i is equal to $-2.5 \log \Sigma_i 10^{-0.4m_i}$

Moon's apparent visual magnitude at phase angle *P* degrees (0° = full Moon) when at its average distance from Earth: $-12.7 + 0.026\,|P| + (4 \times 10^{-9})P^4$

A light source of apparent visual magnitude *m* provides an illuminance *E* (lux) where $E = 10^{-0.4(m + 13.99)}$ or $m = -13.99 - 2.5 \log E$
A diffuse (matt) surface with albedo *A* subject to illuminance *E* (lux) will have luminance *L* (visual surface brightness): $L = AE \div \pi$ (cd/m^2)
To convert luminance *S* (magnitude/arcsecond^2) to luminance *L* (μcd/m^2): $L = 108.5\, e^{(20.7233 - 0.92104\, S)}$ or $S = (20.7233 + \ln(108.5/L))/0.92104$

DOPPLER RELATIONS FOR LIGHT

α ≡ angle between velocity of source and line from source to observer
$\beta \equiv v/c$ $\gamma \equiv (1 - \beta^2)^{-0.5}$
Frequency: $\nu = \nu_0 \gamma^{-1}(1 - \beta \cos \alpha)^{-1}$ $z \equiv (\lambda - \lambda_0)/\lambda_0 = \gamma(1 - \beta \cos \alpha) - 1$
For $\alpha = \pi$ radians: $z = (1 + \beta)^{0.5}(1 - \beta)^{-0.5} - 1$ ($\approx \beta$ if $\beta << 1$)
$\beta = [(1 + z)^2 - 1][(1 + z)^2 + 1]^{-1}$

OPTICAL WAVELENGTH DATA

Bright-adapted (photopic) visible range ≈ 400 – 750 nm ($L \approx 0.005 - 10^5$ cd/m^2)
Dark-adapted (scotopic) visible range ≈ 400 – 620 nm ($L \approx 1 - 5000$ μcd/m^2)
Wavelength of peak sensitivity of eye: ≈ 555 nm (photopic), 507 nm (scotopic)
Mechanical equivalent of light: 1 lm ≡ 1/683 W at 540 THz (λ ≈ 555 nm)
i.e. 1.46 W/klm (A 60-W incandescent light bulb emits about 1 klm = 1000 lm. Compared to an optimum light source that delivers all its energy as light at 540 THz, a 60-W incandescent light bulb is 1.46/60 ≈ 2.4% efficient.)
Colours (representative wavelength, nm):
violet (420), blue (470), green (530), yellow (580), orange (610), red (660)

Some useful wavelengths (element, spectral designation or colour and/or (Fraunhofer line)):

H Lyman α	121.6 nm	N_2^+ blue†	465.2	Hg yellow	579.1
Ca (K solar)	393.4	Hβ (F solar)*	486.1	Na (D_2 solar)	589.0
Ca (H solar)	396.8	O^{++} green*	495.9	Na (D_1 solar)	589.6
Hg violet	404.7	O^{++} green*	500.7	O red†	630.0
Hδ (h solar)	410.2	Hg green	546.1	He-Ne laser	632.8
Hγ (g solar)	434.0	O yel.-green†	557.7	O red†	636.4
Hg deep blue	435.8	Hg yellow	577.0	Hα (C solar)	656.3

* Strong contributor to the visual light of gaseous nebulae
† Strong auroral lines

ANGULAR RELATIONS

2π radians = 360° $\pi = 3.141\,592\,653\,589\,793\,2\ldots \approx (113 \div 355)^{-1}$
Number of square degrees on a sphere = 41 253

For 360° = 24 h, 15° = 1 h, 15′ = 1 min, 15″= 1 s (Earth turns 360° in 86 164.1 s)

Relations between sidereal time t, right ascension α, hour angle h, declination δ, azimuth A (measured east of north), altitude a, and latitude φ:

$h = t - \alpha$
$\sin a = \sin\delta \sin\phi + \cos h \cos\delta \cos\phi$
$\cos\delta \sin h = -\cos a \sin A$
$\sin\delta = \sin a \sin\phi + \cos a \cos A \cos\phi$
Annual precession in α ≈ 3.0750 + 1.3362 sin α tan δ seconds
Annual precession in δ ≈ 20.043″ cos α
(α must be in degrees)

SOME SI SYMBOLS AND PREFIXES

m	metre	N	newton (kg·m/s^2)	a	atto	10^{-18}
kg	kilogram	J	joule (N·m)	f	femto	10^{-15}
s	second	W	watt (J/s)	p	pico	10^{-12}
min	minute	Pa	pascal (N/m^2)	n	nano	10^{-9}
h	hour	t	tonne (10^3 kg)	μ	micro	10^{-6}
d	day	L	litre (10^{-3} m^3)	m	milli	10^{-3}
a	year	Hz	hertz (s^{-1})	c	centi	10^{-2}
A	ampere	C	coulomb (A·s)	h	hecto	10^2
rad	radian	V	volt (J/C)	k	kilo	10^3
mas	milliarcsecond	Wb	weber (V·s)	M	mega	10^6
sr	steradian	T	tesla (Wb/m^2)	G	giga	10^9
K	kelvin (temperature)	lm	lumen	T	tera	10^{12}
ha	hectare (10^4 m^2)	cd	candela (lm/sr)	P	peta	10^{15}
b	barn (10^{-28} m^2)	lx	lux (lm/m^2)	E	exa	10^{18}

VOYAGES IN OUR SOLAR SYSTEM

BY RANDY ATTWOOD

During the second half of the 20th century, humankind began its reconnaissance of the solar system. Although people have travelled only as far as the Moon, robotic space probes have been sent to all the planets but one—Pluto—plus a few asteroids and comets. Our understanding of the solar neighbourhood is increasing at a tremendous pace as a result of the improving sophistication of these spacecraft.

The following is a list of some of the important firsts in the short history of the exploration of our solar system. Note that all space missions are not recorded, not even all the space firsts. A short list of upcoming missions to watch for is also included.

Year	Name	Significance
1957	*Sputnik 1*	First artificial satellite of Earth (Oct. 4); USSR
1957	*Sputnik 2*	First living being in Earth orbit (a dog named Laika); USSR
1959	*Luna 1*	First to escape Earth's gravity; USSR
1959	*Luna 2*	First to impact on the Moon; USSR
1959	*Luna 3*	First to image the far side of the Moon; USSR
1961	*Vostok 1*	First human in Earth orbit (Yuri Gagarin, Apr. 12); USSR
1962	*Mariner 2*	First to fly by another planet, Venus; USA
1965	*Mariner 4*	First to fly by Mars and take pictures; USA
1966	*Luna 9*	First soft landing on the Moon; USSR
1966	*Venera 3*	First to impact on another planet, Venus; USSR
1966	*Luna 10*	First to orbit the Moon; USSR
1968	*Apollo 8*	First humans to orbit the Moon; USA (Frank Borman, James Lovell, William Anders, Dec. 24)
1969	*Apollo 11*	First humans to land and walk on the Moon; USA (Neil Armstrong, Edwin Aldrin, Jul. 20)
1970	*Venera 7*	First soft landing on another planet, Venus; USSR
1971	*Mariner 9*	First to orbit another planet, Mars; USA
1971	*Mariner 9*	First close views of outer satellites (Phobos, Deimos); USA
1972	*Apollo 17*	Last 2 of 12 men to walk on the Moon; USA
1973	*Pioneer 10*	First to fly by Jupiter, reach solar escape speed; USA
1974	*Mariner 10*	First to fly by and study Mercury; USA
1975	*Venera 9*	First to return surface pictures of Venus; USSR
1976	*Viking 1*	First to softly land on Mars, return pictures; USA
1979	*Voyager 1*	First close-up study of Jupiter and its moons; USA
1979	*Pioneer 11*	First to fly by Saturn; USA
1980	*Voyager 1*	First close-up study of Saturn and its moons; USA
1985	*ICE*	*International Cometary Explorer;* first to study a comet; USA
1986	*Voyager 2*	First close-up study of Uranus and its moons; USA
1986	*Giotto*	First images taken of a comet nucleus, Halley; ESA
1989	*Voyager 2*	First close-up study of Neptune and its moons; USA
1991	*Galileo*	First flyby, close-up photos of an asteroid, 951 Gaspra; USA
1995	*Ulysses*	First flyby above the Sun's south/north poles; ESA
1995	*Galileo*	First probe into Jupiter's atmosphere; USA
2001	*NEAR Shoemaker*	First to orbit and soft land on an asteroid, Eros; USA
2003	*MOST*	First Canadian space telescope launched into Earth orbit
2004	*Mars Rovers*	First long-range surface exploration of Mars; USA
2004	*Stardust*	First collection and return of cometary material, Wild 2; USA
2004	*Cassini*	First to orbit Saturn; USA
2005	*Huygens*	First to land on Titan; USA/ESA
2005	*Deep Impact*	First to impact on and study the interior of a comet, Tempel 1; USA
2010	*Hayabusa*	First asteroid-sample return mission; Japan (Rendezvous completed in 2005, return delayed due to spacecraft problems)
2010	*Dawn**	First spacecraft to orbit an asteroid (Vesta, and Ceres in 2015); USA
2011	*Messenger*	First spacecraft to orbit and study Mercury; USA
2014	*Rosetta*	First to orbit, soft land on a comet; ESA
2015	*New Horizons*	First to fly by Pluto, its moon, Charon, Kuiper Belt Objects (2016–2020); USA

* Mission not yet launched

TABLE OF PRECESSION FOR ADVANCING 50 YEARS

RA for Dec – h m	RA for Dec + h m	Prec in Dec ′	85° m	80° m	75° m	70° m	60° m	50° m	40° m	30° m	20° m	10° m	0° m	Prec in Dec ′	RA for Dec + h m	RA for Dec – h m
			Precession in right ascension for declination in row immediately below													
12 00	0 00	16.7	2.56	2.56	2.56	2.56	2.56	2.56	2.56	2.56	2.56	2.56	2.56	–16.7	12 00	*24 00*
12 30	0 30	16.6	4.22	3.39	3.10	2.96	2.81	2.73	2.68	2.64	2.61	2.59	2.56	–16.6	11 30	*23 30*
13 00	1 00	16.1	5.85	4.20	3.64	3.35	3.06	2.90	2.80	2.73	2.67	2.61	2.56	–16.1	11 00	*23 00*
13 30	1 30	15.4	7.43	4.98	4.15	3.73	3.30	3.07	2.92	2.81	2.72	2.64	2.56	–15.4	10 30	*22 30*
14 00	2 00	14.5	8.92	5.72	4.64	4.09	3.53	3.22	3.03	2.88	2.76	2.66	2.56	–14.5	10 00	*22 00*
14 30	2 30	13.3	10.31	6.41	5.09	4.42	3.73	3.37	3.13	2.95	2.81	2.68	2.56	–13.3	9 30	*21 30*
15 00	3 00	11.8	11.56	7.03	5.50	4.72	3.92	3.50	3.22	3.02	2.85	2.70	2.56	–11.8	9 00	*21 00*
15 30	3 30	10.2	12.66	7.57	5.86	4.99	4.09	3.61	3.30	3.07	2.88	2.72	2.56	–10.2	8 30	*20 30*
16 00	4 00	8.4	13.58	8.03	6.16	5.21	4.23	3.71	3.37	3.12	2.91	2.73	2.56	–8.4	8 00	*20 00*
16 30	4 30	6.4	14.32	8.40	6.40	5.39	4.34	3.79	3.42	3.15	2.94	2.74	2.56	–6.4	7 30	*19 30*
17 00	5 00	4.3	14.85	8.66	6.57	5.52	4.42	3.84	3.46	3.18	2.95	2.75	2.56	–4.3	7 00	*19 00*
17 30	5 30	2.2	15.18	8.82	6.68	5.59	4.47	3.88	3.49	3.20	2.96	2.76	2.56	–2.2	6 30	*18 30*
18 00	6 00	0.0	15.29	8.88	6.72	5.62	4.49	3.89	3.50	3.20	2.97	2.76	2.56	0.0	6 00	*18 00*
0 00	12 00	–16.7	2.56	2.56	2.56	2.56	2.56	2.56	2.56	2.56	2.56	2.56	2.56	16.7	24 00	*12 00*
0 30	12 30	–16.6	0.90	1.74	2.02	2.16	2.31	2.39	2.44	2.48	2.51	2.54	2.56	16.6	23 30	*11 30*
1 00	13 00	–16.1	–0.73	0.93	1.49	1.77	2.06	2.22	2.32	2.39	2.46	2.51	2.56	16.1	23 00	*11 00*
1 30	13 30	–15.4	–2.31	0.14	0.97	1.39	1.82	2.05	2.20	2.31	2.41	2.49	2.56	15.4	22 30	*10 30*
2 00	14 00	–14.5	–3.80	–0.60	0.48	1.03	1.60	1.90	2.09	2.24	2.36	2.46	2.56	14.5	22 00	*10 00*
2 30	14 30	–13.3	–5.19	–1.28	0.03	0.70	1.39	1.75	1.99	2.17	2.31	2.44	2.56	13.3	21 30	*9 30*
3 00	15 00	–11.8	–6.44	–1.90	–0.38	0.40	1.20	1.62	1.90	2.11	2.27	2.42	2.56	11.8	21 00	*9 00*
3 30	15 30	–10.2	–7.54	–2.45	–0.74	0.13	1.03	1.51	1.82	2.05	2.24	2.41	2.56	10.2	20 30	*8 30*
4 00	16 00	–8.4	–8.46	–2.91	–1.04	–0.09	0.89	1.41	1.75	2.00	2.21	2.39	2.56	8.4	20 00	*8 00*
4 30	16 30	–6.4	–9.20	–3.27	–1.28	–0.27	0.78	1.33	1.70	1.97	2.19	2.38	2.56	6.4	19 30	*7 30*
5 00	17 00	–4.3	–9.73	–3.54	–1.45	–0.39	0.70	1.28	1.66	1.94	2.17	2.37	2.56	4.3	19 00	*7 00*
5 30	17 30	–2.2	–10.06	–3.70	–1.56	–0.47	0.65	1.25	1.63	1.92	2.16	2.37	2.56	2.2	18 30	*6 30*
6 00	18 00	0.0	–10.17	–3.75	–1.59	–0.50	0.63	1.23	1.63	1.92	2.16	2.36	2.56	0.0	18 00	*6 00*

If declination is positive, use inner RA scale; *if declination is negative, use outer RA scale and reverse the sign of the precession in declination.* To avoid interpolation in this table, which becomes increasingly inaccurate for large |Dec|, precession formulae may be used (see p. 32).

TIME

TIME AND TIME SCALES

BY ROY BISHOP

Time has been said to be nature's way of keeping everything from happening at once. In 1687, Sir Isaac Newton (1642–1727) perceived time as being separate from and more fundamental than the spinning of changeable planets or the oily mechanisms of clocks: "Absolute, true, and mathematical time, of itself, and from its own nature flows equably without regard to anything external." This is the common sense or intuitive view most people have of time.

Albert Einstein (1879–1955) was the first to understand that time is but an abstraction that does not exist independently of clocks. In his special theory of relativity (1905) Einstein predicted that clocks moving relative to an observer run slower. This is called time dilation or the second-order Doppler effect. For example, relative to a clock fixed beside a road the wristwatch of a person driving past at a speed of 100 km/h loses 0.26 ps per minute (ps = picosecond = 10^{-12} s; see p. 32). A decade later, in his theory of gravitation, the general theory of relativity, Einstein predicted that clocks lower or higher than the observer in a gravitational field run slower or faster, respectively, than the observer's clock. In the case of a lower clock this is called the gravitational redshift. For example, an alarm clock on the floor a metre below your bed loses 3.1 ps per 8-h night relative to a watch on your wrist. These counterintuitive effects are not only real, but in recent years they have found their way into the consumer marketplace in the form of GPS (Global Positioning System) receivers. These handheld units receive signals from orbiting atomic clocks and rely on programs that allow for time dilation and gravitational redshift (see *Physics Today,* May 2002, p. 41). In astronomy the general theory of relativity was mostly ignored until the last few decades of the 20th century, when increasing precision of clocks and advances in theoretical astrophysics and cosmology demanded its use.

As to understanding time, Lord Kelvin (1824–1907) said that you know a physical quantity if you can measure it. Time can indeed be measured, with mind-boggling precision. For those who feel compelled to state "We still don't know what time actually is," perhaps the mystery resides merely in the meaning of this statement.

The essence of time is that isolated material changes occur in invariant ratios one with respect to another. That is, as Sir Hermann Bondi has put it: "Time is that which is manufactured by clocks." Thus, to deal with time, clocks must be devised and units and time scales established. Readers who wish to pursue this topic beyond the brief overview presented here should consult *The Measurement of Time,* by C. Audoin and B. Guinot, Cambridge University Press, 2001, and the *Explanatory Supplement to the Astronomical Almanac,* by P.K. Seidelmann (ed.), University Science Books, 1992. For less-technical descriptions of many aspects of time see *A Matter of Time*, a special edition of *Scientific American* (vol. 16, no. 1, 2006) that includes ten articles from the September 2002 issue of that magazine.

Periodic Time Intervals and Clocks

There are three obvious, natural, periodic time intervals on Earth: the seasonal cycle (year), the cycle of lunar phases (month), and the day–night cycle (day). The cycle of the seasons is called the *tropical year* and contains 365.242 190 days. The cycle of lunar phases is known as the *synodic month* and equals 29.530 589 days. The average day–night (diurnal) cycle is the *mean solar day* and presently contains approximately

86 400.0004 s. Other types of year, month, and day have been defined and are listed along with brief definitions and durations on p. 29.

The problem of accurately subdividing these natural intervals to make time locally available at any moment (i.e. timekeeping) was satisfactorily solved in 1657 by Christiaan Huygens, who invented the first practical pendulum clock. Through successive refinements the pendulum clock reigned supreme for nearly three centuries, until it was surpassed in precision by the quartz oscillator in the 1940s. Within another 20 years the quartz clock was, in turn, superseded by the cesium atomic clock, which, using the technique of *laser cooling* of atomic beams (see *Physics Today,* December 1997, p. 17, February 1998, p. 21, and March 2001, p. 37), today has a precision near 2 in 10^{15} (one second in 16 million years).

Earth's Rotation and Time Scales

Of the three obvious, natural, periodic time intervals on Earth (year, month, and day), the day dominates our lives and determines the various time scales we have created. The day is caused primarily by Earth's rotation on its axis. To count rotations, a reference or fiducial point is required. Four such points are of interest, and three of these are the basis of five time scales:

(1) Earth's rotation relative to the distant stars: Although the distant stars (or better, extragalactic sources) provide a reference frame to determine the "true" period of Earth's rotation (presently about 86 164.0993 s), because of Earth's orbital motion and its rotational precession, this true period is not that of either the solar day or the RA/Dec coordinate grid used to specify astronomical positions. Hence no time scales are based on Earth's true rotational period.

(2) Earth's rotation relative to the equinox: The equator and poles of the RA/Dec celestial coordinate grid are aligned with Earth's mean equator and poles. ("Mean" denotes that small, periodic variations caused by the nutation of Earth's axis have been averaged out. Nutation involves the true pole moving relative to the mean pole with an amplitude of about 9″ and a variety of short periods up to 18.6 years.) Hence the RA/Dec grid slowly shifts relative to the distant stars as Earth's rotation axis precesses, a motion caused primarily by the torques exerted by the Moon and Sun on Earth's equatorial bulge. The gravitational influence of the other planets causes the plane of the ecliptic also to precess, although this *planetary precession* is far smaller than the *lunisolar precession* of the mean equator. The sum of these two precessions is called *general precession.* General precession causes the zero point of right ascension (the "Greenwich of the skies," the vernal equinox, or "first point of Aries") to drift westward (retrograde) along the ecliptic about 50″ per year. As a result, Earth's rotation period relative to the equinox (called the *mean sidereal day,* currently 86 164.0909 s) is 8.4 ms shorter than the time for one rotation (see p. 29). At any longitude on Earth the RA of a star on the meridian (corrected for nutation) is the ***Local Mean Sidereal Time*** **(LMST)** at that instant. At the Greenwich meridian (0° longitude) this is called ***Greenwich Mean Sidereal Time*** **(GMST).** LMST may be used to set a telescope on an object of known right ascension. The hour angle of the object equals the sidereal time less the right ascension. LMST may be available from a sidereal clock, or it can be calculated as explained in the middle of p. 41. Because Earth makes one more rotation with respect to the other stars than it does with respect to the Sun during a year, sidereal time gains relative to time scales linked to the Sun (see below) by about 3 min 56 s per day, or 2 h per month.

(3) Earth's rotation relative to the real Sun: A common misconception is that the Sun is highest in the sky and lies on the local north–south meridian at 12:00 noon. However, time based on the position of the Sun in the sky, known as local ***apparent solar***

time or *sundial time,* can differ by up to an hour or more from civil time (the time that we normally use). There are two reasons for this discrepancy. One reason is that the Sun's eastward annual apparent motion around the sky is far from uniform both because of Earth's elliptical orbit and because of the inclination of the celestial equator to the ecliptic. Thus apparent solar time does not have a uniform rate (see the next paragraph). The second reason for the difference between sundial time and civil time is addressed in the penultimate paragraph of this article.

(4) Earth's rotation relative to the mean Sun: If the Sun is replaced by a fictitious mean sun moving uniformly along the celestial equator, Earth's rotation relative to this mean sun defines ***Local Mean (solar) Time*** **(LMT).** Apparent solar time can differ by up to 16 min from LMT depending upon the time of year (see the diagram on p. 158). Small, periodic shifts of Earth's crust relative to the axis of rotation *(polar motion)* affect astronomical time determinations through the resulting east–west shift in the meridian at latitudes away from the equator. LMT at the Greenwich meridian (0° longitude) when corrected for this polar motion is called ***Universal Time*** **(UT1,** or often simply **UT).** UT1 is determined using very-long-baseline interferometry, satellite laser-ranging data, lunar laser-ranging data, and GPS data (via the International GPS Service).

All the above mean time scales (LMST, GMST, LMT, and UT1), being based upon Earth's rotation, are only as uniform as this rotation. By the mid-19th century discrepancies between theory and the observed motion of the Moon indicated that, over the long term, Earth's rotation is slowing down. However, not until clocks became better timekeepers than the spinning Earth (c. 1940, when crystal-controlled clocks exceeded precisions of 1 in 10^{10}) was it realized how complex is the variable rotation of our planet. There are (i) long-, (ii) medium-, and (iii) short-term accelerations:

(i) Over many centuries there is a *secular* slowing caused by tidal friction of about 8 parts in 10^{13} per day (i.e. the day becomes one second longer about every 40 000 years).

(ii) Over a few decades there are *random* accelerations (positive and negative), apparently caused by core–mantle interactions and possibly by changes in ocean currents. These are about 10 times larger than the tidal deceleration and thus completely obscure the latter effect over time intervals of less than a century or so.

(iii) The largest accelerations in Earth's rotation rate are short-term ones: *periodic components* are associated mainly with lunar-induced tides (over two-week and monthly intervals) and seasonal meteorological factors (over semiannual and annual intervals); *nonperiodic* (chaotic) high-frequency variations are associated mainly with the global atmospheric wind and pressure distributions. These short-term accelerations are typically one or two orders of magnitude larger again than the random, decade fluctuations on which they are superimposed (see the article by John Wahr in the June 1986 issue of *Sky & Telescope,* p. 545).

Uniform Time Scales

(1) Based on orbital motion: Although Earth's axial rotation is not sufficiently predictable to serve as a precise clock, the orbital motions of our Moon, Earth, and the other planets are predictable to high accuracy. Through the dynamical equations describing these motions plus extended astronomical observations, a uniform time scale can be derived. Such a scale, known as *Ephemeris Time* (ET), was for several years (1954–1984) the basis of astronomical ephemerides. The ephemeris second, defined as a certain fraction of the tropical year 1900.0, was the fundamental unit of time. Early in the 20th century the UT1 and ET scales coincided, but because Earth's rotation rate has been generally slower than the ET rate, by 1984 UT1 was 54 s behind ET and was losing about half a second per year. From 1985 until 1999 Earth's rotation rate was fairly steady, losing about 0.7 s per year relative to ET (actually TT, see three paragraphs ahead). Since 1999 the rotation rate has been increasing (part of the random decade fluctuations), and the annual loss is presently less than 0.2 s.

(2) Based on atomic motion: The quantum nature of matter gives atoms a permanence and stability that macroscopic objects such as quartz crystals, planets, and pendulums do not possess. The idea of an atomic clock was proposed by the American physicist Isidor Rabi in 1945. In 1967, the second was given an atomic definition: 9 192 631 770 periods of the radiation involved in the transition between the two hyperfine levels of the ground state of the cesium 133 atom. This is known as the SI (for Système International) second (abbreviation s, *not* sec). The number 9 192 631 770 was chosen so that on the rotating geoid (i.e. for clocks fixed on Earth at mean sea level), the SI second is identical to the older ET second to within the precision of measurement.

The previous sentence implies that clocks on the geoid run at the same rate. What about Earth's rotation? Clocks nearer the equator move faster, so does time dilation not make them run slower relative to clocks at higher latitudes? Ignoring the Moon and Sun, if Earth did not rotate and had an isotropic density distribution, its geoid (mean sea-level surface) would be spherical, and clocks fixed on this geoid would, by symmetry, all run at the same rate (they would all be at rest and have similar positions in Earth's gravitational field). For a rotating Earth the equatorial bulge is such that clocks away from the poles are just enough higher in Earth's gravitational field that the resulting gravitational blueshift exactly cancels the time dilation associated with their rotational speed. This simple, elegant, and convenient result is a consequence of Einstein's principle of equivalence: A body at rest in a gravitational field is equivalent to a body being accelerated in a field-free space. As described by general relativity, gravitation is geometry, not a force, which is why no one has ever felt a force of gravity. The only force acting on Earth-based clocks, or on any stationary Earth-based objects, is the electromagnetic contact force supporting them. Any two nearby clocks located on the same surface perpendicular to the direction of this contact force (the plumb-bob direction) will have identical rates. Thus *all* clocks on the geoid run at the same rate. Whether or not the planet beneath is rotating is immaterial.

Because of several difficulties surrounding both the original concept of ET and its determination, and because atomic clocks had become readily available, in 1984 ET was abandoned in favour of *Terrestrial Dynamical Time* (TDT). The unit of TDT was the SI second on the rotating geoid, and its scale was chosen to agree with the 1984 ET scale. In 1991, TDT was renamed simply ***Terrestrial Time*** **(TT).** Because of uncertainties surrounding the realization of the geoid (the geoid would coincide with Earth's sea surface *if* the waters of the oceans were homogeneous and at rest), in 2000 TT was redefined in terms of TCG (see below). The unit of TT is very close to the SI second on the rotating geoid. TT is the time reference for apparent geocentric ephemerides, and it is realized via TAI.

International Atomic Time (**TAI** = Temps Atomique International) is based on a weighted average of atomic clocks in many countries and presently is the most precise *achievable* time scale. Not even atomic clocks are perfect timekeepers, so TAI shifts unpredictably relative to the TT rate by a few microseconds over several years. TAI was arbitrarily set to agree with UT1 at the beginning of 1958, which led to the definition that TT be exactly 32.184 s ahead of TAI on 1977 Jan. 1.0 TAI. This ensured continuity of TT with ET.

In 1991, when the general theory of relativity was explicitly adopted as the theoretical background for spacetime reference frames, two new time scales were introduced: ***Geocentric Coordinate Time*** (**TCG**) and ***Barycentric Coordinate Time*** (**TCB**) for nonrotating coordinate frames with origins located at the centres of mass of Earth and of the solar system, respectively. TCG is not influenced by Earth's gravitation, and TCB is not influenced by *any* gravitational fields of the solar system. These coordinate time scales provide a means to unambiguously date events. TCG is used for analyzing the motions of Earth-orbiting satellites, and TCB is used to study planet and space probe motions. Both TCG and TCB use the SI second.

The gravitational redshift causes TT to lose 22 ms per year relative to TCG (clocks on Earth are deep within Earth's gravitational well). In turn, TCG loses about 467 ms per year relative to TCB because of time dilation and gravitational redshift (the geocentric coordinate frame orbits with Earth deep within the Sun's gravitational well). Thus TCB gains nearly half a second per year relative to TT. The origins of TCG and TCB were chosen so that TCG, TCB, and TT had the same reading at Earth's centre of mass on 1977 Jan. 1.0 (TAI), all three scales being set to be exactly 32.184 s ahead of TAI at that point in spacetime. TCB and TCG (and hence TT) are realized via TAI.

Another time scale, Barycentric Dynamical Time (TDB), was introduced in 1976 when it became necessary to acknowledge relativistic effects but before the general theory of relativity was accepted by astronomers. It is similar to TCB except its scale unit was adjusted to approximate TT. TDB is a needlessly complex time scale; however, because it has been used extensively (e.g. by the Jet Propulsion Laboratory for ephemerides used in planetary exploration), it was not totally abandoned when TCB was introduced in 1991.

(3) Based on pulsars: Millisecond radio pulsars (old, rapidly spinning neutron stars) display extraordinary stability in their rotation. Their stability, after allowing for spin-down, is almost as good as the best atomic clocks. However, uncertainties in predicting the spin-down rate of a pulsar and in Earth's motion relative to a pulsar, the elaborate equipment needed to observe a pulsar, and the complex data analysis required all make it unlikely that a pulsar will ever replace cesium clocks as the basis for a uniform time scale. Like quartz crystals, planets, and pendulums, pulsars do not possess the permanence and stability of atoms.

Uniform Time Scales with Steps (to track the mean Sun)

Closely related to UT1 (which follows Earth's variable rotation relative to the mean Sun) is ***Coordinated Universal Time* (UTC),** introduced in its present form in 1972. UTC, the basis of the world system of civil time, runs at the TAI rate and is offset an integral number of seconds from TAI so that it approximates UT1. When required (usually on Jun. 30 or Dec. 31), "leap seconds" are inserted into (or, if necessary, deleted from) UTC so that the difference UT1 − UTC = ΔUT1 does not exceed ±0.9 s. The most recent leap second occurred on 2005 December 31 (the previous one occurred seven years earlier), making the difference TAI − UTC = ΔAT = 33 s. Hence TT − UTC = 33 s + 32.184 s = 65.184 s exactly during 2006, 2007 and likely for the following few years (see the diagram overleaf). UTC is readily available via radio time signals and GPS receivers. (Note: The term *Greenwich Mean Time* (GMT) over the years has had three different meanings: the same as UT1, UTC, and mean solar time at the Greenwich meridian with 0 h corresponding to noon. To avoid confusion, the term *Greenwich Mean Time* should not be used.)

Anyone in North America can keep track of Earth's varying rotation by listening to the CHU or WWV radio time signals in which is coded the difference ΔUT1 − (UT1 − UTC) (see TIME SIGNALS on p. 41). Also, see the Web site tf.nist.gov/pubs/bulletin/leapsecond.htm. It is interesting to record ΔUT1 about once a month and use these data to make a graphical display of (TT − UT1) as a function of time over several years. Note that during 2007, TT − UT1 = 65.184 − (UT1 − UTC).

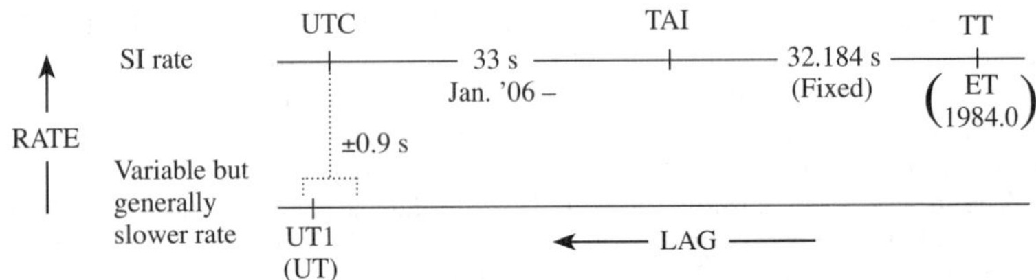

This diagram displays the rate and scale relations between Earth-based time scales that run at or near the SI rate at sea level and that are not longitude dependent.

Local Mean (solar) Time (LMT) would suffice for the inhabitants of an isolated village, but with the advent in the 19th century of rapid travel and communication (railways, steamships, and the telegraph), it became essential that clocks over a range of longitudes indicate the same time. To keep these clocks reasonably in phase with the day–night cycle and yet avoid the inconvenience to travellers of a local time that varies continuously with longitude, in 1884 Earth was divided into 24 ***Standard Time*** zones, adjacent zones generally differing by one hour and each ideally 15° wide (see the time-zone map on p. 43). All clocks within the same zone read the same time. The Canadian railway surveyor and construction engineer Sir Sandford Fleming (1827–1915) was instrumental in establishing this system of standard time zones. The zero zone is centred on the Greenwich meridian (longitude 0°), and, since 1972, standard time in that zone is UTC. Thus the world system of civil time is based on UTC and includes the "leap seconds," which keep UTC near UT1. Depending upon an observer's location within his or her standard time zone, standard time may differ by up to an hour or so from LMT (see the third paragraph on p. 164). This is the second reason why the Sun seldom, if ever, is on the observer's meridian at 12:00 noon, standard time.

Humans generally have an awake/asleep cycle that is delayed by a few hours relative to the day/night cycle. Consequently in higher latitudes during the spring and summer when the Sun rises before humans do, more energy is needed for lighting in the evening than would be the case if the two cycles coincided. To shift the lifestyles of their citizens more in phase with the day/night cycle many countries adopt ***Daylight Saving Time,*** advancing clocks by one hour during the spring and summer (A better term would be *Energy Saving Time* because it is energy that is being saved, not daylight). With the shorter daylight of autumn and winter, the evening energy saving associated with advancing clocks by one hour is cancelled by the accompanying need for more lighting in the morning. In tropical regions the duration of daylight varies little with the seasons so there is no reason to use Daylight Saving Time during part of the year.

For most of Canada and the United States,[(1)] beginning in 2007 the duration of Daylight Saving Time is being increased by four weeks. Clocks will be advanced by one hour at 2:00 local time on the second Sunday in March, and return to standard time at 2:00 local time on the first Sunday in November: "spring ahead, fall back."

[(1)] Some regions, such as Saskatchewan, southeastern British Columbia, Hawaii, and most of Arizona, do not observe Daylight Saving Time. For more information see webexhibits.org/daylightsaving.

TIME SIGNALS

National time services distribute Coordinated Universal Time (UTC). UTC is coordinated through the Bureau International des Poids et Mesures (BIPM) in Sèvres, France so that most time services are synchronized to a tenth of a millisecond. Radio time signals available in North America include:

CHU Ottawa, Ontario, Canada 3.330, 7.335, 14.670 MHz
WWV Fort Collins, Colorado, USA 2.5, 5, 10, 15, 20 MHz

For CHU, each minute starts at the *beginning* of the tone following the voice announcement, the tone for the 29th second is omitted, and the tones for seconds 31 through 39 have a different sound from the others.

The difference ΔUT1 = UT1 – UTC to the nearest tenth of a second is coded in the signals. If UT1 is ahead of UTC, second markers beginning at the 1-second mark of each minute are doubled, the number of doubled markers indicating the number of tenths of a second UT1 is ahead of UTC. If UT1 is behind UTC, the doubled markers begin at the 9-second point.

Time signals are also available by telephone from the National Research Council in Ottawa. Within Canada, call (800) 363-5409; outside Canada, call (613) 745-1576. See also www.boulder.nist.gov/timefreq for an Internet time service.

MEAN SIDEREAL TIME, 2007

The following is the Greenwich Mean Sidereal Time (GMST) in hours on day 0 at 0h UT of each month ("day 0" is the last day of the previous month):

Jan. 6.6188	Apr. 12.5327	Jul. 18.5123	Oct. 0.5576
Feb. 8.6558	May 14.5040	Aug. 20.5493	Nov. 2.5946
Mar. 10.4957	Jun. 16.5410	Sep. 22.5863	Dec. 4.5659

GMST (in hours) at hour t UT on day d of the month =
GMST at 0h UT on day 0 + $0.065710\,d + 1.002738\,t$
LMST (Local Mean Sidereal Time) = GMST – west longitude (or + east longitude)

LMST computed by this method is accurate to ±0.2 s provided t is stated to ±0.1 s or better and the observer's longitude is known to ±1″. Note that t must be expressed in decimal hours UT and longitude in hours, not degrees. Also, to achieve ±0.1 s accuracy in t, the correction ΔUT1 must be applied to UTC. See TIME SIGNALS above.

JULIAN DATE (JD), 2007

The Julian Date (JD) is commonly used by astronomers to refer to the time of astronomical events, because it avoids some of the annoying complexities of the civil calendar. Julian Date 0.0 was the instant of Greenwich mean noon on 4713 Jan. 1 BC (see "The Origin of the Julian Day System" by G. Moyer, *Sky & Telescope,* April 1981).

The Julian day **commences at noon** (12h) UT. To find the Julian Date at any time during 2007, determine the day of the month and time at the Greenwich meridian, convert this to a decimal day, and add it to one of the following numbers according to the month (these numbers are the Julian Dates for 0h UT on the 0th day of each month):

Jan. ... 245 4100.5	Apr. ..245 4190.5	Jul. 245 4281.5	Oct. ...245 4373.5
Feb. ...245 4131.5	May ..245 4220.5	Aug. ..245 4312.5	Nov. ..245 4404.5
Mar. ..245 4159.5	Jun. ...245 4251.5	Sep. ...245 4343.5	Dec. ..245 4434.5

For example, 21:36 EDT on May 18 = 1:36 UT on May 19 = May 19.07 UT = 245 4220.5 + 19.07 = JD 245 4239.57.

The Julian Dates for 0h UT Jan. 0 for the three previous years are 245 0000.5 plus: 3004 (2004), 3370 (2005), and 3735 (2006).

STANDARD TIME ZONES

The map at the right shows the world system of standard time zones. It was prepared and provided by Her Majesty's Nautical Almanac Office. Over the open oceans, the time zones are uniformly spaced and are bounded by lines of longitude 15° apart. In populated regions, political and other considerations have considerably modified the ideal geometry.

As Earth rotates with sunlight shining from one side, at some line of longitude the day of the week must jump discontinuously ahead by one day (otherwise, Monday would be followed by Monday!). The line chosen for this jump is in the relatively unpopulated central part of the Pacific Ocean and approximates longitude 180°. It is called the International Date Line. A person travelling westward across this line has to advance the calendar date by one day, while an eastward-bound traveller moves back one day on the calendar.

The standard time zones are generally designated by letters of the alphabet. The zero time zone, centred on the longitude 0° meridian passing through the Airy Transit Circle at the Old Royal Observatory in Greenwich, England, is denoted Z. Standard time within this zone is Coordinated Universal Time (UTC). Zones A, B, C,…, M (J excluded), run eastward at one-hour intervals to the International Date Line, while zones N, O, P,…, Y run westward to the same boundary. Zones M and Y are only one-half hour wide. Also, as indicated on the map, there are several partial zones that are one-half hour different from the adjacent main zones.

In North America there are six standard time zones and one partial zone. In terms of their name (and letter designation, hours behind the Greenwich zone, and the west longitude of the reference or standard meridian), these are:

(1)	Newfoundland	(P*,	3 h 30 min,	52.5°)
(2)	Atlantic	(Q,	4 h,	60°)
(3)	Eastern	(R,	5 h,	75°)
(4)	Central	(S,	6 h,	90°)
(5)	Mountain	(T,	7 h,	105°)
(6)	Pacific	(U,	8 h,	120°)
(7)	Alaska	(V,	9 h,	135°)

Note: Caution is advised when relying on the time-zone information given in this map. The zones are drawn based on the best information available as of June 2005 and are subject to change. Also, local jurisdictions, especially those near depicted zone boundaries, often adopt a different time. For current official Canadian and U.S. time zones visit inms-ienm.nrc-cnrc.gc.ca/en/time_services/time_services_e.php and www.time.gov respectively.

WORLD MAP OF TIME ZONES

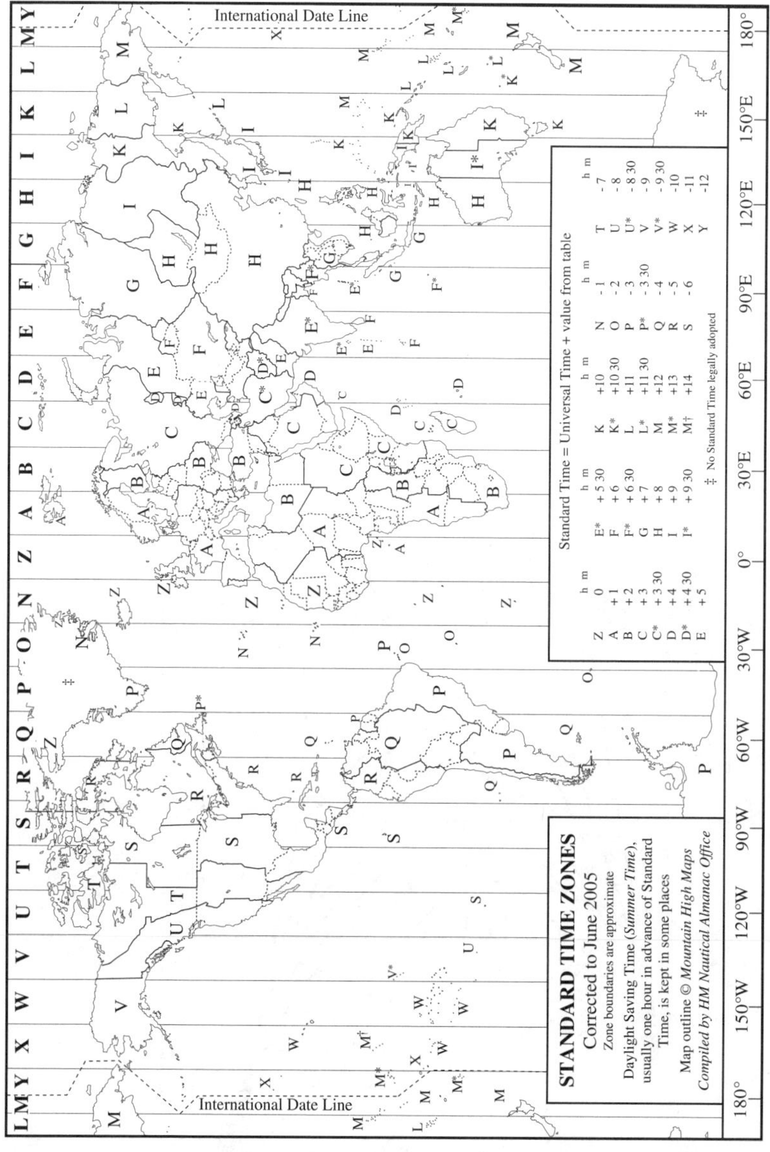

	h m		h m		h m		h m		h m
Z	0	E*	+5 30	K	+10	N	-1	T	-7
A	+1	F	+6	K*	+10 30	O	-2	U	-8
B	+2	F*	+6 30	L	+11	P	-3	U*	-8 30
C	+3	G	+7	L*	+11 30	P*	-3 30	V	-9
C*	+3 30	H	+8	M	+12	Q	-4	V*	-9 30
D	+4	I	+9	M*	+13	R	-5	W	-10
D*	+4 30	I*	+9 30	M†	+14	S	-6	X	-11
E	+5							Y	-12

‡ No Standard Time legally adopted

ASTRONOMICAL TWILIGHT AND SIDEREAL TIME

By Randall Brooks

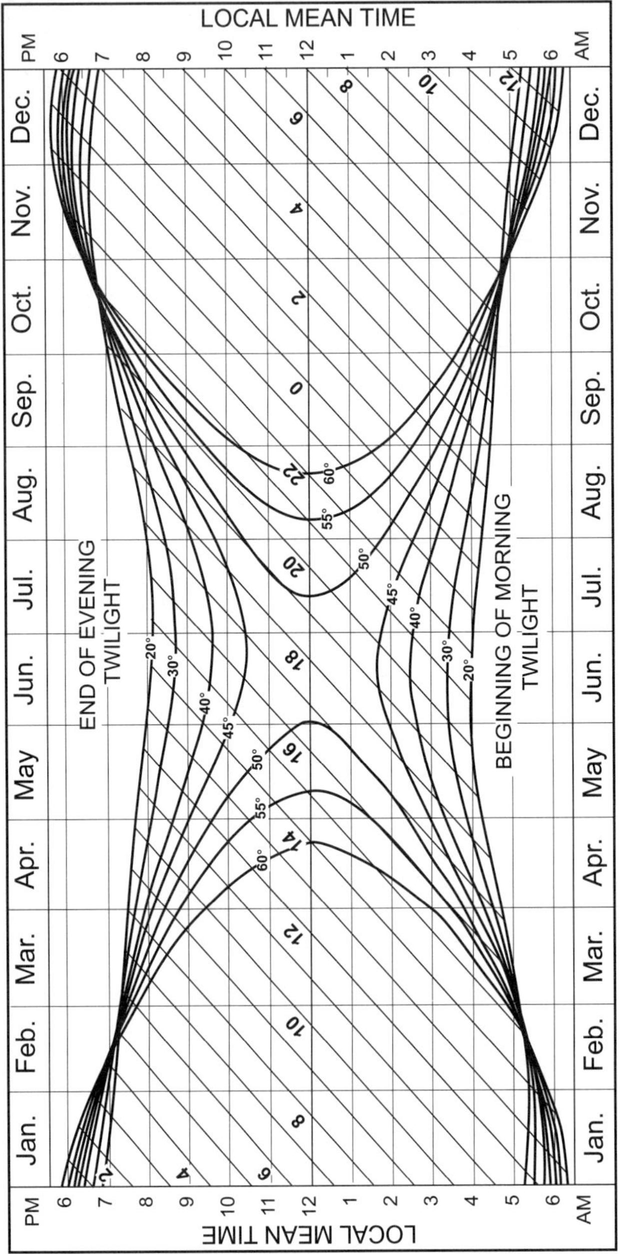

The diagram gives for any day of the year: **(1)** *the local mean time (LMT) of the end and beginning of astronomical twilight at seven specified northern latitudes (curved lines);* **(2)** *the local mean sidereal time (LMST = right ascension at the observer's meridian) as a function of LMT (diagonal lines).*

OPTICS AND OBSERVING

TELESCOPE PARAMETERS

Equations

Objective: f_o = focal length
D = diameter
FR = focal ratio

Eyepiece: f_e = focal length
d_f = diameter of field stop
θ_p = apparent angular field

Whole Instrument: M = angular magnification
d_p = diameter of exit pupil
θ_c = actual angular field

$M = f_o/f_e = D/d_p \approx \theta_p/\theta_c$ FR $= f_o/D$ $d_f{}^* = f_o\theta_c \approx f_e\theta_p$

*(θ_c and θ_p must be expressed in radians.)

Performance

D is assumed to be expressed in millimetres.

Light Grasp (LG) is the ratio of the light flux intercepted by a telescope's objective lens or mirror to that intercepted by a human eye having a 7-mm-diameter entrance pupil.

Limiting Visual Magnitude $m \approx 2.7 + 5 \log D$, assuming transparent, dark-sky conditions and magnification $M \geq 1D$. (See *Sky & Telescope, 45,* 401, 1973; *77,* 332, 1989; *78,* 522, 1989).

Smallest Resolvable Angle $\alpha \approx 116/D$ seconds of arc (Dawes's limit). However, atmospheric conditions seldom permit values less than 0.5″.

Useful Magnification Range ≈ 0.2D to 2D. The lower limit (0.2D) guarantees that, for most observers, all the light exiting a telescope can reach the retina. (The reciprocal of the coefficient to D is the diameter (in mm) of the telescope's exit pupil. Also, see the next section concerning exit pupils and magnification.) The upper limit (2D) is determined by the wave nature of light and the optical limitations of the eye, although atmospheric turbulence usually limits the maximum magnification to 400× or less. For examination of double stars, detection of faint stars, and studying structure in bright nebulae, magnifications of up to 3D are sometimes useful.

Values for some common apertures are:

D (mm):	60	100	125	150	200	250	330	444
LG:	73	200	320	460	820	1300	2200	4000
m:	11.6	12.7	13.2	13.6	14.2	14.7	15.3	15.9
α:	1.93″	1.16″	0.93″	0.77″	0.58″	0.46″	0.35″	0.26″
0.2D:	12×	20×	25×	30×	40×	50×	66×	89×
2D:	120×	200×	250×	300×	400×	500×	660×	890×

TELESCOPE EXIT PUPILS

BY ROY BISHOP

The performance of a visual telescope is constrained by Earth's atmosphere, the wave aspect of light, the design of the telescope and imperfections in its optical system, and the properties of the human visual system. Telescope and eye meet at the *exit pupil* of the telescope, which is the image of the telescope's objective lens or mirror formed by its eyepiece. When a telescope is pointed at a bright area, such as the daytime sky, the exit pupil appears as a small disk of light hovering in the space just behind the eyepiece. (Insert a small piece of paper in this vicinity to prove that this disk of light *really is* located behind the eyepiece.) Since the exit pupil is the narrowest point in the beam of light emerging from the telescope, it is here that the observer's eye must be located to make optimum use of the light passing through the telescope.

The diagram on p. 48 may be used to display the relation between the diameter of the exit pupil (d_p) of a telescope and the focal lengths (f_e) of various eyepieces. Both d_p and f_e are expressed in millimetres. The numbered scale around the upper right-hand corner of the diagram indicates the focal ratio (FR) of the objective lens or mirror of the telescope. (The FR equals the focal length of the objective divided by its diameter; see p. 45.) To prepare the diagram for a particular telescope, locate the FR of the telescope's objective on the FR scale, and draw a straight diagonal line from there to the origin (the lower left-hand corner). The diagram provides a visual display of the standard relation $d_p = f_e/\text{FR}$. One can see at a glance what range of eyepiece focal lengths is suitable for a particular telescope. Concerning the "AGE" scale on the diagram, see the section Very Low (RFT) Magnifications below.

To determine, for example, the eyepiece focal length required to produce a 3-mm exit pupil on a certain telescope, locate $d_p = 3$ on the ordinate, run horizontally across to the diagonal line corresponding to the FR of that telescope, and from there drop vertically downward to the abscissa to find f_e. This procedure may, of course, be reversed: for a given f_e, find the corresponding d_p.

Magnification Ranges

The ranges H, M, L, and RFT blocked off along the ordinate of the diagram break the d_p scale into four sections, starting at 0.5 mm and increasing by factors of 2. Although this sectioning is somewhat arbitrary, it does correspond closely to what are usually considered to be the high (H), medium (M), low (L), and "richest-field telescope" (RFT) magnification ranges of any visual telescope—and the associated d_p ranges are easy to remember. Note that these magnification ranges are defined by d_p, not by the numerical value of the magnification; for example, a magnification of 100× is "high" for a telescope of aperture $D = 70$ mm, "medium" for $D = 150$ mm, "low" for $D = 300$ mm, "very low (RFT)" for $D = 600$ mm, and "ultra-low" for D larger than 0.8 m.

High Magnifications: In the case of the Moon, the planets, and all but the dimmest stars, the highest useful magnification is the point at which blurring due to diffraction (caused by the wave nature of light) becomes noticeable. This corresponds approximately to $d_p = 0.5$ mm, assuming good optics and negligible atmospheric turbulence (i.e. excellent "seeing"). Higher magnifications will not reveal any more detail in these images and will cause reductions in four desirable features: sharpness, brightness, field of view, and eye relief (the space between the eye and eyepiece). However, for double stars and for some objects requiring the use of averted vision (e.g. faint stars) very high magnifications ($d_p < 0.5$ mm) can sometimes be used to advantage.

Medium Magnifications: A problem with high magnifications is that exit-pupil diameters of about 1 mm and smaller cause "floaters" (mobile debris in the vitreous humour of the eye in front of the retina) to interfere with vision. This problem increases with the age of the observer and with decreasing d_p. To avoid the distraction of floaters, an observer might choose to keep exit-pupil diameters no smaller than 1.5 mm (i.e. in the "medium" magnification range). For this lower limit the diagram indicates a minimum eyepiece focal length of, for example, 7 mm for a FR = 4.5 telescope, 15 mm for a FR = 10 telescope, and 24 mm for a FR = 16 telescope. With this restriction, to achieve a magnification of 250× for observing planets, a telescope would need an aperture of at least $D = M \times d_p = 250 \times 1.5 = 375$ mm. Hence, in addition to providing more light and greater resolution, a large-aperture telescope makes floaters less noticeable and magnifications in the "high" range less necessary.

With magnifications greater than very low (RFT) magnifications and also possibly greater than low magnifications, structure in dim, extended objects, such as galaxies and bright and dark nebulae, will be more easily seen. To see such objects, observers use averted vision, which places the image on the peripheral retina, which is composed primarily of the very sensitive "rod" photoreceptor cells. However, the number of rod cells far exceeds the number of nerve axons available to carry the signals to the visual centres in the brain. To accommodate this limitation and to cope with spontaneous thermal noise in the rod cells, the cells are grouped into detector units of various sizes (analogous to binning of pixels in a CCD chip). Because of the thermal noise, only those signals triggered by almost simultaneous photon hits in several rod cells are allowed to produce a conscious sensation. Thus in very dim light only large retinal detector units receive enough photon hits to respond. As a consequence, our ability to see detail is greatly reduced in dim light. Hence extra magnification helps to reveal structure in galaxies and nebulae.

Low Magnifications: Low magnifications have several advantages over certain other magnification ranges:

(1) For most observers an exit-pupil diameter between 2 mm and 4 mm results in the sharpest optical image because the combined influence of optical aberrations in the eye of the observer (which increase with increasing d_p) and blurring due to diffraction (which decreases with increasing d_p) is at a minimum. Assuming, for example, that the optimum d_p for a "typical observer" is 2.5 mm, then to realize this and achieve a magnification of 250× for observing planets, a telescope needs an aperture of $D = M \times d_p = 250 \times 2.5 = 625$ mm. Once again, the superiority of a large telescope (by amateur standards) is apparent. Another example: the reason for the crisp images provided by Canon's image-stabilized binoculars is that their d_p is in the "low magnification" range, and their optical quality is up to the challenge.

(2) Low magnifications provide greater luminance than high or medium magnifications, enabling the eye to discern contrast variations over a wider range of spatial frequencies.

(3) Viewing is more comfortable than with very low (RFT) magnifications, since the observer can move a bit (move the head and/or scan the field) without cutting into the light beam and dimming the image. As mentioned below, ultra-low magnifications have the same advantage, but light is wasted.

(4) Light entering near the edge of the pupil of the dark-adapted eye is not as effective in stimulating the rod cells in the retina—the "scotopic Stiles-Crawford effect" (see VanLoo and Enoch, *Vision Research, 15* (1975), p. 1005,). Thus low magnifications make more effective use of the light than very low (RFT) magnifications.

(5) Low magnifications provide a darker sky background than very low (RFT) magnifications, producing views that some observers consider to be aesthetically more pleasing.

(text continues on p. 49)

EXIT-PUPILS DIAGRAM

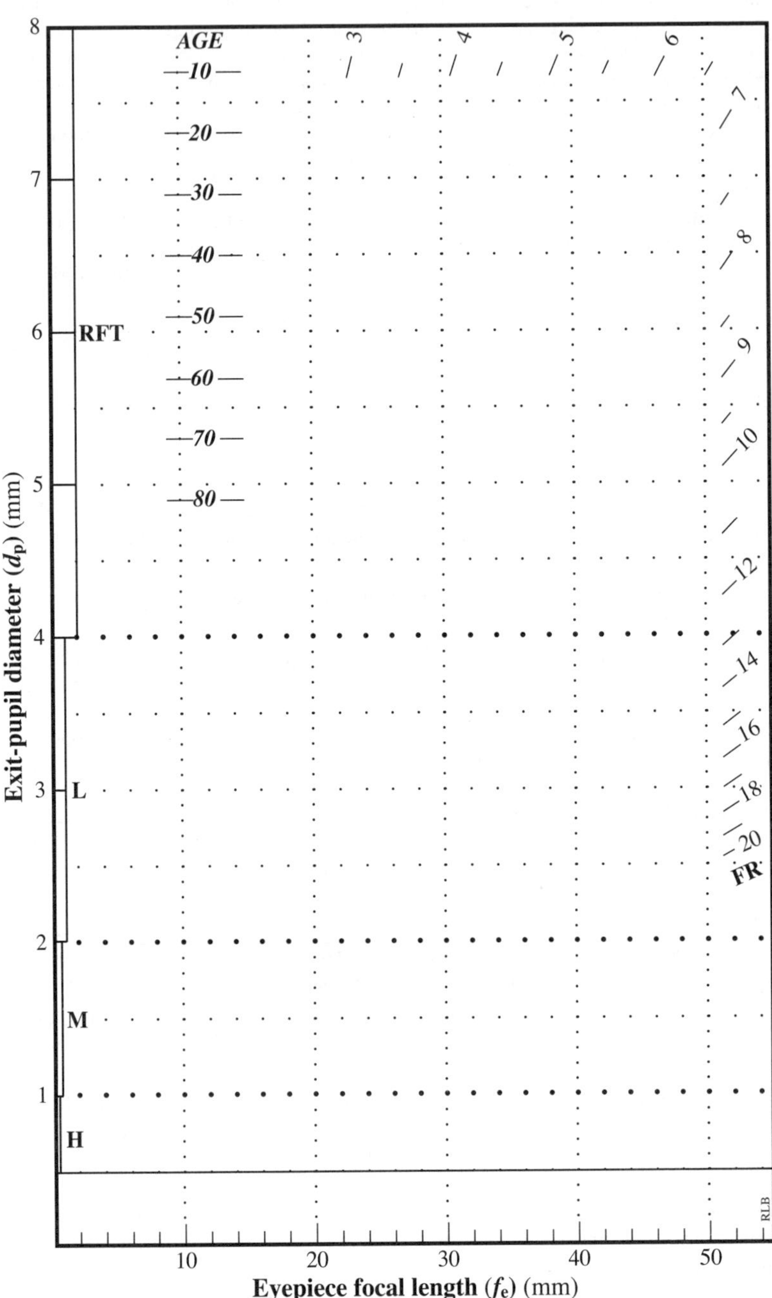

Very Low (RFT) Magnifications: Magnifications in the RFT range are useful because they yield wide fields of view, the brightest (greatest luminance) images of extended objects, and for common telescope apertures, the most stars visible in one view (hence the term *richest field*). The lowest magnification that still makes use of the full aperture of a telescope is determined by the point at which the diameter of the telescope's exit pupil matches the diameter of the *entrance pupil* of the observer's eye.

For the dark-adapted eye, the entrance-pupil diameter seldom equals the often-quoted figure of 7 mm, but depends, among other things, upon the age of the observer as indicated by the scale in the upper-left portion of the diagram (see Kadlecová et al., *Nature, 182* (1958), p. 1520; *Sky & Telescope,* May 1992, p. 502). Note that this scale indicates *average* values; the maximum diameter of the entrance pupil of the eye of any *one* individual may differ by up to a millimetre from these values. A horizontal line should be drawn across the diagram corresponding to the maximum diameter of one's own entrance pupil. This line will be an upper bound on d_p in the same sense that the line at $d_p = 0.5$ mm is a lower bound. Note that in daylight, the entrance pupil of the eye has a diameter in the range of 2 mm to 4 mm. Thus for daylight use of telescopes, the upper bound on d_p will be correspondingly reduced.

Ultra-Low Magnifications: If a d_p value larger than the entrance pupil of the eye is used, the iris of the observer's eye will cut off some of the light passing through the telescope to the retina; that is, the iris will have become the light-limiting aperture *(aperture stop)* of the system rather than the edge of the telescope's objective. In this case, the cornea of the eye together with the lenses of the telescope's eyepiece form an image of the observer's iris at the objective of the telescope; to the incoming starlight, a highly magnified image of the iris hovers as an annular skirt covering the outer region of the objective of the telescope! A telescope can be used at such "ultra-low" magnifications, but obviously a telescope of smaller aperture would perform as well. However, ultra-low magnifications have two advantages:

(1) A wider actual field of view, assuming the field stop of the eyepiece will permit this (an eyepiece having a 2-in. barrel diameter is usually necessary).

(2) Ease of alignment of the entrance pupil of the eye with the exit pupil of the telescope, an aspect of viewing that is usually troublesome when these two pupils are nearly the same size. An oversize exit pupil provides "slop," making alignment less critical. This is particularly helpful when using binoculars during activities involving motion, such as boating or bird watching. This is one advantage of using 7 × 50 (= $M \times D$) binoculars rather than 7 × 35 binoculars for daytime activities, although less than half of the light entering the larger binoculars can reach the observer's retinas.

Some examples using the diagram:

(1) Consider the common 8-in. Schmidt-Cassegrain telescopes. These have $D = 200$ mm and (usually) FR = 10. The diagram indicates that eyepieces with focal lengths from 5 mm to 55 mm are usable for most observers. With a 32-mm eyepiece, the diagram gives $d_p = 3.2$ mm, in the L magnification range, and the magnification $M = D/d_p = 200/3.2 = 62\times$.

(2) If an observer wishes to use the full aperture of an FR = 4.5 telescope, a 40-mm eyepiece is ruled out. Similarly, a 70-year-old observer should probably not use even a 27-mm eyepiece on such a telescope and should not bother with 7 × 50 or 11 × 80 binoculars, unless ease of eye/exit-pupil alignment is the main consideration.

(3) There is no point in using extremely short focal length eyepieces, especially when combined with Barlow lenses, on telescopes having large FRs. This is a common fault (among many others!) with camera/department store "junk telescopes."

MAGNIFICATION AND CONTRAST IN DEEP-SKY OBSERVING

By Lee Johnson and William Roberts

One of the main challenges of deep-sky observing is to distinguish faint, extended objects from the light of the background night sky. As we shall see below, the visibility of an object is a function of its apparent size and contrast, where contrast is the ratio of the object's surface brightness (neglecting the contribution of the background sky) to that of the background sky. As an object's apparent size increases, its minimum detectable surface brightness decreases. As the background sky surface brightness decreases, so does an object's minimum detectable surface brightness. This article addresses the consequences for the visibility of faint deep-sky objects and the effect of magnification thereon.

Surface Brightness and Exit Pupils

Table 1 lists the surface brightness (luminance) of three representative deep-sky objects expressed in magnitude per square arcsecond (mag/sq″). (For more details on these objects, see, respectively, pp. 263, 257, and 263.) When these surface brightnesses are compared to those of skies corresponding to mountain-top observatories (22 mag/sq″), dark country sites (21 mag/sq″), sites with magnitude 5 stars visible (19.5 mag/sq″), and a suburban setting with magnitude 4 stars visible (18.5 mag/sq″), it is clear that the surface brightness of an object can be lower than the sky background, thus leading to very low values of contrast.

TABLE 1—SURFACE BRIGHTNESS OF OBJECTS

Object	m_V	Size ′	Surface Brightness mag/sq″
NGC 7317 (galaxy)	13.6	0.5 × 0.5	20.7
M97 (planetary nebula)	9.9	3.2 × 3.2	21.1
Jones 1 (planetary nebula)	12.1	5.5 × 5.5	24.4

Sizes and magnitudes of deep-sky objects can be found in *The Deep Sky Field Guide to Uranometria 2000.0*. The surface brightnesses of several nebulae are also given in the section GALACTIC NEBULAE, p. 254. For any extended deep-sky object, the surface brightness, S, in magnitude per square arcsecond can be approximated by

$$S = m_V + 2.5\log(2827ab),$$

where a and b are, respectively, the object's major and minor diameters in arcminutes (′), assuming an elliptical shape. (To convert magnitude per square arcminute to magnitude per square arcsecond, add 8.89.)

The exit pupil of a telescope, which equals (objective diameter)/magnification, determines the image brightness through the telescope (see TELESCOPE EXIT PUPILS, pp. 46–49). When an extended object is magnified to the point that the exit pupil is smaller than the eye's entrance pupil—which is nominally 7 mm—its brightness decreases relative to the naked-eye view. The decrease in brightness is the same for both the object and the background sky. In other words, magnification does not alter contrast. Table 2 shows how the degree to which an object's surface brightness or that of the sky decreases as the exit pupil becomes smaller than 7 mm.

TABLE 2—DIMMING WITH RESPECT TO A 7-MM EXIT PUPIL

Exit Pupil (mm)	7	6	5	4	3	2	1	0.5
Dimming (mag)	0.0	0.3	0.7	1.2	1.8	2.7	4.2	5.7

Human binocular vision has a lower surface-brightness limit of approximately 1 μcd/m^2, which, when adjusted for monocular vision, is about 27 mag/sq″. When the dimming due to smaller exit pupils, as given in Table 2, is added to the sky brightness, it is apparent that the magnified sky may approach the detection limit of the eye; for example, a 1-mm exit pupil in a 22 mag/sq″ sky lowers the apparent sky brightness to 26.2 mag/sq″, which is near the eye's limit.

The Relation Between Size and Threshold Surface Brightness

Blackwell (*J. Opt. Soc. Am., 36* (1946), p. 624), in a massive World War II study that is still the only one of its kind, analyzed approximately 450 000 observations of threshold contrast under varying background illuminations. Table 3, derived from Blackwell's data, which goes down to 26 mag/sq″, gives the minimum detectable surface brightness of an object as the object's apparent size and the brightness of the sky vary. The values are corrected for monocular vision and presuppose a 50% probability of detection; for 90% probability, subtract 0.5 from the entries in the table.

TABLE 3—THRESHOLD SURFACE BRIGHTNESS FOR SIZE AND SKY BRIGHTNESS

	Sky Surface Brightness (mag/sq″)							
Size (′)	26	25	24	23	22	21	20	19
360	26.3	26.0	25.6	25.0	24.4	23.7	23.0	22.3
240	26.1	25.8	25.4	24.8	24.2	23.5	22.8	22.2
120	25.5	25.3	24.9	24.4	23.7	23.1	22.4	21.8
60	24.7	24.5	24.2	23.7	23.1	22.5	21.9	21.3
30	23.8	23.8	23.3	22.8	22.3	21.7	21.1	20.6
15	22.5	22.3	22.0	21.6	21.1	20.6	20.1	19.7

As magnification is increased, one moves up and to the left in the table. For a fixed apparent sky brightness, large objects are more easily detected than small ones of equal surface brightness. In addition, low-surface-brightness objects are more easily seen against darker backgrounds and by using higher magnifications, in agreement with experience. However, note that differences in thresholds from increases in magnification are relatively smaller toward the upper-left portion of the table. With sufficient magnification a point may be reached where a further increase in magnification reduces an object's surface brightness faster than the improvement in threshold brightness due to the increase in size. Thus the object will become more difficult to detect, although the increased magnification makes it easier to see any bright detail within the object.

It is important to note that the values in this table are guidelines only. If Table 3 suggests that the detection of an object is marginal, do not be discouraged; try anyway. Other factors that affect the detection of an object are atmospheric extinction, a telescope's efficiency of light transmission, the differences between the eye's nighttime and daytime response (see FILTERS, pp. 58–61), and the observer's visual acuity. Typically, the cumulative effect of these factors is between –0.5 and +0.5 magnitudes; see Schaefer (*PASP, 102* (1990), pp. 213–215) for further details.

An example using Table 3

(1) Consider NGC 7317 under a 21 mag/sq″ sky. A magnification of 148× with a 445-mm telescope gives a size of 74′ and an exit pupil of 3 mm. The dimming due to a 3-mm exit pupil is 1.8 magnitudes (Table 2), which when added to both the object's and sky's surface brightness results in brightnesses of 22.5 mag/sq″ and 22.8 mag/sq″, respectively. The entry in Table 3 for a sky of surface brightness 23 mag/sq″ and size 60′ gives a threshold surface brightness of 23.7 mag/sq″. This is more than one magnitude dimmer than the brightness of NGC 7317, which should therefore be clearly visible under the specified conditions. A 130-mm telescope with a magnification of 43×, on the other hand, gives a size of 22′ and the same surface brightnesses and exit pupil. From the interpolated value 22.2 in the fourth column of Table 3 we see that the object will likely not be visible in this smaller instrument at this magnification. Alternatively, finding the object brightness in the 23 mag/sq″ column we see that the minimum apparent size is almost 30′, and since 22′ is less than this, the object is unlikely to be seen.

Some examples using Figure 1

Figure 1 is a graphical representation of the data in Table 3, whose columns are depicted as a set of correlative curves. The *y*-axis represents the minimum apparent size of the object for visibility, and the *x*-axis is the contrast between the object and the sky. Whereas Table 3 emphasizes the visibility of the object as a function of its brightness and apparent size, Figure 1 emphasizes the visibility of the object as a function of the contrast between it and the sky in relation to its apparent size.

(2) An example with a larger object shows that magnification can be increased without dropping the object below the threshold surface brightness. Consider M97 viewed with a 200-mm aperture under a 20 mag/sq″ sky. The contrast between the object and sky surface brightnesses of 21.1 mag/sq″ and 20 mag/sq″ is 1.1 mag/sq″, which does not change with magnification. A 5-mm exit pupil (40×) gives a sky surface brightness of 20.7 mag/sq, with a 128′ apparent size. Starting at the 1.1 mag/sq″ point on the *x*-axis, move vertically to the curve (21 mag/sq″) most closely corresponding to the sky surface brightness and then horizontally to get the minimum apparent object size on the *y*-axis (40′). Since the apparent size is greater than the minimum, M97 should be visible. If the magnification is increased to 100×, resulting in an exit pupil of 2 mm and apparent size of 320′, the sky brightness changes to 22.7 mag/sq″ and the minimum size to 80′. The object is still visible, but the apparent size is 2.5 times greater, thus resulting in a more detailed view.

The contrast of emission nebulae is a special case and can be increased with bandpass filters (see FILTERS, pp. 58–61). Bandpass filters such as the UHC, OIII, and Hβ increase contrast by passing light near the emission wavelengths and rejecting broad-spectrum light from light pollution and natural skyglow, effectively reducing the sky's surface brightness by about 1.6 magnitudes for the UHC and about 2.6 magnitudes for the OIII and Hβ filters. The visible light from emission nebulae is mainly in the OIII and Hβ wavelengths, which lie close to the peak response of the dark-adapted eye. Filters such as the UHC pass all the light from these lines and do not significantly dim the nebulae. These filters therefore do not require an increase in exit pupils in order to maintain an object's surface brightness. OIII and especially Hβ filters, on the other hand, may pass only a portion of the light from a nebula and result in a dimming of the nebula. Here, the restoration of the object's surface brightness requires an increase in exit pupil and thus a decrease in magnification. The OIII filter passes most of the light from a typical planetary nebula and thus does not require an increase in exit pupil; it is therefore the filter of choice for these objects. The situation for other emission nebulae is not so clear.

(3) Consider viewing the planetary nebula Jones 1 with a 250-mm aperture under a 21 mag/sq″ sky. Exit pupils of 2 mm and smaller reduce the surface brightness below the eye's absolute threshold of 27 mag/sq″; larger exit pupils do not dim the sky sufficiently to make the object visible. A magnification of 50× gives an exit pupil of 5 mm, which results in a contrast of 3.4 mag/sq″, sky brightness of 21.7 mag/sq″, and an object size of 275′. Figure 1 shows the minimum apparent size to be greater than 360′ and that Jones 1 is not visible under these conditions. An OIII filter will reduce the sky surface brightness by 2.6 magnitudes without dimming Jones 1 appreciably and results in a sky surface brightness of 24.3 mag/sq″. The contrast is now 0.1 mag/sq″, and the minimum apparent size is approximately 70′. The planetary nebula should be visible when viewed with the filter.

FIGURE 1—CRITICAL SIZE VS. CONTRAST BY SKY BRIGHTNESS

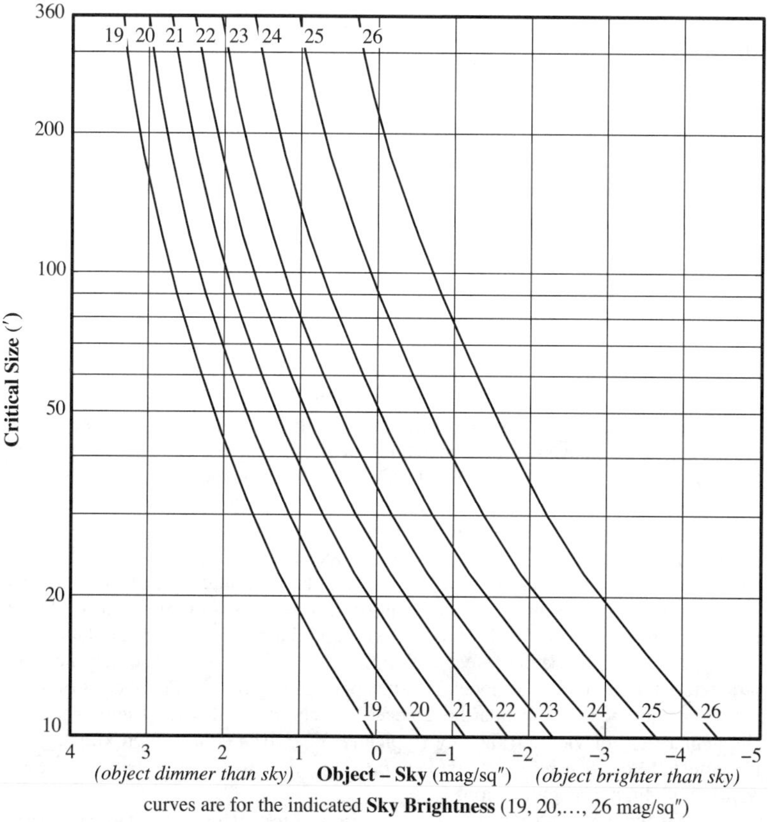

Critical Size (′)

(*object dimmer than sky*) **Object – Sky** (mag/sq″) (*object brighter than sky*)

curves are for the indicated **Sky Brightness** (19, 20,…, 26 mag/sq″)

Summary

Generally, experienced deep-sky observers select eyepieces that result in exit pupils in the range of 2 mm to 3 mm when viewing a faint deep-sky object. This range of exit pupils corresponds to the middle of Table 3 and to the central sections of the middle curves in Figure 1. Larger exit pupils correspond to the lower right of the table, where small, faint objects may fall below the threshold of visibility; and smaller exit pupils to the upper left, where excessive magnification may dim the object to invisibility. At any fixed apparent size, moving from right to left across the table results in a decrease in threshold brightness, which shows the benefit of observing in increasingly dark skies or with the aid of a filter. The corresponding values for Figure 1 show that the threshold size of an object decreases in relation to the darker skies represented by curves further along the *x*-axis.

BINOCULARS

By Roy Bishop

For an experienced observer, binoculars are indispensable. For a beginning observer, binoculars are preferable to an astronomical telescope. For a beginner unfamiliar with the large-scale features of the sky, who cannot yet identify a dozen constellations on any clear night, a telescope's narrow field of view, confusing image orientations, and unfamiliar controls will quickly cause more frustration than fun. The beginner is at a double disadvantage because he or she also does not know enough about astronomical telescopes to distinguish those that are worthy of the name from the common camera/department-store "junk telescopes"—the $299 wonders with poor optics and wobbly mounts. How many such telescopes are gathering dust in closets, their young owners turned off astronomy and their parents a few hundred dollars poorer? Far better had the same investment been made in a good pair of binoculars. With their ease of use, wide field of view, and unreversed, upright images, binoculars are a great help in finding one's way around the sky, and provide many unique views of the heavens.

Binoculars magnifying 6 to 8 times are ideal for locating planets in the twilight, scanning the constellations, studying the larger dark nebulae and star fields of our galaxy, and viewing bright comets. Binoculars magnifying 10 to 20 times provide the best views of objects spanning a few degrees, such as the Hyades, the Pleiades, the North America Nebula, and the Andromeda Galaxy; they also give the finest view of the slender crescent Moon, or of the full Moon with broken clouds blowing by.

Binoculars permit us to view the universe with both eyes, thereby providing more advantages: an improved sense of reality and depth (although parallax is negligible when viewing the heavens); more relaxed viewing; a complete view in the sense that the blind areas of one eye (associated with blood vessels and the region where the optic nerve attaches to the retina) are compensated by the field provided by the other eye; and dim objects appear brighter when viewed with two eyes.

Sizes: Binocular sizes are specified by numbers, for example, 7 × 50 and 8 × 30. The first number, including the "×," is the angular magnification or "power"; the second number is the diameter of the front (objective) lenses in millimetres. That is, in the notation on p. 45: $M \times D$. Thus the exit pupil diameter is easily calculated from $D \div M$ (e.g. 7 × 35 binoculars have exit pupils of 35 ÷ 7 = 5 mm). Another important parameter is field of view. Binoculars have apparent angular field diameters of about 50° when equipped with standard eyepieces, to near 70° with wide-angle eyepieces. The actual field of view on the sky (typically 3° to 10°) equals approximately the apparent field divided by the magnification. Thus the area of sky visible decreases rapidly with higher magnifications.

What is the best binocular size for astronomical use? There is no simple answer. Almost *any* pair of binoculars will show far more than can be seen with the unaided eyes; however, for astronomical use the objective lenses should be at least 30 mm in diameter. Also, small binoculars of high quality are more enjoyable to use than a large pair of low quality. For maximum light transmission and high-contrast images, binoculars with *multicoated* optics are preferable to those with merely *coated* optics (the former give greenish or deep red reflections from their surfaces, the latter bluish or violet).

Caveat emptor! Low-quality binoculars (and telescopes) are common. Images seen through low-quality binoculars are slightly fuzzy (usually not apparent to the inexperienced observer), one's eyes will be strained in trying to compensate for imperfectly aligned optics, and the focusing mechanism is usually flexible and crackling with an excess of grease used to mask poor workmanship. Avoid both zoom (variable magnification) binoculars and binoculars that do not have an adjustable focus—invariably these are of low quality.

Considering that binoculars contain at least 14 pieces of glass with 36 optical surfaces, antireflection coatings on (hopefully) all air-to-glass surfaces, plus two focusing mechanisms and an interpupillary adjustment, it is not surprising that top-quality instruments are in the same price range as video cameras. Such prices buy crisp, high-contrast images, accurately aligned optics, precise, rugged, dust- and moisture-proof construction, and pleasurable service for a lifetime. Nevertheless, there is a big market for $99 binoculars and $299 telescopes, and manufacturers are happy to satisfy the demand. When it comes to optical equipment, quality usually matches price.

Stability: One aspect of binocular use not often appreciated is how much more can be seen if the binoculars are mounted on a stable support, such as a camera tripod. This eliminates the constant jiggling associated with hand-holding and also supports the weight of the instrument. Adapters for attaching binoculars to a tripod are available, although usually it is not difficult to make your own. A recent major advance in binocular design is "image stabilization," an active optical system built into binoculars that compensates for the tremor associated with hand-holding. For example, the Canon company has introduced microprocessor-controlled binocular image stabilization that gives almost tripod-like stability with the convenience of hand-holding. Canon has produced 10 × 30, 10 × 42, 12 × 36, 15 × 45, 15 × 50, and 18 × 50 models, the latter three being particularly impressive for astronomy (see *SkyNews,* July/August 1998, p. 12; and *Sky & Telescope,* July 2000, p. 59).

Rating Binoculars

A frequently cited figure for binocular performance is "Relative Brightness," which equals the square of the diameter (in millimetres) of the instrument's exit pupils. For example, for 7 × 50 binoculars this figure is $(50 \div 7)^2 \approx 51$. Although this is a measure of the surface brightness *(luminance)* of an extended object seen through the binoculars under nighttime conditions, it is a totally inadequate measure of binocular performance on the night sky. For instance, using this figure of merit, large 14 × 100 binoculars have practically the same rating as the unaided eyes (which, when young and in dim light, are effectively 1 × 7 binoculars)!

Since seeing depends upon light, and the amount of light passing through a pair of binoculars depends primarily upon the *area* of the objective lenses (diameter D), a D^2 dependence appears reasonable. However, although the amount of light going into the point images of stars increases as D^2, assuming constant magnification the increase in the luminance of the background sky as D increases leads to a somewhat slower improvement in the visibility of these stars. A similar muted improvement occurs for dim extended images, resulting in an approximately D^1 dependence, rather than D^2.

Also, for constant D the detail that can be seen in the night sky increases with the magnification M. The resulting lower luminance of the background sky allows fainter stars to be seen, and the visibility of structure in extended images improves as M increases because the image is larger and of fixed contrast relative to the sky background.

The simplest figure of merit for the performance of binoculars in low-light conditions that combines both variables is the mathematical product $M \times D$ (which happens to look the same as the binocular size specification). In the case of two pairs of binoculars, one having twice the M and twice the D of the other, $M \times D$ indicates that "four times as much" should be visible in the larger instrument (e.g. 16 × 60 versus 8 × 30 binoculars). This is to be expected, since in the larger instrument stars will be four times brighter and extended images will have four times the area from which the eyes can glean information, with luminances being the same in both instruments.

For many decades the venerable Carl Zeiss optical company has cited $\sqrt{(M \times D)}$ as a "Twilight Performance Factor" for binoculars, its value said to be proportional to the distance at which various binoculars will show the same detail. This is equivalent to $M \times D$ being proportional to *the amount of detail that can be seen at the same distance*. The latter situation is relevant for astronomy since, unlike a bird or other object on Earth, a star or a galaxy is always at essentially the *same distance* from the observer. $M \times D$ could be called the *visibility factor.*

Binocular Performance Diagram

The diagram at the right enables one to quickly compare binoculars in terms of their ability to reveal detail in the night sky. The vertical axis is magnification *M;* the horizontal axis is aperture *D*. The uniform grid of small dots is a guide to reading the diagram. The five straight lines indicate constant exit pupil diameters of 3, 4, 5, 6, and 7 mm, as indicated both by numbers and by circles of these diameters near the top ends of the lines. The five curved arcs indicate constant values of $M \times D$ (the visibility factor), increasing by successive powers of 2 toward the upper right (100, 200, 400, 800, and 1600). Each large dot represents a common size of binoculars. The arrows in the lower right corner indicate the directions on the diagram in which various quantities increase most rapidly.

Each straight line (constant exit-pupil diameter) also corresponds to constant luminance of extended areas, such as the Orion Nebula or the background sky glow, with the luminance being proportional to the square of the exit-pupil diameter (provided the entrance pupils of the observer's eyes are large enough to accommodate the exit pupils of the binoculars). However, exit pupils of 3 to 5 mm ensure that (1) all the light transmitted by the binoculars can enter the dark-adapted eyes no matter what the observer's age; (2) alignment of exit pupils with dark-adapted eye pupils is relatively easy to achieve; (3) the background sky glow will be subdued; and (4) star images will be less distorted by aberrations in the observer's eyes (see TELESCOPE EXIT PUPILS, pp. 46–49).

Examples: Some examples apparent from the diagram: for viewing the night sky 10 × 50 binoculars will show about twice as much detail as 7 × 35s; 11 × 80 and 15 × 60 binoculars are equally capable, as are 8 × 30s and 6 × 42s (assuming one's eye pupils can accommodate the exit pupils of the instrument with the larger *D*); 10 × 50 binoculars are appreciably better than 7 × 50s for visibility (although, assuming equal apparent angular fields, 7 × 50s will show about twice as much sky area as will 10 × 50s). Canon's image-stabilized 15 × 45 binoculars are nearly equivalent to tripod-mounted 10 × 70s, with the *triple* advantage of smaller size, accommodating observers whose pupils will not open to 7 mm, and not requiring a tripod!

The visibility factor ($M \times D$) is applicable to the usual range of binocular sizes (exit pupils between about 2 mm and 7 mm), but should not be extrapolated indefinitely. For instance, as the magnification is increased on a telescope and the exit pupil approaches 1 mm or less, a point will be reached (dependent upon the darkness of the sky) where the background sky glow is imperceptible. Also, stars will begin to show either seeing disks or diffraction disks. A further increase in *M* will not cause a noticeable improvement in the visibility of stars, and the perceived contrast between an extended object and the sky will decrease. In addition, the angular size of an extended object must be kept in mind. Once *M* is increased to the point at which the object fills the field of view of the instrument, the object may not be visible at all! For example, a large, dim comet coma may be visible in 15 × 60 binoculars ($M \times D = 900$) but *invisible* in a 45 × 200 telescope ($M \times D = 9000$).

BINOCULAR PERFORMANCE DIAGRAM

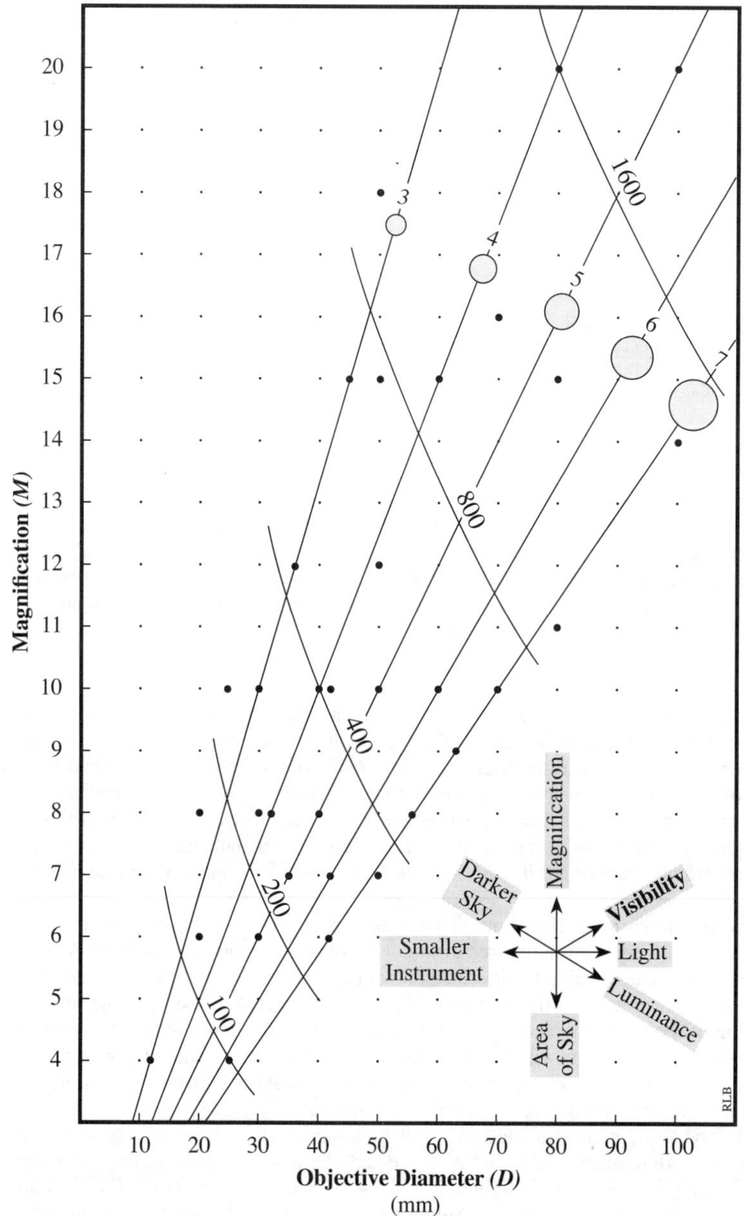

FILTERS

By Roy Bishop

Optical filters reflect and absorb some portion of the incident light. *Neutral-density filters* reflect and absorb light more or less uniformly across the visible spectrum. *Coloured (dye) filters* typically pass only one or two moderately broad portions of the spectrum. *Interference filters* are more selective and typically pass only one or two well-defined, narrow segments of the spectrum. All three types of filter are invaluable in astronomy.

In addition to categorization by physical type, filters may be categorized according to their intended use: lunar and planetary (neutral-density and dye filters), solar (neutral-density and interference filters), and nebula (interference filters).

Lunar and Planetary Filters

As viewed in a telescope, the Moon and the planets Venus, Mars, and Jupiter are often uncomfortably bright. A neutral-density filter, which passes only 13% to 25% of the light, solves this problem while avoiding the loss in resolution that would accompany stopping down the aperture of the telescope to decrease the brightness to the same level. With a less-glaring image, light scattering in the observer's eye is reduced and fine details are easier to see. A neutral-density filter is typically about 26 mm in diameter and is attached to the forward-facing end of an eyepiece.

Dye filters can enhance the visibility of various planetary features. For instance, a red or yellow filter will absorb bluish light scattered by the Martian atmosphere and thereby improve the contrast of features on the surface of Mars. A green filter will increase the visibility of pale red and blue areas in the atmosphere of Jupiter (although the entire image will then appear green). Also, since they absorb an appreciable fraction of the light, dye filters or polarizing filters have the same advantage as a weak neutral-density filter when viewing bright objects.

Solar Filters

A filter is essential when observing the Sun. Solar filters must be designed not only to reduce the brightness of the solar surface to a comfortable level, but to block out the invisible but damaging infrared and ultraviolet radiation. Just because a filter makes the Sun dim enough to view comfortably is no guarantee that it is not transmitting damaging amounts of invisible radiation! This is no place to experiment with do-it-yourself filter designs—use only a proper solar filter from a reputable manufacturer. *Failure to use a proper filter when observing the Sun can cause immediate and irreversible damage to vision.*

A special warning: Heavy atmospheric haze near sunrise or sunset often dims the Sun so that it appears as a dull red disk, not uncomfortably bright to the eye. At such times resist the temptation to view the Sun with a telescope without using a solar filter. The atmosphere at such times is still relatively transparent in the invisible infrared portion of the spectrum, and the great light grasp of a telescope can result in thermal retinal damage! With the unaided eyes the retinal solar image, although just as bright, is much smaller and the eye can better dissipate the heat. Also, with unaided vision, one is less apt to fixate on the Sun for a prolonged period.

For white-light views of the Sun a dark, broad-spectrum, neutral-density solar filter is needed. Aluminized Mylar and metal-coated glass are common designs, although they usually do not attenuate light uniformly across the visible spectrum (i.e. they are not perfect neutral-density filters). Aluminized Mylar gives a bluish colour to the solar image, while metal-coated glass filters usually give an orange colour.

The filter should be 50 mm or more in diameter and must be positioned to cover the *front* of the telescope. Ensure that the filter is *securely attached* so that a gust of wind or a bump cannot dislodge it. (Some small telescopes are sold with a "sun filter" designed to attach to the eyepiece, just before the observer's eye. Sunlight concentrated by the telescope can overheat and shatter a filter of this design. Such filters should be thrown in the garbage!)

For direct viewing of the Sun (not using binoculars or a telescope) shade #14 (no other shade) rectangular welder's glass may be used; this is available for a few dollars at welding supplies shops. These filters are not suitable for attaching to the front of binoculars or a telescope simply because their poor optical quality results in a fuzzy image.

Red, flame-like prominences at the Sun's limb and much structure in its chromosphere across the solar disk can be seen in hydrogen-alpha (Hα) light, a strong spectral line emitted by atomic hydrogen. This light is totally overwhelmed by the rest of the solar spectrum, so a neutral-density filter will not work. Advances in vacuum thin-film technology have made possible interference filters, filters that operate on the same principle as Fabry-Perot interferometers, involving the interference of multiply reflected beams of light. These filters can be constructed so they are transparent only to light having an extremely narrow range of wavelengths, typically 0.15 to 0.05 nm for solar viewing, although band-passes of up to 1 nm are used in solar-prominence viewers designed to occult the solar disk. If this band-pass is centred on the Hα wavelength (656.3 nm), nearly all the Sun's light will be blocked, leaving an image in Hα light.

Hα filters are expensive, particularly for band-passes near 0.05 nm that are needed for high-contrast images of the solar disk. These filters may be located either in front of the objective of a telescope or between the objective and the eyepiece. In the latter case, because the wavelength of the centre of the narrow band-pass varies with the angle at which light rays enter the filter (a characteristic of interference filters), the focal ratio of the imaging telescope must be near f/20 for 0.15-nm band-pass filters and f/30 or higher for filters with narrower band-passes. Temperature control is usually required to keep the band-pass centred on the Hα wavelength, although some Hα filters are designed to be tilted in order to tune them to the Hα wavelength (the wavelength of peak transmittance is shifted toward shorter wavelengths when the filter is tilted away from 90° incidence).

Hα filters require a broadband "energy-rejection prefilter," located at the front of the telescope. The prefilter has a band-pass of about 100 nm in the red part of the spectrum and blocks essentially all the infrared, ultraviolet, and much of the visible part of the solar radiation from entering the telescope.

Nebula Filters

From the surface of Earth, the night sky is not completely dark. Even in the absence of light pollution (human-made and lunar), the air itself emits a feeble light called airglow. In higher latitudes, aurorae can also contribute to the glow of the atmosphere. Two other components of the light of the night sky are the zodiacal light and background starlight. The diffuse glow from all four sources reduces the contrast of celestial objects and, in the case of dim comets, galaxies, and nebulae, the object may be completely obscured by the brightness of the sky.

Filters transmit only a fraction of the incident light. Thus employing them to see faint objects may seem counterproductive. However, there are objects in the heavens that emit light only at certain wavelengths. This behaviour is characteristic of plasmas—excited gases, matter composed of separate atoms energized either by ultraviolet radiation from nearby hot stars or by collisions such as occur in supernova explosion shock fronts. Such regions are called emission nebulae and include star-forming regions, planetary nebulae, and some supernova remnants. A filter that selectively blocks most of the background sky glow but is transparent to the wavelengths at which such objects emit most of their visible light will darken the sky background without appreciably dimming the object of interest. With narrow-band-pass interference-type filters the effect can be dramatic, improving contrast and revealing details that otherwise are completely invisible. It is the next best thing to observing these objects from above Earth's atmosphere!

Dark-adapted (scotopic) human vision responds to light having wavelengths from approximately 400 to 620 nm. In bright light (photopic vision) the spectral range extends to somewhat longer wavelengths, about 750 nm. For both types of vision the response curve (sensitivity versus wavelength) is "bell-shaped," the wavelength of maximum sensitivity being in the middle of the visible range—near 507 nm for scotopic vision and 555 nm for photopic vision (see the figure "Nebular Filter Transmission" at the right). The photopic sensation produced by 555-nm light is green; for scotopic vision colour is not produced, but at photopic levels 507-nm light appears blue-green.

Hydrogen is the predominant element in the universe. Atomic hydrogen, when excited by ultraviolet radiation from a nearby hot star, emits light in the visible spectrum at only four discrete wavelengths: 656, 486, 434, and 410 nm (designated as Hα, Hβ, Hγ, and Hδ, respectively, part of the *Balmer spectrum* of hydrogen). Scotopic vision is blind to 656-nm (Hα) light and relatively insensitive to the less intense 434- and 410-nm light. However, 486 nm (Hβ) lies near the 507-nm peak sensitivity of scotopic vision, and an Hβ ("H-beta") filter having a narrow band-pass at this wavelength will greatly reduce the surrounding sky brightness and reveal Hβ-emitting nebulae.

The classic example is the Horsehead Nebula, a dark, silhouetted column of dust just southeast of the east end of Orion's belt. The surrounding hydrogen gas, excited probably by the nearby hot star ζ Orionis, fluoresces dimly with Hβ light. If the obscuring airglow is blocked by an Hβ filter, the dark Horsehead can distinctly be seen in a telescope having an aperture of 400 mm or greater. However, the number of objects that can be viewed advantageously with an Hβ filter is very limited, apparently because few nebulae emit strongly in Hβ light.

Two other strong nebular emission lines lie at 496 and 501 nm, nearly at the peak sensitivity of scotopic vision. Originally detected in 1864 by the British astronomer William Huggins, the origin of these lines was unknown at that time, and they were attributed to a hypothetical new element, "nebulium." In 1927, the American astrophysicist Ira Bowen identified the lines as due to doubly ionized oxygen (O^{++} or OIII), which glows brightly when very low-density nebular gas is strongly excited (high temperature). A filter that has a narrow band-pass spanning these two wavelengths gives striking views of highly excited nebulae. A good example is the Veil Nebula, a supernova remnant in eastern Cygnus. Through an OIII filter on a dark, transparent night, the direct view of the Veil in a large amateur telescope is more spectacular than any photograph or CCD image. Planetary nebulae (fluorescing, low-density shells of gas surrounding hot central stars) also show up well with an OIII filter; examples include the Helix Nebula, the Owl Nebula (M97), the Dumbbell Nebula (M27), and the Ring Nebula (M57).

Because of their narrow band-passes, Hβ and OIII filters are sometimes called *line filters,* although their band-passes are much wider than that of an Hα filter. Filters encompassing both the Hβ and OIII lines, such as the Lumicon Ultra High Contrast (UHC) filter, are termed *narrowband filters*. These filters also enhance views of many emission nebulae, although with the wider band-pass the sky background is brighter. With a large telescope under dark skies I find that the single most useful filter is the OIII line filter. With smaller apertures (less than about 200 mm), the narrowband Lumicon

UHC filter (or equivalent filter from other manufacturers) may be preferable since it dims the stars less.

Some other nebulae that are greatly enhanced by OIII and narrowband filters include the Omega or Loon Nebula (M17), the Trifid Nebula (M20), the Lagoon Nebula (M8), the Rosette Nebula, the Eagle Nebula (M16), the North America Nebula, and the Eta Carinae Nebula.

Nebular Filter Transmission

The dotted, dashed, and continuous curves show the transmission versus wavelength characteristic of four interference filters (in descending order in the legend): two line filters, a narrowband filter, and a broadband filter. The bell-shaped curves composed of small open and solid circles show the relative response of bright-adapted (photopic) vision and dark-adapted (scotopic) vision. In ascending sequence above the curves are spectral colours, nebula emission lines, and light-pollution lines (M = mercury, S = high-pressure sodium, and LPS = low-pressure sodium). High-pressure sodium light sources emit an additional broad continuum spectrum that is not shown. The two unlabelled light-pollution lines are strong airglow/auroral lines produced by atomic oxygen. (David Lane used a "Varian Model Cory 50 Conc. UV-Visible Spectrophotometer" owned by the Chemistry Department at Saint Mary's University to obtain the filter curves; he also prepared the diagram.)

Stars emit light across the entire visible spectrum. Thus line filters and narrowband filters impair views of single stars, reflection nebulae, star clusters, and galaxies. Filters with wide band-passes extending from about 450 to 530 nm are called *broadband filters*. Examples are the Lumicon Deep Sky filter, the Orion SkyGlow filter, and the Meade Broadband filter. These decrease the airglow somewhat and block several of the brighter wavelengths emitted by sodium- and mercury-vapour streetlights, without dimming stars and galaxies too much. Thus they provide a modest improvement in the visibility of some objects from light-polluted sites. Because of their wide band-pass and high transmission at the Hα line, they are also useful for photography of emission nebulae. However, under dark skies an unfiltered view is preferable to that through a broadband filter.

LIMITING MAGNITUDES

By Douglas Pitcairn

Limiting Visual Magnitudes

One of the many difficulties with visual observing from the surface of our planet is the variability of the atmosphere. In any record of observations it is important to note the condition of the sky. Parameters such as brightness and contrast are greatly affected by the transparency of the sky and the presence of light pollution or aurorae.

One of the simplest ways to quantify local sky conditions is to note the magnitude of the faintest star visible with the unaided eye—the *limiting visual magnitude* (LVM). Although individuals differ in their ability to detect faint stars, these differences are generally small, and for any one observer such observations provide a consistent measure of sky quality.

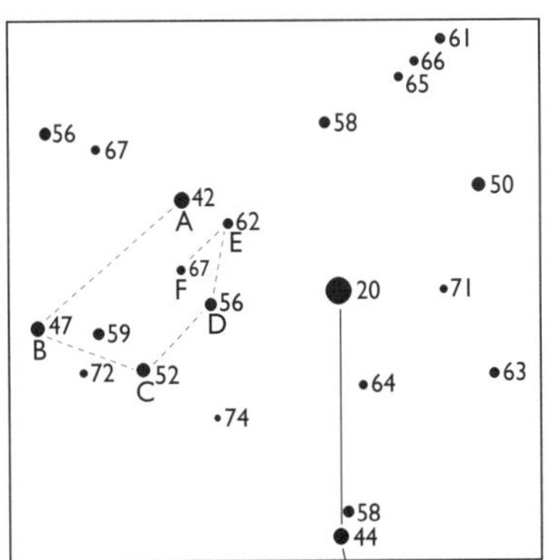

The chart at the left shows a 9°-wide field in the vicinity of Polaris (the brightest star on the chart) and is useful for observers at latitude 20°N or higher. For orientation, the solid lines mark the beginning of the handle of the Little Dipper, as in the ALL-SKY MAPS on pp. 275–280. Several stars have their visual magnitudes indicated (with decimal points omitted). Using this field to determine your LVM has several advantages: it is always above the horizon in midnorthern latitudes; its altitude does not change with the time of night or year, so the variation of atmospheric extinction with altitude is not a consideration; there are no bright stars or planets in the field to dazzle the eye; the faint stars are quite well spaced and therefore easy to identify; and being a simple field, it can be memorized. Especially note the dashed spiral of descending magnitudes labelled "A" through "F."

Limiting Telescopic Magnitudes

Aperture, telescope design, eyepiece design, magnification, and the quality of optical surfaces are a few of the many variables that will determine the faintest stars visible through a given telescope and eyepiece. By determining an instrument's limiting magnitude—the *limiting telescopic magnitude* (LTM)—you can effectively assess the effect of these variables. The quality of the night sky will also affect the LTM. Therefore, changes in the LVM should be taken into account when determining the LTM. (The relationship between LTM and LVM is complex; readers may explore it using the excellent Web-based calculator at www.go.ednet.ns.ca/~larry/astro/maglimit.html.) The LTM is a useful guide when attempting faint targets (Pluto in a 150-mm scope?), comparing the performance of different instruments ("Can my scope see as faint as yours?"), or determining whether a mirror or lens needs cleaning (many people clean their optics too often, assuming that dust degrades optical performance more than it actually does).

To help determine the LTM of your instrument, use the charts at the right, which show an 8′-wide section of the northwest quadrant of M67 centred at RA 8h 50.1m and Dec +11°53′. This old open cluster lies 8° south-southeast of M44, Cancer's famous Beehive cluster. The accompanying table lists the visual magnitudes and the $B-V$ colour indices of the labelled stars. The diagram was constructed from a photograph

STAR	VISUAL	B – V
A	10.60	1.10
B	11.19	0.43
C	11.59	0.42
D	12.01	0.57
E	12.26	0.68
F	12.57	0.59
G	13.04	0.85
H	13.35	0.59
I	13.61	0.59
J	13.96	0.62
K	14.34	0.56
L	14.66	0.67
M	14.96	0.69
N	15.30	0.79
O	15.58	0.84
P	16.06	0.74
Q	16.31	0.99
R	16.62	0.81
S	17.05	1.26
T	17.38	1.17
U	17.64	1.31
V	18.04	1.27
W	18.38	0.76
X	18.69	1.17
Y	19.07	1.56
Z	19.29	0.61
a	19.42	1.34
b	20.10	0.00
c	20.35	0.83
d	20.61	1.55
e	21.03	0.32

"Left-Right Correct" View

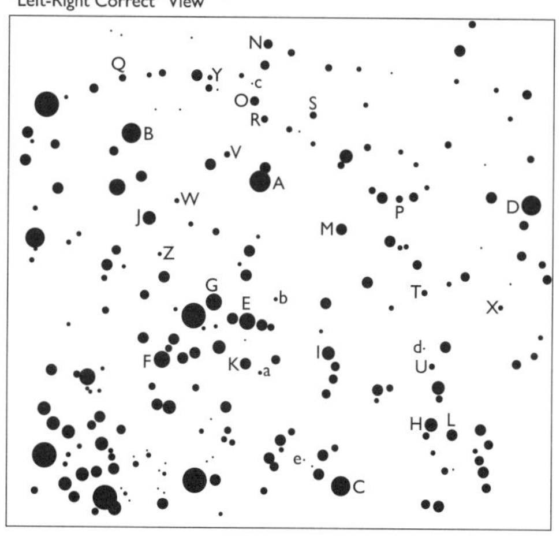

"Mirror Reversed" View

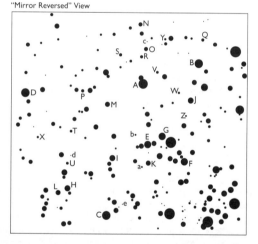

The "left-right correct" chart is for telescopes with an even number of reflecting surfaces (e.g. Newtonian reflectors) and the "mirror-reversed" chart is for telescopes with an odd number of reflecting surfaces (e.g. a refractor with a diagonal). North is at top in both of these charts.

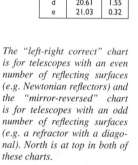

taken by René Racine of the Université de Montréal, who exposed a 103a-D plate at the f/3.67 focus of the Hale Reflector. The magnitudes are based on work by Racine and Ronald Gilliland of the Space Telescope Science Institute.

Correction for Atmospheric Extinction

Atmospheric extinction varies with altitude above the horizon. To normalize observations to the zenith (altitude 90°), the following values should be added to estimates of faintest visible magnitude obtained using the charts (format: altitude range/**correction**):

18° – 20°/**0.5;** 20° – 24°/**0.4;** 24° – 29°/**0.3;** 29° – 36°/**0.2;** 36° – 52°/**0.1;** 52° – 90°/**0.0**

These corrections are for near sea level and would be reduced at higher elevations. Also, excellent sky conditions are assumed; under less than ideal conditions the corrections are generally larger and can be quite uncertain, especially when the target area is closer to the horizon.

POLAR ALIGNMENT

BY RAJIV GUPTA

The charts for the north celestial pole at the right can be used to align an equatorial mount in the northern hemisphere. To polar align a mount, that is, to point the polar axis of the mount at the north celestial pole, select a telescope/eyepiece combination for which you know, or have carefully measured, the diameter of the field of view. Depending on the accuracy required (see below), you can use the finderscope, guidescope, or main telescope. Point the chosen telescope in the same direction as the mount's polar axis. Simply adjusting the mount's declination until the setting circle reads 90° is not sufficient; instead, rotate the mount 180° in RA, and check whether the field rotates in the eyepiece without shifting. If not, make adjustments in declination until the amount of shift is minimal. To reduce the shift to an acceptable level, you may have to make further, one-time transverse adjustments, leaving the declination fixed. For example, on a German equatorial mount, shims can be inserted between a mounting ring and the mounting plate.

Next, using one of the charts, adjust the mount's altitude and azimuth so that the starfield seen in the eyepiece is centred at the pole. Circles corresponding to various field diameters are indicated on both charts; you can draw a circle corresponding to your own exact field size using a compass if you prefer.

Precise polar alignment is necessary for long-exposure photography; otherwise, the stars will be elongated as a result of "field rotation." With good guiding on a system that is free of mechanical flexure, the guidestar will remain stationary on the film or imaging CCD chip. However, because of polar misalignment, all other stars will trace tiny arcs about the guidestar. The length of a particular star's arc a depends upon the amount of polar misalignment p (in arcminutes), the length of the exposure t (in hours), the distance d (in millimetres) in the imaging plane between the star and the guidestar, the declination of the guidestar δ (in degrees), and the geometrical circumstances of the exposure. An approximate formula for a (in μm (microns)), assuming the worst possible geometry, is

$$a \approx ptd/(14 \cos \delta).$$

For example, with $p = 5'$, $t = 1$ h, $d = 20$ mm, and $\delta = 20°$, we have $a \approx 7.6$ μm. You can use this formula to determine the value of p needed to keep a within a specified tolerance (such as 10 μm, a good target for high-resolution imaging), and then achieve the required polar-alignment accuracy using the above method. For example, to keep a under 5 μm with $t = 30$ min (0.5 h), $d = 20$ mm, and $\delta = 60°$, the required accuracy is $p \approx (5)(14)(\cos 60°)/(0.5)(20) = 3.5'$. If you need very high polar-alignment accuracy, you may want to shift the mount down by the amount of atmospheric refraction at the altitude of the pole (see p. 30 for some values of atmospheric refraction), so that the mount is aligned on the true pole instead of the refracted pole.

An alternative method for precise polar alignment is the *star drift method,* which involves alternately detecting the drift in declination of two stars near the celestial equator, one in the south and the other rising in the east, and making azimuth and altitude adjustments accordingly. If the first star drifts north, the mount's axis is pointing west of the true pole; if it drifts south, the axis is east of the pole. If the second star drifts north, the axis is pointing too high; if it drifts south, the axis is too low. The amount of misalignment p (in arcminutes) in terms of the amount of drift d (in arcseconds) and the length of time t the star is observed (in minutes) is given by

$$p \approx 3.8d/t.$$

For example, if a star drifts 10″ in 5 min, the misalignment is ≈7.6′; a rate of drift of 1″/min corresponds to a misalignment of ≈3.8′.

CHARTS FOR THE NORTH CELESTIAL POLE

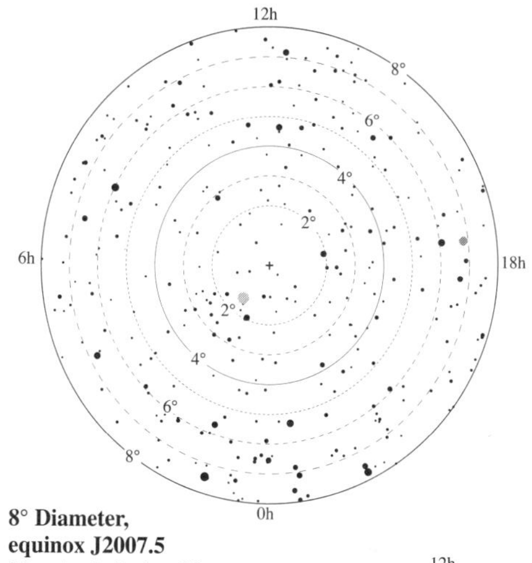

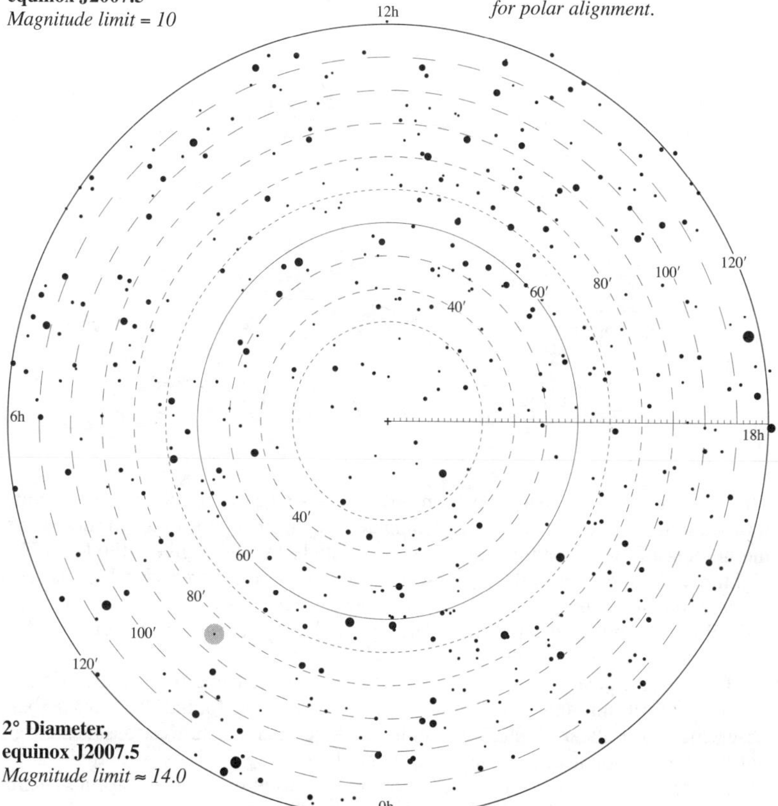

The charts are precessed to equinox J2007.5. Polaris is drawn in light grey in both charts; the penultimate "handle" star in Ursa Minor, δ UMi, is drawn in dark grey in the 8° chart at an RA of approximately 17.5h. The north celestial pole is indicated with a crosshair in both charts.

Circles corresponding to various diameters are drawn. A scale with tick marks separated by 1′ is provided on the 2° chart to facilitate the drawing of a circle of any other diameter using a compass; note that at a separation of 43′ from the pole, Polaris lies just within the 90′-diameter circle.

See the accompanying text for instructions on using these charts for polar alignment.

12h
8°
6°
4°
2°
6h
18h
2°
4°
6°
8°
0h

8° Diameter, equinox J2007.5
Magnitude limit = 10

12h
120′
100′
80′
60′
40′
6h
18h
40′
60′
80′
100′
120′
0h

2° Diameter, equinox J2007.5
Magnitude limit ≈ 14.0

FREQUENCY OF NIGHTTIME CLOUD COVER

BY JAY ANDERSON

APRIL–MAY MEAN NIGHTTIME CLOUD COVER IN PERCENT

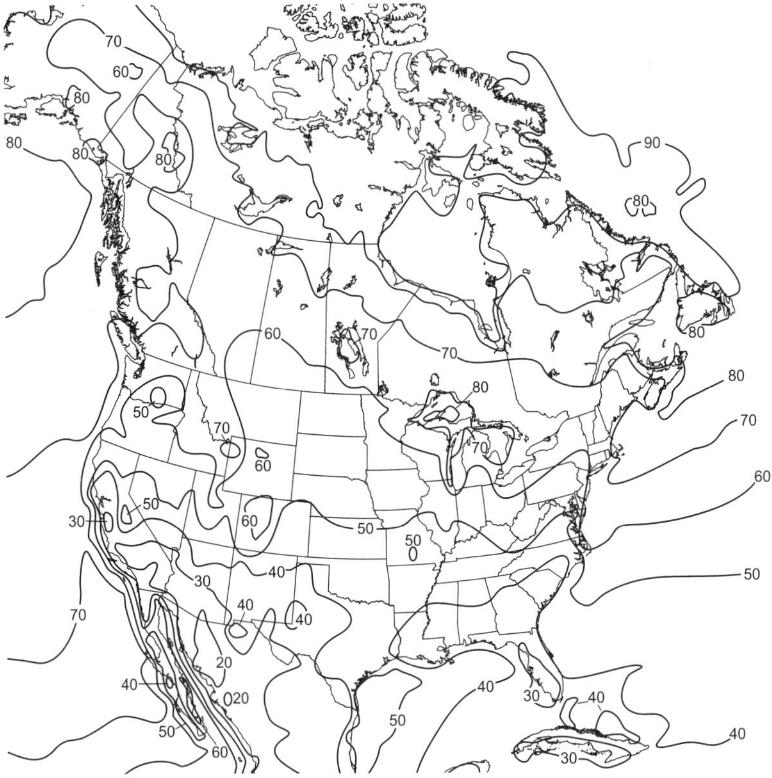

The above maps are constructed from observations taken from 19 years of satellite observations beginning in 1981. Computer algorithms are used to determine the amount of cloud within a one-degree longitude by one-degree latitude bin for nighttime satellite passages using observations in several infrared wavelengths. The observations suffer from small biases over snow and ice fields and lose some of their reliability at high latitudes in spring. The chart at left is an average of April and May observations; that on the right is for July and August.

In spring the clearest skies can be found in a band stretching from central Mexico north-westward through Arizona and into southern California. In Canada best observing prospects are found over southeast Alberta and southwest Saskatchewan, but the cloud amounts are considerably larger than along the Mexico border. Cloud cover is relatively uniform at Canadian latitudes, a result of the many storm systems that travel along and near the border as warmer weather arrives.

JULY–AUGUST MEAN NIGHTTIME CLOUD COVER IN PERCENT

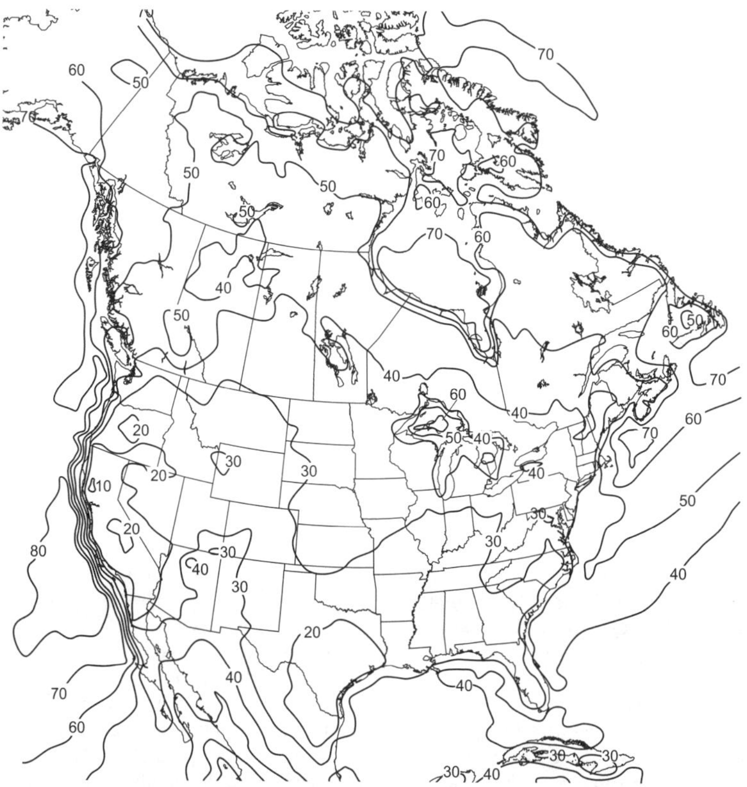

High cloud frequencies are found along the Atlantic coast, the California shoreline (mostly low cloud and fog), over the higher parts of the Rocky Mountain chain (where cirrus cloudiness is endemic), and, to a lesser extent, over the Appalachians. Resolution of the cloud cover within the narrow valleys of the western mountains is not possible at the scale of the observations, although in April the heavy cloudiness of winter is mostly over.

In July and August the clear springtime skies of the southwestern deserts of the United States give way to an increased cloudiness as the "monsoon season" brings moisture and frequent thunderstorms into Arizona, New Mexico, and Colorado. California's interior retains its reputation as the sunniest location, but clearer skies return to the midwestern plains, extending northward into the Prairie provinces. Almost all regions are clearer than in the April–May chart, although the Appalachians and the Atlantic provinces continue to be among the cloudiest locations. As in the spring, the Cypress Hills area of Alberta and Saskatchewan experiences the most reliable nighttime skies in Canada.

The maps may be used for planning travel to star parties and sunnier climates and to special astronomical events. During April and May, cloud cover is changing rapidly across the centre of the continent, and the average cloudiness shown in the chart at the left is likely too optimistic for April and too pessimistic for May.

WEATHER RESOURCES ON THE INTERNET

BY ALLAN RAHILL

Despite public skepticism, weather forecasts are in fact quite accurate, provided they are from informed sources. Specialized weather services—usually involving a fee—are available for aviation, agriculture, forestry, and marine applications. Until recently there was no such service for astronomy, likely because there was no directly related economy. However, the Canada-France-Hawaii Observatory at Mauna Kea has been using a seeing and transparency forecast for more than five years to "queue schedule" observing activities. This marks a new era in which professional observatories are making the best use of weather conditions and changing planned observing activities accordingly.

Similar information has been freely available to amateur and professional astronomers worldwide through the Internet for several years. With light pollution becoming more and more pervasive, amateur astronomers must drive long distances to get to dark skies. They can avoid frustration by using the information and URLs below to plan their observing sessions.

Satellite Images

Many astronomers rely on satellite images to predict nighttime cloud cover. Real-time images are available from GOES satellites for eastern and western America; other satellites such as Meteosat give the same service for Europe and Africa. These satellites give three main types of images: visible, infrared (IR), and water vapour. Visible images are easy to interpret, but they are available only during the day; for nighttime tracking of clouds, IR images are available. Water vapour images do not track clouds; they indicate the total moisture in the air mass. Usually the darkest areas in those images have good correlation with the best sky transparency.

Particularly useful for short-term forecasting are IR satellite loops, which are available at many Web sites. IR images show the radiance emission from Earth and indicate the temperature of the ground and/or clouds. During cold seasons, the ground can be as cold as, if not colder than, the air mass, and single IR satellite images are not very helpful in identifying low-level clouds such as stratocumulus. One way to separate clouds from the ground in these situations is to use a time-lapse loop and look for motion: the ground doesn't move but clouds do. Those in northern latitudes from late fall to early spring should keep this trick in mind.

There are many IR image enhancements available at various Web sites, and you should be aware that many of them do not display *any* low clouds, even with the trick mentioned above. One way to familiarize yourself with low-cloud detection is to compare visible GOES images to IR enhancements in the early morning, when the ground is still cold. In some situations, you may be surprised by the amount of low cloud not displayed in the IR satellite images. By comparing IR and visible images, you can select a Web site that you feel gives accurate images and one that you are comfortable with. I recommend the following Web site for IR satellite images because it provides the ability to zoom into your region, to choose different satellite image enhancements, and to do animation easily:

weather.unisys.com/satellite/sat_ir_hem.html

To make the best use of weather satellite images, you also should be aware of the behaviour of certain types of cloud. Low-level clouds such as stratus usually develop locally and generally move much more slowly than high clouds. These clouds appear during the night and usually get burned off by the Sun during the day. Coastal regions will usually see the low clouds moving inland in the evening and out to sea in the morning.

In addition, cumulus, towering cumulus, and cumulonimbus clouds arise with daytime convective heating if the air mass is unstable. The depth or height of the cloud structure is related to the level of instability and can reach up to 20 000 m for severe thunderstorms. On satellite loops, these clouds appear as clear areas that are gradually filled with clouds during the day and that slowly vanish in the evening. In the summer, some of the most unstable cumulonimbus clouds will survive at night. Even though thunderstorms, associated with cumulonimbus clouds, can be far from your location, cirrus blowoff from these cells may reach you quite quickly, depending on the upper wind direction, and thus ruin your observing session. Satellite and radar loops are good ways to keep track of these thunderstorm lines.

Radar

Remote-controlled observatories, where the operator is not physically present, and star parties, where telescopes are often left set up and exposed, are becoming more popular. When the sky conditions are variable, there is one common worry: is there a fast-moving precipitation band approaching the observing site? The best way to track precipitation in the short term is with radar. The radar network is extensive across the United States; it also covers populated regions of Canada.

Radar images require careful interpretation. During the night, the air cools near the ground and creates a temperature inversion. On some nights with strong inversions, radar signals are refracted, or bent, toward the ground and scattered back to the radar, thus appearing as precipitation on the graphical displays. Similar situations occur in mountainous areas, where higher terrain interrupts the radar signal. A radar loop will help you distinguish these areas: sometimes they are nearly motionless; at other times they shift around in a chaotic jumble. Precipitation moves in a smoother fashion, at times linearly. The best Web sites for access to radar loops for Canada and the United States, respectively, are:

www.weatheroffice.ec.gc.ca/radar/index_e.html
www.intellicast.com (click on "radar")

Weather Forecasts for Astronomy

Cloud Forecasts: Local media and television "experts" cannot always be relied upon when conditions are uncertain. Usually their forecasts cover a large area, and the weather can be quite different within the region. Also, for most people, including many local weather forecasters, skies are considered clear despite thin, high cloudiness that may interfere with observing.

The best forecasts for clouds are from the direct output of numerical models. Weather models are not perfect, but they are surprisingly good at capturing local effects and predicting cloud formation and dissipation. The biggest problem with numerical forecasting is convection (thunderstorms): it is like trying to predict the next bubble in boiling water. Complex thunderstorm cells can be forecast much farther away than they actually appear, leading to poor cloud progression forecasts for regions hundreds of kilometres ahead.

Some weather channels and Web sites use animated forecasts to show cloud progression for the next day, but these animations generally have low resolution and are not very useful for astronomy. The only North American high-resolution cloud forecast I still know of is produced at the Canadian Meteorological Centre (CMC):

www.weatheroffice.ec.gc.ca/astro/clds_vis_e.html

Occasionally, especially in the fall when low clouds (stratocumulus) are omnipresent, a weather balloon can be launched into a cloud hole, and the resulting cloud forecast may be too optimistic for the surrounding regions. To avoid a bad forecast, always compare the cloud cover forecast with the latest satellite picture. In these situations, an old forecast may be a better choice. This is why the most recent old forecast, in addition to the current forecast, is available at this Web site; hourly forecasts are now available.

Sky Transparency Forecasts: For deep-sky observing, sky transparency is critical because it largely determines how dark the sky will be. Aerosols—particles suspended in the atmosphere—and moisture reduce sky transparency and brighten the sky by diffusing the light in the sky. Aerosols include volcanic ash, pollen, sea salts, and smoke from forest fires. Spectacular examples of events that introduced aerosols into the atmosphere are the Mount St. Helens volcanic eruption, which spread roughly 109 tonnes of ash into the atmosphere in 1980, and the more recent large forest fires: in summer 2003 over British Columbia, which spread smoke over large areas, and in 2002 in northern Québec, which spread smoke over all of northeastern North America. Specialized weather numerical models handle aerosol phenomena; Web sites that track aerosol envelopes with up to five-day forecasts across the world are:

toms.gsfc.nasa.gov/aerosols/today_aero.html
www.nrlmry.navy.mil/aerosol/#currentaerosolmodeling

Moisture is the only weather element affecting sky transparency that can be forecast with confidence. For many northern-latitude residents, moisture is the most important contributor to reduced sky transparency; despite clear skies, very often high-level ice crystals (extremely thin clouds) are present and can be seen only at sunset and sunrise. In addition, moisture from open waters, vegetation (evapo-transpiration), or moist soil can keep the low-level atmosphere humid.

Over the years, I have compared water-vapour satellite images to various observers' estimates of background sky brightness. The resulting hourly sky transparency forecasts can be found at:

www.weatheroffice.ec.gc.ca/astro/transparence_e.html

There is a good correlation between the darkest areas in water-vapour images and the darkest observed sky conditions. There are some cases where the sky background is brighter than expected due to moisture trapped by a temperature inversion. Based on this observation and others, the forecasts in the previous Web site emphasize humidity near the surface and also near the tropopause (cirrus heights).

Seeing Forecasts: Seeing conditions determine the steadiness of images through a telescope and are relevant for planetary as well as deep-sky observing. When highest resolution is necessary for planetary imaging or visual observing, seeing should be at its best.

Conditions are favourable when the atmosphere is turbulence-free all across the path of the light. The best weather pattern is weak wind circulation at all levels. These conditions occur more frequently over the southeastern United States than any other region of North America, with Atlantic Canada generally having the worst conditions among populated North American regions. Canadian and U.S. central prairies often experience blocking weather systems that give weak upper wind circulation and excellent seeing conditions.

Another pattern for excellent seeing takes place when moderate winds blow from the same direction at all levels, that is, when horizontal and vertical wind shear are weak at all levels. In other words, no jet stream (strong winds reaching 200 km/h–400 km/h at an altitude of 10 km–12 km) or sudden shifts or increase in wind speed with height are present.

At locations downwind from mountains when winds are moderate, it is best to be far away from the mountains, since "gravity waves"—vertical air-mass oscillations caused by the mountains—can downgrade seeing. In general, topography is quite important because rough terrain increases the wind shear in the low-level atmosphere, due to friction and gravity waves.

Temperature variation at the surface also plays a role in seeing conditions. Nights of excellent wind conditions as described above may nevertheless have marginal seeing. On such nights, temperatures quickly and steadily fall, and large telescopes have trouble cooling at the same rate as the surrounding air. This creates what is called "local seeing": thermal heat released from the optics (despite good ventilation) ruins the seeing despite the excellent weather pattern. The opposite is also true: the best planetary observations with a large telescope often take place just before thick clouds roll in or when looking through thin cirrostratus cloud. Under these conditions the temperature usually rises a few degrees before the clouds appear. Thin cirrostratus clouds usually keep the temperature steady, eliminating any negative local seeing effects. Thin clouds also play the role of a neutral-density filter, increasing fine detail and contrast on bright planets. Ground fog can also be associated with excellent seeing conditions (until the fog thickens) if you can keep your optics dry.

Predicting favourable seeing conditions requires the ability to interpret weather charts, something that is difficult for most observers to do. The Canadian weather service now has an experimental seeing forecast, available at their astro-weather Web site, which attempts to simulate wind shears, topography, and temperature effects:

www.weatheroffice.ec.gc.ca/astro/seeing_e.html

The Clear Sky Clock

The Canadian Meteorological Centre's numerical weather forecasts, given in the URLs above, are unique because they are specifically designed for astronomers. In June 2005, these forecasts became official; they can be found in the weather map section of the Environment Canada Web site:

www.weatheroffice.ec.gc.ca/canada_e.html

We took this opportunity to add a few more products for the astronomy community. We added hourly humidity, temperature, and wind forecast images. However, they include 842 forecast images per day, covering all of North America, so it can be a chore to find the one you want. All the above weather forecasts for astronomy can be viewed at a glance for any particular observing site in North America using Attila Danko's excellent Clear Sky Clock:

www.cleardarksky.com/csk

Editor's Note: Attila Danko, a member of the Ottawa Centre of the Royal Astronomical Society of Canada, received the Ken Chilton Prize from the Society in 2005 for his creation of the Clear Sky Clock, which uses the Canadian Meteorological Centre's forecasts for astronomers created by Allan Rahill. Most popular observing locations in North America now have an associated Clock, and many amateur astronomers rely on these forecasts to plan their observing sessions.

LIGHT POLLUTION

By David L. Crawford

A Lost Heritage: During the last several decades, most people have lost the spectacular view of the universe that our ancestors enjoyed on clear nights. The development of electrical lighting technology and the increase in urban population have caused a rapid increase in sky glow above towns and cities. As a result, fewer and fewer members of the general public ever see a prime dark sky; our children and grandchildren may never. For urban dwellers, star-studded nights are limited to planetarium simulations. Even in rural areas, poorly designed yard lights often obscure the splendour of the night sky. As Leslie Peltier, one of the most famous amateur astronomers of the 20th century, stated eloquently in his autobiography *Starlight Nights:*

> *The moon and the stars no longer come to the farm. The farmer has exchanged his birthright in them for the wattage of his all-night sun. His children will never know the blessed dark of night.*

A nighttime satellite view of central North America

The increased sky glow that adversely affects the environment is called *light pollution,* for it originates mainly from excess light that does nothing to increase useful nighttime illumination. It is light that sprays horizontally and upward into the sky from poorly designed lighting fixtures. It is light that glares into the eyes of motorists and homeowners, compromising visibility, safety, and security. It is light that depresses property values by reducing the aesthetic quality of a neighbourhood. It is light that can seriously affect the circadian rhythm of all living things, including humans, as well as creating other hazards for many species (birds, sea turtles, etc.). In the United States and Canada, over a billion dollars plus large amounts of energy are lost annually in generating this wasted light.

A Threat to Astronomy: Light pollution poses special perils to astronomy. Many observations, including most of those of cosmological interest, can be made only from prime observing sites, far removed from centres of population. Some older observatories, such as the David Dunlap in Ontario and Mount Wilson in California, are severely affected by light pollution from nearby urban centres. New observatories usually are located at remote sites, and amateur astronomers routinely drive long distances to escape the glare of towns and cities. The argument that all astronomy can be done from space is incorrect because it does not make sense to do in space, at much higher costs, what can be done from the ground. There are observations that can only be done from space, but more than three decades of space astronomy have greatly increased the need for ground-based observatories.

Solutions: There are solutions to the problem of light pollution: Outdoor lighting ordinances have been instituted in a number of communities, particularly near large observatories, such as Tucson, Arizona, San Diego, California, and Hawaii. *The main solution is the use of full-cutoff lighting fixtures that direct all their light below the horizontal, such that the light source itself is not directly visible from the side—an* *almost universal fault with street and yard lights. Since this places the light where it is needed, less total light, and thus less electrical energy, is required.*

Inefficient street lighting

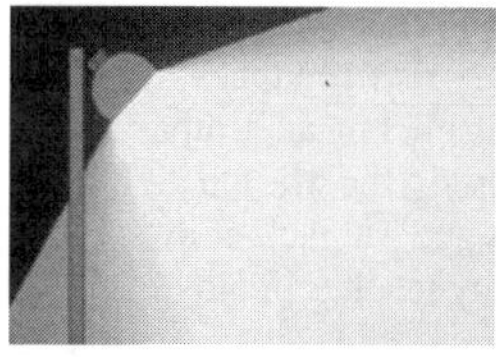

Although full-cutoff, efficient lighting fixtures sometimes have a higher capital cost than polluting fixtures, this cost is quickly recovered through the lower operating costs. Quite a few cities worldwide are realizing substantial savings each year through extensive use of low-pressure sodium (LPS) street lighting. For example, one can usually replace a 175-W mercury vapour lighting fixture with a full-cutoff, 35-W LPS fixture and get the same amount of useful light, with none of the glare and light trespass. The energy saving is remarkable, as is the better visibility. In addition to providing light at the lowest cost, LPS lights are nearly monochromatic, with the result that most of their light can be filtered out by astronomers. Low-pressure sodium lights are especially good for street lighting, parking lot lighting, security lighting, and any application where colour rendering is not important.

Common Types of Outdoor Lights
(in increasing order of efficiency)

Type	**Power** (W/klm)
incandescent (ordinary bulbs)	60
mercury vapour (violet-white light)	24
metal halide (white)	17
high-pressure sodium (orange-gold)	12
low-pressure sodium (yellow)	8

A full-cutoff, efficient light fixture

Even less light pollution and more savings can be realized by using *no more light than is required, and ordinances usually regulate the maximum amount of light that can be used for different tasks*. Too much light and/or poorly shielded lights can ruin adaptation to night lighting, blinding us just when we need to see. When we go from too bright to too dark or vice versa, "transient adaptation" is impaired, and we have poor visibility for a while. Do not exceed IESNA (Illuminating Engineering Society of North America, www.iesna.org) recommended lighting levels. Overkill never helps; it usually just adds glare, and it always wastes energy. In addition, lights should be used only when necessary (timers are useful for controlling lights). Curfews are usually also included in lighting ordinances.

Another common inclusion in lighting ordinances is the use of lighting zones. Different areas have different requirements for lighting; downtown Toronto is not the same as rural Ontario. In addition, some locales have officially declared themselves to be a Dark-Sky Preserve, a region where lighting is strictly controlled or prohibited. A number of these are located in Canada, and the RASC has been instrumental in helping establish these.

Increased lighting generally gives a perception of greater security, yet there is no statistically significant evidence that more lighting results in less crime. Criminals need light. "Security lights" provide this. Furthermore, security lights may draw attention to a house or business that would otherwise not be noticed and mask any additional light that criminals may need to do their work. Our cities and towns are far more brightly lit than ever, yet there has been little or no reduction in the crime rate. We just see more and more bright and glary lights. Security can best be provided by shielded, motion-activated lights that come on only when triggered by movement nearby. These serve to frighten criminals, alert others that there is a potential problem, and provide glare-free visibility (when properly installed so they are glare-free); they also use insignificant amounts of energy.

Lack of Awareness: The biggest problem in controlling light pollution is lack of awareness rather than resistance. After all, it costs money to light pollute! Unlike the case with many other forms of pollution, simple solutions are available; moreover, *everyone benefits* in applying these solutions. Most people are not yet aware of the expense, the waste, and the harm associated with excess lighting. They put up with distant lights that shine directly into their eyes, not realizing that not only does this do *nothing* to illuminate the area near the light but that it also produces a veiling glare. The pollution usually involves not only the light itself but also other forms of environmental pollution associated with the production of the wasted light: the extraction, transportation, and burning of coal and oil. This general lack of awareness has been summarized nicely by Doug Pitcairn, an astronomy teacher in Nova Scotia:

> *It surprises me how someone who would never think of leaving a plastic bottle on the ground at a picnic site will pay extra money each month to illuminate half the neighbourhood with unnecessary, distracting light.*

Education: Educating the public, government officials, lighting professionals, and astronomers is a major thrust of current programs. These efforts have helped. Most committees in the IESNA have been addressing these issues, and Recommended Practices and other documents reflect these concerns. As they are issued, one will see them implemented, albeit on a slow time schedule. Astronomers and environmentalists should do all they can to both learn from these documents and to help publicize them and thereby get them into existing practices in our communities.

The International Dark-Sky Association: The International Dark-Sky Association (IDA) is a tax-exempt, nonprofit membership organization dedicated to overcoming this awareness problem. Its goal is to preserve dark skies while at the same time maximizing the quality and efficiency of nighttime outdoor lighting. The IDA needs your help. Membership begins at $30 U.S. per year. To join this effort or to obtain further information on any aspect of the issue, contact the International Dark-Sky Association, 3225 N First Ave, Tucson AZ 85719, USA (phone: (520) 293-3198; fax: (520) 293-3192; email: ida@darksky.org; Web site: www.darksky.org). Plenty of useful information is on the Web site, including images, and content is added regularly. The IDA has many information sheets available to assist you in educating others—in several languages in addition to English and French—and can provide examples of lighting ordinances that have been enacted in many communities to enforce high-quality, effective nighttime lighting. For more information, see the July 1990 (p. 23) and September 1998 issues of *Sky & Telescope*.

Within Canada, the Royal Astronomical Society of Canada has an active Light-Pollution Abatement Committee under the chairmanship of Robert Dick (contact information: PO Box 79, Rideau Ferry ON K0G 1W0, email: rdick@ccs.carleton.ca); or you may contact the RASC directly (see p. 7). Also, some Centres of the RASC have taken action to address poor lighting practices in their areas.

Editor's Note: An indication that the IDA is making its message heard where it counts is the election of its executive director, David Crawford, as a Fellow of the Illuminating Engineering Society of North America in 1997. The IDA has members in 72 countries, and its total membership as of June 2006 was 11 258 (with 237 from Canada). Of these, 582 are organizational members and 197 are individual lifetime members. This is still well less than 10% of the community of amateur and professional astronomers. As Daniel Green of the Smithsonian Astrophysical Observatory has put it (see *Sky & Telescope,* May 1998, p. 10): "Where are all the astronomers?" Anyone who values the night sky should support this unique and deserving organization. *You* can help make a difference. Please do!

DEEP-SKY OBSERVING HINTS

BY ALAN DYER

In the 1960s and 1970s, few observers owned telescopes larger than 200-mm aperture. Today, 250-mm to 600-mm Dobsonian-mounted reflectors are commonplace. Using computerized telescopes, observers can now find thousands of objects at the push of a button. As a result, deep-sky observing has soared in popularity.

However, owners of less sophisticated, small-aperture instruments shouldn't think they are shut out of deep-sky viewing. In a dark sky an 80-mm to 100-mm telescope will show all the Messier objects and reveal hundreds of brighter NGC (New General Catalogue) objects. In fact, many large objects are best seen in fast (f/4 to f/6), small-aperture telescopes or in giant 70-mm and 80-mm binoculars. Contrary to popular belief, even slow f-ratio instruments (f/11 to f/16) are useful; their only disadvantage is the difficulty of achieving a low-power wide field. No matter what telescope you use, follow these techniques to get the most out of a night's deep-sky viewing:

- Always plan each night's observing: Prepare a list of a dozen or so objects for the night. Hunt them down on star charts or with computer programs first during the day to become familiar with their location.
- Seek out dark skies; a black sky improves contrast and makes up for lack of aperture.
- To preserve night vision, always use a dim red flashlight for reading charts.
- Avoid prolonged exposure to bright sunlight earlier in the day (such as a day at the beach); it will reduce your ability to dark adapt and make for tired eyes at night.
- Use averted vision; looking to one side of an object places it on a more sensitive part of the retina.
- Another technique for picking out faint objects is to jiggle the telescope (and the image) slightly.
- Don't be afraid to use high power; it often brings out small, faint objects such as planetary nebulae and galaxies and resolves detail in globulars, in small, rich open clusters, and in bright galaxies.
- Use a nebula filter on emission and planetary nebulae (see the section FILTERS on pp. 58–61); even in a dark sky, filters can dramatically enhance the view of these kinds of objects, often making obvious an otherwise elusive nebula.
- Be comfortable; sit down while at the eyepiece and be sure to dress warmly.
- Collimate and clean your optics; a poorly maintained telescope will produce distorted star images, reduce image contrast, and make it more difficult to see faint stars and other threshold objects.
- Don't expect to use analog setting circles; in a portable telescope "dial-type" circles will rarely be accurate.
- Digital setting circles and Go To telescopes can find objects precisely. While they are wonderful observing aids, they can overwhelm observers with thousands of targets, often supplying scant information about each one. When making a list for a night's viewing, books such as the three-volume *Burnham's Celestial Handbook* and the two-volume *Night Sky Observer's Guide* by Kepple and Sanner are still the best guides.
- Don't be in a rush to check off targets; take time to examine each object, and take notes or make drawings. Both will help train your eye to see subtle detail; you'll learn to see the most through your telescope.
- Consider keeping a logbook or journal of your nightly tours of the sky; including eyepiece impressions and drawings provides a record of your improving observing skills that is fun to look back upon in future years. See the section THE OBSERVING LOGBOOK (immediately following) for suggestions on organizing a journal.

THE OBSERVING LOGBOOK

By Paul Markov

There are many good reasons for maintaining an observing logbook: A logbook is useful for recalling the details of previous observations and comparing past observations with current ones; maintaining one will make your observing organized and methodical; and having to describe an object forces you to *look* for more details, thus sharpening your observing skills. Finally, if you are planning to apply for an observing certificate (e.g. the RASC's Explore the Universe, Messier, or Finest NGC Certificate; see p. 255), then a logbook with your observations may be required when submitting your application.

Logbooks can be chronological or sectional. In a chronological logbook all observations are listed sequentially by date, regardless of object type. In a sectional logbook observations are grouped by object type, such as open clusters and galaxies. With either format, you may want to keep a master index of objects for cross referencing to the correct page in your logbook.

What about the book itself? Typical choices are the simple three-ring binder with standard lined paper, spiral bound notebooks, and hardcover record/accounting books. In my opinion, the most practical is the three-ring binder because it allows you to insert auxiliary materials into your logbook with the help of a three-hole punch. With this choice, entering observations out of sequence is never an issue because you can easily rearrange the sheets. Also, should you wish to make a copy of your logbook for safekeeping, it's much easier with loose sheets.

For recording observations, using a preprinted observing form offers these advantages: the fill-in-the-blank fields remind you to record the relevant data; many of these forms have a space for making a drawing of the observed object; and they give your book a neat and organized look. An example of an observing form can be found at www.rasc.ca/handbook/obsform.pdf; you may prefer to design your own observing form by using the fields suggested below. However, you can also use plain lined paper: you will never have to worry about running out of forms, and you will not need different forms for different types of objects.

There are two choices for recording your observations: using full sentences and using acronyms and abbreviations. Using full sentences is the preferred method if you enjoy re-reading your observations from past years, or if you want others to be able to easily read your logbook. But if your intent is to keep a data book for reference purposes only, then acronyms and abbreviations are the recommended choices.

It is useful to record the following information for each observing session: date; time of arrival and departure (if you have travelled somewhere to observe); location; names of other people at the observing site; sky transparency (i.e. clarity of the atmosphere, which is generally noted by faintest visible stellar magnitude; see pp. 62–63); seeing (i.e. the steadiness of the atmosphere: if stars and planets appear to shimmer, that indicates poor seeing; if they appear sharp and steady, that indicates good seeing), and environmental conditions (e.g. temperature, dew, wind, sources of light pollution, snow cover, and mosquitoes). You can also number each observing session sequentially for easy referencing within your logbook.

Be sure to standardize your time/date format. For recording time, choose either the military time or a.m./p.m. format. In addition, use alpha characters to specify the month rather than numbers. For example, use 2007 Aug. 5 instead of 8/5/2007; this will avoid ambiguity in reading the date.

For each object observed, record the following information as a minimum: date and time of observation, object name or designation, type of object, constellation, telescope and magnification used, type of filter (if any), and visual description. Making drawings is highly recommended and adds substantially to the appearance of your logbook. It is also important to record failed observations because these entries will remind you to try again in your next observing session.

If you are able to write neatly while observing, it is best to enter observations directly into your logbook. However, if this proves too difficult given the environmental circumstances, you can record your observations in a temporary notebook and transcribe them into your logbook the next day. An audio recorder can also be used if you are careful to ensure its mechanical integrity while in the field and if you are diligent enough to transcribe the recorded observations into your observing logbook regularly. Below are some suggestions on what to look for when observing deep-sky objects.

All Object Types: What is the shape of the object? What is its size (based on the field of view of your eyepiece)? Is averted vision required to see the object? Does averted vision allow you to see more detail? (If yes, describe the extra detail.) Is the object near (or in the same field of view as) other deep-sky objects or bright stars? What magnification gives the best view of the object? Does a filter improve the view? (See the section FILTERS on pp. 58–61.)

Open Cluster: Is there a greater concentration of stars in a specific part of the cluster? Is it fully resolved into its component stars, or are there any unresolved stars causing the cluster to appear nebulous? How many stars can you see (only if reasonable to count them)? Are there any bright stars within the cluster? Are there any coloured stars? (If so, describe their tints and locations within the cluster.) Does the cluster stand out from the background star field?

Globular Cluster: What is the degree of star concentration (high, medium, low)? How much can be resolved to component stars (none, outer edges, middle, to the core)?

Galaxy: Is it uniform in brightness, or does it have a brighter nucleus? Is it diffuse or stellar? Can any detail or mottling be seen in the arms? Are there any stars visible within the arms?

Emission or Reflection Nebula: Is the brightness even, or are there brighter/darker areas? Are the edges of the nebula well defined? Are there any stars within the nebula? Is there a hint of any colour?

Planetary Nebula: Is it stellar in appearance, or can a disk be seen? Are the edges well defined or diffuse? Are there any brighter/darker areas? Can a central star be seen? Is there a hint of any colour?

Dark Nebula: Is it easy or difficult to discern the dark nebula from the background sky? Are there any stars within the nebula?

Logbooks and Databases

If you enjoy using computers, an electronic database can be a helpful complement to an observing logbook. You can obtain commercially available deep-sky databases that allow you to enter your own observations for any object. These databases are also useful for creating observing lists and planning observing sessions. A highly recommended database, which also happens to be freeware, is the Saguaro Astronomy Club (SAC) deep-sky database, available at www.saguaroastro.org. With minimal tweaking, the SAC database can be formatted to accept your own observations.

You can transcribe complete observations from your logbook into the database or simply enter four valuable pieces of information for each observed object: seen (Y/N), date, telescope used, and location. With these fields filled in, in a matter of seconds you can determine which and how many objects you have observed, and the date field for any object will direct you to the correct page in your observing logbook. You can also determine interesting facts such as from which observing location you observed the most objects or which telescope produced the most observations.

THE SKY MONTH BY MONTH

LEFT-HAND PAGES BY
DAVID LANE (TABLES) AND ALAN WHITMAN (TEXT)

INTRODUCTION

In the descriptions on the left-hand monthly pages (pp. 82–104), the right ascension **(RA),** declination **(Dec)** (both for equinox J2000.0), distance from Earth's centre in astronomical units **(Dist),** visual magnitude **(Mag),** and equatorial angular diameter **(Size)** are tabulated for seven planets for 0h UT on the 1st, 11th, and 21st day of each month. The RA, Dec, distance, and diameter of the Sun are also given. **Any stated planet visibility times are in local mean time, which may differ significantly from standard or Daylight Saving Time (see pp. 37, 40).** "Northern observers" and "southern observers" are assumed to be at latitudes 45°N and 30°S, respectively. Unless otherwise stated, descriptions are given first for northern observers and then for southern observers. AT refers to astronomical twilight, NT to nautical twilight, and CT to civil twilight (see p. 167).

Sun

Data concerning the position, transit, orientation, rotation, and activity of the Sun plus times of sunrise and sunset appear on pp. 157–166. For detailed information on this year's solar eclipses, see ECLIPSES IN 2007 on pp. 110–124.

Moon

Conjunctions of the Moon with the naked-eye planets and the bright Messier objects that lie near the ecliptic—the Beehive Cluster (M44), the Lagoon Nebula (M8), M35, and the Pleiades Cluster (M45)—are given in the right-hand monthly tables (pp. 83–105). Only events for which the elongation of the Moon is at least 14° are included, and only selected such events involving the Messier objects are listed. See p. 16 for the definition of conjunction and elongation.

The Moon's phases and perigees and apogees (distances from *Astronomical Tables of the Sun, Moon, and Planets,* by Jean Meeus, 2nd ed., Willmann-Bell, 1995) are also given in the right-hand tables. The phases new Moon, first quarter, full Moon, and last quarter correspond, respectively, to the Moon having a longitude 0°, 90°, 180°, and 270° east of that of the Sun. The age of the Moon is the time since the new phase; first quarter, full, and last quarter phases correspond approximately to 7.4, 14.8, and 22.1 days, respectively. For times of moonrise and moonset, see pp. 128–135.

The Sun's selenographic colongitude (SSC), given on the left-hand monthly pages, indicates the position of the sunrise terminator as it moves across the face of the Moon and provides a method of ascertaining the angle of illumination of features on the Moon's surface. The SSC is the angle of the sunrise terminator measured toward the observer's east (i.e. westward on the Moon) starting from the lunar meridian that passes through the mean centre of the apparent disk. Its value increases by nearly 12.2° per day, or about 0.5° per hour, and is approximately 0°, 90°, 180°, and 270° at the first quarter, full, last quarter, and new phases, respectively. Values of the SSC are given on pp. 82–104 for the beginning of each month.

Selenographic longitude (λ) is measured toward the observer's west (i.e. eastward on the Moon) from the mean central lunar meridian. Thus sunrise will occur at a given point on the Moon when SSC = 360° – λ; values of 360° – λ for several lunar features are listed in the MAP OF MOON on pp. 126–127. The longitude of the sunset terminator differs by 180° from that of the sunrise terminator.

Libration, also given on the left-hand pages, is the apparent rocking motion of the Moon as it orbits Earth. As a consequence, over time, about 59% of the lunar surface can be viewed from Earth (see *Sky & Telescope,* July 1987, p. 60). Libration in longitude (up to ±8°) results from the nearly uniform axial rotation of the Moon combined with its varying orbital speed along its elliptical orbit, while libration in latitude (±7°) is caused by the tilt of the Moon's equator to its orbital plane. A smaller contribution (up to ±1°), called *diurnal libration,* is associated with the shifting of the observer due to Earth's rotation.

When the libration in longitude is positive, more of the Moon's east limb, the limb near Mare Crisium, is exposed to view (in reference to the lunar limbs, *east* and *west* are used in this lunar sense; see also the "E" and "W" labels on the MAP OF MOON). When the libration in latitude is positive, more of the Moon's north limb is exposed to view. The monthly dates of the greatest positive and negative values of the libration in longitude and latitude and the dates of greatest northern and southern declination are given on the left-hand pages.

The lunar graphics on the right-hand pages give the geocentric appearance of the Moon at 0h UT on odd-numbered days of the month. They depict the Moon's phase, size, and libration. A small dot of size proportional to the amount of libration appears near the limb that is exposed. The graphics were prepared by Rajiv Gupta using images and data provided by Roger Fell, who generated the data using the *Lunar Calculator* computer program written by Alister Ling (see www3.telus.net/public/aling/lunarcal/lunarcal.htm).

The Moon's orbit is inclined 5°09′ to the ecliptic. The gravitational influences of Earth and the Sun cause (1) the orbital plane to wobble and (2) the major axis of the orbit to precess. (1) The wobble shifts the line of nodes (see below) westward (retrograde) along the ecliptic with a period of 18.61 years. During 2007, the ascending node regresses from longitude 349.7° to 330.4°, remaining in Aquarius for the entire year. The monthly range of the Moon's declination begins to decrease from its 2006 maximum of ±29°. (2) The precession shifts the perigee point eastward (direct) with a period of 8.85 years, although the positions of successive perigees fluctuate considerably from the mean motion. The Moon's mean equatorial plane, its mean orbital plane, and the plane of the ecliptic intersect along a common line of nodes, the equator being inclined at 1°32′ to the ecliptic and at 1°32′ + 5°09′ = 6°41′ to the orbit (i.e. the ascending node of the equator on the ecliptic coincides with the descending node of the orbit).

Jupiter's Satellites

The configurations of Jupiter's Galilean satellites, provided by Larry Bogan, are given on the right-hand monthly pages. In these diagrams the vertical double line represents the equatorial diameter of the disk of Jupiter. Time is shown on the vertical scale, successive horizontal lines indicating 0h UT on the various days of the month. The relative east–west positions of the four satellites with respect to the disk of Jupiter are given by the four curves, where I = Io, II = Europa (dashed curve), III = Ganymede, and IV = Callisto. Note the "West–East" orientation given at the top of each diagram; these directions are those of the observer's sky, not Jupiter's limbs, and correspond to the view in an inverting telescope.

Double shadow transits of Jupiter's Galilean satellites that are not within 1.5 months of Jupiter's conjunction with the Sun are listed. Double satellite transits that are not accompanied by a double-shadow event are generally also listed. For more information about the various transits, occultations, and eclipses of Jupiter's Galilean satellites, see PHENOMENA OF THE GALILEAN SATELLITES on pp. 183–189.

Occultations Involving the Moon, Stars, Planets, and Asteroids

Occultations by the Moon of the bright stars that lie near the ecliptic—Aldebaran, Antares, Regulus, and Spica—and of the planets and bright asteroids—Ceres, Pallas, Juno, and Vesta—are given in the right-hand tables. If the elongation of the Moon is less than 14° the event is not listed. Footnotes give areas of visibility; for more details on occultations visible in North America, including several involving members of the Pleiades (M45), see pp. 136–151 and pp. 197–200.

Minima of Algol

Predicted times of mideclipse are based on the formula heliocentric minimum = 245 2253.567 + 2.867 321E and are expressed as geocentric times for comparison with observations. The first number is the Julian Date for the minimum of 2001 Dec. 10.067, and the second is the period of Algol in days; E is an integer.

Planets

Conjunctions of the planets (except for Pluto) with each other and the bright ecliptic stars and Messier objects are listed in the right-hand tables, with the elongation of the inner planet indicated in parentheses. Only events for which the elongation of the inner planet is greater than 11° are included, and not all events involving the Messier objects are listed. Also included are oppositions, conjunctions with the Sun, greatest elongations, and stationary times. See pp. 16–17 for definitions of these terms and CONTENTS or the INDEX for the location of more information on each of the planets. The diagrams below and to the right give an overview of the circumstances of the planets in 2007.

Miscellaneous Entries

Peaks of major meteor showers (see also p. 219), equinoxes and solstices, heliocentric phenomena of the planets, phenomena of the bright asteroids, and a few other events and occasional notes are also given in the right-hand tables.

MAGNITUDES OF NAKED-EYE PLANETS IN 2007

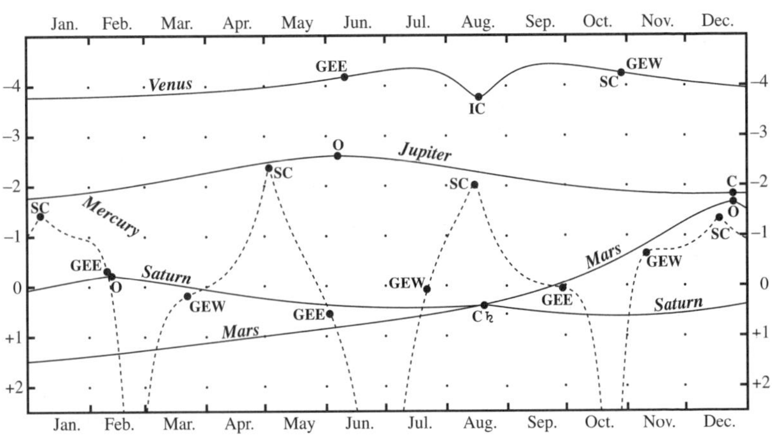

The visual magnitudes of the five, classical (naked-eye) planets during 2007 are given. Oppositions (O), conjunctions (C), inferior and superior conjunctions (IC, SC), and greatest elongations east and west (GEE, GEW) are indicated. A diagram explaining these terms is on p. 17.

RIGHT ASCENSIONS OF THE SUN AND PLANETS IN 2007

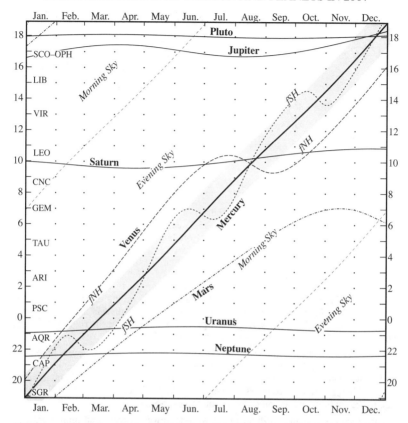

This diagram shows the variation during the year in the right ascension (vertical axis) of the Sun and the planets. The slightly curved, heavy diagonal line represents the Sun; the shaded regions approximately indicate parts of the night sky affected by twilight. The two thin, dashed diagonal lines at the upper left and bottom right represent the boundary between the evening sky and the morning sky.

The diagram may be used to determine in what part of the sky a planet may be found (including in which constellation—note the abbreviations along the vertical axis), when a superior planet is in conjunction with the Sun or at opposition (opposition is approximately where its curve intersects the dashed diagonal lines, and note that, due to retrograde motion, this point is also where the planet's curve has its maximum negative slope), when Mercury and Venus have their various greatest elongations and conjunctions, and when there are conjunctions of planets—that is, when the curves for two planets intersect. For example, note the conjunction of Mars with Neptune in late March (and then with Uranus in late April), the opposition of Jupiter in early June, the conjunction of Saturn and Venus in early July and again in mid October., and the opposition of Mars in late December.

For observers in midlatitudes, at certain times of the year the ecliptic stands steeply to the horizon in the western evening sky or the eastern morning sky, making apparitions of planets in these parts of the sky favourable from the Northern Hemisphere ("fNH" on the diagram) or favourable from the Southern Hemisphere ("fSH").

For more information on all these events, see the following 24 monthly pages and THE PLANETS FOR 2007 *(pp. 170–182).*

THE SKY FOR 2007 JANUARY

		Mercury	Venus	Mars	Jupiter	Saturn	Uranus	Neptune	Sun
RA	1	18^h28^m	19^h53^m	17^h09^m	16^h26^m	9^h48^m	22^h53^m	21^h22^m	18^h44^m
	11	19^h39^m	20^h45^m	17^h41^m	16^h34^m	9^h46^m	22^h54^m	21^h23^m	19^h28^m
	21	20^h50^m	21^h36^m	18^h13^m	16^h42^m	9^h44^m	22^h56^m	21^h25^m	20^h11^m
Dec	1	−24°45′	−22°16′	−23°14′	−20°58′	+14°32′	−7°58′	−15°38′	−23°03′
	11	−23°33′	−19°36′	−23°47′	−21°17′	+14°45′	−7°49′	−15°32′	−21°55′
	21	−19°49′	−16°00′	−23°56′	−21°32′	+14°59′	−7°39′	−15°26′	−20°03′
Dist	1	1.44	1.62	2.38	6.17	8.45	20.54	30.82	0.983
	11	1.42	1.59	2.34	6.08	8.34	20.68	30.91	0.983
	21	1.33	1.56	2.29	5.96	8.27	20.81	30.98	0.984
Mag	1	−1.0	−3.8	1.5	−1.8	0.2	5.9	8.0	
	11	−1.3	−3.8	1.5	−1.8	0.2	5.9	8.0	
	21	−1.0	−3.8	1.4	−1.8	0.1	5.9	8.0	
Size	1	4.7″	10.3″	3.9″	31.9″	19.7″	3.4″	2.2″	32′32″
	11	4.7″	10.5″	4.0″	32.4″	19.9″	3.4″	2.2″	32′32″
	21	5.1″	10.7″	4.1″	33.1″	20.1″	3.4″	2.2″	32′30″

Moon—On Jan. 1.0 UT, the age of the Moon is 11.4 d. The Sun's selenographic colongitude is 53.67° and increases by 12.2° each day thereafter. The libration in longitude is maximum (east limb exposed) on Jan. 4 and 31 (+5°), and minimum (west limb exposed) on Jan. 16 (–6°). (See the two paragraphs concerning libration on p. 79) The libration in latitude is maximum (north limb exposed) on Jan. 16 (+7°), and minimum (south limb exposed) on Jan. 1 and 28 (–7°). The Moon reaches its greatest northern declination on Jan. 2 and 29 (+28°), and its greatest southern declination on Jan. 16 (–28°). The waning crescent slides past Antares on the morning of Jan. 15. This year the Moon occults an unusually high number of planets and bright stars: Saturn, Venus, Mercury, Mars, Regulus, Spica, and Antares. See the right-hand pages and OCCULTATIONS BY THE MOON on pp. 136–151.

Mercury is in superior conjunction on Jan. 7. It is poorly placed for observation until late in the month when it becomes visible to northern observers at magnitude –1.2, 7° below Venus in evening twilight. The Jan.-Feb. evening apparition is moderately favourable for northern observers. The planet remains difficult for southern observers due to the shallow inclination of the ecliptic to the horizon.

Venus decorates evening twilight in the west-southwest, except that more northerly observers view it in the southwest for the first half of the month. It begins January fairly low in bright twilight and for southern observers the planet's altitude only increases slightly by Jan. 31, but before month end northern observers will see it setting in a fully dark sky.

Mars begins the month in Ophiuchus and crosses into Sagittarius on Jan. 11. On Jan. 1 it rises in the east-southeast about 1.5 h before sunrise in both hemispheres. Only the southern hemisphere sees a significant increase in the altitude of the Red Planet during the month. Mars remains a morning planet for much of the year, until its rather distant opposition on Dec. 24.

Jupiter spends the first 11 months of the year in Ophiuchus so that its Jun. 5 opposition will be an unfavourable one from Canadian latitudes. In January it is a beacon in the morning sky, rising an hour before twilight on Jan. 5 when it passes 5° N of Antares. By midmonth it rises at 2:00. at latitude 30°S and 4:30 at 45°N.

Saturn, in Leo all year, rises about half an hour after the end of evening AT by midmonth for northern observers and at AT for southern observers. It transits near 2:00 at an altitude of 60° at latitude 45°N, 75° at 30°N, and 45° (in the North) at latitude 30°S. The southern side of the rings is visible this year and next. The tilt of the rings increases from 12.6° in early January to 15.4° in mid-April, and then closes to only 6.6° in mid-December. At year-end they will have reopened to 6.7°.

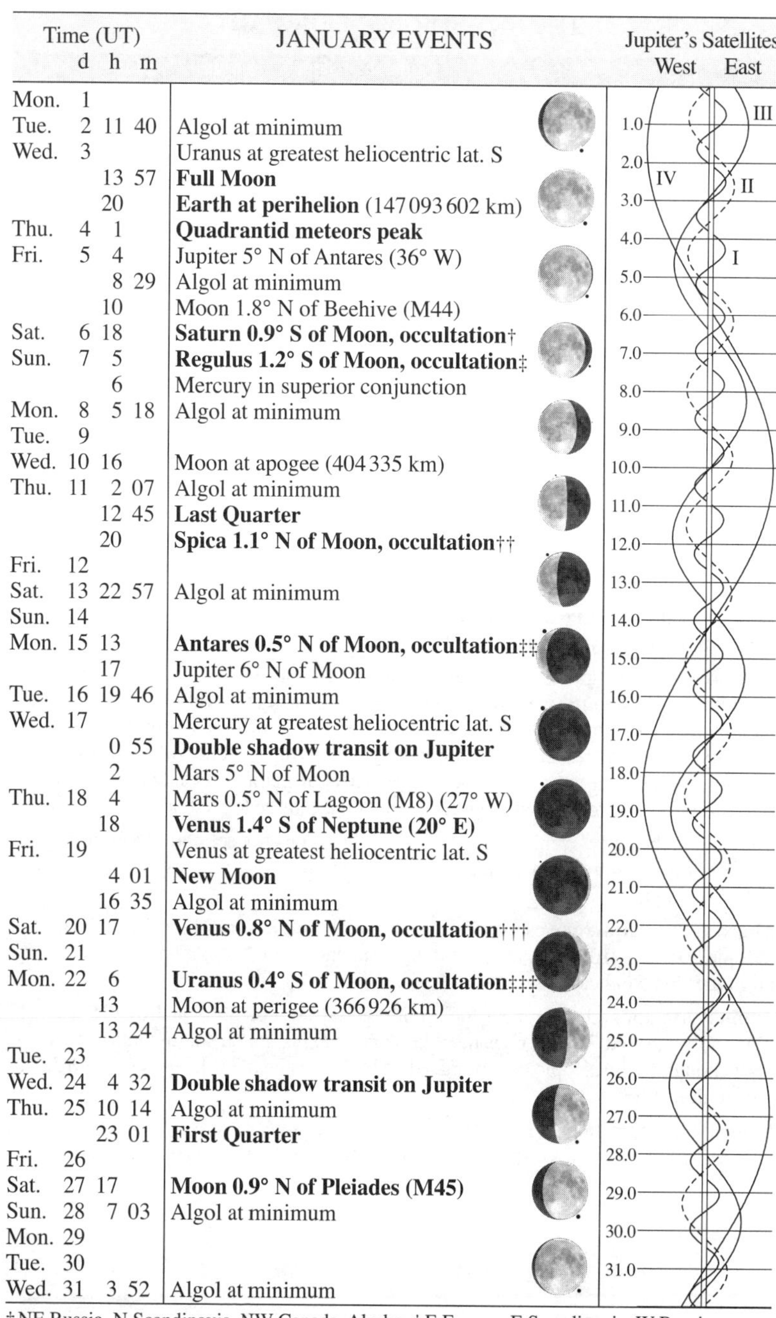

Time (UT)	d	h	m	JANUARY EVENTS
Mon.	1			
Tue.	2	11	40	Algol at minimum
Wed.	3			Uranus at greatest heliocentric lat. S
		13	57	**Full Moon**
		20		**Earth at perihelion** (147 093 602 km)
Thu.	4	1		**Quadrantid meteors peak**
Fri.	5	4		Jupiter 5° N of Antares (36° W)
		8	29	Algol at minimum
		10		Moon 1.8° N of Beehive (M44)
Sat.	6	18		**Saturn 0.9° S of Moon, occultation**†
Sun.	7	5		**Regulus 1.2° S of Moon, occultation**‡
		6		Mercury in superior conjunction
Mon.	8	5	18	Algol at minimum
Tue.	9			
Wed.	10	16		Moon at apogee (404 335 km)
Thu.	11	2	07	Algol at minimum
		12	45	**Last Quarter**
		20		**Spica 1.1° N of Moon, occultation**††
Fri.	12			
Sat.	13	22	57	Algol at minimum
Sun.	14			
Mon.	15	13		**Antares 0.5° N of Moon, occultation**‡‡
		17		Jupiter 6° N of Moon
Tue.	16	19	46	Algol at minimum
Wed.	17			Mercury at greatest heliocentric lat. S
		0	55	**Double shadow transit on Jupiter**
		2		Mars 5° N of Moon
Thu.	18	4		Mars 0.5° N of Lagoon (M8) (27° W)
		18		**Venus 1.4° S of Neptune (20° E)**
Fri.	19			Venus at greatest heliocentric lat. S
		4	01	**New Moon**
		16	35	Algol at minimum
Sat.	20	17		**Venus 0.8° N of Moon, occultation**†††
Sun.	21			
Mon.	22	6		**Uranus 0.4° S of Moon, occultation**‡‡‡
		13		Moon at perigee (366 926 km)
		13	24	Algol at minimum
Tue.	23			
Wed.	24	4	32	**Double shadow transit on Jupiter**
Thu.	25	10	14	Algol at minimum
		23	01	**First Quarter**
Fri.	26			
Sat.	27	17		**Moon 0.9° N of Pleiades (M45)**
Sun.	28	7	03	Algol at minimum
Mon.	29			
Tue.	30			
Wed.	31	3	52	Algol at minimum

† NE Russia, N Scandinavia, NW Canada, Alaska ‡ E Europe, E Scandinavia, W Russia
†† Most of Antarctica, SE Indian Ocean ‡‡ S tips of S. America and Africa, part of Antarctica
††† SW Africa, most of Antarctica, S tip of S. America
‡‡‡ Japan, Philippines, Indonesia, E Indian Ocean, S tip of India

THE SKY FOR 2007 FEBRUARY

		Mercury	Venus	Mars	Jupiter	Saturn	Uranus	Neptune	Sun
RA	1	22^h01^m	22^h28^m	18^h48^m	16^h51^m	9^h40^m	22^h58^m	21^h26^m	20^h56^m
	11	22^h41^m	23^h15^m	19^h21^m	16^h57^m	9^h37^m	23^h00^m	21^h28^m	21^h37^m
	21	22^h27^m	23^h59^m	19^h53^m	17^h03^m	9^h34^m	23^h02^m	21^h29^m	22^h15^m
Dec	1	−13°02′	−11°12′	−23°37′	−21°47′	+15°17′	−7°27′	−15°18′	−17°18′
	11	−6°44′	−6°19′	−22°54′	−21°57′	+15°34′	−7°14′	−15°11′	−14°15′
	21	−5°48′	−1°10′	−21°47′	−22°05′	+15°50′	−7°02′	−15°04′	−10°48′
Dist	1	1.13	1.52	2.24	5.82	8.22	20.92	31.03	0.985
	11	0.86	1.48	2.18	5.67	8.20	21.00	31.04	0.987
	21	0.66	1.44	2.13	5.52	8.22	21.05	31.02	0.989
Mag	1	−0.9	−3.8	1.4	−1.9	0.0	5.9	8.0	
	11	−0.1	−3.8	1.3	−1.9	−0.0	5.9	8.0	
	21	4.4	−3.8	1.3	−2.0	−0.0	5.9	8.0	
Size	1	5.9″	11.0″	4.2″	33.9″	20.2″	3.3″	2.2″	32′28″
	11	7.8″	11.3″	4.3″	34.7″	20.3″	3.3″	2.2″	32′25″
	21	10.2″	11.6″	4.4″	35.7″	20.2″	3.3″	2.2″	32′21″

Moon—On Feb. 1.0 UT, the age of the Moon is 12.8 d. The Sun's selenographic colongitude is 70.54° and increases by 12.2° each day thereafter. The libration in longitude is maximum (east limb exposed) on Feb. 26 (+6°), and minimum (west limb exposed) on Feb. 13 (–7°). The libration in latitude is maximum (north limb exposed) on Feb. 12 (+7°), and minimum (south limb exposed) on Feb. 25 (–7°). The Moon reaches its greatest northern declination on Feb. 25 (+29°), and its greatest southern declination on Feb. 13 (–29°). Regulus is occulted in large parts of North America on Feb. 3, unfortunately by a nearly full Moon.

Mercury reaches greatest elongation east (18°) on Feb. 7 when it shines at magnitude –0.6 about 7° below Venus in evening twilight. Mid-northern observers will find it at an altitude of 8° in the west-southwest 45 min after sunset. By midmonth Mercury, a waning crescent, is fading rapidly and diving back down towards the Sun. Inferior conjunction is on Feb. 23. The planet is difficult for southern observers in early February due to the shallow inclination of the ecliptic to the horizon.

Venus is in the early evening sky. At midmonth it does not set until 37 minutes after the end of AT at latitude 45°N. Less favoured southern observers see it set in the west in late twilight.

Mars, in Sagittarius, moves into Capricornus on Feb. 25. At morning AT on Feb. 15 at latitude 30°S it is 16° high, at 30°N it is 6° up, and at 45°N it is minutes from rising, all in the east-southeast.

Jupiter at midmonth rises near local midnight at latitude 30°S and by CT it is 61° high in the east. At 30°N it rises near 2:00 and is at 36° in the south-southeast by CT, high enough for telescopic observing. At 45°N it rises near 3:00, but is only up 22° in the south-southeast at CT.

Saturn is at opposition on Feb. 10 when it rises near sunset, transits at local midnight, and sets near sunrise. (See January for culmination altitudes and ring inclination.)

Time (UT)	d	h	m	FEBRUARY EVENTS
Thu.	1			Pallas in conjunction with the Sun
		18		Moon 1.8° N of Beehive (M44)
Fri.	2	5	45	**Full Moon**
		23		**Saturn 0.9° S of Moon, occultation**†
Sat.	3	0	42	Algol at minimum
		14		**Regulus 1.1° S of Moon, occultation**‡
Sun.	4			**Zodiacal Light** vis. in N lat. in W after evening twilight for next two weeks
Mon	5			Mercury at ascending node
		21	31	Algol at minimum
Tue.	6			
Wed.	7	13		Moon at apogee (404 992 km)
		13		**Venus 0.7° S of Uranus (24° E)**
		17		**Mercury greatest elongation E (18°)**
Thu.	8	4		**Spica 1.3° N of Moon, occultation**††
		16		Neptune in conjunction with the Sun
		18	20	Algol at minimum
Fri.	9			
Sat.	10			Mercury at perihelion
		9	51	**Last Quarter**
		19		**Saturn at opposition**
Sun.	11	15	10	Algol at minimum
		22		**Antares 0.7° N of Moon, occultation**‡‡
Mon	12	10		Jupiter 6° N of Moon
Tue.	13	14		Mercury stationary
Wed.	14	11	59	Algol at minimum
Thu.	15	1		Mars 4° N of Moon
Fri.	16			
Sat.	17	8	48	Algol at minimum
		16	14	**New Moon**
Sun.	18			
Mon	19			Juno stationary
		10		Moon at perigee (361 436 km)
		17		**Venus 2° S of Moon**
Tue.	20			Mercury at greatest heliocentric lat. N
		5	37	Algol at minimum
Wed.	21			
Thu.	22			
Fri.	23	2	27	Algol at minimum
		5		Mercury in inferior conjunction
		23		**Moon 1.0° N of Pleiades (M45)**
Sat.	24	7	56	**First Quarter**
Sun.	25	23	16	Algol at minimum
Mon.	26			
Tue.	27			
Wed.	28	20	05	Algol at minimum

Jupiter's Satellites
West East

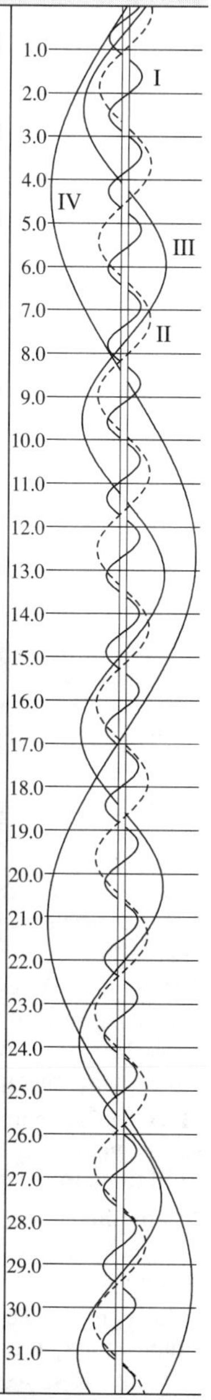

† Central Asia, Eastern Scandinavia, Arctic regions ‡ NW North America, N Greenland
†† Drake Passage, South of South America
‡‡ Southern oceans, Antarctica

THE SKY FOR 2007 MARCH

		Mercury	Venus	Mars	Jupiter	Saturn	Uranus	Neptune	Sun
RA	1	21h57m	0h35m	20h18m	17h07m	9h32m	23h03m	21h31m	22h46m
	11	21h51m	1h20m	20h50m	17h11m	9h29m	23h05m	21h32m	23h23m
	21	22h18m	2h05m	21h21m	17h14m	9h27m	23h08m	21h33m	23h59m
Dec	1	−9°06′	+3°00′	−20°36′	−22°10′	+16°02′	−6°51′	−14°59′	−7°51′
	11	−12°03′	+8°07′	−18°49′	−22°14′	+16°16′	−6°38′	−14°52′	−3°59′
	21	−11°36′	+12°57′	−16°43′	−22°17′	+16°27′	−6°25′	−14°46′	−0°02′
Dist	1	0.64	1.40	2.09	5.39	8.25	21.08	30.98	0.991
	11	0.75	1.35	2.04	5.23	8.32	21.08	30.91	0.993
	21	0.90	1.29	1.98	5.07	8.42	21.05	30.82	0.996
Mag	1	2.8	−3.8	1.3	−2.0	0.0	5.9	8.0	
	11	0.7	−3.8	1.2	−2.1	0.1	5.9	8.0	
	21	0.2	−3.9	1.2	−2.2	0.1	5.9	8.0	
Size	1	10.5″	11.9″	4.5″	36.5″	20.1″	3.3″	2.2″	32′17″
	11	9.0″	12.4″	4.6″	37.7″	20.0″	3.3″	2.2″	32′12″
	21	7.5″	12.9″	4.7″	38.9″	19.7″	3.3″	2.2″	32′07″

Moon—On Mar. 1.0 UT, the age of the Moon is 11.3 d. The Sun's selenographic colongitude is 51.26° and increases by 12.2° each day thereafter. The libration in longitude is maximum (east limb exposed) on Mar. 26 (+7°), and minimum (west limb exposed) on Mar. 13 (−8°). The libration in latitude is maximum (north limb exposed) on Mar. 11 (+7°), and minimum (south limb exposed) on Mar. 24 (−7°). The Moon reaches its greatest northern declination on Mar. 25 (+29°), and its greatest southern declination on Mar. 12 (−29°).

There is a **total lunar eclipse** on Mar. 3–4 visible from the eastern half of North America, South America, Africa, Europe, and much of Asia. Europe and Africa are favoured. There is a **partial solar eclipse** for the extreme northwestern Yukon and much of both Alaska and Asia on Mar. 19. (See ECLIPSES IN 2007 pp. 110–124).

Mercury reaches greatest elongation west (28°) on Mar. 22. It becomes a reasonable target in morning twilight for observers at latitude 30°N after the first week of March, but this is a very unfavourable apparition for observers at Canadian latitudes (except for daytime observing with Go-To telescopes). For **southern hemisphere observers this is the finest morning apparition of the year** and it illustrates why they are puzzled when they read that Mercury is a difficult planet to observe—on Mar. 23 the 0.2-magnitude planet is 10° high before AT begins! It dominates the fully dark eastern sky, a magnitude brighter than its only rivals, Mars and Fomalhaut.

Venus bejewels the early evening sky in both hemispheres. Favoured northern hemisphere observers will see its striking glitter path across lakes and bays after twilight ends. On the other hand, Venus will somewhat inhibit viewing of the zodiacal light.

Mars, in Capricornus, rises in the east-southeast. At morning AT on Mar. 15 it has vaulted up to 23° altitude at latitude 30°S and climbed to 7° at 30°N, but at 45°N it is still 11 min from rising.

Jupiter, in Ophiuchus, rises at midmonth around 1:00 at mid-northern latitudes and 23:00 at latitude 30°S. It transits during CT at these altitudes: 23° at latitude 45°N, 38° at latitude 30°N, and 82° (in the north) at latitude 30°S.

Saturn crosses the meridian near 22:00 at midmonth. (See January for culmination altitudes and ring inclination.) It sets in the west-northwest half an hour after morning AT begins, at latitude 45°N, shortly before AT at 30°N, and shortly after 3:00 at 30°S.

Time (UT)	d	h	m	MARCH EVENTS
Thu.	1	1		Moon 1.9° N of Beehive (M44)
Fri.	2	2		**Saturn 1.1° S of Moon, occultation†**
		21		**Regulus 1.1° S of Moon, occultation‡**
Sat.	3	16	55	Algol at minimum
		23	17	**Full Moon, total eclipse** (p. 110)
Sun.	4			
Mon.	5	16		Uranus in conjunction with the Sun
Tue.	6			**Zodiacal Light** vis. in N lat. in W after evening twilight for next two weeks
		1		Mars 4° N of Moon
		13	44	Algol at minimum
Wed.	7	4		Moon at apogee (405 853 km)
		10		Mercury stationary
		11		**Spica 1.3° N of Moon**
Thu.	8			
Fri.	9	10	33	Algol at minimum
Sat.	10			
Sun.	11			**Daylight Saving Time begins**
		6		**Antares 0.7° N of Moon, occultation††**
Mon.	12	0		Jupiter 6° N of Moon
		3	54	**Last Quarter**
		7	22	Algol at minimum
Tue.	13			
Wed.	14			
Thu.	15			Mercury at descending node
		4	12	Algol at minimum
Fri.	16			Venus at ascending node
		1		**Mars 1.9° N of Moon**
Sat.	17			
		3		**Mercury 1.4° N of Moon, occultation‡‡**
Sun.	18	1	01	Algol at minimum
Mon.	19	2	43	**New Moon, partial solar eclipse** (p. 110)
		19		Moon at perigee (357 814 km) **Large tides**
Tue.	20	21	50	Algol at minimum
Wed.	21	0	7	**Equinox**
		15		Venus 4° S of Moon
Thu.	22			Ceres in conjunction with the Sun
		2		**Mercury greatest elongation W (28°)**
		14	04	**Double shadow transit on Jupiter**
Fri.	23	6		**Moon 1.0° N of Pleiades (M45)**
		18	39	Algol at minimum
Sat.	24			
Sun.	25	7		**Mars 1.0° S of Neptune (44° W)**
		18	16	**First Quarter**
Mon.	26			Mercury at aphelion
		15	28	Algol at minimum
Tue.	27			
Wed.	28	6		Moon 1.8° N of Beehive (M44)
Thu.	29	4		**Saturn 1.2° S of Moon, occultation†††**
		12	18	Algol at minimum
		16	36	**Double shadow transit on Jupiter**
Fri.	30	3		**Regulus 1.1° S of Moon, occultation‡‡‡**
Sat.	31			

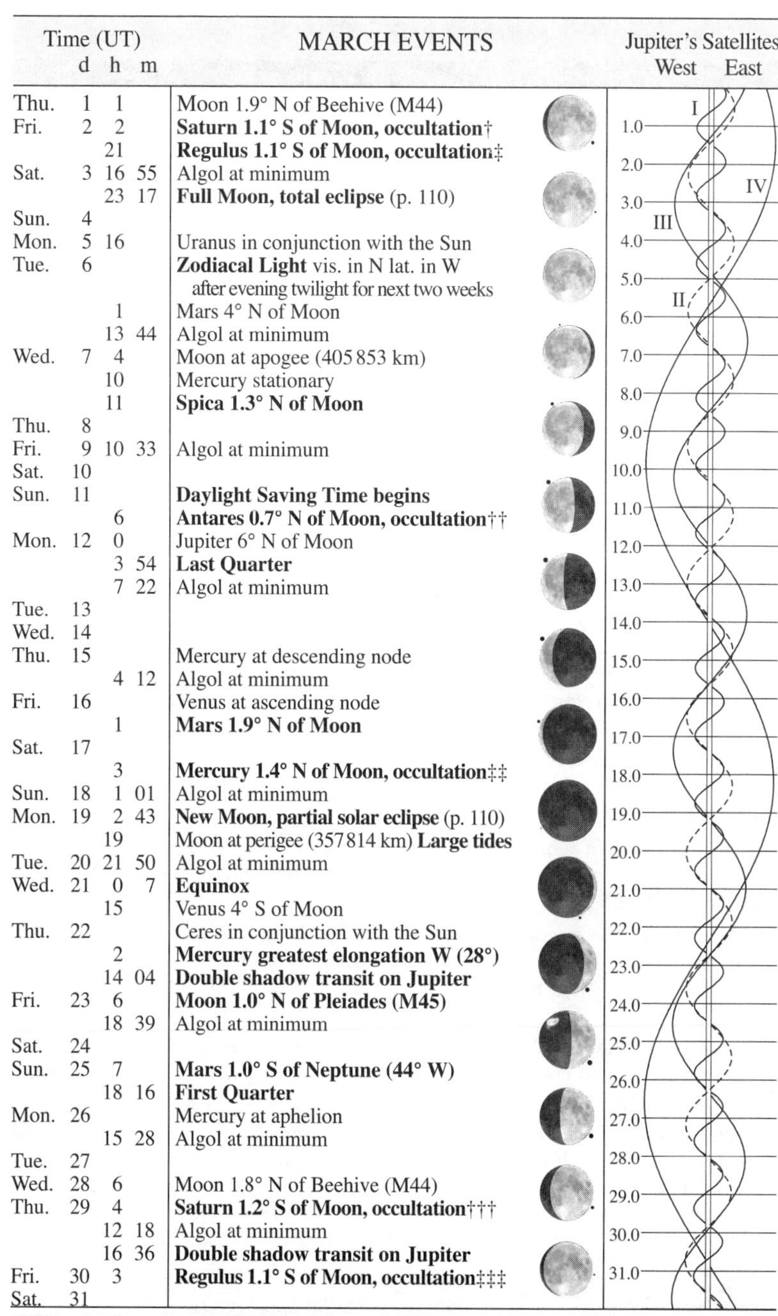

† W Russia, Europe except W British Isles, and SW Europe ‡ E Central Asia, Arctic regions
†† Antarctica, southern part of S. America ‡‡ Southern Ocean south of New Zealand
††† N British Isles, N Scandinavia, N Atlantic Ocean, E Greenland
‡‡‡ W Europe including British Isles, Scandinavia, Arctic regions

THE SKY FOR 2007 APRIL

		Mercury	Venus	Mars	Jupiter	Saturn	Uranus	Neptune	Sun
RA	1	23^h08^m	2^h56^m	21^h54^m	17^h15^m	9^h25^m	23^h10^m	21^h35^m	0^h40^m
	11	0^h04^m	3^h44^m	22^h23^m	17^h15^m	9^h24^m	23^h12^m	21^h35^m	1^h16^m
	21	1^h07^m	4^h33^m	22^h52^m	17^h14^m	9^h24^m	23^h14^m	21^h36^m	1^h53^m
Dec	1	−7°56′	+17°40′	−14°05′	−22°18′	+16°35′	−6°11′	−14°40′	+4°16′
	11	−2°17′	+21°12′	−11°28′	−22°18′	+16°39′	−5°59′	−14°36′	+8°03′
	21	+5°06′	+23°51′	−8°40′	−22°16′	+16°40′	−5°48′	−14°32′	+11°37′
Dist	1	1.05	1.22	1.93	4.90	8.55	20.99	30.69	0.999
	11	1.18	1.16	1.87	4.75	8.70	20.91	30.55	1.002
	21	1.28	1.09	1.82	4.62	8.85	20.81	30.40	1.005
Mag	1	0.0	−3.9	1.1	−2.3	0.2	5.9	8.0	
	11	−0.3	−3.9	1.1	−2.3	0.3	5.9	7.9	
	21	−0.8	−3.9	1.0	−2.4	0.3	5.9	7.9	
Size	1	6.4″	13.6″	4.9″	40.2″	19.4″	3.3″	2.2″	32′01″
	11	5.7″	14.4″	5.0″	41.5″	19.1″	3.3″	2.2″	31′56″
	21	5.2″	15.3″	5.1″	42.7″	18.8″	3.4″	2.2″	31′50″

Moon—On Apr. 1.0 UT, the age of the Moon is 12.9 d. The Sun's selenographic colongitude is 68.84° and increases by 12.2° each day thereafter. The libration in longitude is maximum (east limb exposed) on Apr. 23 (+8°), and minimum (west limb exposed) on Apr. 11 (−8°). The libration in latitude is maximum (north limb exposed) on Apr. 7 (+7°), and minimum (south limb exposed) on Apr. 20 (−7°). The Moon reaches its greatest northern declination on Apr. 21 (+28°), and its greatest southern declination on Apr. 8 (−29°). On Apr. 25 **Saturn is occulted** northwest of a line from Edmonton to Seattle (the Moon is very low at both cities). The altitude is 3° at Vancouver, 5° at Prince George, and 21° at Anchorage. On the next night a larger part of northwestern North America enjoys an **occultation of Regulus**. At Vancouver the altitude is 15°. (See also Venus.)

Mercury continues its fine morning apparition for southern observers until midmonth, brightening as it sinks lower in the dawn. It is poorly placed for northern observers.

Venus continues its striking evening apparition, setting in the west-northwest well after full dark in both hemispheres. On Apr. 18 it passes less than a degree northwest of the outlying northern arc of the Hyades. On the following evening the 2.5-day-old crescent Moon with earthshine joins the scene.

Mars moves from Capricornus to Aquarius on Apr. 2. At morning AT on Apr. 15 the planet has already risen to 30° altitude in the east at latitude 30°S due to the nearly vertical ecliptic and to 9° in the east-southeast at latitude 30°N, but at 45°N it is still a quarter hour from rising.

Jupiter begins its retrograde loop on Apr. 6. On Apr. 15 it rises in late evening at mid-northern latitudes and near 21:00 at mid-southern. It transits near 3:30. (See March for altitudes at transit.)

Saturn, which has been retrograding in Leo for four months, has almost reached the Cancer border, but it is stationary on Apr. 20 and then resumes direct (eastward) motion. At culmination, just before 20:00 at midmonth, Saturn is now 2° higher than it was in January for northern observers and 2° lower for southern observers. It sets in the west-northwest near 3:00 at latitude 45°N, 2:30 at 30°N, and 1:00 at 30°S.

Time (UT)	d	h	m	APRIL EVENTS
Sun.	1	0		Pluto stationary
		7		**Mercury 1.6° S of Uranus (26° E)**
		9	07	Algol at minimum
Mon.	2	17	15	**Full Moon (smallest in 2007)**
Tue.	3	9		Moon at apogee (406 329 km)
		17		**Spica 1.3° N of Moon**
Wed.	4	5	56	Algol at minimum
Thu.	5	20	07	**Double shadow transit on Jupiter**
Fri.	6	2		Jupiter stationary
Sat.	7	2	45	Algol at minimum
		13		**Antares 0.6° N of Moon, occultation†**
Sun.	8	9		Jupiter 6° N of Moon
Mon.	9	23	34	Algol at minimum
Tue.	10			Juno at opposition
		18	04	**Last Quarter**
Wed.	11	13		**Venus 3° S of Pleiades (M45) (38° E)**
Thu.	12	20	23	Algol at minimum
Fri.	13	0	05	**Double shadow transit on Jupiter**
Sat.	14	2		**Mars 0.5° S of Moon, occultation‡**
		20		**Uranus 1.0° S of Moon, occultation††**
Sun.	15			Mercury at greatest heliocentric lat. S
		17	12	Algol at minimum
Mon.	16	11		Mercury 5° S of Moon
Tue.	17	6		Moon at perigee (357 136 km) **Large tides**
		11	36	**New Moon**
Wed.	18			Vesta stationary
		14	01	Algol at minimum
Thu.	19			Venus at perihelion
		16		**Moon 0.9° N of Pleiades (M45)**
Fri.	20	1		Saturn stationary
		8		**Venus 3° S of Moon**
Sat.	21	10	50	Algol at minimum
		12		Venus 7° N of Aldebaran (39° E)
Sun.	22	22		Lyrid meteors peak
Mon.	23			
Tue.	24	6	36	**First Quarter**
		7	39	Algol at minimum
		13		**Moon 1.7° N of Beehive (M44)**
Wed.	25	10		**Saturn 1.1° S of Moon, occultation‡‡**
Thu.	26	9		**Regulus 1.0° S of Moon, occultation†††**
Fri.	27	4	28	Algol at minimum
Sat.	28	19		**Mars 0.7° S of Uranus (51° W)**
Mon.	30	1	17	Algol at minimum
		11		Moon at apogee (406 209 km)
		23		**Spica 1.3° N of Moon**

Jupiter's Satellites — West / East

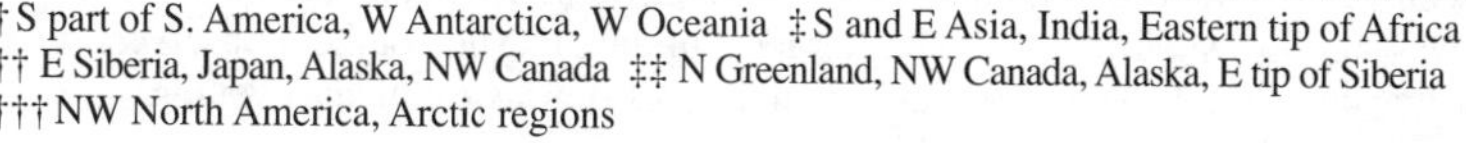
† S part of S. America, W Antarctica, W Oceania ‡ S and E Asia, India, Eastern tip of Africa
†† E Siberia, Japan, Alaska, NW Canada ‡‡ N Greenland, NW Canada, Alaska, E tip of Siberia
††† NW North America, Arctic regions

THE SKY FOR 2007 MAY

		Mercury	Venus	Mars	Jupiter	Saturn	Uranus	Neptune	Sun
RA	1	2h22m	5h23m	23h21m	17h11m	9h24m	23h15m	21h37m	2h31m
	11	3h46m	6h13m	23h49m	17h07m	9h25m	23h16m	21h37m	3h10m
	21	5h08m	7h01m	0h17m	17h03m	9h27m	23h18m	21h38m	3h49m
Dec	1	+13°32′	+25°29′	−5°46′	−22°14′	+16°37′	−5°38′	−14°29′	+14°52′
	11	+21°06′	+26°00′	−2°47′	−22°09′	+16°32′	−5°30′	−14°27′	+17°42′
	21	+25°07′	+25°26′	+0°12′	−22°04′	+16°23′	−5°23′	−14°26′	+20°02′
Dist	1	1.33	1.02	1.77	4.51	9.01	20.68	30.23	1.007
	11	1.26	0.94	1.72	4.41	9.18	20.54	30.07	1.010
	21	1.08	0.86	1.68	4.35	9.34	20.39	29.90	1.012
Mag	1	−2.0	−4.0	1.0	−2.5	0.4	5.9	7.9	
	11	−1.4	−4.0	0.9	−2.5	0.4	5.9	7.9	
	21	−0.6	−4.1	0.9	−2.6	0.5	5.9	7.9	
Size	1	5.1″	16.4″	5.3″	43.7″	18.5″	3.4″	2.2″	31′45″
	11	5.3″	17.7″	5.4″	44.6″	18.1″	3.4″	2.2″	31′41″
	21	6.2″	19.3″	5.6″	45.3″	17.8″	3.4″	2.2″	31′37″

Moon—On May 1.0 UT, the age of the Moon is 13.5 d. The Sun's selenographic colongitude is 74.76° and increases by 12.2° each day thereafter. The libration in longitude is maximum (east limb exposed) on May 21 (+7°), and minimum (west limb exposed) on May 9 (–7°). The libration in latitude is maximum (north limb exposed) on May 5 (+7°), and minimum (south limb exposed) on May 17 (–7°). The Moon reaches its greatest northern declination on May 18 (+28°), and its greatest southern declination on May 6 (–28°).

Mercury reaches superior conjunction on May 3 and remains poorly placed until it appears in the evening twilight low in the west-northwest late in the month for observers near latitudes 30°S or 45°N. At the more favoured latitude of 30°N it may become visible by about May 18. The May–June evening apparition is moderately favourable for northern observers. Mercury is brighter in late May than in early June when at the same altitude, so May is the better part of this apparition for finding the planet.

Venus is well up in the evening twilight sky for both hemispheres as its elongation from the Sun increases to 45° by May 31. It then sets about 1 h 45 min after the end of AT at latitudes 30°S and 30°N, and one hour after at latitude 45°N. Twilight's other ornament, the three-day-old crescent Moon with earthshine, is paired with Venus on the evening of May 19.

Mars begins May in Aquarius, moves into Pisces on May 9, slips into Cetus on May 24, and finally returns to Pisces on May 29. At morning AT on May 15 it stands at 35° altitude in the east-northeast at latitude 30°S and at 13° in the east at 30°N, but at 45°N it does not rise until shortly after AT.

Vesta is magnitude 5.4 at opposition on May 30, making it an easy naked-eye target. On May 1 and Jun. 30 it is mag. 6.0 so it is a naked-eye asteroid from a dark location for two months.

Jupiter rises in mid-evening on May 15 at mid-northern latitudes and before 19:00 at latitude 30°S. It transits near 1:30. (See March for altitudes at transit.)

Saturn is at quadrature in the second week of May. This is when the planet's shadow on the rings is most prominent and Saturn looks most three-dimensional. On May 15, when it becomes observable near the end of CT, it is at 67° altitude in the west-southwest as seen from latitude 30°N, and 51° high in the southwest at latitude 45°N. It sets in the west-northwest during the hour after local midnight. Mid-southern observers see it transit at 44° altitude near 18:00 and set in the west-northwest in late evening.

Time (UT)	d	h	m	MAY EVENTS
Tue.	1			
Wed.	2	10	09	**Full Moon**
		22	06	Algol at minimum
Thu.	3	4		Mercury in superior conjunction
Fri.	4	18		**Antares 0.5° N of Moon, occultation**†
				Mercury at ascending node
Sat.	5			Juno stationary
		11		η-Aquarid meteors peak
		12		Jupiter 6° N of Moon
		18	55	Algol at minimum
Sun.	6			
Mon.	7			
Tue.	8	15	44	Algol at minimum
Wed.	9			Mercury at perihelion
				Mars at greatest heliocentric lat. S
Thu.	10	4	27	**Last Quarter**
		5		Venus 1.7° N of M35 (42° E)
Fri.	11			Venus at greatest heliocentric lat. N
		12	33	Algol at minimum
Sat.	12	7		**Uranus 1.3° S of Moon, occultation**‡
Sun.	13	1		Mars 3° S of Moon
Mon.	14	9	22	Algol at minimum
Tue.	15	15		Moon at perigee (359 390 km)
Wed.	16	19	27	**New Moon**
		21		Mercury 7° N of Aldebaran (15° E)
Thu.	17	6	11	Algol at minimum
Fri.	18	0		Mercury 3° S of Moon
Sat.	19			Mercury at greatest heliocentric lat. N
Sun.	20	1		**Venus 1.7° S of Moon**
		3	00	Algol at minimum
Mon.	21	21		**Moon 1.4° N of Beehive (M44)**
Tue.	22	19		**Saturn 0.8° S of Moon, occultation**††
		23	49	Algol at minimum
Wed.	23	16		**Regulus 0.7° S of Moon, occultation**‡‡
		21	03	**First Quarter**
Thu.	24			
Fri.	25	6		Neptune stationary
		20	38	Algol at minimum
Sat.	26			
Sun.	27	22		Moon at apogee (405 460 km)
Mon.	28	6		**Spica 1.4° N of Moon**
		17	27	Algol at minimum
Wed.	30			Vesta at opposition
		19		Venus 4° S of Pollux (45° E)
		20		Mercury 1.1° N of M35 (23° E)
Thu.	31	14	15	Algol at minimum

Jupiter's Satellites
West East

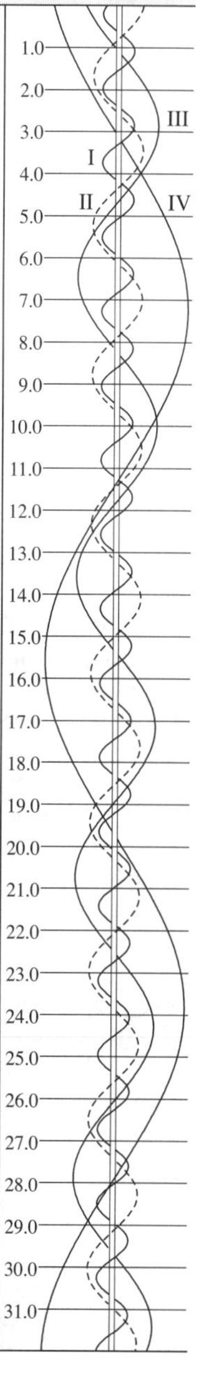

† New Zealand, Tasmania, part of Antarctica, SE Africa
‡ N Atlantic Ocean, British Isles, except SE, E Greenland
†† Europe inc. British Isles, NE Africa, NW Asia, Arctic regions, NW Canada
‡‡ Asia except E part, NE Europe including British Isles, Greenland, NE tip of Canada

THE SKY FOR 2007 JUNE

		Mercury	Venus	Mars	Jupiter	Saturn	Uranus	Neptune	Sun
RA	1	6^h15^m	7^h51^m	0^h48^m	16^h57^m	9^h30^m	23^h18^m	21^h37^m	4^h34^m
	11	6^h46^m	8^h32^m	1^h15^m	16^h52^m	9^h33^m	23^h19^m	21^h37^m	5^h15^m
	21	6^h45^m	9^h08^m	1^h43^m	16^h46^m	9^h36^m	23^h19^m	21^h37^m	5^h56^m
Dec	1	+25°16′	+23°41′	+3°27′	−21°56′	+16°09′	−5°18′	−14°27′	+21°57′
	11	+23°08′	+21°14′	+6°18′	−21°49′	+15°54′	−5°15′	−14°28′	+23°02′
	21	+20°28′	+18°12′	+9°02′	−21°41′	+15°37′	−5°14′	−14°31′	+23°26′
Dist	1	0.85	0.77	1.62	4.31	9.52	20.21	29.72	1.014
	11	0.68	0.69	1.58	4.31	9.67	20.05	29.56	1.015
	21	0.58	0.61	1.53	4.33	9.81	19.88	29.42	1.016
Mag	1	0.4	−4.1	0.8	−2.6	0.5	5.9	7.9	
	11	1.5	−4.2	0.8	−2.6	0.5	5.8	7.9	
	21	3.7	−4.2	0.8	−2.6	0.5	5.8	7.9	
Size	1	7.9″	21.5″	5.8″	45.7″	17.5″	3.5″	2.3″	31′33″
	11	9.9″	24.0″	5.9″	45.8″	17.2″	3.5″	2.3″	31′30″
	21	11.7″	27.2″	6.1″	45.5″	17.0″	3.5″	2.3″	31′29″

Moon—On June 1.0 UT, the age of the Moon is 15.2 d. The Sun's selenographic colongitude is 93.28° and increases by 12.2° each day thereafter. The libration in longitude is maximum (east limb exposed) on June 18 (+6°), and minimum (west limb exposed) on June 5 (–6°). The libration in latitude is maximum (north limb exposed) on Jun. 1 and 28 (+7°), and minimum (south limb exposed) on Jun. 14 (–7°). The Moon reaches its greatest northern declination on Jun. 15 (+28°), and its greatest southern declination on Jun. 2 and 29 (–28°). On Jun. 19 much of North America has a **daytime occultation of Regulus**. See also Saturn.

Mercury continues to be visible in both hemispheres on early June evenings, reaching greatest elongation east (23°) on Jun. 2, but its magnitude plummets, making it harder to find, as the waning crescent planet closes in on the Sun and inferior conjunction on Jun. 28.

Venus continues to be very well placed in the evening sky, reaching greatest elongation east (45°) on Jun. 9. (See also May.) It skims by the northern edge of the Beehive Cluster (M44) on Jun. 12 and 13.

Mars, in Pisces for most of June, enters Aries on Jun. 26. At morning AT at midmonth mid-northern observers view it in the eastern sky, only 3° up at latitude 45°N, but 23° high at latitude 30°N. Mid-southern observers will find it in the northeast at 39° altitude.

Vesta continues to be an easy naked-eye asteroid. See May.

Jupiter is at opposition on Jun. 5 when it rises near sunset, transits at midnight, and sets near sunrise. In Ophiuchus, it is too far south for most Canadians to have many nights of steady seeing. (See March.)

Saturn on Jun. 15 lies in the west at the end of CT at mid-northern latitudes, at an altitude of 40° for observers at latitude 30°N, but only 27° high at latitude 45°N. It sets in the west-northwest in late evening. Mid-southern observers find it 39° up in the north-northwest at CT, and it sets in the west-northwest near 21:00. On the evening of Jun. 18 the crescent Moon is very close to Saturn for North Americans.

Pluto reaches opposition on Jun. 19, located in the Sagittarius Milky Way just south of the Serpens border. See the finder chart for Pluto on p. 182.

Time (UT) d h m				JUNE EVENTS
Fri.	1	1		**Antares 0.4° N of Moon, occultation†**
		1	04	**Full Moon**
		12		Jupiter 6° N of Moon
Sat.	2	10		Mercury greatest elongation E (23°)
Sun.	3	11	04	Algol at minimum
Mon.	4			
Tue.	5			Mars at perihelion
		23		**Jupiter at opposition**
Wed.	6	7	53	Algol at minimum
Thu.	7			
Fri.	8	11	43	**Last Quarter**
Sat.	9	3		**Venus greatest elongation E (45°)**
		4	42	Algol at minimum
		9	18	**Double shadow transit on Jupiter**
Sun.	10	22		Mars 5° S of Moon
Mon.	11			Mercury at descending node
Tue.	12	1	30	Algol at minimum
		17		Moon at perigee (363 779 km)
Wed.	13	5		**Venus 0.6° N of Beehive (M44) (45° E)**
		13		**Moon 0.9° N of Pleiades (M45)**
Thu.	14	22	19	Algol at minimum
Fri.	15	3	13	**New Moon**
		16		Mercury stationary
Sat.	16	9		Mercury 6° S of Moon
		11	48	**Double shadow transit on Jupiter**
Sun.	17	19	08	Algol at minimum
Mon.	18	6		**Moon 1.2° N of Beehive (M44)**
		15		**Venus 0.6° S of Moon, occultation‡**
Tue.	19	7		Pluto at opposition
		8		**Saturn 0.4° S of Moon, occultation††**
Wed.	20	0		**Regulus 0.4° S of Moon, occultation‡‡**
		15	57	Algol at minimum
Thu.	21	18	06	**Solstice**
Fri.	22			Mercury at aphelion
		13	15	**First Quarter**
Sat.	23	12	45	Algol at minimum
		23		Uranus stationary
Sun.	24	13		**Spica 1.6° N of Moon**
		14		Moon at apogee (404 540 km)
Mon.	25			
Tue.	26	9	34	Algol at minimum
Wed.	27			
Thu.	28	8		**Antares 0.5° N of Moon, occultation†††**
		14		Jupiter 6° N of Moon
		19		Mercury in inferior conjunction
Fri.	29	6	23	Algol at minimum
Sat.	30	13	49	**Full Moon**

Jupiter's Satellites
West East
IV III I II
1.0 2.0 3.0 4.0 5.0 6.0 7.0 8.0 9.0 10.0 11.0 12.0 13.0 14.0 15.0 16.0 17.0 18.0 19.0 20.0 21.0 22.0 23.0 24.0 25.0 26.0 27.0 28.0 29.0 30.0 31.0

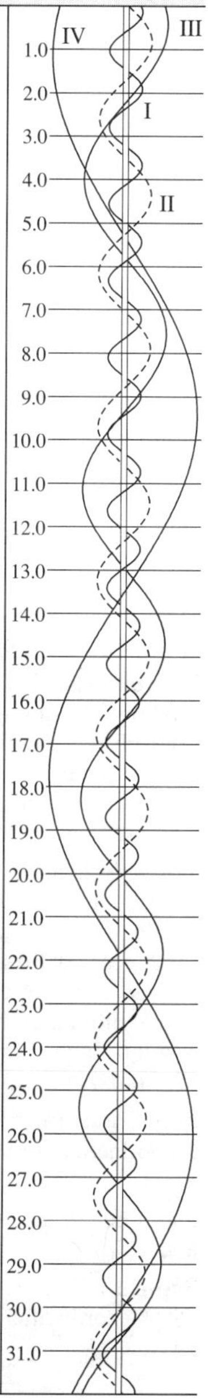

† S half of S. America, part of Antarctica, SW Indian Ocean
‡ W Asia, Europe including British Isles except S Iberia, Greenland, N Canada
†† Japan, Central Asia, E part of Europe ‡‡ E Siberia, N. America except NE, Caribbean, NW South America
††† W Oceania, W tip of Antarctica, S part of South America

THE SKY FOR 2007 JULY

		Mercury	Venus	Mars	Jupiter	Saturn	Uranus	Neptune	Sun
RA	1	6^h22^m	9^h38^m	2^h10^m	16^h42^m	9^h40^m	23^h19^m	21^h36^m	6^h38^m
	11	6^h10^m	10^h00^m	2^h38^m	16^h38^m	9^h44^m	23^h19^m	21^h35^m	7^h19^m
	21	6^h33^m	10^h12^m	3^h05^m	16^h35^m	9^h49^m	23^h18^m	21^h34^m	7^h59^m
Dec	1	+18°45′	+14°51′	+11°35′	−21°35′	+15°18′	−5°15′	−14°34′	+23°09′
	11	+19°05′	+11°27′	+13°56′	−21°29′	+14°56′	−5°18′	−14°38′	+22°12′
	21	+20°52′	+8°24′	+16°02′	−21°25′	+14°33′	−5°22′	−14°43′	+20°36′
Dist	1	0.57	0.53	1.48	4.38	9.93	19.72	29.29	1.017
	11	0.67	0.46	1.43	4.46	10.04	19.57	29.19	1.017
	21	0.87	0.39	1.38	4.57	10.12	19.43	29.11	1.016
Mag	1	5.2	−4.3	0.7	−2.5	0.6	5.8	7.9	
	11	2.1	−4.3	0.6	−2.5	0.6	5.8	7.8	
	21	0.2	−4.3	0.6	−2.4	0.6	5.8	7.8	
Size	1	11.8″	31.2″	6.3″	44.9″	16.7″	3.6″	2.3″	31′28″
	11	10.0″	36.4″	6.5″	44.2″	16.6″	3.6″	2.3″	31′28″
	21	7.7″	42.7″	6.8″	43.2″	16.4″	3.6″	2.3″	31′29″

Moon—On July 1.0 UT, the age of the Moon is 15.9 d. The Sun's selenographic colongitude is 99.87° and increases by 12.2° each day thereafter. The libration in longitude is maximum (east limb exposed) on Jul. 15 (+6°), and minimum (west limb exposed) on Jul. 1 and 28 (−5°). The libration in latitude is maximum (north limb exposed) on Jul. 25 (+7°), and minimum (south limb exposed) on Jul. 11 (−7°). The Moon reaches its greatest northern declination on Jul. 12 (+28°), and its greatest southern declination on Jul. 26 (−28°). On the evening of Jul. 16 there is a **binocular grouping of the young crescent Moon, Venus, Saturn, and Regulus.**

Mercury has a morning apparition. It reaches greatest elongation west (20°) on Jul. 20 and brightens throughout the month. It rises in the east-northeast for observers in both hemispheres and should be visible with the unaided eye at latitude 30°S by about Jul. 15, and by about Jul. 19 for latitude 30°N. Observers at latitude 45°N will have to view the planet in much brighter twilight and may require binoculars. Nonetheless, this is the best morning apparition of the year for northern observers.

Venus, brilliant at magnitude −4.4 for most of July, begins the month still high in the evening sky, but after midmonth it dives down towards the Sun and its Aug. 18 inferior conjunction. By Jul. 31, Venus's position in Sextans, well south of the ecliptic, combines with the angle of the ecliptic to cause dramatic differences in visibility with latitude: at 45°N Venus is only at 5° altitude in the west at sunset; while at 30°N Venus is at 6° altitude at the end of CT and sets just before the end of NT; and at 30°S Venus is still 6° high at the end of AT! Venus is in conjunction with Saturn on Jul. 2 (Jul. 1 for North America).

Mars passes from Aries into Taurus on Jul. 27. At morning AT it is well up, in the east for northern observers and in the northeast for southern astronomers.

Jupiter transits at 21:00 on Jul. 15 and sets in the west-southwest near 2:00 at mid-northern latitudes and 4:00 at mid-southern latitudes. (See March for altitudes at transit.)

Saturn, in Leo, sets in the west-northwest near the end of evening NT at latitude 45°N, shortly after the end of AT at 30°N, and an hour after AT at 30°S. See Venus above.

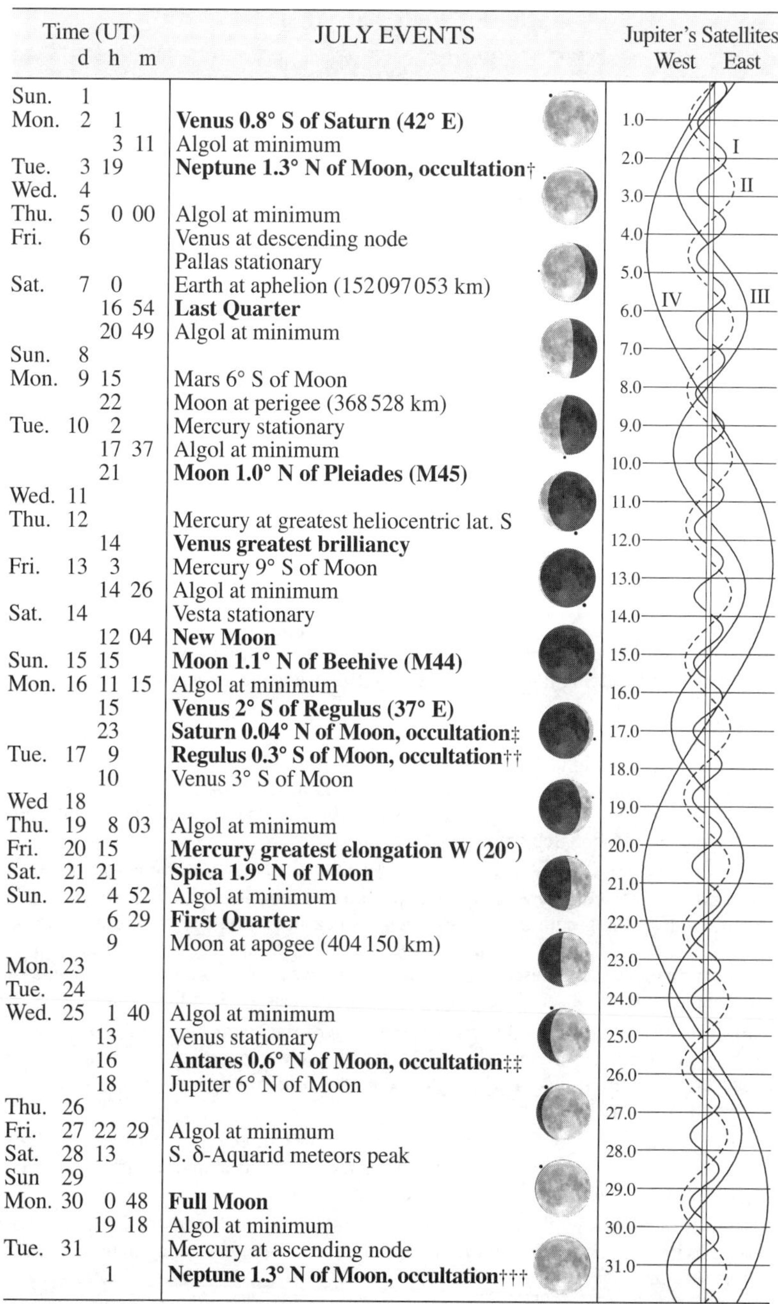

Time (UT)	d	h	m	JULY EVENTS
Sun.	1			
Mon.	2	1		**Venus 0.8° S of Saturn (42° E)**
		3	11	Algol at minimum
Tue.	3	19		**Neptune 1.3° N of Moon, occultation†**
Wed.	4			
Thu.	5	0	00	Algol at minimum
Fri.	6			Venus at descending node
				Pallas stationary
Sat.	7	0		Earth at aphelion (152 097 053 km)
		16	54	**Last Quarter**
		20	49	Algol at minimum
Sun.	8			
Mon.	9	15		Mars 6° S of Moon
		22		Moon at perigee (368 528 km)
Tue.	10	2		Mercury stationary
		17	37	Algol at minimum
		21		**Moon 1.0° N of Pleiades (M45)**
Wed.	11			
Thu.	12			Mercury at greatest heliocentric lat. S
		14		**Venus greatest brilliancy**
Fri.	13	3		Mercury 9° S of Moon
		14	26	Algol at minimum
Sat.	14			Vesta stationary
		12	04	**New Moon**
Sun.	15	15		**Moon 1.1° N of Beehive (M44)**
Mon.	16	11	15	Algol at minimum
		15		**Venus 2° S of Regulus (37° E)**
		23		**Saturn 0.04° N of Moon, occultation‡**
Tue.	17	9		**Regulus 0.3° S of Moon, occultation††**
		10		Venus 3° S of Moon
Wed	18			
Thu.	19	8	03	Algol at minimum
Fri.	20	15		**Mercury greatest elongation W (20°)**
Sat.	21	21		**Spica 1.9° N of Moon**
Sun.	22	4	52	Algol at minimum
		6	29	**First Quarter**
		9		Moon at apogee (404 150 km)
Mon.	23			
Tue.	24			
Wed.	25	1	40	Algol at minimum
		13		Venus stationary
		16		**Antares 0.6° N of Moon, occultation‡‡**
		18		Jupiter 6° N of Moon
Thu.	26			
Fri.	27	22	29	Algol at minimum
Sat.	28	13		S. δ-Aquarid meteors peak
Sun	29			
Mon.	30	0	48	**Full Moon**
		19	18	Algol at minimum
Tue.	31			Mercury at ascending node
		1		**Neptune 1.3° N of Moon, occultation†††**

† Bellingshausen Sea (Antarctica) ‡ Hawaiian Islands, W parts of South America
†† Europe including British Isles, S and W Asia, Indonesia, S Philippines, NW Australia
‡‡ S tip of Africa, most of Antarctica, S parts of Australia and New Zealand
††† Part of Antarctica, Kerguelen Islands

THE SKY FOR 2007 AUGUST

		Mercury	Venus	Mars	Jupiter	Saturn	Uranus	Neptune	Sun
RA	1	7ʰ39ᵐ	10ʰ11ᵐ	3ʰ35ᵐ	16ʰ33ᵐ	9ʰ54ᵐ	23ʰ17ᵐ	21ʰ33ᵐ	8ʰ43ᵐ
	11	9ʰ02ᵐ	9ʰ55ᵐ	4ʰ02ᵐ	16ʰ33ᵐ	9ʰ59ᵐ	23ʰ16ᵐ	21ʰ32ᵐ	9ʰ21ᵐ
	21	10ʰ21ᵐ	9ʰ31ᵐ	4ʰ28ᵐ	16ʰ34ᵐ	10ʰ04ᵐ	23ʰ15ᵐ	21ʰ31ᵐ	9ʰ59ᵐ
Dec	1	+21°40′	+6°00′	+18°03′	−21°24′	+14°07′	−5°28′	−14°48′	+18°11′
	11	+18°32′	+5°16′	+19°35′	−21°26′	+13°42′	−5°36′	−14°53′	+15°28′
	21	+12°03′	+6°07′	+20°50′	−21°30′	+13°16′	−5°44′	−14°59′	+12°21′
Dist	1	1.14	0.33	1.32	4.70	10.19	19.30	29.05	1.015
	11	1.31	0.30	1.27	4.83	10.23	19.21	29.03	1.014
	21	1.36	0.29	1.21	4.98	10.24	19.14	29.04	1.012
Mag	1	−0.9	−4.2	0.5	−2.4	0.6	5.8	7.8	
	11	−1.7	−3.9	0.5	−2.3	0.6	5.7	7.8	
	21	−1.4	−3.9	0.4	−2.2	0.6	5.7	7.8	
Size	1	5.9″	50.5″	7.1″	41.9″	16.3″	3.6″	2.3″	31′31″
	11	5.1″	56.3″	7.4″	40.8″	16.3″	3.6″	2.3″	31′33″
	21	4.9″	57.7″	7.7″	39.6″	16.2″	3.7″	2.3″	31′37″

Moon—On Aug. 1.0 UT, the age of the Moon is 17.5 d. The Sun's selenographic colongitude is 118.69° and increases by 12.2° each day thereafter. The libration in longitude is maximum (east limb exposed) on Aug. 11 (+5°), and minimum (west limb exposed) on Aug. 25 (−6°). The libration in latitude is maximum (north limb exposed) on Aug. 21 (+7°), and minimum (south limb exposed) on Aug. 7 (−7°). The Moon reaches its greatest northern declination on Aug. 8 (+28°), and its greatest southern declination on Aug. 23 (−28°). The first-quarter Moon slides past Antares on the night of Aug. 21/22. There is a **deep total lunar eclipse on Aug. 28** visible from the Pacific Rim, North America except for the Atlantic Provinces (which see a partial eclipse), and South America except for Brazil and the Guyanas. (See ECLIPSES IN 2007 on pp. 110–124).

Mercury remains visible for northern observers for the first few mornings of the month in bright twilight. It is very low in the east-northeast, but is also very bright, shining at magnitude −1.3 on Aug. 3. Mercury is at superior conjunction Aug. 15. Southern observers can spot it low in the west in bright evening twilight at month end, the beginning of a fine September–October apparition.

Venus reaches inferior conjunction on Aug. 18, 8° south of the Sun. Southern observers will have fine telescopic views of the razor-thin crescent. Interestingly, Venus spends the first half of the month in Sextans, then a week in Hydra, before returning to the Zodiac in Leo and Cancer. See July for the planet's visibility on Aug. 1. After inferior conjunction the waxing crescent is visible low in the eastern morning sky for southern observers. Northern observers can spot it during the last week of the month.

Mars, in Taurus, passes by the northernmost arc of the Hyades on Aug. 19, 5° from fainter Aldebaran. At midmonth it rises shortly before midnight for mid-northern observers and at morning AT it is high in the east. Mid-southern observers will see it rise about 1:30 and transit at sunrise.

Jupiter is stationary on Aug. 7, and then resumes direct (eastward) motion. At mid-northern latitudes on Aug. 15 it is near the meridian at sunset and sets in the west-southwest before local midnight. At 30°S it sets near 2:00.

Saturn is overtaken by the Sun's glare early in the month. At mid-southern latitudes it is still visible in bright twilight for part of the second week. Its conjunction with the Sun is on Aug. 21.

Neptune, in Capricornus all year, is at opposition on Aug. 13. See the finder chart for Neptune on page 181.

Time (UT)	d	h	m	AUGUST EVENTS
Wed.	1	19		Mercury 6° S of Pollux (14° W)
Thu.	2	16	06	Algol at minimum
Fri.	3	2		Venus 6° S of Regulus (21° E)
		24		Moon at perigee (368 891 km)
Sat.	4			
Sun.	5			Mercury at perihelion
		11		Mars 5° S of Pleiades (M45) (73° W)
		12	55	Algol at minimum
		21	20	**Last Quarter**
Mon.	6			
Tue.	7	2		**Moon 1.1° N of Pleiades (M45)**
		4		Mars 6° S of Moon
		6		Jupiter stationary
Wed.	8	9	43	Algol at minimum
Thu.	9			
Fri.	10			Venus at aphelion
Sat.	11	6	32	Algol at minimum
Sun.	12	23	02	**New Moon**
Mon.	13	5		**Perseid meteors peak**
		18		**Neptune at opposition**
Tue.	14	3	21	Algol at minimum
Wed.	15			Mercury at greatest heliocentric lat. N
		20		Mercury in superior conjunction
Thu.	16			
Fri.	17	0	09	Algol at minimum
Sat.	18	4		**Venus in inferior conjunction (8° S of Sun)**
		5		**Spica 2.0° N of Moon**
Sun.	19	3		Moon at apogee (404 618 km)
		20	58	Algol at minimum
Mon.	20	23	54	**First Quarter**
Tue.	21	23		Saturn in conjunction with the Sun
Wed.	22	1		**Antares 0.7° N of Moon, occultation**†
		3		Jupiter 6° N of Moon
		17	46	Algol at minimum
Thu.	23			
Fri.	24	0		Mars 5° N of Aldebaran (79° W)
Sat.	25	14	35	Algol at minimum
Sun.	26			
Mon.	27			
Tue.	28	10	35	**Full Moon, total lunar eclipse** (p. 110)
		11	23	Algol at minimum
Wed.	29			
Thu.	30			
Fri.	31	0		Moon at perigee (364 171 km)
		8	12	Algol at minimum

Jupiter's Satellites: West / East

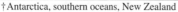

† Antarctica, southern oceans, New Zealand

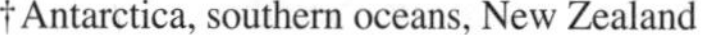

THE SKY FOR 2007 SEPTEMBER

		Mercury	Venus	Mars	Jupiter	Saturn	Uranus	Neptune	Sun
RA	1	$11^{h}34^{m}$	$9^{h}11^{m}$	$4^{h}56^{m}$	$16^{h}37^{m}$	$10^{h}09^{m}$	$23^{h}13^{m}$	$21^{h}30^{m}$	$10^{h}39^{m}$
	11	$12^{h}30^{m}$	$9^{h}08^{m}$	$5^{h}20^{m}$	$16^{h}41^{m}$	$10^{h}14^{m}$	$23^{h}12^{m}$	$21^{h}29^{m}$	$11^{h}15^{m}$
	21	$13^{h}19^{m}$	$9^{h}20^{m}$	$5^{h}43^{m}$	$16^{h}45^{m}$	$10^{h}19^{m}$	$23^{h}10^{m}$	$21^{h}28^{m}$	$11^{h}51^{m}$
Dec	1	+3°40′	+8°01′	+21°53′	−21°38′	+12°47′	−5°54′	−15°04′	+8°32′
	11	−3°44′	+9°34′	+22°35′	−21°47′	+12°22′	−6°03′	−15°09′	+4°50′
	21	−10°16′	+10°19′	+23°04′	−21°58′	+11°57′	−6°13′	−15°13′	+0°59′
Dist	1	1.32	0.31	1.15	5.15	10.23	19.10	29.08	1.009
	11	1.24	0.36	1.09	5.30	10.20	19.09	29.15	1.007
	21	1.12	0.42	1.03	5.45	10.14	19.11	29.25	1.004
Mag	1	−0.5	−4.2	0.3	−2.2	0.6	5.7	7.8	
	11	−0.1	−4.4	0.2	−2.1	0.7	5.7	7.8	
	21	−0.0	−4.4	0.1	−2.1	0.7	5.7	7.8	
Size	1	5.1″	53.1″	8.1″	38.3″	16.3″	3.7″	2.3″	31′41″
	11	5.4″	46.4″	8.6″	37.2″	16.3″	3.7″	2.3″	31′46″
	21	6.0″	39.8″	9.1″	36.2″	16.4″	3.7″	2.3″	31′51″

Moon—On Sep. 1.0 UT, the age of the Moon is 19.0 d. The Sun's selenographic colongitude is 137.31° and increases by 12.2° each day thereafter. The libration in longitude is maximum (east limb exposed) on Sep. 7 (+6°), and minimum (west limb exposed) on Sep. 22 (−7°). The libration in latitude is maximum (north limb exposed) on Sep. 18 (+7°), and minimum (south limb exposed) on Sep. 3 (−7°). The Moon reaches its greatest northern declination on Sep. 5 (+28°), and its greatest southern declination on Sep. 19 (−28°). There is a **partial solar eclipse** on Sep. 11 visible from southern South America. (See ECLIPSES IN 2007 on pp. 110–124)

Mercury is well placed for southern observers in the evening sky throughout September and well into October. At greatest elongation east on Sep. 29 (26°) it is at 8° altitude at the end of AT, dominating the western sky. **This is the best evening apparition of the year for southern observers.** This is an unfavourable apparition for northern observers, but those at latitude 30°N may succeed in spotting the planet with binoculars in very bright twilight. **Mercury passes very close to Spica on Sep. 22.**

Venus, brilliant in morning skies, climbs much higher this month for northern observers who see the planet at 11° altitude when AT begins on Sep. 15, increasing to 20° on Sep. 30. At 30°S on those dates the corresponding altitudes are 9° and 11°. Look for its glitter path across calm bodies of water.

Mars, in Taurus, passes into Gemini on Sep. 29. At midmonth it rises in late evening for mid-northern observers and at about 1:00 for mid-southern observers. It transits near sunrise.

Jupiter sets in mid-evening in the west-southwest for mid-northern observers and at midnight at 30°S.

Saturn was in conjunction with the Sun on Aug. 21. Due to the steep inclination of the ecliptic for mid-northern observers, Saturn becomes visible in bright morning twilight low in the east-northeast by about Sep. 2, only 50′ NNE of Regulus. They are closer than at their (invisible) conjunction in RA in August. **This is an attractive pairing since the star is only 0.8 magnitudes fainter than the planet.** On Sep. 8 they are still within 1.2° and rise before NT. Less favoured southern observers may be able to spot the pairing by that date at the beginning of CT. At midmonth Saturn rises in the east-northeast near 4:00 for mid-northern locations, and near 5:00 at 30°S.

Uranus, in Aquarius all year, is at opposition on Sep. 9. It is relatively easy to spot the 5.7–magnitude planet with the unaided eye at any dark site. See the finder chart for Uranus on p. 180.

Time (UT)	d	h	m	SEPTEMBER EVENTS
Sat.	1			Venus at greatest heliocentric lat. S
		12		Aurigids peak. Possible enhanced activity
Sun.	2			
Mon.	3			Pallas at opposition
		5	01	Algol at minimum
		8		**Moon 1.2° N of Pleiades (M45)**
Tue.	4	2	32	**Last Quarter**
		14		Mars 6° S of Moon
Wed.	5			
Thu.	6	1	49	Algol at minimum
Fri.	7			Mercury at descending node
		14		Venus stationary
		22		Pluto stationary
Sat.	8	6		**Moon 1.1° N of Beehive (M44)**
		19		Venus 9° S of Moon
		22	38	Algol at minimum
Sun.	9	19		**Uranus at opposition**
Mon.	10	1		**Regulus 0.2° S of Moon, occultation**†
		4		**Saturn 0.8° N of Moon, occultation**‡
Tue.	11	12	44	**New Moon, partial solar eclipse** (p. 110)
		19	27	Algol at minimum
Wed	12			
Thu.	13	14		**Mercury 2° N of Moon**
Fri.	14	13		**Spica 2.0° N of Moon**
		16	15	Algol at minimum
Sat.	15	21		Moon at apogee (405 642 km)
Sun.	16			
Mon.	17	13	04	Algol at minimum
Tue.	18			Mercury at aphelion
		8		**Antares 0.7° N of Moon, occultation**††
		15		Jupiter 6° N of Moon
Wed.	19	16	48	**First Quarter**
Thu.	20	9	53	Algol at minimum
Fri.	21			Ceres stationary
				Zodiacal Light vis. in N lat. in E before morning twilight for next two weeks
Sat.	22	9		**Mercury 0.08° N of Spica (24° E)**
Sun.	23	6	41	Algol at minimum
		9	51	**Equinox**
		23		**Venus greatest brilliancy**
Mon.	24			
Tue.	25			
Wed.	26	3	30	Algol at minimum
		19	45	**Full Moon**
Thu.	27			
Fri.	28	2		Moon at perigee (359 419 km)
Sat.	29	0	19	Algol at minimum
		16		**Mercury greatest elongation E (26°)**
Sun.	30	15		**Moon 1.1° N of Pleiades (M45)**

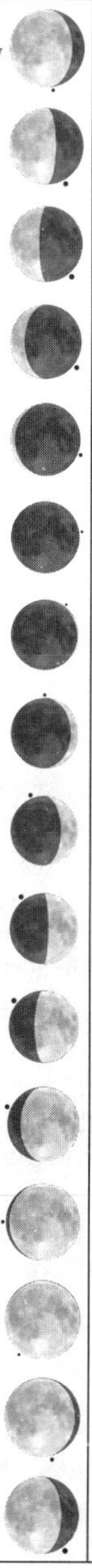

Jupiter's Satellites
West East

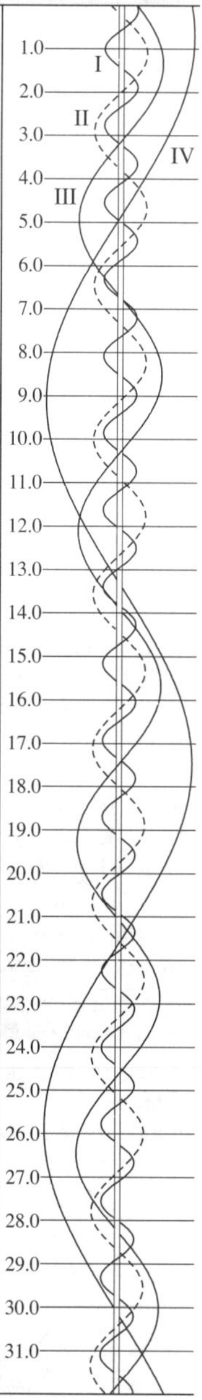

I II III IV

1.0 2.0 3.0 4.0 5.0 6.0 7.0 8.0 9.0 10.0 11.0 12.0 13.0 14.0 15.0 16.0 17.0 18.0 19.0 20.0 21.0 22.0 23.0 24.0 25.0 26.0 27.0 28.0 29.0 30.0 31.0

† Polynesia, Japan, Central Asia
‡ S Indian Ocean, W tip of Australia, part of Antarctica
†† Antarctica, southern oceans, S Madagascar

THE SKY FOR 2007 OCTOBER

		Mercury	Venus	Mars	Jupiter	Saturn	Uranus	Neptune	Sun
RA	1	13^h59^m	9^h43^m	6^h03^m	16^h51^m	10^h23^m	23^h09^m	21^h28^m	12^h27^m
	11	14^h21^m	10^h13^m	6^h21^m	16^h58^m	10^h27^m	23^h08^m	21^h27^m	13^h03^m
	21	14^h03^m	10^h48^m	6^h36^m	17^h05^m	10^h31^m	23^h07^m	21^h27^m	13^h41^m
Dec	1	−15°19′	+10°07′	+23°22′	−22°09′	+11°33′	−6°21′	−15°17′	−2°55′
	11	−17°43′	+8°56′	+23°34′	−22°21′	+11°10′	−6°29′	−15°19′	−6°45′
	21	−14°40′	+6°52′	+23°44′	−22°33′	+10°50′	−6°36′	−15°21′	−10°27′
Dist	1	0.97	0.49	0.97	5.59	10.06	19.16	29.36	1.001
	11	0.79	0.56	0.90	5.73	9.95	19.24	29.50	0.999
	21	0.67	0.63	0.84	5.85	9.83	19.34	29.66	0.996
Mag	1	0.1	−4.4	−0.1	−2.0	0.7	5.7	7.9	
	11	0.5	−4.4	−0.2	−2.0	0.8	5.8	7.9	
	21	3.9	−4.3	−0.4	−1.9	0.8	5.8	7.9	
Size	1	7.0″	34.2″	9.7″	35.2″	16.5″	3.7″	2.3″	31′57″
	11	8.5″	29.8″	10.4″	34.4″	16.7″	3.6″	2.3″	32′02″
	21	10.0″	26.3″	11.2″	33.7″	16.9″	3.6″	2.3″	32′08″

Moon—On Oct. 1.0 UT, the age of the Moon is 19.5 d. The Sun's selenographic colongitude is 143.35° and increases by 12.2° each day thereafter. The libration in longitude is maximum (east limb exposed) on Oct. 4 (+7°), and minimum (west limb exposed) on Oct. 20 (–7°). The libration in latitude is maximum (north limb exposed) on Oct. 15 (+7°), and minimum (south limb exposed) on Oct. 1 and 28 (–7°). The Moon reaches its greatest northern declination on Oct. 2 and 29 (+28°), and its greatest southern declination on Oct. 16 (–28°).

Mercury continues to be well placed in the west-southwest evening twilight for southern observers until midmonth, after a fine September display. It does fade rapidly in the second week as it moves towards inferior conjunction on Oct. 24. Mercury is poorly placed for northern observers this month.

Venus, Saturn, and Regulus form an attractive triangle for the unaided eye or binoculars for several days around Oct. 13. Venus dominates the morning sky. On Oct. 15 it rises over two hours before AT begins at latitude 45°N and almost an hour before AT at 30°S. Greatest elongation west (46°) is Oct. 28.

Mars, in Gemini, grows large enough to usefully observe this month as its Dec. 24 opposition nears. Rising in mid-evening for northern observers and near midnight for southern ones, it transits near 5:00.

Jupiter, at midmonth, sets in the west-southwest an hour after AT ends at latitude 45°N, almost two hours after AT at 30°N, and in late evening at 30°S.

Saturn rises in the east-northeast shortly after 2:00 for mid-northern observers at midmonth, and an hour later for mid-southern observers. By CT it is nearing 40° altitude for mid-northern observers, but has only risen 20° at latitude 30°S.

Time (UT)	d	h	m	OCTOBER EVENTS
Mon.	1	21	07	Algol at minimum
Tue.	2	20		Mars 5° S of Moon
Wed.	3	10	06	**Last Quarter**
				Mars at ascending node
		20		**Mars 0.9° S of M35 (98° W)**
Thu.	4	17	56	Algol at minimum
Fri.	5	11		**Moon 1.1° N of Beehive (M44)**
Sat.	6			
Sun.	7	3		Venus 3° S of Moon
		7		**Regulus 0.2° S of Moon, occultation**†
		14	45	Algol at minimum
		16		**Saturn 1.3° N of Moon, occultation**‡
Mon.	8			Mercury at greatest heliocentric lat. S
		19		Draconid meteors peak
Tue.	9	11		Venus 3° S of Regulus (44° W)
Wed.	10	11	34	Algol at minimum
Thu.	11	5	01	**New Moon**
Fri.	12	7		Mercury stationary
Sat.	13	1		**Mercury 1.3° N of Moon**
		8	22	Algol at minimum
		10		Moon at apogee (406 492 km)
Sun.	14			
Mon.	15	14		Venus 3° S of Saturn (45° W)
		15		**Antares 0.6° N of Moon, occultation**††
Tue.	16	5	11	Algol at minimum
		6		Jupiter 5° N of Moon
Wed.	17			
Thu.	18	8	42	**Double shadow transit on Jupiter**
Fri.	19	2	00	Algol at minimum
		8	33	**First Quarter**
Sat.	20			**Zodiacal Light** vis. in N lat. in E before morning twilight for next two weeks
Sun.	21	3		**Neptune 1.3° N of Moon, occultation**‡‡
		21	39	**Double shadow transit on Jupiter**
		22		Orionid meteors peak
		22	49	Algol at minimum
Mon.	22			Pallas stationary
Tue.	23			
Wed.	24	0		Mercury in inferior conjunction
		19	38	Algol at minimum
Thu.	25	10	36	**Double shadow transit on Jupiter**
Fri.	26	4	52	**Full Moon (largest in 2007)**
		12		Moon at perigee (356 753 km) **Large tides**
Sat.	27			Mercury at ascending node
				Venus at ascending node
		16	27	Algol at minimum
Sun.	28	1		**Moon 1.0° N of Pleiades (M45)**
		15		**Venus greatest elongation W (46°)**
		23	34	**Double shadow transit on Jupiter**
Mon.	29			
Tue.	30	13	16	Algol at minimum
		18	02	**Double shadow transit on Jupiter**
		19		Mars 3° S of Moon
Wed.	31	20		Neptune stationary

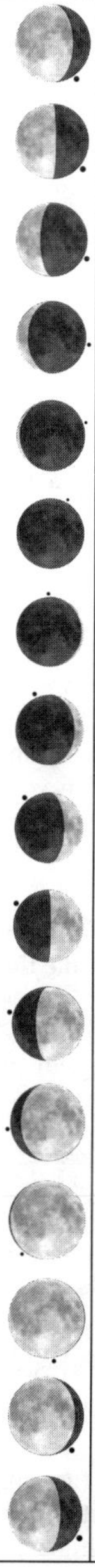

Jupiter's Satellites
West East

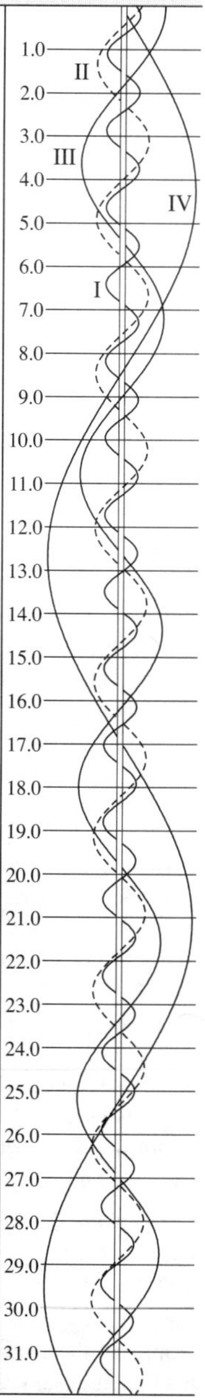

† Europe including S British Isles, N and E Africa, Middle East
‡ Southern Ocean S of Polynesia †† Larger part of Antarctica, S half of South America
‡‡ Part of Antarctica, South Georgia

THE SKY FOR 2007 NOVEMBER

		Mercury	Venus	Mars	Jupiter	Saturn	Uranus	Neptune	Sun
RA	1	13^h28^m	11^h30^m	6^h48^m	17^h14^m	10^h35^m	23^h06^m	21^h27^m	14^h23^m
	11	13^h53^m	12^h10^m	6^h54^m	17^h23^m	10^h38^m	23^h05^m	21^h27^m	15^h03^m
	21	14^h46^m	12^h51^m	6^h53^m	17^h32^m	10^h40^m	23^h05^m	21^h27^m	15^h44^m
Dec	1	−7°46′	+3°44′	+23°57′	−22°45′	+10°31′	−6°41′	−15°21′	−14°12′
	11	−9°11′	+0°17′	+24°17′	−22°55′	+10°16′	−6°44′	−15°21′	−17°13′
	21	−14°26′	−3°32′	+24°46′	−23°03′	+10°05′	−6°46′	−15°19′	−19°45′
Dist	1	0.79	0.72	0.77	5.97	9.68	19.48	29.84	0.993
	11	1.05	0.79	0.71	6.06	9.53	19.63	30.01	0.990
	21	1.26	0.87	0.66	6.14	9.37	19.79	30.18	0.988
Mag	1	0.8	−4.2	−0.6	−1.9	0.8	5.8	7.9	
	11	−0.7	−4.2	−0.8	−1.8	0.8	5.8	7.9	
	21	−0.7	−4.1	−1.1	−1.8	0.8	5.8	7.9	
Size	1	8.6″	23.3″	12.2″	33.0″	17.2″	3.6″	2.2″	32′13″
	11	6.4″	21.0″	13.2″	32.5″	17.5″	3.6″	2.2″	32′18″
	21	5.3″	19.3″	14.2″	32.1″	17.8″	3.5″	2.2″	32′23″

Moon—On Nov. 1.0 UT, the age of the Moon is 20.8 d. The Sun's selenographic colongitude is 161.06° and increases by 12.2° each day thereafter. The libration in longitude is maximum (east limb exposed) on Nov. 1 and 29 (+8°), and minimum (west limb exposed) on Nov. 18 (–7°). The libration in latitude is maximum (north limb exposed) on Nov. 11 (+7°), and minimum (south limb exposed) on Nov. 24 (–6°). The Moon reaches its greatest northern declination on Nov. 26 (+28°), and its greatest southern declination on Nov. 13 (–28°). On Nov. 3 much of the southern half of the USA enjoys an **occultation of Regulus**.

Mercury reaches greatest elongation west (19°) on Nov. 8. This morning apparition favours northern observers due to the steep inclination of the ecliptic. Look low in the east-southeast through about Nov. 28. At latitude 30°N the innermost planet rises above a sea horizon just before the beginning of AT for a few days around greatest elongation. For southern observers Mercury is a binocular object very low in the east in very bright twilight for about ten days centred on Nov. 10.

Venus continues to rule the morning sky in both hemispheres, with little change from October. On Nov. 15 it rises almost 2.5 h before AT begins at latitude 45°N and 40 minutes before AT at 30°S. The respective altitudes at AT are 24° and 8°. On Nov. 5 the adjacent Moon will make it **easy to spot Venus in the midday sky** with the unaided eye.

Mars, in Gemini, begins its retrograde loop on Nov. 15 when it rises around 20:00 for northern observers and 22:00 for southern ones. It transits near 3:00 when its altitude is 85° at latitude 30°N, 70° at latitude 45°N, and only 36° at latitude 30°S. By month end it is magnitude –1.2, bright enough to carefully follow with the unaided eye until minutes after sunrise!

Ceres reaches opposition on Nov. 9, brightening to magnitude 7.2.

Jupiter sets in the west-southwest at the end of evening twilight for observers at latitude 45°N at midmonth, half an hour after twilight ends at 30°N, and only 45 minutes after twilight even at 30°S. See December.

Saturn rises in the east-northeast at midmonth about half an hour after local midnight at mid-northern latitudes and an hour later at mid-southern. It transits at 7:00 which is about sunrise at latitude 45°N, half an hour after sunrise at 30°N, and two hours after sunrise at 30°S. It is at quadrature Dec. 1 (see May).

Time (UT)	d	h	m	NOVEMBER EVENTS	Jupiter's Satellites West East
Thu.	1			Mercury at perihelion	
		12	31	**Double shadow transit on Jupiter**	
		13		Mercury stationary	
		18		**Moon 0.8° N of Beehive (M44)**	
		21	18	**Last Quarter**	
Fri.	2	10	04	Algol at minimum	
Sat.	3	13		**Regulus 0.03° N of Moon, occultation**†	
Sun.	4			**Daylight Saving Time ends**	
		3		**Saturn 1.8° N of Moon**	
Mon.	5	1	28	**Double shadow transit on Jupiter**	
		6	53	Algol at minimum	
		20		Venus 3° N of Moon	
		22		S. Taurid meteors peak	
Tue.	6	19	57	**Double shadow transit on Jupiter**	
Wed.	7				
Thu.	8	2		**Spica 1.9° N of Moon**	
		3	42	Algol at minimum	
		11		Mercury 7° N of Moon	
		14	25	**Double shadow transit on Jupiter**	
		21		**Mercury greatest elongation W (19°)**	
Fri.	9			Ceres at opposition	
		13		Moon at apogee (406 671 km)	
		23	03	**New Moon**	
Sat.	10				
Sun.	11			Mercury at greatest heliocentric lat. N	
		0	31	Algol at minimum	
		21		**Antares 0.4° N of Moon, occultation**‡	
Mon.	12	3	38	**Double shadow transit on Jupiter**	
		21		N. Taurid meteors peak	
		22		Jupiter 5° N of Moon	
Tue.	13	21	20	Algol at minimum	
		23	30	**Double shadow transit on Jupiter**	
Wed.	14			Juno in conjunction with the Sun	
Thu.	15	16		Mars stationary	
		16	56	**Double shadow transit on Jupiter**	
Fri.	16	18	09	Algol at minimum	
Sat.	17	11		**Neptune 1.0° N of Moon, occultation**††	
		22	32	**First Quarter**	
Sun.	18	4		Leonid meteors peak	
Mon.	19	6	15	**Double shadow transit on Jupiter**	
		14	58	Algol at minimum	
Tue.	20				
Wed.	21				
Thu.	22	11	47	Algol at minimum	
		19	34	**Double shadow transit on Jupiter**	
Fri.	23				
Sat.	24	0		Moon at perigee (357 194 km) **Large tides**	
		12		**Moon 0.9° N of Pleiades (M45)**	
		14	30	**Full Moon**	
		18		Uranus stationary	
Sun.	25	8	36	Algol at minimum	
Mon.	26	8	53	**Double shadow transit on Jupiter**	
Tue.	27	6		**Mars 1.7° S of Moon**	
Wed.	28	5	25	Algol at minimum	
		22		Venus 4° N of Spica (43° W)	
Thu.	29	2		**Moon 0.6° N of Beehive (M44)**	
		22	11	**Double shadow transit on Jupiter**	
Fri.	30			Venus at perihelion	
		20		**Regulus 0.3° N of Moon, occultation**‡‡	

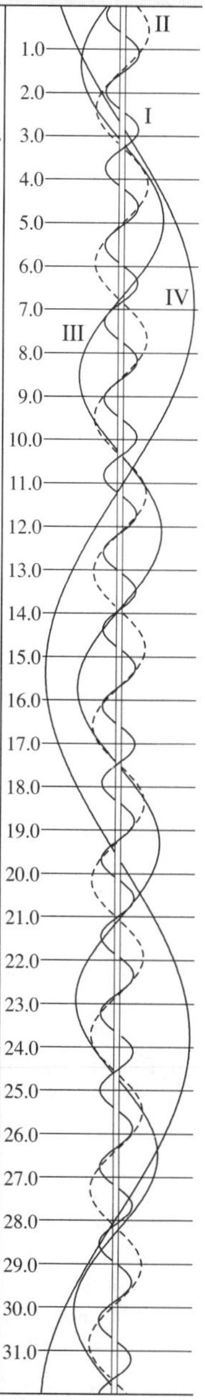

† S North America, Caribbean, N of South America

‡ S part of South America, S Pacific Ocean, most of New Zealand, Polynesia

†† Antarctica, southern Australia, New Zealand

‡‡ E India, SE Asia, NE Australia, New Zealand, Micronesia, Melanesia

THE SKY FOR 2007 DECEMBER

		Mercury	Venus	Mars	Jupiter	Saturn	Uranus	Neptune	Sun
RA	1	15^h48^m	13^h34^m	6^h47^m	17^h42^m	10^h42^m	23^h05^m	21^h28^m	16^h26^m
	11	16^h53^m	14^h19^m	6^h34^m	17^h52^m	10^h43^m	23^h05^m	21^h28^m	17^h10^m
	21	18^h02^m	15^h05^m	6^h18^m	18^h02^m	10^h43^m	23^h06^m	21^h29^m	17^h54^m
Dec	1	−19°34′	−7°31′	+25°24′	−23°09′	+9°58′	−6°45′	−15°17′	−21°41′
	11	−23°17′	−11°26′	+26°04′	−23°13′	+9°54′	−6°42′	−15°13′	−22°56′
	21	−25°03′	−15°04′	+26°37′	−23°15′	+9°55′	−6°38′	−15°08′	−23°26′
Dist	1	1.38	0.94	0.62	6.19	9.20	19.96	30.35	0.986
	11	1.44	1.01	0.60	6.22	9.04	20.13	30.51	0.985
	21	1.44	1.08	0.59	6.23	8.88	20.30	30.65	0.984
Mag	1	−0.8	−4.1	−1.3	−1.8	0.7	5.8	7.9	
	11	−1.1	−4.0	−1.5	−1.8	0.7	5.9	7.9	
	21	−1.2	−4.0	−1.6	−1.8	0.6	5.9	8.0	
Size	1	4.9″	17.8″	15.1″	31.8″	18.1″	3.5″	2.2″	32′26″
	11	4.7″	16.5″	15.7″	31.7″	18.4″	3.5″	2.2″	32′29″
	21	4.7″	15.5″	15.9″	31.6″	18.7″	3.4″	2.2″	32′31″

Moon—On Dec. 1.0 UT, the age of the Moon is 21.0 d. The Sun's selenographic colongitude is 166.13° and increases by 12.2° each day thereafter. As December opens, the Moon's libration has receded slightly from the Nov. 29 maximum. The libration in longitude is maximum (east limb exposed) on Dec. 1 (+8°) and Dec. 27 (+7°), and minimum (west limb exposed) on Dec. 16 (−6°). The libration in latitude is maximum (north limb exposed) on Dec. 8 (+7°), and minimum (south limb exposed) on Dec. 21 (−7°). The Moon reaches its greatest northern declination on Dec. 23 (+28°), and its greatest southern declination on Dec. 10 (−28°). The last-quarter Moon passes Saturn on Dec. 1. (See Mars.)

Mercury is difficult to observe this month since it reaches superior conjunction on Dec. 17.

Venus decorates the morning sky in both hemispheres, with only a slow change from October and November. (See November.) By Dec. 31 at latitude 45°N Venus rises 75 min before AT begins and is then 11° high; at latitude 30°S Venus rises an hour before AT and is also 11° high at AT.

Mars, in Gemini, retrogrades into Taurus on Dec. 30. It is at opposition on Dec. 24 when it rises near sunset, transits about midnight, and sets near sunrise, but closest approach is on Dec 19. (See November.) **Mars's 16″ disk is occulted by the full Moon on Dec. 23/24** northwest of a line from Calgary to Portland, at an adequate altitude.

Jupiter has been in Ophiuchus all year. On Dec. 2 it passes into Sagittarius, headed towards conjunction with the Sun three weeks later. The giant planet sinks rapidly into the west-southwestern evening twilight and becomes lost in the glare of the Sun during the second week.

Saturn is at quadrature on Dec. 1 (see May). Also, the last-quarter Moon passes Saturn on Dec. 1. At midmonth the planet rises in the east-northeast near 22:30 at mid-northern latitudes, and in the east an hour later at latitude 30°S. Saturn crosses the meridian at 5:00 at these altitudes: 55° at latitude 45°N, 70° at latitude 30°N, and 50° at latitude 30°S. Its retrograde loop begins on Dec 20.

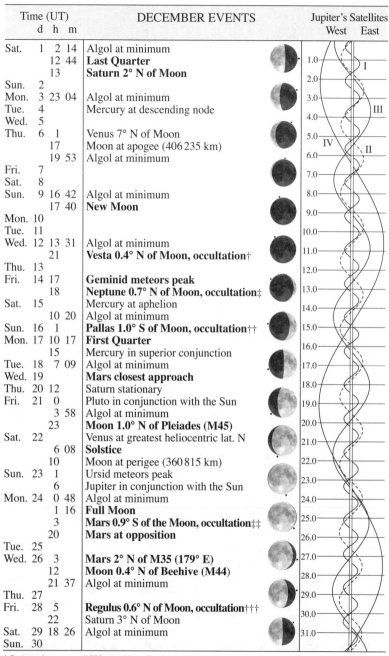

Time (UT) d	h	m	DECEMBER EVENTS
Sat. 1	2	14	Algol at minimum
	12	44	**Last Quarter**
	13		**Saturn 2° N of Moon**
Sun. 2			
Mon. 3	23	04	Algol at minimum
Tue. 4			Mercury at descending node
Wed. 5			
Thu. 6	1		Venus 7° N of Moon
	17		Moon at apogee (406 235 km)
	19	53	Algol at minimum
Fri. 7			
Sat. 8			
Sun. 9	16	42	Algol at minimum
	17	40	**New Moon**
Mon. 10			
Tue. 11			
Wed. 12	13	31	Algol at minimum
	21		**Vesta 0.4° N of Moon, occultation**†
Thu. 13			
Fri. 14	17		**Geminid meteors peak**
	18		**Neptune 0.7° N of Moon, occultation**‡
Sat. 15			Mercury at aphelion
	10	20	Algol at minimum
Sun. 16	1		**Pallas 1.0° S of Moon, occultation**††
Mon. 17	10	17	**First Quarter**
	15		Mercury in superior conjunction
Tue. 18	7	09	Algol at minimum
Wed. 19			**Mars closest approach**
Thu. 20	12		Saturn stationary
Fri. 21	0		Pluto in conjunction with the Sun
	3	58	Algol at minimum
	23		**Moon 1.0° N of Pleiades (M45)**
Sat. 22			Venus at greatest heliocentric lat. N
	6	08	**Solstice**
	10		Moon at perigee (360 815 km)
Sun. 23	1		Ursid meteors peak
	6		Jupiter in conjunction with the Sun
Mon. 24	0	48	Algol at minimum
	1	16	**Full Moon**
	3		**Mars 0.9° S of the Moon, occultation**‡‡
	20		**Mars at opposition**
Tue. 25			
Wed. 26	3		**Mars 2° N of M35 (179° E)**
	12		**Moon 0.4° N of Beehive (M44)**
	21	37	Algol at minimum
Thu. 27			
Fri. 28	5		**Regulus 0.6° N of Moon, occultation**†††
	22		Saturn 3° N of Moon
Sat. 29	18	26	Algol at minimum
Sun. 30			

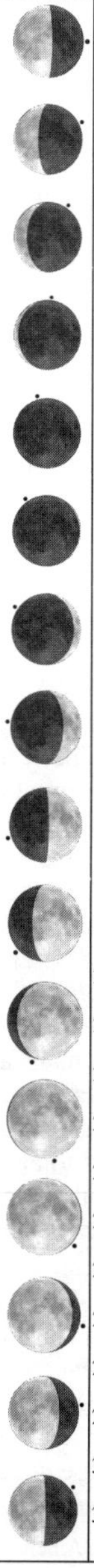

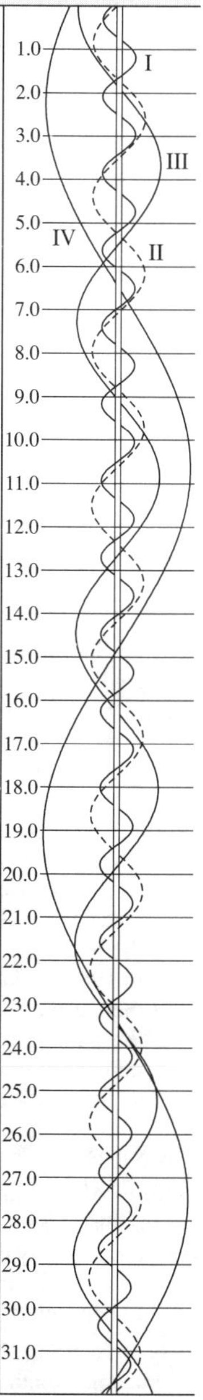

† S. America except NW part, New Zealand ‡ Part of Antarctica, S tip of S. America, S Africa
†† NW Canada, Alaska, E tip of Siberia, Hawaiian Islands
‡‡ NW Canada, Alaska, Arctic regions, N Russia, E Europe, NE British Isles
††† S. America except S part, S Atlantic Ocean

ECLIPSES

ECLIPSE PATTERNS

BY ROY BISHOP

Eclipse Seasons

The plane of the Moon's orbit is tilted about 5° to the plane of Earth's orbit, the ecliptic. Since 5° is considerably larger than both the north–south range of lunar parallax for various localities on Earth (≈1.9°) and the angular radii of the Sun and Moon (each ≈0.25°), solar eclipses can occur only when the Sun is near (within about

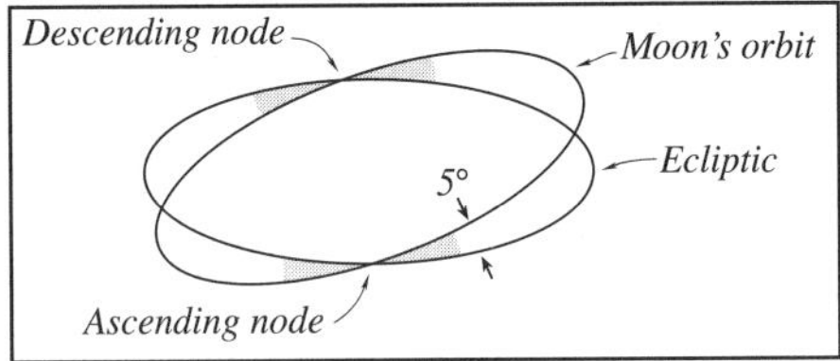

±15° to ±18°) one of the two points at which the Moon's orbit crosses the ecliptic (nodes). Lunar eclipses have a comparable restriction. The *ascending* node is the one at which the Moon crosses to the *north* side of the ecliptic.

The Sun moves eastward along the ecliptic about 1° per day; thus the interval during which an eclipse can occur is at most about (2 × 18°) ÷ 1°/d = 36 d, an *eclipse season*. Since the interval between new moons (29.5 days) is somewhat less, one or two solar eclipses will occur in each eclipse season. Six months later, when the Sun is near the other node, another eclipse season occurs. However, the plane of the Moon's orbit wobbles, making the nodes regress slowly westward along the ecliptic with a period of 18.61 years; thus the two eclipse seasons drift backward through the year, occurring about 19 days earlier each year. *The eclipse seasons of 2007 occur in March and August–September.*

In a calendar year,

- there can be as many as seven eclipses (solar and lunar combined, as last occurred in 1982) and as few as four (the usual number, as in 2007);
- there can be as many as five solar or lunar eclipses and as few as two;
- the number of total or annular solar eclipses can range from zero to two, the number of total lunar eclipses from zero to three.

In 2007, there are four eclipses: two lunar (both total) and two solar (both partial).

The Saros

Eclipses of the Sun and Moon recur with various periodicities that are more or less approximate. These periodicities are interesting both as numerical curiosities and because they may be used to predict eclipses. The most famous periodicity, the *Saros*, has been known since ancient times. It is a consequence of a remarkable commensurability between three lunar average periods:

Synodic month *(S)* (new to new)	= 29.530 589 d, 223S	= 6585.3213 d
Draconic month *(N)* (node to node)	= 27.212 221 d, 242N	= 6585.3575 d
Anomalistic month *(P)* (perigee to perigee)	= 27.554 550 d, 239P	= 6585.5375 d

Several aspects of this arithmetic are relevant to the pattern of eclipses (for brevity, the following comments are restricted primarily to the case of solar eclipses):

(1) An integer number of *S*s (223) ensures a new Moon and hence the possibility of a second solar eclipse.

(2) $242N \approx 223S$ means that the new Moon will be at almost the same position relative to a node, ensuring that an eclipse *will* occur again and that it will occur on Earth's globe about the same distance north or south of the ecliptic plane as did the first eclipse.

(3) The Saros (223*S*) = 6585.3213 d = 18 years + *only* 10.3213 d or 11.3213 d (depending on the number of intervening leap years). Thus one Saros later Earth will be at almost the same point in its elliptical orbit and hence at nearly the same distance from the Sun. Moreover, the inclination of Earth toward the Sun (season) will be nearly the same; thus the same latitude region of Earth will be exposed to the eclipse.

(text continues on next page)

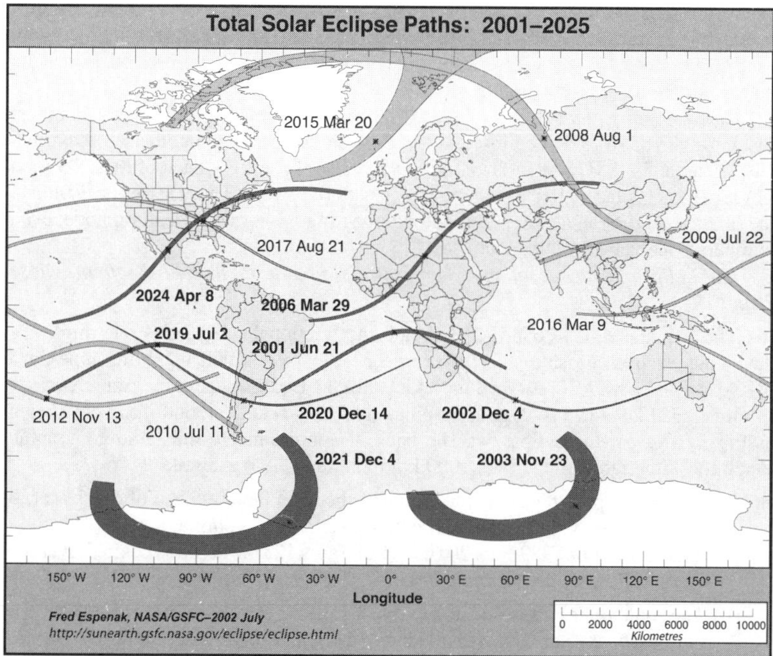

The figure shows the paths of all total solar eclipses, excluding hybrid annular/total eclipses, occurring during the years 2001–2025. There are 15 eclipses, one in each of the years 2001, 2002, 2003, 2006, 2008, 2009, 2010, 2012, 2015, 2016, 2017, 2019, 2020, 2021, and 2024. Because the 25-year period covered by the figure is somewhat longer than the 18-year Saros interval, the first four and last four eclipses, drawn with heavy shading and with labels in bold type, make up four Saros pairs, with Saros numbers 127, 142, 152, and 139, respectively. Note that the members of each pair are both total eclipses, are separated in time by one Saros, have similar path shapes, and occur at similar latitudes; note also that the later member is shifted 120° westward in longitude (see items (2) through (6) of the text explaining these features). The figure was produced by Fred Espenak and is presented here with his permission. For figures showing total solar eclipses, annular eclipses, and hybrid annular/total eclipses for the period 1801–2200, see sunearth.gsfc.nasa.gov/eclipse/SEatlas/SEatlas.html.

(4) $239P \approx 223S$ means that one Saros later the new Moon will be at almost the same point in its elliptical orbit and thus at the same distance from Earth. With the same lunar and solar distances, the type of eclipse (total or annular) will be the same. Since the eclipse will occur near the same geographic latitude (see (2) and (3)), the duration of totality or annularity, or the magnitude of partial eclipse if the eclipse is not central, will be almost the same as it was one Saros earlier.

(5) $242N - 223S = 0.0361$ d = 0.87 h. This, together with the 0.55°/h eastward speed of the Moon in its orbit, means that after one Saros the Moon will be about 0.5° west of its former position relative to its node. Thus a Saros series does not last forever; there will be about 36°/0.5° ≈ 72 eclipses in a Saros series (the number ranges from 69 to 86). Furthermore, any one Saros series will last for about 72 × 18 ≈ 1300 years (the range is 1226 to 1532 years).

A Saros series begins with about 10 partial eclipses of increasing magnitude in the north or south polar region, depending upon whether the eclipses are occurring near the ascending or descending lunar node, respectively. These are followed by about 50 central eclipses (either total or annular), which over many centuries progressively shift southward or northward across Earth (an approximate 300-km shift in latitude with each successive eclipse). The series ends with 10 or so partial eclipses of decreasing magnitude in the opposite polar region.

Currently, for solar eclipses, 39 Saros series are running simultaneously, numbers 117 through 155 (for lunar eclipses, 41 Saros series are running, numbers 109 through 149). That is, in any 18-year 11-day interval, one eclipse from each of these 39 (and 41) series takes place, after which the whole pattern repeats. Those series occurring at the lunar ascending node are given odd numbers; those at the descending node, even numbers (vice versa for lunar eclipses).

The eclipse sequence of the year 2007 is similar to that of the four-eclipse year 1989.

(6) The Saros = $223S$ = 6585.3213 d, and the fractional 0.3213 d ≈ one-third of a day. Thus each successive solar eclipse in a Saros series will be shifted one-third of the way westward (120° in longitude) around Earth. After three Saros periods (3 × 6585.3213 d ≈ 19 756 d, or approximately 54 years and 1 month), a cycle known as the *Exeligmos,* the eclipse will be back at approximately the same geographic longitude, although shifted about 1000 km in latitude. Two examples follow.

(a) The geographic region of visibility of the total lunar eclipse of 2007 Mar. 3 (no. 52 of Saros 123) which is centred over Africa is similar to that of the total lunar eclipse of 1989 Feb. 20 (no. 51 of Saros 123) which was centred over the western Pacific, 120° further east.

(b) The total solar eclipse of 2024 Apr. 8 (no. 30 of Saros 139), which sweeps northeastward across eastern North America, will be geographically similar to that of 1970 Mar. 7 (no. 27 of Saros 139), which followed the eastern seaboard of North America one Exeligmos earlier. Also, one Saros earlier we had the similar total solar eclipse of 2006 Mar. 29 (no. 29 of Saros 139), which occurred about 120° to the east, across Africa and the Mediterranean (see the figure on the previous page). You, the reader, should now be able to figure out the date, the shape of the path of totality, and the geographic location of solar eclipse no. 28 of Saros 139!

The Metonic Cycle

The sequence of lunar phases and the year repeat their relative pattern at 19-year intervals, a cycle known to astronomers in ancient Babylon and which was discovered independently around 430 BC by Meton, a Greek astronomer. We have

$235S = 235 \times 29.530\,589 = 6939.6884$ d;
19 years = 6939 d or 6940 d (depending on leap years).

Moreover, $255N$ is also very close to 19 years:

$255N = 255 \times 27.212\,221 = 6939.1164$ d.

Thus solar and lunar eclipses also repeat on a 19-year "Metonic" cycle. Since $255N$ is less than $235S$, the Moon does not reach the same phase (new or full for an eclipse) until it has moved eastward relative to the node by

$(235S - 255N) \times 24\text{ h} \times 0.55°/\text{h} = 7.5°$.

Thus a Metonic eclipse series will have only

eclipse season width on the ecliptic $(36°) \div 7.5° \approx 4$ or 5 eclipses;

and the geographic latitude of successive solar eclipses in a series will change substantially (north or south, depending upon whether the Moon is at its ascending node or descending node, respectively).

What about the Moon's position in its orbit relative to its perigee? Using the anomalistic month P (the Moon returns to perigee on average every 27.554 550 d),

$235S \div P = 251.85$, which is *not* near an integer.

Thus in a Metonic series the Moon's distance is not the same from one eclipse to another. Hence the type of solar eclipse (total or annular) will vary within the series.

With only about four eclipses in a series, a mix of eclipse types, and scattered geographic occurrence, a Metonic eclipse series is not as elegant or useful as a Saros series. The main feature of a Metonic eclipse series is that, like lunar phases, the successive eclipses occur on (almost) the *same day* of the year.

Examples of the Metonic cycle for a lunar phase, lunar eclipses, and two recent Western Hemisphere total solar eclipses are given below. The numbers in parentheses are Saros numbers.

Full Moon	**Lunar Eclipses**	**Solar Eclipses**
1950 Dec. 24	1969 Mar. 3 (no eclipse)	1960 Feb. 26 (no eclipse)
1969 Dec. 23	1988 Mar. 3 Partial (113)	**1979** Feb. 26 Total (120)
1988 Dec. 23	2007 Mar. 3 Total (123)	**1998** Feb. 26 Total (130)
2007 Dec. 24	2026 Mar. 3 Total (133)	2017 Feb. 26 Annular (140)
2026 Dec. 24	2045 Mar. 3 Penumbral (143)	2036 Feb. 27 Partial (150)
2045 Dec. 24	2064 Mar. 3 (no eclipse)	2055 Feb. 27 (no eclipse)

ECLIPSES IN 2007

By Fred Espenak

Two partial solar and two total lunar eclipses occur in 2007 as follows:

2007 Mar. 3:Total lunar eclipse
2007 Mar. 19:Partial solar eclipse
2007 Aug. 28:Total lunar eclipse
2007 Sep. 11:Partial solar eclipse

Predictions for the eclipses are summarized in Figures 1 through 4 (pp. 121–124). World maps show the regions of visibility for each eclipse. The lunar eclipse diagrams also include the path of the Moon through Earth's shadows. Contact times for each principal phase are tabulated along with the magnitudes and geocentric coordinates of the Sun and Moon at greatest eclipse.

Total Lunar Eclipse of March 3

The first of two total lunar eclipses in 2007 is unique in that it is partly visible from every continent. The eclipse occurs at the descending node, 3.2 days before apogee and 1.9 days after the Moon occults Saturn (northern and eastern Europe). During the eclipse, the Moon is in southern Leo, about 13° east of the 1.3-magnitude star Regulus (α Leo).

The Moon's orbital trajectory takes it through the northern half of Earth's umbral shadow. Although the eclipse is not central, the total phase still lasts 73 min. The timings of the major phases of the eclipse are listed below:

Penumbral eclipse begins:	20:18:11 UT
Partial eclipse begins:	21:30:22 UT
Total eclipse begins:	22:44:13 UT
Greatest eclipse:	23:20:56 UT
Total eclipse ends:	23:57:37 UT
Partial eclipse ends:	1:11:28 UT
Penumbral eclipse ends:	2:23:44 UT

The Moon's path through Earth's shadows as well as a map illustrating worldwide visibility of the event are shown in Figure 1 (p. 121).

At the instant of greatest eclipse (23:21 UT) the Moon will lie in the zenith for observers in Nigeria and Cameroon. At this time, the umbral magnitude peaks at 1.2331 as the Moon's southern limb passes 2.4′ north of the shadow's central axis. In contrast, the Moon's northern limb will lie 6.9′ from the northern edge of the umbra and 32.2′ from the shadow centre. Thus the northern sections of the Moon will appear much brighter than the southern part, which lies deeper in the shadow. Since the Moon samples a large range of umbral depths during totality, its appearance will change dramatically with time. It is not possible to predict the exact brightness distribution in the umbra, so observers are encouraged to estimate the Danjon value at different times during totality (see Danjon Scale of Lunar Eclipse Brightness below). Note that it may also be necessary to assign different Danjon values to different portions of the Moon (i.e. north vs. south).

During totality, the spring constellations will be well placed for viewing, so a number of bright stars can be used for magnitude comparisons. Spica (m_V = +0.98) is 40° southeast of the eclipsed Moon, while Arcturus (m_V = –0.05) is 49° to the northeast. Alphard or α Hya (m_V = +1.99) is 28° to the southwest, and Procyon (m_V = –0.05) is 50° to the west. Saturn shines at magnitude +0.8 about 24° northwest of the Moon near the western border of Leo.

The entire event will be visible from Europe, Africa, and western Asia. In eastern Asia, moonset occurs during various stages of the eclipse. For example, the Moon sets while in total eclipse from central China and southeast Asia. Western Australia catches part of the initial partial phases, but the Moon sets before totality. Observers in eastern North and South America will find the Moon already partially or totally eclipsed at moonrise. From western North America, only the final penumbral phases are visible.

Table 1 (p. 118) lists predicted umbral immersion and emersion times for 20 well-defined lunar craters. The timing of craters is useful in determining the atmospheric enlargement of Earth's shadow (see Crater Timings During Lunar Eclipses below).

Partial Solar Eclipse of March 19

The first solar eclipse of 2007 occurs at the Moon's ascending node in Pisces and is visible from eastern Asia and parts of northern Alaska (Figure 2, p. 122). Greatest eclipse(1) takes place at 2:31:56 UT, when the eclipse magnitude(2) will reach 0.8754. The penumbral contact times with Earth are listed below:

Partial eclipse begins:	0:38:26 UT
Partial eclipse ends:	4:25:00 UT

Local circumstances for a number of cities within the zone of partial eclipse are given in Universal Time in Table 2 (pp. 118–119). The Sun's altitude and azimuth, the eclipse magnitude, and obscuration(3) are all given at the instant of local maximum eclipse.

This event is the 20th partial eclipse of Saros series 149. After one more partial eclipse, the series will produce its first total solar eclipse on 2043 Apr. 9.

Total Lunar Eclipse of August 28

The second lunar eclipse of the year is another total eclipse. It is a deeper event, since it is the first central total eclipse since 2000. The eclipse occurs at the ascending node of Luna's orbit in southern Aquarius. Since the Moon is 2.6 days shy of perigee, it will appear 8% larger (= 1.2′) than it was during March's eclipse. The Moon's trajectory takes it deep into the southern umbral shadow, resulting in a total eclipse that lasts 90 min. At midtotality the Moon's centre passes just 12.8′ south of the shadow axis. This places the Moon's northern limb only 3.4′ north of the axis, while the southern limb is 15.4′ from the umbra's southern edge.

Since different parts of the Moon will probe radically different portions of Earth's umbral shadow, a large variation in shadow brightness can be expected. As a consequence of this geometry, the southern half of the totally eclipsed Moon will appear considerably brighter than the northern half. Observers are encouraged to estimate the Danjon value at midtotality (see Danjon Scale of Lunar Eclipse Brightness below).

The penumbral phase of August's eclipse begins at about 7:54 UT, but most observers will not be able to visually detect the shadow until about 8:30 UT. A timetable for the major phases of the eclipse is listed below:

Penumbral eclipse begins:	7:53:39 UT
Partial eclipse begins:	8:51:16 UT
Total eclipse begins:	9:52:22 UT
Greatest eclipse:	10:37:22 UT
Total eclipse ends:	11:22:24 UT
Partial eclipse ends:	12:23:30 UT
Penumbral eclipse ends:	13:21:01 UT

(1) The instant of greatest eclipse occurs when the distance between the Moon's shadow axis and Earth's geocentre reaches a minimum.

(2) Eclipse magnitude is defined as the fraction of the Sun's diameter occulted by the Moon.

(3) Eclipse obscuration is defined as the fraction of the Sun's surface area occulted by the Moon.

The Moon's path through Earth's shadows as well as a map illustrating worldwide visibility of the event are shown in Figure 3 (p. 123).

At the instant of midtotality (10:37 UT) the Moon will stand near the zenith for observers in French Polynesia. At that time, the umbral eclipse magnitude will be 1.4760.

All of North America will witness some portion of the eclipse, but western observers are favoured. The early penumbral or umbral phases will be in progress at moonset for observers in Maritime Canada. From the eastern United States, the Great Lakes region, and Ontario, the Moon sets in total eclipse. Only observers to the west of the Rockies (including Alaska) will be treated to the entire event. All phases of the eclipse are also visible from islands of the Pacific Ocean, New Zealand, and eastern Australia. Various stages of the eclipse are in progress at moonrise for eastern Asia. No eclipse is visible from Europe, Africa, and western Asia.

Table 3 (p. 120) lists predicted umbral immersion and emersion times for 20 well-defined lunar craters. The timing of craters is useful in determining the atmospheric enlargement of Earth's shadow (see Crater Timings During Lunar Eclipses below).

Partial Solar Eclipse of September 11

The last eclipse of 2007 is a partial solar eclipse at the Moon's descending node in southern Leo. Its visibility is confined to parts of South America, Antarctica, and the South Atlantic (Figure 4, p. 124). Greatest eclipse takes place at 12:31:21 UT, when the eclipse magnitude will reach 0.7505. The penumbral contact times with Earth are as follows:

Partial eclipse begins:	10:25:46 UT
Partial eclipse ends:	14:36:33 UT

Local circumstances for a number of cities within the zone of partial eclipse are given in Table 4 (p. 120). All times are given in Universal Time. The Sun's altitude and azimuth, the eclipse magnitude, and obscuration are all given at the instant of maximum eclipse.

This event is the sixth partial eclipse of Saros series 154. After one more partial eclipse (2025 Sep. 25) the series will produce the first of many annular eclipses on 2043 Oct. 3.

Solar Eclipse Figures

An orthographic projection map of Earth shows the path of penumbral (partial) eclipse for each event. North is up, and the daylight terminator is plotted for the instant of greatest eclipse. An asterisk (*) indicates the subsolar point[(4)] on Earth.

The limits of the Moon's penumbral shadow delineate the region of visibility of the partial eclipse. This irregular or saddle-shaped region often covers nearly half the daylight hemisphere of Earth and consists of several distinct zones, or limits. At the northern and/or southern boundaries lie the limits of the penumbra's path. Partial eclipses have only one of these limits. Great loops at the western and eastern extremes identify the areas where the eclipse begins and ends at sunrise and sunset, respectively. The curves are connected in a distorted figure 8. Bisecting the "eclipse begins/ends" loops is the curve of maximum eclipse at sunrise (western loop) and sunset (eastern loop). The points P1 and P4 mark the coordinates where the penumbral shadow first contacts (partial eclipse begins) and last contacts (partial eclipse ends) Earth's surface.

A curve of maximum eclipse is the locus of all points where the eclipse is at maximum at a given time. The curves are plotted at each half hour Universal Time.

(4) The subsolar point is the geographic location where the Sun appears directly overhead (zenith).

Curves of constant eclipse magnitude delineate the locus of all points where the magnitude at maximum eclipse is constant. These curves run exclusively between the curves of maximum eclipse at sunrise and sunset. Furthermore, they run parallel to the northern and southern penumbral limits. In fact, the northern and southern limits of the penumbra can be thought of as curves of constant magnitude of 0.0. The adjacent curves are for magnitudes of 0.2, 0.4, 0.6, and 0.8 (i.e. 20%, 40%, 60%, and 80%).

Greatest eclipse is the instant when the axis of the Moon's shadow passes closest to Earth's centre. For partial eclipses, the shadow axis misses Earth entirely. The point on Earth's surface closest to the axis is marked by an asterisk. This point lies on the day/night terminator, so the Sun appears on the horizon.

Each map includes data pertinent to the eclipse. The instant of conjunction of the Sun and Moon in right ascension and the instant of greatest eclipse are expressed as both Universal Times and Julian Dates. The eclipse magnitude is defined as the fraction of the Sun's diameter obscured by the Moon at greatest eclipse. Gamma is the minimum distance of the Moon's shadow axis from Earth's centre in Earth radii at greatest eclipse. The Saros series of the eclipse is listed, followed by the member position. The first member number identifies the sequence position of the eclipse in the Saros, while the second is the total number of eclipses in the series.

In the upper left and right corners are the geocentric coordinates of the Sun and the Moon, respectively, at the instant of greatest eclipse. They are

R.A. Right ascension
Dec. Declination
S.D. Apparent semi-diameter
H.P. Horizontal parallax

To the lower left in the figures are exterior/interior contact times of the Moon's penumbral shadow with Earth, which are defined as follows:

P1 Instant of first exterior tangency of penumbra with Earth's limb (partial eclipse begins)
P4 Instant of last exterior tangency of penumbra with Earth's limb (partial eclipse ends)

At bottom left is a list of parameters used in the eclipse predictions. The list at bottom right gives the Moon's geocentric libration (optical + physical) at greatest eclipse.

Lunar Eclipse Figures

Each lunar eclipse has two diagrams associated with it along with data pertinent to the eclipse. The top figure shows the path of the Moon through Earth's penumbral and umbral shadows. Above this figure are listed the instant of conjunction in right ascension of the Moon with Earth's shadow axis and the instant of greatest eclipse, expressed as both Universal Times and Julian Dates. The penumbral and umbral magnitudes are defined as the fraction of the Moon's diameter immersed in the two shadows at greatest eclipse. The radii of the penumbral and umbral shadows, P. Radius and U. Radius, are also listed. Gamma is the minimum distance in Earth radii of the Moon's centre from Earth's shadow axis at greatest eclipse, and Axis is the same parameter expressed in degrees. The Saros series of the eclipse is listed, followed by a pair of numbers. The first number identifies the sequence position of the eclipse in the Saros; the second is the total number of eclipses in the series.

In the upper left and right corners are the geocentric coordinates of the Sun and the Moon, respectively, at the instant of greatest eclipse, defined as in the solar-eclipse diagrams.

To the lower left are the semi, or half, durations of the penumbral, umbral (partial), and total eclipses. Below them are the Sun/Moon ephemerides used in the predictions, followed by the extrapolated value of ΔT (the difference between Terrestrial Dynamical Time and Universal Time). To the lower right are the contact times of the Moon with Earth's penumbral and umbral shadows, defined as follows:

- P1 Instant of first exterior tangency of Moon with penumbra (penumbral eclipse begins)
- U1 Instant of first exterior tangency of Moon with umbra (partial umbral eclipse begins)
- U2 Instant of first interior tangency of Moon with umbra (total umbral eclipse begins)
- U3 Instant of last interior tangency of Moon with umbra (total umbral eclipse ends)
- U4 Instant of last exterior tangency of Moon with umbra (partial umbral eclipse ends)
- P4 Instant of last exterior tangency of Moon with penumbra (penumbral eclipse ends)

The bottom figure is a cylindrical equidistant projection map of Earth that shows the regions of visibility for each stage of the eclipse. In particular, the moonrise/moonset terminator is plotted for each contact and is labelled accordingly. The point where the Moon is in the zenith at greatest eclipse is indicated by an asterisk. Observers in the region that is completely unshaded will observe the entire eclipse, while those in the darkly shaded area will witness no eclipse. Observers in the remaining lightly shaded areas will experience moonrise or moonset while the eclipse is in progress. Those in the shaded zones east of the asterisk will witness moonset before the eclipse ends, and those in the shaded zones west will witness moonrise after the eclipse has begun.

Shadow Diameters and Lunar Eclipses

Chauvenet [1891] is credited with the introduction of an empirical enlargement of 1/50 to the diameters of the umbral and penumbral shadows to compensate for Earth's atmosphere when calculating the circumstances of a lunar eclipse. This rule has been used by long tradition in many of the national institutes in their official eclipse predictions (including the author's work at NASA). However, the French astronomer André-Louis Danjon [1951] pointed out that the correct procedure is to enlarge Earth's diameter by 1/85 to compensate for the atmosphere. The umbral and penumbral shadow diameters are then calculated based on this modified geometry. The French almanac *Connaissance des Temps* has used the Danjon rule in its eclipse predictions since 1951. The resulting umbral and penumbral eclipse magnitudes are approximately 0.005 and 0.026 magnitudes smaller, respectively, than predictions using the traditional 1/50 rule.

Beginning with ECLIPSES IN 2007, we will use the Danjon rule rather than the traditional (and flawed) 1/50 rule in calculating lunar eclipse circumstances.

Danjon Scale of Lunar Eclipse Brightness

The Moon's appearance during a total lunar eclipse can vary enormously from one eclipse to the next. Obviously, the geometry of the Moon's path through the umbra plays an important role. Not as apparent is the effect that Earth's atmosphere has on total eclipses. Although the physical mass of Earth blocks all direct sunlight from the umbra, the planet's atmosphere refracts some of the Sun's rays into the shadow. Earth's atmosphere contains varying amounts of water (clouds, mist, precipitation) and solid particles (meteoric dust, organic debris, volcanic ash). This material significantly filters and attenuates the sunlight before it is refracted into the umbra. For instance, large or frequent volcanic eruptions dumping huge quantities of ash into the atmosphere are often followed by very dark, red eclipses for several years. Extensive cloud cover along Earth's limb also tends to darken the eclipse by blocking sunlight.

Danjon proposed a useful five-point scale for evaluating the visual appearance and brightness of the Moon during total lunar eclipses. L values for various luminosities are defined as follows:

$L = 0$ Very dark eclipse
(Moon almost invisible, especially at midtotality)
$L = 1$ Dark eclipse, grey or brownish in colouration
(details distinguishable only with difficulty)
$L = 2$ Deep red or rust-coloured eclipse
(very dark central shadow, while outer umbra is relatively bright)
$L = 3$ Brick-red eclipse
(umbral shadow usually has a bright or yellow rim)
$L = 4$ Very bright copper-red or orange eclipse
(umbral shadow has a bluish, very bright rim)

The assignment of an L value to lunar eclipses is best done with the naked eye, binoculars, or a small telescope near the time of midtotality. It's also useful to examine the Moon's appearance just after the beginning and just before the end of totality. The Moon is then near the edge of the shadow, providing an opportunity to assign an L value to the outer umbra. In making any evaluations, the instrumentation used and the time should both be recorded. Also note any variations in colour and brightness in different parts of the umbra, as well as the apparent sharpness of the shadow's edge. Pay attention to the visibility of lunar features within the umbra. Notes and sketches made during the eclipse are often invaluable in recalling important details, events, and impressions.

Crater Timings During Lunar Eclipses

In 1702, Pierre de La Hire made a curious observation about Earth's umbra. In order to accurately predict the duration of a lunar eclipse, he found it necessary to increase the radius of the shadow about 1% more than is warranted by geometric considerations. Although the effect is clearly related to Earth's atmosphere, it is not completely understood, since the shadow enlargement seems to vary from one eclipse to the next. The enlargement can be measured through careful timings of lunar craters as they enter and exit the umbra.

Such observations are best made using a low-power telescope and a clock or watch synchronized with radio time signals. Timings should be made to a precision of 0.1 min. Record the instant when the most abrupt gradient at the umbra's edge crosses the apparent centre of the crater. In the case of large craters such as Tycho and Copernicus, record the times when the shadow touches the two opposite edges of the crater. The average of these times is equal to the instant of crater bisection.

As a planning guide, Tables 2 and 4 list 20 well-defined craters with predicted umbral immersion and emersion times during the two lunar eclipses of 2007. You should be thoroughly familiar with these features before viewing an eclipse in order to prevent confusion and misidentification. The four umbral contacts with the Moon's limb can also be used in determining the shadow's enlargement. However, these events are less distinct and therefore difficult to time accurately. Observers are encouraged to make crater timings and to send their results to *Sky & Telescope* (Sky Publishing Corporation, 49 Bay State Road, Cambridge MA 02138-1200, USA) for analysis.

Note that all predictions presented here use Danjon's rule of shadow enlargement (see Shadow Diameters and Lunar Eclipses). In particular, the diameter of the umbral shadow has been calculated assuming an enlargement of Earth's radius of 1/85 to account for the opacity of the terrestrial atmosphere. The effects of Earth's oblateness have also been included.

Eclipse Altitudes and Azimuths

The altitude a and azimuth A of the Sun or Moon during an eclipse depend on the time and the observer's geographic coordinates. They are calculated as follows:

$$h = 15\,(\mathrm{GST} + \mathrm{UT} - \alpha) + \lambda$$
$$a = \arcsin\,[\sin\delta\,\sin\phi + \cos\delta\,\cos h\,\cos\phi]$$
$$A = \arctan\,[-(\cos\delta\,\sin h)/(\sin\delta\,\cos\phi - \cos\delta\,\cos h\,\sin\phi)]$$

where

h = hour angle of Sun or Moon
a = altitude
A = azimuth
GST = Greenwich Sidereal Time at 0:00 UT
UT = Universal Time
α = right ascension of Sun or Moon
δ = declination of Sun or Moon
λ = observer's longitude (east +, west –)
ϕ = observer's latitude (north +, south –)

During the eclipses of 2007, the values for GST and the geocentric right ascension and declination of the Sun or the Moon (at greatest eclipse) are as follows:

Eclipse	Date	GST	α	δ
Total lunar	2007 Mar. 3	10.757	10.964	6.934
Partial solar	2007 Mar. 19	11.751	23.884	–0.751
Total lunar	2007 Aug. 28	22.418	22.447	–9.955
Partial solar	2007 Sep. 11	23.343	11.289	4.587

Eclipses In 2008

Next year, there will be two solar and two lunar eclipses:

2008 Feb. 7: Annular solar eclipse
2008 Feb. 21: Total lunar eclipse
2008 Aug. 1: Total solar eclipse
2008 Aug. 16: Partial lunar eclipse

A full report on eclipses in 2008 will be published next year in the *Observer's Handbook 2008*.

NASA Solar Eclipse Bulletins

Special bulletins containing detailed predictions and meteorological data for future solar eclipses of interest are prepared by Fred Espenak and Jay Anderson and are published through NASA's Publication series. The bulletins are provided as a public service to both the professional and lay communities, including educators and the media. A list of currently available bulletins and an order form can be found at:

sunearth.gsfc.nasa.gov/eclipse/SEpubs/RPrequest.html

The most recent bulletin of the series covers the total solar eclipse of 2008 Aug. 1, which is visible from northern Canada, Russia, Mongolia, and China. Single copies of the eclipse bulletins are available at no cost by sending a 9 × 12-in. self-addressed envelope stamped with postage for 11 oz. (310 g). Please print the eclipse year on the envelope's lower left corner. Use stamps only, since cash and cheques cannot be accepted. Requests from outside the United States and Canada may include 10 international postal coupons. Mail requests to: Fred Espenak, NASA's Goddard Space Flight Center, Code 693, Greenbelt MD 20771, USA.

The NASA eclipse bulletins are also available over the Internet, including out-of-print bulletins. Using a Web browser, they can be read or downloaded through the World Wide Web from the GSFC/SDAC (Solar Data Analysis Center) eclipse page:

umbra.nascom.nasa.gov/eclipse/index.html

Eclipse Web sites

The NASA Eclipse Home Page is available at:

sunearth.gsfc.nasa.gov/eclipse/eclipse.html

The site features predictions and maps for all solar and lunar eclipses well into the 21st century, with special emphasis on eclipses occurring during the next two years. Detailed path maps, tables, graphs, and meteorological data are included. A world atlas of solar eclipses provides maps of all central eclipse paths from 2000 BC to 3000 AD. Additional catalogues list every solar and lunar eclipse over a 5000-year period.

Detailed information on solar and lunar eclipse photography and tips on eclipse observing and eye safety may be found at:

www.MrEclipse.com

Acknowledgments

All eclipse predictions were generated on an Apple G4 iMac computer using algorithms developed from the *Explanatory Supplement* (1974) with additional algorithms from Meeus, Grosjean, and Vanderleen (1966). The solar and lunar ephemerides were generated from Newcomb and the *Improved Lunar Ephemeris* by Eckert, Jones, and Clark (1954). For lunar eclipses, the diameters of the umbral and penumbral shadows were calculated using Danjon's rule of enlarging Earth's radius by 1/85 to compensate for the opacity of the terrestrial atmosphere; corrections for the effects of oblateness have also been included.

All calculations, diagrams, tables, and opinions presented in this paper are those of the author, and he assumes full responsibility for their accuracy.

This publication is available electronically through the Internet along with additional information and updates at:

sunearth.gsfc.nasa.gov/eclipse/OH/OH2007.html

References

Chauvenet, W., *Manual of Spherical and Practical Astronomy, Vol. 1,* 1891, Dover edition, 1961.

Danjon, A., "Les éclipses de Lune par la pénombre en 1951," *L'Astronomie, 65,* 51–53, Feb. 1951.

Eckert, W.J., Jones, R., and Clark, H.K., *Improved Lunar Ephemeris 1952–1959,* U.S. Naval Observatory, Washington, D.C., 1954.

Espenak, F., *Fifty Year Canon of Solar Eclipses: 1986–2035,* Sky Publishing Corp., Cambridge, Mass., 1988.

Espenak, F., *Fifty Year Canon of Lunar Eclipses: 1986–2035,* Sky Publishing Corp., Cambridge, Mass., 1989.

Explanatory Supplement to the Astronomical Ephemeris and the American Ephemeris and Nautical Almanac, Her Majesty's Nautical Almanac Office, London, 1974.

Littmann, M., Willcox, K., and Espenak, F., *Totality—Eclipses of the Sun,* Oxford University Press, New York, 1999.

Meeus, J., Grosjean, C.C., and Vanderleen, W., *Canon of Solar Eclipses,* Pergamon Press, New York, 1966.

Meeus, J. and Mucke, H., *Canon of Lunar Eclipses: –2002 to +2526,* Astronomisches Buro, Wien, 1979.

Newcomb, S., "Tables of the Motion of the Earth on its Axis Around the Sun," *Astron. Papers Amer. Eph., Vol. 6, Part I,* 1895.

TABLE 1—CRATER IMMERSION AND EMERSION TIMES FOR THE TOTAL LUNAR ECLIPSE OF 2007 MARCH 3

Immersion	Crater Name	Emersion	Crater Name
21:35	Grimaldi	00:06	Grimaldi
21:37	Billy	00:06	Aristarchus
21:43	Campanus	00:13	Kepler
21:49	Kepler	00:13	Billy
21:49	Tycho	00:17	Plato
21:54	Aristarchus	00:19	Pytheas
21:57	Copernicus	00:22	Timocharis
22:02	Pytheas	00:22	Copernicus
22:08	Timocharis	00:26	Campanus
22:13	Dionysius	00:28	Aristoteles
22:13	Manilius	00:30	Eudoxus
22:17	Menelaus	00:36	Tycho
22:21	Plinius	00:37	Manilius
22:22	Goclenius	00:41	Menelaus
22:23	Plato	00:45	Dionysius
22:27	Taruntius	00:45	Plinius
22:27	Langrenus	00:56	Proclus
22:28	Eudoxus	00:59	Taruntius
22:31	Aristoteles	01:01	Goclenius
22:31	Proclus	01:07	Langrenus

All times are Universal Time. Predictions include 2% enlargement of the umbral shadow due to Earth's atmosphere.

TABLE 2—LOCAL CIRCUMSTANCES FOR PARTIAL SOLAR ECLIPSE OF 2007 MARCH 19

Geographic Location		Eclipse Begins h:m	Max. Eclipse h:m	Eclipse Ends h:m	Sun Alt °	Sun Azm °	Ecl. Mag.	Ecl. Obs.
AFGHANISTAN	Kabul	--- r	01:46	02:40	3	93	0.676	0.602
BANGLADESH	Chittagong	00:43	01:31	02:23	21	100	0.399	0.288
	Dacca	00:43	01:33	02:26	19	100	0.434	0.324
CAMBODIA	Phnum Pénh	00:58	01:21	01:44	32	98	0.065	0.020
CHINA	Beijing	01:28	02:23	03:21	41	139	0.394	0.283
	Chengdu	01:00	01:54	02:51	33	114	0.431	0.321
	Chongqing	01:01	01:54	02:50	36	115	0.385	0.273
	Canton	01:07	01:47	02:30	43	115	0.189	0.097
	Harbin	01:53	02:45	03:39	42	161	0.320	0.210
	Nanjing	01:24	02:11	03:00	46	133	0.249	0.145
	Shanghai	01:29	02:12	02:56	49	136	0.192	0.099
	Shenyang	01:42	02:35	03:28	44	152	0.314	0.204
	Shuicheng	00:56	01:47	02:41	34	111	0.360	0.248
	Tianjin	01:28	02:23	03:20	42	139	0.373	0.261
	Wuhan	01:13	02:03	02:55	43	125	0.297	0.187
	Xi'an	01:09	02:05	03:03	37	123	0.424	0.313
	Zibo	01:27	02:19	03:14	44	138	0.329	0.218
HONG KONG	Kowloon	01:09	01:47	02:26	44	114	0.161	0.077
	New Kowloon	01:09	01:47	02:27	44	114	0.162	0.077
	Tsuen Wan	01:09	01:47	02:27	44	114	0.163	0.078
	Victoria	01:09	01:47	02:26	44	114	0.161	0.077
INDIA	Ahmadabad	--- r	01:28	02:17	2	92	0.474	0.366
	Bangalore	--- r	01:15	01:52	4	92	0.247	0.143
	Bombay	--- r	01:23	02:07	2	91	0.388	0.275
	Calcutta	00:42	01:30	02:22	17	98	0.423	0.312
	Delhi	--- r	01:37	02:31	8	95	0.573	0.479
	Hyderabad	--- r	01:20	02:05	6	93	0.348	0.236

All times are Universal Time.
"r" indicates eclipse in progress at sunrise.

TABLE 2—LOCAL CIRCUMSTANCES FOR PARTIAL SOLAR ECLIPSE OF 2007 MARCH 19 (continued)

Geographic Location		Eclipse Begins h:m	Max. Eclipse h:m	Eclipse Ends h:m	Sun Alt °	Sun Azm °	Ecl. Mag.	Ecl. Obs.
INDIA (continued)	Kanpur	––– r	01:34	02:27	10	96	0.527	0.426
	Madras	––– r	01:15	01:53	7	92	0.246	0.142
	Nagpur	––– r	01:26	02:14	8	94	0.428	0.317
	Pune	––– r	01:22	02:07	2	91	0.378	0.265
IRAN	Mashhad	––– r	02:10 r	02:42	0	91	0.505	0.401
KAZAKHSTAN	Alma-Ata	01:06	02:02	03:02	11	101	0.766	0.713
KOREA, NORTH	P'yongyang	01:45	02:32	03:21	47	153	0.238	0.136
KOREA, SOUTH	Pusan	01:54	02:29	03:05	51	154	0.120	0.049
	Seoul	01:48	02:31	03:16	49	153	0.195	0.102
	Taegu	01:52	02:30	03:09	51	155	0.140	0.063
KYRGYZSTAN	Frunze (Bishkek)	––– r	02:01	03:00	9	99	0.768	0.716
MONGOLIA	Ulaanbaatar	01:28	02:29	03:32	31	134	0.597	0.508
MYANMAR	Yangon	00:43	01:24	02:08	24	99	0.258	0.153
PAKISTAN	Karachi	––– r	01:40 r	02:20	0	91	0.483	0.376
	Lahore	––– r	01:41	02:36	6	95	0.626	0.541
RUSSIA	Chelyabinsk	––– r	02:21	03:18	2	94	0.865	0.838
	Kazan	––– r	02:54 r	03:17	0	91	0.417	0.306
	Kujbysev	––– r	02:49 r	03:12	0	91	0.409	0.297
	Novosibirsk	01:28	02:26	03:28	15	113	0.812	0.772
	Omsk	01:26	02:23	03:23	9	105	0.846	0.815
	Perm	––– r	02:26	03:22	0	91	0.873	0.848
	Samara	––– r	02:49 r	03:12	0	91	0.409	0.297
	Saratov	––– r	03:06 r	03:09	0	91	0.062	0.018
	Ufa	––– r	02:26 r	03:16	0	91	0.826	0.788
SRI LANKA	Colombo	––– r	01:08	01:31	5	91	0.091	0.033
TAIWAN	Kaohsiung	01:27	01:54	02:21	50	121	0.068	0.021
	T'aipei	01:30	02:00	02:31	51	127	0.089	0.032
TAJIKISTAN	Dusanbe	––– r	01:52	02:49	4	94	0.731	0.669
THAILAND	Bangkok	00:48	01:22	01:57	28	98	0.157	0.074
UZBEKISTAN	Taskent	––– r	01:57	02:54	5	95	0.762	0.708
VIETNAM	Hai Phong	00:55	01:38	02:23	36	107	0.237	0.135
	Hanoi	00:54	01:37	02:23	35	107	0.250	0.146
	Ho Chi Minh City	01:05	01:21	01:36	34	98	0.027	0.005

All times are Universal Time.
"r" indicates eclipse in progress at sunrise.

TABLE 3—CRATER IMMERSION AND EMERSION TIMES FOR THE TOTAL LUNAR ECLIPSE OF 2007 AUGUST 28

Immersion	Crater Name	Emersion	Crater Name
08:58	Grimaldi	11:26	Grimaldi
08:59	Aristarchus	11:31	Billy
09:04	Kepler	11:36	Aristarchus
09:05	Billy	11:38	Kepler
09:10	Pytheas	11:39	Campanus
09:11	Copernicus	11:45	Tycho
09:12	Timocharis	11:47	Copernicus
09:13	Plato	11:47	Pytheas
09:18	Campanus	11:51	Timocharis
09:22	Aristoteles	11:53	Plato
09:22	Eudoxus	12:01	Aristoteles
09:24	Manilius	12:01	Manilius
09:27	Menelaus	12:02	Eudoxus
09:30	Tycho	12:05	Menelaus
09:30	Dionysius	12:05	Dionysius
09:31	Plinius	12:08	Plinius
09:39	Proclus	12:15	Goclenius
09:41	Taruntius	12:17	Proclus
09:44	Goclenius	12:17	Taruntius
09:48	Langrenus	12:20	Langrenus

All times are Universal Time. Predictions include 2% enlargement of the umbral shadow due to Earth's atmosphere.

TABLE 4—LOCAL CIRCUMSTANCES FOR PARTIAL SOLAR ECLIPSE OF 2007 SEPTEMBER 11

Geographic Location		Eclipse Begins h:m	Max. Eclipse h:m	Eclipse Ends h:m	Sun Alt °	Sun Azm °	Ecl. Mag.	Ecl. Obs.
ANTARCTICA								
ANTARCTICA	Palmer Station	11:38	12:47	14:00	11	53	0.698	0.610
SOUTH AMERICA								
ARGENTINA	Buenos Aires	10:42	11:49	13:02	21	68	0.522	0.409
	Córdoba	10:36	11:39	12:48	16	75	0.507	0.392
	Rosario	10:39	11:44	12:56	19	71	0.513	0.399
	San Justo	10:43	11:49	13:02	21	68	0.524	0.411
BOLIVIA	La Paz	--- r	11:11	12:01	9	83	0.256	0.147
BRAZIL	Belford Roxo	10:43	11:37	12:35	35	66	0.241	0.135
	Belo Horizonte	10:41	11:30	12:24	35	69	0.200	0.103
	Brasília	10:36	11:19	12:05	30	75	0.161	0.074
	Campinas	10:38	11:34	12:35	32	69	0.279	0.167
	Cava	10:43	11:37	12:35	35	66	0.240	0.134
	Curitiba	10:37	11:37	12:42	30	68	0.336	0.219
	Goiânia	10:34	11:20	12:09	28	75	0.188	0.093
	Japeri	10:42	11:36	12:35	35	66	0.242	0.136
	Mesquita	10:43	11:37	12:35	35	66	0.242	0.136
	Nova Iguaçu	10:43	11:37	12:35	35	66	0.241	0.135
	Pinheirinhos	10:40	11:35	12:34	34	68	0.252	0.144
	Porto Alegre	10:41	11:45	12:56	28	66	0.418	0.299
	Queimados	10:42	11:36	12:35	35	66	0.242	0.136
	Rio de Janeiro	10:43	11:37	12:36	36	66	0.242	0.135
	Salvador	11:06	11:21	11:37	40	73	0.016	0.002
	Santos	10:39	11:37	12:39	32	67	0.289	0.175
	São Paulo	10:39	11:35	12:37	32	68	0.285	0.172
CHILE	Santiago	--- r	11:40	12:48	10	78	0.550	0.440
PARAGUAY	Asuncion	10:31	11:30	12:36	21	74	0.389	0.269
PERU	Lima	--- r	11:08 r	11:41	0	85	0.150	0.067
URUGUAY	Montevideo	10:44	11:51	13:05	23	66	0.512	0.398

All times are Universal Time.
"r" indicates eclipse in progress at sunrise.

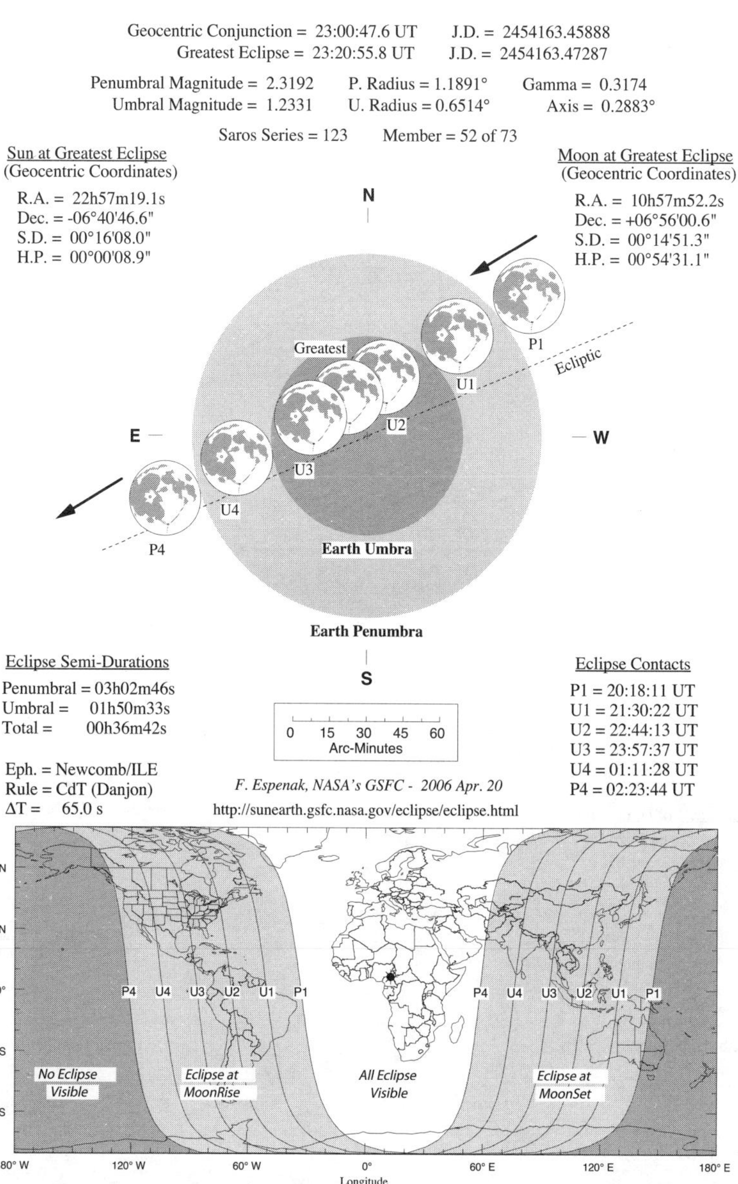
FIGURE 1—TOTAL LUNAR ECLIPSE OF 2007 MARCH 3
Geocentric Conjunction = 23:00:47.6 UT J.D. = 2454163.45888
Greatest Eclipse = 23:20:55.8 UT J.D. = 2454163.47287
Penumbral Magnitude = 2.3192 P. Radius = 1.1891° Gamma = 0.3174
Umbral Magnitude = 1.2331 U. Radius = 0.6514° Axis = 0.2883°
Saros Series = 123 Member = 52 of 73
Sun at Greatest Eclipse
(Geocentric Coordinates)
R.A. = 22h57m19.1s
Dec. = -06°40'46.6"
S.D. = 00°16'08.0"
H.P. = 00°00'08.9"
Moon at Greatest Eclipse
(Geocentric Coordinates)
R.A. = 10h57m52.2s
Dec. = +06°56'00.6"
S.D. = 00°14'51.3"
H.P. = 00°54'31.1"
N
E
W
S
Greatest
P1
U1
U2
U3
U4
P4
Ecliptic
Earth Umbra
Earth Penumbra
Eclipse Semi-Durations
Penumbral = 03h02m46s
Umbral = 01h50m33s
Total = 00h36m42s
0 15 30 45 60
Arc-Minutes
Eclipse Contacts
P1 = 20:18:11 UT
U1 = 21:30:22 UT
U2 = 22:44:13 UT
U3 = 23:57:37 UT
U4 = 01:11:28 UT
P4 = 02:23:44 UT
Eph. = Newcomb/ILE
Rule = CdT (Danjon)
ΔT = 65.0 s
F. Espenak, NASA's GSFC - 2006 Apr. 20
http://sunearth.gsfc.nasa.gov/eclipse/eclipse.html
60° N
30° N
0°
30° S
60° S
Latitude
No Eclipse Visible
Eclipse at MoonRise
All Eclipse Visible
Eclipse at MoonSet
180° W
120° W
60° W
0°
60° E
120° E
180° E
Longitude

See pp. 112–113 for an explanation of this figure.

FIGURE 2—PARTIAL SOLAR ECLIPSE OF 2007 MARCH 19

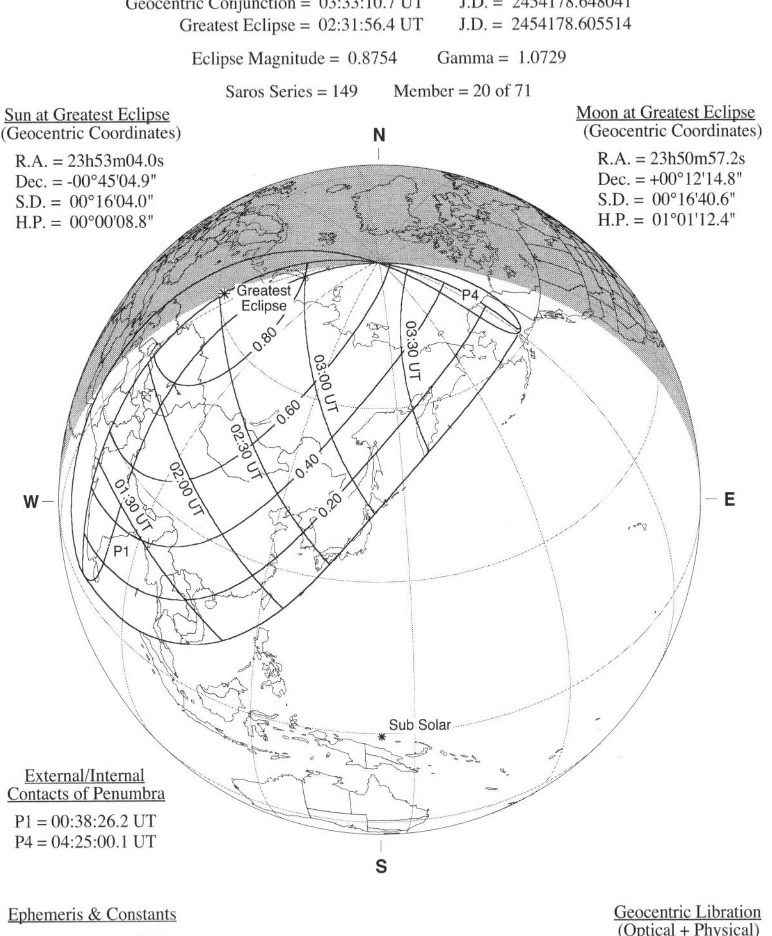

Ephemeris & Constants

Eph. = Newcomb/ILE
ΔT = 65.0 s
k1 = 0.2724880
k2 = 0.2722810
Δb = 0.0" Δl = 0.0"

0 1000 2000 3000 4000 5000
Kilometres

Geocentric Libration
(Optical + Physical)

l = -1.78°
b = -1.40°
c = -21.95°

Brown Lun. No. = 1042

F. Espenak, NASA's GSFC - 2006 Apr. 21

http://sunearth.gsfc.nasa.gov/eclipse/eclipse.html

See pp. 113–114 for an explanation of this figure.

FIGURE 3—TOTAL LUNAR ECLIPSE OF 2007 AUGUST 28

Geocentric Conjunction = 10:25:41.6 UT J.D. = 2454340.93451
Greatest Eclipse = 10:37:22.3 UT J.D. = 2454340.94262

Penumbral Magnitude = 2.4528 P. Radius = 1.2677° Gamma = -0.2145
Umbral Magnitude = 1.4760 U. Radius = 0.7400° Axis = 0.2126°

Saros Series = 128 Member = 40 of 71

Sun at Greatest Eclipse
(Geocentric Coordinates)
R.A. = 10h26m26.8s
Dec. = +09°45'57.0"
S.D. = 00°15'50.0"
H.P. = 00°00'08.7"

Moon at Greatest Eclipse
(Geocentric Coordinates)
R.A. = 22h26m50.4s
Dec. = -09°57'18.5"
S.D. = 00°16'12.5"
H.P. = 00°59'29.2"

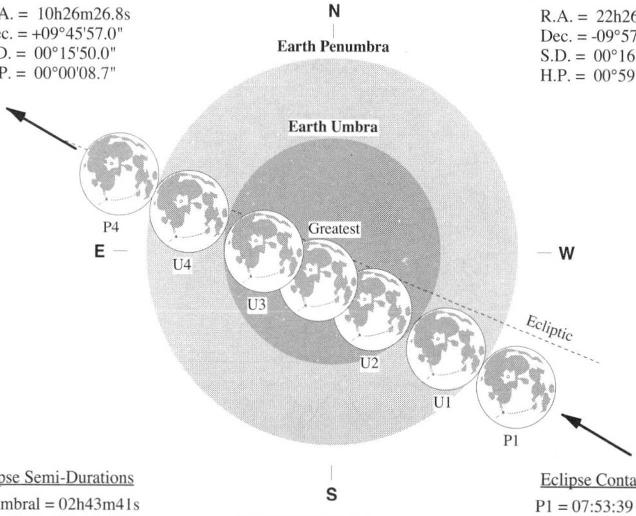

Eclipse Semi-Durations
Penumbral = 02h43m41s
Umbral = 01h46m07s
Total = 00h45m01s

Eclipse Contacts
P1 = 07:53:39 UT
U1 = 08:51:16 UT
U2 = 09:52:22 UT
U3 = 11:22:24 UT
U4 = 12:23:30 UT
P4 = 13:21:01 UT

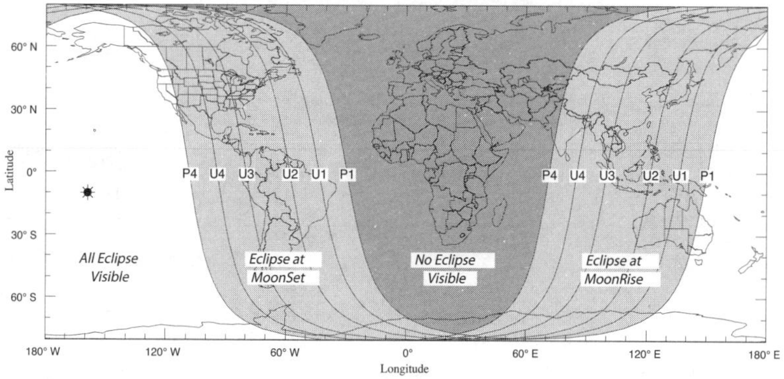

Eph. = Newcomb/ILE
Rule = CdT (Danjon)
ΔT = 65.0 s

F. Espenak, NASA's GSFC - 2006 Apr. 20
http://sunearth.gsfc.nasa.gov/eclipse/eclipse.html

See pp. 112–113 for an explanation of this figure.

FIGURE 4—PARTIAL SOLAR ECLIPSE OF 2007 SEPTEMBER 11

Geocentric Conjunction = 13:42:43.4 UT J.D. = 2454355.071336
Greatest Eclipse = 12:31:21.2 UT J.D. = 2454355.021773

Eclipse Magnitude = 0.7505 Gamma = -1.1256

Saros Series = 154 Member = 6 of 71

Sun at Greatest Eclipse
(Geocentric Coordinates)

R.A. = 11h17m20.7s
Dec. = +04°35'13.5"
S.D. = 00°15'53.2"
H.P. = 00°00'08.7"

Moon at Greatest Eclipse
(Geocentric Coordinates)

R.A. = 11h15m21.9s
Dec. = +03°40'57.2"
S.D. = 00°15'00.5"
H.P. = 00°55'05.0"

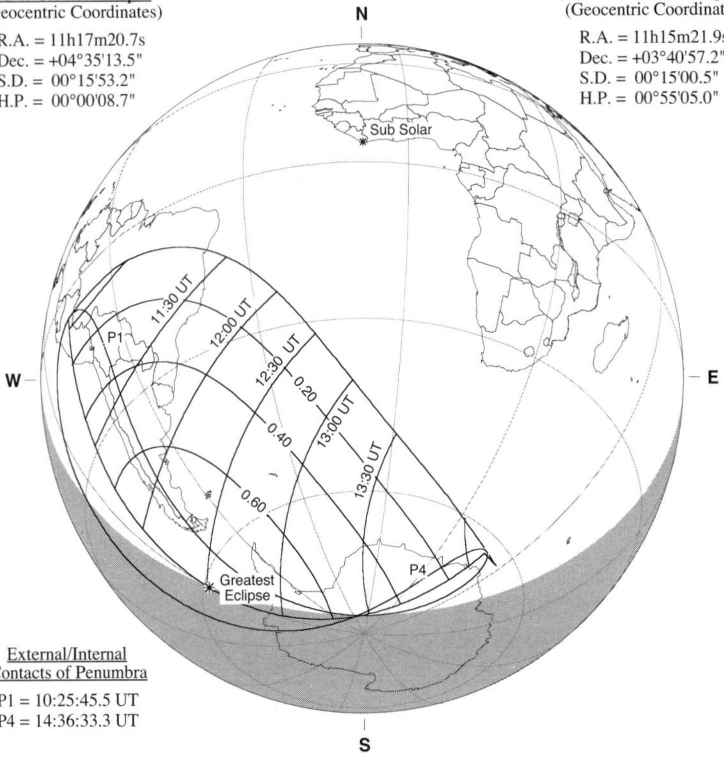

External/Internal
Contacts of Penumbra

P1 = 10:25:45.5 UT
P4 = 14:36:33.3 UT

Ephemeris & Constants

Eph. = Newcomb/ILE
ΔT = 65.1 s
k1 = 0.2724880
k2 = 0.2722810
Δb = 0.0" Δl = 0.0"

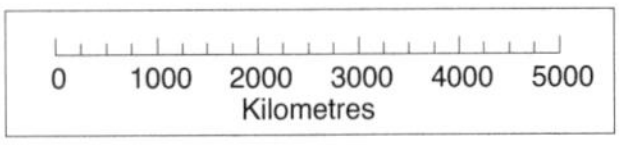

Geocentric Libration
(Optical + Physical)

l = 3.98°
b = 1.38°
c = 21.47°

Brown Lun. No. = 1048

F. Espenak, NASA's GSFC - 2006 Apr. 21

http://sunearth.gsfc.nasa.gov/eclipse/eclipse.html

See pp. 113–114 for an explanation of this figure.

VIEWING A SOLAR ECLIPSE—A WARNING

Solar eclipses are among the most widely publicized and observed celestial events. It is essential to be aware of the visual danger associated with a solar eclipse. The safety rule is simple but not widely appreciated: **Never look at the surface of the Sun, either directly with the unaided eyes or through binoculars or a telescope.** To do so one risks permanent partial blindness, and this can occur almost instantly in the case of telescopic viewing. Viewing our Sun is just as dangerous on any clear day, but at the time of an eclipse people have a reason to want to look at it—and often resort to dangerous methods.

A direct view of the Sun is safe only if a suitable filter is used in a proper manner. In the case of binoculars or a telescope, the filter must be one that attaches *securely* to the *front* end of the instrument, never one that attaches to the eyepiece end (the heat developed near the eyepiece can shatter such a filter).

Filters specifically designed for solar viewing include aluminized Mylar and glass filters plated with a slightly transparent, metallic film. Such filters may be purchased at telescope supply stores. Shade #14 (no other shade) rectangular welder's glass may be used; however, since these filters are of low optical quality, they are useful only for views not involving binoculars or a telescope. All of these are commercial items and cannot be replaced with ordinary household items. For example, layers of photographic colour film, coloured glass, stacked sunglasses, crossed polarizers, smoked glass, or photographic neutral-density filters must never be used. Although one may devise a combination that dims the *visible* sunlight to a comfortable level, the makeshift filter may be quite transparent in the infrared part of the solar spectrum, and this invisible radiation will damage the retina of the observer's eye. For the same reason, one must never rely on clouds or heavy atmospheric haze to dim the solar image when using a telescope. Two layers of fully exposed and developed, silver-based, black and white photographic film provides adequate protection, but many modern films, including all colour films, are based on dyes that do not provide protection in the infrared. Thus it is best to avoid using filters made of photographic film.

One of the simplest, safest, and least known ways to observe the partial phases of a solar eclipse is *pinhole mirror projection*. Take a small pocket mirror and, with masking tape, cover all but a small section of the mirror's surface. The shape and size of the small opening are not critical, but a square about 6 mm on a side works well. Prop the mirror up on a sunny windowsill and orient the mirror so the reflected sunlight shines on the ceiling or a wall of the room—but not directly into anyone's eyes! The spot of light on the viewing surface will be a *pinhole image* of the solar disk. The mirror has a great advantage over the usual "pinhole-in-a-box arrangement" in that the image can be aimed across a substantial distance to a convenient viewing screen. The greater the projection distance, the larger, but dimmer, the Sun's image. The size of the mirror aperture should be adjusted for the best compromise between image brightness and image sharpness. With this simple device the progress of a solar eclipse can be viewed in complete safety by a group of children in a darkened room.

A sharper and brighter image of the solar disk may be projected onto a white viewing screen placed 30 or 40 cm behind the eyepiece of binoculars or a small telescope (the telescope aperture should be stopped down to about 50 mm in order to limit the intensity of sunlight passing through the instrument, and the viewing screen should be shielded from direct sunlight). However, one must *not* look through the instrument when aiming it, and, especially if children are present, a physical barrier should be used to prevent anyone from attempting to look into the eyepiece. If the telescope has a finderscope, it should be either covered or removed.

THE MOON

MAP OF MOON

BY ROY BISHOP

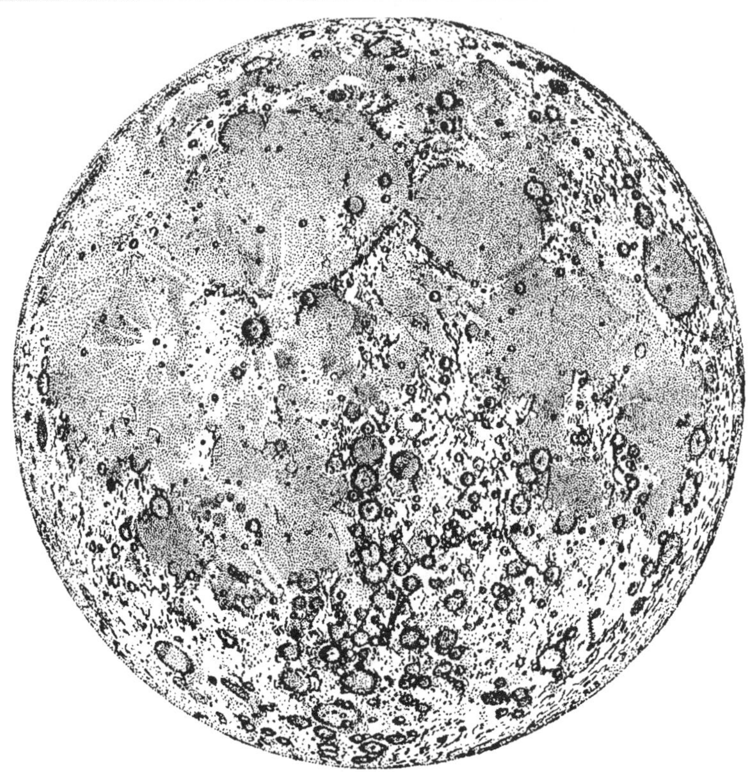

Maria	**Lunar Probes**
LS Lacus Somniorum (Lake of Dreams) (330°)	2 *Luna 2*, First to reach Moon (1959.9.13) (0°)
MC Mare Crisium (Sea of Crises) (300°)	7 *Ranger 7*, First close pictures (1964.7.31) (21°)
MFe Mare Fecunditatis (Sea of Fertility) (310°)	9 *Luna 9*, First soft landing (1966.2.3) (64°)
MFr Mare Frigoris (Sea of Cold) (0°)	11 *Apollo 11*, First men on Moon (1969.7.20) (337°)
MH Mare Humorum (Sea of Moisture) (40°)	12 *Apollo 12* (1969.11.19) (23°)
MI Mare Imbrium (Sea of Rains) (20°)	14 *Apollo 14* (1971.2.5) (17°)
MNe Mare Nectaris (Sea of Nectar) (325°)	15 *Apollo 15* (1971.7.30) (356°)
MNu Mare Nubium (Sea of Clouds) (15°)	16 *Apollo 16* (1972.4.21) (344°)
MS Mare Serenitatis (Sea of Serenity) (340°)	17 *Apollo 17* (1972.12.11) (329°)
MT Mare Tranquillitatis (Sea of Tranquillity) (330°)	
MV Mare Vaporum (Sea of Vapours) (355°)	
OP Oceanus Procellarum (Ocean of Storms) (50°)	
SA Sinus Aestuum (Seething Bay) (8°)	
SI Sinus Iridum (Bay of Rainbows) (32°)	
SM Sinus Medii (Central Bay) (0°)	
SR Sinus Roris (Bay of Dew) (60°)	

Angles in parentheses equal 360°– λ, where λ is the selenographic longitude of the centre of the feature. 0° marks the mean centre of the lunar disk and the angles increase toward the observer's east (i.e. westward on the Moon). These angles facilitate locating the feature on the accompanying map, and may be correlated with the Sun's selenographic colongitude (see THE SKY MONTH BY MONTH *(pp. 78–105)) to determine the optimum times for viewing the feature.*

MAP OF MOON (continued)

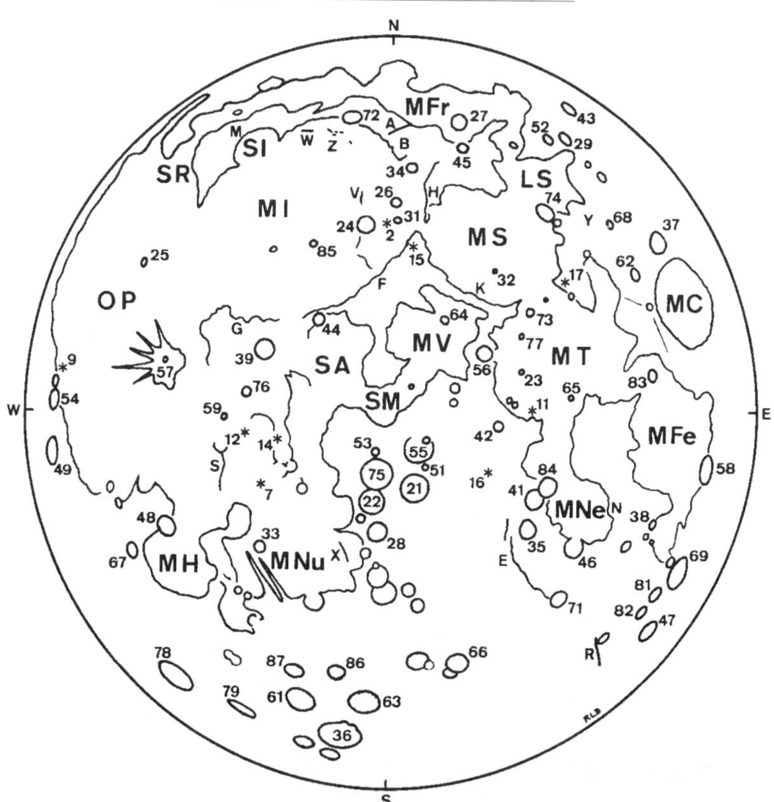

Craters

21 Albategnius (356°)
22 Alphonsus (3°)
23 Arago (338°)
24 Archimedes (4°)
25 Aristarchus (47°)
26 Aristillus (358°)
27 Aristoteles (342°)
28 Arzachel (2°)
29 Atlas (315°)
31 Autolycus (358°)
32 Bessel (342°)
33 Bullialdus (22°)
34 Cassini (355°)
35 Catharina (336°)
36 Clavius (15°)
37 Cleomedes (304°)
38 Cook (311°)
39 Copernicus (20°)
41 Cyrillus (336°)
42 Delambre (342°)
43 Endymion (305°)
44 Eratosthenes (11°)
45 Eudoxus (343°)
46 Fracastorius (326°)
47 Furnerius (299°)
48 Gassendi (40°)
49 Grimaldi (68°)
51 Halley (354°)
52 Hercules (321°)
53 Herschel (2°)
54 Hevelius (66°)
55 Hipparchus (354°)
56 Julius Caesar (345°)
57 Kepler (38°)
58 Langrenus (299°)
59 Lansberg (27°)
61 Longomontanus (21°)
62 Macrobius (314°)
63 Maginus (6°)
64 Manilius (351°)
65 Maskelyne (330°)
66 Maurolycus (345°)
67 Mersenius (49°)
68 Newcomb (316°)
69 Petavius (298°)
71 Piccolomini (327°)
72 Plato (10°)
73 Plinius (336°)
74 Posidonius (330°)
75 Ptolemaeus (2°)
76 Reinhold (23°)
77 Ross (338°)
78 Schickard (55°)
79 Schiller (40°)
81 Snellius (304°)
82 Stevinus (305°)
83 Taruntius (313°)
84 Theophilus (333°)
85 Timocharis (13°)
86 Tycho (11°)
87 Wilhelm (20°)

Mountains

A Alpine Valley (356°)
B Alps Mts. (359°)
E Altai Mts. (336°)
F Apennine Mts. (2°)
G Carpathian Mts. (24°)
H Caucasus Mts. (352°)
K Haemus Mts. (349°)
M Jura Mts. (34°)
N Pyrenees Mts. (319°)
R Rheita Valley (312°)
S Riphaeus Mts. (27°)
V Spitzbergen (5°)
W Straight Range (20°)
X Straight Wall (8°)
Y Taurus Mts. (319°)
Z Teneriffe Mts. (13°)

UNIVERSAL TIME OF NEW MOON DATES

2007			2008		
Jan. 19.2	May 16.8	Sep. 11.5	Jan. 8.5	May 5.5	Aug. 30.8
Feb. 17.7	Jun. 15.1	Oct. 11.2	Feb. 7.2	Jun. 3.8	Sep. 29.3
Mar. 19.1	Jul. 14.5	Nov. 10.0	Mar. 7.7	Jul. 3.1	Oct. 29.0
Apr. 17.5	Aug. 13.0	Dec. 9.7	Apr. 6.2	Aug. 1.4	Nov. 27.7
					Dec. 27.5

These dates will be useful for planning observing sessions, determining favourable dates for observing very thin lunar crescents, and setting Moon dials on clocks. The dates are indicated to lower precision in the calendar on the inside back cover.

TIMES OF MOONRISE AND MOONSET

By Rajiv Gupta

The table on pp. 130–135 gives the times of moonrise and moonset for locations ranging from 20°N to 60°N latitude. Dates of New Moon and Full Moon are given in **bold** and *italic* respectively. The table may be interpolated linearly for nontabular latitudes and can be extrapolated beyond the 20° and 60° limits a few degrees without significant loss of accuracy. "Rise" and "Set" correspond to the upper limb of the Moon appearing at the horizon for an observer at sea level. The times are local mean time (LMT) for the Greenwich meridian (i.e. UT at 0° longitude). Because of the relatively rapid eastward motion of the Moon, unlike the sunrise and sunset table, for observers not near 0° longitude the times cannot be read directly as LMT; the table must be interpolated according to the observer's longitude. Also, to convert from the observer's LMT to standard time, the observer's longitude correction relative to his or her standard meridian must be applied. After it is prepared for a given location, the chart at the right enables the sum of these two corrections to be determined in one step.

To prepare the **Moonrise/Moonset Correction Diagram,** first mark your longitude on the *West or East Longitude* scale. Draw a diagonal line from this mark to the 0,0 point. Next, the *Correction in minutes* axis (which is subdivided at two-minute intervals) must be labelled. As a guide, the first three divisions have been tentatively labelled 0, ±2, ±4 *(use + if you are west of the prime meridian in Greenwich, England, – if east);* but, to these numbers must be added your longitude correction relative to your standard meridian (see the third paragraph on p. 164). As an aid both for labelling and for reading the chart, the vertical lines at 10-min intervals are wider. **Examples:** For Toronto, which is 4.5° W of its standard meridian of 75°W, the longitude correction is +18 min, so an observer in Toronto would label the Correction axis 18, 20, 22, 24,...; an observer in Boston (longitude correction –16) would label the axis –16, –14, –12,...; an observer in Hong Kong (east longitude, longitude correction +24) would label the axis 24, 22, 20,...; an observer in Vienna (longitude correction –6) would label the axis –6, –8, –10,....

The chart is now ready for use on any day from your position. Interpolating for nontabular latitudes, from the table obtain today's time for the event (moonrise, or moonset) and tomorrow's time if you are west of Greenwich, yesterday's time if east, enter the difference on the *Tabular Delay* axis, and run horizontally across to meet the diagonal line. The correction, to the nearest minute, can then be read directly below off the Correction axis. This correction is applied to the tabular "today's time" and results in the standard time of the event for your position. **Example:** The latitude of Toronto is 44°N. Interpolating the 40°N and 45°N entries, the table gives for 44°N a moonset time of 20:53 on May 17 and 22:04 on May 18. The Correction corresponding to a 71-min Tabular Delay, when the chart is prepared for Toronto as described above, is +33 min; hence the time of moonrise is 20:53 + 33 min = 21:26 EST May 17 or 22:26 EDT May 17

Note: Due to a difference in height between the observer and the actual horizon, the observed time may differ by several minutes from the predicted time.

MOONRISE/MOONSET CORRECTION DIAGRAM

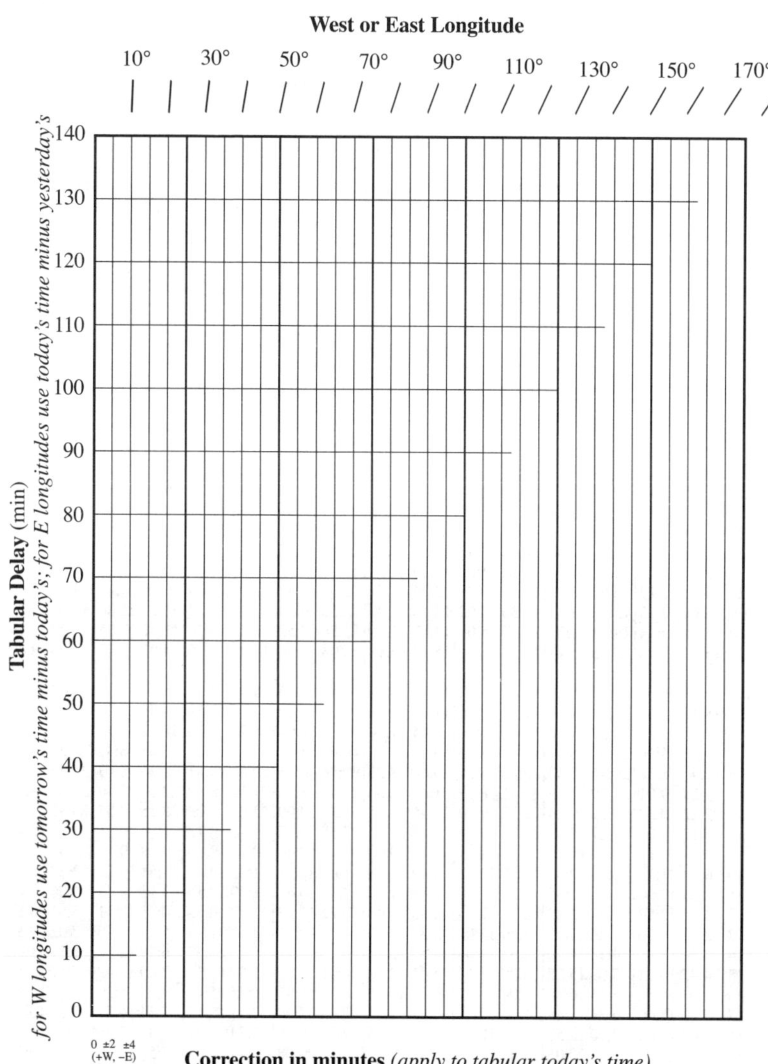

MOONRISE AND MOONSET, 2007 JANUARY, FEBRUARY
UNIVERSAL TIME AT GREENWICH MERIDIAN

Latitude:	+20°		+30°		+35°		+40°		+45°		+50°		+55°		+60°	
Event:	**RISE**	**SET**	**RISE**	**SET**	**RISE**	**SET**	**RISE**	**SET**	**RISE**	**SET**	**RISE**	**SET**	**RISE**	**SET**	**RISE**	**SET**
Jan. 1	15:32	4:30	15:04	4:57	14:48	5:13	14:29	5:31	14:06	5:53	13:37	6:22	12:58	7:01	11:52	8:06
2	16:31	5:34	16:03	6:02	15:46	6:19	15:26	6:38	15:02	7:02	14:32	7:33	13:49	8:16	12:32	9:33
3	17:32	6:33	17:05	7:00	16:50	7:17	16:31	7:36	16:09	7:59	15:40	8:28	15:00	9:08	13:53	10:16
4	18:33	7:26	18:10	7:51	17:56	8:05	17:40	8:22	17:20	8:42	16:56	9:07	16:24	9:41	15:35	10:31
5	19:31	8:12	19:12	8:33	19:01	8:45	18:48	8:59	18:33	9:15	18:15	9:35	17:50	10:00	17:16	10:36
6	20:25	8:52	20:12	9:08	20:04	9:17	19:54	9:28	19:44	9:40	19:31	9:55	19:14	10:13	18:51	10:38
7	21:17	9:28	21:08	9:39	21:03	9:45	20:58	9:52	20:51	10:00	20:43	10:10	20:33	10:22	20:20	10:38
8	22:06	10:01	22:02	10:06	22:00	10:10	21:58	10:13	21:56	10:18	21:53	10:23	21:49	10:29	21:44	10:37
9	22:53	10:31	22:55	10:32	22:56	10:32	22:58	10:33	22:59	10:33	23:01	10:34	23:03	10:35	23:06	10:36
10	23:41	11:02	23:48	10:57	23:52	10:55	23:57	10:52	—	10:49	—	10:45	—	10:40	—	10:34
11	—	11:33	—	11:23	—	11:18	—	11:12	0:02	11:05	0:09	10:57	0:17	10:46	0:28	10:33
12	0:30	12:06	0:42	11:51	0:49	11:43	0:57	11:34	1:07	11:23	1:18	11:10	1:33	10:54	1:52	10:32
13	1:21	12:42	1:38	12:23	1:48	12:12	2:00	12:00	2:13	11:45	2:30	11:27	2:51	11:04	3:21	10:32
14	2:15	13:23	2:37	13:00	2:49	12:46	3:04	12:31	3:22	12:12	3:44	11:49	4:13	11:19	4:56	10:34
15	3:12	14:11	3:37	13:44	3:52	13:28	4:10	13:10	4:31	12:48	4:58	12:20	5:36	11:42	6:36	10:41
16	4:10	15:04	4:39	14:36	4:55	14:19	5:15	13:59	5:38	13:35	6:09	13:05	6:52	12:21	8:10	11:03
17	5:09	16:04	5:38	15:36	5:55	15:19	6:15	15:00	6:38	14:36	7:09	14:06	7:53	13:22	9:11	12:05
18	6:06	17:08	6:33	16:42	6:48	16:27	7:06	16:10	7:28	15:48	7:56	15:22	8:34	14:45	9:34	13:46
19	6:58	18:12	7:21	17:51	7:34	17:39	7:49	17:25	8:08	17:08	8:30	16:47	8:59	16:19	9:41	15:39
20	7:46	19:16	8:03	19:01	8:13	18:52	8:25	18:42	8:38	18:30	8:55	18:15	9:16	17:56	9:44	17:30
21	8:28	20:17	8:40	20:08	8:47	20:03	8:54	19:57	9:03	19:50	9:14	19:42	9:27	19:31	9:44	19:17
22	9:08	21:17	9:14	21:15	9:17	21:13	9:20	21:12	9:25	21:10	9:29	21:07	9:36	21:04	9:43	21:00
23	9:46	22:16	9:45	22:20	9:45	22:22	9:45	22:25	9:44	22:28	9:44	22:31	9:43	22:36	9:42	22:41
24	10:24	23:16	10:17	23:26	10:13	23:32	10:09	23:38	10:04	23:46	9:58	23:56	9:51	—	9:42	—
25	11:03	—	10:51	—	10:43	—	10:35	—	10:25	—	10:14	—	10:00	0:07	9:41	0:23
26	11:46	0:16	11:27	0:32	11:17	0:42	11:05	0:53	10:50	1:05	10:33	1:21	10:11	1:41	9:42	2:08
27	12:33	1:19	12:09	1:40	11:56	1:53	11:40	2:07	11:22	2:25	10:59	2:47	10:29	3:15	9:45	3:57
28	13:25	2:22	12:58	2:48	12:42	3:03	12:24	3:21	12:02	3:42	11:34	4:09	10:56	4:46	9:55	5:46
29	14:21	3:25	13:53	3:53	13:36	4:09	13:16	4:29	12:52	4:53	12:22	5:23	11:39	6:06	10:22	7:22
30	15:21	4:24	14:53	4:52	14:37	5:09	14:17	5:28	13:54	5:52	13:24	6:22	12:42	7:05	11:29	8:19
31	16:21	5:18	15:56	5:44	15:41	6:00	15:24	6:18	15:03	6:39	14:37	7:06	14:02	7:42	13:06	8:40
Feb. 1	17:20	6:06	16:59	6:29	16:47	6:42	16:32	6:57	16:16	7:15	15:55	7:37	15:27	8:06	14:48	8:47
2	18:15	6:48	17:59	7:06	17:50	7:16	17:39	7:28	17:27	7:42	17:12	7:59	16:52	8:20	16:25	8:49
3	19:08	7:25	18:57	7:38	18:51	7:46	18:44	7:54	18:36	8:04	18:26	8:16	18:13	8:30	17:57	8:49
4	19:58	7:59	19:52	8:07	19:49	8:11	19:46	8:16	19:42	8:22	19:37	8:29	19:31	8:37	19:23	8:48
5	20:46	8:31	20:46	8:33	20:46	8:35	20:46	8:36	20:46	8:38	20:46	8:41	20:46	8:43	20:46	8:47
6	21:34	9:01	21:39	8:59	21:42	8:57	21:45	8:56	21:49	8:54	21:54	8:52	22:00	8:49	22:07	8:46
7	22:22	9:32	22:32	9:24	22:38	9:20	22:45	9:15	22:53	9:09	23:03	9:03	23:15	8:55	23:31	8:44
8	23:12	10:03	23:27	9:51	23:36	9:44	23:46	9:36	23:58	9:27	—	9:15	—	9:01	—	8:43
9	—	10:38	—	10:21	—	10:11	—	10:00	—	9:46	0:13	9:30	0:32	9:10	0:57	8:42
10	0:04	11:17	0:24	10:55	0:36	10:42	0:49	10:28	1:05	10:11	1:25	9:49	1:51	9:22	2:29	8:43
11	0:58	12:00	1:23	11:35	1:37	11:20	1:54	11:02	2:13	10:42	2:39	10:16	3:13	9:41	4:06	8:47
12	1:55	12:50	2:23	12:22	2:39	12:05	2:58	11:46	3:21	11:23	3:50	10:53	4:31	10:11	5:43	8:59
13	2:53	13:46	3:22	13:17	3:39	13:00	3:59	12:40	4:23	12:16	4:55	11:45	5:39	11:00	7:02	9:37
14	3:50	14:47	4:18	14:20	4:35	14:04	4:54	13:45	5:17	13:22	5:47	12:53	6:29	12:12	7:39	11:02
15	4:45	15:51	5:09	15:28	5:24	15:14	5:41	14:58	6:01	14:39	6:27	14:15	7:00	13:42	7:51	12:53
16	5:34	16:56	5:55	16:38	6:06	16:27	6:20	16:15	6:36	16:01	6:55	15:43	7:20	15:20	7:55	14:47
17	6:20	18:00	6:34	17:48	6:43	17:41	6:52	17:33	7:03	17:24	7:17	17:12	7:34	16:58	7:56	16:39
18	7:02	19:02	7:10	18:57	7:15	18:54	7:20	18:50	7:27	18:46	7:34	18:41	7:43	18:35	7:55	18:26
19	7:42	20:04	7:44	20:05	7:45	20:06	7:46	20:07	7:48	20:08	7:49	20:09	7:52	20:10	7:54	20:12
20	8:21	21:05	8:16	21:13	8:14	21:18	8:11	21:23	8:08	21:29	8:04	21:36	7:59	21:45	7:53	21:57
21	9:01	22:08	8:50	22:22	8:44	22:30	8:37	22:40	8:29	22:51	8:20	23:04	8:08	23:21	7:53	23:45
22	9:43	23:11	9:27	23:31	9:17	23:43	9:06	23:56	8:53	—	8:38	—	8:19	—	7:53	—
23	10:30	—	10:08	—	9:55	—	9:40	—	9:23	0:12	9:02	0:32	8:34	0:59	7:55	1:36
24	11:21	0:15	10:55	0:40	10:39	0:55	10:22	1:12	10:00	1:32	9:34	1:58	8:57	2:33	8:01	3:28
25	12:16	1:19	11:48	1:47	11:31	2:03	11:12	2:22	10:48	2:46	10:18	3:16	9:35	3:58	8:21	5:12
26	13:15	2:19	12:46	2:48	12:30	3:05	12:10	3:25	11:46	3:49	11:16	4:19	10:32	5:03	9:14	6:22
27	14:14	3:14	13:48	3:42	13:33	3:58	13:15	4:16	12:53	4:39	12:25	5:07	11:47	5:46	10:44	6:49
28	15:13	4:04	14:50	4:28	14:37	4:42	14:22	4:58	14:04	5:17	13:41	5:41	13:10	6:12	12:26	6:59

MOONRISE AND MOONSET, 2007 MARCH, APRIL

UNIVERSAL TIME AT GREENWICH MERIDIAN

Latitude:	+20°		+30°		+35°		+40°		+45°		+50°		+55°		+60°	
Event:	**RISE**	**SET**	**RISE**	**SET**	**RISE**	**SET**	**RISE**	**SET**	**RISE**	**SET**	**RISE**	**SET**	**RISE**	**SET**	**RISE**	**SET**
Mar. 1	16:08	4:47	15:51	5:06	15:40	5:18	15:28	5:31	15:14	5:46	14:57	6:05	14:35	6:29	14:04	7:01
2	17:01	5:25	16:49	5:40	16:41	5:48	16:33	5:58	16:23	6:09	16:11	6:23	15:56	6:40	15:36	7:02
3	17:52	5:59	17:45	6:09	17:40	6:15	17:35	6:21	17:30	6:28	17:23	6:37	17:15	6:47	17:04	7:01
4	18:41	6:31	18:39	6:36	18:37	6:38	18:36	6:41	18:34	6:45	18:33	6:49	18:30	6:54	18:27	7:00
5	19:28	7:02	19:32	7:01	19:33	7:01	19:36	7:01	19:38	7:00	19:41	7:00	19:45	6:59	19:49	6:58
6	20:16	7:32	20:25	7:27	20:30	7:24	20:35	7:20	20:42	7:16	20:49	7:11	20:59	7:05	21:12	6:57
7	21:06	8:04	21:19	7:53	21:27	7:47	21:36	7:40	21:46	7:32	21:59	7:23	22:15	7:11	22:37	6:55
8	21:56	8:37	22:15	8:22	22:25	8:13	22:38	8:02	22:52	7:51	23:10	7:36	23:34	7:18	—	6:54
9	22:49	9:14	23:12	8:54	23:26	8:42	23:41	8:29	—	8:13	—	7:54	—	7:29	0:06	6:54
10	23:45	9:55	—	9:30	—	9:16	—	9:00	0:00	8:41	0:23	8:16	0:54	7:44	1:40	6:56
11	—	10:41	0:11	10:14	0:26	9:58	0:45	9:39	1:07	9:17	1:34	8:48	2:13	8:09	3:17	7:03
12	0:41	11:33	1:09	11:04	1:26	10:47	1:46	10:27	2:10	10:03	2:41	9:32	3:25	8:48	4:46	7:27
13	1:37	12:30	2:06	12:02	2:23	11:46	2:42	11:26	3:06	11:02	3:37	10:32	4:21	9:48	5:40	8:29
14	2:31	13:32	2:58	13:06	3:13	12:51	3:32	12:34	3:54	12:12	4:21	11:45	4:59	11:09	5:59	10:09
15	3:22	14:35	3:44	14:14	3:58	14:01	4:13	13:47	4:31	13:30	4:54	13:09	5:23	12:41	6:06	12:00
16	4:08	15:38	4:26	15:23	4:36	15:14	4:48	15:04	5:01	14:52	5:18	14:37	5:39	14:18	6:07	13:52
17	4:51	16:41	5:03	16:32	5:10	16:27	5:18	16:21	5:26	16:14	5:37	16:06	5:50	15:55	6:07	15:41
18	5:32	17:43	5:38	17:41	5:41	17:40	5:44	17:38	5:48	17:37	5:53	17:34	5:59	17:32	6:07	17:28
19	6:12	18:46	6:11	18:51	6:11	18:53	6:10	18:56	6:09	19:00	6:08	19:04	6:07	19:09	6:06	19:16
20	6:53	19:50	6:45	20:01	6:41	20:08	6:36	20:15	6:30	20:24	6:24	20:35	6:15	20:48	6:05	21:06
21	7:36	20:55	7:22	21:13	7:14	21:23	7:05	21:35	6:54	21:49	6:41	22:06	6:25	22:29	6:05	22:59
22	8:22	22:02	8:02	22:25	7:51	22:39	7:38	22:55	7:22	23:14	7:03	23:37	6:39	—	6:06	—
23	9:13	23:09	8:49	23:36	8:34	23:52	8:17	—	7:57	—	7:33	—	7:00	0:09	6:11	0:56
24	10:09	—	9:41	—	9:25	—	9:06	0:10	8:43	0:33	8:13	1:01	7:33	1:42	6:24	2:49
25	11:08	0:12	10:40	0:41	10:23	0:58	10:03	1:17	9:39	1:41	9:08	2:12	8:24	2:56	7:05	4:16
26	12:08	1:10	11:41	1:38	11:25	1:54	11:07	2:14	10:44	2:37	10:15	3:06	9:35	3:47	8:27	4:56
27	13:08	2:02	12:44	2:27	12:30	2:41	12:14	2:58	11:54	3:19	11:30	3:44	10:57	4:18	10:07	5:09
28	14:04	2:47	13:45	3:08	13:34	3:20	13:21	3:34	13:05	3:50	12:46	4:11	12:22	4:37	11:47	5:13
29	14:57	3:26	14:43	3:42	14:35	3:52	14:26	4:02	14:14	4:15	14:01	4:30	13:44	4:49	13:20	5:14
30	15:48	4:01	15:39	4:13	15:34	4:19	15:28	4:26	15:21	4:35	15:13	4:45	15:02	4:58	14:48	5:14
31	16:37	4:34	16:33	4:40	16:31	4:43	16:29	4:47	16:26	4:52	16:22	4:57	16:18	5:04	16:12	5:13
Apr. 1	17:25	5:04	17:26	5:05	17:27	5:06	17:28	5:07	17:29	5:08	17:30	5:09	17:32	5:10	17:34	5:11
2	18:13	5:35	18:19	5:31	18:23	5:28	18:27	5:26	18:32	5:23	18:39	5:20	18:46	5:15	18:56	5:10
3	19:01	6:05	19:13	5:57	19:20	5:51	19:28	5:46	19:37	5:39	19:48	5:31	20:02	5:21	20:20	5:09
4	19:52	6:38	20:08	6:24	20:18	6:16	20:29	6:07	20:42	5:57	20:58	5:44	21:19	5:28	21:48	5:08
5	20:44	7:14	21:05	6:55	21:18	6:44	21:32	6:32	21:49	6:18	22:11	6:00	22:39	5:38	23:20	5:07
6	21:38	7:53	22:03	7:30	22:18	7:17	22:35	7:02	22:56	6:43	23:22	6:21	23:58	5:51	—	5:09
7	22:34	8:37	23:01	8:11	23:18	7:56	23:37	7:38	—	7:16	—	6:49	—	6:12	0:56	5:14
8	23:29	9:27	23:58	8:58	—	8:42	—	8:22	0:00	7:58	0:30	7:28	1:13	6:46	2:27	5:30
9	—	10:21	—	9:53	0:15	9:36	0:34	9:16	0:59	8:52	1:30	8:21	2:14	7:37	3:35	6:16
10	0:23	11:19	0:50	10:53	1:06	10:37	1:25	10:18	1:48	9:56	2:17	9:28	2:57	8:48	4:04	7:42
11	1:13	12:20	1:37	11:57	1:52	11:43	2:08	11:28	2:28	11:09	2:53	10:45	3:25	10:14	4:14	9:26
12	2:00	13:21	2:20	13:03	2:31	12:52	2:44	12:40	3:00	12:26	3:19	12:08	3:44	11:45	4:18	11:14
13	2:43	14:22	2:57	14:10	3:06	14:03	3:15	13:55	3:26	13:45	3:40	13:34	3:56	13:19	4:19	13:00
14	3:23	15:23	3:32	15:17	3:37	15:14	3:42	15:10	3:49	15:05	3:57	15:00	4:06	14:53	4:18	14:45
15	4:03	16:24	4:05	16:25	4:06	16:26	4:08	16:26	4:10	16:27	4:12	16:28	4:14	16:29	4:18	16:30
16	4:42	17:27	4:38	17:35	4:36	17:39	4:33	17:44	4:30	17:50	4:27	17:57	4:22	18:06	4:17	18:18
17	5:24	18:32	5:14	18:47	5:08	18:55	5:01	19:04	4:53	19:16	4:43	19:29	4:32	19:47	4:17	20:10
18	6:09	19:40	5:53	20:01	5:43	20:13	5:32	20:26	5:19	20:43	5:03	21:03	4:44	21:30	4:18	22:08
19	7:00	20:49	6:37	21:14	6:24	21:29	6:09	21:47	5:51	22:08	5:30	22:34	5:01	23:10	4:21	—
20	7:55	21:57	7:29	22:25	7:13	22:41	6:55	23:01	6:33	23:24	6:06	23:55	5:29	—	4:30	0:08
21	8:56	22:59	8:27	23:28	8:10	23:44	7:51	—	7:27	—	6:56	—	6:14	0:37	4:58	1:52
22	9:58	23:55	9:30	—	9:14	—	8:54	0:04	8:31	0:28	8:01	0:58	7:20	1:40	6:07	2:53
23	10:59	—	10:34	0:21	10:20	0:37	10:03	0:55	9:42	1:16	9:16	1:43	8:41	2:19	7:45	3:15
24	11:58	0:44	11:37	1:06	11:25	1:19	11:11	1:34	10:54	1:52	10:34	2:14	10:07	2:42	9:28	3:23
25	12:53	1:26	12:37	1:43	12:28	1:54	12:17	2:05	12:05	2:19	11:50	2:36	11:31	2:57	11:04	3:25
26	13:45	2:02	13:34	2:15	13:28	2:23	13:21	2:31	13:13	2:41	13:03	2:52	12:50	3:07	12:34	3:26
27	14:34	2:36	14:29	2:43	14:25	2:48	14:22	2:53	14:18	2:59	14:13	3:06	14:07	3:14	13:59	3:25
28	15:22	3:07	15:22	3:09	15:22	3:11	15:21	3:13	15:21	3:15	15:21	3:17	15:21	3:20	15:21	3:24
29	16:09	3:37	16:14	3:35	16:17	3:33	16:20	3:32	16:24	3:30	16:29	3:28	16:35	3:26	16:42	3:22
30	16:58	4:08	17:08	4:00	17:14	3:56	17:20	3:51	17:28	3:46	17:37	3:40	17:49	3:32	18:05	3:21

MOONRISE AND MOONSET, 2007 MAY, JUNE

UNIVERSAL TIME AT GREENWICH MERIDIAN

Latitude:	+20°		+30°		+35°		+40°		+45°		+50°		+55°		+60°	
Event:	RISE	SET	RISE	SET	RISE	SET	RISE	SET	RISE	SET	RISE	SET	RISE	SET	RISE	SET
May 1	17:47	4:40	18:02	4:27	18:11	4:20	18:21	4:13	18:33	4:03	18:48	3:52	19:06	3:38	19:31	3:20
2	18:39	5:14	18:59	4:57	19:11	4:48	19:24	4:36	19:40	4:23	19:59	4:07	20:25	3:47	21:02	3:20
3	19:33	5:53	19:57	5:31	20:11	5:19	20:27	5:04	20:47	4:48	21:12	4:27	21:45	4:00	22:36	3:22
4	20:29	6:35	20:55	6:10	21:11	5:56	21:30	5:39	21:53	5:18	22:21	4:53	23:01	4:18	—	3:26
5	21:24	7:24	21:52	6:56	22:09	6:40	22:29	6:21	22:53	5:58	23:24	5:28	—	4:48	0:10	3:39
6	22:18	8:16	22:46	7:48	23:02	7:31	23:21	7:12	23:45	6:48	—	6:17	0:07	5:33	1:26	4:14
7	23:09	9:13	23:34	8:46	23:49	8:30	—	8:11	—	7:48	0:14	7:19	0:56	6:38	2:06	5:28
8	23:56	10:12	—	9:48	—	9:34	0:06	9:17	0:27	8:57	0:53	8:32	1:28	7:58	2:21	7:06
9	—	11:11	0:17	10:52	0:30	10:40	0:44	10:27	1:01	10:11	1:22	9:52	1:49	9:26	2:27	8:50
10	0:39	12:11	0:55	11:56	1:05	11:48	1:15	11:39	1:28	11:27	1:43	11:14	2:03	10:56	2:29	10:33
11	1:19	13:09	1:30	13:01	1:36	12:56	1:43	12:51	1:51	12:44	2:01	12:37	2:13	12:27	2:29	12:14
12	1:57	14:08	2:02	14:06	2:05	14:05	2:08	14:03	2:12	14:02	2:16	14:00	2:22	13:58	2:29	13:55
13	2:35	15:08	2:34	15:13	2:33	15:15	2:33	15:18	2:32	15:21	2:31	15:25	2:30	15:30	2:28	15:37
14	3:15	16:11	3:07	16:21	3:03	16:28	2:58	16:35	2:53	16:44	2:46	16:54	2:38	17:07	2:28	17:24
15	3:57	17:16	3:43	17:33	3:36	17:44	3:27	17:55	3:16	18:09	3:04	18:26	2:49	18:48	2:28	19:18
16	4:44	18:25	4:25	18:48	4:13	19:01	4:00	19:17	3:45	19:35	3:27	19:59	3:03	20:30	2:31	21:17
17	5:38	19:34	5:13	20:01	4:59	20:17	4:42	20:35	4:22	20:58	3:58	21:26	3:25	22:06	2:37	23:12
18	6:37	20:41	6:09	21:09	5:53	21:26	5:34	21:46	5:11	22:09	4:42	22:40	4:02	23:22	2:55	—
19	7:40	21:42	7:12	22:09	6:55	22:25	6:36	22:44	6:12	23:06	5:42	23:34	4:59	—	3:44	0:38
20	8:44	22:35	8:18	22:59	8:03	23:13	7:45	23:29	7:23	23:48	6:55	—	6:17	0:13	5:15	1:16
21	9:46	23:21	9:24	23:40	9:11	23:52	8:56	—	8:37	—	8:15	0:12	7:45	0:43	7:00	1:29
22	10:44	—	10:27	—	10:16	—	10:05	0:05	9:51	0:20	9:34	0:38	9:12	1:02	8:41	1:34
23	11:38	0:01	11:26	0:15	11:19	0:23	11:11	0:33	11:01	0:44	10:49	0:57	10:35	1:14	10:15	1:36
24	12:29	0:36	12:22	0:45	12:18	0:50	12:13	0:56	12:08	1:04	12:01	1:12	11:53	1:22	11:43	1:36
25	13:18	1:08	13:16	1:12	13:15	1:15	13:14	1:17	13:12	1:21	13:10	1:24	13:08	1:29	13:06	1:35
26	14:05	1:38	14:09	1:38	14:11	1:37	14:13	1:37	14:15	1:36	14:18	1:36	14:22	1:35	14:27	1:34
27	14:53	2:09	15:02	2:03	15:07	2:00	15:12	1:56	15:19	1:52	15:26	1:47	15:36	1:41	15:49	1:33
28	15:42	2:40	15:56	2:30	16:04	2:24	16:13	2:17	16:23	2:09	16:36	1:59	16:52	1:47	17:14	1:32
29	16:34	3:14	16:52	2:59	17:03	2:50	17:15	2:40	17:29	2:28	17:47	2:14	18:10	1:56	18:43	1:32
30	17:27	3:51	17:50	3:31	18:03	3:20	18:18	3:07	18:37	2:51	19:00	2:32	19:31	2:07	20:16	1:33
31	18:22	4:33	18:48	4:09	19:04	3:55	19:22	3:39	19:43	3:20	20:11	2:56	20:49	2:24	21:51	1:37
Jun. *1*	19:19	5:20	19:47	4:53	20:03	4:37	20:23	4:19	20:46	3:56	21:16	3:28	21:59	2:50	23:15	1:47
2	20:14	6:12	20:42	5:44	20:58	5:27	21:18	5:07	21:41	4:44	22:11	4:13	22:53	3:31	—	2:14
3	21:06	7:08	21:32	6:41	21:47	6:24	22:05	6:05	22:27	5:42	22:53	5:12	23:30	4:31	0:07	3:17
4	21:54	8:07	22:17	7:42	22:30	7:27	22:45	7:10	23:03	6:49	23:25	6:23	23:54	5:47	0:28	4:51
5	22:38	9:06	22:56	8:46	23:06	8:33	23:18	8:19	23:32	8:02	23:48	7:41	—	7:14	0:35	6:34
6	23:18	10:05	23:31	9:49	23:38	9:40	23:46	9:30	23:55	9:17	—	9:02	0:10	8:43	0:38	8:16
7	23:56	11:03	—	10:53	—	10:47	—	10:40	—	10:33	0:07	10:23	0:21	10:11	0:39	9:56
8	—	12:00	0:03	11:56	0:07	11:54	0:11	11:51	0:16	11:48	0:22	11:44	0:30	11:40	0:39	11:34
9	0:33	12:58	0:34	13:00	0:34	13:01	0:35	13:02	0:36	13:04	0:36	13:06	0:37	13:09	0:39	13:12
10	1:10	13:57	1:05	14:05	1:02	14:10	0:59	14:16	0:55	14:22	0:51	14:30	0:45	14:40	0:38	14:53
11	1:50	14:59	1:39	15:14	1:33	15:22	1:25	15:32	1:17	15:44	1:07	15:58	0:55	16:15	0:39	16:40
12	2:34	16:04	2:17	16:25	2:07	16:37	1:56	16:51	1:43	17:07	1:27	17:28	1:07	17:55	0:40	18:33
13	3:23	17:12	3:01	17:37	2:48	17:52	2:33	18:10	2:15	18:30	1:53	18:57	1:25	19:33	0:44	20:29
14	4:19	18:20	3:53	18:48	3:37	19:05	3:19	19:24	2:57	19:47	2:30	20:17	1:53	20:59	0:56	22:12
15	5:20	19:24	4:52	19:52	4:36	20:09	4:16	20:28	3:53	20:51	3:22	21:21	2:40	22:02	1:27	23:12
16	6:25	20:22	5:58	20:47	5:42	21:02	5:23	21:20	5:00	21:40	4:31	22:06	3:50	22:41	2:41	23:34
17	7:29	21:12	7:05	21:33	6:51	21:46	6:34	22:00	6:14	22:17	5:49	22:38	5:16	23:04	4:24	23:42
18	8:30	21:55	8:11	22:12	7:59	22:21	7:46	22:32	7:30	22:45	7:11	23:00	6:46	23:19	6:10	23:45
19	9:27	22:33	9:13	22:44	9:05	22:51	8:55	22:58	8:44	23:06	8:30	23:17	8:13	23:29	7:49	23:46
20	10:21	23:06	10:12	23:13	10:06	23:16	10:00	23:20	9:53	23:25	9:45	23:30	9:35	23:37	9:21	23:45
21	11:11	23:38	11:07	23:39	11:05	23:40	11:03	23:40	11:00	23:41	10:56	23:42	10:52	23:43	10:47	23:45
22	11:59	—	12:01	—	12:02	—	12:03	—	12:04	23:57	12:05	23:54	12:07	23:49	12:09	23:44
23	12:47	0:09	12:54	0:05	12:58	0:03	13:02	0:00	13:07	—	13:14	—	13:21	23:56	13:31	23:43
24	13:36	0:40	13:48	0:31	13:55	0:26	14:02	0:20	14:12	0:13	14:23	0:05	14:37	—	14:55	23:42
25	14:26	1:13	14:43	0:59	14:53	0:51	15:04	0:42	15:17	0:32	15:33	0:19	15:54	0:03	16:22	23:43
26	15:19	1:49	15:40	1:30	15:53	1:20	16:07	1:07	16:24	0:53	16:45	0:36	17:13	0:13	17:54	23:45
27	16:14	2:29	16:39	2:06	16:54	1:53	17:11	1:38	17:31	1:19	17:57	0:57	18:33	0:28	19:29	23:53
28	17:10	3:14	17:38	2:48	17:54	2:32	18:13	2:15	18:36	1:53	19:06	1:26	19:47	0:50	21:00	—
29	18:06	4:04	18:34	3:36	18:51	3:20	19:11	3:00	19:34	2:37	20:05	2:07	20:48	1:25	22:04	0:12
30	19:00	5:00	19:27	4:32	19:43	4:15	20:02	3:56	20:24	3:32	20:52	3:02	21:31	2:19	22:34	1:03

MOONRISE AND MOONSET, 2007 JULY, AUGUST

UNIVERSAL TIME AT GREENWICH MERIDIAN

Latitude:	+20°		+30°		+35°		+40°		+45°		+50°		+55°		+60°	
Event:	**RISE**	**SET**	**RISE**	**SET**	**RISE**	**SET**	**RISE**	**SET**	**RISE**	**SET**	**RISE**	**SET**	**RISE**	**SET**	**RISE**	**SET**
Jul. 1	19:51	5:59	20:14	5:33	20:28	5:18	20:44	5:00	21:03	4:38	21:27	4:10	21:58	3:32	22:45	2:30
2	20:36	6:59	20:56	6:37	21:07	6:24	21:20	6:09	21:35	5:51	21:53	5:28	22:16	4:58	22:49	4:13
3	21:18	7:59	21:32	7:42	21:40	7:32	21:49	7:20	22:00	7:07	22:13	6:50	22:29	6:28	22:50	5:58
4	21:57	8:58	22:05	8:47	22:10	8:40	22:15	8:32	22:22	8:23	22:29	8:12	22:38	7:58	22:50	7:40
5	22:34	9:56	22:36	9:50	22:38	9:47	22:39	9:43	22:41	9:39	22:43	9:33	22:46	9:27	22:50	9:18
6	23:11	10:53	23:07	10:53	23:05	10:53	23:03	10:54	23:00	10:54	22:57	10:55	22:54	10:55	22:49	10:56
7	23:49	11:51	23:39	11:57	23:34	12:01	23:28	12:05	23:21	12:10	23:13	12:17	23:02	12:24	22:49	12:34
8	—	12:50	—	13:03	—	13:10	23:56	13:19	23:44	13:29	23:30	13:41	23:13	13:56	22:50	14:17
9	0:30	13:53	0:15	14:11	0:06	14:22	—	14:35	—	14:50	23:53	15:08	23:28	15:32	22:52	16:05
10	1:16	14:58	0:55	15:22	0:43	15:35	0:29	15:52	0:13	16:11	—	16:35	23:51	17:08	23:00	17:58
11	2:08	16:04	1:42	16:31	1:28	16:47	1:11	17:06	0:50	17:29	0:25	17:58	—	18:38	23:20	19:46
12	3:05	17:09	2:38	17:37	2:21	17:54	2:02	18:13	1:39	18:37	1:10	19:07	0:29	19:50	—	21:04
13	4:08	18:09	3:40	18:35	3:23	18:51	3:04	19:10	2:40	19:32	2:10	19:59	1:28	20:37	0:14	21:38
14	5:12	19:02	4:46	19:25	4:31	19:39	4:13	19:54	3:52	20:13	3:25	20:36	2:48	21:06	1:48	21:50
15	6:15	19:48	5:53	20:06	5:40	20:17	5:25	20:30	5:08	20:44	4:46	21:02	4:17	21:24	3:34	21:55
16	7:14	20:28	6:57	20:41	6:47	20:49	6:36	20:58	6:23	21:08	6:07	21:21	5:46	21:36	5:18	21:56
17	8:09	21:04	7:58	21:12	7:52	21:17	7:44	21:22	7:35	21:28	7:25	21:36	7:11	21:45	6:54	21:56
18	9:01	21:36	8:56	21:39	8:52	21:41	8:48	21:43	8:44	21:45	8:39	21:48	8:32	21:51	8:23	21:56
19	9:51	22:08	9:51	22:06	9:50	22:04	9:50	22:03	9:50	22:02	9:49	22:00	9:49	21:57	9:48	21:55
20	10:40	22:39	10:45	22:32	10:47	22:28	10:51	22:23	10:54	22:18	10:59	22:11	11:04	22:04	11:11	21:54
21	11:29	23:11	11:38	22:59	11:44	22:52	11:51	22:44	11:58	22:35	12:08	22:24	12:19	22:11	12:35	21:53
22	12:18	23:46	12:33	23:29	12:42	23:19	12:52	23:08	13:03	22:55	13:18	22:39	13:36	22:19	14:00	21:53
23	13:10	—	13:29	—	13:41	23:50	13:54	23:36	14:10	23:19	14:29	22:59	14:54	22:32	15:30	21:54
24	14:03	0:24	14:27	0:02	14:41	—	14:57	—	15:17	23:50	15:41	23:24	16:14	22:50	17:04	21:59
25	14:59	1:06	15:26	0:41	15:42	0:27	16:00	0:10	16:22	—	16:51	—	17:31	23:19	18:38	22:11
26	15:55	1:54	16:23	1:27	16:40	1:11	17:00	0:52	17:24	0:29	17:54	0:00	18:38	—	19:56	22:47
27	16:50	2:48	17:18	2:20	17:35	2:03	17:54	1:43	18:17	1:19	18:46	0:49	19:28	0:05	20:38	—
28	17:43	3:46	18:08	3:19	18:23	3:03	18:40	2:44	19:01	2:21	19:26	1:52	20:01	1:12	20:54	0:02
29	18:31	4:47	18:52	4:23	19:04	4:09	19:19	3:53	19:35	3:33	19:56	3:08	20:22	2:34	21:00	1:43
30	19:15	5:48	19:31	5:29	19:40	5:18	19:51	5:05	20:03	4:49	20:18	4:30	20:37	4:05	21:01	3:30
31	19:56	6:49	20:06	6:35	20:12	6:27	20:18	6:18	20:26	6:08	20:35	5:54	20:47	5:38	21:02	5:15
Aug. 1	20:34	7:48	20:38	7:41	20:41	7:36	20:43	7:31	20:47	7:25	20:51	7:18	20:55	7:09	21:01	6:57
2	21:11	8:47	21:09	8:45	21:09	8:44	21:07	8:44	21:06	8:42	21:05	8:41	21:03	8:39	21:01	8:37
3	21:49	9:45	21:41	9:50	21:37	9:53	21:32	9:56	21:26	10:00	21:19	10:04	21:11	10:10	21:00	10:17
4	22:29	10:45	22:16	10:56	22:08	11:02	21:59	11:10	21:49	11:18	21:36	11:29	21:21	11:42	21:01	11:59
5	23:13	11:46	22:54	12:03	22:43	12:13	22:30	12:25	22:15	12:38	21:57	12:55	21:34	13:16	21:02	13:46
6	—	12:50	23:39	13:13	23:24	13:26	23:08	13:41	22:49	13:59	22:25	14:22	21:54	14:52	21:07	15:37
7	0:03	13:55	—	14:22	—	14:37	23:55	14:55	23:33	15:17	23:04	15:45	22:25	16:24	21:21	17:27
8	0:57	14:59	0:30	15:28	0:14	15:44	—	16:04	—	16:28	23:58	16:58	23:15	17:41	21:59	18:57
9	1:57	16:00	1:29	16:27	1:12	16:44	0:52	17:03	0:29	17:26	—	17:55	—	18:35	23:20	19:43
10	3:00	16:54	2:33	17:19	2:17	17:34	1:58	17:50	1:36	18:11	1:07	18:36	0:27	19:09	—	20:00
11	4:02	17:42	3:38	18:03	3:25	18:15	3:08	18:28	2:49	18:45	2:25	19:05	1:53	19:30	1:03	20:06
12	5:02	18:24	4:43	18:39	4:32	18:49	4:19	18:59	4:04	19:11	3:46	19:25	3:22	19:44	2:48	20:08
13	5:58	19:01	5:45	19:11	5:37	19:17	5:28	19:24	5:17	19:32	5:05	19:41	4:48	19:53	4:26	20:08
14	6:52	19:35	6:44	19:40	6:39	19:43	6:34	19:46	6:28	19:50	6:20	19:55	6:11	20:00	5:58	20:07
15	7:43	20:07	7:40	20:07	7:38	20:07	7:37	20:07	7:35	20:07	7:32	20:07	7:29	20:07	7:25	20:06
16	8:32	20:38	8:35	20:33	8:36	20:30	8:38	20:27	8:40	20:23	8:42	20:18	8:46	20:13	8:50	20:05
17	9:21	21:10	9:29	21:00	9:33	20:54	9:38	20:47	9:45	20:40	9:52	20:30	10:01	20:19	10:13	20:04
18	10:10	21:43	10:23	21:28	10:31	21:20	10:39	21:10	10:49	20:58	11:02	20:44	11:17	20:27	11:38	20:04
19	11:01	22:19	11:19	22:00	11:29	21:49	11:41	21:36	11:55	21:20	12:13	21:02	12:35	20:38	13:06	20:04
20	11:53	23:00	12:15	22:36	12:29	22:22	12:44	22:06	13:02	21:48	13:24	21:24	13:54	20:53	14:39	20:07
21	12:48	23:45	13:13	23:18	13:29	23:03	13:46	22:44	14:08	22:22	14:35	21:55	15:12	21:16	16:13	20:15
22	13:43	—	14:11	—	14:28	23:51	14:47	23:31	15:10	23:07	15:41	22:37	16:23	21:54	17:40	20:37
23	14:38	0:36	15:06	0:07	15:23	—	15:43	—	16:07	—	16:37	23:33	17:20	22:50	18:38	21:33
24	15:31	1:31	15:58	1:03	16:14	0:47	16:32	0:27	16:54	0:04	17:22	—	18:00	—	19:02	23:06
25	16:21	2:31	16:44	2:05	16:58	1:50	17:14	1:32	17:32	1:11	17:55	0:44	18:26	0:06	19:10	—
26	17:07	3:32	17:26	3:10	17:36	2:58	17:49	2:43	18:03	2:25	18:21	2:03	18:43	1:34	19:13	0:52
27	17:50	4:33	18:03	4:17	18:10	4:08	18:18	3:57	18:28	3:44	18:40	3:28	18:55	3:07	19:14	2:39
28	18:30	5:34	18:37	5:24	18:41	5:18	18:45	5:11	18:50	5:03	18:56	4:53	19:04	4:41	19:14	4:25
29	19:08	6:34	19:09	6:30	19:09	6:28	19:10	6:25	19:10	6:22	19:11	6:18	19:12	6:14	19:13	6:08
30	19:47	7:34	19:41	7:37	19:38	7:38	19:35	7:40	19:31	7:42	19:26	7:44	19:20	7:47	19:13	7:50
31	20:27	8:35	20:16	8:44	20:09	8:49	20:02	8:55	19:53	9:02	19:42	9:11	19:29	9:21	19:13	9:35

MOONRISE AND MOONSET, 2007 SEPTEMBER, OCTOBER

UNIVERSAL TIME AT GREENWICH MERIDIAN

Latitude:	+20°		+30°		+35°		+40°		+45°		+50°		+55°		+60°	
Event:	RISE	SET	RISE	SET	RISE	SET	RISE	SET	RISE	SET	RISE	SET	RISE	SET	RISE	SET
Sep. 1	21:11	9:38	20:54	9:53	20:43	10:02	20:32	10:12	20:18	10:24	20:02	10:39	19:41	10:57	19:14	11:23
2	21:59	10:43	21:37	11:03	21:23	11:16	21:08	11:30	20:50	11:47	20:28	12:08	19:59	12:35	19:17	13:15
3	22:53	11:48	22:26	12:14	22:11	12:29	21:53	12:46	21:31	13:07	21:03	13:34	20:26	14:10	19:27	15:08
4	23:51	12:53	23:23	13:21	23:06	13:38	22:47	13:57	22:23	14:21	21:53	14:51	21:10	15:33	19:55	16:47
5	—	13:54	—	14:23	—	14:39	23:49	14:59	23:26	15:22	22:57	15:52	22:15	16:34	21:03	17:47
6	0:53	14:50	0:25	15:16	0:09	15:31	—	15:49	—	16:10	—	16:37	23:36	17:13	22:41	18:09
7	1:54	15:39	1:29	16:01	1:15	16:14	0:58	16:29	0:37	16:47	0:11	17:09	—	17:37	—	18:17
8	2:54	16:22	2:34	16:40	2:21	16:50	2:08	17:01	1:51	17:15	1:30	17:31	1:04	17:52	0:25	18:20
9	3:51	17:00	3:35	17:13	3:26	17:20	3:16	17:28	3:04	17:37	2:49	17:48	2:30	18:02	2:04	18:21
10	4:45	17:35	4:35	17:42	4:29	17:46	4:22	17:51	4:14	17:56	4:05	18:02	3:53	18:10	3:37	18:20
11	5:36	18:07	5:31	18:09	5:28	18:10	5:25	18:11	5:22	18:13	5:17	18:14	5:12	18:17	5:05	18:19
12	6:25	18:38	6:26	18:35	6:26	18:33	6:27	18:31	6:27	18:29	6:28	18:26	6:29	18:23	6:30	18:18
13	7:14	19:10	7:20	19:01	7:24	18:57	7:27	18:51	7:32	18:45	7:37	18:38	7:44	18:29	7:53	18:17
14	8:03	19:42	8:14	19:29	8:21	19:22	8:28	19:13	8:37	19:03	8:47	18:51	9:00	18:36	9:18	18:16
15	8:54	20:18	9:10	20:00	9:19	19:49	9:30	19:38	9:42	19:24	9:58	19:07	10:17	18:46	10:44	18:17
16	9:45	20:56	10:06	20:34	10:18	20:21	10:32	20:06	10:48	19:49	11:09	19:27	11:36	18:59	12:15	18:18
17	10:38	21:39	11:03	21:13	11:17	20:58	11:34	20:41	11:54	20:20	12:20	19:54	12:54	19:18	13:48	18:24
18	11:33	22:27	12:00	21:59	12:16	21:42	12:35	21:23	12:58	21:00	13:27	20:30	14:08	19:49	15:18	18:38
19	12:27	23:19	12:55	22:51	13:12	22:34	13:32	22:14	13:56	21:50	14:27	21:20	15:10	20:36	16:29	19:17
20	13:20	—	13:48	23:49	14:04	23:33	14:23	23:14	14:46	22:52	15:15	22:23	15:56	21:43	17:05	20:34
21	14:10	0:16	14:35	—	14:50	—	15:07	—	15:27	—	15:53	23:37	16:27	23:04	17:19	22:14
22	14:57	1:15	15:18	0:51	15:30	0:37	15:44	0:21	16:01	0:01	16:21	—	16:47	—	17:24	23:59
23	15:41	2:15	15:56	1:56	16:05	1:45	16:16	1:32	16:28	1:17	16:43	0:58	17:01	0:33	17:25	—
24	16:21	3:16	16:31	3:02	16:37	2:54	16:44	2:45	16:51	2:35	17:00	2:22	17:11	2:06	17:26	1:44
25	17:01	4:16	17:05	4:09	17:07	4:04	17:09	4:00	17:12	3:54	17:16	3:47	17:20	3:39	17:25	3:28
26	17:40	5:16	17:38	5:16	17:36	5:15	17:35	5:15	17:33	5:14	17:31	5:13	17:28	5:12	17:25	5:11
27	18:21	6:18	18:12	6:24	18:07	6:27	18:01	6:31	17:54	6:36	17:47	6:41	17:37	6:48	17:25	6:56
28	19:04	7:22	18:49	7:34	18:40	7:41	18:31	7:50	18:19	7:59	18:05	8:11	17:48	8:26	17:26	8:46
29	19:52	8:28	19:31	8:47	19:19	8:57	19:06	9:10	18:49	9:25	18:30	9:43	18:04	10:07	17:28	10:40
30	20:46	9:36	20:20	10:00	20:06	10:14	19:48	10:30	19:28	10:50	19:02	11:14	18:28	11:47	17:36	12:38
Oct. 1	21:44	10:43	21:16	11:11	21:00	11:27	20:41	11:46	20:17	12:08	19:48	12:38	19:07	13:18	17:57	14:27
2	22:46	11:48	22:18	12:16	22:01	12:33	21:42	12:52	21:18	13:16	20:48	13:46	20:06	14:29	18:52	15:43
3	23:48	12:46	23:23	13:13	23:07	13:29	22:50	13:47	22:28	14:09	22:01	14:37	21:24	15:15	20:24	16:16
4	—	13:37	—	14:01	—	14:15	23:59	14:30	23:42	14:49	23:20	15:12	22:50	15:43	22:07	16:27
5	0:49	14:22	0:27	14:41	0:14	14:52	—	15:05	—	15:19	—	15:37	—	16:00	23:47	16:31
6	1:46	15:01	1:29	15:15	1:19	15:23	1:08	15:32	0:55	15:43	0:38	15:56	0:17	16:12	—	16:33
7	2:40	15:36	2:29	15:45	2:22	15:50	2:14	15:56	2:05	16:03	1:54	16:10	1:40	16:20	1:21	16:33
8	3:32	16:09	3:25	16:12	3:22	16:15	3:17	16:17	3:12	16:20	3:06	16:23	2:59	16:27	2:49	16:32
9	4:21	16:40	4:20	16:39	4:19	16:38	4:19	16:37	4:18	16:36	4:17	16:35	4:15	16:33	4:14	16:31
10	5:10	17:11	5:14	17:05	5:16	17:01	5:19	16:57	5:22	16:52	5:26	16:46	5:31	16:39	5:37	16:30
11	5:59	17:43	6:08	17:32	6:13	17:25	6:19	17:18	6:26	17:09	6:35	16:59	6:46	16:46	7:00	16:30
12	6:48	18:18	7:03	18:01	7:11	17:52	7:20	17:41	7:31	17:29	7:45	17:14	8:02	16:55	8:26	16:30
13	7:39	18:55	7:58	18:34	8:09	18:22	8:22	18:09	8:37	17:52	8:56	17:33	9:20	17:07	9:54	16:31
14	8:32	19:36	8:55	19:12	9:09	18:58	9:24	18:41	9:43	18:21	10:07	17:57	10:39	17:24	11:26	16:35
15	9:26	20:22	9:52	19:55	10:08	19:39	10:26	19:20	10:47	18:58	11:15	18:30	11:54	17:51	12:57	16:46
16	10:20	21:12	10:48	20:44	11:04	20:27	11:24	20:08	11:47	19:44	12:17	19:14	13:00	18:31	14:16	17:15
17	11:12	22:06	11:40	21:39	11:57	21:22	12:16	21:03	12:39	20:40	13:09	20:11	13:51	19:29	15:04	18:17
18	12:02	23:03	12:29	22:38	12:44	22:23	13:02	22:06	13:23	21:45	13:50	21:19	14:26	20:43	15:24	19:47
19	12:49	—	13:12	23:40	13:25	23:27	13:40	23:13	13:58	22:56	14:21	22:35	14:50	22:07	15:32	21:27
20	13:33	0:01	13:51	—	14:01	—	14:13	—	14:27	—	14:44	23:55	15:06	23:35	15:35	23:08
21	14:13	0:59	14:26	0:43	14:33	0:34	14:42	0:23	14:51	0:10	15:03	—	15:17	—	15:36	—
22	14:52	1:58	14:59	1:47	15:03	1:41	15:08	1:35	15:13	1:27	15:19	1:17	15:27	1:05	15:36	0:49
23	15:31	2:56	15:31	2:52	15:32	2:50	15:33	2:47	15:33	2:44	15:34	2:40	15:35	2:35	15:36	2:29
24	16:10	3:57	16:05	3:59	16:02	4:00	15:58	4:02	15:54	4:04	15:49	4:06	15:44	4:08	15:36	4:12
25	16:52	4:59	16:41	5:08	16:34	5:13	16:26	5:19	16:17	5:26	16:07	5:34	15:54	5:45	15:37	5:58
26	17:39	6:05	17:21	6:20	17:11	6:29	16:59	6:40	16:45	6:52	16:29	7:07	16:08	7:25	15:39	7:51
27	18:31	7:14	18:08	7:35	17:55	7:48	17:39	8:02	17:21	8:19	16:58	8:41	16:28	9:09	15:45	9:50
28	19:30	8:24	19:03	8:50	18:47	9:05	18:29	9:23	18:07	9:44	17:39	10:12	17:01	10:49	16:00	11:49
29	20:33	9:33	20:05	10:01	19:48	10:17	19:29	10:37	19:06	11:00	18:35	11:30	17:53	12:12	16:40	13:25
30	21:38	10:36	21:11	11:03	20:55	11:20	20:37	11:38	20:15	12:01	19:47	12:30	19:08	13:10	18:03	14:15
31	22:41	11:32	22:18	11:56	22:04	12:11	21:49	12:27	21:30	12:47	21:06	13:12	20:34	13:45	19:47	14:34

MOONRISE AND MOONSET, 2007 NOVEMBER, DECEMBER

UNIVERSAL TIME AT GREENWICH MERIDIAN

Latitude:	+20°		+30°		+35°		+40°		+45°		+50°		+55°		+60°	
Event:	RISE	SET	RISE	SET	RISE	SET	RISE	SET	RISE	SET	RISE	SET	RISE	SET	RISE	SET
Nov. 1	23:41	12:20	23:22	12:40	23:11	12:52	22:59	13:05	22:44	13:21	22:26	13:41	22:03	14:06	21:30	14:41
2	—	13:01	—	13:17	—	13:26	—	13:36	23:56	13:47	23:44	14:02	23:28	14:20	23:06	14:43
3	0:36	13:38	0:23	13:48	0:15	13:54	0:07	14:01	—	14:08	—	14:18	—	14:29	—	14:44
4	1:29	14:11	1:21	14:16	1:16	14:19	1:11	14:22	1:05	14:26	0:57	14:31	0:48	14:37	0:36	14:44
5	2:18	14:43	2:16	14:43	2:14	14:43	2:12	14:43	2:10	14:43	2:08	14:43	2:05	14:43	2:01	14:43
6	3:07	15:14	3:10	15:09	3:11	15:06	3:13	15:03	3:15	14:59	3:17	14:55	3:20	14:49	3:23	14:42
7	3:55	15:45	4:03	15:35	4:07	15:30	4:12	15:23	4:18	15:16	4:25	15:07	4:34	14:56	4:46	14:42
8	4:44	16:19	4:57	16:04	5:04	15:56	5:13	15:46	5:23	15:35	5:35	15:21	5:50	15:04	6:10	14:42
9	5:35	16:55	5:52	16:36	6:03	16:25	6:14	16:12	6:28	15:57	6:45	15:39	7:07	15:15	7:37	14:43
10	6:27	17:35	6:49	17:12	7:02	16:58	7:16	16:43	7:34	16:24	7:56	16:01	8:25	15:31	9:08	14:47
11	7:21	18:19	7:46	17:53	8:01	17:38	8:18	17:20	8:39	16:59	9:05	16:32	9:41	15:55	10:39	14:57
12	8:15	19:08	8:42	18:41	8:58	18:24	9:17	18:05	9:40	17:42	10:10	17:12	10:51	16:31	12:02	15:19
13	9:08	20:01	9:36	19:34	9:52	19:17	10:11	18:58	10:35	18:35	11:05	18:05	11:46	17:23	13:00	16:11
14	9:58	20:57	10:25	20:31	10:41	20:16	10:59	19:58	11:21	19:37	11:48	19:09	12:26	18:32	13:27	17:32
15	10:46	21:53	11:09	21:31	11:23	21:18	11:39	21:03	11:58	20:45	12:22	20:22	12:53	19:52	13:39	19:07
16	11:29	22:50	11:49	22:32	12:00	22:22	12:13	22:10	12:28	21:56	12:47	21:38	13:11	21:16	13:44	20:45
17	12:09	23:46	12:24	23:34	12:32	23:27	12:42	23:18	12:53	23:09	13:07	22:57	13:23	22:42	13:46	22:22
18	12:47	—	12:56	—	13:02	—	13:08	—	13:15	—	13:23	—	13:33	—	13:46	23:58
19	13:24	0:42	13:28	0:36	13:30	0:32	13:32	0:28	13:35	0:22	13:38	0:16	13:42	0:08	13:47	—
20	14:02	1:40	13:59	1:39	13:58	1:39	13:56	1:38	13:55	1:38	13:52	1:37	13:50	1:36	13:47	1:35
21	14:41	2:39	14:33	2:44	14:28	2:48	14:22	2:51	14:16	2:56	14:08	3:01	13:59	3:07	13:47	3:16
22	15:25	3:41	15:10	3:53	15:01	4:00	14:52	4:08	14:41	4:17	14:27	4:29	14:11	4:43	13:49	5:02
23	16:14	4:47	15:53	5:05	15:41	5:16	15:28	5:28	15:12	5:43	14:52	6:01	14:27	6:24	13:53	6:56
24	17:09	5:57	16:44	6:21	16:30	6:35	16:13	6:51	15:52	7:10	15:27	7:34	14:53	8:07	14:03	8:56
25	18:12	7:08	17:44	7:35	17:28	7:51	17:09	8:10	16:46	8:32	16:17	9:01	15:36	9:41	14:29	10:48
26	19:18	8:16	18:51	8:44	18:35	9:01	18:16	9:20	17:53	9:43	17:23	10:12	16:43	10:54	15:33	12:04
27	20:25	9:18	20:00	9:44	19:46	9:59	19:29	10:17	19:08	10:38	18:43	11:04	18:08	11:40	17:14	12:35
28	21:29	10:11	21:08	10:33	20:56	10:46	20:43	11:01	20:26	11:18	20:06	11:40	19:40	12:08	19:02	12:47
29	22:28	10:57	22:13	11:14	22:04	11:24	21:54	11:35	21:42	11:48	21:27	12:04	21:09	12:25	20:44	12:52
30	23:22	11:36	23:13	11:48	23:07	11:55	23:01	12:03	22:53	12:12	22:44	12:23	22:33	12:36	22:18	12:54
Dec. 1	—	12:11	—	12:18	—	12:22	—	12:26	—	12:31	23:57	12:37	23:52	12:45	23:46	12:54
2	0:14	12:44	0:10	12:45	0:07	12:46	0:04	12:47	0:01	12:48	—	12:50	—	12:52	—	12:54
3	1:03	13:15	1:04	13:12	1:05	13:10	1:05	13:07	1:06	13:05	1:07	13:02	1:08	12:58	1:10	12:53
4	1:52	13:47	1:58	13:38	2:01	13:33	2:05	13:28	2:10	13:22	2:16	13:14	2:23	13:05	2:32	12:53
5	2:41	14:19	2:52	14:06	2:58	13:59	3:05	13:50	3:14	13:40	3:25	13:28	3:38	13:13	3:55	12:53
6	3:30	14:55	3:46	14:37	3:56	14:27	4:06	14:15	4:19	14:01	4:34	13:44	4:54	13:23	5:21	12:54
7	4:22	15:34	4:42	15:12	4:54	14:59	5:08	14:44	5:25	14:27	5:45	14:05	6:12	13:37	6:50	12:57
8	5:15	16:17	5:39	15:52	5:54	15:37	6:10	15:20	6:30	14:59	6:55	14:33	7:29	13:58	8:21	13:05
9	6:10	17:05	6:36	16:37	6:52	16:21	7:11	16:02	7:33	15:40	8:02	15:11	8:41	14:31	9:48	13:23
10	7:03	17:57	7:31	17:29	7:48	17:13	8:07	16:53	8:30	16:30	9:00	16:00	9:42	15:19	10:55	14:06
11	7:55	18:52	8:22	18:26	8:38	18:10	8:57	17:52	9:19	17:30	9:47	17:02	10:26	16:24	11:31	15:20
12	8:44	19:49	9:08	19:25	9:22	19:12	9:39	18:56	9:59	18:37	10:24	18:13	10:57	17:41	11:46	16:53
13	9:28	20:45	9:49	20:26	10:01	20:15	10:15	20:02	10:31	19:47	10:51	19:29	11:17	19:04	11:53	18:30
14	10:09	21:41	10:25	21:27	10:34	21:19	10:45	21:10	10:57	20:59	11:12	20:46	11:30	20:29	11:55	20:06
15	10:47	22:36	10:58	22:28	11:04	22:23	11:11	22:18	11:19	22:11	11:29	22:03	11:41	21:53	11:56	21:41
16	11:23	23:31	11:28	23:29	11:31	23:27	11:35	23:25	11:39	23:23	11:44	23:21	11:49	23:18	11:57	23:14
17	11:59	—	11:59	—	11:58	—	11:58	—	11:58	—	11:58	—	11:57	—	11:57	—
18	12:36	0:27	12:30	0:31	12:26	0:33	12:22	0:35	12:18	0:37	12:12	0:40	12:06	0:44	11:57	0:49
19	13:16	1:26	13:04	1:35	12:57	1:41	12:49	1:47	12:40	1:54	12:29	2:03	12:16	2:14	11:58	2:29
20	14:00	2:28	13:42	2:43	13:32	2:52	13:20	3:03	13:07	3:15	12:50	3:30	12:29	3:49	12:01	4:15
21	14:51	3:34	14:28	3:55	14:15	4:07	13:59	4:21	13:41	4:38	13:19	5:00	12:49	5:28	12:07	6:08
22	15:49	4:42	15:23	5:08	15:07	5:23	14:49	5:41	14:27	6:02	14:00	6:29	13:22	7:05	12:23	8:04
23	16:54	5:52	16:26	6:19	16:09	6:36	15:50	6:55	15:27	7:18	14:57	7:48	14:16	8:29	13:05	9:40
24	18:01	6:57	17:35	7:24	17:19	7:40	17:01	7:59	16:39	8:21	16:12	8:50	15:33	9:29	14:31	10:32
25	19:08	7:55	18:46	8:20	18:32	8:34	18:17	8:50	17:59	9:09	17:36	9:33	17:05	10:05	16:20	10:52
26	20:11	8:46	19:54	9:05	19:44	9:17	19:32	9:30	19:18	9:45	19:01	10:03	18:39	10:27	18:09	11:00
27	21:10	9:29	20:58	9:44	20:51	9:52	20:43	10:01	20:34	10:12	20:22	10:25	20:08	10:41	19:49	11:03
28	22:04	10:07	21:58	10:16	21:54	10:21	21:50	10:27	21:45	10:34	21:39	10:42	21:32	10:51	21:22	11:04
29	22:56	10:42	22:55	10:45	22:54	10:47	22:54	10:50	22:53	10:52	22:52	10:55	22:51	10:59	22:50	11:04
30	23:45	11:14	23:50	11:13	23:52	11:12	23:55	11:11	23:58	11:09	—	11:08	—	11:06	—	11:04
31	—	11:46	—	11:39	—	11:36	—	11:31	—	11:26	0:02	11:20	0:07	11:13	0:14	11:03

OCCULTATIONS BY THE MOON

By David W. Dunham

The Moon often passes between Earth and a star, an event called an *occultation.* During an occultation, a star suddenly disappears as the east limb of the Moon crosses the line between the star and the observer. The star reappears from behind the west limb some time later. Because the Moon moves through an angle about equal to its own diameter every hour, the longest time for an occultation is about an hour. The time is shorter if the occultation is not central. Solar eclipses are actually occultations: the star being occulted by the Moon is the Sun.

Since observing occultations is rather easy, amateur astronomers should try to observe one. The slow, majestic drift of the Moon in its orbit is an interesting part of such observations, and the disappearance or reappearance of a star at the Moon's limb is a remarkable sight, particularly when it occurs as a *graze* near the Moon's northern or southern limb. During a graze, a star may disappear and reappear several times in succession as mountains and valleys in the Moon's polar regions drift by it. On rarer occasions the Moon occults a planet. During 2007 the planets Mercury, Venus, Mars, Saturn, and Uranus, and the first-magnitude star Regulus, are occulted. Also occulted are 1.6-magnitude β Tauri (El Nath) and several stars in the Pleiades.

Lunar occultation and graze observations refine our knowledge of the shape of the lunar profile and the fundamental star coordinate system. These observations complement those made by other techniques, such as Clementine laser ranging and photographs. Improved knowledge of the lunar profile is useful in determinations of the Sun's diameter from solar eclipse records. Occultation observations are also useful for detecting double stars and measuring their separations. Binaries with separations as small as 0.02″ have been discovered visually during grazes. Doubles with separations in this range are useful for filling the gap between doubles that can be directly resolved and those whose duplicity has been discovered spectroscopically.

Observations

The **International Lunar Occultation Centre (ILOC)** analyzes lunar occultation observations and is the world clearinghouse for such observations. Anyone interested in pursuing a systematic program of lunar occultation observations should write to the ILOC, Geodesy and Geophysics Division, Hydrographic Department, Tsukiji 5-3-1, Chuo-ku, Tokyo 104-0045, Japan, email iloc@jodc.go.jp, for their booklet *Guide to Lunar Occultation Observations.* ILOC's Web site is www1.kaiho.mlit.go.jp/KOHO/iloc/obsrep.

Observers in North America should also contact the **International Occultation Timing Association (IOTA),** 5403 Bluebird Trail, Stillwater OK 74074-7600, USA; email: business@occultations.org. IOTA provides predictions and coordination services for occultation observers. Detailed predictions for any grazing occultation are available ($1.50 U.S. each; free by email); instructions explaining the use of predictions are also available ($5 U.S.; free at iota.jhuapl.edu/ocmangrz.htm). Annual membership in IOTA is $30 U.S. in North America, $35 U.S. overseas. Less expensive online rates are available. Membership includes free graze predictions, descriptive materials, and a subscription to *Occultation Newsletter* (available separately for $20 U.S. in North America, $25 overseas). IOTA's administrative Web site is www.occultations.org, and its site for predictions, updates, observations, and other technical information is www.lunar-occultations.com/iota.

For observers in the southwestern Pacific (New Zealand, Australia, Papua New Guinea, and nearby areas), the Royal Astronomical Society of New Zealand

(RASNZ) provides occultation data (total lunar, lunar grazing, planetary, and Jupiter's satellites), plus comprehensive instructions for new observers. See the RASNZ Web page: occsec.wellington.net.nz/sitemap.htm.

Two main pieces of information are required in a lunar occultation observation: the time of the event and the observer's location. Supplementary data include the seeing conditions, telescope size, timing method, estimate of the observer's reaction time and the accuracy of the timing, and whether or not the reaction time correction has been applied. The timing should be accurate to 0.5 s or better (a shortwave radio time signal and audio recorder provide a simple, permanent time record, but a video record provides higher accuracy). The observer's longitude, latitude, and altitude should be reported to the nearest tenth of an arcsecond and 10 m, respectively, and should be accurate to at least 0.5″ or 16 m. These can be determined from either GPS measurements (10 min of position averaging and an unobstructed view of the sky above 15° altitude are needed) or a suitable topographical map. For Canada, the maps are available from the Policy and Product Promotion Office, Centre for Topographic Information, Natural Resources Canada, 615 Booth St, Room 711, Ottawa ON K1A 0E9. For the United States (except Alaska), write to US Geological Survey, Map Sales, PO Box 25286, Denver CO 80225, asking for an index to topographical maps in the desired state, or call (800) USA-MAPS. For Alaska, write to US Geological Survey, Map Sales, 4230 University Dr, Room 101, Anchorage AK 99508-4664, or phone (907) 786-7011. Parts of USGS maps can be viewed and printed at www.topozone.com. Detailed imagery and maps are available at other Web sites, such as www.terraserver.com and maps.google.com. IOTA is starting to exploit these resources for prediction purposes, but the maps do not provide accurate enough positions for reporting observations.

Observers are encouraged to learn how to videotape occultations in order to obtain reliable and accurate timings. Inexpensive yet sensitive video cameras are now available. Visual timings must be accurate to ±0.2 s to be good enough for further improvement of the lunar profile and other parameters, except for grazes, where ±0.5 s is adequate. Information about videotaping occultations is on IOTA's technical Web site given above.

Pages 142–151 give tables of occultation predictions and a table and maps of northern or southern limits for grazing occultations.

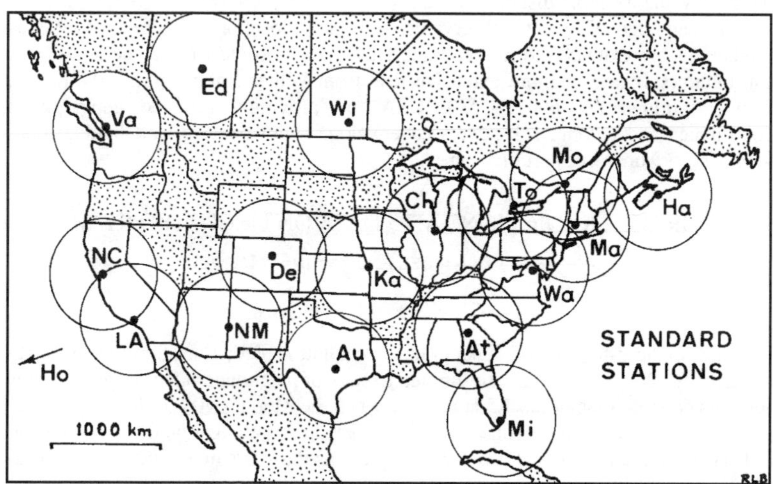

1. TOTAL OCCULTATION PREDICTIONS

PREDICTIONS BY THE INTERNATIONAL LUNAR OCCULTATION CENTRE, JAPAN

The total occultation predictions, as given in the tables on pp. 142–145, are for the 18 standard stations identified on the map on the previous page; the longitudes and latitudes of these stations are given in the table headings.

The predictions are limited to stars of magnitude 5.0 and brighter. The first five columns give for each occultation the date, the Zodiacal Catalogue (ZC) number of the star, its magnitude, the phenomenon, and the elongation of the Moon from the Sun in degrees. Under each station are given the Universal Time of the event, factors A and B (see below), and the position angle P (from the north point, eastward around the Moon's limb to the point of occurrence of the phenomenon). If no data are given for an occultation for a given station, the reason is specified. If A and B give an unrealistic representation, as in the case of near grazes, they are omitted.

The terms A and B are for determining corrections to the times of the events for stations within 300 km of the standard stations. If Lo* and La* represent the longitude and latitude of the standard station, and Lo and La those of the observer, then for the observer,

UT of event = UT of event at the standard station + A(Lo – Lo*) + B(La – La*),

where Lo, etc., are expressed in degrees, and A and B are in minutes of time per degree. Longitude measured *west* of Greenwich is assumed to be *positive* (which is opposite to the IAU convention and that used by IOTA's *Occult* software). Due regard must be paid to the algebraic signs of the terms. To convert UT to the standard time of the observer, see the section STANDARD TIME ZONES on pp. 42–43.

As an example, consider the occultation of ZC 2383 (τ Scorpii) on 2007 Jan. 15 as seen from Ottawa, Ontario. For Ottawa, Lo = 75.70° and La = 45.44°. The nearest standard station is Montréal, for which Lo* = 73.60° and La* = 45.50°. Therefore, the UT of the disappearance at the bright limb (DB) is:

16:06.1 – 1.8 × (75.70° – 73.60°) min – 1.7 × (45.44° - 45.50°) min = 16:02.4.

The elongation of the Moon is 316°, which corresponds to the waning crescent phase (between last quarter and new Moon). The position angle of disappearance is approximately 135° by roughly interpolating between the 135° value for Montréal and the 134° value for more distant Toronto.

The number of events observable from any location increases *rapidly* as predictions are extended to fainter stars. Observers who wish to pursue such work can obtain software or more extensive lists from Walter Robinson, 515 W Kump, Bonner Springs KS 66012–1439, USA, by providing accurate geographical coordinates and a long, self-addressed envelope (with postage); or, better, email webmaster@lunar-occultations.com.

2. GRAZE PREDICTIONS AND DATA ON OCCULTED STARS

BY EBERHARD RIEDEL AND DAVID W. DUNHAM

(A) GRAZE PREDICTIONS

The table on pp. 146–147 lists lunar grazing occultation predictions for much of North America for 2007. The events are limited to stars of magnitude 6.5 or brighter (paths for stars down to magnitude 7.5 are shown when the Moon is 40% or less sunlit) that will graze the limb of the Moon when it is at a favourable elongation from the Sun and at least as high above a land horizon in degrees as the star's magnitude (e.g. a third-magnitude star is included only if its altitude is at least 3°). The star's USNO reference number is the ZC number, unless the number is prefixed with an X. In the latter case, the star is not in the ZC and its number is from the XZ catalogue, a more extensive catalogue of zodiacal stars prepared originally at the U.S. Naval Observatory but now updated by David Herald in Australia.

The maps on pp. 148–151 show the predicted graze tracks. The maps are "false" projections, since the latitude and longitude scales are both linear. This makes it much easier for measuring coordinates or plotting locations with known coordinates than is possible with any other type of projection. The longitude scale is compressed by a factor of cos 50°. The maps are not detailed enough for locating oneself in the 2- or 3-km-wide zone where multiple disappearances of the star may occur. To obtain detailed predictions of any graze for plotting on larger-scale maps of your region, write to (or email) IOTA (see p. 136). For grazes of very bright stars, IOTA overlays the predicted limit line on the very detailed maps and imagery of maps.google.com, available at IOTA's main Web site, but further corrections are needed based on the predicted lunar profile and the observer's height above sea level.

Each track is keyed to the sequential number in the table. The computer-drawn number appears at the east and west ends of the track and is aligned parallel to it. Some overlapping numbers have been omitted for legibility; in these cases, check the other end of the track for the number. Conditions are represented by three different types of lines:

solid line = dark limb, night
dashed line = bright limb, night
dotted line = dark or bright limb, day

Thicker lines are drawn for first-magnitude stars and planets. Many tracks begin and/or end with the letter A, B, or S: A denotes that the Moon is at a low altitude, B that the bright limb interferes, and S that sunlight or twilight interferes. The tick marks along the tracks indicate multiples of 10 min of every hour. For example, if the time for the west end of the track is 3:16.2, the tick marks proceeding eastward correspond to 3:20, 3:30, etc. Time always increases from west to east along the path. *The time ticks, track numbers, and the* A, B, *and* S *letters are on the side of the limit with an occultation,* that is north of southern limits and south of northern limits. The locations for the North American standard stations for lunar total occultation predictions are indicated by asterisks on the graze maps (see the map on p. 137). For grazes of planets, a *partial occultation* of the object will occur at the northern or southern limit. The line plotted is the centre of the partial occultation zone, typically several kilometres wide.

(B) NAMES OF OCCULTED STARS

The stars that are occulted by the Moon are stars that lie along the zodiac; hence they are known by their number in the ZC compiled by James Robertson and published in the *Astronomical Papers Prepared for the Use of the American Ephemeris and Nautical Almanac, Vol. 10,* Part 2 (U.S. Government Printing Office, Washington, 1940). Robertson's ZC has been out of print for several years. In 1986, Isao Sato, a member of the Lunar Occultation Observers Group in Japan, republished the ZC. This new edition is based on the epoch J2000 and includes much new data, particularly on double stars. Since stars are not usually recognized by their ZC numbers, the equivalent Bayer designations or Flamsteed numbers of the stars occulted during the year are given in the table on p. 140. The ZC and XZ (now version XZ80Q) catalogues, updated in 2005 by D. Herald using HIPPARCOS, Tycho-2, and UCAC-2 data, are available through IOTA's Web site.

ZC	Name	ZC	Name	ZC	Name
105	δ Psc	1061	39 Gem	1853	ψ Vir
370	26 Ari	1062	40 Gem	1884	49 Vir
399	μ Ari	1088	47 Gem	2051	CS Vir
440	ε Ari	1117	57 Gem	2276	4 Sco
518	7 Tau	1170	κ Gem	2287	π Sco
536	16 Tau (Celaeno)	1221	9 Cnc	2383	τ Sco
538	18 Tau	1277	η Cnc	2609	W Sgr
539	19 Tau (Taygeta)	1308	γ Cnc (Asellus Borealis)	2784	τ Sgr
541	20 Tau (Maia)	1370	80 Cnc	3031	17 Cap
542	21 Tau (Asterope)	1383	83 Cnc	3078	η Cap (Chow)
543	22 Tau	1420	11 Leo	3113	30 Cap
545	23 Tau (Merope)	1434	ψ Leo	3171	γ Cap (Nashira)
552	η Tau (Alcyone)	1449	23 Leo	3181	45 Cap
560	27 Tau (Atlas)	1466	ν Leo	3190	δ Cap (Deneb Algedi)
561	28 Tau (Pleione)	1487	α Leo (Regulus)	3237	ι Aqr
616	44 Tau	1531	45 Leo	3307	σ Aqr
647	χ Tau	1547	ρ Leo	3324	64 Aqr
810	β Tau (El Nath)	1589	56 Leo	3353	λ Aqr
890	136 Tau	1600	59 Leo	3360	78 Aqr
1008	49 Aur	1652	79 Leo	3383	82 Aqr
1022	54 Aur	1660	83 Leo	3459	11 Psc
1026	25 Gem	1815	χ Vir	3474	14 Psc

(C) OCCULTED STARS KNOWN TO BE DOUBLE

In the table at the right are data on double stars for which graze predictions are given. This information is from DSFILE, a comprehensive file of zodiacal double-star data compiled by Don Stockbauer, Henk Bulder, Mitsuru Sôma, David Herald, and David Dunham; most of the data for the ZC stars are in the Sato ZC catalogue. The successive columns give the USNO reference number of the star, the number of the graze track, the double-star code (d), the magnitudes of the brighter (A) and dimmer (B) components, the separation in arcseconds, and the position angle (PA) of B from A measured eastward from north. If the star is triple, the third component's magnitude is given under C, and its separation and PA from A are given in the last columns. XZ numbers are given for the last seven non-ZC stars.

The parameters are given for the epoch of the occultation, computed from orbital elements when available or from extrapolations from a long series of observations. If there is little change in the available observations, the last-observed separation and PA are used. Components fainter than magnitude 11.5 are not listed, and some very close doubles whose parameters are not known, generally with separations less than 0.2″, are also not listed. The latter include spectroscopic binaries (code J, U, or sometimes V) and visual occultation doubles (most codes K and X, and many Vs).

The codes have the following meanings:

A, C, or G.. visual double
B or V........ close double, usually discovered by occultation
D................ primary of wide pair; secondary has separate catalogue entry
E................ secondary star of wide pair
F................ prediction is for the following component of a visual double
H................ triple, with close occultation pair and third visual component; prediction uses a mean position
I................. data for B component computed from orbital elements, but B component is itself a close double, with data for C component referred to B rather than A
K................ possible double from occultation
L................ close triple star (only two stars often listed because inner pair is often spectroscopic)

M............... mean position (centre of light) of a close pair is used by the ZC and/or XZ catalogue
N................ northern component of nearly equal double star
O................ orbital elements available and used to calculate the separation and PA
Q................ = O, but A component may be close double (if triple, C-component data are computed from orbital elements)
R................ triple; close pair = O and C component also has orbit relative to centre of close pair
S................ southern component of nearly equal double star
T................ visual triple star
W............... = A or C, but A component is a spectroscopic binary
X................ probable double from occultation
Y................ triple, K or X (B component) and A or C (C component)
Z................ triple, O (B component) and V (C component)

Some close pairs have rapid orbital motion so the current PA is unknown.

USNO	Graze #	d	A	B	Sep. ″	PA °	C	Sep. ″	PA °
166	36, 98	D	6.7	10.8	80.8	136			
196	15	O	7.4	8.0	0.5	101			
399	112	Z	6.3	6.8	0.02	188	8.3	0.2	0
438	39, 138	O	7.4	7.5	0.5	271			
440	38, 241	M	5.2	5.6	1.5	208			
470	17	D	6.8	10.4	42.7	35			
518	67, 181	O	6.6	6.7	0.7	351			
548	44, 120	K	6.8	9.8	0.3	173			
569	47, 161	O	5.8	6.2	0.1	184			
647	1, 182, 246	Y	6.3	6.3	0.1	90	7.6	19.4	24
701	165, 183	W	8.0	8.0	0.1		7.4	4.4	10
746	143	A	6.8	8.3	20.5	205			
771	19, 53, 84, 145, 200	T	6.1	9.1	0.28	90	8.6	11.8	27
773	146	C	7.1	8.7	14.0	352			
909	201	T	6.2	8.2	0.0	194	12.4	239.3	242
1013	185	O	7.1	8.7	0.7	292			
1022	71	M	6.2	7.8	0.9	36			
1026	72	C	6.5	11.7	30.7	46	10.4	55.9	57
1105	86	V	7.0	7.7	0.2	231			
1170	2, 188	A	3.7	8.2	7.5	241			
1208	104	M	6.5	9.8	2.1	326			
1221	220	V	5.9	10.0	0.4	110			
1304	189	M	7.0	8.4	0.5	85			
1329	105, 175	M	7.3	7.9	0.2	45			
1487	123, 208	A	1.4	8.2	217.0	274			
1531	107	Y	6.7	6.7	0.02	18	10.9	33.6	132
1660	89	A	6.2	7.9	28.4	149	9.9	90.3	188
1692	4	M	7.0	10.0	0.8	131			
1845	231	A	6.5	9.3	28.9	298			
2045	25	M	6.4	10.5	0.7	99			
2066	28, 132	Y	6.8	7.7	0.1	0	7.3	35.1	296
2108	61	O	7.0	7.2	0.2	218			
2609	32	V	5.1	5.1	0.1	153	13.6	33.4	233
3078	177	M	5.0	7.4	0.3	281			
3333	214	M	6.7	8.0	2.5	307	11.0	70.2	357
X03537	111	V	7.5	8.5	0.3	70			
X04845	117	M	8.4	10.1	0.3	4			
X06319	100	V	7.6	10.1	0.1	82			
X10660	148	X	8.1	8.5	0.1	21			
X12068	173	M	7.4	11.0	1.3	170			
X20283	27, 131	M	7.1	8.4	1.3	89			
X29959	237	A	7.1	11.4	17.5	104			

TABLE OF TOTAL LUNAR OCCULTATION PREDICTIONS

					HALIFAX 63.6°W, 44.6°N				MONTRÉAL 73.6°W, 45.5°N				TORONTO 79.4°W, 43.7°N			
DATE	ZC	MAG	PH	ELG °	TIME (UT)	A m	B m	P °	TIME (UT)	A m	B m	P °	TIME (UT)	A m	B m	P °
Jan. 15	2383	2.9	DB	316	After Moonset				16:06.1	–1.8	–1.7	135	15:58.2	–1.9	–1.5	134
15	2383	2.9	RD	317	After Moonset				After Moonset				17:00.7	–1.0	–0.5	236
27	552	3.0	RB	112	16:51.4	0.4	1.5	238	After Moonrise				After Moonrise			
Feb. 18	Uran.	5.9	DD	14	17:06.2	–0.6	1.7	16	17:06.2			351	Bright Limb			
23	440	4.6	DD	75	After Moonset				4:11.9	0.2	–1.2	90	4:15.3	0.1	–1.6	101
23	539	4.4	DD	85	22:9.6			140	After Sunset				After Sunset			
Mar. 1	1308	4.7	DD	147	1:06.4	–2.4	2.4	65	0:48.3	–1.7	2.4	68	0:35.4	–1.4	1.9	77
11	2383	2.9	DB	261	8:07.4	–1.6	0.4	107	7:54.7	–1.0	0.5	119	7:49.0	–0.7	0.3	130
11	2383	2.9	RD	261	9:33.2	–1.9	–0.2	284	9:14.4	–1.8	0.4	276	9:02.5	–1.9	0.8	267
Apr. 30	1853	4.9	DD	157	7:00.4	–0.7	–1.7	96	6:49.5	–1.1	–1.7	99	6:45.5	–1.3	–1.7	104
May 4	2287	3.0	DB	200	No Occultation				3:18.7	–2.2	2.4	60	3:04.7	–1.4	1.8	78
4	2287	3.0	RD	200	No Occultation				4:04.2	0.1	–1.1	347	4:04.4	–0.4	–0.4	330
10	3171	3.8	RD	273	Bright Twilight				Bright Twilight				9:16.9			311
10	3190	3.0	DB	274	No Occultation				12:58	–2.8	–1.9	113	12:45.1	–2.6	–1.0	103
10	3190	3.0	RD	275	No Occultation				13:36	0.6	2.3	176	13:34.3	0.1	1.7	185
19	890	4.5	DD	32	After Moonset				2:00.4	0.2	–1.0	80	2:03.4	0.2	–1.1	90
27	1815	4.8	DD	127	5:21.6	–0.5	–2.2	142	5:13.5	–0.7	–2.2	144	5:13.3	–0.8	–2.3	149
Jun. 18	Ven.	–4.4	DD	44	13:7.7	–0.5	–0.8	153	After Moonrise				After Moonrise			
18	Ven.	–4.4	RB	44	13:49.7	0.2	3.0	237	13:54.3	0.3	2.1	251	13:52.7	0.4	1.9	251
Jul. 3	3078	4.9	RD	212	4:50.6	–1.8	0.8	274	4:35.1	–1.4	1.1	280	4:25.5	–1.2	1.2	279
5	3353	3.8	RD	239	Bright Twilight				7:59.7	–1.9	0.7	262	7:47.2	–2.0	0.8	269
Aug. 1	3307	4.9	RD	207	3:08.7	–0.8	2.0	206	3:02.7	–0.7	2.0	213	2:55.0	–0.6	2.1	213
6	440	4.6	RD	275	6:20.9	–0.2	2.0	226	6:20.4	–0.2	1.8	240	6:16.5	–0.1	1.7	244
12	Merc.	–1.8	DB	356	14:59.3	–2.7	1.0	88	14:36.4	–2.1	1.0	95	14:23.9	–1.8	0.7	105
12	Merc.	–1.8	RD	356	16:19.4	–0.8	–3.4	343	16:5.7	–1.4	–2.5	329	16:0.2	–1.8	–1.6	316
31	105	4.6	RD	217	3:37.2	0.2	2.7	180	3:39.1	–0.2	2.2	199	3:34.1	–0.2	2.2	204
Sep. 3	541	4.0	RD	259	No Occultation				No Occultation				6:24.6			180
3	539	4.4	RD	259	6:36.1	0.0	3.2	198	6:36.7	–0.3	2.3	219	6:31.2	–0.2	2.2	224
23	3171	3.8	DD	141	22:29.1			138	After Sunset				After Moonrise			
Oct. 15	2383	2.9	DD	49	17:22.3			180	No Occultation				No Occultation			
15	2383	2.9	RB	50	17:45.9			213	No Occultation				No Occultation			
24	105	4.6	DD	162	23:31.9	–1.4	1.0	103	23:23.0	–0.7	1.4	88	23:16.8	–0.5	1.5	85
27	537	3.8	RD	206	23:00.6	0.3	1.3	254	23:05.1	0.4	1.1	263	After Moonrise			
27	552	3.0	DB	206	23:07.4	–0.1	0.8	114	23:09.4	0.3	1.0	102	After Moonrise			
27	545	4.3	RD	206	23:09.8			187	23:20.2	0.7	1.8	204	After Moonrise			
27	541	4.0	RD	206	23:20.2	–0.1	0.9	292	23:19.9	–0.1	0.6	307	After Moonrise			
27	552	3.0	RD	206	23:44.2	0.6	2.0	208	23:51.0	0.5	1.7	221	23:51.2	0.6	1.6	224
Nov. 26	890	4.5	RD	206	10:15.0	0.2	–2.6	323	10:12.2	–0.3	–2.3	310	10:13.1	–0.7	–1.9	297
Dec. 21	552	3.0	DD	149	No Occultation				No Occultation				21:17.4			142
21	552	3.0	RB	150	No Occultation				No Occultation				21:34.1			179

					WINNIPEG 97.2°W, 49.9°N				EDMONTON 113.4°W, 53.6°N				VANCOUVER 123.1°W, 49.2°N			
DATE	ZC	MAG	PH	ELG °	TIME (UT)	A m	B m	P °	TIME (UT)	A m	B m	P °	TIME (UT)	A m	B m	P °
Jan. 0	537	3.8	DD	140	After Moonset				11:13.7	0.0	–1.1	71	11:19.2	0.0	–1.4	91
0	545	4.3	DD	140	After Moonset				11:48.8	0.5	–1.9	119	12:07.0			150
0	541	4.0	DD	140	No Occultation				No Occultation				11:51.8	–0.4	–0.1	39
0	552	3.0	DD	141	After Moonset				12:11.3	0.4	–1.2	91	12:21.6	0.5	–1.6	111
15	2383	2.9	DB	316	15:22.4	–1.4	–0.4	132	15:04.1	–0.8	0.1	142	15:00.4	0.1	–0.7	165
15	2383	2.9	RD	316	16:32.4	–1.6	–0.4	250	16:04.7	–1.7	0.4	246	15:40.7	–2.5	1.8	229
Feb. 3	1487	1.3	DB	196	After Moonset				14:32.7	0.2	–2.0	146	14:43.2	0.2	–2.1	156
3	1487	1.3	RD	196	After Moonset				After Moonset				15:30.2	0.0	–1.5	263
7	1853	4.9	DD	238	Bright Limb				Bright Limb				10:19.5			
7	1853	4.9	RD	238	11:36.2	–1.6	–1.1	290	11:06.1	–1.9	0.1	271	10:31.7			228
23	440	4.6	DD	75	4:03.0	–0.4	–1.7	96	3:47.1	–0.8	–1.4	90	3:44.7	–1.2	–2.0	108
Mar. 1	1308	4.7	DD	147	0:39.5			37	No Occultation				No Occultation			
16	3190	3.0	DB	328	19:47.0	–0.7	–0.6	63	19:36.5	–0.5	0.3	33	19:28.9	–0.6	0.7	27
16	3190	3.0	RD	329	After Moonset				20:35.3	–0.9	–1.1	262	20:28.6	–1.3	–0.9	265
23	537	3.8	DD	58	After Moonset				6:17.3	0.8	–2.5	137	No Occultation			
23	539	4.4	DD	58	After Moonset				6:20.5	0.0	–0.7	57	6:24.6	0.0	–1.0	77
23	541	4.0	DD	58	After Moonset				6:30.0	0.2	–1.2	82	6:38.4	0.3	–1.5	102
25	890	4.5	DD	85	After Moonset				8:06.6	0.8	–2.1	146	No Occultation			
Apr. 19	552	3.0	DD	31	14:47.3	–0.2	1.3	99	14:53.1	0.2	1.4	80	14:50.5	0.4	1.2	77
19	552	3.0	RB	31	15:34.6	0.2	2.0	220	15:43.6	0.2	1.7	241	15:39.0	0.3	1.5	245
26	1487	1.3	DD	114	After Moonset				9:17.2	0.1	–1.8	115	9:25.4	0.0	–1.9	123
26	1487	1.3	RB	115	After Moonset				After Moonset				10:23.4	0.2	–1.7	296
30	1853	4.9	DD	156	6:10.3	–1.5	–1.2	117	5:45.8	–1.1	–0.7	134	5:40.8	–0.7	–1.2	156
May 10	3190	3.0	DB	274	12:13.0	–1.4	0.8	64	11:57.7	–1.0	1.4	48	11:41.1	–1.0	1.7	46
10	3190	3.0	RD	275	13:27.3	–1.1	0.5	230	13:08.4	–1.4	0.7	253	12:50.6	–1.4	1.1	258

TABLE OF TOTAL LUNAR OCCULTATION PREDICTIONS (continued)

					WINNIPEG (cont) 97.2°W, 49.9°N				EDMONTON (cont) 113.4°W, 53.6°N				VANCOUVER (cont) 123.1°W, 49.2°N			
DATE	ZC	MAG	PH	ELG °	TIME (UT)	A m	B m	P °	TIME (UT)	A m	B m	P °	TIME (UT)	A m	B m	P °
May 27	1815	4.8	DD	126	4:45.8	–0.7	–2.0	161	4:32.2	0.1	–2.1	183	No Occultation			
Jun. 19	1487	1.3	DD	61	No Occultation				23:47.6	–2.1	0.6	78	23:28.7	–1.6	0.0	105
20	1487	1.3	RB	62	No Occultation				0:39.1	–0.2	–2.7	352	0:42.9	–1	–1.8	325
Jul. 5	3353	3.8	RD	239	7:17.3			309	No Occultation				No Occultation			
Aug. 6	440	4.6	RD	275	6:25.3	0.0	1.4	269	6:32.2	0.2	1.3	284	After Moonrise			
12	Merc.	–1.8	DB	355	14:10.1	–0.8	2.2	84	14:13.1	–0.1	3.5	62	14:0.8	0.2	2.5	72
12	Merc.	–1.8	RD	356	15:25.0	–1.3	–1.0	324	15:03.8	–0.9	–1.4	339	14:59.3	–0.7	–0.4	325
22	2383	2.9	DD	103	After Moonset				3:13.2	–1.5	–0.6	87	2:58.4	–1.8	–0.1	92
22	2383	2.9	RB	103	After Moonset				After Moonset				4:22.6	–1.7	–1.0	285
31	105	4.6	RD	217	3:43.2	–0.1	1.8	226	3:49.4	0.1	1.7	235	After Moonrise			
Sep. 3	537	3.8	RD	259	5:56.8			174	6:18.3	0.5	1.9	210	6:15.8	0.6	1.7	214
3	539	4.4	RD	259	6:37.6	–0.3	1.6	258	6:39.9	–0.1	1.4	280	6:34.0	0.1	1.1	285
3	541	4.0	RD	259	6:46.0	0.0	2.0	227	6:53.2	0.1	1.7	249	6:47.7	0.2	1.5	253
5	890	4.5	RD	286	8:02.7	0.1	2.0	240	8:11.0	0.1	1.5	264	8:07.2	0.3	1.2	267
21	2784	3.4	DD	107	No Occultation				After Moonset				4:32.1	–1.8	–0.8	102
23	3078	4.9	DD	133	No Occultation				After Moonset				8:14.4			129
Oct. 4	1170	3.7	RD	283	10:38.5	–1.1	1.7	259	10:29.2	–0.7	1.3	278	10:17.7	–0.4	1.4	272
27	440	4.6	RD	196	6:39.1	–0.8	2.3	208	6:32.2	–0.9	1.5	238	6:17.2	–0.8	1.7	241
28	560	3.8	RD	206	0:31.5	0.7	1.6	206	After Moonrise				After Moonrise			
Nov. 26	890	4.5	RD	206	9:45.8	–1.1	–1.7	297	9:20.2	–1.3	–1.4	303	9:10.0	–1.6	–0.4	287
Dec. 21	440	4.6	DD	139	No Occultation				3:47.5			134	3:30.0			132
21	552	3.0	DD	149	21:17.7	0.2	1.1	104	After Moonrise				After Moonrise			
21	552	3.0	RB	150	22:00.0	0.4	1.8	221	22:12.7	0.4	1.4	238	After Moonrise			
24	Mars	–1.6	DD	184	No Occultation				1:48.6			153	1:41.8			149
24	Mars	–1.6	RD	184	No Occultation				2:10.5			202	2:05.5			205

					MASSACHUSETTS 72.5°W, 42.5°N				WASHINGTON, DC 77.0°W, 38.9°N				CHICAGO 87.7°W, 41.9°N			
DATE	ZC	MAG	PH	ELG °	TIME (UT)	A m	B m	P °	TIME (UT)	A m	B m	P °	TIME (UT)	A m	B m	P °
Jan. 15	2383	2.9	DB	316	16:13.8	–2.0	–2.1	140	16:11.9	–2.2	–2.2	144	15:44.7	–1.9	–1.3	136
15	2383	2.9	RD	317	17:06.7	–0.6	–0.2	226	17:04.0	–0.7	0.1	224	16:51.0	–1.5	–0.3	239
Feb. 7	1853	4.9	RD	238	Bright Twilight				Bright Twilight				12:02.5	–1.5	–1.6	293
18	Uran.	5.9	DD	14	16:58.5	–0.1	2.4	1	16:48.9	–0.1	2.7	358	No Occultation			
23	440	4.6	DD	75	4:15.6	0.3	–1.3	97	4:22.7	0.4	–1.8	114	4:19.8	0.1	–2.2	116
Mar. 1	1308	4.7	DD	147	0:44.3	–1.8	1.6	81	0:32.4	–1.6	0.9	96	0:22.0	–1.0	1.7	83
11	2383	2.9	DB	261	7:54.7	–1.1	0.3	122	7:50.4	–0.7	–0.2	137	After Moonrise			
11	2383	2.9	RD	261	9:15.3	–2.0	0.4	274	9:03.4	–2.3	0.9	262	8:44.2	–2.0	1.7	251
16	3190	3.0	DB	328	After Moonset				No Occultation				20:03.8	–1.1	–1.9	103
Apr. 19	552	3.0	DD	31	No Occultation				No Occultation				14:45.3			130
19	552	3.0	RB	31	No Occultation				No Occultation				15:11.3			185
30	1853	4.9	DD	157	6:55.8	–1.1	–1.7	101	6:56.8	–1.3	–1.7	108	6:36.4	–1.6	–1.6	114
May 4	2287	3.0	DB	200	3:14.3	–2.1	2.1	67	3:00.6	–1.4	1.3	87	After Moonrise			
4	2287	3.0	RD	200	4:07.6	–0.2	–1.0	341	4:07.9	–0.7	–0.5	323	4:00.5	–0.6	0.1	311
10	3171	3.8	RD	273	Bright Twilight				9:22.2	–2.3	0.2	296	9:01.1			315
10	3190	3.0	DB	275	13:15.7			141	No Occultation				12:25.9	–2.3	0.0	89
10	3190	3.0	RB	275	13:19.5			147	No Occultation				13:29.6	–0.5	1.3	199
19	890	4.5	DD	32	2:03.0	0.3	–1.0	84	2:08.1	0.3	–1.1	96	2:07.2	0.2	–1.4	103
27	1815	4.8	DD	127	5:21.1	–0.7	–2.3	147	5:26.6	–0.7	–2.5	154	5:10.8	–0.8	–2.4	158
Jun. 18	Ven.	–4.4	RB	44	13:46.9	0.5	2.6	238	After Moonrise				After Moonrise			
Jul. 3	3078	4.9	RD	212	4:33.6	–1.5	1.0	276	4:23.1	–1.4	1.1	272	4:14.7	–0.9	1.3	275
5	3353	3.8	RD	239	7:59.5	–1.9	0.8	255	7:47.5	–2.0	1.0	257	7:29.2	–1.9	0.9	280
Aug. 1	3307	4.9	RD	207	2:57.3	–0.7	2.1	209	2:46.1	–0.7	2.3	205	After Moonrise			
6	440	4.6	RD	275	6:15.2	–0.1	1.8	235	6:08.5	0.0	1.7	235	6:13.5	0.0	1.5	251
12	Merc.	–1.8	DB	355	14:36.6	–2.1	0.4	105	14:27.6	–1.9	–0.4	121	14:09.8	–1.4	0.4	114
12	Merc.	–1.8	RD	356	16:14.4	–1.6	–2.3	322	16:12.2	–2.3	–1.4	304	15:46.2	–2.0	–0.6	301
31	105	4.6	RD	217	3:32.3	–0.1	2.4	193	3:23.4	0.0	2.4	194	3:29.1	–0.1	2.0	211
Sep. 3	539	4.4	RD	259	6:29.6	–0.1	2.6	210	6:20.2	0.1	2.5	209	6:25.9	–0.2	1.9	233
3	541	4.0	RD	259	No Occultation				No Occultation				6:25.6	0.6	2.8	196
5	890	4.5	RD	286	No Occultation				No Occultation				7:38.6			199
Oct. 4	1170	3.7	RD	283	Bright Twilight				No Occultation				10:27.7			217
24	105	4.6	DD	162	23:19.7	–0.8	1.3	94	23:11.8	–0.7	1.2	94	23:11.2	–0.2	1.4	81
27	545	4.3	RD	206	23:13.5	0.9	2.0	196	After Moonrise				After Moonrise			
27	541	4.0	RD	206	23:18.1	0.0	0.6	299	After Moonrise				After Moonrise			
27	552	3.0	RD	206	23:45.3	0.6	1.8	215	23:41.9	0.7	1.7	214	After Moonrise			
Nov. 26	890	4.5	RD	206	10:19.0	–0.4	–2.0	303	10:23.0	–0.7	–1.5	287	10:08.7	–1.1	–1.3	281
Dec. 21	552	3.0	DD	149	No Occultation				No Occultation				21:11.2	–0.3	0.3	128
21	552	3.0	RB	150	No Occultation				No Occultation				21:38.2	0.9	2.5	193

DB/DD = Disappearance at Bright/Dark limb; RB/RD = Reappearance at Bright/Dark limb

See p. 138 for additional explanation of these tables.

TABLE OF TOTAL LUNAR OCCULTATION PREDICTIONS (continued)

					MIAMI 80.3°W, 25.8°N				ATLANTA 84.3°W, 33.8°N				AUSTIN 97.8°W, 30.2°N			
DATE	ZC	MAG	PH	ELG °	TIME (UT)	A m	B m	P °	TIME (UT)	A m	B m	P °	TIME (UT)	A m	B m	P °
Jan. 15	2383	2.9	DB	316	No Occultation				16:07.0	-2.5	-2.7	153	15:49.4			171
15	2383	2.9	RD	317	No Occultation				16:54.3	-1.2	1.0	218	16:22.1			212
Feb. 7	1853	4.9	RD	238	Bright Twilight				Bright Twilight				11:53.0	-3.7	-0.1	257
11	2287	3.0	RD	280	7:48.7	-0.8	0.6	280	After Moonrise				After Moonrise			
18	Uran.	5.9	DD	14	16:13.4	-0.9	2.4	21	16:33.8	0.1	3.3	353	No Occultation			
23	440	4.6	DD	75	No Occultation				4:45.6			161	No Occultation			
Mar. 1	1308	4.7	DD	147	0:32.7	-1.9	-2.1	146	0:18.9	-1.4	0.1	114	After Sunset			
11	2383	2.9	DB	261	No Occultation				7:54.1	0.8	-2.1	169	No Occultation			
11	2383	2.9	RD	261	No Occultation				8:36.1	-3.3	2.8	234	No Occultation			
24	810	1.8	DD	78	19:39.3			13	No Occultation				No Occultation			
24	810	1.8	RB	79	20:14.8			319	No Occultation				No Occultation			
Apr. 10	2784	3.4	RD	264	6:56.3	-0.7	0.5	282	After Moonrise				After Moonrise			
30	1853	4.9	DD	157	7:17.3	-1.3	-2.1	131	6:55.8	-1.5	-1.9	121	6:42.2	-1.5	-2.2	144
May 4	2287	3.0	DB	199	2:51.2	-0.4	-0.4	130	2:49.3	-0.5	0.4	114	After Moonrise			
4	2287	3.0	RD	200	4:06.2	-1.7	0.2	285	4:02.1	-1.1	0.2	298	3:43.8	-1.3	1.4	262
10	3171	3.8	RD	272	9:08.2	-2.0	0.8	270	9:05.6	-1.8	0.4	291	8:46.1	-0.9	0.7	284
10	3190	3.0	DB	274	No Occultation				12:43.8			124	11:57.0	-2.8	0.4	93
10	3190	3.0	RB	275	No Occultation				13:08.9			160	13:02.2	-0.7	2.3	194
19	890	4.5	DD	32	After Moonset				2:17.0	0.5	-1.4	116	2:31.1	0.8	-2.3	148
27	1815	4.8	DD	127	6:08.0			193	5:35.1	-0.7	-3.0	169	No Occultation			
Jun. 10	105	4.6	RD	295	8:53.9	-1.0	1.1	262	8:57.3	-1.2	0.7	286	8:43.7	-0.6	0.3	295
20	1487	1.3	DD	62	1:15.1	-2.0	-0.4	76	1:04.5			60	0:35.1	-2.0	-1.4	107
20	1487	1.3	RB	62	1:58.3	0.5	-3.2	357	1:32.7			13	1:46.5	-0.4	-2.5	332
Jul. 3	3078	4.9	RD	212	4:01.7	-1.4	1.5	248	4:07.8	-1.1	1.3	263	After Moonrise			
5	3353	3.8	RD	239	7:24.3	-1.8	1.6	239	7:27.6	-1.9	1.2	261	7:00.4	-1.4	1.1	271
Aug. 1	3307	4.9	RD	207	No Occultation				2:28.8	-0.6	2.7	195	No Occultation			
6	440	4.6	RD	275	5:45.8	0.4	1.9	214	6:00.7	0.2	1.6	235	After Moonrise			
12	Merc.	-1.8	DB	356	14:55.9	-1.0	-6.8	181	14:19.7	-1.7	-1.7	144	14:06.6	-1.5	-3.0	160
12	Merc.	-1.8	RD	356	15:58.9	-5.6	3.7	248	15:55.5	-3.1	0.5	276	15:10.3	-2.2	3.5	246
22	2383	2.9	DD	103	No Occultation				After Moonset				4:08.8	-2.2	-2.2	127
22	2383	2.9	RB	104	No Occultation				After Moonset				5:10.9	-0.3	0.2	230
31	105	4.6	RD	216	2:41.5			153	3:11.3	0.1	2.4	194	3:04.7	0.2	2.2	198
Sep. 3	541	4.0	RD	259	No Occultation				No Occultation				5:59.5			180
3	539	4.4	RD	259	Bright Limb				6:08.9	0.3	2.3	210	6:05.1	0.3	1.8	225:
17	2287	3.0	RB	68	17:15.9	-0.2	-0.3	307	After Moonrise				After Moonrise			
Oct. 24	105	4.6	DD	162	23:01.5			125	After Sunset				After Moonrise			
Nov. 3	1487	1.3	DB	289	11:37.5	-3.6	0.9	84	No Occultation				10:55.5	-1.8	0.8	95
3	1487	1.3	RD	289	12:39.2	-0.1	-4.0	358	No Occultation				12:09.6	-1.3	-2.3	333
26	890	4.5	RD	206	10:28.8	-1.8	0.4	241	10:21.1	-1.4	-0.6	261	9:51.1	-2.9	2.3	224

					KANSAS CITY 94.5°W, 39.0°N				DENVER 105.0°W, 39.8°N				NEW MEX., ARIZ. 109.0°W, 34.0°N			
DATE	ZC	MAG	PH	ELG °	TIME (UT)	A m	B m	P °	TIME (UT)	A m	B m	P °	TIME (UT)	A m	B m	P °
Jan. 15	2383	2.9	DB	316	15:35.3	-1.8	-1.3	144	15:18.2	-1.2	-1.2	153	15:28.8			181
15	2383	2.9	RD	316	16:39.5	-2.0	0.1	237	16:15.9	-2.6	0.7	235	15:52.5			212
Feb. 7	1853	4.9	RD	238	11:54.5	-2.1	-1.3	281	11:26.9	-3.2	0.0	261	No Occultation			
23	440	4.6	DD	75	4:30.3			141	No Occultation				No Occultation			
Mar. 11	2383	2.9	RD	261	8:20.1			222	No Occultation				No Occultation			
16	3190	3.0	DB	328	20:00.6	-1.4	-1.8	102	19:45.3	-1.3	-0.6	78	19:43.0	-1.9	-0.8	87
16	3190	3.0	RD	329	20:43.5	0.3	1.5	191	20:44.9	-0.2	0.6	212	20:49.0	-0.2	1.0	207
Apr. 19	552	3.0	DD	30	14:38.1	-0.7	0.4	123	14:35.6	0.0	0.9	105	After Moonrise			
19	552	3.0	RB	31	15:08.9	0.8	2.7	192	15:16.9	0.5	2.0	213	15:07.7	0.7	2.0	206
30	1853	4.9	DD	156	6:30.3	-1.6	-1.7	126	6:12.8	-1.4	-1.7	141	6:19.1	-1.0	-2.3	159
May 4	2287	3.0	RD	200	3:55.0	-0.7	0.6	293	After Moonrise				After Moonrise			
10	3171	3.8	RD	272	8:53.2			307	After Moonrise				After Moonrise			
10	3190	3.0	DB	274	12:09.8	-2.2	0.6	82	11:50.2	-1.7	1.2	67	11:35.6	-1.8	1.3	71
10	3190	3.0	RD	275	13:20.8	-0.9	1.4	207	13:08.8	-1.5	1.1	227	12:54.9	-1.6	1.5	223
19	890	4.5	DD	32	2:12.9	0.2	-1.6	118	After Sunrise				2:30.6.	1.0	-3.4	160
27	1815	4.8	DD	127	5:13.3	-0.6	-2.8	172	5:09.4			193	No Occultation			
Jun. 20	1487	1.3	DD	62	0:34.2	-2.7	-0.5	77	0:08.6	-2.2	-0.9	101	0:07.6	-1.9	-1.6	123
20	1487	1.3	RB	62	1:21.9	0.3	-3.2	359	1:18.3	-0.5	-2.6	337	1:29.0	-1.1	-2.2	318
Jul. 5	3353	3.8	RD	239	7:14.1	-1.7	0.9	284	6:59.4	-1.2	0.7	297	6:51.1	-0.9	0.8	286
Aug. 6	440	4.6	RD	275	6:10.1	0.2	1.3	253	After Moonrise				After Moonrise			
12	Merc.	-1.8	DB	355	14:0.5	-1.2	0.0	124	13:50.9	-0.7	0.5	117	13:47.9	-0.8	-0.5	135
12	Merc.	-1.8	RD	356	15:32.5	-2.0	0.5	286	15:14.9	-1.4	0.8	286	15:02.0	-1.2	1.9	264
22	2383	2.9	DD	103	3:58.9	-1.6	-1.6	111	3:39.0	-1.9	-1.1	102	3:37.3	-2.3	-1.2	109
22	2383	2.9	RB	103	After Moonset				5:00.3	-1.1	-1.1	262	5:00.7	-1.3	-0.7	255
31	105	4.6	RD	217	3:22.7	0.0	2.0	212	3:24.7	0.1	1.8	219	After Moonrise			
Sep. 3	539	4.4	RD	259	6:20.0	0.0	1.7	237	6:21.3	0.0	1.4	252	6:13.7	0.2	1.4	247

TABLE OF TOTAL LUNAR OCCULTATION PREDICTIONS (continued)

					KANSAS CITY (cont) 94.5°W, 39.0°N				DENVER (cont) 105.0°W, 39.8°N				NEW MEX., ARIZ (cont) 109.0°W, 34.0°N			
DATE	ZC	MAG	PH	ELG °	TIME (UT)	A m	B m	P °	TIME (UT)	A m	B m	P °	TIME (UT)	A m	B m	P °
Sep. 3	541	4.0	RD	259	6:21.6	0.5	2.5	202	6:27.6	0.3	1.9	221	6:18.4	0.6	1.9	215
5	890	4.5	RD	286	7:35.9	1.0	3.1	204	7:45.6	0.6	2.0	227	7:36.9	0.9	2.1	217
Oct. 4	1170	3.7	RD	282	No Occultation				10:03.5			218	No Occultation			
27	440	4.6	RD	196	No Occultation				6:04.7	0.3	4.1	183	5:39.2			163
Nov. 3	1487	1.3	DB	288	No Occultation				11:05.2			51	10:42.8	−1.2	1.5	86
3	1487	1.3	RD	289	No Occultation				11:32.3			10	11:47.6	−1.2	−1.9	333
26	890	4.5	RD	206	10:02.3	−1.6	−0.6	265	9:43.1	−1.9	0.0	258	9:29.1	−2.5	2.0	231
Dec. 21	552	3.0	RB	150	21:37.5	0.9	2.2	197	After Moonrise				After Moonrise			

					LOS ANGELES 118.3°W, 34.1°N				N. CALIFORNIA 122.0°W, 38.0°N				HONOLULU 157.9°W, 21.3°N			
DATE	ZC	MAG	PH	ELG °	TIME (UT)	A m	B m	P °	TIME (UT)	A m	B m	P °	TIME (UT)	A m	B m	P °
Jan. 0	537	3.8	DD	140	After Moonset				11:37.2	0.5	−2.0	123	No Occultation			
0	539	4.4	DD	140	After Moonset				11:49.4	−0.4	0.2	43	No Occultation			
0	541	4.0	DD	140	After Moonset				11:56.4	0.0	−0.6	70	No Occultation			
5	1308	4.7	RD	203	No Occultation				No Occultation				11:35.4	−3.8	1.5	254
22	3353	3.8	DD	41	After Moonset				After Moonset				5:21.6	−0.5	0.8	45
29	810	1.8	DD	134	No Occultation				No Occultation				9:40.6	−3.0	2.0	48
29	810	1.8	RB	134	No Occultation				No Occultation				10:34.8	−0.3	−3.4	325
Feb. 3	1487	1.3	DB	196	After Moonset				15:8.5	0.4	−2.5	171	No Occultation			
Mar. 10	2263	4.8	RD	251	No Occultation				No Occultation				12:06.8	−1.3	0.1	288
16	3190	3.0	DB	328	19:26.5	−1.7	0.2	67	19:22.5	−1.3	0.6	51	18:04.2	−1.4	2.5	27
16	3190	3.0	RD	329	20:35.6	−0.7	0.7	218	20:34.1	−1.0	0.2	235	19:13.1	−2.7	0.5	269
23	539	4.4	DD	58	After Moonset				6:37.5	0.4	−1.3	104	No Occultation			
28	1308	4.7	DD	120	No Occultation				No Occultation				7:27.1	−2.3	−1.6	120
Apr. 19	552	3.0	RB	31	15:14.0	0.6	1.6	218	15:22.2	0.5	1.5	229	After Moonrise			
26	1487	1.3	DD	114	After Moonset				9:46.4	0.1	−1.9	134	No Occultation			
30	1853	4.9	DD	156	6:13.9	0.2	−3.2	182	6:02.7	0.2	−2.9	182	No Occultation			
May 7	2784	3.4	RD	239	Bright Twilight				Bright Twilight				14:12	−2.9	0.8	253
10	3190	3.0	DB	274	11:20.8	−1.4	1.6	65	11:22.5	−1.2	1.7	58	After Moonrise			
10	3190	3.0	RD	274	12:39.2	−1.7	1.5	236	12:38.5	−1.7	1.4	245	After Moonrise			
31	2287	3.0	DD	172	After Moonset				After Moonset				10:48.9	−3.5	0.9	66
31	2287	3.0	RB	172	After Moonset				After Moonset				12:7.4	−2.7	−2.7	322
Jun. 19	1487	1.3	DD	61	23:51.7	−1.5	−1.9	141	23:39.2	−1.5	−1.5	136	No Occultation			
20	1487	1.3	RB	62	1:15.4	−1.8	−1.6	300	1:02.8	−1.8	−1.5	301	No Occultation			
Jul. 5	3353	3.8	RD	238	6:45.5	−0.4	0.8	288	After Moonrise				After Moonrise			
16	Sat.	0.6	DD	29	No Occultation				No Occultation				20:35.7	−1.2	−1.0	133
16	Sat.	0.6	RB	30	No Occultation				No Occultation				21:52.6	−2.0	0.1	282
Aug. 12	Merc.	−1.8	DB	355	13:42.8	−0.3	0.0	127	13:43.4	−0.1	0.7	110	After Moonrise			
12	Merc.	−1.8	RD	355	14:53.7	−0.7	1.6	268	14:56.2	−0.6	1.0	284	After Moonrise			
22	2383	2.9	DD	103	3:14.6	−2.5	−0.8	108	3:03.4	−2.3	−0.4	103	No Occultation			
22	2383	2.9	RB	103	4:45.8	−1.9	−0.7	264	4:35.3	−2.0	−0.9	272	No Occultation			
Sep. 3	539	4.4	RD	259	6:16.3	0.3	1.1	257	6:21.6	0.3	1.0	268	After Moonrise			
3	541	4.0	RD	259	6:23.6	0.5	1.6	227	6:31.2	0.5	1.4	237	After Moonrise			
21	2784	3.4	DD	107	No Occultation				4:49	−3.3	−2.2	127	After Sunrise			
23	3078	4.9	DD	133	No Occultation				No Occultation				7:18.2			131
23	3078	4.9	RD	133	No Occultation				No Occultation				7:38.6			158
Oct. 4	1170	3.7	RD	282	9:40.5			204	9:56.7	0.1	2.6	234	After Moonrise			
27	440	4.6	RD	196	5:47.2	0.0	2.9	197	5:56.2	−0.4	2.3	215	5:22.6	0.3	1.3	235
Nov. 3	1487	1.3	DB	288	10:34.2	−0.7	1.4	87	10:39.6	−0.5	2.6	69	After Moonrise			
3	1487	1.3	RD	289	11:37.0	−1.1	−1.3	327	11:27.0	−0.8	−2.1	343	After Moonrise			
26	890	4.5	RD	205	9:07.7	−2.2	2.5	229	9:07.3	−1.9	1.4	246	7:52.4	−0.1	2.1	227
Dec. 4	1853	4.9	RD	304	No Occultation				No Occultation				13:26.5	−0.1	−0.6	309
31	1815	4.8	RD	272	No Occultation				No Occultation				12:42.5	−0.7	−0.9	314

DB/DD = Disappearance at Bright/Dark limb; RB/RD = Reappearance at Bright/Dark limb

See p. 138 for additional explanation of these tables.

TABLE OF GRAZING LUNAR OCCULTATION PREDICTIONS

The table below and on p. 147 lists lunar grazing occultation predictions for much of North America for 2007. The eight maps on pp. 148–151 show the graze tracks (see the descriptive text on pp. 138–141).

For each graze is given:

No. .... a chronological sequential number used on the maps
Date .... the date
USNO d... the star's USNO (U.S. Naval Observatory) reference number (see the bottom of p. 139) and its duplicity code (in the **"d"** column—see section (C) on pp. 141–142 concerning double stars)
m.............. its visual magnitude
%sl .... the percent of the Moon sunlit (+ for waxing, – for waning, E for lunar eclipses)
L .... whether the track is a northern (N) or southern (S) limit
W.U.T. ..... the Universal Time at the west end of the track
Lo., La...... the longitude and latitude of the west end of the track

No.	Date	USNO	d	m	%sl	L	W.U.T.	Lo.	La.
1	Jan. 1	647	Y	5.4	92+	S	0:19.0	–116	45
2	4	1170	A	3.6	99–	S	10:37.6	–65	55
3	8	1600		5.0	78–	S	8:52.4	–130	45
4	9	1692	M	6.9	71–	S	6:52.8	–120	39
5	10	1779		6.5	61–	S	7:42.5	–116	46
6	11	1884		5.2	52–	S	9:00.4	–122	44
7	13	2084		6.5	33–	S	7:35.5	–60	51
8	15	2370		6.9	15–	S	12:35.2	–104	44
9	15	2383		2.8	15–	S	15:12.5	–130	49
10	16	2519		7.3	9–	S	12:04.4	–101	25
11	20	3190	J	2.9	4+	S	23:26.7	–94	30
12	21	3324		6.9	9+	S	22:48.0	–79	34
13	22	3470		7.1	17+	S	23:33.6	–91	36
14	24	64		6.5	29+	S	2:31.0	–130	29
15	25	196	O	7.0	40+	S	2:11.9	–124	20
16	25	203		6.8	40+	S	2:59.7	–130	43
17	27	470	D	6.8	63+	N	5:10.6	–100	40
18	28	616		5.4	73+	N	3:47.1	–101	30
19	29	771	T	6.0	82+	N	2:44.3	–87	50
20	29	797	J	6.3	83+	N	7:58.8	–89	55
21	31	1088		5.8	95+	N	2:59.3	–80	52
22	Feb. 6	1735		6.3	86–	S	2:36.1	–78	24
23	6	1744		6.4	86–	S	6:47.6	–86	55
24	7	1853	V	4.8	77–	S	10:17.3	–130	53
25	9	2045	M	6.4	61–	S	6:18.5	–90	32
26	9	2051		5.9	61–	S	7:05.4	–103	31
27	9	X20283	M	6.8	59–	S	11:52.7	–118	55
28	9	2066	Y	6.6	59–	S	11:54.0	–118	55
29	10	2174	K	6.5	50–	S	11:33.8	–101	55
30	11	2297		7.0	41–	S	9:40.9	–105	36
31	13	X24317		7.1	22–	S	10:18.2	–91	29
32	13	2609	V	4.7	21–	S	13:01.1	–116	44
33	14	2784	V	3.3	13–	N	13:15.5	–122	34
34	20	19		7.5	8+	S	1:40.8	–121	53
35	21	145		6.8	15+	S	1:27.6	–114	41
36	21	166	D	6.7	16+	S	4:25.6	–130	40
37	21	X01570		7.3	16+	S	4:23.3	–130	53
38	23	440	M	4.7	36+	S	4:07.0	–130	42
39	23	438	O	6.8	36+	N	4:26.0	–95	55
40	23	536	V	5.5	45+	S	22:02.3	–66	52
41	23	541	V	3.9	45+	S	22:23.5	–74	50
42	23	538	V	5.7	45+	N	22:35.4	–69	55
43	23	543	K	6.4	45+	S	22:37.3	–71	42
44	23	548	K	6.8	45+	S	22:59.0	–77	46
45	23	555		6.4	45+	S	23:34.2	–82	23
46	24	571	J	6.8	46+	S	0:54.2	–101	24
47	24	569	O	5.3	46+	N	0:58.4	–94	29
48	24	574	K	6.8	46+	S	1:11.5	–106	26
49	24	571	J	6.8	46+	N	1:49.1	–60	55
50	24	579		6.3	46+	N	2:36.2	–101	34
51	25	731		6.0	57+	N	1:20.9	–104	41
52	Feb 25	756		6.6	60+	N	6:58.0	–81	55
53	25	771	T	6.0	61+	N	9:19.2	–130	40
54	25	885	Y	5.6	67+	S	23:48.7	–92	49
55	26	897		6.3	68+	N	2:37.0	–105	23
56	Mar. 1	1308	V	4.7	92+	N	0:45.6	–106	50
57	3	1600		5.0	0E	S	23:47.6	–83	37
58	4	X16547		8.9	14E	S	0:02.9	–82	44
59	6	1815	V	4.7	95–	S	10:31.0	–73	55
60	8	2011		6.3	84–	S	6:23.3	–117	42
61	9	2108	O	6.5	77–	S	4:14.4	–83	22
62	9	2109		6.0	77–	S	4:49.2	–90	25
63	11	2383		2.8	58–	S	8:04.5	–100	41
64	12	2538		6.7	47–	S	11:09.9	–126	38
65	13	2688		7.0	38–	S	8:52.8	–81	37
66	22	370	K	6.1	12+	N	1:25.5	–107	21
67	23	518	O	6.0	21+	N	2:31.3	–123	39
68	23	X04688	C	7.1	22+	N	4:39.1	–130	39
69	24	810	Y	1.6	40+	N	19:35.7	–94	20
70	25	1008		5.3	52+	N	23:56.9	–82	49
71	26	1022	M	6.0	53+	N	1:37.4	–109	28
72	26	1026	C	6.5	53+	N	2:21.3	–120	30
73	26	1035	X	6.7	54+	N	4:25.9	–130	53
74	26	1042		6.7	55+	N	6:31.8	–73	55
75	31	1600		5.0	95+	N	7:07.4	–122	55
76	Apr. 8	2496		7.0	73–	S	10:18.7	–130	47
77	12	3081		6.5	33–	N	10:22.9	–97	46
78	13	3237	V	4.3	22–	N	12:44.3	–130	30
79	15	X31927		7.1	6–	N	10:49.7	–92	22
80	20	603		7.5	9+	N	0:44.4	–90	27
81	20	X05382	V	7.2	9+	N	1:20.0	–89	53
82	20	X05494		7.2	10+	N	3:38.5	–128	46
83	20	768		7.0	16+	N	23:47.5	–78	27
84	21	771	T	6.0	17+	N	0:06.5	–78	42
85	21	797	J	6.3	19+	N	4:09.5	–124	55
86	23	1105	V	6.5	36+	N	0:44.3	–89	35
87	23	1108	V	7.0	37+	N	1:42.0	–107	22
88	25	1383		6.6	61+	N	8:09.2	–130	46
89	28	1660	A	6.5	84+	N	2:46.1	–119	34
90	May 4	2287	W	2.9	97–	S	3:13.4	–104	25
91	4	2287	W	2.9	97–	N	3:46.0	–77	55
92	6	2586	K	6.0	86–	N	7:42.8	–127	37
93	7	2784	V	3.3	77–	S	14:48.5	–120	20
94	9	3031		5.9	60–	N	7:40.2	–104	25
95	10	3171	V	3.7	49–	N	8:42.5	–101	46
96	10	3190	J	2.9	47–	S	12:15.9	–97	20
97	11	3307	V	4.8	37–	N	7:53.3	–90	24
98	14	166	D	6.7	9–	N	9:12.5	–81	27
99	14	173		6.5	8–	N	10:34.7	–102	27
100	18	X06319	V	7.3	3+	N	5:04.1	–130	54
101	19	885	Y	5.6	7+	N	1:32.5	–90	45
102	19	X07872		7.0	7+	N	3:01.8	–82	55

TABLE OF GRAZING LUNAR OCCULTATION PREDICTIONS (continued)

No.	Date	USNO	d	m	%sl	L	W.U.T.	Lo.	La.
103	May 20	X10230		7.5	15+	N	3:46.0	−127	37
104	21	1208	M	6.4	24+	N	4:19.2	−91	55
105	22	1329	M	6.8	32+	N	3:35.2	−120	42
106	22	Saturn		0.8	39+	S	17:59.2	−116	52
107	24	1531	Y	6.0	52+	N	2:40.4	−72	55
108	24	1547	M	3.8	53+	N	5:18.6	−130	43
109	Jun. 1	2383		2.8	100−	S	3:18.1	−62	55
110	10	105		4.4	29−	N	8:33.7	−106	34
111	12	X03537	V	7.2	11−	N	8:23.6	−78	24
112	12	399	Z	5.7	10−	N	9:57.0	−104	26
113	13	539	V	4.3	4−	N	10:41.4	−105	28
114	13	536	V	5.5	4−	N	10:45.4	−112	40
115	13	542		5.8	4−	N	10:55.1	−105	25
116	13	543	K	6.4	4−	N	11:00.3	−107	28
117	13	X04845	M	7.2	4−	N	11:05.0	−115	41
118	13	541	V	3.9	4−	N	11:06.2	−118	38
119	13	552	K	2.9	4−	S	11:09.9	−110	23
120	13	548	K	6.8	4−	N	11:25.9	−115	32
121	17	X11340	V	7.4	5+	N	3:24.1	−109	45
122	19	1395		6.3	19+	N	3:58.9	−123	41
123	20	1487	A	1.4	26+	N	0:22.7	−103	55
124	21	1589		5.9	35+	N	2:15.4	−106	29
125	26	2084		6.5	81+	N	1:38.7	−86	43
126	Jul. 3	3113	K	5.4	91−	N	11:40.0	−127	20
127	5	3353		3.7	77−	N	6:45.5	−119	47
128	5	3360		6.2	76−	N	7:22.0	−130	30
129	12	X07045	X	7.4	5−	N	10:59.5	−120	42
130	19	1652	U	5.4	21+	S	3:44.8	−96	33
131	23	X20283	M	6.8	59+	N	6:03.5	−130	50
132	23	2066	Y	6.6	59+	N	6:04.8	−130	50
133	24	2164	C	6.5	67+	S	4:46.1	−94	35
134	25	2276		5.6	75+	N	0:45.6	−72	48
135	Aug. 2	3459		6.3	87−	N	8:30.3	−76	20
136	2	3474		5.9	87−	N	10:24.8	−114	20
137	5	317		6.4	57−	N	8:59.3	−130	47
138	6	438	O	6.8	46−	N	5:40.7	−92	33
139	7	X05148		7.5	34−	N	5:16.5	−77	37
140	7	603		7.5	33−	N	8:46.7	−84	20
141	7	X05382	V	7.2	33−	N	9:46.6	−130	39
142	7	616		5.4	33−	N	10:45.2	−106	20
143	8	746	A	7.0	24−	N	5:55.2	−88	52
144	8	756		6.6	23−	N	7:15.2	−89	30
145	8	771	T	6.0	23−	N	9:05.0	−100	20
146	8	773	C	7.0	23−	N	9:46.2	−130	54
147	8	810	Y	1.6	21−	N	16:50.4	−130	25
148	10	X10660	X	7.4	7−	N	8:38.3	−74	22
149	10	X10805		7.3	7−	N	10:33.1	−102	23
150	10	X10949		7.5	7−	N	12:18.0	−128	24
151	11	1239		6.6	3−	N	10:09.4	−86	30
152	22	2383		2.8	61+	S	4:44.9	−100	20
153	28	3282		7.8	18E	N	9:24.9	−126	38
154	28	3286		7.2	0E	N	10:52.1	−130	20
155	28	3282		7.8	0E	S	9:50.3	−91	20
156	28	X30653		7.8	0E	S	9:53.0	−130	39
157	28	X30642		8.6	0E	S	9:37.5	−130	36
158	28	X30667		8.9	0E	S	10:17.7	−130	53
159	Sep. 3	538	V	5.7	60−	N	5:50.1	−110	25
160	3	555		6.4	59−	N	7:00.5	−127	27
161	3	569	O	5.3	59−	N	8:18.7	−94	20
162	3	571	J	6.8	59−	N	8:30.4	−130	37
163	3	574	K	6.8	59−	N	9:00.0	−130	45
164	3	579		6.3	59−	N	9:25.3	−119	20
165	4	701	G	6.5	49−	N	2:49.9	−63	41
166	4	731		6.0	48−	N	8:12.1	−94	20
167	5	885	Y	5.6	37−	N	6:38.3	−105	40
168	5	890	V	4.6	37−	S	8:01.0	−57	53
169	5	X08040		6.7	36−	N	10:01.6	−130	36
170	6	1056		7.2	26−	N	7:47.3	−82	20
171	6	X10230		7.5	26−	N	9:40.4	−124	31
172	6	1067	K	7.1	26−	N	9:50.1	−106	20
173	7	X12068	M	7.4	16−	N	11:11.6	−130	33
174	8	X13328		7.5	10−	N	7:24.7	−69	46
175	8	1329	M	6.8	9−	N	10:39.3	−110	34
176	Sep. 21	2784	V	3.3	64+	S	4:56.8	−130	27
177	23	3078	M	4.9	84+	S	8:21.7	−130	44
178	23	3171	V	3.7	89+	S	22:28.5	−69	41
179	25	3353		3.7	97+	S	9:26.0	−130	48
180	29	370	K	6.1	91−	N	8:27.0	−129	20
181	30	518	O	6.0	82−	N	9:39.7	−130	35
182	Oct. 1	647	Y	5.4	75−	S	3:26.6	−115	52
183	1	701	G	6.5	73−	S	10:27.2	−92	36
184	2	840	V	6.3	63−	S	7:43.1	−55	48
185	3	1013	O	7.0	52−	N	6:03.2	−112	43
186	3	1035	X	6.7	51−	N	9:29.1	−111	20
187	3	1042		6.7	50−	N	11:19.1	−130	46
188	4	1170	A	3.6	40−	S	9:32.9	−115	35
189	5	1304	M	6.8	29−	S	10:51.9	−108	38
190	6	1395		6.3	21−	N	7:50.8	−96	54
191	14	X21768		7.2	12+	S	22:53.2	−80	43
192	15	2287	W	2.9	13+	N	2:29.0	−120	20
193	15	2406		6.0	18+	S	22:56.3	−82	39
194	17	2702		6.8	36+	S	23:36.2	−90	31
195	22	3383		6.2	85+	S	22:57.5	−85	40
196	24	105		4.4	98+	S	23:05.4	−86	22
197	27	545		4.1	95−	S	22:52.4	−68	38
198	27	561	K	5.0	95−	S	23:52.6	−80	36
199	28	560	U	3.6	95−	S	0:01.1	−88	42
200	29	771	T	6.0	87−	N	5:28.8	−99	20
201	30	909	T	6.0	79−	N	0:20.5	−66	45
202	31	1117	K	5.0	67−	S	7:49.9	−130	44
203	Nov. 1	1269		6.9	55−	S	11:39.8	−130	48
204	2	1370	V	6.9	46−	N	6:48.2	−100	35
205	2	1387	K	7.0	44−	S	12:10.3	−130	38
206	3	1466	V	5.3	36−	S	6:15.9	−84	47
207	3	1476		7.1	35−	S	10:09.5	−74	55
208	3	1487	A	1.4	34−	N	11:00.5	−130	42
209	4	X16391	V	7.4	25−	S	12:07.1	−130	31
210	5	X17525		7.2	16−	S	14:38.0	−130	50
211	6	X18381		7.2	10−	S	14:12.3	−130	40
212	13	2660		6.2	14+	S	23:45.9	−95	22
213	17	3084		6.7	40+	S	1:41.1	−123	20
214	18	3333	M	6.4	61+	S	23:38.2	−78	20
215	19	X31039		7.0	62+	S	3:32.4	−130	22
216	24	552	K	2.9	100+	S	12:51.6	−97	55
217	26	890	V	4.6	96−	S	8:04.7	−130	26
218	27	1061		6.2	90−	S	7:51.4	−130	35
219	27	1062	K	6.4	89−	S	8:23.0	−130	45
220	28	1221	V	6.0	80−	S	11:24.7	−130	35
221	29	1322		6.4	73−	S	5:44.1	−116	53
222	29	1340		6.6	72−	S	9:15.3	−130	49
223	29	1343		6.3	72−	S	9:53.6	−130	55
224	30	1420		6.6	63−	S	3:38.0	−76	47
225	30	1434		5.4	63−	S	6:03.7	−107	31
226	30	1449		6.5	61−	S	10:11.2	−130	43
227	Dec. 2	1652	U	5.4	41−	S	11:22.6	−130	47
228	3	1731		7.5	33−	S	7:01.6	−72	52
229	3	X17979		7.5	32−	S	8:39.8	−102	27
230	3	1747		7.5	31−	S	11:51.5	−130	37
231	4	1845	A	6.5	23−	S	13:21.7	−89	55
232	7	X20931		7.2	5−	S	11:03.7	−74	40
233	7	2174	K	6.5	4−	S	14:55.4	−116	51
234	8	2287	W	2.9	2−	S	11:39.2	−87	23
235	8	2287	W	2.9	2−	N	12:08.2	−64	53
236	12	2899		7.5	9+	S	20:39.6	−61	45
237	15	X29959	A	7.2	25+	S	1:29.3	−78	20
238	15	3181	V	6.0	25+	S	2:11.0	−113	20
239	17	3459		6.3	48+	S	7:00.4	−130	43
240	20	317		6.4	81+	S	8:51.4	−130	54
241	21	440	M	4.7	87+	S	3:25.1	−130	43
242	21	545		4.1	93+	S	21:08.6	−80	51
243	21	552	K	2.9	93+	S	21:18.4	−85	38
244	21	561	K	5.0	93+	S	22:09.4	−90	48
245	21	560	U	3.6	93+	S	22:16.8	−101	54
246	22	647	Y	5.4	96+	S	12:33.5	−110	55
247	24	Mars		−1.4	100−	S	1:46.1	−130	42
248	26	1277		5.3	93−	S	08:26.6	−130	39

GRAZING OCCULTATION MAPS

JANUARY 1 – FEBRUARY 15

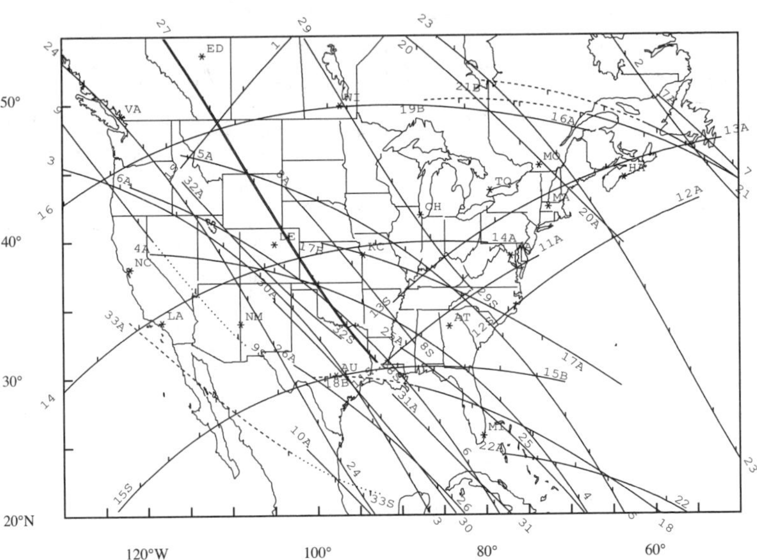

FEBRUARY 16 – MARCH 15

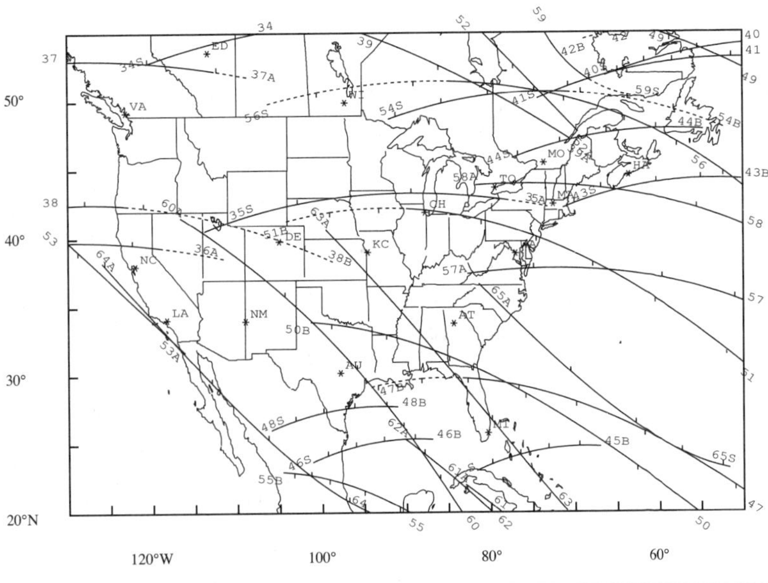

GRAZING OCCULTATION MAPS (continued)

MARCH 16 – MAY 15

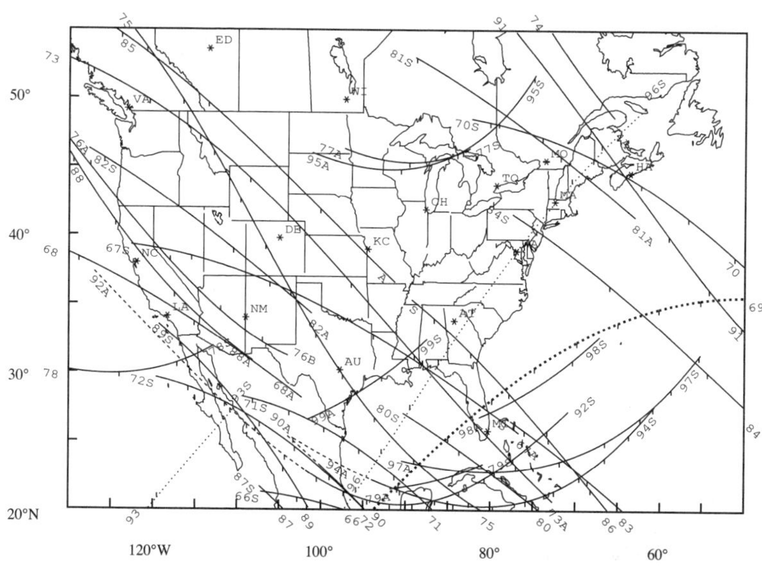

MAY 16 – JUNE 30

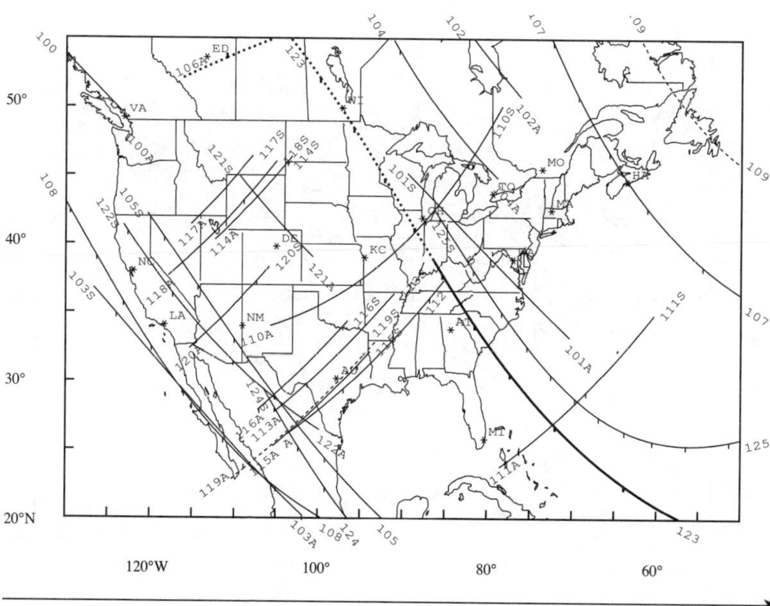

GRAZING OCCULTATION MAPS (continued)

JULY 1 – AUGUST 31

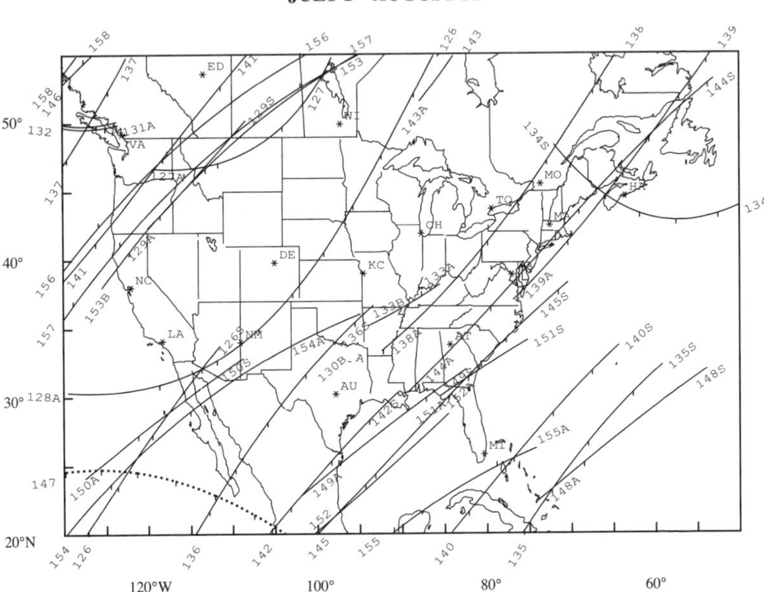

SEPTEMBER 1 – OCTOBER 14

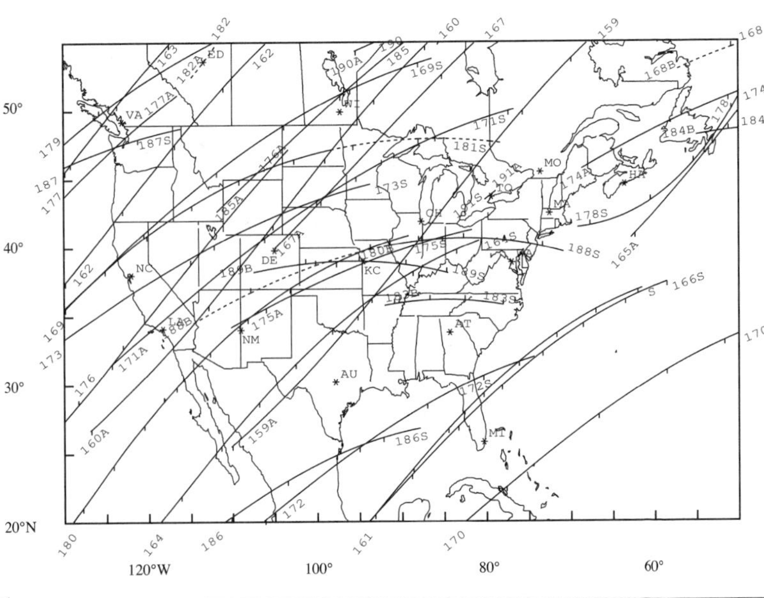

GRAZING OCCULTATION MAPS (continued)

OCTOBER 15 – NOVEMBER 25

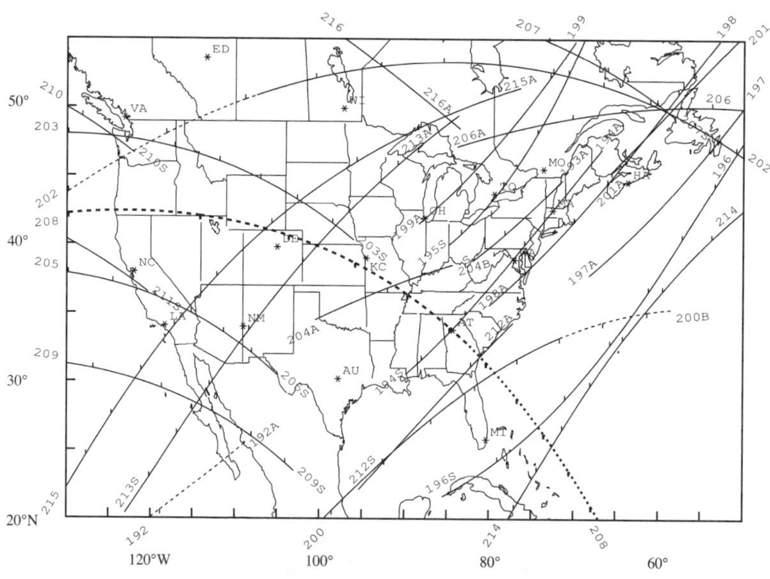

NOVEMBER 26 – DECEMBER 31

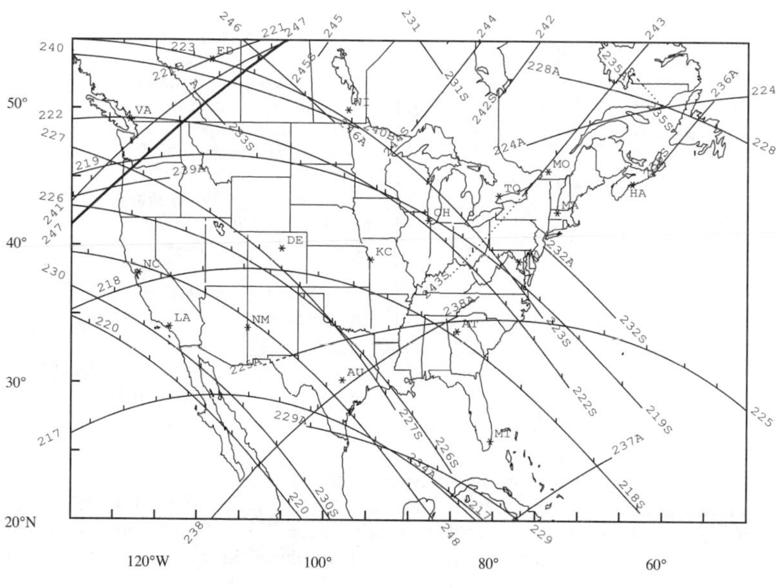

TIDES AND THE EARTH–MOON SYSTEM

BY ROY BISHOP

The tidal aspect of gravitation produces some of the most interesting phenomena in the universe, from the structure of interacting galaxies, such as M51, to the volcanoes of Io, the fragmentation of Comet Shoemaker-Levy 9 by Jupiter in 1992, the synchronous rotation of our Moon, and the pulse of the seas on our planet. Perhaps because they occur at our feet, the tides of the oceans are often overlooked when considering the heavens; yet the pulse of the tides is the heartbeat of a greater universe beyond Earth.

Newtonian Tides

Tides were known to the ancients, but an understanding of their origin came only three centuries ago with the publication of Newton's *Principia* (1687). In the Newtonian context, the decrease of the force of gravity with distance causes the tides. The Moon exerts a force on Earth, and Earth responds by accelerating toward the Moon; however, the waters on the hemisphere facing the Moon, being closer to the Moon, accelerate more and fall ahead of Earth. Similarly, Earth itself accelerates more than the waters on the other hemisphere and falls ahead of these waters; the Moon is yanking Earth out from under the waters on the more distant hemisphere, leaving these waters behind. Thus two tidal bulges are produced, one on the side of Earth facing the Moon and one on the side facing away from the Moon. Because the Moon is quite far from Earth (about 60 Earth radii), these two tidal bulges are essentially equal in size.

Note that the waters directly under the Moon and the waters farthest from the Moon do not rise up because of the slightly larger and smaller, respectively, lunar gravity at these two locations; all that results from the Moon's action on the waters at these two points is a slight decrease in the pressure on the floor of the sea. The two tidal bulges form because the variation in the Moon's gravity causes the *surrounding* waters on each hemisphere to flow horizontally across Earth's surface into these regions:

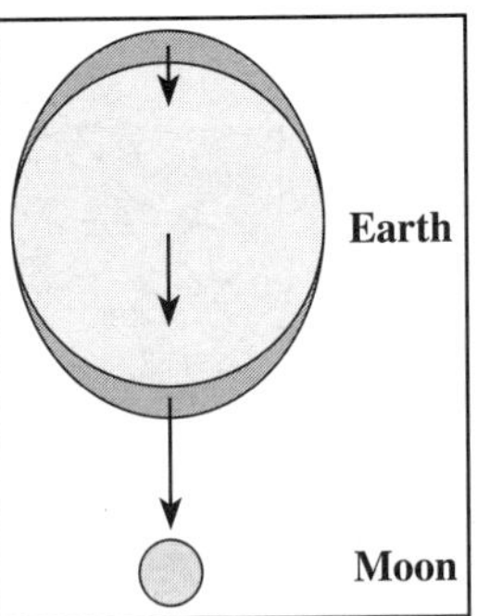

In order of decreasing length, the arrows indicate the force per unit mass (acceleration) produced by the Moon's gravity on the near side, centre, and far side of Earth. It is the resulting horizontal flow of the water across Earth's surface toward the two points nearest and farthest from the Moon that produces the two tidal bulges (indicated by heavy shading).

As Earth rotates on its axis, the orientation of these two bulges in relation to the Moon remains fixed; hence the rise and fall of the oceans on Earth. If Earth had no rigidity, the entire planet would flex freely in the same fashion, and there would be virtually no water tides. The very existence of the ocean tides indicates that on a time scale of several hours our planet displays considerable rigidity.

Because of the Moon's orbital motion, it transits on average 50.47 min later each day. Thus on successive days, high tides recur about 50 min later; or for the many regions experiencing two high tides daily, these tides recur at intervals of 12 h 25 min.

The Sun exerts a gravitational force 180 times stronger than that exerted by the Moon on Earth; however, because the Moon is so much closer, the *variation* in the Moon's force across Earth's diameter is about 2.2 times larger than the variation in the Sun's force. As described above, it is this variation that produces tides; thus the pair of bulges raised by the Moon is considerably larger than the pair raised by the Sun. As the Moon goes through its monthly cycle of phases, these two pairs of tidal bulges get in and out of step, combining in step to produce *spring tides* (no connection with the season) when the Moon is new or full (syzygy) and out of step to produce *neap tides* when the Moon is at first or last quarter (quadrature).

Another factor having a substantial influence on tidal ranges is the elliptical shape of the Moon's orbit. The Moon is only 9% to 12% closer at perigee than at apogee; however, because the *variation* in its gravitational force varies inversely as the cube of its distance (the force itself varies inversely as the square of the distance), the Moon's tidal influence is 31% to 49% greater at perigee than at apogee. Because the Sun tidally influences the shape of the Moon's orbit, exceptionally close perigees coincide with full or new Moon, and the resulting extreme tides are known as *perigean spring tides*. If the lunar orbit were fixed in orientation, such tides would recur at half-year intervals; however, the major axis of the lunar orbit rotates prograde with a period of 8.85 years, making the average interval between perigean spring tides about 23 days longer than half a year (206 days).

Influences on the Tides

Many astronomical factors influence the tides. These can be sorted according to the periods they produce. In ascending order, the periods of the more important components are as follows:

(1) semidiurnal, 12 h 00 min (two solar-induced tidal bulges, as described above);

(2) semidiurnal, 12 h 25 min (two lunar-induced tidal bulges, as described above);

(3) diurnal, 24 h 00 min (the usual nonzero declination of the Sun shifts the pair of solar tidal bulges out of Earth's equatorial plane, resulting in a tidal component with a one-day period);

(4) diurnal, 24 h 50 min (the usual nonzero declination of the Moon shifts the pair of lunar tidal bulges out of Earth's equatorial plane, resulting in a tidal component with a one-day period; this is the dominant tide in some areas, such as parts of the southern coast of Canada's Gulf of St. Lawrence);

(5) semimonthly, 13.66 days (variation in the Moon's declination);

(6) semimonthly, 14.77 days (spring–neap cycle, described above);

(7) monthly, 27.55 days (perigee–apogee cycle, described above);

(8) semiannual, 182.62 days (variation in the Sun's declination);

(9) semiannual, 206 days (perigean spring cycle, described above);

(10) annual, 365.26 days (perihelion–aphelion cycle);

(11) 8.85 years (prograde precession of the lunar perigee); and

(12) 18.61 years (retrograde precession of the nodes of the lunar orbit).

In addition to astronomical factors, the tides on Earth are strongly influenced by the sizes, boundaries, and depths of ocean basins and inlets and by Earth's rotation, winds, and barometric pressure fluctuations. Using Newton's gravitation and laws of motion, the French physicist Pierre-Simon Laplace (1749–1827) developed the dynamical theory of the tides on the rotating Earth (*Mécanique Céleste,* 1799), but because of the complexity of the tides the full application of his theory was not possible until the advent of the digital computer in the last third of the 20th century.

Tides typically have ranges (vertical high to low) of a metre or two, but there are regions in the oceans where the various influences conspire to produce virtually no tides at all and others where the tides are greatly amplified. Among the latter regions are the Sea of Okhotsk, the Gulf of Alaska, the northern coast of Australia, the English Channel, and in Canada, Ungava Bay in northern Québec and the Bay of Fundy between New Brunswick and Nova Scotia. The tidal ranges in these regions are of the order of 10 m.

Fundy Tides

Only two localities on Earth sometimes have a vertical tide range exceeding 16 m (52 ft.), and both are in Canada: Minas Basin, the eastern extremity of the Bay of Fundy in Nova Scotia, and Leaf Basin, a remote inlet on the southwestern side of Ungava Bay in northern Québec. The current best data give Minas Basin a slight edge; however, several years of tide gauge data continuing through the year 2015 are needed to determine which site, if either (to the precision that measurements can be made), has the greater tide range. (In 2015, the 18.61-year lunar cycle will next have its peak effect on the tides; see below.)

The primary cause of the immense tides of Fundy is a resonance of the Bay of Fundy/Gulf of Maine system. The system is effectively bounded at its outer end by the edge of the continental shelf with its approximately 40:1 increase in depth. The system has a natural period of approximately 13 hours, a *Q*-value[(1)] of about 5, and is driven near resonance, not directly by the Moon, but by the dominant semidiurnal tides of the Atlantic Ocean. Like a father pushing his daughter on a swing, the gentle Atlantic tidal pulse pushes the waters of the Bay of Fundy/Gulf of Maine basin at nearly the optimum frequency to cause a large oscillation. The seventh Astronomer Royal, G.B. Airy (1801–1892), first developed the theory of the behaviour of tides in restricted arms of the ocean such as the Fundy system.

Fundy tides are unique in that they respond more to the perigee–apogee influence than they do to the spring–neap influence. This is because the lunar tidal period (12.4 hours) is closer to the system's resonant period than is the solar tidal period (12.0 hours). Although the variation in the Moon's distance is not obvious when viewing the Moon directly, near the head of the Bay of Fundy the 3-m to 6-m *increase* in the vertical tidal range makes it obvious when the Moon is near perigee, clear skies or cloudy!

The most dramatic view of the vertical range of Fundy tides is at the Minas Basin Pulp & Power Company wharf in the town of Hantsport, Nova Scotia. Remarkably, this site is practically unknown; it is not advertised, and no special provisions have been made to accommodate spectators.

Perhaps the most awesome display of the tides on our planet occurs at Cape Split, Nova Scotia, on the southern side of the entrance to Minas Basin. (Cape Split may be reached by a pleasant two-hour walk along a popular hiking trail from the village of Scots Bay.) Here, at the time of the midpoint of an incoming tide, for a considerable distance the forest on the towering cliffs is filled with a hollow roar produced by the turbulence of the waters surging over the submarine ridges below. The currents exceed 8 knots (4 m/s), and the flow in the deep, 5-km-wide channel on the north side of Cape Split equals the combined flow of all the streams and rivers of Earth ($\approx$4 km^3/h). Three hours later the spectacle pauses and then begins flowing in the opposite direction.

The highest of the high tides in the Bay of Fundy occur when a perigean spring high tide coincides with a low barometric-pressure storm system sweeping northward

---

(1) The *Q*-value, or quality-value, of an oscillator indicates its efficiency. A large *Q* means low energy loss per cycle and a well-defined resonant frequency. A *Q* of 5 is relatively small, indicative of considerable damping in the Fundy system, yet it is large enough to make these tides among the highest on Earth.

across New Brunswick, accompanied by hurricane-force southerly winds over the Gulf of Maine and the Bay of Fundy. The close Moon, the in-phase solar tide, the reduced air pressure above the water, and the wind drag pushing more water into the Bay of Fundy (the last two effects are called a storm surge) all contribute to an especially high tide. An additional favourable influence is if all this occurs near an equinox, for then the axis of the tidal bulges of the spring tide is at a right angle to Earth's rotation axis, optimizing the tidal range (if the axes were parallel there would be no tidal cycle). This right-angle-axes enhancement of the tides is strengthened in those years when the declination range of the Moon (±18° to ±29°) is near a minimum, a situation that recurs with the 18.61-year period of the retrograde motion of the nodes of its orbit. (The declination range was at its ±18° minimum in 1959, 1978, and 1997 and will be again in 2015. See p. 79 for the shift in the longitude of the ascending node of the Moon's orbit during 2007.) Furthermore, since perihelion occurs in January, the highest tides of all tend to occur just prior to the March equinox or after the September equinox. The infamous Bay of Fundy "Saxby gale" of 1869 Oct. 5 was a time when all seven of these factors approximately coincided (perigee, spring tide, low pressure, south wind, equinox, minimum declination range, and perihelion enhancement). Since weather is unpredictable, so, too, is the next major tidal flood in the Bay of Fundy.

Paradoxically, the large tides of Fundy protect its shores from flooding associated with most storm surges, since the normal variation in its high tide levels is already several metres. Only those rare storm surges that happen to coincide with a perigean spring high tide will be a problem. In contrast, shorelines with small tides are much more susceptible to storm surges.

Sea level is slowly increasing in the Bay of Fundy region. This is bringing the resonant period of the Fundy/Gulf of Maine system closer to the lunar tidal period which, in turn, is causing Fundy tides to gradually become even larger (by a few centimetres per decade).

Tidal Friction

Tidal friction, which occurs primarily in shallow seas around the margins of the oceans, transforms Earth's rotational kinetic energy into heat at a rate of about 3.5 TW. This is comparable to humankind's total rate of energy use. Approximately 1% of this energy transformation occurs in the Bay of Fundy, and, since 1984, a tiny portion of this (20 MW peak) is being turned into commercial electric power at the Annapolis Basin tidal power plant in Nova Scotia. The only other large-scale tidal power installation is in France on the Rance estuary (240 MW peak).

Tidal friction also transfers angular momentum from Earth to the Moon, lengthening the day and increasing the size of the orbit of the Moon. The day is lengthening by about 1 s every 40 000 years—imperceptible on a human time scale but of profound significance to Earth's rotation over a few billion years. (For example, 900 million years ago, when Earth was already 80% of its present age, there were about 480 18-hour days in a year.) The Moon is receding about 3.8 cm per year, with the result that about one billion years from now total solar eclipses will cease. Presently we are well into the transitional phase: Annular eclipses already outnumber total solar eclipses. New moons occur, on average, almost one day earlier each successive month; however, because of the increasing size of the lunar orbit, in about 300 million years the lunar (synodic) month will have lengthened to equal the average calendar month (although the average month will then contain only about twenty-eight 26-hour days).

If the Sun does not first incinerate our planet, there will come a day that is as long as the lunar month (each then equal to about 40 present days), and a more distant Moon will stand stationary in the sky, as does Earth now in the lunar sky. But this situation will not endure, for solar tides will still be present and will reduce the angular momentum of the Earth–Moon system, causing the Moon to approach Earth once more.

General Relativity and Tides

Einstein's theory of gravitation, general relativity, superseded Newton's theory nearly a century ago, yet descriptions of the tides almost invariably ignore Einstein (as has this article to this point). The reasons for using the older, wrong theory are: (1) Newton's theory describes the gentle tides on Earth to high accuracy; (2) the mathematics involved is much simpler than that of general relativity; (3) the Newtonian description of the tides is compatible with cultivated common sense. Because of this last reason, Newton's concepts regarding motion and gravitation form the essential foundation for anyone attempting to understand the tides. One must climb up on Newton's towering shoulders before it is possible to focus clearly on Einstein.

As mentioned in the section ORBITAL MOTION (see pp. 27–28), Newton's Euclidean universe with its force of gravity never did exist. Although Newton's ideas are more than adequate for describing the tides on Earth, for some purposes, such as the Global Positioning System (GPS), Newton's concepts of space, time, and gravitation are inadequate. We inhabit an Einsteinian universe, a universe in which gravitation is a manifestation of the structure of spacetime, the four-dimensional stage of our existence in which space and time are interwoven. The geometry of spacetime is curved by the mass–energy of matter, and the curvature tells matter how to move.

The Moon's mass alters the structure of spacetime at its location, and this distortion propagates outward, becoming more dilute with the volume encompassed according to the inverse cube of the distance. At Earth, the distortion results in the waters of the oceans following slightly different paths through spacetime than does the rigid planet beneath, producing the characteristic egglike shape of the tidal effect. The tidal heartbeat is that of the very fabric of spacetime. The tides at our feet carry a profound message.

References

For more information, see the superb introduction *The Tides* by E.P. Clancy, Anchor Books, Doubleday and Co., 1969 (now, unfortunately, out of print). For a detailed account of the evolution of our understanding of the tides see *Tides, A Scientific History,* by D.E. Cartwright, Cambridge University Press, 1999. (Note, however, that neither Clancy nor Cartwright mentions general relativity.) For a popular account of general relativity, see *A Journey into Gravity and Spacetime,* by J.A. Wheeler, Scientific American Library, 1990. An article dealing specifically with the tides of Fundy and tidal power installations has been written by Christopher Garrett (*Endeavour, 8* (1984), No. 2, pp. 58–64). The major astronomical factors influencing the tides (the phases, perigees, and apogees of the Moon) are tabulated in THE SKY MONTH BY MONTH section (pp. 83–105) of this Handbook. These may be perused to determine days favourable for large tides. Detailed predictions for tides in Canadian waters, produced by the Department of Fisheries and Oceans Canada, are published in *Canadian Tide and Current Tables,* the six volumes of which are individually available from Canadian Government bookstores and other authorized chart dealers; see www.lau.chs-shc.dfo-mpo.gc.ca for a list of dealers and also for predictions for particular locations.

Editor's Note: Roy Bishop has walked the shores and sailed the waters of Minas Basin for over half a century, and enjoys showing visitors the exceptional tides. He can be contacted at rg@ns.sympatico.ca.

THE SUN

EPHEMERIS FOR THE SUN

Sundial Correction

The **Greenwich Transit** time in the table overleaf may be used to calculate the sundial correction at the observer's position. For example, to find the correction at Halifax on 2007 Aug. 10, determine the following: At Greenwich the Sun transits at 12:05:33 on Aug. 9 and at 12:04:55 on Aug. 13. Thus, to the nearest minute, on Aug. 10 at both Greenwich and Halifax the Sun will transit at 12:05 local mean solar time (LMT), or 12:19 Atlantic Standard Time (AST) since Halifax has a longitude correction of +14 min (see the 3rd paragraph on p. 164). Thus a 5-minute correction must be added to the reading of a simple sundial to obtain LMT, an additional 14 minutes must be added to obtain AST, and a further 1 hour for Atlantic Daylight Time (ADT).

A figure accurate to a second or two can be obtained by interpolating for longitude. The interpolated transit time at Greenwich for Aug. 10 is 12:05:23, the daily change in time being –9.5 s. Adjusting this for the longitude of Halifax:

12 h 5 min 23 s – (9.5 s × 4 h 14 min ÷ 24 h) = 12 h 5 min 21 s.

Thus the sundial correction is 5 min 21 s. To find the standard time of the Sun's transit to the nearest second or two, the observer's longitude must be known to 10″ or better. For example, suppose an observer in Halifax is at longitude 63°25′30″W, or 4 h 13 min 42 s W of Greenwich. The time of transit will be 12:05:21 + 13 min 42 s = 12:19:03 AST or 13:19:03 ADT.

Orientation of the Sun

The table overleaf gives three angles that specify the orientation of the Sun.

P is the position angle of the axis of rotation, measured eastward in the observer's sky from the north point on the disk. Note that P varies between +26° (solar north pole tilted eastward) and –26° (tilted westward) during the year. This tilt is associated mainly with the inclination of the ecliptic in the observer's sky, with a smaller contribution from the Sun's 7.2° inclination to the ecliptic (the longitude of the ascending node of the solar equator on the ecliptic is 76°).

B_0 is the heliographic latitude of the centre of the disk, and is the result of the Sun's 7.2° inclination to the ecliptic. Note that positive values of B_0 correspond to the solar equator passing south of the centre of the disk, with the solar north pole being tipped toward the observer.

L_0 is the heliographic longitude of the centre of the disk measured from Carrington's solar prime meridian in the direction of rotation. L_0 decreases about 13° per day. The dates during the year when L_0 = 0° are given in the table below. The rotation period of the Sun depends upon heliographic latitude. The synodic and sidereal periods of rotation at the solar equator are 27.2753 days and 25.38 days, respectively.

Commencement (UT) of Numbered Synodic Solar Rotations

No*	Commences	No	Commences	No	Commences	No	Commences
2051	'06 Dec. 12.17	2055	Mar. 31.49	2059	Jul. 18.38	2063	Nov. 4.42
2052	'07 Jan. 8.50	2056	Apr. 27.75	2060	Aug. 14.60	2064	Dec. 1.73
2053	Feb. 4.84	2057	May 24.98	2061	Sep. 10.85	2065	Dec. 29.05
2054	Mar. 4.18	2058	Jun. 21.18	2062	Oct. 8.12		

*Based on R.C. Carrington's Greenwich photoheliocentric series in which rotation no. 1 commenced 1853 Nov. 9.

EPHEMERIS FOR THE SUN, 2007

Date 0h UT	Apparent RA (2007) h m	Apparent Dec ° ′	Greenwich Transit UT	Orientation P	Orientation B_0	Orientation L_0
Jan. 1	18 39.8	−23 07	12:03:26	+2.7	−2.9	111.9
5	19 01.9	−22 41	12:05:16	+0.3	−3.4	46.0
9	19 19.4	−22 11	12:06:59	−1.6	−3.9	353.4
13	19 36.8	−21 35	12:08:34	−3.6	−4.3	300.7
17	19 54.0	−20 52	12:10:00	−5.4	−4.7	248.0
21	20 11.0	−20 02	12:11:14	−7.3	−5.1	195.4
25	20 27.8	−19 07	12:12:16	−9.0	−5.4	142.7
29	20 44.5	−18 05	12:13:05	−10.8	−5.8	90.0
Feb. 2	21 00.8	−16 59	12:13:40	−12.4	−6.1	37.4
6	21 17.0	−15 48	12:14:03	−14.0	−6.3	344.7
10	21 33.0	−14 33	12:14:13	−15.5	−6.6	292.0
14	21 48.7	−13 13	12:14:11	−16.9	−6.7	239.4
18	22 04.3	−11 51	12:13:57	−18.3	−6.9	186.7
22	22 19.7	−10 25	12:13:32	−19.5	−7.1	134.0
26	22 34.9	−8 56	12:12:57	−20.6	−7.2	81.3
Mar. 2	22 49.9	−7 26	12:12:13	−21.7	−7.2	28.6
6	23 04.9	−5 54	12:11:20	−22.6	−7.2	335.9
10	23 19.7	−4 21	12:10:22	−23.5	−7.2	283.2
14	23 34.4	−2 46	12:09:18	−24.2	−7.2	230.5
18	23 49.0	−1 11	12:08:10	−24.8	−7.1	177.8
22	0 03.6	+0 24	12:07:00	−25.3	−7.0	125.1
26	0 18.2	+1 58	12:05:47	−25.8	−6.8	72.3
30	0 32.8	+3 32	12:04:35	−26.0	−6.7	19.6
Apr. 3	0 47.3	+5 05	12:03:23	−26.2	−6.5	326.8
7	1 01.9	+6 36	12:02:14	−26.3	−6.2	274.0
11	1 16.6	+8 06	12:01:08	−26.2	−5.9	221.2
15	1 31.3	+9 33	12:00:07	−26.1	−5.6	168.4
19	1 46.2	+10 58	11:59:12	−25.8	−5.3	115.6
23	2 01.1	+12 20	11:58:23	−25.4	−5.0	62.8
27	2 16.2	+13 39	11:57:42	−24.8	−4.6	9.9
May 1	2 31.4	+14 54	11:57:08	−24.2	−4.2	317.1
5	2 46.7	+16 05	11:56:43	−23.5	−3.8	264.2
9	3 02.2	+17 12	11:56:26	−22.6	−3.4	211.3
13	3 17.8	+18 14	11:56:20	−21.6	−2.9	158.4
17	3 33.6	+19 12	11:56:22	−20.5	−2.5	105.5
21	3 49.6	+20 04	11:56:34	−19.3	−2.0	52.6
25	4 05.6	+20 51	11:56:53	−18.0	−1.6	359.7
29	4 21.9	+21 32	11:57:21	−16.7	−1.1	306.8
Jun. 2	4 38.2	+22 07	11:57:55	−15.2	−0.6	253.8
6	4 54.6	+22 35	11:58:36	−13.7	−0.1	200.9
10	5 11.2	+22 58	11:59:21	−12.1	+0.4	148.0
14	5 27.7	+23 14	12:00:11	−10.4	+0.8	95.0
18	5 44.4	+23 24	12:01:03	−8.7	+1.3	42.1
22	6 01.0	+23 26	12:01:56	−6.9	+1.8	349.1
26	6 17.6	+23 23	12:02:47	−5.1	+2.3	296.2
30	6 34.2	+23 12	12:03:36	−3.3	+2.7	243.2
Jul. 4	6 50.8	+22 56	12:04:21	−1.5	+3.2	190.3
8	7 07.2	+22 32	12:05:01	+0.3	+3.6	137.3
12	7 23.6	+22 03	12:05:35	+2.1	+4.0	84.4
16	7 39.8	+21 28	12:06:02	+3.9	+4.4	31.5
20	7 55.9	+20 46	12:06:21	+5.6	+4.8	338.5
24	8 11.9	+19 59	12:06:31	+7.4	+5.1	285.6
28	8 27.7	+19 07	12:06:31	+9.0	+5.4	232.7
Aug. 1	8 43.3	+18 10	12:06:21	+10.6	+5.8	179.8
5	8 58.8	+17 08	12:06:02	+12.2	+6.0	126.9
9	9 14.1	+16 01	12:05:33	+13.7	+6.3	74.0
13	9 29.2	+14 51	12:04:55	+15.2	+6.5	21.1
17	9 44.2	+13 37	12:04:09	+16.5	+6.7	328.2
21	9 59.1	+12 19	12:03:13	+17.8	+6.9	275.4
25	10 13.8	+10 58	12:02:11	+19.0	+7.0	222.5
29	10 28.5	+9 34	12:01:02	+20.2	+7.1	169.7
Sep. 2	10 43.0	+8 08	11:59:47	+21.2	+7.2	116.8
6	10 57.5	+6 40	11:58:28	+22.2	+7.2	64.0
10	11 11.9	+5 10	11:57:05	+23.0	+7.2	11.2
14	11 26.2	+3 38	11:55:41	+23.8	+7.2	318.4
18	11 40.6	+2 06	11:54:16	+24.5	+7.2	265.6
22	11 54.9	+0 33	11:52:50	+25.0	+7.1	212.8
26	12 09.3	−1 00	11:51:26	+25.5	+7.0	160.0
30	12 23.7	−2 34	11:50:05	+25.9	+6.8	107.2
Oct. 4	12 38.2	−4 07	11:48:49	+26.1	+6.6	54.4
8	12 52.8	−5 39	11:47:38	+26.3	+6.4	1.6
12	13 07.5	−7 10	11:46:34	+26.3	+6.1	308.8
16	13 22.3	−8 40	11:45:38	+26.2	+5.8	256.1
20	13 37.3	−10 07	11:44:51	+26.0	+5.5	203.3
24	13 52.4	−11 32	11:44:14	+25.6	+5.2	150.6
28	14 07.7	−12 55	11:43:49	+25.2	+4.8	97.8
Nov. 1	14 23.2	−14 14	11:43:35	+24.6	+4.4	45.0
5	14 38.9	−15 30	11:43:34	+23.8	+4.0	352.3
9	14 54.9	−16 41	11:43:47	+23.0	+3.6	299.6
13	15 11.1	−17 48	11:44:14	+22.0	+3.1	246.8
17	15 27.5	−18 50	11:44:54	+21.0	+2.7	194.1
21	15 44.1	−19 47	11:45:47	+19.8	+2.2	141.4
25	16 01.0	−20 38	11:46:52	+18.4	+1.7	88.6
29	16 18.0	−21 22	11:48:10	+17.0	+1.2	35.9
Dec. 3	16 35.2	−22 01	11:49:39	+15.5	+0.7	343.2
7	16 52.6	−22 32	11:51:18	+13.9	+0.2	290.5
11	17 10.2	−22 57	11:53:05	+12.2	−0.3	237.8
15	17 27.8	−23 14	11:54:58	+10.4	−0.8	185.1
19	17 45.6	−23 24	11:56:56	+8.6	−1.4	132.4
23	18 03.3	−23 26	11:58:54	+6.7	−1.9	79.7
27	18 21.0	−23 21	12:00:53	+4.8	−2.4	27.0
31	18 38.8	−23 08	12:02:50	+2.8	−2.8	334.3

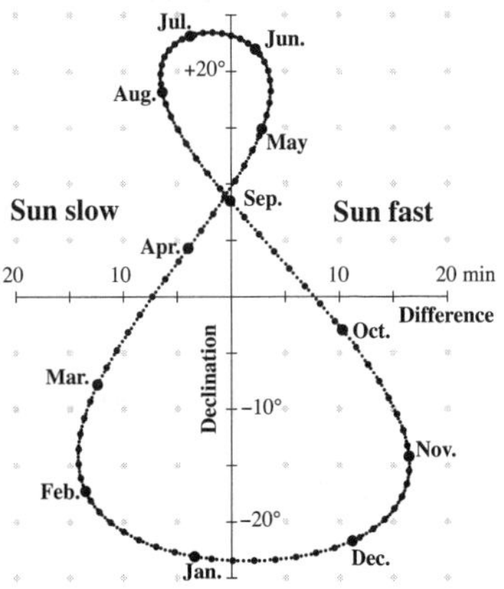

The bowling-pin-shaped analemma depicts the drift of apparent solar time or sundial time relative to local mean time (horizontal axis) and the changing declination of the Sun (vertical axis) during 2007. For points to the left of the vertical axis ("Sun slow") the Sun transits after 12:00 local mean time. To the right ("Sun fast"), the Sun transits before 12:00 local mean time. For each month, a heavy dot marks day 1 with medium dots for days 5, 9, 13, 17, 21, 25, and 29. *See pp. 36–37 for further details.*

SOLAR ACTIVITY
BY KEN TAPPING

Solar Activity Cycle 23*, which peaked in 2000, continues to fall. From the rate of decline apparent in July this year (see the Figure) it is clear we have not yet reached the next activity minimum, which is unlikely to occur before the middle of 2007 at the earliest. Compared with other cycles monitored since 1947, Cycle 23 had a low maximum, barely exceeding 200 solar flux units (sfu, see explanation below). Particularly noteworthy of Cycle 23 was a dramatic resurgence of activity that started in late 2001 and persisted into 2002, when it ended as sharply as it began. This Cycle was markedly different from its two predecessors: Cycles 21 and 22. Its noisy peak and gradual decline with repeated episodes of activity make it more like Cycles 20 and 18.

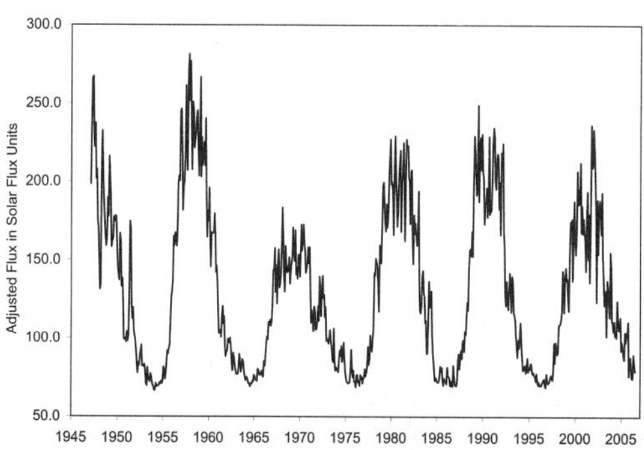

The figure shows solar activity as represented by the adjusted 10.7-cm solar microwave flux activity index (see p. 163) from 1950 to the present. The plotted values are averaged values of the index over each solar (≈27-day) rotation. The ≈11-year activity cycle is clearly evident, as are the dramatic resurgence of activity during 2001 and the frequent resurgences of activity during the Cycle's decline.

Solar activity is fundamentally a magnetic phenomenon. Deep below the photosphere, differential rotation and convection cause the solar material to move in a complex manner. The density of this material is high enough for its movement to drag the magnetic fields along with it. This generates electric currents, which in turn produce magnetic fields. The result is a complex system of subphotospheric "magnetic flux ropes." The penetration of sections of these flux ropes through the photosphere and into the chromosphere and corona gives rise to the many observed forms of solar activity. Above the photosphere the situation is strikingly different: the density is much lower, and the magnetic fields trap and confine the ionized gas of the solar atmosphere, supporting loops and filaments and forming the diverse menagerie of photospheric, chromospheric, and coronal structures with which we are familiar, such as sunspots, active regions, complexes of activity, and systems of loops. Changing emissions in the X-ray and ultraviolet wavelengths, and at radio wavelengths, are due to the changing amount of trapped plasma and the strengths of the magnetic fields containing them. The Sun's total energy output is also affected by magnetic activity, fortunately only slightly.

The organization of the subphotospheric magnetic fields gives rise to a consistent pattern in the magnetic configuration of active regions. Each region is magnetically bipolar, with the bipoles arranged east–west on the disk. All bipoles lying in the same hemisphere are arranged with the same magnetic polarity leading (facing in the direction in which the region appears to move as it is carried across the disk by solar rotation—westward in the observer's sky). In the other hemisphere the leading and following magnetic polarities are reversed.

*The numbering system for solar activity cycles was started by Rudolph Wolf, who arbitrarily designated the activity maximum of 1750 as that of Cycle 1.

Exceptions do occur. Regions are sometimes formed that have a magnetic orientation perpendicular to or even the reverse of the norm for that hemisphere. Such regions usually try to move into the conventional orientation but are impeded by the magnetic linkages formed with their surroundings. These regions tend to produce flares as potential energy builds up in their magnetic structures and is subsequently released catastrophically.

The "conventional" magnetic configurations for active regions reverse on alternate activity cycles. For example, during Cycle 22, active regions in the northern solar hemisphere were oriented with their "negative" (i.e. south-seeking) magnetic polarity ends leading and "positive" (north-seeking) ends following, with the reverse situation in the southern hemisphere. In Cycle 23 this arrangement is reversed. A *magnetic* activity cycle, which is probably a more realistic description of the rhythms of solar activity, is equal to two of Wolf's activity cycles and takes about 22 years to complete.

Active regions are not isolated phenomena; they occur in complexes, comprising several active regions at various stages of development, together with the network of elements remaining from decayed regions. This localization of activity gives rise to a rotational modulation of the 10.7-cm flux as active region clusters are carried across the disk and disappear around the west limb. To smooth out this modulation in long-term studies of solar activity, the data are averaged over solar rotations rather than by month. Active regions can persist for one or more solar rotations and the complexes for a dozen or so.

The large-scale organization of solar magnetic activity is also apparent in the spatial distribution of active regions during the solar cycle. The first activity of the new cycle is marked by the formation of active regions at high latitudes. As activity builds toward the maximum of the cycle, the number of active regions increases, and they tend to form at lower latitudes. As the activity wanes toward the next minimum, the number of regions decreases, but the average latitude continues to decrease until the last activity of the cycle is located near the equator. Then, as the new cycle starts, new active regions form at high latitudes.

The formation of a new active region begins with the emergence through the photosphere into the overlying chromosphere and corona of magnetic loops. This is heralded by the appearance of small pores, about 1000 km across, which coalesce and spread into a patch of magnetic flux that may exceed 50 000 km in length. The average magnetic field strength in such patches is of the order of 0.01 T (100 gauss). The emergence of these magnetic fields modifies the spatial and density structure of the chromosphere, giving rise to enhanced emission in the calcium and magnesium II K spectral lines. These bright patches (called plage), which stand out prominently in filtergrams, are the most conspicuous aspect of active regions. In some areas of the new active region, magnetic field strengths reach or exceed 0.1 T. These magnetic fields are strong enough to impede the transfer of energy from within the Sun, leading to these patches being cooler (3000 K) compared with the surrounding photosphere, which has a temperature of about 6000 K. Although actually quite hot and shining quite brightly, in contrast with their hotter surroundings these flux concentrations appear as dark spots: sunspots. As a region grows, one or more large spots form at the leading end, and a scattering of smaller ones form at the trailing end. Sunspots are a prominent feature of active regions and are the aspect of solar activity that has been longest known.

The growth of the new active region continues through repeated episodes of magnetic flux emergence. In general, the size is directly proportional to the total magnetic flux in the region. Growth stops when the emergence of new magnetic flux ceases. Soon after, the region starts to decay. This proceeds partly by the resubmergence of magnetic flux and partly by fragmentation. The spots disappear, and eventually, all that remains is a large area of magnetic flux arranged in a network pattern, blending in slowly with the remains of other decayed active regions.

Repeated episodes of magnetic-flux emergence, together with motions of the footpoints, which are the photospheric anchors of magnetic loops, lead to the magnetic field overactive regions becoming complex and tangled and storing enormous amounts of energy. The relaxation of these fields is an important aspect of the evolution and dissipation of active regions. In some cases, this can occur noncatastrophically; otherwise, stresses increase until various plasma instabilities allow rapid relaxation and reconnection of the magnetic fields and a rapid release of the stored energy. These energy releases are known as flares.

The Solar Wind and Aurorae

The solar atmosphere is not stable. It is constantly flowing outward as a stream of particles and magnetic fields—the *solar wind*. The flow is strongest where the magnetic loops are very large and impose the least drag on the outwardly flowing particles. Because of their lower coronal densities, these regions produce a lower flux of X-rays and appear in X-ray images as dark patches, known as "coronal holes." The solar wind is not homogeneous or steady; its speed, density, and direction can change according to the positions of coronal holes and the nature of current solar activity.

The solar wind profoundly changes Earth's magnetic field. The wind pressure pushes the field out of its dipole shape into a long teardrop. The magnetic geometry in the tail of the drop makes it the site of many plasma instabilities. The flow of the solar wind over the boundary of Earth's magnetic field (the magnetopause) excites many types of waves, which move along Earth's magnetic field lines and which can be detected on the ground at high magnetic latitudes. Increases in the density or velocity of the solar wind change the pressure equilibrium between the solar wind and the magnetosphere, producing fluctuations in the strength and direction of the magnetic field lines at ground level. If the fluctuations are strong enough, the events are referred to as magnetic storms and substorms. These can disrupt any human activity that involves connected metal networks covering large geographical areas, especially at high magnetic latitudes.

Complex interactions between the solar wind and Earth's magnetic field lead to an accumulation of trapped particles in the magnetosphere. During magnetic storms, instabilities and waves excited in the magnetosphere by the solar wind accelerate some of the trapped particles downward along Earth's magnetic field into increasingly dense atmosphere, where they collide with the atmospheric constituents, exciting them with sufficient energy to produce light. These displays are called aurorae, or the northern and southern lights: *aurora borealis* and *aurora australis,* respectively. Views from space show that aurorae fall in a rough circle (the auroral oval), centred around the magnetic pole, that is, in a definite band of magnetic latitudes. As activity increases, the auroral oval expands, covering lower and lower magnetic latitudes. It also becomes increasingly distorted. During the period of very high activity in March 1989, auroral displays were seen as far south as the Caribbean.

Aurorae occur in many forms and can be steady, moving, or rapidly pulsating, depending upon the nature of the particle streams causing them. Aurorae can appear green or red, although if they are faint, the eye cannot respond in colour and they appear grey. The greenish colour is due to spectral lines from oxygen (558 nm) and a range of lines from nitrogen covering the band 391 nm to 470 nm. Under highly disturbed conditions, red spectral-line emissions at 630 nm and 636 nm and in a series of bands between 650 nm and 680 nm can also be seen. The green emissions are produced at a height of about 110 km; the red, 630-nm and 636-nm emissions, due

AURORAL FORMS

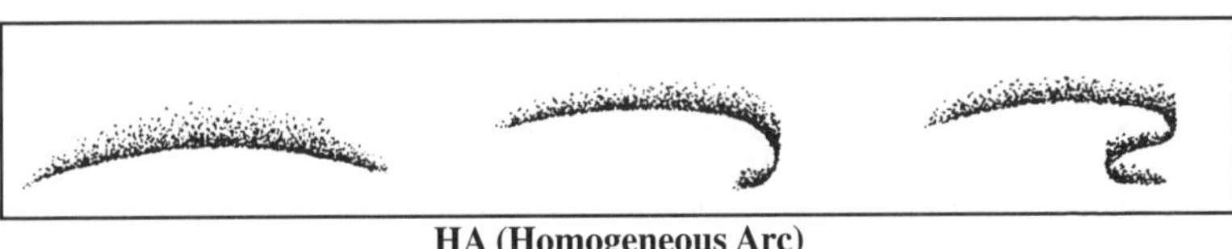

HA (Homogeneous Arc)

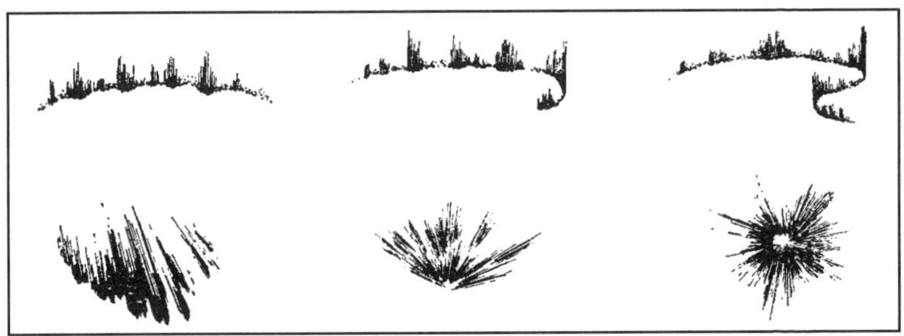

RA (Rayed Arc)

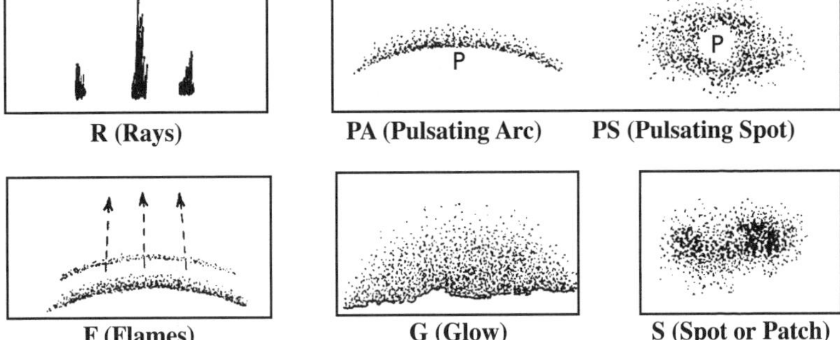

R (Rays) **PA (Pulsating Arc)** **PS (Pulsating Spot)**

F (Flames) **G (Glow)** **S (Spot or Patch)**

The above sketches illustrate standard auroral forms. This simplified classification was devised for visual observers during the International Geophysical Year over five decades ago (1957–58). Although there is great variety in auroral patterns, the sketches emphasize fundamental features and minimize variations that depend on the location of the observer. The light of the aurora is emitted by the upper fringes of Earth's atmosphere (heights of 100 to 400 km) as it is bombarded by electrons of the solar wind (solar wind protons contribute a smaller amount of energy). The modification of the trajectories of these particles by Earth's magnetic field restricts activity to high latitudes, producing the "aurora borealis" in the Northern Hemisphere and the "aurora australis" in the Southern Hemisphere. The wavelengths of four atmospheric molecular and atomic emission lines that can contribute strongly to auroral light are included in the list on p. 32. Whether aurorae appear coloured depends on their luminance—light that is too faint will not activate colour vision and appears white. When the luminance is sufficiently great, the relative contributions of blue, green, and red emission lines can result in a variety of auroral hues.

to atomic oxygen, originate at heights between 200 km and 400 km; the 650-nm to 680-nm emissions are produced at about 90 km.

The Impact and Measurement of Solar Activity

We find evidence of the profound effects of solar activity upon Earth extending as far back in time as we have been able to look. The rhythm of the solar activity cycle is reflected in cores from ocean beds, ice cores, and sediments from lakes that dry up in summer. It is also apparent in the growth rates of trees (determined from the study of tree rings) in recently living timber, wood from medieval buildings, and fossilized trees.

Solar activity can dramatically affect our lives. Magnetic storms due to solar activity induce currents in communications and power transmission systems having long-distance wires, disrupting their operation for hours. The power blackouts in Québec and Scandinavia produced by a large flare on 1989 Mar. 10 are a particularly outstanding example. Railway signalling systems might also be affected. Increased X-ray emissions from flares cause enhanced ionization of Earth's atmosphere at D-region heights (about 90 km), producing blackouts of shortwave communications.

Solar activity heats the upper atmosphere, causing it to expand further into space, increasing the drag experienced by artificial satellites in low orbits. It is ironic that the lifetime of the Solar Max satellite was dramatically shortened in this way. Above the atmosphere, satellites have no protection from high-energy particle fluxes produced by the Sun. Their electronic systems can be damaged, leading to catastrophic failures in some cases, as occurred with two Anik communications satellites in January 1994.

The oldest index of solar activity is the sunspot number. A number of techniques, many empirical, have been developed to combine observations from various observatories and observers to form the International Sunspot Number. This is a rather poor index; however, it has given us a database extending back to at least the 17th century.

Probably the best available index of solar activity, at least covering the last 50 years or so, is the *10.7-cm flux,* or $F_{10.7}$. This index is an objective measurement of the integrated emission at the 10.7-cm wavelength (a frequency of 2.8 GHz) from all sources present on the solar disk. It has been measured daily by the National Research Council of Canada for nearly 60 years and is now used worldwide as a primary index of solar activity. In 2003 the program became a joint one with the Canadian Space Agency. $F_{10.7}$ is expressed in solar flux units (1 sfu = 10^{-22} W·m^{-2}Hz^{-1}). The 10.7-cm flux has the great advantage that it can be measured in all weather conditions and requires no human involvement or "interpretation." When quiet, the Sun produces a 10.7-cm flux of 64 sfu, due to free-free thermal emission from the quiet solar corona. The 10.7-cm flux can be used as an objective proxy for other activity-related quantities. The strength of the radio emission constituting $F_{10.7}$ is modulated by the annual variation in the distance between Earth and Sun. When considering solar-driven phenomena at the Earth and in near-Earth space, this is not important, so the "Observed" value of the flux may be applicable. On the other hand, when considering solar activity this modulation has to be removed from the data. In such instances, the "Adjusted" flux, which is scaled to an Earth–Sun distance of 1 au, should be used.

We are a long way from understanding the nature and the extent of the effects solar activity has upon Earth. Some correlations, like that between the length of miniskirts and solar activity, are probably spurious; others might not be. As we exploit our environment more fully, we become increasingly sensitive to things that might affect it, even slightly.

TIMES OF SUNRISE AND SUNSET

BY RAJIV GUPTA

The table on pp. 165–166 gives the times of sunrise and sunset at four-day intervals for locations ranging from 20° to 60° north latitude. "Rise" and "set" correspond to the upper limb of the Sun appearing at the horizon for an observer at sea level. The times are local mean time (LMT) for the Greenwich meridian (i.e. UT at 0° longitude), although for North American observers the stated values may be read directly as LMT at the observer's position with an error less than 1 min. The table may be interpolated linearly for both nontabular latitudes and dates, and can be extrapolated beyond the 20° and 60° latitude limits a few degrees without significant loss of accuracy.

It is a common misconception that extreme values for sunrise and sunset times occur on the shortest and the longest days of the year. This is not the case and is due to the tilt of Earth's spin axis to the axis of its orbit and to Earth's varying speed along its elliptical orbit (as Kepler described in his second law). At midnorthern latitudes, the earliest sunset occurs early in December and the latest sunrise in early January whereas the shortest day (in the sense of hours of daylight) is Dec. 21 or 22. For more information see *Sky & Telescope,* December 1988, p. 674 and July 1972, p. 20, and an article by Terence Hicks in *JRASC, 88,* p. 86, February 1994.

The standard time of an event at a particular location must take account of the observer's longitude relative to his or her standard meridian (see STANDARD TIME ZONES on pp. 42–43). The table below lists the latitude and the longitude correction (in minutes of time) for a number of cities in Canada and the United States. For example, to find the time of sunrise at Boston on 2007 May 18: the latitude is 42°, and from the table the time of sunrise at 0° longitude is 4:37 UT (after interpolating for latitude). Thus, at Boston, the time of sunrise will be approximately 4:37 LMT. Boston is in the Eastern time zone (E) and is 16 minutes of time east of the standard meridian for this zone (75°W). Thus, sunrise in Boston will occur at 5:21 EDT (Eastern Daylight Time). The longitude correction for any location may be found by converting the difference between the longitude of the place and that of its standard meridian to time (1° = 4 minutes of time), the correction being + if the place is west of its standard meridian, – if east. **Note**: Due to a difference in height between the observer and the actual horizon, the observed time may differ by several minutes from the predicted time.

Canadian Cities						American Cities		
Belleville	44°	+10E	Québec	47°	−15E	Atlanta	34°	+37E
Calgary	51°	+36M	Regina	50°	+58C	Boston	42°	−16E
Charlottetown	46°	+12A	Resolute	75°	+20C	Chicago	42°	−10C
Corner Brook	49°	+22N	Rimouski	48°	−26E	Cincinnati	39°	+38E
Edmonton	54°	+34M	Saint John	45°	+24A	Denver	40°	0M
Halifax	45°	+14A	St. John's	48°	+1N	Fairbanks	65°	+50A
Hamilton	43°	+20E	Sarnia	43°	+29E	Flagstaff	35°	+27M
Kelowna	50°	−3P	Saskatoon	52°	+67C	Kansas City	39°	+18C
Kingston	44°	+6E	Sudbury	47°	+24E	Los Angeles	34°	−7P
Kitchener	43°	+22E	Thunder Bay	48°	+57E	Miami	26°	+21E
London	43°	+25E	Toronto	44°	+18E	Minneapolis	45°	+13C
Moncton	46°	+19A	Vancouver	49°	+12P	New Orleans	30°	0C
Montréal	46°	−6E	Victoria	48°	+13P	New York	41°	−4E
Niagara Falls	43°	+16E	Whitehorse	61°	+60P	San Francisco	38°	+10P
Ottawa	45°	+3E	Windsor, ON	42°	+32E	Seattle	48°	+9P
Pangnirtung	66°	+23A	Winnipeg	50°	+29C	Tucson	32°	+24M
Prince George	54°	+11P	Yellowknife	62°	+38M	Washington	39°	+8E

SUNRISE AND SUNSET, 2007 JANUARY–JUNE

UNIVERSAL TIME AT GREENWICH MERIDIAN

Latitude:	+20°	+30°	+35°	+40°	+45°	+50°	+55°	+60°
Event:	**RISE SET**	**RISE SET**	**RISE SET**	**RISE SET**	**RISE SET**	**RISE SET**	**RISE SET**	**RISE SET**
Jan. -2	6:34 17:30	6:55 17:09	7:07 16:57	7:21 16:43	7:38 16:26	7:58 16:06	8:25 15:39	9:03 15:01
2	6:35 17:33	6:56 17:12	7:08 17:00	7:22 16:46	7:38 16:30	7:59 16:09	8:25 15:43	9:02 15:06
6	6:36 17:35	6:57 17:15	7:09 17:03	7:22 16:50	7:38 16:34	7:58 16:14	8:23 15:49	8:59 15:13
10	6:37 17:38	6:57 17:18	7:08 17:07	7:22 16:53	7:37 16:38	7:56 16:19	8:21 15:55	8:55 15:20
14	6:38 17:40	6:57 17:21	7:08 17:10	7:21 16:58	7:35 16:43	7:54 16:25	8:17 16:01	8:50 15:29
18	6:38 17:43	6:56 17:25	7:07 17:14	7:19 17:02	7:33 16:48	7:51 16:31	8:13 16:08	8:43 15:38
22	6:38 17:46	6:55 17:28	7:05 17:18	7:17 17:07	7:30 16:53	7:47 16:37	8:08 16:16	8:36 15:48
26	6:37 17:48	6:54 17:32	7:03 17:22	7:14 17:11	7:27 16:59	7:42 16:43	8:02 16:24	8:28 15:58
30	6:36 17:50	6:52 17:35	7:01 17:26	7:11 17:16	7:23 17:04	7:37 16:50	7:55 16:32	8:19 16:08
Feb. 3	6:35 17:53	6:49 17:39	6:58 17:30	7:07 17:21	7:18 17:10	7:31 16:57	7:48 16:40	8:10 16:18
7	6:33 17:55	6:47 17:42	6:54 17:34	7:03 17:26	7:13 17:16	7:25 17:04	7:40 16:49	8:00 16:29
11	6:32 17:57	6:44 17:45	6:51 17:38	6:58 17:31	7:07 17:22	7:18 17:11	7:32 16:57	7:50 16:40
15	6:29 17:59	6:40 17:48	6:46 17:42	6:54 17:35	7:02 17:27	7:11 17:18	7:23 17:06	7:39 16:50
19	6:27 18:01	6:37 17:51	6:42 17:46	6:48 17:40	6:55 17:33	7:04 17:25	7:15 17:14	7:28 17:01
23	6:24 18:03	6:33 17:54	6:37 17:50	6:43 17:45	6:49 17:39	6:56 17:31	7:05 17:22	7:17 17:11
27	6:22 18:04	6:29 17:57	6:33 17:53	6:37 17:49	6:42 17:44	6:48 17:38	6:56 17:31	7:06 17:21
Mar. 3	6:19 18:06	6:24 18:00	6:28 17:57	6:31 17:53	6:35 17:49	6:40 17:45	6:46 17:39	6:54 17:31
7	6:16 18:07	6:20 18:03	6:22 18:00	6:25 17:58	6:28 17:55	6:32 17:51	6:36 17:47	6:42 17:41
11	6:12 18:08	6:15 18:05	6:17 18:04	6:19 18:02	6:21 18:00	6:23 17:58	6:26 17:55	6:30 17:51
15	6:09 18:09	6:10 18:08	6:11 18:07	6:12 18:06	6:13 18:05	6:15 18:04	6:16 18:03	6:18 18:01
19	6:05 18:11	6:06 18:11	6:06 18:10	6:06 18:10	6:06 18:11	6:06 18:11	6:06 18:11	6:06 18:11
23	6:02 18:12	6:01 18:13	6:00 18:14	5:59 18:15	5:59 18:16	5:57 18:17	5:56 18:19	5:54 18:21
27	5:58 18:13	5:56 18:15	5:55 18:17	5:53 18:19	5:51 18:21	5:49 18:23	5:46 18:26	5:42 18:31
31	5:55 18:14	5:51 18:18	5:49 18:20	5:46 18:23	5:44 18:26	5:40 18:30	5:36 18:34	5:30 18:40
Apr. 4	5:51 18:15	5:46 18:20	5:43 18:23	5:40 18:27	5:36 18:31	5:31 18:36	5:25 18:42	5:18 18:50
8	5:48 18:16	5:42 18:23	5:38 18:26	5:34 18:31	5:29 18:36	5:23 18:42	5:15 18:50	5:06 19:00
12	5:45 18:17	5:37 18:25	5:33 18:30	5:28 18:35	5:22 18:41	5:14 18:48	5:05 18:58	4:54 19:10
16	5:42 18:18	5:33 18:28	5:27 18:33	5:21 18:39	5:15 18:46	5:06 18:55	4:56 19:05	4:42 19:20
20	5:39 18:20	5:28 18:30	5:22 18:36	5:16 18:43	5:08 18:51	4:58 19:01	4:46 19:13	4:30 19:29
24	5:36 18:21	5:24 18:33	5:18 18:39	5:10 18:47	5:01 18:56	4:50 19:07	4:37 19:21	4:19 19:39
28	5:33 18:22	5:20 18:35	5:13 18:43	5:05 18:51	4:55 19:01	4:43 19:13	4:28 19:29	4:07 19:49
May 2	5:31 18:24	5:17 18:38	5:09 18:46	4:59 18:55	4:49 19:06	4:35 19:20	4:19 19:36	3:56 19:59
6	5:28 18:25	5:13 18:40	5:05 18:49	4:55 18:59	4:43 19:11	4:29 19:26	4:10 19:44	3:46 20:09
10	5:26 18:27	5:10 18:43	5:01 18:52	4:50 19:03	4:38 19:16	4:22 19:32	4:02 19:52	3:36 20:19
14	5:25 18:28	5:08 18:45	4:58 18:55	4:46 19:07	4:33 19:21	4:16 19:37	3:55 19:59	3:26 20:29
18	5:23 18:30	5:05 18:48	4:55 18:59	4:43 19:11	4:28 19:25	4:11 19:43	3:48 20:06	3:17 20:38
22	5:22 18:32	5:03 18:50	4:52 19:02	4:39 19:14	4:24 19:30	4:06 19:48	3:42 20:13	3:08 20:47
26	5:21 18:33	5:01 18:53	4:50 19:04	4:37 19:18	4:21 19:34	4:01 19:53	3:36 20:19	3:00 20:55
30	5:20 18:35	5:00 18:55	4:48 19:07	4:34 19:21	4:18 19:37	3:58 19:58	3:31 20:25	2:53 21:03
Jun. 3	5:20 18:36	4:59 18:57	4:47 19:10	4:33 19:24	4:16 19:41	3:55 20:02	3:27 20:30	2:47 21:10
7	5:20 18:38	4:59 18:59	4:46 19:12	4:31 19:26	4:14 19:44	3:53 20:05	3:24 20:34	2:42 21:16
11	5:20 18:39	4:58 19:01	4:46 19:14	4:31 19:29	4:13 19:46	3:51 20:08	3:22 20:38	2:39 21:21
15	5:20 18:40	4:58 19:02	4:46 19:15	4:31 19:30	4:13 19:48	3:50 20:11	3:21 20:41	2:36 21:25
19	5:21 18:42	4:59 19:04	4:46 19:17	4:31 19:32	4:13 19:50	3:50 20:12	3:20 20:42	2:36 21:27
23	5:22 18:42	5:00 19:04	4:47 19:17	4:32 19:33	4:14 19:51	3:51 20:13	3:21 20:43	2:36 21:28
27	5:23 18:43	5:01 19:05	4:48 19:18	4:33 19:33	4:15 19:51	3:53 20:13	3:23 20:43	2:38 21:27

SUNRISE AND SUNSET, 2007 JULY–DECEMBER
UNIVERSAL TIME AT GREENWICH MERIDIAN

Latitude:	+20°		+30°		+35°		+40°		+45°		+50°		+55°		+60°	
Event:	**RISE**	**SET**	**RISE**	**SET**	**RISE**	**SET**	**RISE**	**SET**	**RISE**	**SET**	**RISE**	**SET**	**RISE**	**SET**	**RISE**	**SET**
Jul. 1	5:24	18:43	5:02	19:05	4:49	19:18	4:35	19:33	4:17	19:50	3:55	20:13	3:25	20:42	2:42	21:25
5	5:25	18:44	5:04	19:05	4:51	19:18	4:37	19:32	4:19	19:49	3:58	20:11	3:29	20:40	2:46	21:22
9	5:27	18:43	5:06	19:04	4:53	19:17	4:39	19:31	4:22	19:48	4:01	20:09	3:33	20:37	2:52	21:17
13	5:28	18:43	5:08	19:03	4:56	19:15	4:42	19:29	4:25	19:46	4:05	20:06	3:38	20:33	2:59	21:11
17	5:30	18:42	5:10	19:02	4:58	19:14	4:45	19:27	4:29	19:43	4:09	20:02	3:43	20:28	3:07	21:04
21	5:31	18:41	5:12	19:00	5:01	19:11	4:48	19:24	4:33	19:39	4:14	19:58	3:50	20:22	3:15	20:56
25	5:33	18:40	5:15	18:58	5:04	19:09	4:52	19:21	4:37	19:35	4:19	19:53	3:56	20:16	3:24	20:48
29	5:34	18:39	5:17	18:56	5:07	19:06	4:55	19:17	4:41	19:31	4:25	19:48	4:03	20:09	3:33	20:39
Aug. 2	5:36	18:37	5:19	18:53	5:10	19:02	4:59	19:13	4:46	19:26	4:30	19:42	4:10	20:02	3:42	20:29
6	5:37	18:35	5:22	18:50	5:13	18:59	5:03	19:09	4:50	19:21	4:36	19:35	4:17	19:54	3:51	20:19
10	5:38	18:32	5:24	18:46	5:16	18:54	5:06	19:04	4:55	19:15	4:42	19:28	4:24	19:45	4:01	20:08
14	5:40	18:30	5:27	18:43	5:19	18:50	5:10	18:59	5:00	19:09	4:47	19:21	4:32	19:36	4:11	19:57
18	5:41	18:27	5:29	18:39	5:22	18:45	5:14	18:53	5:05	19:02	4:53	19:13	4:39	19:27	4:20	19:46
22	5:42	18:24	5:31	18:34	5:25	18:40	5:18	18:47	5:09	18:56	4:59	19:06	4:47	19:18	4:30	19:34
26	5:43	18:21	5:33	18:30	5:28	18:35	5:22	18:42	5:14	18:49	5:05	18:57	4:54	19:08	4:40	19:23
30	5:44	18:17	5:36	18:25	5:31	18:30	5:25	18:35	5:19	18:42	5:11	18:49	5:02	18:59	4:49	19:11
Sep. 3	5:45	18:14	5:38	18:21	5:34	18:25	5:29	18:29	5:24	18:34	5:17	18:41	5:09	18:49	4:59	18:59
7	5:46	18:10	5:40	18:16	5:37	18:19	5:33	18:23	5:28	18:27	5:23	18:32	5:17	18:38	5:08	18:47
11	5:46	18:07	5:42	18:11	5:40	18:13	5:37	18:16	5:33	18:19	5:29	18:23	5:24	18:28	5:17	18:35
15	5:47	18:03	5:44	18:06	5:42	18:08	5:40	18:10	5:38	18:12	5:35	18:15	5:31	18:18	5:27	18:22
19	5:48	17:59	5:46	18:01	5:45	18:02	5:44	18:03	5:43	18:04	5:41	18:06	5:39	18:08	5:36	18:10
23	5:49	17:56	5:49	17:56	5:48	17:56	5:48	17:56	5:48	17:57	5:47	17:57	5:46	17:57	5:45	17:58
27	5:50	17:52	5:51	17:51	5:51	17:50	5:52	17:50	5:52	17:49	5:53	17:48	5:54	17:47	5:55	17:46
Oct. 1	5:51	17:48	5:53	17:46	5:54	17:45	5:56	17:43	5:57	17:41	5:59	17:39	6:01	17:37	6:04	17:34
5	5:52	17:45	5:55	17:41	5:57	17:39	6:00	17:37	6:02	17:34	6:05	17:31	6:09	17:27	6:14	17:22
9	5:53	17:42	5:58	17:37	6:01	17:34	6:04	17:30	6:07	17:27	6:12	17:22	6:17	17:17	6:24	17:10
13	5:54	17:38	6:00	17:32	6:04	17:28	6:08	17:24	6:12	17:19	6:18	17:14	6:25	17:07	6:33	16:58
17	5:55	17:35	6:03	17:28	6:07	17:23	6:12	17:18	6:18	17:13	6:24	17:06	6:33	16:57	6:43	16:47
21	5:57	17:32	6:06	17:23	6:11	17:18	6:16	17:13	6:23	17:06	6:31	16:58	6:41	16:48	6:53	16:35
25	5:58	17:30	6:08	17:20	6:14	17:14	6:21	17:07	6:28	16:59	6:37	16:50	6:49	16:39	7:03	16:24
29	6:00	17:27	6:11	17:16	6:18	17:09	6:25	17:02	6:34	16:53	6:44	16:43	6:57	16:30	7:13	16:13
Nov. 2	6:02	17:25	6:14	17:13	6:21	17:05	6:30	16:57	6:39	16:47	6:51	16:36	7:05	16:22	7:24	16:03
6	6:04	17:23	6:17	17:10	6:25	17:02	6:34	16:53	6:45	16:42	6:57	16:29	7:13	16:13	7:34	15:52
10	6:06	17:22	6:21	17:07	6:29	16:58	6:39	16:49	6:50	16:37	7:04	16:23	7:21	16:06	7:44	15:43
14	6:08	17:21	6:24	17:05	6:33	16:55	6:43	16:45	6:56	16:33	7:10	16:18	7:29	15:59	7:54	15:34
18	6:10	17:20	6:27	17:03	6:37	16:53	6:48	16:42	7:01	16:29	7:17	16:13	7:37	15:53	8:04	15:25
22	6:13	17:19	6:30	17:01	6:41	16:51	6:53	16:39	7:06	16:25	7:23	16:08	7:45	15:47	8:14	15:17
26	6:15	17:19	6:34	17:00	6:45	16:50	6:57	16:37	7:11	16:23	7:29	16:05	7:52	15:42	8:23	15:11
30	6:18	17:19	6:37	17:00	6:48	16:49	7:01	16:36	7:16	16:21	7:35	16:02	7:59	15:38	8:32	15:05
Dec. 4	6:20	17:20	6:40	17:00	6:52	16:48	7:05	16:35	7:21	16:19	7:40	16:00	8:05	15:35	8:40	15:00
8	6:23	17:21	6:43	17:00	6:55	16:48	7:09	16:35	7:25	16:18	7:45	15:59	8:11	15:33	8:47	14:56
12	6:25	17:22	6:46	17:01	6:58	16:49	7:12	16:35	7:29	16:18	7:49	15:58	8:15	15:32	8:53	14:54
16	6:28	17:23	6:49	17:02	7:01	16:50	7:15	16:36	7:32	16:19	7:52	15:58	8:19	15:31	8:58	14:53
20	6:30	17:25	6:51	17:04	7:03	16:52	7:18	16:37	7:34	16:20	7:55	16:00	8:22	15:33	9:01	14:54
24	6:32	17:27	6:53	17:06	7:05	16:54	7:19	16:39	7:36	16:23	7:57	16:02	8:24	15:35	9:03	14:56
28	6:33	17:29	6:55	17:08	7:07	16:56	7:21	16:42	7:38	16:25	7:58	16:05	8:25	15:38	9:04	14:59
32	6:35	17:32	6:56	17:11	7:08	16:59	7:22	16:45	7:38	16:28	7:59	16:08	8:25	15:42	9:03	15:04

TWILIGHT

BY RAJIV GUPTA

There are three definitions for the beginning of morning and ending of evening twilight: (1) *Civil twilight*—centre of the Sun 6° below the horizon, brightest stars visible, artificial illumination required for most outdoor activities, marks the ending or beginning of night for aviation purposes; (2) *Nautical twilight*—centre of the Sun 12° below the horizon, sea horizon no longer visible; (3) *Astronomical twilight*—centre of the Sun 18° below the horizon, amount of sunlight scattered by the atmosphere is negligible.

The table below gives the beginning of morning and ending of evening astronomical twilight in UT at 0° longitude. For observers in North America the times may be handled in the same way as those of sunrise and sunset (see p. 164).

Latitude:	**+20°**		**+30°**		**+35°**		**+40°**		**+45°**		**+50°**		**+55°**		**+60°**	
M–E:	**Morn.**	**Eve.**	**Morn.**	**Eve.**	**Morn.**	**Eve.**	**Morn.**	**Eve.**	**Morn.**	**Eve.**	**Morn.**	**Eve.**	**Morn.**	**Eve.**	**Morn.**	**Eve.**
Jan. 0	5:16	18:50	5:30	18:36	5:37	18:29	5:44	18:22	5:52	18:14	6:00	18:06	6:08	17:58	6:18	17:48
10	5:19	18:56	5:32	18:43	5:39	18:36	5:45	18:30	5:52	18:23	5:59	18:16	6:06	18:09	6:15	18:00
20	5:21	19:01	5:32	18:50	5:38	18:45	5:43	18:39	5:48	18:34	5:54	18:28	6:00	18:23	6:06	18:17
30	5:20	19:06	5:29	18:57	5:34	18:53	5:38	18:49	5:41	18:46	5:45	18:42	5:48	18:39	5:52	18:36
Feb. 9	5:18	19:11	5:24	19:05	5:27	19:02	5:29	19:00	5:31	18:58	5:32	18:57	5:33	18:57	5:32	18:57
19	5:13	19:15	5:17	19:12	5:18	19:11	5:18	19:11	5:17	19:11	5:16	19:13	5:13	19:16	5:09	19:21
Mar. 1	5:07	19:18	5:07	19:18	5:06	19:19	5:04	19:21	5:01	19:24	4:57	19:29	4:51	19:36	4:41	19:45
11	4:59	19:21	4:56	19:25	4:53	19:28	4:49	19:32	4:43	19:38	4:36	19:46	4:25	19:57	4:10	20:13
21	4:50	19:24	4:44	19:32	4:39	19:37	4:32	19:44	4:23	19:52	4:12	20:04	3:57	20:20	3:34	20:43
31	4:41	19:28	4:31	19:39	4:23	19:46	4:14	19:55	4:02	20:07	3:47	20:23	3:25	20:45	2:54	21:18
Apr. 10	4:32	19:31	4:17	19:46	4:08	19:56	3:56	20:08	3:40	20:24	3:20	20:45	2:51	21:14	2:04	22:03
20	4:23	19:36	4:04	19:54	3:52	20:07	3:37	20:22	3:18	20:42	2:52	21:08	2:12	21:49	0:48	23:23
30	4:14	19:41	3:52	20:03	3:38	20:18	3:19	20:36	2:56	21:01	2:22	21:35	1:24	22:35	—	—
May 10	4:07	19:46	3:41	20:12	3:24	20:29	3:03	20:51	2:34	21:21	1:50	22:05	—	—	—	—
20	4:01	19:52	3:32	20:21	3:13	20:41	2:48	21:06	2:14	21:41	1:15	22:41	—	—	—	—
30	3:58	19:57	3:26	20:29	3:05	20:51	2:37	21:19	1:56	22:00	0:28	23:35	—	—	—	—
Jun. 9	3:56	20:02	3:23	20:36	3:00	20:59	2:30	21:29	1:44	22:15	—	—	—	—	—	—
19	3:57	20:06	3:22	20:40	2:59	21:04	2:28	21:35	1:40	22:23	—	—	—	—	—	—
29	4:00	20:07	3:25	20:41	3:02	21:05	2:31	21:36	1:44	22:22	—	—	—	—	—	—
Jul. 9	4:04	20:07	3:31	20:39	3:08	21:01	2:39	21:30	1:56	22:13	—	—	—	—	—	—
19	4:09	20:04	3:38	20:34	3:17	20:54	2:51	21:21	2:13	21:58	1:02	23:07	—	—	—	—
29	4:14	19:59	3:46	20:26	3:28	20:44	3:05	21:07	2:33	21:39	1:41	22:29	—	—	—	—
Aug. 8	4:19	19:52	3:55	20:16	3:39	20:31	3:19	20:51	2:52	21:17	2:13	21:55	0:53	23:10	—	—
18	4:24	19:44	4:03	20:04	3:50	20:17	3:33	20:34	3:11	20:55	2:41	21:25	1:52	22:12	—	—
28	4:28	19:34	4:11	19:51	4:00	20:02	3:46	20:15	3:29	20:32	3:05	20:56	2:31	21:29	1:28	22:29
Sep. 7	4:31	19:25	4:18	19:37	4:10	19:46	3:59	19:56	3:45	20:10	3:27	20:28	3:01	20:53	2:21	21:31
17	4:34	19:15	4:25	19:24	4:19	19:30	4:11	19:38	4:00	19:48	3:46	20:01	3:27	20:20	3:00	20:47
27	4:37	19:05	4:31	19:10	4:27	19:15	4:21	19:20	4:14	19:27	4:04	19:37	3:51	19:50	3:31	20:09
Oct. 7	4:39	18:56	4:37	18:58	4:35	19:00	4:32	19:03	4:27	19:08	4:21	19:14	4:12	19:23	3:59	19:35
17	4:42	18:49	4:43	18:47	4:43	18:47	4:42	18:48	4:40	18:50	4:37	18:53	4:32	18:58	4:24	19:05
27	4:45	18:43	4:49	18:38	4:51	18:36	4:52	18:35	4:52	18:35	4:52	18:35	4:50	18:36	4:47	18:39
Nov. 6	4:48	18:39	4:56	18:31	4:59	18:28	5:02	18:25	5:04	18:22	5:07	18:20	5:08	18:18	5:09	18:17
16	4:53	18:36	5:03	18:26	5:07	18:22	5:12	18:17	5:16	18:13	5:20	18:08	5:25	18:04	5:29	17:59
26	4:58	18:36	5:10	18:24	5:16	18:18	5:21	18:13	5:27	18:07	5:33	18:01	5:40	17:54	5:47	17:47
Dec. 6	5:03	18:38	5:17	18:25	5:23	18:18	5:30	18:11	5:37	18:04	5:44	17:57	5:52	17:49	6:02	17:40
16	5:09	18:42	5:23	18:28	5:30	18:21	5:37	18:13	5:45	18:06	5:53	17:58	6:02	17:49	6:12	17:39
26	5:14	18:47	5:28	18:33	5:35	18:25	5:43	18:18	5:50	18:11	5:58	18:03	6:07	17:54	6:18	17:43
Jan. 5	5:18	18:53	5:32	18:39	5:38	18:32	5:45	18:25	5:52	18:18	6:00	18:11	6:08	18:03	6:17	17:53

MIDNIGHT TWILIGHT AND MIDNIGHT SUN

By Roy Bishop

Astronomers generally desire dark skies, free of moonlight and man-made light pollution. As mentioned on p. 167, the beginning or end of *astronomical twilight* corresponds to the centre of the Sun being 18° below the horizon. At that point the amount of sunlight scattered by the upper layers of Earth's atmosphere is negligible; that is, it is less than the combined illuminance (about 2×10^{-3} lux) from starlight, airglow, and zodiacal light, the three main contributors to the light of the "dark" night sky.

For observers in countries at high latitudes (e.g. the United Kingdom, Norway, southern Argentina and Chile, and most of Canada), around the time of the summer solstice the Sun always lies less than 18° below the horizon, and the sky does not get dark at night. This "midnight twilight" phenomenon can be displayed in a graph as a function of latitude and time of year.

The **diagram** at the right indicates the brightness of the sky at local midnight at any time of the year for any latitude north of 45°N or south of 45°S. Below the lower curve the natural sky is dark. Between the two curves twilight prevails. Above the upper curve the Sun is in the sky. Place names in roman type (left-hand side) are in the Northern Hemisphere; place names in *italic* type (right-hand side) are in the *Southern Hemisphere*. On the horizontal axis use the roman-type months for the former, *italic*-type months for the latter. The diagram is simplified slightly in that the months are assumed to be of equal duration, and the seasonal pattern of months and summer solstices for Earth's two hemispheres are assumed to be identical except for a 6-month phase shift.

The latitude of the Arctic and Antarctic Circles (90° subtract the obliquity of the ecliptic = 66°34′) is indicated by the dashed line. This line is *not* tangent to the Midnight Sun curve because at midnight on the summer solstice at either the Arctic or the Antarctic Circle the Sun is above the horizon. Atmospheric refraction raises the apparent Sun about 34′ above the true Sun. Also, rise/set is defined as the top limb of the Sun at a sea-level horizon; thus the 16′ semidiameter of the Sun must also be taken into account. To see the top limb of the Sun on the horizon at local midnight on the summer solstice, an observer must be 34′ + 16′ = 50′ south of the Arctic Circle (or north of the Antarctic Circle), at latitude 65°44′.

By running a horizontal line across the chart at a selected latitude, the reader can determine the approximate dates when midnight twilight and, possibly, midnight Sun begin and end for any locality at north or south latitudes above 48.6°, the lower limit for midnight twilight on the summer solstice. (Remarkably, when rounded to the nearest degree, the latter figure is the latitude of the longest east–west international border: the 2000-km-long 49th parallel between the United States and western Canada.)

Some examples: The diagram shows that at Grise Fiord (a hamlet on the stunning south coast of Ellesmere Island, and Canada's most northerly community) the sky is never dark from about Mar. 10 until early October, and the midnight Sun lasts from late April until mid-August. Note that Cape Horn at midnight is bathed in dim Antarctic twilight from early November until early February. Even at the latitude of Vancouver there is a period of almost a month each year when the sky never gets astronomically dark—although the natural night sky is obliterated *every* night near any town or city unless there is an electrical power failure! Finally, note that Earth's poles are astronomically dark for less than three months of the year.

MIDNIGHT TWILIGHT AND MIDNIGHT SUN DIAGRAM

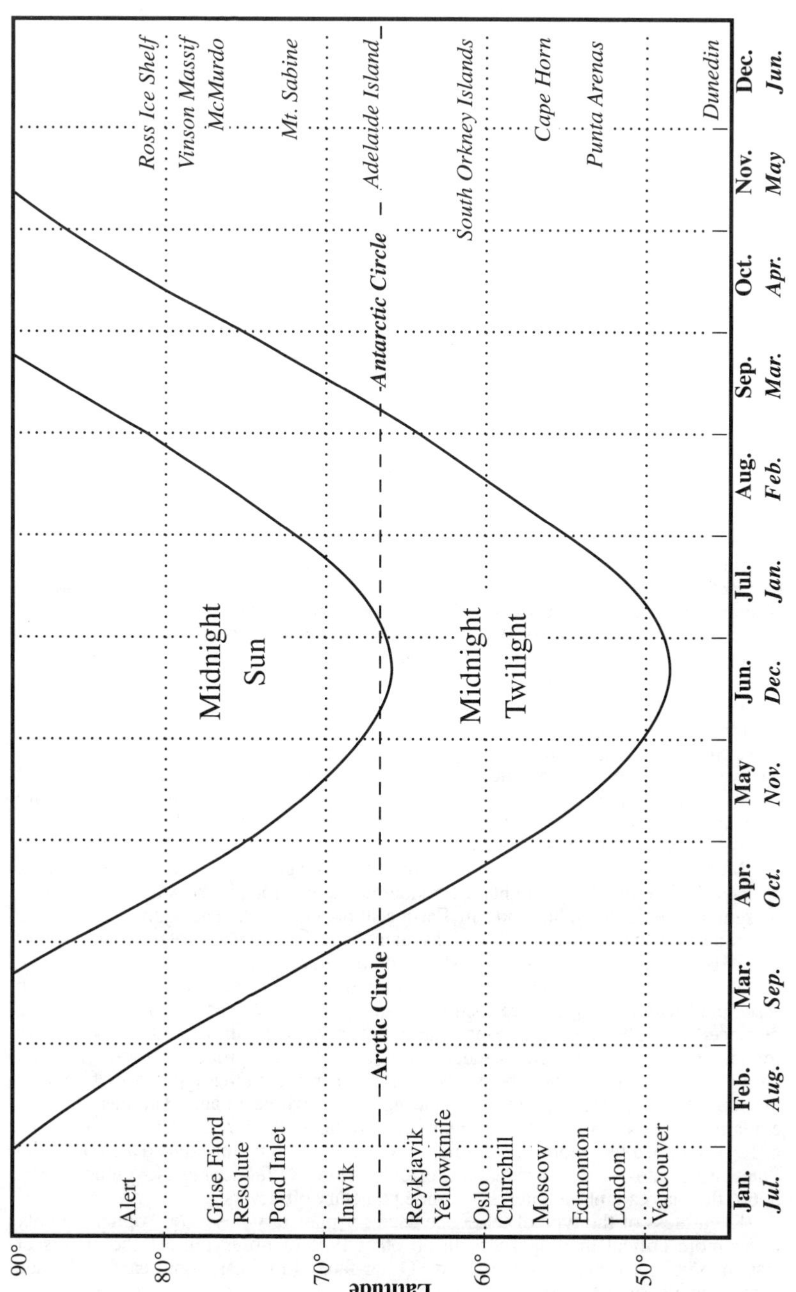

PLANETS AND SATELLITES

THE PLANETS FOR 2007

BY TERENCE DICKINSON

INTRODUCTION

Planetary observing is perhaps the most widely accessible and diversified category of amateur astronomical pursuits. Planets can be seen on almost any clear night of the year. Indeed, in heavily light-polluted cities they are sometimes the *only* celestial objects visible. With dark skies ever more remote from population centres, planetary observing is returning—partly by default—to take its place as an important part of the amateur astronomer's repertoire.

But a factor more important than sky conditions is needed to explain the expanding interest in planetary observing. There is a widespread recognition among amateur astronomers that high-quality optics are essential for good views of the planets; the increased commercial availability of such instruments—especially previously unavailable systems such as apochromatic refractors and Maksutov-Newtonians—means that planetary observing is more accessible than ever.

Planetary observing divides into three distinct categories, each with its opportunities and limitations. *Unaided-eye* observing consists of detecting, identifying, and monitoring the night-to-night and week-to-week motion and visibility of the six brightest planets. *Binoculars* add Neptune along with the Galilean satellites of Jupiter and the crescent phase of Venus. Binoculars are ideal for tracking planetary motion against the backdrop of stars, many of which are too faint for naked-eye detection. But it is only through *telescopic* observing that the planets reveal their uniqueness, and this section concentrates on that aspect. For a listing of unaided-eye highlights such as conjunctions, see THE SKY MONTH BY MONTH section on pp. 78–105.

Urban and suburban locales unsuited for many aspects of astronomy can be perfectly acceptable for telescopic planetary observing. Atmospheric turbulence—seeing—is often no worse, and sometimes better, in urban areas. However, observers should avoid using telescopes on pavement, balconies, or immediately beside a house or substantial building due to the heat radiated to the surrounding atmosphere from these structures. Also, avoid looking over these objects if possible. A typical grassed backyard is fine in most instances. For optimum performance all telescopes (except small refractors) require from ten minutes to an hour to cool to outside temperature when taken outdoors. Hazy but otherwise cloudless nights are usually just as good as, and sometimes better than, clear skies for steady telescopic images of planets.

More than any other class of telescopic observing, planetary observing is most affected by seeing. Many nights are rendered useless for planet watching by ever-present ripples and undulations in Earth's atmosphere. Planets within 15° of the horizon are virtually always afflicted (as many observers of Mars noted in the summer of 2001 from Canadian latitudes). Minimum altitude for expectations of reasonable seeing is 25°. A further problem with low-altitude planetary targets is dispersion associated with atmospheric refraction. Refraction causes celestial objects to appear displaced to higher altitudes. Since the effect is wavelength-dependent (being less for longer wavelengths), for planets at low altitudes this produces a red fringe on the lower side of the planet and a green (or blue) fringe on the upper; the effect also introduces undesirable chromatic smearing to the whole image. Thomas Dobbins explained possible fixes for the problem in an article in *Sky & Telescope* (August 2003, p. 124). Within a few months, Adirondack Video Astronomy introduced a commercial Planetary Atmospheric Dispersion Corrector (*Sky & Telescope,* November 2003, p. 60) that has caught the interest of some planetary observers.

Regardless of the type of telescope used for planetary observing, optical quality is far more critical than aperture. In no other type of observing are the effects of less-than-perfect optics more apparent. Other factors that can significantly degrade a telescope's planetary performance include a large *central obstruction* in the optical system (all Schmidt-Cassegrains, Maksutov-Cassegrains, and Newtonians with secondary mirror diameters exceeding 25% of their apertures), *secondary mirror supports* (most Newtonians), *chromatic aberration* (most achromatic refractors over 90 mm), *internal air currents* (all types, refractors least), optical component *cool-down time* (mostly aperture-dependent, telescopes over 200 mm can take hours), *improperly light-baffled optics*, and *dirty optics*.

In the remarks below, when a planetary phenomenon is stated as being visible in a certain minimum aperture, good seeing and a moderate level of observer experience are assumed. When a specific minimum aperture is cited, an unobstructed optical system (i.e. a refractor) is assumed. Somewhat larger apertures are often required if centrally obstructed systems are used or the observer is inexperienced.

Editor's Note: The tables and figures that appear in this section were prepared by the editor or other contributors; the editor assumes full responsibility for their accuracy.

MERCURY

Of the five planets visible to the unaided eye, Mercury is by far the most difficult to observe and is seldom conveniently located for either unaided eye or telescopic observation. The problem for observers is Mercury's tight orbit, which constrains the planet to a small zone on either side of the Sun as viewed from Earth. When Mercury is east of the Sun we may see it as an evening "star" low in the west just after sunset. When it is west of the Sun we might view Mercury as a morning "star" in the east before sunrise. But due to the celestial geometry of the tilt of Earth's axis and Mercury's orbit, we get much better views of Mercury at certain times of the year.

From midlatitudes, the best time to see the planet in the *evening* sky is within a month or two of the spring equinox and in the *morning* sky within a month or two of the fall equinox. (This applies to both northern and southern latitudes, although the respective seasons are six months out of phase.) Binoculars are of great assistance in searching for the planet about 30 minutes to an hour after sunset or before sunrise during the periods when it is visible. The planet's brightness, which varies by more than two magnitudes, is a more important factor influencing its visibility than its angular distance from the Sun during any particular elongation. Mercury's true colour is almost pure white, but absorption from Earth's atmosphere within 15° of the horizon, where Mercury is most easily seen, usually imparts a yellow or ochre hue to the planet.

Telescopic observers will find the rapidly changing phases of Mercury of interest. The planet zips from gibbous to crescent phase in about three weeks during each of its evening elongations. The phases are accessible to users of 75-mm or larger telescopes; the 30% phase can be detected at 50×. Large apertures (over 200 mm) rarely offer an advantage due to the crippling effects of poor seeing at lower altitudes, especially following sunset when the planet is most frequently observed. Experienced planetary observers often report their most satisfying telescopic observations of Mercury in the morning sky. Near favourable western elongations, the planet may be easily located at least an hour before sunrise, then followed to higher altitudes into the daytime sky. Seeing often remains steady more than an hour after sunrise by which time the planet

MERCURY—MOST FAVOURABLE EVENING VIEW IN 2007 FROM NORTHERN LATITUDES

Date 0h UT	Mag.	Angular Diameter ″	Percent Illuminated	Elongation from Sun °	Apparent RA (2007) h m	Dec ° ′
May 22	−0.5	6.4	64	19	5 15	+25 19
26	−0.2	6.9	54	21	5 42	+25 39
30	+0.1	7.6	45	23	6 05	+25 29
Jun. 3	+0.5	8.3	36	23	6 24	+24 57
7	+0.9	9.1	28	23	6 38	+24 08
11	+1.4	9.9	20	21	6 46	+23 07

may be 30° above the horizon. Under such conditions the phase is sharply defined, and the small disk takes on a unique appearance, paler than Venus, with a vaguely textured surface. Surface details, although suspected in moments of fine seeing, are always elusive. Contrasts between the planet's surface features are lower than on the lunar surface, although in other respects the two bodies are similar.

VENUS

Venus is the only world in the solar system that closely resembles Earth in size and mass. It also comes nearer to Earth than any other planet, at times approaching as close as 0.27 au. Despite the fundamental similarity, surface conditions on Earth and Venus differ greatly. The clouds and haze that cloak the planet are highly reflective, making Venus the brightest natural celestial object in the nighttime sky apart from our Moon. Whenever it is visible, it is readily recognized. Because its orbit is within that of Earth's, Venus is never separated from the Sun by an angle greater than 47°, more than sufficient for the dazzling object to dominate the morning or evening sky.

Like Mercury, Venus exhibits phases, although they are much more easily detected in small telescopes because of Venus's greater size. When it is far from us near the other side of its orbit, we see the planet nearly fully illuminated, but because of its distance it appears small—about 10″ in diameter. As Venus moves closer to Earth, the phase decreases (we see less of the illuminated portion of the planet), but the diameter increases until it is a thin slice nearly a minute of arc in diameter. It takes Venus several months to move from one of these extremes to the other, compared to just a few weeks for Mercury.

As the year opens, Venus is emerging from superior conjunction in October 2006 and becoming visible low in the southwest evening sky at dusk. Visibility improves daily as the brilliant planet's elongation from the Sun increases. By mid-February it is well into a fully dark evening sky for mid-northern latitudes, and remains there through June when conditions reverse and observers in mid-southern latitudes begin to enjoy the dazzling planet well above the western horizon in full evening darkness and northern observers see Venus plunge into twilight glow in late June and July.

Inferior conjunction occurs at 4h UT Aug. 18 when Venus passes 8° south of the Sun. On that day it is a 1% sliver of a crescent, 58″ in apparent diameter. About a week later, Venus is a morning-sky object low on the eastern horizon for southern-hemisphere observers. Southern observers can watch Venus rapidly climb higher into the morning sky during September where it remains in prime position for the rest of the year. Northern observers can glimpse Venus low in the east in bright morning twilight beginning about 10 days after inferior conjunction. By mid-September, it soon becomes a conspicuous morning-sky object and remains so for the rest of the year.

For telescopic observing, the following information will be useful: on Mar. 1, Venus is a 87% illuminated disk 12″ in apparent diameter; May 1, 69%, 16″; Jun. 1, 55%, 21″; Jul. 1, 36%, 31″; Aug. 1, 10%, 50″; Sep. 1, 7%, 53″; Oct. 1, 32%, 34″; Nov. 1, 52%, 23″; Dec 1, 66%, 18″.

When Venus is about a 20% crescent, even rigidly held, good-quality binoculars can be used to distinguish that the planet is not spherical or a point source. The new image-stabilized binoculars beautifully display the crescent Venus. A 60-mm refractor should be capable of revealing the shape of all but the gibbous and full phases. Experienced observers prefer to observe Venus during the daytime, and indeed the planet is bright enough to be seen with the unaided eye if one knows where to look.

Because of Venus's high surface brightness (about 40 times greater than Jupiter's), Venus can accommodate the highest magnifications a telescope can deliver. The author has used magnifications over 4× per millimetre of aperture on occasion and regularly employs 1.5× to 3× per millimetre on the planet, particularly in bright twilight when the sky is moderately dark but Venus is still high enough to avoid low-altitude seeing degradation. Venus's cloud-shrouded surface appears to most observers to be featureless no matter what type of telescope is used or what the planet's phase. Broad streaks and splotches in the clouds, revealed in blue-filtered and ultraviolet images of Venus, may be vaguely detected telescopically using a violet filter (#38A or #47), although sketches of these features seldom match among different observers.

MARS

In late August 2003, Mars made its closest approach to Earth in recorded history. At the following close approach, in October 2005, the red planet was 25% farther from Earth than it was in 2003, however, its more northerly declination positioned the planet about 30° higher in the sky for telescopic observers at mid-northern latitudes, resulting in what many observers say was the finest telescopic viewing of Mars in a generation. This year's close approach of Mars in December is also a high-declination apparition for northern-hemisphere observers, but the planet will be considerably more remote than it was in either 2003 or 2005. Still, observing prospects are better for northern observers in 2007 than they will be until at least 2016.

Mars—2007			
Date UT		**Mag.**	**Equatorial Diameter** ″
Jan.	1.0	+1.5	3.9
Feb.	1.0	+1.4	4.2
Mar.	1.0	+1.3	4.5
Apr.	1.0	+1.1	4.8
May	1.0	+1.0	5.3
Jun.	1.0	+0.8	5.8
Jul.	1.0	+0.7	6.3
Aug.	1.0	+0.5	7.1
Sep.	1.0	+0.3	8.1
Oct.	1.0	–0.1	9.6
Nov.	1.0	–0.6	12.1
Nov.	15.0	–1.0	13.6
Dec.	1.0	–1.3	15.1
Dec.	15.0	–1.5	15.8
Jan.	1.0	–1.5	15.4

Even without any astronomical equipment, Mars is often considered the most interesting planet to observe with the unaided eye. It moves rapidly among the stars—its motion can often be detected after an interval of less than a week—and it varies in brightness over a far greater range than any other outer planet. Mars can be distinguished by its pale orange-red colour, a hue that originates with rust-coloured dust that covers much of the planet. As 2007 opens, Mars is an inconspicuous second-magnitude dawn-sky object buried in twilight glow in the east. By April, it brightens to a first-magnitude morning "star," well seen from southern latitudes, but still quite low for northern observers. From April through October it moves eastward and into easy visibility, passing through Pisces, Aries, Taurus, and into Gemini as it brightens to zero magnitude, and its ochre glow begins to dominate the eastern sky after midnight. Mars remains in Gemini through opposition on Christmas Eve when Mars is magnitude –1 and is visible throughout the night. It will draw attention to itself because of its distinctive rusty hue.

At the 2003 closest approach, Mars reached 25.1″ in apparent diameter, the maximum possible, compared to maximum apparent diameters of 20.2″ in 2005 and 15.9″ this year at closest approach at 18h UT on Dec. 19 at a distance of 0.5895AU, or 88 183 000 km. Opposition this year is on Christmas Eve, at 19h 41m UT the night of Dec. 24, when the red planet shines at magnitude –1.6.

Since the apparent diameter of Mars at its least-favourable (aphelic) oppositions is 13.8″, the red planet will be a more difficult telescopic target in 2007 than the past two more-favourable approaches, but as in other things, size is not everything. Two other factors come into play. The most important is atmospheric turbulence on Earth, which is heavily dependent on the altitude above the horizon of the object being observed. An altitude of at least 30° is usually necessary for even moderately steady seeing; above 45° is much preferred. In this respect, for Mars observers at midnorthern latitudes in 2007, the news is all good. From Halloween through to early February—the prime observing window—an observer at 45°N latitude will see Mars 70° above the horizon when at the meridian. This high opposition altitude for Mars from mid-northern latitudes will not be repeated until 2022.

Although high elevation above the horizon does not make up for the smaller apparent size of Mars this year, planetary observers should be aware that the observing window around the opposition half a century ago, in December 1960, was nearly identical to the one this year. Members of the Toronto and Montreal Centres of the RASC experienced views of Mars that became legendary for good seeing and contrast and clarity of detail. Many pencil sketches of Mars made by observers using10- to 20-cm refractors and Newtonian telescopes at both Centres were combined to produce excellent global maps of Mars.

OPPOSITIONS OF MARS, 2001–2014

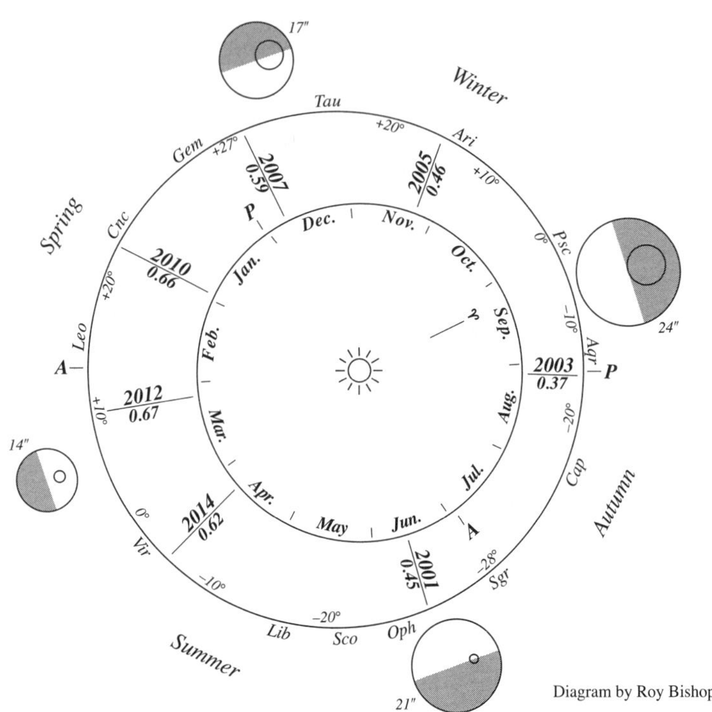

Diagram by Roy Bishop

The above diagram represents the orbits of Earth and Mars as viewed from the north ecliptic pole. Straight lines link simultaneous positions of the two planets for seven successive oppositions of Mars, beginning with that of the year 2001. The separation of the two planets (in astronomical units) at the various oppositions is indicated beside each of the connecting lines. The months inside of Earth's orbit indicate the position of Earth during the year (both planets orbit counterclockwise). For each orbit, two tick marks labelled A and P indicate the aphelion point and the perihelion point, respectively. The direction of the vernal equinox is shown (toward the late September position of Earth). Around the orbit of Mars is indicated its declination (ranges between +27° and –28°) and the constellation in which Mars resides when at opposition.

Four views of Mars are shown—at its two equinoxes and two solstices. These views show the portion of Mars illuminated by the Sun, the location and approximate size of its north polar cap, and the apparent size of Mars (labelled in arcseconds) for oppositions occurring at these points in its orbit. The seasons of the Martian northern hemisphere are indicated around the outer margin of the diagram, and are very nearly one season ahead of those on Earth at the same orbital position. (For the southern hemisphere of Mars, the season and the configuration of the south polar cap are the same as those of the diametrically opposite view.) Note that the maximum angular diameter Mars can attain (25") occurs near its perihelion, at a late-August opposition.

As an example of the information that can be read from this diagram: the 2005 opposition of Mars occurred in early November with Mars 0.46 au from Earth. Mars was about 20" in angular diameter and located near declination +15° in Aries. It was midwinter in the northern hemisphere of Mars, with a large north polar cap beginning to show at the northern limb and a small south polar cap possibly visible near the southern limb.

A second factor that heavily affects the observing outcome during a Mars opposition is also atmospheric turbulence, although in this case the turbulence in question is in the atmosphere of Mars. An example was the opposition of June 2001, which turned into a major disappointment for many fans of Mars observing because just days after the planet's closest approach to Earth, a dust storm spread to envelop 80% of the Martian globe for several months thereafter. It was the biggest dust storm seen on Mars in three decades. Could it happen again? So little is known about the seasonal atmospheric dynamics behind the storms that predicting Martian storm activity months or years in advance has proven only slightly more accurate than flipping coins.

In moments of good seeing, observers using 200-mm or larger telescopes of good optical quality will see an overwhelming amount of fine detail on Mars. The planet's chief characteristic is peach-coloured desert with darker greyish zones, which are also deserts of varying size and prominence. The clarity of the surface features varies depending on the regional transparency of the Martian atmosphere. In addition to local dust storms, ice clouds and haze can lower contrast across large areas of the disk. When the Martian air is clear, and the seeing conditions on Earth permit, the subtle colour and fine detail of the planet's surface are exquisite and compelling in a telescope. In particular, changes in the dark regions from one opposition to the next caused by wind-blown dust have fascinated observers since the late 19th century.

The region within a few degrees latitude of the equator of Mars will be at the centre of the Martian disc throughout the prime observing window. The Martian southern-hemisphere autumn equinox occurs on 2007 Dec. 9. This means that the south polar cap will be at its minimum size and probably undetectable in smaller telescopes. The north polar cap will be near maximum size and likely hidden under an extensive bluish haze called the north polar hood until sometime in December. After that, the north polar hood will gradually break up, exposing the white, mainly frozen carbon-dioxide north polar cap. At times during this apparition, the north polar cap should be the most prominent Martian feature.

Coloured eyepiece filters can improve the visibility of darker Martian surface features and reduce glare in larger-aperture telescopes. Deep yellow, orange, or red filters enhance the contrast of the dark areas. Smaller telescopes benefit most from a #21 or #23A filter; for larger instruments try #23A or #25. These filters also slightly improve the seeing by eliminating shorter (mostly blue) wavelengths of light, which are more susceptible to atmospheric turbulence. For the same reason, these filters also reduce the effects of atmospheric dispersion mentioned in the first section.

Mars observers using achromatic refractors can also consider a minus-violet or planetary-contrast filter, which uses the interference technology of nebula filters to heighten contrast and reduce chromatic aberration on the planets. In recent years, several filters have become available specifically designed to reduce the image-degrading false colour inherent in achromatic refractors of 100-mm aperture and above and thereby sharpen planetary images. A report on these filters by Thomas Dobbins in *Sky & Telescope,* April 2004, p. 54, is essential reading for owners of achromatic refractors in the 100-mm to 200-mm class. These filters sharpen images of the Moon, Jupiter, Saturn, and particularly Mars, however, they are not a complete solution. Each filter dims the view—often significantly—and introduces a colour cast of its own to the planet (usually yellow-green), although it is not as blatant as the hues imparted by the colour filters mentioned above.

Planetary filters are most effective when used after the observer is fully familiar with the planet's appearance without a filter. This is the only way to properly gauge the filters' effectiveness (if any). Small-telescope owners should note that all the filters mentioned here have minimal benefits on telescopes under 100-mm aperture. Further, in the case of Mars there is also an aesthetic issue. Much of the history and lore of Mars connects to the planet's colour in the sky, as well as the hues visible telescopically on its surface. The ideas of Schaparelli and Lowell from the late 19th century stem at least partly from the beautiful mix of coral, greenish-grey, yellow, and white that greets the observer's gaze across the interplanetary gulf that separates Earth from Mars.

JUPITER

Jupiter, the solar system's largest planet, is a colossal ball of hydrogen and helium without any solid surface comparable to land masses on Earth. Jupiter likely has a small rocky core encased in a thick mantle of metallic hydrogen which is enveloped by a massive atmospheric cloak topped by a quilt of multicoloured clouds. These clouds are the visible surface of Jupiter—a realm of constant change characterized by alternating dark belts and brighter zones. The zones are ammonia ice-crystal clouds, the belts mainly ammonium hydrosulphide clouds. Frequently, the belts intrude on the zones with dark rifts or loops called festoons.

The equatorial region of Jupiter's clouds rotates 5 min faster than the rest of the planet: 9 h 50 min compared to 9 h 55 min. This means constant interaction as one region slips by the other at about 400 km/h. It also means that there are basically two rotational systems from the viewpoint of week-to-week telescopic observation. (See Jupiter—Table of Daily Central Meridians, 2007 on p. 178 for daily longitudes of Jupiter's regions System I and System II.) Jupiter's rapid rotation also makes the great globe markedly bulged at the equator.

Jupiter—2007		
Date UT	Mag.	Equatorial Diameter ″
Jan. 1.0	−1.8	31.9
Feb. 1.0	−1.9	33.9
Mar. 1.0	−2.0	36.6
Apr. 1.0	−2.3	40.2
May 1.0	−2.5	43.8
Jun. 1.0	−2.6	45.7
Jul. 1.0	−2.5	45.0
Aug. 1.0	−2.4	42.0
Sep. 1.0	−2.2	38.3
Oct. 1.0	−2.0	35.2
Nov. 1.0	−1.9	33.0
Dec. 1.0	−1.8	31.8
Jan. 1.0	−1.8	31.7

Two dark belts, the North Equatorial Belt and the South Equatorial Belt, are obvious in the smallest telescopes. Larger instruments reveal several more narrow dark belts along with the famous Great Red Spot, a salmon-coloured oval vortex observed for centuries on the south edge of the South Equatorial Belt. Historically, the Red Spot has varied from being blatantly obvious to nearly invisible. For example, in 2006 it was detectable with a 100-mm aperture but could hardly be described as prominent because it closely matched its surroundings in hue and contrast. In 2007, observers should find the Red Spot near longitude 110° in System II. (See Jupiter—Daily Central Meridians and Time of Transit of Great Red Spot at right for instructions to determine when the Great Red Spot crosses Jupiter's central meridian.)

The smallest of telescopes will reveal Jupiter's four large satellites, three of which are larger than Earth's satellite (see p. 21). They provide a never-ending fascination for amateur astronomers. (For the configurations of the Galilean satellites see the right side of the pages in the THE SKY MONTH BY MONTH section on pp. 83–105.) Sometimes the satellites are paired on either side of the belted planet; frequently one is missing—either behind Jupiter, in the planet's shadow, or in front of Jupiter. In the latter case the satellite usually blends in against Jupiter's bright clouds and is difficult to see (more on this below). Even more interesting are the occasions when one of the satellites casts its shadow on the disk of the planet. (See PHENOMENA OF THE GALILEAN SATELLITES on pp. 183–189.) The tiny black shadow can be particularly evident if it is cast on one of the bright zones of Jupiter. This phenomenon sometimes is evident in a 60-mm refractor under good seeing conditions. On rarer occasions, *two* shadows are cast on the face of Jupiter. These "double shadow transits" appear in bold type in the table on pp. 184–189 and are included in the right-hand pages of THE SKY MONTH BY MONTH section on pp. 83–105.

The satellite umbral shadows vary significantly in size from one to another. Mean opposition angular diameters are Io 0.9″, Europa 0.6″, Ganymede 1.1″, and Callisto 0.5″. The enormous contrast between the dark shadows and the bright Jovian clouds makes these tiny features visible even though they are smaller than the nominal resolution limit of a small telescope. Furthermore, the satellites' penumbral shadows are quite large, especially Callisto's, which adds a few tenths of an arcsecond to their effective visual diameters. The satellites themselves have the following mean opposition apparent diameters: Io 1.2″, Europa 1.0″, Ganymede 1.7″, and Callisto 1.6″. A 150-mm telescope reveals the size differences as well as colour variations among the satellites.

JUPITER—DAILY CENTRAL MERIDIANS AND TIME OF TRANSIT OF GREAT RED SPOT

The table on the next page can be used to calculate the longitude of the central meridian of the observed disk of Jupiter during the months January–October (when Jupiter is well placed for observation). System I is the most rapidly rotating region between the middle of the North Equatorial Belt and the middle of the South Equatorial Belt. System II applies to the rest of the planet. The rotation rate of System I is 36.577 ± 0.008 °/h and that of System II is 36.259 ± 0.008 °/h. These figures, together with the closest tabular value, can be used to determine the longitude of a system's central meridian for any given date and time (UT) of observation. **Example:** At 1:00 ADT Aug. 16 = 4:00 UT Aug. 16 the longitude of the central meridian of System I is

$$285.8 + (36.577 \times 4) = 432.1°;$$

putting this angle in the range 0°–360° by subtracting 360° leaves a longitude of 72.1°, accurate to about 0.1°.

The table may also be used to determine when the Great Red Spot (GRS) (near longitude 110° in System II) will cross the central meridian of the disk of Jupiter. **Example:** Suppose an observer in Winnipeg is viewing Jupiter on the evening of Apr. 30 (time zone: CDT, −5 h) . At 0h UT May 1 (19h CDT Apr. 30) the table gives approximately 228° for the longitude of the central meridian in System II. A further rotation of 360° − 228° + 110° = 242° will bring the GRS to the central meridian, which will require 242° ÷ 36.259°/h = 6.67 h = 6 h 40 min. Thus the GRS will transit at 6:40 UT May 1 = 1:40 CDT May 1. Note that the GRS slowly drifts in longitude, so the 110° figure is only a guide. By timing a transit of the GRS and using the table, you can update its longitude.

When the Galilean satellites transit the disk of Jupiter, they are seldom visible in telescopes under 100 mm and are best seen near the planet's limb when entering or leaving the disk. Tracking a satellite transit completely across Jupiter is a challenging observation. Each satellite has a characteristic appearance when superimposed on the Jovian cloudscape. Europa is bright white, similar to the brightest Jovian clouds. When traversing a white cloud zone in the central sector of Jupiter, Europa is usually invisible, however, it stands out well when near the limb or against a dark belt. Callisto, the darkest satellite, is best seen in the reverse circumstances. *[Editor's note: There are no transits of Callisto in 2007.]* When seen against a pale zone this greyish satellite can be mistaken for a satellite shadow, but it is often lost against a dark belt. Ganymede is intermediate in surface brightness, but because of its great size, it is the easiest of the four to track completely across Jupiter's face. Io, innermost of the Galilean satellites, is also the most frequently seen in transit. It is close to Europa in brightness but is generally easier to follow over typical cloud features, probably due to its slightly greater diameter. Near opposition, a transiting satellite often appears adjacent to its own shadow. These events are especially worth a look. Jupiter's other satellites are photographic objects for large instruments.

As 2007 opens, Jupiter is in Scorpius, rising about 2 hours before the Sun. The big planet reaches opposition on Jun. 6, when it is 7° from Anatares. Jupiter remains in Scorpius with excursions into the "foot" of Ophiuchus during the rest of the year before descending into evening twilight in late October. Conjunction with the Sun occurs on Dec. 22.

SATURN

Saturn is the telescopic showpiece of the night sky. The chilling beauty of the ringed orb floating in a field of black is something no photographs or descriptions can adequately duplicate. Any telescope magnifying more than 30× will show the rings. The view is exquisite in 100-mm to 200-mm instruments. The rings consist of billions of particles—largely water ice—that range from microscopic specks to flying boulders the size of houses. The reason "rings" is plural is that gaps and brightness differences define hundreds of distinct rings. However, from Earth only the three most prominent components—known simply as rings A, B, and C—can be distinguished visually. (See the diagram Saturn—Main Ring Features Visible from Earth on p. 179.)

Cassini's Division, a gap between rings A and B discovered in 1675, is visible in small telescopes when the ring system is well inclined to our view. Cassini's Division is a region less densely populated with ring particles than adjacent rings. Ring B, the

JUPITER—TABLE OF DAILY CENTRAL MERIDIANS, 2007

JANUARY

Date 0h UT	System I	System II
0	280.2	198.2
1	77.9	348.3
2	235.7	138.4
3	33.4	288.5
4	191.2	78.6
5	348.9	228.8
6	146.7	18.9
7	304.4	169.0
8	102.2	319.1
9	259.9	109.2
10	57.7	259.4
11	215.4	49.5
12	13.2	199.6
13	170.9	349.7
14	328.7	139.9
15	126.5	290.0
16	284.2	80.2
17	82.0	230.3
18	239.8	20.4
19	37.6	170.6
20	195.3	320.7
21	353.1	110.9
22	150.9	261.0
23	308.7	51.2
24	106.5	201.3
25	264.3	351.5
26	62.0	141.6
27	219.8	291.8
28	17.6	82.0
29	175.4	232.1
30	333.2	22.3
31	131.0	172.5

FEBRUARY

Date 0h UT	System I	System II
1	288.8	322.7
2	86.6	112.8
3	244.4	263.0
4	42.3	53.2
5	200.1	203.4
6	357.9	353.6
7	155.7	143.7
8	313.5	293.9
9	111.4	84.1
10	269.2	234.3
11	67.0	24.5
12	224.8	174.7
13	22.7	324.9
14	180.5	115.1
15	338.3	265.3
16	136.2	55.5
17	294.0	205.8
18	91.9	356.0
19	249.7	146.2
20	47.6	296.4
21	205.4	86.6
22	3.3	236.9
23	161.1	27.1
24	319.0	177.3
25	116.9	327.6
26	274.7	117.8
27	72.6	268.0
28	230.5	58.3

MARCH

Date 0h UT	System I	System II
1	28.4	208.5
2	186.2	358.8
3	344.1	149.0
4	142.0	299.3
5	299.9	89.5
6	97.8	239.8
7	255.7	30.0
8	53.6	180.3
9	211.5	330.6
10	9.4	120.8
11	167.3	271.1
12	325.2	61.4
13	123.1	211.7
14	281.0	2.0
15	78.9	152.2
16	236.8	302.5
17	34.7	92.8
18	192.7	243.1
19	350.6	33.4
20	148.5	183.7
21	306.4	334.0
22	104.4	124.3
23	262.3	274.6
24	60.2	64.9
25	218.2	215.2
26	16.1	5.5
27	174.1	155.8
28	332.0	306.2
29	130.0	96.5
30	287.9	246.8
31	85.9	37.1

APRIL

Date 0h UT	System I	System II
1	243.9	187.5
2	41.8	337.8
3	199.8	128.1
4	357.7	278.5
5	155.7	68.8
6	313.7	219.2
7	111.7	9.5
8	269.6	159.8
9	67.6	310.2
10	225.6	100.5
11	23.6	250.9
12	181.6	41.3
13	339.6	191.6
14	137.6	342.0
15	295.6	132.3
16	93.6	282.7
17	251.6	73.1
18	49.6	223.4
19	207.6	13.8
20	5.6	164.2
21	163.6	314.6
22	321.6	105.0
23	119.6	255.3
24	277.6	45.7
25	75.6	196.1
26	233.6	346.5
27	31.7	136.9
28	189.7	287.3
29	347.7	77.7
30	145.7	228.1

MAY

Date 0h UT	System I	System II
1	303.8	18.4
2	101.8	168.8
3	259.8	319.2
4	57.8	109.6
5	215.9	260.0
6	13.9	50.4
7	171.9	200.9
8	330.0	351.3
9	128.0	141.7
10	286.0	292.1
11	84.1	82.5
12	242.1	232.9
13	40.2	23.3
14	198.2	173.7
15	356.2	324.1
16	154.3	114.5
17	312.3	264.9
18	110.4	55.3
19	268.4	205.8
20	66.5	356.2
21	224.5	146.6
22	22.5	297.0
23	180.6	87.4
24	338.6	237.8
25	136.7	28.2
26	294.7	178.6
27	92.7	329.1
28	250.8	119.5
29	48.8	269.9
30	206.9	60.3
31	4.9	210.7

JUNE

Date 0h UT	System I	System II
1	162.9	1.1
2	321.0	151.5
3	119.0	301.9
4	277.0	92.3
5	75.1	242.7
6	233.1	33.1
7	31.1	183.5
8	189.2	333.9
9	347.2	124.3
10	145.2	274.7
11	303.2	65.1
12	101.3	215.5
13	259.3	5.9
14	57.3	156.3
15	215.3	306.6
16	13.3	97.0
17	171.3	247.4
18	329.3	37.8
19	127.3	188.2
20	285.3	338.5
21	83.3	128.9
22	241.3	279.3
23	39.3	69.6
24	197.3	220.0
25	355.3	10.3
26	153.3	160.7
27	311.3	311.1
28	109.3	101.4
29	267.2	251.7
30	65.2	42.1

JULY

Date 0h UT	System I	System II
1	223.2	192.4
2	21.1	342.8
3	179.1	133.1
4	337.1	283.4
5	135.0	73.8
6	293.0	224.1
7	90.9	14.4
8	248.9	164.7
9	46.8	315.0
10	204.7	105.3
11	2.7	255.6
12	160.6	45.9
13	318.5	196.2
14	116.5	346.5
15	274.4	136.8
16	72.3	287.1
17	230.2	77.4
18	28.1	227.7
19	186.0	18.0
20	343.9	168.2
21	141.8	318.5
22	299.7	108.8
23	97.6	259.0
24	255.5	49.3
25	53.4	199.5
26	211.3	349.8
27	9.1	140.0
28	167.0	290.3
29	324.9	80.5
30	122.7	230.7
31	280.6	21.0

AUGUST

Date 0h UT	System I	System II
1	78.4	171.2
2	236.3	321.4
3	34.1	111.6
4	192.0	261.8
5	349.8	52.0
6	147.7	202.3
7	305.5	352.5
8	103.3	142.7
9	261.1	292.8
10	59.0	83.0
11	216.8	233.2
12	14.6	23.4
13	172.4	173.6
14	330.2	323.8
15	128.0	113.9
16	285.8	264.1
17	83.6	54.3
18	241.4	204.5
19	39.2	354.6
20	197.0	144.8
21	354.8	294.9
22	152.6	85.1
23	310.3	235.2
24	108.1	25.4
25	265.9	175.5
26	63.6	325.6
27	221.4	115.8
28	19.2	265.9
29	176.9	56.0
30	334.7	206.2
31	132.4	356.3

SEPTEMBER

Date 0h UT	System I	System II
1	290.2	146.4
2	87.9	296.5
3	245.7	86.6
4	43.4	236.8
5	201.2	26.9
6	358.9	177.0
7	156.6	327.1
8	314.4	117.2
9	112.1	267.3
10	269.8	57.4
11	67.5	207.5
12	225.3	357.6
13	23.0	147.7
14	180.7	297.7
15	338.4	87.8
16	136.1	237.9
17	293.8	28.0
18	91.5	178.1
19	249.2	328.1
20	46.9	118.2
21	204.6	268.3
22	2.3	58.4
23	160.0	208.4
24	317.7	358.5
25	115.4	148.6
26	273.1	298.6
27	70.8	88.7
28	228.5	238.7
29	26.2	28.8
30	183.9	178.9

OCTOBER

Date 0h UT	System I	System II
1	341.6	328.9
2	139.2	119.0
3	296.9	269.0
4	94.6	59.1
5	252.3	209.1
6	49.9	359.2
7	207.6	149.2
8	5.3	299.2
9	163.0	89.3
10	320.6	239.3
11	118.3	29.4
12	276.0	179.4
13	73.6	329.4
14	231.3	119.5
15	29.0	269.5
16	186.6	59.5
17	344.3	209.6
18	142.0	359.6
19	299.6	149.6
20	97.3	299.7
21	254.9	89.7
22	52.6	239.7
23	210.3	29.8
24	7.9	179.8
25	165.6	329.8
26	323.2	119.8
27	120.9	269.9
28	278.5	59.9
29	76.2	209.9
30	233.8	359.9
31	31.5	150.0

brightest, overpowers ring C to such an extent that ring C, also known as the *crepe ring,* is seen only with difficulty in small telescopes. A Saturn phenomenon easily seen with backyard telescopes is the shadow of the planet on the rings. From one to four months before or after opposition the shadow falling on the rings is very apparent, often giving the scene a powerful three-dimensional aura. The shadow is not easily seen in the weeks near opposition, at which point the shadow is cast straight back from our line of sight

In addition to the rings, Saturn has a family of at least 47 satellites (see pp. 23–25). Titan, the largest, is easily seen in any telescope as an 8th-magnitude object orbiting Saturn in about 16 days. At east and west elongation Titan appears about five ring diameters from the planet. Telescopes over 60 mm in aperture should reveal 10th-magnitude Rhea at less than two ring diameters from Saturn. The satellite Iapetus has the peculiar property of being five times brighter at western elongation (magnitude 10.1) than at eastern elongation (11.9). One side of the satellite has the reflectivity of snow while the other resembles dark rock. When brightest, Iapetus is located about 12 ring diameters west of the parent planet. Of the remaining satellites, Tethys and Dione may be glimpsed in a 150-mm telescope, but the others require

SATURN—MAIN RING FEATURES VISIBLE FROM EARTH

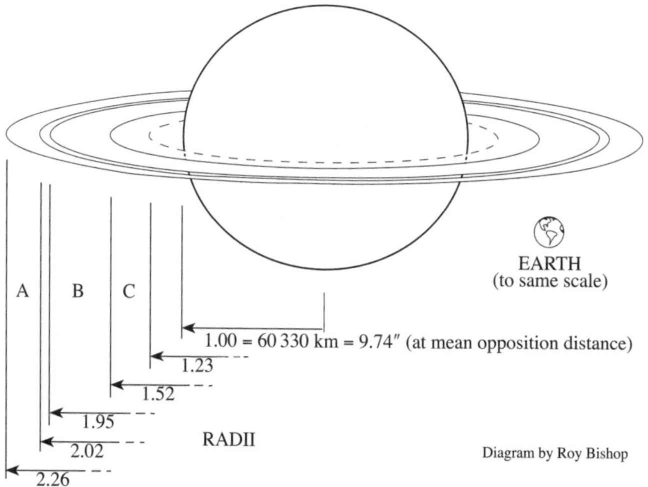

Diagram by Roy Bishop

SATURN'S RING SYSTEM—MAIN STRUCTURAL REGIONS

Ring	Radius**	Discoverer
D	1.11 – 1.23	*Voyager 1* (1980)
C*	1.23 – 1.52	W.C. & G.P. Bond, W.R. Dawes (1850)
B*	1.52 – 1.95	Galileo (1610), C. Huygens (1659),
A*	2.02 – 2.26	G.D. Cassini (1675)
F	2.33	*Pioneer 11* (1979)
G	2.8	*Voyager 1* (1980)
E	3. – 8.	W.A. Feibelman (1966)

*Visible from Earth; also, the E ring can be detected when Saturn's ring system appears edge-on.

**In units of Saturn's equatorial radius (60 330 km)

Saturn—2007				
Date UT		Mag.	Equatorial Diam. ″	Ring Incl. °
Jan.	1.0	+0.3	19.7	−12.6
Feb.	1.0	0.0	20.2	−13.6
Mar.	1.0	0.0	20.1	−14.6
Apr.	1.0	+0.2	19.4	−15.3
May	1.0	+0.4	18.4	−15.4
Jun.	1.0	+0.5	17.5	−14.7
Jul.	1.0	+0.6	16.7	−13.6
Aug.	1.0	+0.6	16.3	−12.0
Sep.	1.0	+0.6	16.2	−10.3
Oct.	1.0	+0.7	16.5	−8.8
Nov.	1.0	+0.8	17.2	−7.4
Dec.	1.0	+0.7	18.1	−6.7
Jan.	1.0	+0.6	19.1	−6.7

larger apertures. (See CONFIGURATIONS OF SATURN'S BRIGHTEST SATELLITES on pp. 190–193.)

The disk of Saturn appears about one-sixth the area of Jupiter through the same telescope with the same magnification. In telescopes less than 75-mm aperture, probably no features will ever be seen on the cloud deck of the planet other than the shadow cast by the rings. As the size of the telescope is increased, the pale equatorial region, a dusky equatorial band, and the darker polar regions become evident. Saturn has a belt system like Jupiter's, but it is much less active and the contrast is reduced. In addition, it is partially obscured by the ring passing in front of the planet. Seldom in telescopes less than 100 mm in aperture do more than one or two belts come into view.

Saturn is at opposition in Leo on Feb. 10, and spends the entire year in that constellation. The Earthbound observer's view of the tilt of Saturn's rings varies from edge-on to "wide open" (about 27°) over a 7 to 8-year cycle. They were edge-on in 1995 and 1996, and open to their maximum extent in 2003. In 2007 the ring tilt varies between 15.4° and 6.7°.

URANUS

At magnitude 5.7–5.9, Uranus can be seen with the unaided eye under a clear, dark sky. However, it is much more easily located with binoculars. A 75-mm telescope will reveal its small, greenish, featureless disk.

Unlike the three other giant planets, the axis of Uranus is tipped almost parallel to the plane of the solar system. This means that we view Uranus nearly pole-on at certain points in its 84-year orbit. The southern (and counterclockwise turning) hemisphere of Uranus is now angled slightly toward Earth. Its south pole appeared

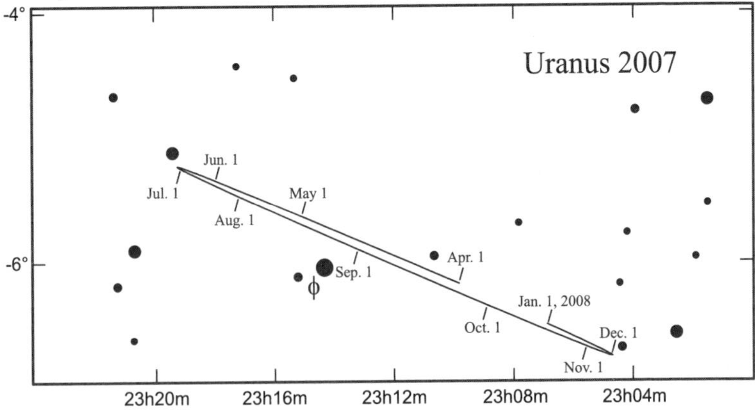

The finder chart above, provided by David Lane, shows the path of Uranus in Aquarius during the nine-month period 2007 April–December. Coordinates are for equinox J2000.0, and the magnitude limit is approximately 8.5. Tick marks are drawn along the path at the beginning of each month. The brightest star in the chart is 4th-magnitude ϕ Aqr.

Along the five-month retrograde portion of its track, from Jun. 23 to Nov. 24 and centred at its Sep. 9 opposition, Uranus ranges between 5.7 and 5.8 in magnitude.

nearest to (and slightly south of) the centre of its disk in 1985. Uranus has at least 27 satellites (see p. 25), all smaller than Earth's Moon, none of which can be detected in small or moderate-sized telescopes.

Uranus is at opposition in Aquarius on Sep. 7, when it is magnitude 5.7 and 3.7″ in apparent diameter. Use the chart on the previous page to locate this distant planet.

NEPTUNE

Neptune is an 8th-magnitude binocular object—an easy target in 7 × 50 or larger glasses—but seeing the planet as a disk rather than a point of light is a different matter. Magnifications over 200× are usually necessary, and even then Neptune is just a tiny bluish dot with no hard edge due to limb darkening. Neptune's large satellite, Triton, can be seen by an experienced observer using a 300-mm telescope. Triton varies between 8″ and 17″ from Neptune.

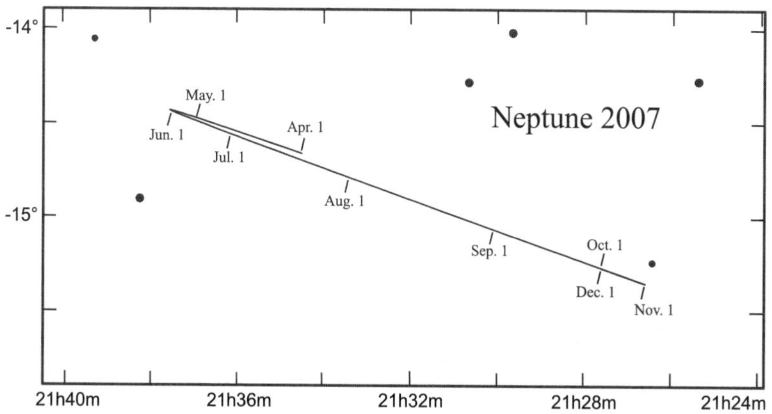

The finder chart above, provided by David Lane, shows the path of Neptune in Capricornus during the eight-month period 2007 April–November. Coordinates are for equinox J2000.0, and the magnitude limit is approximately 8.5. Tick marks are drawn along the path at the beginning of each month. The brightest star in the chart is 6th-magnitude HIPPARCOS 106199.

Along the five-month retrograde portion of its track, from May 25 to Oct. 31 and centred at its Aug. 13 opposition, Neptune ranges between 7.8 and 7.9 in magnitude.

In 2007, Neptune is in Capricornus and may be easily identified using the chart below. At opposition on Aug. 13, Neptune is magnitude 7.8 and 2.3″ in diameter.

PLUTO

Besides being the solar system's smallest planet, Pluto is different from the other eight in almost every respect. Its unique characteristics include its orbit, which is so elliptical that the planet was closer to the Sun than was Neptune from 1980 through 1999.

Opposition is on Jun. 19, when the planet is at magnitude 13.9. It can be identified using the chart overleaf and a 200-mm or larger telescope. Pluto was near perihelion throughout the 1980s and 1990s and as bright as it ever gets. At that time, a few observers (with good optics, transparent skies, steady seeing, and high magnifications) succeeded in sighting Pluto with telescopes as small as 100-mm refractors.

In 2006 the International Astronomical Union formally reclassified Pluto as a dwarf planet. Nonetheless it remains an object of interest for amateur astronomers.

FINDER CHART FOR PLUTO

BY IAN CAMERON

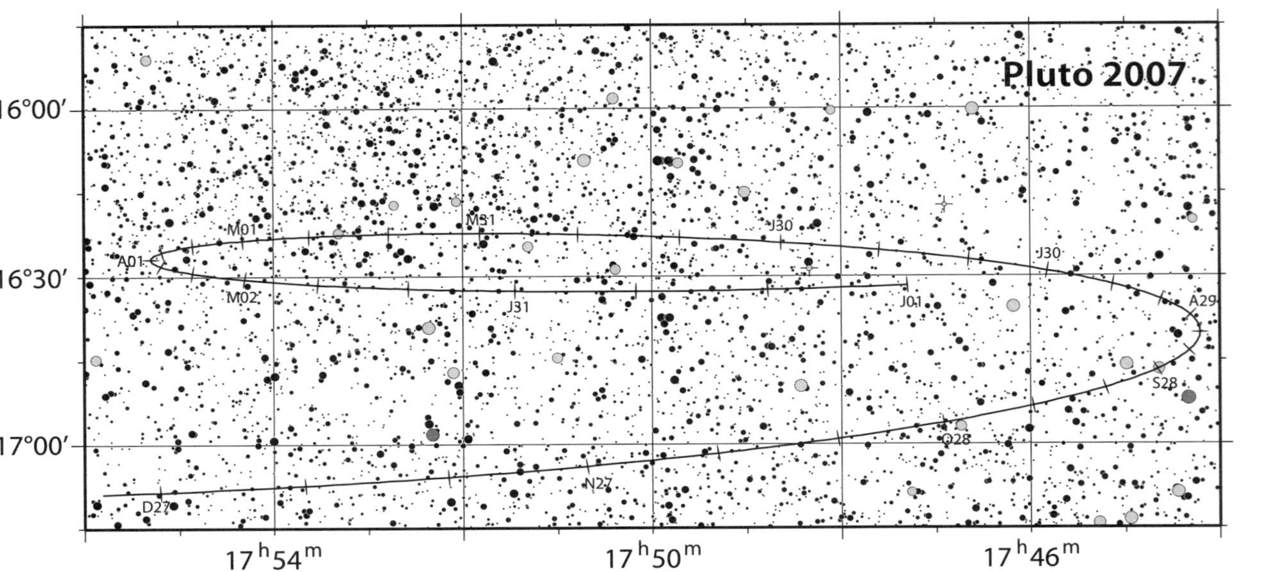

This chart shows the path of Pluto in the constellation Sagittarius during 2007. Pluto's position is marked at 10-day intervals beginning January 1 (J01) and ending on December 31.

To locate the field: *The gray disks all appear in* Uranometria *(1st edition, vol. II, chart no. 293) and only the dark-gray ones appear in Tirion's* Sky Atlas 2000.0 *(1st edition, chart no. 15). The brightest star in the chart has a magnitude of 7.55 and is located in the bottom right corner. The two planetary nebulae NGC 6439 (just inside the open end of the smaller loop), and PK 11+6.1 (located at RA $17^h 46^m 54^s$ Dec –16° 17′) are indicated by crosses through open circles.*

Pluto is at opposition on Jun. 19 at magnitude 13.9. The chart limit is magnitude 14.5 using the Guide Star Catalog as the criterion. Caution is thus advised when star hopping, since not all faint visible stars appear in this catalogue.

The chart was generated mainly using the free public-domain Generic Mapping Tools *program.*

PHENOMENA OF THE GALILEAN SATELLITES

The table on pp. 184–189 gives the various transits, occultations, and eclipses of the four great satellites of Jupiter during January–October 2007. Jupiter is not well-placed for observing during the final two months since it is in conjunction with the Sun on Dec. 23. Double shadow transits and satellite transits are indicated in **bold.**

Since the satellite phenomena are not instantaneous but take up to several minutes, the predicted times are for the middle of each event. The predictions were generated by the Institut de Mécanique Céleste et de Calcul des Ephémérides in Paris.

Satellites are denoted using the standard designations: I = Io; II = Europa; III = Ganymede; IV = Callisto. Events are denoted using the following abbreviations:

Ec = eclipse; Oc = occultation; Tr = transit of satellite; Sh = transit of shadow;
I = ingress; E = egress; D = disappearance; R = reappearance

The general motion of the satellites and the successive phenomena are shown in the diagram at right, which is a view of Jupiter and the orbit of one of its satellites looking down from the north side. Satellites move from east to west across the face of the planet and from west to east behind it (here "east" and "west" are used in the sense of the observer's sky, not in the Jovian sense). Before opposition, shadows fall to the west and after opposition, to the east (as in the diagram).

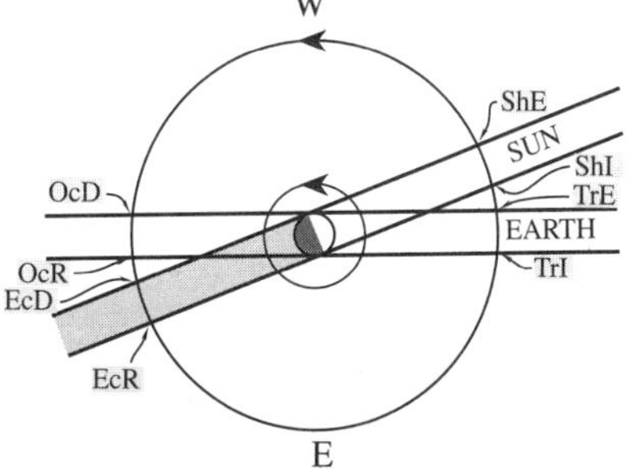

The sequence of phenomena for the outer satellite shown in the diagram, counterclockwise beginning at the lower right, is transit ingress (TrI), transit egress (TrE), shadow ingress (ShI), shadow egress (ShE), occultation disappearance (OcD), occultation reappearance (OcR), eclipse disappearance (EcD), and eclipse reappearance (EcR). The actual sequence will depend on the actual Sun–Jupiter–Earth angle and the size of the satellite's orbit.

Over three-quarters of the phenomena listed will not be visible from any one location because they occur when Jupiter is near or below the horizon or when daylight interferes. In practice, an observer usually knows when Jupiter will be conveniently placed in the night sky; if not, he or she can check THE SKY MONTH BY MONTH section (pp. 82–104) for this information. The table can then be scanned to see if there are any events during the intended observing period. For example, an observer in Halifax would know that Jupiter is well placed near midnight in early June, with opposition occurring on Jun. 5. If planning to observe from 22:00 Jun. 3 to 2:00 Jun. 4 ADT (3 h behind UT), he or she could scan the table for events in the interval 1:00 to 5:00 UT Jun. 4 and find that there are four events, beginning at 22:51 ADT with the ingress of Io's shadow, closely followed at 22:54 by a transit of Io. Two hours later Io's shadow egresses at 1:03 (Jun. 4) followed by the end of Io's transit a few minutes later. The configuration of the four Galilean satellites during that night is given in the diagram on the right-hand side of p. 93 in the THE SKY MONTH BY MONTH section.

Callisto is the only Galilean satellite that is not eclipsed during each of its revolutions. It is only eclipsed during about half of Jupiter's orbit around the Sun. No eclipses of Callisto occur this year; the next one will occur on 2008 Jan. 9.

A total of 1881 events (341 eclipse, 339 occultation, 601 transit, and 600 shadow) appear in the table, an average of one event every 3 h 53 min.

SATELLITES OF JUPITER, UT OF 2007 GEOCENTRIC PHENOMENA

JANUARY

Day	UT	Sat.	Phen.
0	0:27	II	TrE
	5:30	I	ECD
	8:19	I	OcR
	23:59	I	ECD
1	2:38	I	ShI
	3:17	I	TrI
	4:48	I	ShE
	5:28	I	TrE
	14:48	II	ECD
	18:43	II	OcR
2	2:49	I	OcR
	16:37	III	ShI
	18:32	III	ShE
	19:19	III	TrI
	21:07	I	ShI
	21:23	III	TrE
	21:47	I	TrI
	23:17	I	ShE
	23:58	I	TrE
3	9:55	II	ShI
	11:17	II	TrI
	12:27	II	ShE
	13:50	II	TrE
	18:27	I	ECD
	21:19	I	OcR
4	15:35	I	ShI
	16:17	I	TrI
	17:45	I	ShE
	18:28	I	TrE
5	4:06	II	ECD
	8:07	II	OcR
	12:55	I	ECD
	15:49	I	OcR
6	6:48	III	ECD
	8:46	III	EcR
	9:43	III	OcD
	10:04	I	ShI
	10:47	I	TrI
	11:48	III	OcR
	12:14	I	ShE
	12:58	I	TrE
	23:12	II	ShI
7	0:41	II	TrI
	1:44	II	ShE
	3:13	II	TrE
	7:24	I	ECD
	10:19	I	OcR
8	4:32	I	ShI
	5:17	I	TrI
	6:42	I	ShE
	7:28	I	TrE
	17:23	II	ECD
	21:30	II	OcR
9	1:52	I	ECD
	4:49	I	OcR
	20:35	III	ShI
	22:31	III	ShE
	23:00	I	ShI
	23:43	III	TrI
	23:47	**I**	**TrI**
10	1:10	I	ShE
	1:47	III	TrE
	1:58	I	TrE
	12:29	II	ShI
	14:04	II	TrI
	15:01	II	ShE
	16:36	II	TrE
	20:21	I	ECD
	23:19	I	OcR
11	17:29	I	ShI
	18:17	I	TrI
	19:39	I	ShE
	20:28	I	TrE
12	6:41	II	ECD
	10:54	II	OcR
	14:49	I	ECD
	17:49	I	OcR
13	10:45	III	ECD
	11:57	I	ShI
	12:44	III	EcR
	12:47	I	TrI
	14:05	III	OcD
	14:07	I	ShE
	14:57	I	TrE
	16:10	III	OcR
14	1:46	II	ShI
	3:26	II	TrI
	4:18	II	ShE
	5:59	II	TrE
	9:17	I	ECD
	12:18	I	OcR
15	6:26	I	ShI
	7:17	I	TrI
	8:36	I	ShE
	9:27	I	TrE
	19:58	II	ECD
16	0:18	II	OcR
	3:46	I	ECD
	6:48	I	OcR
17	0:33	III	ShI
	0:54	**I**	**ShI**
	1:47	I	TrI
	2:30	III	ShE
	3:04	I	ShE
	3:57	I	TrE
	4:05	III	TrI
	6:08	III	TrE
	15:03	II	ShI
	16:49	II	TrI
	17:35	II	ShE
	19:21	II	TrE
	22:14	I	ECD
18	1:18	I	OcR
	19:23	I	ShI
	20:16	I	TrI
	21:32	I	ShE
	22:27	I	TrE
19	9:16	II	ECD
	13:41	II	OcR
	16:42	I	ECD
	19:47	I	OcR
20	13:51	I	ShI
	14:42	III	ECD
	14:46	I	TrI
	16:01	I	ShE
	16:41	III	EcR
	16:57	I	TrE
	18:25	III	OcD
	20:30	III	OcR
21	4:20	II	ShI
	6:11	II	TrI
	6:52	II	ShE
	8:43	II	TrE
	11:11	I	ECD
	14:17	I	OcR
22	8:19	I	ShI
	9:16	I	TrI
	10:29	I	ShE
	11:26	I	TrE
	22:33	II	ECD
23	3:04	II	OcR
	5:39	I	ECD
	8:47	I	OcR
24	2:48	I	ShI
	3:45	I	TrI
	4:31	**III**	**ShI**
	4:58	I	ShE
	5:56	I	TrE
	6:29	III	ShE
	8:25	III	TrI
	10:28	III	TrE
	17:37	II	ShI
	19:33	II	TrI
	20:09	II	ShE
	22:05	II	TrE
25	0:07	I	ECD
	3:16	I	OcR
	21:16	I	ShI
	22:15	I	TrI
	23:26	I	ShE
26	0:25	I	TrE
	11:51	II	ECD
	16:27	II	OcR
	18:35	I	ECD
	21:46	I	OcR
27	15:45	I	ShI
	16:45	I	TrI
	17:55	I	ShE
	18:39	III	ECD
	18:55	I	TrE
	20:39	III	EcR
	22:43	III	OcD
28	0:47	III	OcR
	6:54	II	ShI
	8:54	II	TrI
	9:25	II	ShE
	11:26	II	TrE
	13:04	I	ECD
	16:15	I	OcR
29	10:13	I	ShI
	11:14	I	TrI
	12:23	I	ShE
	13:25	I	TrE
30	1:09	II	ECD
	5:49	II	OcR
	7:32	I	ECD
	10:44	I	OcR
31	4:42	I	ShI
	5:44	I	TrI
	6:51	I	ShE
	7:54	I	TrE
	8:29	III	ShI
	10:27	III	ShE
	12:42	III	TrI
	14:44	III	TrE
	20:11	II	ShI
	22:16	II	TrI
	22:42	II	ShE

FEBRUARY

Day	UT	Sat.	Phen.
1	0:47	II	TrE
	2:00	I	ECD
	5:14	I	OcR
	23:10	I	ShI
2	0:13	I	TrI
	1:20	I	ShE
	2:24	I	TrE
	14:27	II	ECD
	19:12	II	OcR
	20:29	I	ECD
	23:43	I	OcR
3	17:38	I	ShI
	18:43	I	TrI
	19:48	I	ShE
	20:53	I	TrE
	22:37	III	ECD
4	0:38	III	EcR
	2:59	III	OcD
	5:04	III	OcR
	9:28	II	ShI
	11:36	II	TrI
	11:59	II	ShE
	14:07	II	TrE
	14:57	I	ECD
	18:12	I	OcR
5	12:07	I	ShI
	13:12	I	TrI
	14:17	I	ShE
	15:22	I	TrE
6	3:44	II	ECD
	8:33	II	OcR
	9:25	I	ECD
	12:42	I	OcR
7	6:35	I	ShI
	7:41	I	TrI
	8:45	I	ShE
	9:52	I	TrE
	12:26	III	ShI
	14:25	III	ShE
	16:56	III	TrI
	18:58	III	TrE
	22:44	II	ShI
8	0:57	II	TrI
	1:15	II	ShE
	3:28	II	TrE
	3:53	I	ECD
	7:11	I	OcR
9	1:04	I	ShI
	2:11	I	TrI
	3:13	I	ShE
	4:21	I	TrE
	17:02	II	ECD
	21:55	II	OcR
	22:22	I	ECD
10	1:40	I	OcR
	19:32	I	ShI
	20:40	I	TrI
	21:42	I	ShE
	22:50	I	TrE
11	2:35	III	ECD
	4:36	III	EcR
	7:12	III	OcD
	9:16	III	OcR
	12:01	II	ShI
	14:17	II	TrI
	14:32	II	ShE
	16:48	II	TrE
	16:50	I	ECD
	20:09	I	OcR
12	14:00	I	ShI
	15:09	I	TrI
	16:10	I	ShE
	17:20	I	TrE
13	6:20	II	ECD
	11:16	II	OcR
	11:18	I	ECD
	14:38	I	OcR
14	8:29	I	ShI
	9:38	I	TrI
	10:39	I	ShE
	11:49	I	TrE
	16:23	III	ShI
	18:23	III	ShE
	21:08	III	TrI
	23:10	III	TrE
15	1:18	II	ShI
	3:37	II	TrI
	3:49	II	ShE
	5:46	I	ECD
	6:07	II	TrE
	9:07	I	OcR
16	2:57	I	ShI
	4:08	I	TrI
	5:07	I	ShE
	6:18	I	TrE
	19:38	II	ECD
17	0:15	I	ECD
	0:37	II	OcR
	3:36	I	OcR
	21:26	I	ShI
	22:37	I	TrI
	23:35	I	ShE
18	0:47	I	TrE
	6:32	III	ECD
	8:35	III	EcR
	11:22	III	OcD
	13:26	III	OcR
	14:34	II	ShI
	16:56	II	TrI
	17:05	II	ShE
	18:43	I	ECD
	19:26	II	TrE
	22:05	I	OcR

SATELLITES OF JUPITER, UT OF 2007 GEOCENTRIC PHENOMENA (cont)

19	15:54	I	ShI
	17:06	I	TrI
	18:04	I	ShE
	19:16	I	TrE
20	8:55	II	ECD
	13:11	I	ECD
	13:57	II	OcR
	16:34	I	OcR
21	10:22	I	ShI
	11:35	I	TrI
	12:32	I	ShE
	13:45	I	TrE
	20:21	III	ShI
	22:21	III	ShE
22	1:16	III	TrI
	3:18	III	TrE
	3:51	II	ShI
	6:15	II	TrI
	6:22	II	ShE
	7:39	I	ECD
	8:45	II	TrE
	11:03	I	OcR
23	4:51	I	ShI
	6:04	I	TrI
	7:01	I	ShE
	8:14	I	TrE
	22:13	II	ECD
24	2:08	I	ECD
	3:18	II	OcR
	5:31	I	OcR
	23:19	I	ShI
25	0:32	I	TrI
	1:29	I	ShE
	2:43	I	TrE
	10:29	III	ECD
	12:32	III	EcR
	15:28	III	OcD
	17:07	II	ShI
	17:32	III	OcR
	19:33	II	TrI
	19:38	II	ShE
	20:36	I	ECD
	22:03	II	TrE
26	0:00	I	OcR
	17:47	I	ShI
	19:01	I	TrI
	19:57	I	ShE
	21:11	I	TrE
27	11:31	II	ECD
	15:04	I	ECD
	16:37	II	OcR
	18:29	I	OcR
28	12:16	I	ShI
	13:30	I	TrI
	14:26	I	ShE
	15:40	I	TrE

MARCH

1	0:19	III	ShI
	2:20	III	ShE
	5:22	III	TrI
	6:24	II	ShI
	7:24	III	TrE
	8:51	II	TrI
	8:55	II	ShE
	9:32	I	ECD
	11:21	II	TrE
	12:57	I	OcR
2	6:44	I	ShI
	7:59	I	TrI
	8:54	I	ShE
	10:09	I	TrE
3	0:49	II	ECD
	4:01	I	ECD
	5:57	II	OcR
	7:26	I	OcR
4	1:13	I	ShI
	2:27	I	TrI
	3:23	I	ShE
	4:38	I	TrE
	14:26	III	ECD
	16:30	III	EcR
	19:30	III	OcD
	19:40	II	ShI
	21:34	III	OcR
	22:09	II	TrI
	22:11	II	ShE
	22:29	I	ECD
5	0:39	II	TrE
	1:54	I	OcR
	19:41	I	ShI
	20:56	I	TrI
	21:51	I	ShE
	23:06	I	TrE
6	14:06	II	ECD
	16:41	II	EcR
	16:41	II	OcD
	16:57	I	ECD
	19:15	II	OcR
	20:22	I	OcR
7	14:09	I	ShI
	15:25	I	TrI
	16:19	I	ShE
	17:35	I	TrE
8	4:17	III	ShI
	6:18	III	ShE
	8:57	II	ShI
	9:24	III	TrI
	11:25	I	ECD
	11:25	III	TrE
	11:26	II	TrI
	11:28	II	ShE
	13:55	II	TrE
	14:51	I	OcR
9	8:38	I	ShI
	9:53	I	TrI
	10:48	I	ShE
	12:03	I	TrE
10	3:25	II	ECD
	5:53	I	ECD
	5:59	II	EcR
	6:00	II	OcD
	8:33	II	OcR
	9:19	I	OcR
11	3:06	I	ShI
	4:21	I	TrI
	5:16	I	ShE
	6:32	I	TrE
	18:23	III	ECD
	20:27	III	EcR
	22:13	II	ShI
	23:29	III	OcD
12	0:22	I	ECD
	0:42	II	TrI
	0:44	II	ShE
	1:33	III	OcR
	3:12	II	TrE
	3:47	I	OcR
	21:35	I	ShI
	22:50	I	TrI
	23:45	I	ShE
13	1:00	I	TrE
	16:42	II	ECD
	18:50	I	ECD
	19:16	II	EcR
	19:17	II	OcD
	21:51	II	OcR
	22:15	I	OcR
14	16:03	I	ShI
	17:18	I	TrI
	18:13	I	ShE
	19:28	I	TrE
15	8:15	III	ShI
	10:17	III	ShE
	11:30	II	ShI
	13:18	I	ECD
	13:21	III	TrI
	13:58	**II**	**TrI**
	14:01	II	ShE
	15:23	III	TrE
	16:28	II	TrE
	16:44	I	OcR
16	10:31	I	ShI
	11:46	I	TrI
	12:41	I	ShE
	13:56	I	TrE
17	6:00	II	ECD
	7:46	I	ECD
	8:35	II	EcR
	8:35	II	OcD
	11:08	II	OcR
	11:12	I	OcR
18	5:00	I	ShI
	6:14	I	TrI
	7:10	I	ShE
	8:25	I	TrE
	22:20	III	ECD
19	0:25	III	EcR
	0:46	II	ShI
	2:15	I	ECD
	3:14	II	TrI
	3:17	II	ShE
	3:24	III	OcD
	5:27	III	OcR
	5:40	I	OcR
	5:43	II	TrE
	23:28	I	ShI
20	0:42	I	TrI
	1:38	I	ShE
	2:53	I	TrE
	19:18	II	ECD
	20:43	I	ECD
21	0:07	I	OcR
	0:25	II	OcR
	17:56	I	ShI
	19:11	I	TrI
	20:07	I	ShE
	21:21	I	TrE
22	12:12	III	ShI
	14:03	**II**	**ShI**
	14:15	III	ShE
	15:11	I	ECD
	16:29	II	TrI
	16:34	II	ShE
	17:14	**III**	**TrI**
	18:35	I	OcR
	18:58	II	TrE
	19:15	III	TrE
23	12:25	I	ShI
	13:38	I	TrI
	14:35	I	ShE
	15:49	I	TrE
24	8:36	II	ECD
	9:39	I	ECD
	13:03	I	OcR
	13:41	II	OcR
25	6:53	I	ShI
	8:06	I	TrI
	9:03	I	ShE
	10:17	I	TrE
26	2:18	III	ECD
	3:19	II	ShI
	4:07	I	ECD
	4:24	III	EcR
	5:43	II	TrI
	5:50	II	ShE
	7:15	III	OcD
	7:31	I	OcR
	8:13	II	TrE
	9:18	III	OcR
27	1:22	I	ShI
	2:34	I	TrI
	3:32	I	ShE
	4:44	I	TrE
	21:54	II	ECD
	22:36	I	ECD
28	1:58	I	OcR
	2:56	II	OcR
	19:50	I	ShI
	21:02	I	TrI
	22:00	I	ShE
	23:12	I	TrE
29	16:09	III	ShI
	16:35	**II**	**ShI**
	17:04	I	ECD
	18:13	III	ShE
	18:57	II	TrI
	19:06	II	ShE
	20:26	I	OcR
	21:03	**III**	**TrI**
	21:27	II	TrE
	23:03	III	TrE
30	14:18	I	ShI
	15:30	I	TrI
	16:29	I	ShE
	17:40	I	TrE
31	11:12	II	ECD
	11:32	I	ECD
	14:53	I	OcR
	16:12	II	OcR

APRIL

1	8:47	I	ShI
	9:57	I	TrI
	10:57	I	ShE
	12:08	I	TrE
2	5:52	II	ShI
	6:00	I	ECD
	6:15	III	ECD
	8:10	II	TrI
	8:22	III	EcR
	8:23	II	ShE
	9:21	I	OcR
	10:40	II	TrE
	11:01	III	OcD
	13:04	III	OcR
3	3:15	I	ShI
	4:25	I	TrI
	5:25	I	ShE
	6:35	I	TrE
4	0:29	I	ECD
	0:30	II	ECD
	3:48	I	OcR
	5:26	II	OcR
	21:44	I	ShI
	22:52	I	TrI
	23:54	I	ShE
5	1:03	I	TrE
	18:57	I	ECD
	19:08	II	ShI
	20:06	**III**	**ShI**
	21:23	II	TrI
	21:39	II	ShE
	22:11	III	ShE
	22:16	I	OcR
	23:53	II	TrE
6	0:47	III	TrI
	2:47	III	TrE
	16:12	I	ShI
	17:20	I	TrI
	18:22	I	ShE
	19:30	I	TrE
7	13:25	I	ECD
	13:48	II	ECD
	16:43	I	OcR
	18:40	II	OcR
8	10:40	I	ShI
	11:47	I	TrI
	12:51	I	ShE
	13:57	I	TrE
9	7:53	I	ECD
	8:24	II	ShI
	10:12	III	ECD
	10:36	II	TrI
	10:56	II	ShE
	11:10	I	OcR
	12:20	III	EcR
	13:05	II	TrE
	14:43	III	OcD
	16:46	III	OcR
10	5:09	I	ShI
	6:14	I	TrI
	7:19	I	ShE
	8:25	I	TrE

→

SATELLITES OF JUPITER, UT OF 2007 GEOCENTRIC PHENOMENA (cont)

APRIL (cont)

Day	UT	Sat.	Phen.
11	2:22	I	ECD
	3:06	II	ECD
	5:37	I	OcR
	7:53	II	OcR
	23:37	I	ShI
12	0:42	I	TrI
	1:48	I	ShE
	2:52	I	TrE
	20:50	I	ECD
	21:41	II	ShI
	23:47	II	TrI
13	0:04	I	OcR
	0:04	**III**	**ShI**
	0:12	II	ShE
	2:10	III	ShE
	2:17	II	TrE
	4:26	III	TrI
	6:27	III	TrE
	18:05	I	ShI
	19:09	I	TrI
	20:16	I	ShE
	21:19	I	TrE
14	15:18	I	ECD
	16:24	II	ECD
	18:31	I	OcR
	21:06	II	OcR
15	12:34	I	ShI
	13:36	I	TrI
	14:45	I	ShE
	15:46	I	TrE
16	9:46	I	ECD
	10:57	II	ShI
	12:58	I	OcR
	12:59	II	TrI
	13:29	II	ShE
	14:09	III	ECD
	15:29	II	TrE
	16:18	III	EcR
	18:20	III	OcD
	20:22	III	OcR
17	7:02	I	ShI
	8:03	I	TrI
	9:13	I	ShE
	10:13	I	TrE
18	4:15	I	ECD
	5:42	II	ECD
	7:25	I	OcR
	10:18	II	OcR
19	1:31	I	ShI
	2:30	I	TrI
	3:41	I	ShE
	4:40	I	TrE
	22:43	I	ECD
20	0:14	II	ShI
	1:52	I	OcR
	2:09	II	TrI
	2:46	II	ShE
	4:02	III	ShI
	4:39	II	TrE
	6:09	III	ShE
	8:02	III	TrI
	10:02	III	TrE
	19:59	I	ShI
	20:57	I	TrI
	22:10	I	ShE
	23:07	I	TrE
21	17:11	I	ECD
	19:00	II	ECD
	20:18	I	OcR
	23:30	II	OcR
22	14:27	I	ShI
	15:24	I	TrI
	16:38	I	ShE
	17:34	I	TrE
23	11:39	I	ECD
	13:30	II	ShI
	14:45	I	OcR
	15:20	II	TrI
	16:02	II	ShE
	17:50	II	TrE
	18:06	III	ECD
	20:16	III	EcR
	21:52	III	OcD
	23:54	III	OcR
24	8:56	I	ShI
	9:50	I	TrI
	11:07	I	ShE
	12:01	I	TrE
25	6:08	I	ECD
	8:18	II	ECD
	9:12	I	OcR
	12:41	II	OcR
26	3:24	I	ShI
	4:17	I	TrI
	5:35	I	ShE
	6:28	I	TrE
27	0:36	I	ECD
	2:47	II	ShI
	3:38	I	OcR
	4:30	II	TrI
	5:19	II	ShE
	7:00	II	TrE
	8:00	III	ShI
	10:08	III	ShE
	11:33	III	TrI
	13:33	III	TrE
	21:53	I	ShI
	22:44	I	TrI
28	0:04	I	ShE
	0:54	I	TrE
	19:04	I	ECD
	21:36	II	ECD
	22:05	I	OcR
29	1:52	II	OcR
	16:21	I	ShI
	17:10	I	TrI
	18:32	I	ShE
	19:21	I	TrE
30	13:33	I	ECD
	16:03	II	ShI
	16:31	I	OcR
	17:39	II	TrI
	18:36	II	ShE
	20:09	II	TrE
	22:03	III	ECD

MAY

Day	UT	Sat.	Phen.
1	0:14	III	EcR
	1:21	III	OcD
	3:23	III	OcR
	10:50	I	ShI
	11:37	I	TrI
	13:01	I	ShE
	13:48	I	TrE
2	8:01	I	ECD
	10:54	II	ECD
	10:58	I	OcR
	15:02	II	OcR
3	5:18	I	ShI
	6:04	I	TrI
	7:29	I	ShE
	8:14	I	TrE
4	2:29	I	ECD
	5:20	II	ShI
	5:24	I	OcR
	6:48	II	TrI
	7:52	II	ShE
	9:18	II	TrE
	11:58	III	ShI
	14:07	III	ShE
	15:00	III	TrI
	17:00	III	TrE
	23:46	I	ShI
5	0:30	I	TrI
	1:58	I	ShE
	2:41	I	TrE
	20:58	I	ECD
	23:50	I	OcR
6	0:12	II	ECD
	4:12	II	OcR
	18:15	I	ShI
	18:56	I	TrI
	20:26	I	ShE
	21:07	I	TrE
7	15:26	I	ECD
	18:17	I	OcR
	18:36	II	ShI
	19:56	II	TrI
	21:09	II	ShE
	22:27	II	TrE
8	2:01	III	ECD
	4:12	III	EcR
	4:45	III	OcD
	6:47	III	OcR
	12:43	I	ShI
	13:23	I	TrI
	14:55	I	ShE
	15:33	I	TrE
9	9:54	I	ECD
	12:43	I	OcR
	13:30	II	ECD
	17:21	II	OcR
10	7:12	I	ShI
	7:49	I	TrI
	9:23	I	ShE
	10:00	I	TrE
11	4:23	I	ECD
	7:09	I	OcR
	7:53	II	ShI
	9:04	II	TrI
	10:26	II	ShE
	11:35	II	TrE
	15:56	III	ShI
	18:06	III	ShE
	18:23	III	TrI
	20:23	III	TrE
12	1:40	I	ShI
	2:15	I	TrI
	3:52	I	ShE
	4:26	I	TrE
	22:51	I	ECD
13	1:35	I	OcR
	2:48	II	ECD
	6:30	II	OcR
	20:09	I	ShI
	20:42	I	TrI
	22:20	I	ShE
	22:52	I	TrE
14	17:19	I	ECD
	20:01	I	OcR
	21:10	II	ShI
	22:12	II	TrI
	23:43	II	ShE
15	0:43	II	TrE
	5:59	III	ECD
	10:10	III	OcR
	14:37	I	ShI
	15:08	I	TrI
	16:49	I	ShE
	17:18	I	TrE
16	11:48	I	ECD
	14:27	I	OcR
	16:06	II	ECD
	19:38	II	OcR
17	9:06	I	ShI
	9:34	I	TrI
	11:17	I	ShE
	11:45	I	TrE
18	6:16	I	ECD
	8:53	I	OcR
	10:27	II	ShI
	11:20	II	TrI
	13:00	II	ShE
	13:50	II	TrE
	19:53	III	ShI
	21:43	III	TrI
	22:05	III	ShE
	23:43	III	TrE
19	3:34	I	ShI
	4:00	I	TrI
	5:46	I	ShE
	6:11	I	TrE
20	0:44	I	ECD
	3:19	I	OcR
	5:25	II	ECD
	8:47	II	OcR
	22:03	I	ShI
	22:26	I	TrI
21	0:14	I	ShE
	0:37	I	TrE
	19:13	I	ECD
	21:45	I	OcR
	23:43	II	ShI
22	0:27	II	TrI
	2:17	II	ShE
	2:58	II	TrE
	9:57	III	ECD
	13:29	III	OcR
	16:31	I	ShI
	16:52	I	TrI
	18:43	I	ShE
	19:03	I	TrE
23	13:41	I	ECD
	16:11	I	OcR
	18:42	II	ECD
	21:55	II	OcR
24	11:00	I	ShI
	11:18	I	TrI
	13:11	I	ShE
	13:29	I	TrE
25	8:10	I	ECD
	10:37	I	OcR
	13:00	II	ShI
	13:34	II	TrI
	15:34	II	ShE
	16:05	II	TrE
	23:51	III	ShI
26	1:01	III	TrI
	2:04	III	ShE
	3:02	III	TrE
	5:28	I	ShI
	5:44	I	TrI
	7:40	I	ShE
	7:55	I	TrE
27	2:38	I	ECD
	5:03	I	OcR
	8:01	II	ECD
	11:03	II	OcR
	23:57	I	ShI
28	0:10	I	TrI
	2:09	I	ShE
	2:21	I	TrE
	21:07	I	ECD
	23:29	I	OcR
29	2:17	II	ShI
	2:41	II	TrI
	4:51	II	ShE
	5:12	II	TrE
	13:55	III	ECD
	16:47	III	OcR
	18:25	I	ShI
	18:36	I	TrI
	20:37	I	ShE
	20:47	I	TrE
30	15:35	I	ECD
	17:55	I	OcR
	21:19	II	ECD
31	0:10	II	OcR
	12:54	I	ShI
	13:02	I	TrI
	15:06	I	ShE
	15:13	I	TrE

SATELLITES OF JUPITER, UT OF 2007 GEOCENTRIC PHENOMENA (cont)

JUNE			
1	10:03	I	ECD
	12:21	I	OcR
	15:34	II	ShI
	15:48	II	TrI
	18:08	II	ShE
	18:19	II	TrE
2	3:49	III	ShI
	4:17	III	TrI
	6:03	III	ShE
	6:19	III	TrE
	7:22	I	ShI
	7:28	I	TrI
	9:34	I	ShE
	9:39	I	TrE
3	4:32	I	ECD
	6:47	I	OcR
	10:37	II	ECD
	13:18	II	OcR
4	1:51	I	ShI
	1:54	I	TrI
	4:03	I	ShE
	4:05	I	TrE
	23:00	I	ECD
5	1:13	I	OcR
	4:51	II	ShI
	4:55	II	TrI
	7:25	II	ShE
	7:26	II	TrE
	17:53	III	ECD
	20:09	III	EcR
	20:20	I	ShI
	20:20	I	TrI
	22:31	I	ShE
	22:31	I	TrE
6	17:28	I	OcD
	19:40	I	EcR
	23:53	II	OcD
7	2:30	II	EcR
	14:46	I	TrI
	14:48	I	ShI
	16:57	I	TrE
	17:00	I	ShE
8	11:54	I	OcD
	14:09	I	EcR
	18:02	II	TrI
	18:09	II	ShI
	20:33	II	TrE
	20:43	II	ShE
9	7:34	III	TrI
	7:49	III	ShI
	9:12	**I**	**TrI**
	9:17	**I**	**ShI**
	9:37	III	TrE
	10:03	III	ShE
	11:23	I	TrE
	11:29	I	ShE
10	6:20	I	OcD
	8:37	I	EcR
	13:01	II	OcD
	15:49	II	EcR
11	3:38	I	TrI
	3:45	I	ShI
	5:49	I	TrE
	5:57	I	ShE
12	0:46	I	OcD
	3:06	I	EcR
	7:08	II	TrI
	7:26	II	ShI
	9:40	II	TrE
	10:00	II	ShE
	21:15	III	OcD
	22:04	I	TrI
	22:14	I	ShI
13	0:07	III	EcR
	0:15	I	TrE
	0:26	I	ShE
	19:12	I	OcD
	21:34	I	EcR
14	2:08	II	OcD
	5:07	II	EcR
	16:30	I	TrI
	16:43	I	ShI
	18:41	I	TrE
	18:55	I	ShE
15	13:38	I	OcD
	16:03	I	EcR
	20:16	II	TrI
	20:43	II	ShI
	22:47	II	TrE
	23:17	II	ShE
16	10:51	III	TrI
	10:56	**I**	**TrI**
	11:11	I	ShI
	11:47	**III**	**ShI**
	12:55	III	TrE
	13:07	I	TrE
	13:23	I	ShE
	14:03	III	ShE
17	8:04	I	OcD
	10:32	I	EcR
	15:16	II	OcD
	18:25	II	EcR
18	5:22	I	TrI
	5:40	I	ShI
	7:33	I	TrE
	7:52	I	ShE
19	2:30	I	OcD
	5:00	I	EcR
	9:23	II	TrI
	10:01	II	ShI
	11:55	II	TrE
	12:35	II	ShE
	23:49	I	TrI
20	0:09	I	ShI
	0:32	III	OcD
	2:00	I	TrE
	2:20	I	ShE
	4:06	III	EcR
	20:56	I	OcD
	23:29	I	EcR
21	4:24	II	OcD
	7:43	II	EcR
	18:15	I	TrI
	18:37	I	ShI
	20:26	I	TrE
	20:49	I	ShE
22	15:22	I	OcD
	17:57	I	EcR
	22:30	II	TrI
	23:18	II	ShI
23	1:03	II	TrE
	1:52	II	ShE
	12:41	I	TrI
	13:06	I	ShI
	14:08	**III**	**TrI**
	14:52	I	TrE
	15:18	I	ShE
	15:46	III	ShI
	16:14	III	TrE
	18:03	III	ShE
24	9:48	I	OcD
	12:26	I	EcR
	17:32	II	OcD
	21:01	II	EcR
25	7:07	I	TrI
	7:35	I	ShI
	9:18	I	TrE
	9:46	I	ShE
26	4:14	I	OcD
	6:54	I	EcR
	11:38	II	TrI
	12:36	II	ShI
	14:11	II	TrE
	15:10	II	ShE
27	1:34	I	TrI
	2:03	I	ShI
	3:44	I	TrE
	3:50	III	OcD
	4:15	I	ShE
	8:06	III	EcR
	22:41	I	OcD
28	1:23	I	EcR
	6:41	II	OcD
	10:19	II	EcR
	20:00	I	TrI
	20:32	I	ShI
	22:11	I	TrE
	22:44	I	ShE
29	17:07	I	OcD
	19:52	I	EcR
30	0:47	II	TrI
	1:53	II	ShI
	3:19	II	TrE
	4:28	II	ShE
	14:26	I	TrI
	15:01	I	ShI
	16:37	I	TrE
	17:12	I	ShE
	17:28	III	TrI
	19:35	III	TrE
	19:45	III	ShI
	22:02	III	ShE
JULY			
1	11:33	I	OcD
	14:20	I	EcR
	19:50	II	OcD
	23:38	II	EcR
2	8:53	I	TrI
	9:29	I	ShI
	11:04	I	TrE
	11:41	I	ShE
3	6:00	I	OcD
	8:49	I	EcR
	13:55	II	TrI
	15:11	II	ShI
	16:28	II	TrE
	17:45	II	ShE
4	3:19	I	TrI
	3:58	I	ShI
	5:30	I	TrE
	6:09	I	ShE
	7:12	III	OcD
	9:23	III	OcR
	9:47	III	ECD
	12:06	III	EcR
5	0:26	I	OcD
	3:18	I	EcR
	8:59	II	OcD
	12:56	II	EcR
	21:46	I	TrI
	22:27	I	ShI
	23:57	I	TrE
6	0:38	I	ShE
	18:52	I	OcD
	21:46	I	EcR
7	3:04	II	TrI
	4:29	II	ShI
	5:37	II	TrE
	7:03	II	ShE
	16:12	I	TrI
	16:55	I	ShI
	18:23	I	TrE
	19:07	I	ShE
	20:50	III	TrI
	23:00	III	TrE
	23:43	III	ShI
8	2:01	III	ShE
	13:19	I	OcD
	16:15	I	EcR
	22:08	II	OcD
9	2:14	II	EcR
	10:39	I	TrI
	11:24	I	ShI
	12:50	I	TrE
	13:35	I	ShE
10	7:46	I	OcD
	10:44	I	EcR
	16:14	II	TrI
	17:46	II	ShI
	18:47	II	TrE
	20:21	II	ShE
11	5:06	I	TrI
	5:53	I	ShI
	7:17	I	TrE
	8:04	I	ShE
	10:37	III	OcD
	12:49	III	OcR
	13:46	III	ECD
	16:06	III	EcR
12	2:12	I	OcD
	5:12	I	EcR
	11:18	II	OcD
	15:32	II	EcR
	23:33	I	TrI
13	0:21	I	ShI
	1:43	I	TrE
	2:33	I	ShE
	20:39	I	OcD
	23:41	I	EcR
14	5:24	II	TrI
	7:04	II	ShI
	7:57	II	TrE
	9:39	II	ShE
	17:59	I	TrI
	18:50	I	ShI
	20:10	I	TrE
	21:01	I	ShE
15	0:17	III	TrI
	2:28	III	TrE
	3:42	III	ShI
	6:01	III	ShE
	15:06	I	OcD
	18:10	I	EcR
16	0:29	II	OcD
	4:50	II	EcR
	12:26	I	TrI
	13:19	I	ShI
	14:37	I	TrE
	15:30	I	ShE
17	9:33	I	OcD
	12:39	I	EcR
	18:34	II	TrI
	20:22	II	ShI
	21:07	II	TrE
	22:57	II	ShE
18	6:53	I	TrI
	7:47	I	ShI
	9:04	I	TrE
	9:59	I	ShE
	14:06	III	OcD
	16:19	III	OcR
	17:45	III	ECD
	20:07	III	EcR
19	4:00	I	OcD
	7:07	I	EcR
	13:40	II	OcD
	18:08	II	EcR
20	1:20	I	TrI
	2:16	I	ShI
	3:31	I	TrE
	4:28	I	ShE
	22:27	I	OcD
21	1:36	I	EcR
	7:45	II	TrI
	9:40	II	ShI
	10:19	II	TrE
	12:15	II	ShE
	19:47	I	TrI
	20:45	I	ShI
	21:58	I	TrE
	22:56	I	ShE

SATELLITES OF JUPITER, UT OF 2007 GEOCENTRIC PHENOMENA (cont)

JULY (cont)

Day	UT	Sat.	Event
22	3:47	III	TrI
	6:00	III	TrE
	7:41	III	ShI
	10:01	III	ShE
	16:54	I	OcD
	20:05	I	EcR
23	2:51	II	OcD
	7:26	II	EcR
	14:15	I	TrI
	15:14	I	ShI
	16:25	I	TrE
	17:25	I	ShE
24	11:21	I	OcD
	14:33	I	EcR
	20:57	II	TrI
	22:58	II	ShI
	23:30	II	TrE
25	1:33	II	ShE
	8:42	I	TrI
	9:42	I	ShI
	10:53	I	TrE
	11:54	I	ShE
	17:38	III	OcD
	19:54	III	OcR
	21:44	III	ECD
26	0:06	III	EcR
	5:48	I	OcD
	9:02	I	EcR
	16:03	II	OcD
	20:44	II	EcR
27	3:09	I	TrI
	4:11	I	ShI
	5:20	I	TrE
	6:22	I	ShE
28	0:15	I	OcD
	3:31	I	EcR
	10:09	II	TrI
	12:17	II	ShI
	12:43	II	TrE
	14:51	II	ShE
	21:37	I	TrI
	22:40	I	ShI
	23:47	I	TrE
29	0:51	I	ShE
	7:22	III	TrI
	9:37	III	TrE
	11:41	III	ShI
	14:02	III	ShE
	18:43	I	OcD
	22:00	I	EcR
30	5:16	II	OcD
	10:02	II	EcR
	16:04	I	TrI
	17:09	I	ShI
	18:15	I	TrE
	19:20	I	ShE
31	13:10	I	OcD
	16:29	I	EcR
	23:22	II	TrI

AUGUST

Day	UT	Sat.	Event
1	1:35	II	ShI
	1:56	II	TrE
	4:09	II	ShE
	10:31	I	TrI
	11:37	I	ShI
	12:42	I	TrE
	13:48	I	ShE
	21:14	III	OcD
	23:32	III	OcR
2	1:42	III	ECD
	4:06	III	EcR
	7:38	I	OcD
	10:57	I	EcR
	18:29	II	OcD
	23:20	II	EcR
3	4:59	I	TrI
	6:06	I	ShI
	7:10	I	TrE
	8:17	I	ShE
4	2:05	I	OcD
	5:26	I	EcR
	12:36	II	TrI
	14:53	II	ShI
	15:10	II	TrE
	17:28	II	ShE
	23:27	I	TrI
5	0:35	I	ShI
	1:37	I	TrE
	2:46	I	ShE
	11:02	III	TrI
	13:18	III	TrE
	15:40	III	ShI
	18:02	III	ShE
	20:33	I	OcD
	23:55	I	EcR
6	7:43	II	OcD
	12:38	II	EcR
	17:54	I	TrI
	19:03	I	ShI
	20:05	I	TrE
	21:15	I	ShE
7	15:01	I	OcD
	18:24	I	EcR
8	1:49	II	TrI
	4:11	II	ShI
	4:24	II	TrE
	6:46	II	ShE
	12:22	I	TrI
	13:32	I	ShI
	14:33	I	TrE
	15:43	I	ShE
9	0:55	III	OcD
	3:15	III	OcR
	5:41	III	ECD
	8:06	III	EcR
	9:28	I	OcD
	12:53	I	EcR
	20:57	II	OcD
10	1:56	II	EcR
	6:50	I	TrI
	8:01	I	ShI
	9:01	I	TrE
	10:12	I	ShE
11	3:56	I	OcD
	7:21	I	EcR
	15:04	II	TrI
	17:30	II	ShI
	17:39	II	TrE
	20:04	II	ShE
12	1:18	I	TrI
	2:30	I	ShI
	3:29	I	TrE
	4:41	I	ShE
	14:46	III	TrI
	17:04	III	TrE
	19:40	III	ShI
	22:03	III	ShE
	22:24	I	OcD
13	1:50	I	EcR
	10:12	II	OcD
	15:14	II	EcR
	19:46	I	TrI
	20:58	I	ShI
	21:57	I	TrE
	23:09	I	ShE
14	16:52	I	OcD
	20:19	I	EcR
15	4:19	II	TrI
	6:48	II	ShI
	6:54	II	TrE
	9:23	II	ShE
	14:14	I	TrI
	15:27	I	ShI
	16:25	I	TrE
	17:38	I	ShE
16	4:41	III	OcD
	7:03	III	OcR
	9:41	III	ECD
	11:20	I	OcD
	12:07	III	EcR
	14:48	I	EcR
	23:27	II	OcD
17	4:32	II	EcR
	8:42	I	TrI
	9:56	I	ShI
	10:53	I	TrE
	12:07	I	ShE
18	5:49	I	OcD
	9:17	I	EcR
	17:35	II	TrI
	20:06	II	ShI
	20:10	II	TrE
	22:41	II	ShE
19	3:10	I	TrI
	4:25	I	ShI
	5:21	I	TrE
	6:36	I	ShE
	18:34	III	TrI
	20:54	III	TrE
	23:38	III	ShI
20	0:17	I	OcD
	2:02	III	ShE
	3:45	I	EcR
	12:43	II	OcD
	17:50	II	EcR
	21:39	I	TrI
	22:53	I	ShI
	23:49	I	TrE
21	1:04	I	ShE
	18:45	I	OcD
	22:14	I	EcR
22	6:51	II	TrI
	9:25	II	ShI
	9:26	II	TrE
	12:00	II	ShE
	16:07	I	TrI
	17:22	I	ShI
	18:18	I	TrE
	19:33	I	ShE
23	8:33	III	OcD
	10:56	III	OcR
	13:14	I	OcD
	13:41	III	ECD
	16:08	III	EcR
	16:43	I	EcR
24	1:59	II	OcD
	7:08	II	EcR
	10:35	I	TrI
	11:51	I	ShI
	12:46	I	TrE
	14:02	I	ShE
25	7:42	I	OcD
	11:12	I	EcR
	20:08	II	TrI
	22:43	II	ShI
	22:43	II	TrE
26	1:19	II	ShE
	5:04	I	TrI
	6:20	I	ShI
	7:14	I	TrE
	8:30	I	ShE
	22:26	III	TrI
27	0:48	III	TrE
	2:10	I	OcD
	3:37	III	ShI
	5:41	I	EcR
	6:02	III	ShE
	15:16	II	OcD
	20:26	II	EcR
	23:32	I	TrI
28	0:48	I	ShI
	1:43	I	TrE
	2:59	I	ShE
	20:39	I	OcD
29	0:10	I	EcR
	9:26	II	TrI
	12:01	II	TrE
	12:02	II	ShI
	14:37	II	ShE
	18:01	I	TrI
	19:17	I	ShI
	20:12	I	TrE
	21:28	I	ShE
30	12:28	III	OcD
	14:52	III	OcR
	15:08	I	OcD
	17:40	III	ECD
	18:38	I	EcR
	20:08	III	EcR
31	4:33	II	OcD
	9:44	II	EcR
	12:30	I	TrI
	13:46	I	ShI
	14:40	I	TrE
	15:57	I	ShE

SEPTEMBER

Day	UT	Sat.	Event
1	9:36	I	OcD
	13:07	I	EcR
	22:44	II	TrI
2	1:19	II	TrE
	1:21	II	ShI
	3:56	II	ShE
	6:58	I	TrI
	8:14	I	ShI
	9:09	I	TrE
	10:25	I	ShE
3	2:23	III	TrI
	4:05	I	OcD
	4:46	III	TrE
	7:36	I	EcR
	7:36	III	ShI
	10:03	III	ShE
	17:51	II	OcD
	23:01	II	EcR
4	1:27	I	TrI
	2:43	I	ShI
	3:38	I	TrE
	4:54	I	ShE
	22:34	I	OcD
5	2:05	I	EcR
	12:02	II	TrI
	14:38	II	TrE
	14:39	II	ShI
	17:14	II	ShE
	19:56	I	TrI
	21:12	I	ShI
	22:06	I	TrE
	23:23	I	ShE
6	16:27	III	OcD
	17:03	I	OcD
	18:53	III	OcR
	20:34	I	EcR
	21:40	III	ECD
7	0:09	III	EcR
	7:09	II	OcD
	12:19	II	EcR
	14:25	I	TrI
	15:41	I	ShI
	16:35	I	TrE
	17:52	I	ShE
8	11:32	I	OcD
	15:03	I	EcR
9	1:22	II	TrI
	3:57	II	TrE
	3:58	II	ShI
	6:34	II	ShE
	8:53	I	TrI
	10:09	I	ShI
	11:04	I	TrE
	12:20	I	ShE
10	6:01	I	OcD
	6:24	III	TrI
	8:49	III	TrE
	9:32	I	EcR
	11:36	III	ShI
	14:03	III	ShE
	20:27	II	OcD

SATELLITES OF JUPITER, UT OF 2007 GEOCENTRIC PHENOMENA (cont)

Day	UT	Sat.	Phen.
SEP. (cont)			
11	1:37	II	EcR
	3:22	I	TrI
	4:38	I	ShI
	5:33	I	TrE
	6:49	I	ShE
12	0:30	I	OcD
	4:00	I	EcR
	14:41	II	TrI
	17:16	II	ShI
	17:17	II	TrE
	19:52	II	ShE
	21:51	I	TrI
	23:07	I	ShI
13	0:02	I	TrE
	1:18	I	ShE
	18:59	I	OcD
	20:30	III	OcD
	22:29	I	EcR
	22:57	III	OcR
14	1:39	III	ECD
	4:09	III	EcR
	9:46	II	OcD
	14:55	II	EcR
	16:21	I	TrI
	17:36	I	ShI
	18:31	I	TrE
	19:47	I	ShE
15	13:28	I	OcD
	16:58	I	EcR
16	4:01	II	TrI
	6:35	II	ShI
	6:37	II	TrE
	9:11	II	ShE
	10:50	I	TrI
	12:04	I	ShI
	13:01	I	TrE
	14:15	I	ShE
17	7:57	I	OcD
	10:29	III	TrI
	11:27	I	EcR
	12:56	III	TrE
	15:36	III	ShI
	18:04	III	ShE
	23:06	II	OcD
18	4:12	II	EcR
	5:19	I	TrI
	6:33	I	ShI
	7:30	I	TrE
	8:44	I	ShE
19	2:27	I	OcD
	5:56	I	EcR
	17:21	II	TrI
	19:54	II	ShI
	19:58	II	TrE
	22:30	II	ShE
	23:48	I	TrI
20	1:02	I	ShI
	1:59	I	TrE
	3:13	I	ShE
	20:56	I	OcD
21	0:25	I	EcR
	0:36	III	OcD
	3:05	III	OcR
	5:38	III	ECD
	8:09	III	EcR
	12:26	II	OcD
	17:30	II	EcR
	18:17	I	TrI
	19:30	I	ShI
	20:28	I	TrE
	21:42	I	ShE
22	15:25	I	OcD
	18:54	I	EcR
23	6:43	II	TrI
	9:13	II	ShI
	9:19	II	TrE
	11:49	II	ShE
	12:47	I	TrI
	13:59	I	ShI
	14:58	I	TrE
	16:10	I	ShE
24	9:55	I	OcD
	13:22	I	EcR
	14:38	III	TrI
	17:05	III	TrE
	19:35	III	ShI
	22:05	III	ShE
25	1:46	II	OcD
	6:48	II	EcR
	7:16	I	TrI
	8:28	I	ShI
	9:27	I	TrE
	10:39	I	ShE
26	4:24	I	OcD
	7:51	I	EcR
	20:04	II	TrI
	22:31	II	ShI
	22:40	II	TrE
27	1:08	II	ShE
	1:45	I	TrI
	2:57	I	ShI
	3:56	I	TrE
	5:08	I	ShE
	22:54	I	OcD
28	2:20	I	EcR
	4:46	III	OcD
	7:16	III	OcR
	9:38	III	ECD
	12:10	III	EcR
	15:06	II	OcD
	20:05	II	EcR
	20:15	I	TrI
	21:25	I	ShI
	22:26	I	TrE
	23:37	I	ShE
29	17:24	I	OcD
	20:49	I	EcR
30	9:26	II	TrI
	11:51	II	ShI
	12:03	II	TrE
	14:27	II	ShE
	14:44	I	TrI
	15:54	I	ShI
	16:55	I	TrE
	18:05	I	ShE
OCTOBER			
1	11:53	I	OcD
	15:18	I	EcR
	18:50	III	TrI
	21:19	III	TrE
	23:34	III	ShI
2	2:05	III	ShE
	4:27	II	OcD
	9:14	I	TrI
	9:23	II	EcR
	10:23	I	ShI
	11:25	I	TrE
	12:34	I	ShE
3	6:23	I	OcD
	9:47	I	EcR
	22:48	II	TrI
4	1:09	II	ShI
	1:25	II	TrE
	3:43	I	TrI
	3:46	II	ShE
	4:51	I	ShI
	5:54	I	TrE
	7:03	I	ShE
5	0:53	I	OcD
	4:16	I	EcR
	8:59	III	OcD
	11:31	III	OcR
	13:37	III	ECD
	16:10	III	EcR
	17:48	II	OcD
	22:13	I	TrI
	22:40	II	EcR
	23:20	I	ShI
6	0:24	I	TrE
	1:31	I	ShE
	19:22	I	OcD
	22:44	I	EcR
7	12:11	II	TrI
	14:28	II	ShI
	14:48	II	TrE
	16:42	I	TrI
	17:05	II	ShE
	17:49	I	ShI
	18:54	I	TrE
	20:00	I	ShE
8	13:52	I	OcD
	17:13	I	EcR
	23:03	III	TrI
9	1:34	III	TrE
	3:33	III	ShI
	6:05	III	ShE
	7:10	II	OcD
	11:12	I	TrI
	11:58	II	EcR
	12:17	I	ShI
	13:23	I	TrE
	14:29	I	ShE
10	8:22	I	OcD
	11:42	I	EcR
11	1:33	II	TrI
	3:47	II	ShI
	4:11	II	TrE
	5:42	I	TrI
	6:24	II	ShE
	6:46	I	ShI
	7:53	I	TrE
	8:58	I	ShE
12	2:52	I	OcD
	6:11	I	EcR
	13:16	III	OcD
	15:49	III	OcR
	17:37	III	ECD
	20:12	III	EcR
	20:31	II	OcD
13	0:11	I	TrI
	1:15	I	ShI
	1:16	II	EcR
	2:23	I	TrE
	3:26	I	ShE
	21:22	I	OcD
14	0:40	I	EcR
	14:57	II	TrI
	17:06	II	ShI
	17:35	II	TrE
	18:41	I	TrI
	19:43	II	ShE
	19:43	I	ShI
	20:53	I	TrE
	21:55	I	ShE
15	15:52	I	OcD
	19:09	I	EcR
16	3:20	III	TrI
	5:52	III	TrE
	7:32	III	ShI
	9:53	II	OcD
	10:05	III	ShE
	13:11	I	TrI
	14:12	I	ShI
	14:33	II	EcR
	15:23	I	TrE
	16:24	I	ShE
17	10:22	I	OcD
	13:37	I	EcR
18	4:20	II	TrI
	6:24	II	ShI
	6:58	II	TrE
	7:41	I	TrI
	8:41	**I**	**ShI**
	9:02	II	ShE
	9:52	I	TrE
	10:52	I	ShE
19	4:52	I	OcD
	8:06	I	EcR
	17:34	III	OcD
	20:09	III	OcR
	21:37	III	ECD
	23:16	II	OcD
20	0:12	III	EcR
	2:11	I	TrI
	3:09	I	ShI
	3:50	II	EcR
	4:22	I	TrE
	5:21	I	ShE
	23:22	I	OcD
21	2:35	I	EcR
	17:44	II	TrI
	19:44	II	ShI
	20:22	II	TrE
	20:41	I	TrI
	21:38	**I**	**ShI**
	22:21	II	ShE
	22:52	I	TrE
	23:50	I	ShE
22	17:52	I	OcD
	21:04	I	EcR
23	7:39	III	TrI
	10:13	III	TrE
	11:31	III	ShI
	12:38	II	OcD
	14:06	III	ShE
	15:10	I	TrI
	16:07	I	ShI
	17:08	II	EcR
	17:22	I	TrE
	18:19	I	ShE
24	12:22	I	OcD
	15:33	I	EcR
25	7:08	II	TrI
	9:02	II	ShI
	9:40	**I**	**TrI**
	9:46	II	TrE
	10:35	**I**	**ShI**
	11:40	II	ShE
	11:52	I	TrE
	12:47	I	ShE
26	6:52	I	OcD
	10:02	I	EcR
	21:56	III	OcD
27	0:31	III	OcR
	1:36	III	ECD
	2:01	II	OcD
	4:10	I	TrI
	4:13	III	EcR
	5:04	I	ShI
	6:22	I	TrE
	6:25	II	EcR
	7:16	I	ShE
28	1:22	I	OcD
	4:30	I	EcR
	20:33	II	TrI
	22:21	II	ShI
	22:40	**I**	**TrI**
	23:11	II	TrE
	23:33	**I**	**ShI**
29	0:52	I	TrE
	0:59	II	ShE
	1:45	I	ShE
	19:53	I	OcD
	22:59	I	EcR
30	12:00	III	TrI
	14:35	III	TrE
	15:24	II	OcD
	15:30	III	ShI
	17:10	I	TrI
	18:01	**I**	**ShI**
	18:06	III	ShE
	19:22	I	TrE
	19:43	II	EcR
	20:13	I	ShE
31	14:23	I	OcD
	17:28	I	EcR
JUPITER NEAR CONJUNCTION			

CONFIGURATIONS OF SATURN'S BRIGHTEST SATELLITES

BY LARRY D. BOGAN

The diagrams on pp. 191–193 give the relative locations of Saturn's five brightest satellites for January through June and October through December 2007. The names and magnitudes of these satellites, in order of increasing distance from Saturn, are Enceladus 11.8, Tethys 10.3, Dione 10.4, Rhea 9.7, and Titan 8.4.

The curves in the diagrams show the elongations of the satellites from Saturn for day 0.0 UT to day 32.0 UT for each month. The dashed curves represent Enceladus and Dione, the first and third out from Saturn. The narrow, central, vertical band represents the disk of Saturn, and the wider band the outer edge of Saturn's A ring.

At the top of each monthly diagram is a scale drawing of Saturn, its rings, and the orbits of four of the five brightest satellites as seen through an inverting telescope (in the Northern Hemisphere). South is up. Because of the small size of the scale drawing, no orbit is shown for Enceladus, the innermost satellite. Due to its faintness and proximity to the bright rings, Enceladus is best seen when near a maximum elongation, but even then good seeing, good optics, and an aperture of at least 250 mm are required.

During 2007 we see Saturn and its satellites from south of the ring plane. The tilt for 2007 varies between −15° and −7° during the year. The direction of motion of the satellites is clockwise as viewed with a telescope having an even number (0, 2, 4, ...) of reflections in its optics.

A particular configuration of the satellites may be determined by drawing a horizontal line across the monthly curves at the time (UT) of interest. The intersection of this line with the curves gives the relative elongations of the satellites. Project these elongations onto the drawing of the orbits at the top of the diagram. The east side of the A ring vertical band has been extended up to the drawing to facilitate transfer of each elongation. A millimetre scale, a pair of dividers, or a strip of paper on which to mark enables one to do this quickly and accurately.

The direction of the orbital motion of a satellite determines on which side of its orbit (north or south) a satellite is located. A satellite *moving right* (east) will be *above* (south of) Saturn in the scale drawing, and a satellite *moving left* (west) will be *below* (north of) Saturn in the drawing. The January diagram shows an example configuration for Jan. 2 at 17:00 EST (Jan. 2 at 22h UT).

Greatest Elongations and Conjunctions for Iapetus

While the magnitude of Iapetus is comparable to the five plotted satellites, it varies from 10.1 (western elongation) to 11.9 (eastern elongation). This moon's orbit is about 2.9 times the size of Titan's and is tilted 15° to Saturn's ring plane; its period is 79 days. Iapetus is easiest to find near conjunctions when it is just north or south of Saturn. The table below lists times (UT) of greatest elongations and conjunctions during 2007.

Eastern Elong.	Inferior Conj.	Western Elong.	Superior Conj.
—	Jan. 7 4.2h	Jan. 26 1.1h	Feb. 14 5.6h
Mar. 6 9.7h	Mar. 26 9.9h	Apr. 14 1.8h	May 3 21.8h
May 24 10.7h	Jun. 14 3.8h	Jul. 3 9.9h	Jul. 23 16.1h
Aug. 13 19.5h	Sep. 3 9.3h	Sep. 23 2.2h	Oct. 13 4.2h
Nov. 3 10.2h	Nov. 23 7.3h	Dec. 12 20.0h	Dec. 32 8.1h

Note: Three freeware computer programs that display the configurations of Saturn's satellites are *SATSAT2* (DOS) by Dan Bruton (www.physics.sfasu.edu/astro/dansoftware.html), *Meridian* (Windows) by Claude Duplessis (www.merid.cam.org/meridian/index.html), and *The Planets* (Java) by Benden Murphy (www.cpac.org.uk).

CONFIGURATIONS OF SATURN'S SATELLITES 2007 JANUARY–MARCH

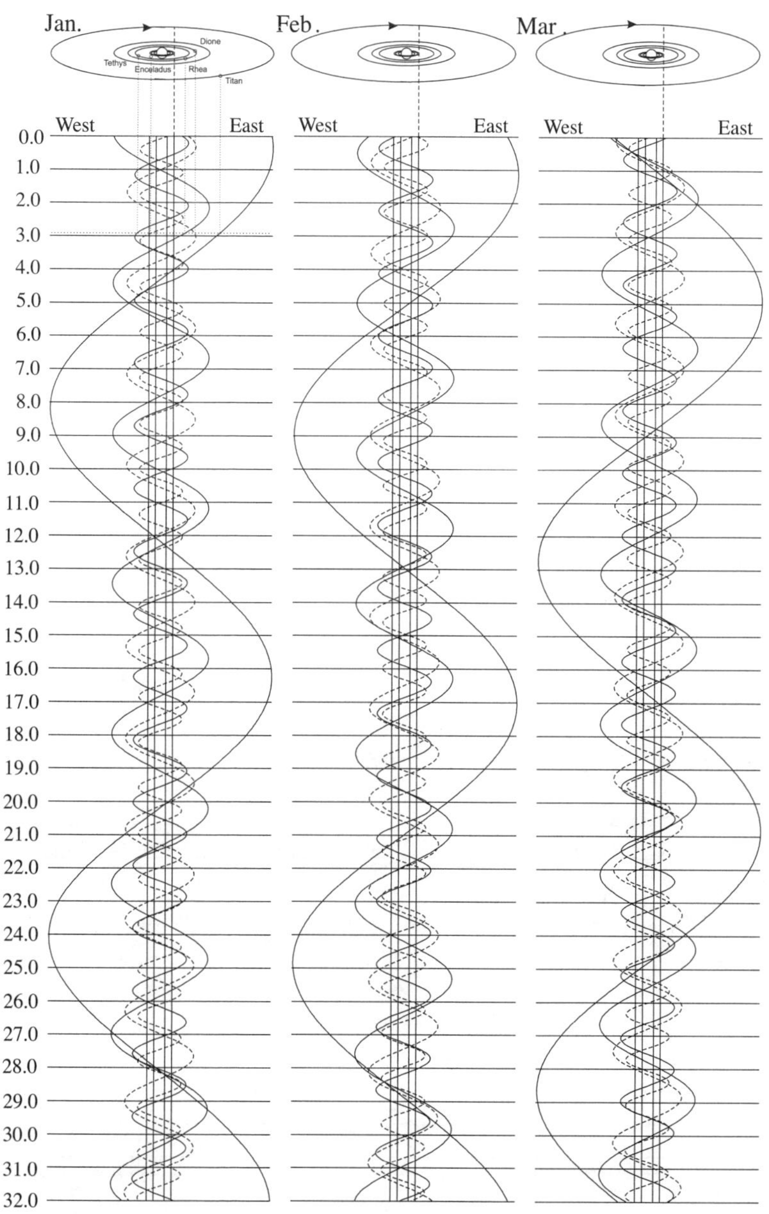

CONFIGURATIONS OF SATURN'S SATELLITES
2007 APRIL–JUNE

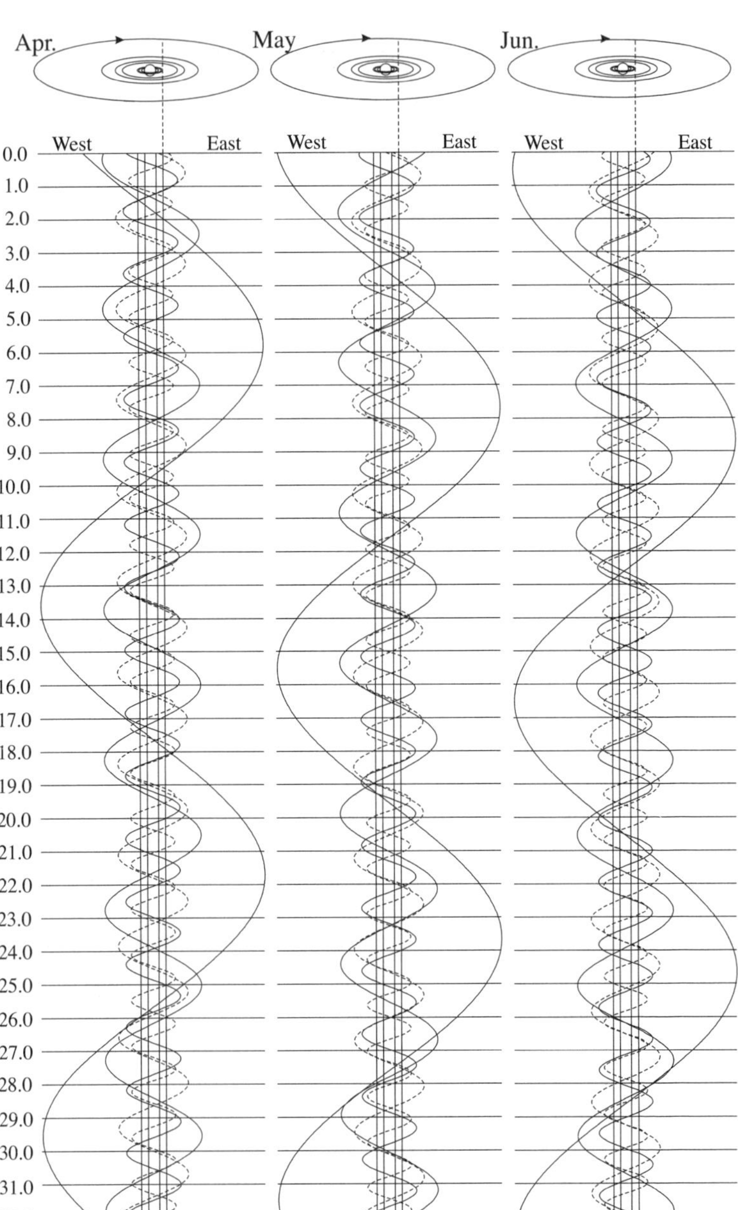

CONFIGURATIONS OF SATURN'S SATELLITES
2007 OCTOBER–DECEMBER

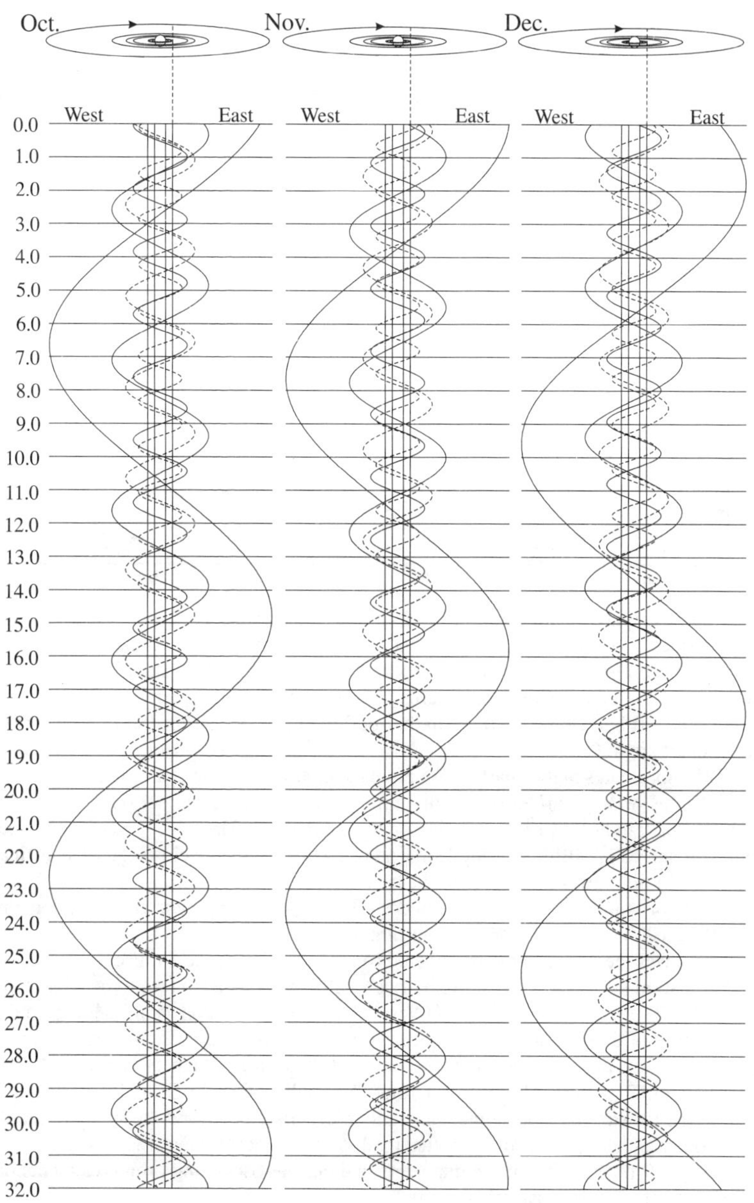

ASTEROIDS

THE BRIGHTEST ASTEROIDS

On pp. 195–196 are ephemerides for asteroids (identified by number and name) that will be brighter than or equal to visual magnitude 10.0 and more than 90° from the Sun during 2007. The positions are based on TT, which differs by about one minute from UT (see TIME AND TIME SCALES on pp. 35–40). "Mag" is visual magnitude. These data were derived from current osculating elements.

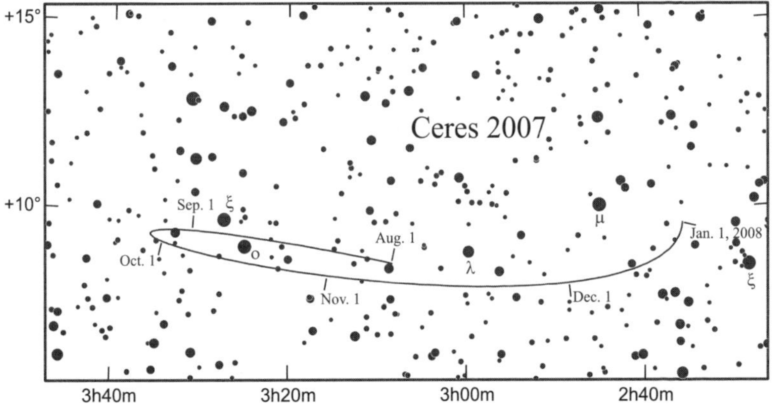

Charts displaying the motion of each asteroid can be produced by using the ephemerides provided and an appropriate star atlas, or on a computer by using a planetarium program. For example, the chart above, provided by David Lane, shows the path of (1) Ceres in Cetus and Taurus between August and December. The labelled stars in the left half of the chart are in the southwest part of Taurus, those in right half of the chart are in Cetus.

The coordinates in the chart are for equinox J2000.0, and the chart magnitude limit is 9.0; Ceres remains brighter than this limit during the depicted period. Tick marks along the path indicate Ceres's position on the given dates. The stars ξ and ο Tau can be found on the NOVEMBER ALL-SKY MAP on p. 280. They are the close pair of stars that are several millimetres below and to the right of the "S" in "TAURUS."

Ceres brightens to visual magnitude 7.3 in November when at opposition on Nov. 9. It will have an angular diameter of about 0.7″.

Ceres was the first asteroid discovered (on the first day of the 19th century), hence its designation (1) Ceres. It was originally classified as a planet, as were the next three asteroids, (2) Pallas, (3) Juno, and (4) Vesta. About 50 years after its initial discovery, and as more of these small bodies continued to be discovered, these objects lost their planetary status. In a way, the recent demotion of Pluto from a planet to a dwarf planet, follows a similar pattern. The term "asteroid," originally coined by Sir William Herschel to describe the star-like appearance of small objects like these (and the smaller moons of the outer planets), came to be applied to all of the objects in this area of space.

See p. 19 for a listing of the diameters and current osculating orbital elements of the 30 largest main-belt asteroids.

EPHEMERIDES FOR THE BRIGHTEST ASTEROIDS IN 2007

BY BRIAN MARSDEN

Date 0h TT	RA (2000) h m	Dec ° ′	Mag.
(1) Ceres			
Aug. 18	3 22.5	+9 13	8.8
28	3 28.7	+9 24	8.7
Sep. 7	3 33.0	+9 28	8.5
17	3 35.2	+9 24	8.3
27	3 35.0	+9 14	8.1
Oct. 7	3 32.3	+9 00	7.9
17	3 27.0	+8 42	7.7
27	3 19.7	+8 24	7.5
Nov. 6	3 10.8	+8 09	7.3
16	3 01.4	+8 00	7.3
26	2 52.4	+8 00	7.5
Dec. 6	2 44.8	+8 11	7.7
16	2 39.3	+8 35	7.9
26	2 36.2	+9 10	8.1
(2) Pallas			
Jun. 29	22 54.1	+10 55	10.0
Jul. 9	22 54.6	+10 50	9.8
19	22 53.2	+10 28	9.7
29	22 49.9	+9 45	9.5
Aug. 8	22 44.9	+8 40	9.3
18	22 38.5	+7 12	9.1
28	22 31.3	+5 25	8.9
Sep.. 7	22 23.7	+3 23	8.8
17	22 16.6	+1 13	9.0
27	22 10.7	–0 56	9.1
Oct. 7	22 06.4	–2 57	9.3
17	22 04.2	–4 46	9.5
27	22 04.0	–6 18	9.6
Nov. 6	22 06.0	–7 32	9.7
16	22 09.9	–8 28	9.9
(3) Juno			
Mar. 21	13 41.9	–1 35	9.9
31	13 35.0	–0 14	9.8
Apr. 10	13 27.2	+1 06	9.7
20	13 19.4	+2 18	9.8
30	13 12.2	+3 17	10.0
(4) Vesta			
Mar. 1	16 24.1	–14 04	7.3
11	16 36.0	–14 14	7.1
21	16 45.8	–14 17	6.9
31	16 53.1	–14 14	6.7
Apr. 10	16 57.6	–14 08	6.5
20	16 58.8	–14 00	6.3
30	16 56.7	–13 54	6.1
May 10	16 51.3	–13 50	5.8
20	16 43.2	–13 53	5.6
30	16 33.5	–14 02	5.4
Jun. 9	16 23.4	–14 21	5.6
19	16 14.5	–14 49	5.8
29	16 08.0	–15 26	6.0
Jul. 9	16 04.6	–16 12	6.2
19	16 04.4	–17 04	6.4
29	16 07.6	–18 01	6.6

Date 0h TT	RA (2000) h m	Dec ° ′	Mag.
(4) Vesta (continued)			
Aug. 8	16 13.7	–19 01	6.8
18	16 22.5	–20 01	7.0
28	16 33.7	–21 00	7.2
(7) Iris			
Jan. 10	3 07.5	+18 07	8.5
20	3 17.4	+18 07	8.7
30	3 29.9	+18 20	9.0
Feb. 9	3 44.4	+18 42	9.2
19	4 00.5	+19 08	9.4
(8) Flora			
Aug. 18	3 18.6	+10 41	9.9
28	3 33.6	+11 05	9.7
Sep. 7	3 46.7	+11 18	9.5
17	3 57.3	+11 18	9.3
27	4 04.9	+11 08	9.1
Oct. 7	4 09.1	+10 49	8.9
17	4 09.3	+10 25	8.7
27	4 05.5	+9 59	8.4
Nov. 6	3 58.1	+9 38	8.2
16	3 48.3	+9 26	8.0
26	3 37.9	+9 28	8.1
Dec. 6	3 28.6	+9 48	8.3
16	3 22.1	+10 26	8.6
26	3 19.2	+11 21	8.9
(9) Metis			
Jun. 9	18 20.7	–26 18	10.0
19	18 10.4	–26 43	9.8
29	17 59.5	–27 03	9.8
Jul. 9	17 49.1	–27 16	10.0
(12) Victoria			
Aug. 28	1 05.1	+19 45	10.0
Sep. 7	1 02.5	+19 35	9.8
17	0 56.8	+18 52	9.6
27	0 48.9	+17 37	9.5
Oct. 7	0 40.2	+15 57	9.3
17	0 32.2	+14 05	9.5
27	0 26.1	+12 15	9.8
(15) Eunomia			
Oct. 17	7 39.6	+27 36	9.7
27	7 49.5	+26 56	9.6
Nov. 6	7 56.7	+26 18	9.5
16	8 00.9	+25 43	9.3
26	8 01.7	+25 12	9.1
Dec. 6	7 58.9	+24 45	9.0
16	7 52.8	+24 20	8.8
26	7 43.7	+23 56	8.6

EPHEMERIDES FOR THE BRIGHTEST ASTEROIDS IN 2007 (cont)

Date 0h TT		RA (2000) h m	Dec ° ′	Mag.
(18) Melpomene				
Jan.	10	8 25.2	+9 46	9.4
	20	8 14.8	+11 02	9.2
	30	8 04.4	+12 27	9.4
Feb.	9	7 55.3	+13 52	9.6
	19	7 48.7	+15 11	9.9
(20) Massalia				
Jan.	10	9 03.3	+15 29	9.0
	20	8 54.9	+16 02	8.7
	30	8 45.1	+16 42	8.4
Feb.	9	8 35.4	+17 21	8.8
	19	8 27.4	+17 54	9.1
Mar.	1	8 22.3	+18 17	9.4
	11	8 20.6	+18 29	9.6
	21	8 22.3	+18 28	9.9
(23) Thalia				
Feb.	19	12 45.1	+13 36	10.0
Mar.	1	12 40.5	+14 36	9.8
	11	12 33.1	+15 31	9.6
	21	12 23.9	+16 11	9.6
	31	12 14.4	+16 27	9.7
Apr.	10	12 06.1	+16 16	10.0
(29) Amphitrite				
Sep.	17	3 48.1	+25 25	10.0
	27	3 51.2	+26 14	9.8
Oct.	7	3 51.1	+26 55	9.6
	17	3 47.7	+27 27	9.4
	27	3 41.1	+27 45	9.2
Nov.	6	3 31.9	+27 49	8.9
	16	3 21.3	+27 36	8.8
	26	3 10.8	+27 09	8.9
Dec.	6	3 01.8	+26 34	9.1
	16	2 55.5	+25 58	9.3
	26	2 52.4	+25 27	9.6
(40) Harmonia				
Jul.	9	21 16.5	–19 32	10.0
	19	21 09.8	–20 33	9.7
	29	21 00.8	–21 37	9.4
Aug.	8	20 50.9	–22 39	9.4
	18	20 41.3	–23 29	9.7
	28	20 33.7	–24 03	10.0
(44) Nysa				
Jan.	10	6 19.9	+19 53	9.2
	20	6 11.7	+20 25	9.4
	30	6 06.6	+20 56	9.6
Feb.	9	6 05.2	+21 26	9.8
	19	6 07.6	+21 54	10.0
(115) Thyra				
Aug.	28	22 46.0	+4 21	10.0
Sep.	7	22 35.1	+4 33	9.8
	17	22 24.5	+4 29	10.0
(192) Nausikaa				
Jun.	29	19 10.0	–33 20	10.0
Jul.	9	18 58.1	–33 27	9.9
	19	18 46.1	–33 16	10.0
(194) Prokne				
Aug.	8	21 46.8	–1 04	9.8
	18	21 41.1	–3 56	9.6
	28	21 35.5	–7 03	9.7
Sep.	7	21 31.3	–10 06	10.0
(349) Dembowska				
Nov.	6	4 47.1	+28 45	9.9
	16	4 39.1	+29 07	9.8
	26	4 29.3	+29 20	9.6
Dec.	6	4 19.0	+29 21	9.6
	16	4 09.4	+29 14	9.8
	26	4 01.8	+29 00	10.0

PLANETARY AND ASTEROIDAL OCCULTATIONS

BY DAVID W. DUNHAM AND JAMES STAMM

As planets, satellites, asteroids, and comets move across the sky, they occasionally pass directly between an observer and a distant star, thereby producing an *occultation*. Astronomers have learned much about various solar system bodies by carefully monitoring the changing apparent brightness of stars during the immersion and emersion phases of occultations. If the occulting body does not have an atmosphere, the occultation is virtually instantaneous; if there is an atmosphere, it causes the star's disappearance and reappearance to occur gradually. If a planet has rings or other debris in its environs, the extent and degree of transparency of this material can be precisely mapped. The rings of Uranus, the ring arcs of Neptune, and the atmosphere of Pluto were all discovered by occultation observations. In addition, if an occultation is observed at several appropriately distributed sites, it is often possible to determine the size and shape of the occulting body more accurately than by other Earth-based techniques.

Amateur astronomers can sometimes make important contributions to occultation observing campaigns. This is particularly true for asteroid occultations, for which the event path across Earth is often very narrow and uncertain in location (due to uncertainties in both the star's position and the ephemeris of the asteroid). By recording the times of the star's disappearance and reappearance as seen from several sites (i.e. by noting the edges of the asteroid's shadow as it sweeps across Earth), the asteroid's profile can be directly determined. Often timings of adequate accuracy can be made by visual observers using modest telescopes.

When observing an occultation, it is important that an observer know his or her location to within a fraction of a kilometre. Geographic longitude and latitude as well as the altitude of an observing site can be determined with a GPS receiver, from a high-quality topographic map, or from some map Web sites. If observations are to be of maximum value, the times of immersion and emersion must be determined as accurately as possible—certainly to better than 0.5 s, and better than 0.2 s for the shortest events (those less than about 10 s in duration). Photoelectric equipment with high-speed digital recording systems is well suited for this work. Attaching a low-light-level video camera to a telescope is a less expensive method for accurately timing these events. Visual observers equipped with audio recorders and shortwave time-signal receivers can also make useful contributions. Even simple measurements of the duration of an occultation made with an ordinary stopwatch can be of value. CCD observers should be aware that most of these systems are incapable of timing accuracies better than about 2 s; hence visual observation may be better. A trick that some CCD observers have used is to turn off the telescope clock drive shortly before the predicted time and let the images trail. The occultation will appear as a break in the trail that can be measured to a few tenths of a second if the moment the drive is turned off is accurately timed.

Occultation observations are coordinated in North America by the International Occultation Timing Association (IOTA). IOTA member or not, IOTA wants to inform you and others in your area able to locate stars to 11th magnitude of last-minute prediction updates. Please email the longitude and latitude (or location from the nearest town) of convenient observing sites, telescope size(s), and an indication of whether you are mobile to dunham@starpower.net. Individuals interested in joining IOTA should refer to OCCULTATIONS BY THE MOON, p. 136, for membership information.

More information is in the *Solar System Photometry Handbook* (Willmann-Bell, Inc., 1983), *Sky & Telescope* (usually the February issue), and occasional papers in the *Astronomical Journal, Icarus,* and other scientific journals.

Observations of asteroidal and planetary occultations, *including* negative observations, should be sent to Jan Manek, Stefanik Observatory, Petrin 205, 118 46 Praha (Prague) 1, Czech Republic (email: jmanek@mbox.vol.cz; copy positive observations to dunham@starpower.net) for analysis and publication by IOTA. When reporting timings, describe your geographic longitude, latitude, and altitude (to the nearest second of arc and 30 m, respectively), telescope size, timing method, the start and end time of observation, an estimate of the observer's reaction time (if applicable) and the accuracy of the timing, and whether the reaction time correction has been applied.

The following two-page table of predictions of asteroidal and planetary satellite occultations visible from North America for 2007 is based on predictions by Edwin Goffin, Scott Donnell, Steve Preston, and David Herald.

The successive columns in the table list (1) the date and central time of the event; (2) the name of the occulting body; (3) the apparent magnitude of the asteroid or planet; (4) the catalogue number of the occulted star; (5) the apparent visual magnitude of the star; (6) the right ascension and (7) declination of the star; (8) the expected magnitude change from the combined brightness; (9) the predicted maximum duration of the occultation in seconds; and (10) the approximate region from which the occultation is predicted to be visible. Due to uncertainties in the catalogue positions of the stars and the ephemerides of the asteroids from which these predictions are derived, the exact region of visibility of an occultation cannot be derived until CCD observations link the star and asteroid to the new HIPPARCOS reference frame, usually a few weeks prior to the event.

Note that the times are mostly geocentric; for specific locations in North America, the time may be many minutes earlier. Within a few weeks of each event, improved predictions and the latest path maps may be obtained from Steve Preston's asteroidal occultation Web site: www.asteroidoccultation.com. See also the *2007 Planetary Occultation Supplement to Occultation Newsletter* available from IOTA.

Notes regarding some of the events in the table:

Jan. 26: The combination of a nearly naked-eye star (easy with binoculars) and wide path crossing North America from coast to coast makes this the best asteroidal occultation of the year for us; mark your calendars! Observers far from the path throughout the continent are encouraged to monitor the star for a possible occultation by a satellite of Palma. The star, 32 Lyncis, is SAO 60896 = HIP 41975.

Feb. 21: SAO 97654 has a 12th-magnitude companion 1.3″ away in position angle (PA) 318°. The star is about the same magnitude as Thisbe and will be close enough that most observers will not be able to resolve it from the asteroid, so when SAO 97654's primary star disappears, the apparent magnitude drop will be about 1.9 rather than 2.6, but still quite noticeable. The secondary star will be occulted along a parallel path passing over Angola, Tobago, Aruba, northern Nicaragua, southern Honduras, and El Salvador, but the event will probably not be noticed since the 9.5-mag. primary star will remain unocculted and its light will overwhelm that of the faint secondary star.

Mar. 27: 1999 HC12 is a Kuiper Belt object, estimated to be 100 km in diameter. The path location is very uncertain so observers throughout North America have a chance for an occultation.

Apr. 18: The star, ι Cancri = SAO 80416 = HIP 43103, has a 6.6-mag. companion, SAO 80415, 30.6″ away in PA 307° that will not be occulted as seen from the Earth's surface.

Jun. 5: Jupiter's 45.7″ disk will be fully sunlit. Since one square arc second of Jupiter will be mag. 5.4, it will be very difficult to detect this occultation unless one has an infrared detector and can observe with a filter in a methane absorption band that would considerably decrease the brightness of Jupiter relative to the star.

Jul. 13: (45) Eugenia, 215 km in diameter, has a 13-km satellite about 1190 km from Eugenia that could occult the star briefly in a narrow path parallel to the main occultation path.

Aug. 21: (146) Lucina may have a small satellite several hundred kilometres from the asteroid, based on a brief occultation video recorded outside the main path during an occultation by Lucina observed on 1982 Apr. 18. SAO 77528 has an 11.3-magnitude companion 6.3″ away in PA 335° that will not be occulted from the Earth's surface.

Aug. 30: (602) Marianna may have an unusual dumbbell shape according to observations of an occultation observed on Mar. 12 last year.

Nov. 18: 2002 XV93 is a Kuiper Belt object, estimated to be 330 km in diameter. The path location is very uncertain so observers throughout North America have a chance for an occultation

Dec. 18: (602) Marianna may have an unusual dumbbell shape according to observations of an occultation observed on Mar. 12 last year.

Dec. 29: (772) Tanete may have a satellite a few hundred kilometres away based on separate occultations of another star observed during an occultation on 2004 Apr. 18.

IOTA SELECTED LIST OF NORTH AMERICAN OCCULTATIONS BY SOLAR SYSTEM OBJECTS FOR THE YEAR 2007

Date	UT	Occulting Body	(Mag.)	Star	(Mag.)	RA (2000) h m s	Dec ° ′ ″	ΔMag.	Dur. s	Nominal Path
Jan. 3	13:18	51 Nemausa	11.0	SAO 117996	9.7	09 55 43	01 11 15	1.6	130.2	Northern Kansas to central California
10	1:21	44 Nysa	9.2	TYC 1323–00422–1	9.7	06 19 53	19 52 53	0.5	10.0	South Carolina to northern Mexico
25	10:40	313 Chaldea	13.3	SAO 158835	7.2	14 50 36	–12 01 06	6.1	4.0	Nunavut to Newfoundland
26*	9:50	372 Palma	10.5	32 Lyncis	6.3	08 33 22	36 26 11	4.2	14.4	Delaware thru n. CA to north of Hawaii
31	2:44	247 Eukrate	11.6	TYC 3798–01944–1	11.5	08 49 28	54 10 11	0.8	11.1	Southern Greenland to central Mexico
Feb. 5	2:19	37 Fides	10.4	TYC 1916–00059–1	10.6	07 42 34	26 06 44	0.6	15.4	Newfoundland to northern California
5	23:47	419 Aurelia	13.6	UCAC2 38405787	11.3	06 22 20	18 54 55	2.4	14.8	Florida Keys
18	6:09	70 Pandora	12.0	SAO 99189	9.9	10 35 07	15 58 42	2.3	5.0	Northern Florida to southern California
21*	1:50	88 Thisbe	12.0	SAO 97654	9.5	08 12 59	15 47 01	2.6	20.5	Southern Florida to Baja Sur
28	8:43	51 Nemausa	10.3	SAO 117582	8.7	09 18 21	07 04 24	1.8	16.2	Western Mexico to eastern Alaska
Mar. 3	7:38	494 Virtus	14.6	SAO 57982	9.4	05 24 28	30 11 31	5.2	9.0	Western Alaska to western Texas
4	2:08	57 Mnemosyne	11.8	TYC 4878–01239–1	9.6	09 00 22	–01 09 38	2.3	9.6	Costa Rica to Baja Norte
5	3:20	404 Arsinoe	12.6	TYC 2495–00457–1	10.3	09 03 02	34 56 32	2.4	16.0	Northern Nova Scotia to s. British Columbia
8	8:49	165 Loreley	12.5	TYC 0247–00083–1	11.3	10 01 44	02 37 38	1.5	11.8	Northern Florida to southern California
24	12:43	194 Prokne	12.4	UCAC2 30097085	11.0	19 47 22	–05 08 37	1.6	5.2	Central Baja to northern Louisiana
27*	8:36	1999 HC12	23.8	UCAC2 25549222	13.1	15 19 34	–16 33 50	10.7	6.0	North America
28	4:29	72 Feronia	13.8	SAO 96108	7.6	06 47 14	16 55 35	6.2	6.5	Baja Sur to Yucatan
Apr. 13	5:05	19 Fortuna	11.3	TYC 0272–00940–1	11.0	11 40 50	00 55 26	0.9	14.9	North Carolina thru Chicago to Alaska
18*	0:55	411 Xanthe	14.7	Iota Cancri	4.2	08 46 42	28 45 35	10.5	8.6	Northern Florida
23	10:46	702 Alauda	13.2	TYC 5783–01031–1	10.0	21 08 24	–13 42 02	3.3	8.7	Southern Mexico to southern Florida
27	2:45	Venus †	–4.1	SAO 76929	7.4	05 03 52	24 58 21		340.0	Central North America
27	10:50	225 Henrietta	13.6	TYC 0483–01195–1	11.1	19 43 21	02 42 34	2.6	6.6	Western Mexico thru southern Texas
May 4	7:15	1424 Sundmania	14.4	SAO 184276	8.5	16 16 23	–25 03 47	5.9	7.0	Northern Florida to central Baja
7	3:28	451 Patientia	12.4	TYC 1293–00947–1	11.1	05 03 18	22 22 47	1.6	5.2	Southern California to nw. Texas
20	3:08	Venus ‡	–4.2	SAO 78893	8.9	06 56 45	25 31 33		436.0	Central North America
22	7:32	85 Io ††	11.0	UCAC2 29123142	11.2	17 27 33	–07 58 07	0.7	19.8	Panama to central California
Jun. 5*	10:52	Jupiter	–2.6	SAO 184782	8.0	16 54 38	–21 52 47		8611.0	Southern Mexico to Hawaii
16	2:13	579 Sidonia	13.6	SAO 99931	9.0	12 05 01	11 20 09	4.6	6.0	Northern Mississippi to Cuba
25	8:57	192 Nausikaa	10.1	PPM 750520	9.8	19 13 55	–33 13 43	0.9	12.3	Iowa to Baja Norte
26	13:28	10 Hygiea	11.5	SAO 109353	9.5	00 39 31	08 13 34	2.2	21.6	Hawaii
Jul. 10	4:17	192 Nausikaa	9.9	SAO 210738	8.7	18 56 39	–33 26 54	1.5	11.2	Northern Florida to eastern Texas
13*	11:49	45 Eugenia	13.5	TYC 1251–00631–1	11.3	04 12 42	15 38 12	2.3	5.9	Central California to eastern Québec

* See the preceding note.

† 70% of Venus's 16.0″ disk will be sunlit; the disappearance will be on the dark side. The star is number 753 in Robertson's *Zodiacal Catalog*.

‡ 60% of Venus's 19.2″ disk will be sunlit; the disappearance will be on the dark side.

†† The object is the asteroid (85) Io, not the Galilean satellite of Jupiter.

IOTA SELECTED LIST OF NORTH AMERICAN OCCULTATIONS BY SOLAR SYSTEM OBJECTS FOR THE YEAR 2007 (continued)

Date	UT	Occulting Body	(Mag.)	Star	(Mag.)	RA (2000) h m s	Dec ° ′ ″	ΔMag.	Dur. s	Nominal Path
Jul. 16	4:46	225 Henrietta	12.5	TYC 1065–00745–1	10.6	19 42 59	12 49 41	2.1	15.7	Newfoundland to southern California
16	6:20	2920 Automedon ‡‡	16.0	SAO 126257	8.0	20 49 33	08 41 48	8.0	8.0	Puerto Rico to southern Mexico
20	6:58	85 Io ††	11.3	TYC 5058–00663–1	11.4	16 46 52	–05 14 10	0.7	61.6	Northern Ontario to southern California
24	1:07	137 Meliboea	11.5	SAO 124555	9.1	19 22 22	00 36 48	2.5	18.0	Southern Georgia to northern Florida
29	6:13	27 Euterpe	10.6	TYC 6362–00617–1	11.0	21 37 41	15 55 12	0.6	11.4	Northern Québec to southern California
30	3:28	31 Euphrosyne	12.5	SAO 81682	9.4	11 07 46	20 24 31	3.2	5.9	Arizona to northern Mexico
Aug. 7	11:11	1356 Nyanza	15.2	SAO 110317	9.8	02 04 00	04 05 38	5.5	7.0	Vancouver to northern Labrador
15	10:33	558 Carmen	14.3	SAO 110534	8.2	02 27 03	06 13 35	6.2	6.0	Baja Norte to Florida Keys
21*	8:59	146 Lucina	14.0	SAO 77528	8.2	05 46 00	20 15 00	5.8	4.6	Wyoming to Labrador
22	6:59	176 Iduna	12.2	TYC 1681–00869–1	10.8	22 15 53	15 28 51	1.6	11.1	Hudson Bay to northern California
29	9:34	409 Aspasia	13.1	TYC 1327–00077–1	10.3	06 21 10	20 55 53	2.9	5.3	Baja Sur to southern Georgia
30*	9:18	602 Marianna	12.6	TYC 2329–01580–1	11.2	02 49 34	32 29 06	1.7	9.6	Western Mexico to Hudson Bay
Sep. 9	9:45	704 Interamnia	11.6	TYC 2410–00061–1	11.5	05 53 55	32 58 40	0.8	15.1	Baja Norte to Newfoundland
20	10:52	146 Lucina	13.8	SAO 78252	7.9	06 20 32	21 05 27	5.9	7.0	Northern California to Labrador
28	11:47	84 Klio	12.8	TYC 2381–00537–1	11.0	04 30 47	35 08 23	2.0	11.7	Southern California to North Dakota
Oct. 7	7:51	261 Prymno	12.7	TYC 0032–00886–1	10.3	01 41 20	04 14 04	2.5	5.0	Delaware to Baja Sur
26	9:46	203 Pompeja	14.5	TYC 1410–00470–1	10.9	09 44 33	15 49 28	3.7	4.0	Northern California to Massachusetts
29	13:09	663 Gerlinde	14.5	TYC 0728–01958–1	9.5	05 57 51	14 48 12	5.0	13.0	Southern Saskatchewan to southern California
Nov. 10	8:39	15 Eunomia	9.4	SAO 79832	9.5	07 58 56	26 01 52	0.7	43.7	Central Baja to Puerto Rico
16	6:35	792 Metcalfia	10.1	PPM 92603	10.1	03 33 28	26 25 16	3.4	6.0	Nova Scotia to Baja Norte
18*	3:04	2002 XV93	21.1	UCAC2 43927695	13.5	05 04 31	34 32 49	7.6	14.0	North Carolina to Mexico
24	6:01	351 Yrsa	12.6	TYC 1316–01762–1	9.9	05 54 54	18 04 51	2.8	6.0	Nova Scotia to Oregon
Dec. 1	3:42	444 Gyptis	11.3	TYC 0666–00574–1	11.0	04 07 04	08 14 17	0.9	15.5	Cuba to southern Mexico
8	10:42	419 Aurelia	13.8	TYC 4935–00372–1	11.1	11 52 21	–03 07 13	2.8	5.0	Oregon to Georgia
9	4:51	409 Aspasia	11.7	TYC 0770–01302–1	11.2	07 16 13	12 29 53	1.1	17.2	Dominican Republic to Nicaragua
9	22:29	105 Artemis	13.5	UCAC2 29943970	11.5	00 26 46	–05 27 49	2.1	16.5	Southwestern Ontario to Labrador
10	0:09	971 Alsatia	12.5	TYC 1288–00498–1	10.0	04 55 38	19 13 37	2.6	6.3	Delaware to Missouri
18*	5:00	602 Marianna	12.3	TYC 2320–01358–1	11.3	02 01 09	35 58 29	1.4	21.5	Nunavut through e. Arizona to Baja Sur
18	5:13	219 Thusnelda	13.2	SAO 115966	6.7	07 48 59	04 20 01	6.6	4.4	Southern Florida to western Mexico
20	5:10	187 Lamberta	12.6	PPM 70611	9.4	05 36 41	37 23 23	3.2	9.2	Virginia thru s. California to s. of Hawaii
21	3:39	334 Chicago	13.7	TYC 5807–00471–1	10.7	22 27 40	–12 27 03	3.7	6.0	Oregon to central Alberta
29*	11:50	772 Tanete	13.3	TYC 3442–00145–1	10.6	10 38 01	46 43 29	2.8	8.6	Guatemala to Labrador

* See the preceding note.
‡‡ (2920) Automedon is a Trojan asteroid
†† The object is the asteroid (85) Io, not the Galilean satellite of Jupiter.

METEORS, COMETS, AND DUST

METEORS

BY MARGARET CAMPBELL-BROWN AND PETER BROWN

A *meteor* (from the Greek *meteoros,* meaning high in the air) is the light, heat, ionization, and, occasionally, sound phenomena produced when a solid body (a *meteoroid*) collides with molecules in Earth's upper atmosphere. These collisions heat the surface of the object; then at a height typically between 120 km and 80 km the meteoroid begins to ablate, or lose mass. Typically, ablation takes the form of vapourization, although melting and quasicontinuous fragmentation may also contribute. It is these ablated meteoric atoms that collide with air molecules to produce atomic excitations, or ionization, leading to the emission of light we see in the night sky. Typical visual meteors are produced by meteoroids the size of a small pebble, although the relationship between mass–brightness and velocity is complex (Figure 1). The faintest meteors visible to the naked eye are due to meteoroids the size of the tip of a ballpoint pen; the brightest meteors are due to meteoroids whose diameters roughly match the thickness of a pen.

Larger and low-velocity meteoroids are favoured to pass through Earth's atmosphere, although rarely as a single monolithic body. When these ponderable masses reach the ground, they are called *meteorites*. At the other extreme, very small meteoroids (micrometres in size) efficiently radiate heat from their surface and do not reach ablation temperatures; such particles reach Earth's surface without having been fully ablated, although most are heated many hundreds of degrees.

Meteoroids can be divided broadly into two groups: stream and sporadic meteoroids. *Stream* meteoroids follow similar orbits around the Sun, many of which can be linked to a particular parent object, in most cases a comet. When Earth intersects the orbit of a stream, a meteor shower occurs. Since all the meteoroids in a stream move along nearly identical orbits, their paths in the atmosphere are parallel. This creates a perspective effect: the meteor trails on the celestial sphere appear to radiate from a fixed location, called the meteor *radiant*. *Sporadic* meteoroids, in contrast, are much more loosely associated and are not part of tightly grouped streams.

Meteor showers are named for the constellation from which they appear to radiate. When several showers have radiants in the same constellation, nearby bright stars are used in naming. The Quadrantid shower is named for the obsolete constellation Quadrans Muralis, but now has a radiant in Boötes.

The sporadic complex as seen at Earth, however, is structured and shows definite directionalities as well as annual variations in activity levels. Sporadic meteor radiants are concentrated in six major source regions throughout the sky. These sources are in fixed locations with respect to the Sun. Variations in the strengths of these sources throughout the year have been observed; it is the elevation of these sources at a particular location plus the intrinsic strength of each source at a given time of the year that determine the average background sporadic rate. Figure 2 shows the expected sporadic rate as a function of the altitude of the apex of Earth's way throughout the year. The apex is the instantaneous direction of travel of Earth around the Sun; it is the point on the ecliptic that transits at 6:00 apparent solar time (see pp. 36–37). The altitude of the apex for a given time of year, latitude ϕ, and apparent solar time t approximately equals the sum $\pm 23.5 \sin(\lambda - 90) + (90 - |\phi|) \sin(t/24 \times 360)$, where λ is the solar longitude and $\pm$ is the sign of ϕ (except if the sum lies outside the range -90 to $+90$).

In general, meteoroid streams are formed when particles are ejected from comets as they approach the Sun. The parent objects of many showers have been identified from the similarity of the orbits of the object and the stream. Cometary associations include the η-Aquarids and Orionids, which are derived from 1P/Halley, the Leonids, which originate from 55P/Tempel-Tuttle, and the Perseids, from 109P/Swift-Tuttle. One asteroid is known to be associated with a stream: 3200 Phaethon and the Geminid stream, while 2003 EH1 has been tentatively linked to the Quadrantid shower. All of these particles have orbits that coincide closely with that of the parent object, but their orbits are gradually shifted through radiative effects and planetary perturbations. Such effects lead to a broadening of the stream over time, resulting in an increased duration of the meteor shower as seen from Earth—older streams tend to be more long-lived—and eventually transform stream meteoroids into sporadic meteoroids.

The visual strength of a meteor shower is measured by its Zenithal Hourly Rate (ZHR), defined as the number of meteors a single average observer would see if the radiant were directly overhead and the sky dark and transparent with a limiting stellar magnitude of +6.5 (conditions that are rarely met in reality). A more physical measure is the flux of a meteoroid stream, measured in numbers of meteors of absolute brightness (referenced to a range of 100 km) brighter than +6.5 per square kilometre per second perpendicular to the radiant direction. While an observer will tend to see the largest number of meteors by looking at the shower radiant, the most useful counts are obtained by looking some distance away from the radiant.

Most data on meteor showers are currently gathered visually by amateur observers. It is crucial to observe from a dark-sky location with a clear view of the sky, and to allow at least 20 min before the start of observations to allow dark adaptation of the eyes. One should choose an area of the sky to observe, preferably with an elevation greater than 40°. The limiting magnitude should be carefully recorded for each session, along with the UT and the centre of the field of view of the observer. The most basic

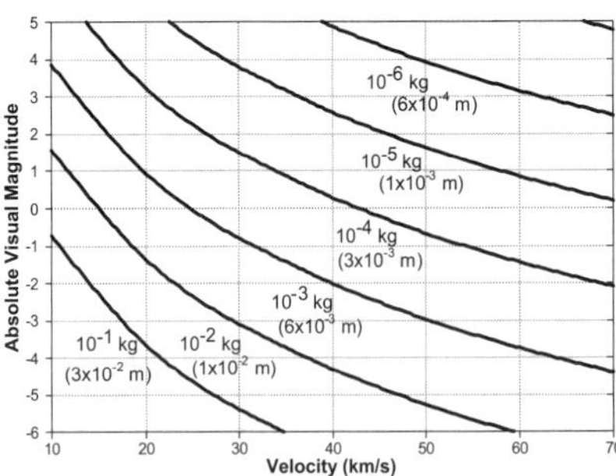

FIGURE 1 *Magnitude as a function of velocity for meteoroids of different sizes. Uncertainties in the mass scale are largest at high velocities and small masses, and may be as large as an order of magnitude in mass at the extremes.*

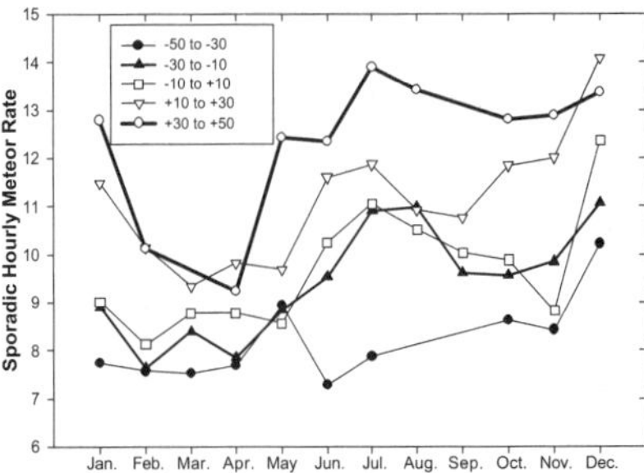

FIGURE 2 *The observed visual rate of sporadic meteors as a function of various elevations of the apex of Earth's way throughout the year. The equivalent hourly rate (like ZHR) is measured for a sky with a limiting stellar magnitude of +6.5. The position of the apex is 90° west of the Sun along the ecliptic plane. Total meteor rates on a given night may be somewhat higher due to contributions from minor showers. Data courtesy of the International Meteor Organization and R. Arlt.*

observations should include an estimate of the brightness of the meteor, the time of observation, and a shower association (based on the radiant and apparent speed of the meteor). Information on collecting and reporting scientifically useful observations can be found at the International Meteor Organization's Web site, www.imo.net.

TABLE OF METEOR SHOWERS FOR 2007

The table lists the major visual showers as well as those detectable by radio/radar methods during the day. The Moon is favourable for two of the three main annual nighttime showers of the year, namely the Perseids and Geminids. The Perseids may experience slightly heightened activity in the 4-6 hours prior to the normal maximum in 2007 from more recent ejections from the parent comet 109P/Swift-Tuttle, though the magnitude of that increase is uncertain.

Shower	Max Date UT	λ 2000	*D*	ZHR	θ $\times 10^{-6}$	*R*	Moon %	*r*	RA h m	Dec °	*v* km/s
Quadrantid	Jan. 4 1h	283.16	0.6	120	8.4	✓	99–	2.1	15 20	+49	41
Lyrid	Apr. 22 22h	32.3	1.3	20	4.6	✓	37+	2.9	18 10	+34	48
η-Aquarid	May 5 11h	44.5	5	60	6.4	>03	90–	2.4	22 30	−2	65
S. δ-Aquarid	Jul. 28 13h	125	8	20	6.2	>23	97+	3.2	22 40	−16	41
Perseid	Aug. 13 5h	140.0	2	90	6.0	✓	0+	2.1	3 08	+58	60
Draconid	Oct. 8 19h	195	<0.1	?	?	✓	5–	2.6	17 28	+54	20
Orionid	Oct. 21 22h	208	2	20	2.2	>23	75+	2.4	6 20	+16	66
S. Taurid	Nov. 5 22h	223	15	10	1.0	✓	13–	2.3	3 28	+14	27
N. Taurid	Nov. 12 21h	230	15	15	1.4	✓	7+	2.3	4 00	+22	29
Leonid	Nov. 18 4h	235.3	1	15	1.9	>00	52–	2.5	10 12	+22	71
Geminid	Dec. 14 17h	262.2	1	120	11.0	✓	22+	2.3	7 28	+33	35
Ursid	Dec. 23 1h	270.7	0.5	10	2.2	✓	98+	3.0	14 28	+76	33
Arietid	Jun. 9 20h	78.5	20	≈60	—	day	—	—	2 52	+26	39
ζ-Perseid	Jun. 14 13h	83	23	≈40	—	day	—	—	4 12	+26	29
β-Taurid	Jun. 30 14h	98.3	20	≈25	—	day	—	—	5 16	+21	31
D Sextantid	Sep. 28 15h	185	7	≈20	—	day	—	—	10 12	−2	32

The column **Max Date** lists the date and hour (in Universal Time) when Earth intersects the densest part of the stream, based on the solar longitude λ (J2000.0) given in the third column.

The fourth column, ***D*,** gives the duration of the shower in days, which is the total number of days for which the activity level is over half the maximum activity.

The **ZHR,** or Zenithal Hourly Rate, is given for the peak of the shower. The **θ** column gives the meteoroid flux at the time of maximum (see text for explanation).

The ***R*** column gives the local times for which the radiant is above the horizon for an observer at 43°N latitude (and therefore meteors from the shower are visible); a ✓ symbol indicates that the radiant is up throughout the night hours, while "day" indicates that the shower is not visible at night.

The **Moon** column gives the percent illumination of the Moon at the time of the shower peak (+ for waxing, – for waning). The population index, ***r*,** at the time of the maximum is a measure of the size distribution of particles in the stream. A larger *r* value indicates an excess of small particles, while smaller *r* values indicate larger numbers of brighter meteors. A shower with a higher *r* value will therefore suffer more from background light such as moonlight or light pollution. Sporadic meteors at observable visual magnitudes have an *r* value near 3.0.

The **RA** and **Dec** are given in the next two columns: They give the position in the sky of the radiant at the time of the shower peak. The position of the radiant will vary from these values away from the time of the peak; tables published by the International Meteor Organization in their annual shower calendar provide details of radiant drift. The last column, ***v*,** gives the geocentric speed of the meteors in the shower.

RADIO DETECTION OF METEORS

BY PHILIP GEBHARDT

The term *meteor* applies not only to the streak of light produced by a meteoroid, but also to the column of ionized atoms and molecules along the path behind the meteoroid. These meteor trails are capable of scattering radio signals from terrestrial stations. Radio detection rates tend to be higher than visual observation rates because particles down to 10^{-5} kg can be detected visually, while particles down to 10^{-10} kg can be detected by radio. Assuming a density of 1 t/m^3, these mass limits correspond to diameters of about 3 mm and 0.06 mm, respectively.

Two types of meteor trails exist: *underdense* and *overdense;* they are determined by the density of free electrons. Reradiated signals from underdense trails (fewer than 2×10^{14} electrons per metre) rise above the receiver noise almost instantaneously and then decay exponentially. The duration of many meteor bursts is about a second or less. Reflected signals from overdense trails may have higher amplitude and longer duration, but destructive interference due to reflection from different parts of the trail can produce fluctuations in the signal.

Data for selected meteor showers appear in the Table of Meteor Showers on the previous page. These data are for visual observations and should only be considered as guidelines for radio purposes. The sporadic meteor rate (visual and radio) peaks about 6:00 local time (i.e. on the advancing side of Earth in its orbit) and is minimum near 18:00. The rate will vary from a few per hour for off-peak times for sporadic meteors to several hundred per hour during a very active shower. Unlike visual observation, radio detection of sporadic meteors or shower meteors can be undertaken in daylight and during inclement weather. Four daytime showers are listed in the Table of Meteor Showers. Frequencies between 20 MHz and 150 MHz are typically used for meteor detection. Both amplitude and duration of meteor bursts are frequency-dependent—they decrease with increasing frequency. At the lower frequencies, however, galactic as well as human-made noise (particularly in urban areas) become limiting factors. Also, as the wavelength becomes comparable to the width of the meteor trail, the echo strength decreases.

The commercial FM broadcast band (88 MHz to 108 MHz) provides a good introductory opportunity for meteor detection. The abundance of over-the-horizon stations transmitting 24 hours a day ensures that a meteor burst can be heard from a suitably positioned meteor regardless of the time of day.

The technique involves listening on a frequency not used by a local FM station. A receiver with a digital frequency readout is therefore an asset. Frequencies throughout North America are assigned at 200-kHz intervals between 88.1 MHz and 107.9 MHz. Alternatively, a TV set (channels 2 through 6) can be used, provided the set is connected to an antenna rather than through cable TV. Long bursts can be heard from WWV (20 MHz, Fort Collins, Colorado) or CHU (14.670 MHz, Ottawa, Ontario), provided there is no ionospheric propagation between the station and your receiving site. In all cases, an outdoor antenna is preferable. It is also possible to listen using the FM radio in your car. Note that other means of signal propagation may be heard, but only meteor signals have their characteristic fast rise-time and short duration.

Further information can be found on the following Web sites:

www.imo.net/calendar/2007/tables
www.spaceweather.com/glossary/nasameteorradar.html
www.iap-kborn.de/radar/Radars/Skiymet/sky_main.htm

Also see *Sky & Telescope, 94* (December 1997), No. 6, p. 108.

FIREBALLS

BY DAMIEN LEMAY AND ALAN HILDEBRAND

Exceptionally bright meteors (above magnitude –5) that are spectacular enough to light up a wide area and attract public attention are generally referred to as *fireballs*. The main reasons to report the observation of a fireball are the following: (1) to assist with meteorite recovery; (2) to help provide orbital information for recovered meteorites; (3) to rule out other catastrophic events, such as airplane crashes and satellite re-entries; and (4) to help calibrate infrasound arrays deployed to monitor the Comprehensive Test Ban Treaty.

Rapid recovery of freshly fallen meteorites—as well as careful handling and storage—before they have been exposed too long to the terrestrial atmosphere is highly desirable. This allows meteorite researchers to study water-soluble minerals (such as salt), organic phases, and physical properties (such as porosity and seismic velocities). Rapid recovery is also essential for the study of short-lived radioactive isotopes induced by space exposure.

Fireballs no brighter than magnitude –6 can produce small meteorites. A slow fireball with or without terminal breakup is a good candidate for dropping meteorites. A delayed sonic boom associated with a fireball indicates that it is relatively nearby and often that it has penetrated into the lower atmosphere with an associated meteorite fall.

The scientific value of a meteorite is significantly greater when its prefall orbit is known. Under favourable circumstances, visual data can be used to obtain an approximate atmospheric trajectory, which, coupled with satellite or video observations, can be used to derive a prefall orbit.

The Meteorites and Impacts Advisory Committee (MIAC) of the Canadian Space Agency maintains an informative Web site: miac.uqac.uquebec.ca. The preferred method for submitting fireball reports is via the web:

Canada (only): miac.uqac.uquebec.ca/MIAC/fireball.htm
United States (AMS): www.amsmeteors.org/fireball/report.html
Global (IMO): www.imo.net/fireball/report.html
North American Meteor Network (NAMN):
visual: www.namnmeteors.org/fireball_form.html
photographic: www.namnmeteors.org/photo_form.html

Reports of fireballs seen over Canada can also be faxed to the Canadian Fireball Reporting Centre at (403) 284-0074. Reports should include the following information (making notes immediately, at least of the precise time, is recommended):

(1) The name, telephone number/email, and address of the observer(s).
(2) The time of occurrence (and uncertainty in this time); an accurate time is required to search instrumental databases.
(3) The location of the observer at the time the fireball was seen (preferably in precise longitude and latitude).

(4) The beginning and ending points of the fireball, in terms of either right ascension and declination or azimuth and elevation. Indicate whether the true beginning was observed and whether the ending point was blocked by an object on the horizon.
(5) An estimate of the apparent magnitude; or compare the fireball brightness to that of the Moon. Was the ground lit up?
(6) The duration of the fireball and the persistent train (if any).
(7) A qualitative description of the event (e.g. colour, flares, fragmentation, dust clouds persisting after the fireball, and sound). If sound was heard, report the time delay between the fireball and the arrival of the sound or the precise time of the sound arrival as well as that of the fireball.
(8) The existence of any video, audio, or photographic records.

METEORITE IDENTIFICATION

By Richard K. Herd

Meteorites are rocks from space that have fallen on Earth. Some have lain for many thousands of years before discovery. Fossil meteorites are found in ancient strata; others are recent arrivals. Those observed to traverse Earth's atmosphere, and recovered based on those observations, are called meteorite *falls*. Those with no record of arrival are meteorite *finds* when recognized. Meteorites are named for where they are found. Over 25 000 meteorites are known worldwide: 18 000 are from Antarctica and a few thousand from deserts in Africa and Asia. See *The Cambridge Encyclopedia of Meteorites* by O.R. Norton, Cambridge University Press, 2002, and *Meteorites from A to Z* (2nd ed) by M.R. Jensen et al., published by Michael R. Jensen, 2004.

Often there is confusion over when and where meteorites have fallen or have been preserved, and also over what they are and look like, even though Web sites now provide ready access to meteorite research, photos, and data. All are significantly different than Earth rocks. Samples sent to experts for identification, even by other scientists, are usually "meteorwrongs"—terrestrial rocks or minerals, human-made slag, metals, alloys, or concrete—that rarely resemble meteorites. Over 60 identified meteorites are known in Canada. There have been three falls since 1994: Tagish Lake, British Columbia, 2000 Jan. 18; Kitchener, Ontario, 1998 Jul. 12; and St-Robert, Québec, 1994 Jun. 14.

Meteorites probably begin as streams of fragments *(meteoroids)* that are debris from collisions between larger objects. The calculated orbits of several falls intersect the asteroid belt; their ultimate origin in space and time may be elsewhere. About 30 meteorites have come from the Moon. The petrological and isotopic evidence is compelling that a similar number are from Mars, blasted off the surface by impacts. Based on the meteorites' reflectance spectra or density, links have been suggested between other types or groups of meteorites and specific asteroids or asteroid types or comets, but the provenance of most is uncertain. Yet they are an unparalleled source of information about our solar system, from its primitive beginnings to the present. Many preserve presolar mineral grains; some contain primordial compounds made in other stars, yielding information about the origin of the universe. To prepare for space exploration, they are scientifically invaluable. Meteorite researchers are called *meteoriticists*. The Meteoritical Society (www.meteoriticalsociety.org) sets international research standards.

Popular ideas about when and where meteorites fall are connected with the observation of *meteors,* the brief streaks of light produced when high-speed, interplanetary particles enter Earth's upper atmosphere. Sporadic meteors and *meteor showers* do not produce meteorites; their fragile cometary debris fragments are reduced to dust high in the atmosphere. Earth collects over 100 tonnes of cosmic dust debris per day. In contrast, stronger, larger space rocks can survive a fiery passage through the atmosphere and result in meteorites. These first appear as bright *fireballs,* are slowed to terminal speeds by atmospheric friction, and cease to show a bright trail long before they reach Earth's surface. Fireballs, which may seem very close, are usually quite high in the atmosphere, 50 km or more from the observer. Even if an extraterrestrial object does reach the surface, it is likely to plunge into the 70% that is water or to be lost among forests, jungles, or mountainous regions. In only uncommonly recorded cases have meteorites struck or landed within a few metres of humans (see "Possible Hazards of Meteorite Falls" by C.E. Spratt, *JRASC, 85* (October 1991), p. 263). Rare meteoroids of masses exceeding 100 tonnes are not slowed appreciably by Earth's atmosphere and produce impact craters. The larger impacts may have dramatically altered the history of life on our planet, but they do not result in meteorites—the kinetic energy is sufficiently high to vapourize the impacting body completely and to deform and melt the target area

in a fraction of a second. Crater diameters are typically 10 times the diameter of the impacting body. Glassy *tektites* found scattered over several continents may be evidence of such impacts, but they do not have meteorite compositions or characteristics.

Meteorites are divided into three groups that vary widely both in appearance and properties: *stones* or *stony meteorites (aerolites), stony-irons (siderolites),* and *irons* or *iron meteorites (siderites).* All usually contain metallic nickel-iron compounds (with traces of other metals) and are mildly to strongly magnetic. Those that have lain on Earth's surface for long periods may be rusted almost beyond recognition; some require laboratory tests to confirm their identity. Specimens generally have a quite soft, dull black to brown fusion crust; more prevalent on stones and stony-irons, it may have partially flaked off. Meteorites only rarely contain bubble-like cavities; they are never almost perfectly spherical and smooth. During atmospheric entry, only their surface is affected. Surfaces of irons and stony-irons are dimpled rather than bulbous. They rust easily so there may be no bright metal showing. Stony meteorites do not show protuberances; weathered varieties are rusty, even on broken surfaces. Fresh stony meteorites may have a whitish rock interior, with bright metal specks. Their crusts are black or smoky grey, varying from quite glassy to dull; telltale lines and bubbled patches orient their flight through the air. More metallic samples may also be oriented.

Stones are the most abundant; they resemble some terrestrial rocks but are denser. Most (called *chondrites*) consist of spheres of silicate minerals (called *chondrules*) visible on broken, cut, or polished surfaces and scattered grains of metal. Chondrites are the oldest, most primitive, and least altered meteorites. Rare stony meteorites without chondrules are called *achondrites;* these are thought to be melt products from chondrites, samples of younger volcanic planetary surfaces. In August 1996, NASA scientists announced the discovery of fossil and chemical evidence of bacterial life in an ancient achondrite from Mars, but other scientists disagree. This controversy has resulted in renewed interest in missions to Mars and in finding water and life on Mars and elsewhere, even in extreme conditions on Earth. Irons and stony-irons are dense, with up to equal amounts of silicates and iron, and are often irregular in shape. They are thought to be core/mantle material of planets formed by melting chondrites.

Rare *carbonaceous chondrites* are grey to black, some resembling charcoal with silicate inclusions. The dark colour is from iron oxides and sulphides. They contain a few percent carbon in very fine-grained carbonates, carbides, graphite, diamonds, and primitive organic molecules, detectable mainly by isotopic analyses. They may have had biologically significant roles in providing seeds for the origin of life. They probably come from comet nuclei or similar ice-rich asteroids. Their organic molecules originate in interstellar space as coatings on dust. The study of interplanetary and interstellar dust particles has become important in deciphering the origins of meteorites and, therefore, of our solar system and everything in it. We are all composed of recycled stardust.

The Geological Survey of Canada (GSC) maintains the National Meteorite Collection of about 2700 specimens of 1100 different meteorites, identifies meteorites, and supports research on them. It also offers to pay the owner a minimum of $500 for the first specimen of any new Canadian meteorite. Should you find a suspected meteorite, you may forward it to Geological Survey of Canada, Natural Resources Canada, Attention: Meteorite Identification, 601 Booth St, Ottawa ON K1A 0E8 (telephone: (613) 992-4042; fax: (613) 943-1286; email: herd@nrcan.gc.ca). The specimen will be examined and reported on free of charge. If it is too large for mailing, a description of its appearance (or a photograph) and its exact location should be sent. The GSC also makes available a free brochure on meteorites, with pictures of meteorites and comparative nonmeteorites. Write to the GSC's Publication Office at the above address. Meteorites of Canadian origin are subject to the provisions of the Cultural Property Export and Import Act and may not be exported from Canada without a permit.

METEORITE IMPACT CRATERS OF NORTH AMERICA

By John Spray, Jason Hines, Richard Grieve, and James Whitehead

Since its inception 4.6 Ga ago, Earth has endured the hypervelocity impact of planetary materials, just like any other planet in our solar system, however, in contrast to the Moon, Mercury, Mars, and many asteroids, the Earth shows relatively few impact craters on its surface. The Moon's surface is saturated with craters, as is Mercury's, and 42 000 craters have been catalogued from Mars. On Earth, currently 174 are proven; see the Web site below. Our inventory is limited because Earth (like Venus) is an active planet. This means that most craters are destroyed or buried due to plate tectonics, volcanic activity, and weathering. Of the 174 known craters on Earth, 57 are known from North America (see the table pp. 209–210), 29 of which are in Canada, 27 in the United States, and 1 in Mexico (see map p.211). This total thus represents about a third of the world inventory. North American craters range in diameter from as small as 170 m, for the largest of the Odessa crater field (Texas), up to ~250 km for Sudbury (Ontario).

The principal criteria for determining if a geological feature is an impact structure formed by the hypervelocity impact of a meteorite or comet are listed below. Criteria are divided into megascopic (overview—bird's eye/satellite scale), macroscopic (can be seen easily with the naked eye), and microscopic (requires a microscope to see) features:

1. Presence of *in situ* shatter cones (macroscopic evidence);
2. Presence of multiple planar deformation features (PDFs) in minerals within *in situ* lithologies (microscopic evidence);
3. Presence of high-pressure mineral polymorphs within *in situ* lithologies (microscopic evidence and requiring proof via X-ray diffraction, etc.);
4. Morphometry—on some planetary bodies, such as the Moon and Mars, we rely on the shape of the impact structure to determine its presence and type. This is a megascopic quality (i.e. too big to be seen unaided by the human eye, thus requiring remote sensing, etc.). On Earth, recognizing impact structures solely by their morphometry is complicated by two factors: (a) weathering, erosion, burial processes, and tectonic deformation; and (b) certain terrestrial features having comparable shape (e.g. volcanoes, salt diapirs, glacigenic features), such that a circular structure alone is not sufficient to claim impact structure status;
5. Presence of an impact-melt sheet and/or dikes, and impact-melt breccias that were generated due to hypervelocity impact (macroscopic)—melt sheets may be overlain by so-called fallback breccias (referred to as "suevite" by some workers), and material blasted out of the crater may form ejecta blankets about the original central cavity. For large impact events, ejecta can be distributed globally;
6. Pseudotachylyte—is a rock generated by faulting at either microscopic or macroscopic scales. Some peudotachylytes are associated with endogenic seismic faulting (e.g. earthquakes due to isostatic rebound and plate tectonics), so they are not exclusively impact generated; however, in association with features 1-3 above, they can be a contributory criterion.

In terms of relative importance, criteria 1–3 above are definitive, with contributory evidence being added by 4–6. For well-preserved buried structures, as revealed by detailed geophysical techniques (especially seismic data), some workers consider this as strong evidence in favour of an impact origin. Normally, buried craters are verified by drilling and sampling for evaluation using criteria 1–3 above.

For more information, visit www.unb.ca/passc/ImpactDatabase.

TABLE OF METEORITE IMPACT CRATERS OF NORTH AMERICA

#	Name, Location	Lat. (N) ° ′	Long. (W) ° ′	Diam. km	Age* Ma	Surface Expression	Visible Geologic Features
1	Ames, Oklahoma, USA	36 15	98 12	16.	470. (30)	buried 3 km	none
2	Avak, Alaska, USA	71 15	156 38	12.	3–95.	buried 30 m	none
3	Barringer (Meteor) Crater, Arizona, USA	35 02	111 01	1.2	0.049 (0.003)	rimmed polygonal crater	fragments of meteorite, highly shocked sandstone
4	Beaverhead, Montana, USA	44 36	113 00	60.	≈600.	oval area of crushed sandstone, and shatter cones	shatter cones
5	Brent, Ontario	46 05	78 29	3.8	396. (20)	sediment-filled shallow depression	fracturing
6	Calvin, Michigan, USA	41 50	85 57	8.5	450. (10)	buried 400 m	none
7	Carswell, Saskatchewan	58 27	109 30	39.	115. (10)	discontinuous circular ridge	shatter cones, breccia, impact melt
8	Charlevoix, Québec	47 32	70 18	54.	342. (15)	semicircular trough, central peak	breccia, shatter cones, impact melt
9	Chesapeake Bay, Virginia, USA	37 17	76 01	90.	35.5 (0.3)	buried 400–500 m, ring structure	none
10	Chicxulub, Mexico	21 20	89 30	170.	64.98 (0.05)	buried 1 km, ring of sink holes	none (related to the K/T mass extinction event)
11	Clearwater East, Québec	56 05	74 07	26.	290. (20)	circular lake	sedimentary float
12	Clearwater West, Québec	56 13	74 30	36.	290. (20)	island ring in circular lake	impact melt, breccias
13	Cloud Creek, Wyoming, USA	43 07	106 45	7.	190. (30)	buried 1.1 km	none
14	Couture, Québec	60 08	75 20	8.	430. (25)	circular lake	breccia float
15	Crooked Creek, Missouri, USA	37 50	91 23	7.	320. (80)	oval area of disturbed rocks, shallow marginal depression	breccia, shatter cones
16	Decaturevillle, Missouri, USA	37 54	92 43	6.	<300.	slight oval depression	breccia, shatter cones
17	Deep Bay, Saskatchewan	56 24	102 59	13.	99. (4)	circular bay	sedimentary float
18	Des Plaines, Illinois, USA	42 03	87 52	8.	<280.	buried, 15–100 m	none
19	Eagle Butte, Alberta	49 42	110 30	10.	<65.	minor structural disturbance	shatter cones
20	Elbow, Saskatchewan	50 59	106 43	8.	395. (25)	buried, small mound	none
21	Flynn Creek, Tennessee, USA	36 17	85 40	3.8	360. (20)	sediment-filled shallow depression with small central peak	breccia, shatter cones
22	Glasford, Illinois, USA	40 36	89 47	4.	<430.	buried 350 m	none
23	Glover Bluff, Wisconsin, USA	43 58	89 32	8.	<500.	disturbed dolomite exposed	shatter cones
24	Gow, Saskatchewan	56 27	104 29	5.	<250.	lake and central island	breccia, impact melt
25	Haughton, Nunavut	75 22	89 41	23.	39.	shallow circular depression	shatter cones, breccia
26	Haviland, Kansas, USA	37 35	99 10	0.015	<0.001	excavated depression	fragments of meteorite
27	Holleford, Ontario	44 28	76 38	2.4	550. (100)	sediment-filled shallow depression	sedimentary fill
28	Île Rouleau, Québec	50 41	73 53	4.	<300.	island is central peak of submerged structure	shatter cones, breccia dykes
29	Kentland, Indiana, USA	40 45	87 24	13.	<97.	central peak exposed in quarries, rest buried	breccia, shatter cones, disturbed rocks

*Numbers in parentheses are possible errors.

TABLE OF METEORITE IMPACT CRATERS OF NORTH AMERICA (cont)

#	Name, Location	Lat. (N) ° ′	Long. (W) ° ′	Diam. km	Age* Ma	Surface Expression	Visible Geologic Features
30	La Moinerie, Québec	57 26	66 37	8.	400. (50)	lake-filled depression	breccia float
31	Manicouagan, Québec	51 23	68 42	100.	214. (1)	circumferential lake, central peak	impact melt, breccia
32	Manson, Iowa, USA	42 35	94 33	35.	73.8 (0.3)	none, central elevation buried 30 m	none
33	Maple Creek, Saskatchewan	49 48	109 06	6.	<75.	buried, small mound	disturbed rocks
34	Marquez, Texas, USA	31 17	96 18	12.7	58. (2)	circular area of disturbed rock	shatter cones
35	Middlesboro, Kentucky, USA	36 37	83 44	6.	<300.	circular depression	disturbed rocks
36	Mistastin, Labrador	55 53	63 18	28.	36.4. (4)	elliptical lake and central island	breccia, impact melt
37	Montagnais, Nova Scotia	42 53	64 13	45.	50.5 (0.8)	none, under water (115 m) and sediment	none
38	New Québec, Québec	61 17	73 40	3.4	1.4 (0.1)	rimmed, circular lake	raised rim, impact melt
39	Newporte, North Dakota, USA	48 58	101 58	3.2	<500.	none, buried 3 km	none
40	Nicholson, NWT	62 40	102 41	12.5	<400.	irregular lake with islands	breccia
41	Odessa, Texas, USA	31 45	102 29	0.17	<0.05	sediment-filled depression with very slight rim, 4 others buried & smaller	fragments of meteorite
42	Pilot, NWT	60 17	111 01	6.	445. (2)	circular lake	fracturing, breccia float
43	Presqu'île, Québec	49 43	74 48	24.	<500.	none, heavily eroded	shatter cones
44	Red Wing, North Dakota, USA	47 36	103 33	9.	200. (25)	none, buried 1.5 km	none
45	Rock Elm, Wisconsin, USA	44 43	92 14	6.	<505.	circular rim depression, central dome	shatter cones, breccia
46	St. Martin, Manitoba	51 47	98 32	40.	220. (32)	none, partially buried	impact melt
47	Serpent Mound, Ohio, USA	39 02	83 24	8.	<320.	circular area of disturbed rock, slight central peak	breccia, shatter cones
48	Sierra Madera, Texas, USA	30 36	102 55	13.	<100.	central hills, annular depression, outer ring of hills	breccia, shatter cones
49	Slate Islands, Ontario	48 40	87 00	30.	≈450.	islands are central peak of submerged structure	shatter cones, breccia dykes
50	Steen River, Alberta	59 30	117 38	25.	91. (7)	none, buried 200 m	none
51	Sudbury, Ontario	46 36	81 11	250.	1850. (3)	deformed elliptical basin	breccia, impact melt, shatter cones, breccia dykes
52	Upheaval Dome, Utah, USA	38 26	109 54	10.	<170.	circular area of disturbed rock	breccia dykes
53	Viewfield, Saskatchewan	49 35	103 04	2.5	190. (20)	buried 1 km	none
54	Wanapitei, Ontario	46 45	80 45	7.5	37. (1.2)	lake-filled depression	breccia float
55	Wells Creek, Tennessee, USA	36 23	87 40	12.	200. (100)	basin with central hill, inner and outer annular valleys, ridges	breccia, shatter cones
56	West Hawk Lake, Manitoba	49 46	95 11	2.4	351. (20)	circular lake	none
57	Wetumpka, Alabama, USA	32 31	86 10	6.5	81. (1.5)	arcuate outer ridge, central depression	breccia

*Numbers in parentheses are possible errors.

MAP OF NORTH AMERICAN METEORITE IMPACT STRUCTURES

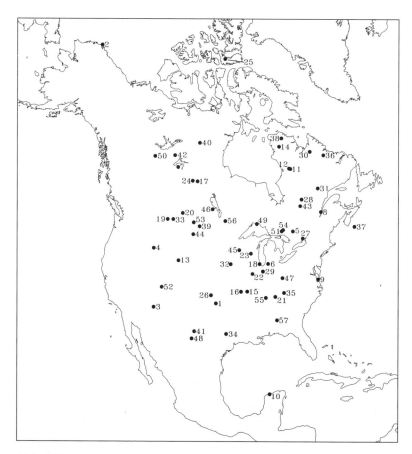

Of the 170 plus impact structures identified on Earth, 57 are in North America (29 in Canada, 27 in the United States, and 1 in Mexico). These are identified on the above map; the numbers correspond to the listing in the table on pp. 209–210. Although the oceans cover 70% of Earth, only two impact structures have been identified on the seafloor (#37 and Mjølnir, in the Barents Sea). Also, with the exception of structure #51, all of those shown occurred within approximately the last 10% of Earth's history. Evidence of many earlier craters has been erased by geologic processes. It is possible, however, to calculate a terrestrial cratering rate by focusing only on geologically stable areas of Earth (known as cratons), with low erosion and sedimentation rates. One such area is the North American craton. These rate calculations indicate that Earth has received at least 10 000 impacts sufficient to result in craters greater than 20 km in diameter over the last 3.5 billion years. Very early in Earth history, the cratering rate was even higher, perhaps as high as 100 times the current rate. Doubtless some of these impacts have had profound influence upon the evolution of life on this planet. For example, Chicxulub (#10), the very large structure in Mexico, is linked to a major extinction event 65 million years ago. Some impact craters are the source of considerable economic resources: in North America, hydrocarbons are extracted from #1, 2, 6, 34, 39, 44, 48, 50, 53; #7 produces uranium; and #51 is the site of a world-class nickel and copper mining camp.

COMETS IN 2007

BY BRIAN G. MARSDEN

Listed below are the periodic comets expected at perihelion in 2007. The orbital elements are given with sufficient precision to allow an ephemeris computation good to about 1′. The angular elements are referred to the ecliptic and mean equinox J2000.0.

Comet	Perihelion Date *T* TT	Perihelion Dist. *q* au	Eccen. *e*	Rev. Per. *P* a	Arg. Peri. ω °	Asc. Node Ω °	Incl. *i* °
99P	Jan. 15.71	4.7183	0.2272	15.1	172.83	28.40	4.35
P/2001 W2	Feb. 6.19	0.9797	0.6659	5.0	51.45	75.06	16.91
P/2001 Q2	Feb. 24.62	0.9376	0.6981	5.5	181.92	214.10	13.97
106P	Apr. 2.22	1.5561	0.5868	7.3	355.83	50.61	20.11
96P	Apr. 4.62	0.1246	0.9587	5.2	14.62	94.55	59.96
2P	Apr. 19.31	0.3393	0.8470	3.3	186.52	334.57	11.75
17P	May 4.50	2.0532	0.4324	6.9	24.26	326.87	19.11
P/1998 Q4	May 12.19	1.8799	0.5520	8.6	30.33	341.81	17.71
135P	May 31.00	2.7112	0.2911	7.5	22.32	213.30	6.05
128P	Jun. 13.65	3.0689	0.3199	9.6	210.45	214.42	4.36
156P	Jun. 17.36	1.5931	0.5576	6.8	357.68	39.05	20.75
87P	Jul. 7.24	2.1733	0.3764	6.5	24.24	182.19	2.58
P/1998 U2	Jul. 7.87	2.0319	0.5206	8.7	49.73	336.12	2.19
108P	Jul. 18.04	1.7191	0.5415	7.3	357.98	53.74	13.08
P/2002 O5	Jul. 26.27	1.1734	0.5977	5.0	15.27	282.20	20.40
125P	Aug. 10.73	1.5236	0.5127	5.5	87.34	153.20	9.99
70P	Oct. 5.94	2.0119	0.4532	7.1	2.11	119.26	6.60
136P	Oct. 22.24	2.9607	0.2930	8.6	224.87	137.56	9.43
50P	Nov. 1.18	1.9244	0.5292	8.3	49.04	355.34	19.15
P/1995 A1	Dec. 4.10	4.0873	0.3079	14.4	295.47	115.85	19.87
P/1990 V1	Dec. 12.89	1.4639	0.7733	16.4	312.73	51.66	24.56
P/1998 S1	Dec. 16.11	2.5521	0.4159	9.1	26.44	359.15	10.55
93P	Dec. 17.35	1.7047	0.6118	9.2	74.67	339.92	12.22

For an explanation of these elements, see p. 18; the elements are for an epoch within 20 days of perihelion.

The returns of 50P/Arend, 93P/Lovas, 96P/Machholz, 99P/Kowal, 135P/Shoemaker–Levy, 136P/Mueller, P/1995 A1 (Jedicke), P/1998 S1 (LINEAR–Mueller), P/2001 W2 (LONEOS), and P/2002 O5 (NEAT) are favourable, and those of 2P/Encke, 17P/Holmes, 87P/Bus, 125P/Spacewatch, 128P/Shoemaker–Holt, P/1990 V1 (Shoemaker–Levy), P/1998 Q4 (LONEOS-Tucker), and P/1998 U2 (Mueller) are fair. The returns of 70P/Kojima, 108P/Ciffréo, and 156P/Russell-LINEAR are poor, and those of 106P/Schuster and P/2001 Q2 (Petriew) are very poor.

For current ephemerides for all comets listed here, visit

www.cfa.harvard.edu/iau/Ephemerides/Comets

OBSERVING COMETS

BY DAVID H. LEVY

Each comet has its own unique, changing appearance. Observationally, comets are very much like deep-sky objects. Even in large telescopes an observer can confuse a comet with a galaxy or a diffuse planetary nebula. Comets near a telescope's limit are virtually impossible to spot without an accurate position extracted from a detailed atlas like *Uranometria* or *Millennium*. It is difficult to define a telescope's limiting magnitude for comets because the more diffuse a comet, the more difficult it is to find. Typically, under a dark sky a 150-mm telescope will catch a 9th-magnitude comet, a 200-mm telescope will see 10th, and a 400-mm should capture a 13th-magnitude comet.

If you are sure you have discovered a comet, follow the procedure in REPORTING OF ASTRONOMICAL DISCOVERIES, p. 7. For more information on comet observing and hunting, read *David Levy's Guide to Observing and Discovering Comets* (Cambridge, 2003).

Magnitude Estimates

The brightness of the coma can be estimated using a variety of methods, the most common of which is the "In-Out" method:

(1) Study the coma until you are familiar with its "average" brightness, an easy process if the coma is of uniform brightness but rather difficult if there is a strong central condensation.

(2) With the help of a variable-star chart or some source in which star magnitudes are listed, find a comparison star at approximately the same altitude as the comet.

(3) Defocus the star to the size of the in-focus coma.

(4) Compare the star's out-of-focus brightness with that of the coma.

Repeat the last three steps with a second star, or more if needed, until an interpolation can be made.

Physical Characteristics

An estimate of a comet's magnitude is more useful if an estimate of the coma diameter is made at the same time. An observer seeing a 3′ coma, for example, will estimate much brighter than one who sees only a 1′ coma at the same time. The simplest way of estimating coma size is to draw the coma with the embedded and surrounding field stars and then compare the drawing to an atlas, using its scale to determine the size.

A nightly measurement of a comet's degree of condensation is a good way of studying its changing behaviour. A comet undergoing an outburst of dust from its nucleus might begin its display by showing almost overnight the development of an increased condensation. Use an integer scale from 0 to 9, where 0 means a diffuse coma with absolutely uniform brightness, 3 means a diffuse coma with gradually increasing brightness toward the centre, 6 involves a definite central condensation, and 9 refers to an almost stellar image.

Because of the changing Earth–Sun–comet geometry and the changing activity in a comet, the length and position angle of a tail should be measured. A rough way to measure the length of a tail is to sketch it and compare with a detailed atlas, as with the coma. Observers can also measure the position angle using an atlas and a protractor.

Visual Comet Hunting

The key ingredient to a successful comet search is perseverance, especially in this time of automated searches. The chances for a visual discovery have plummeted in the last few years. Although there are stories of people finding comets very quickly (Mark Whitaker discovered Comet Whitaker-Thomas 1968 V after three nights of comet hunting), these are the exception. Don Machholz searched for some 1700 hours for each of his first two comets, and I spent more than 917 hours before my first discovery. In contrast, neither Alan Hale nor Tom Bopp was comet hunting when they independently discovered what later became the Great Comet of 1997.

It is important to know the sky well before beginning a comet search program, but it is more important to know the difference between the fuzzy appearances of comets compared to galaxies, nebulae, and clusters. Observing all the objects in Messier's Catalogue (see pp. 255–258) provides an excellent education in what these distant objects look like, and observing as many known comets as possible is good preparation for recognizing an interloper. Generally, comets lack the bilateral symmetry of spiral galaxies and the mottled appearance of globular clusters. More important, they usually have unsharp edges, fading off into space so that it is often difficult to tell where the comet ends and the sky begins.

Although most comet hunters still use traditional star atlases to check their suspects, some are moving into a new mode of comet hunting. These hunters have attached encoders to their telescopes that allow an instant reading of the suspect's position in right ascension and declination. If the telescope has been properly set up, this approach is faster. However, a sense of the nature of the fuzzy object in the field of view is still important since thousands of nonstellar objects dot the sky.

Comets may appear at any time, but they are usually found within 90° of the Sun. Good areas to search are in the evening western sky during the week after full Moon and in the morning eastern sky before dawn around new Moon. Although comet hunters differ in their approaches to searching, one way is to use an altazimuth mount and make horizontal sweeps. In the western sky, begin near the end of evening twilight at the horizon, sweep across, then return to the point of origin, move upward about half a field of view and sweep again, etc. In the morning reverse the process.

In June 2006 the author captured this image of Comet 73P Schwassmann-Wachmann 3b and 3c using a 250-mm lens and a Meade Pictor CCD camera. Fragments 3b (left) and 3c (right) are seen in the image, which is a combination of four separate 90-second exposures.

Photographic and Electronic Comet Hunting

While still possible, it is now very difficult to discover comets photographically because the sky is so well covered by the professional surveys. With film and a wide-angle camera like a Schmidt camera, take photographs of selected areas of sky, then repeat these exposures after at least 45 min. Using a stereomicroscope or a blink microscope, it is then possible to spot moving objects. Through a stereomicroscope, the comet will appear to "float" above or "sink" below the stellar background. If a blink microscope is used, the comet will appear to jump back and forth.

Using a CCD, take at least three images of each field, then examine either visually or using a moving-object detection program. Visual inspection is like blinking, so moving objects appear to move steadily through the three pictures, then jump back and begin moving again.

Finally, it is possible to discover comets over the Internet. Since images from the SOHO spacecraft are made available soon after they are taken, amateur astronomers can scan these images for Sun-grazing comets. RASC member Michael Boschat won the 2001 Ken Chilton Prize for his discoveries of several SOHO comets in this way.

Designation of Comets

At the International Astronomical Union's 22nd General Assembly in The Hague in 1994, Commission 20 of the IAU approved a resolution that changes the way comets are designated. Under the old system, a comet was designated according to its order of discovery or recovery in a given year (e.g. 1982i, Comet Halley, was the ninth comet to appear in 1982). After cometary information was complete for a given year, each comet also received a Roman numeral designation based on the order of perihelion passage (e.g. Halley at its last return was also known as 1986 III). Although the new designation went into effect in January 1995, it is retroactive to every comet for which a reasonable orbit is available.

Under the new system, a comet is assigned only one designation which is similar, although not identical, to the provisional designation system for asteroids. With this system the year is divided into periods called *half-months* beginning with A (the first half of January) and concluding with Y (the last half of December), omitting the letter I. In addition, there is a letter indicating the comet's status: C for a long-period comet, P for a "periodic comet" (defined as having a period of less than 200 years), X for a comet for which a reasonable orbit cannot be computed, and D for a disappeared comet. Once the orbit of a periodic comet is well known, that comet receives a permanent number according to the order in which the comet's periodicity was recognized. Thus Comet Hale-Bopp, as the first comet to be found in the O part of 1995, is labelled C/1995 O1. Comet Shoemaker-Levy 9 was 1993e; its new designation as the second comet to be found in the F part of 1993 is D/1993 F2. The new designation for Comet Halley is 1P/Halley.

When a comet becomes well known, the vast majority of scientists, press, and public ignore the official designation, preferring instead to use more easily remembered names. Our experience with comets Hale-Bopp and Hyakutake (C/1996 B2) showed clearly that people were more comfortable with proper names. However, with 2 comets named Hyakutake, more than 200 named SOHO, and more than 50 named LINEAR, we need to become familiar with the official designation in order to separate one comet from another.

A handful of comets are named not for their discoverers but for the persons who computed their orbits. The most famous of these is P/Halley, which has been well observed since at least 240 BC. It was finally identified as a comet appearing every 76 years or so by Sir Edmund Halley in 1705. Two others are 2P/Encke and 27P/Crommelin.

In the event that the cometary nature of an object is established after it was originally given an asteroidal designation, the original designation remains. When Gene and Carolyn Shoemaker and I discovered Asteroid 1990 UL3 using the Palomar 18-in. telescope, for example, its orbit appeared to be more cometary than asteroidal. A few weeks after discovery, Steve Larson and I took a series of images through the Kuiper 61-in. telescope that clearly showed a tail, and the identification was changed to periodic comet Shoemaker-Levy 2. The mixed designation C/1990 UL3 applies.

INTERPLANETARY DUST

By Roy Bishop

Outside of the astronomical community it is not generally realized that the inner solar system contains a vast cloud of dust. The particles in this cloud are concentrated near the plane of the ecliptic and toward the Sun, their spatial particle density in the ecliptic falling off somewhat more rapidly than the reciprocal of their distance from the Sun. Measurements from spacecraft indicate that the cloud extends well beyond the orbit of Mars but is negligible in the vicinity of Jupiter's orbit and beyond.

The particles composing the cloud have a continuum of sizes, from pebble-sized clumps down to specks with diameters comparable to the wavelength of visible light and smaller. The smaller particles are the more numerous, although the mass distribution appears to peak near 10^{-8} kg, corresponding to a particle diameter of a few tenths of a millimetre. The total mass of the cloud is small, amounting to perhaps 10^{-14} of the mass of the solar system. It is as if the satellites of Mars had been pulverized and spread throughout the inner solar system.

Like the planetary system, the interplanetary dust cloud is not static; its particles generally move in orbits about the Sun. In addition, the particles undergo continual fragmentation due to collisions, sputtering associated with bombardment by the solar wind, electrostatic bursting, and sublimation. This progression toward smaller and smaller sizes is of crucial significance for the cloud, since particles with diameters appreciably less than a tenth of a millimetre have a sufficiently large surface-to-volume ratio that the radiation pressure of sunlight has a significant effect upon their motion—aberration of sunlight results in a small backward force that slows the dust particles (the Poynting–Robertson Effect), and they slowly spiral inward toward the Sun. During a total solar eclipse in 1983, instruments carried by a balloon detected a ringlike concentration of dust only a couple of solar diameters from the Sun. Its inner edge apparently marks the point at which solar heat vapourizes the infalling particles. The resulting tiny gas molecules, like the smallest particles of dust, are blown out of the solar system by the dominant radiation pressure and interactions with the solar wind.

Because of the above-mentioned influences on the sizes and motions of the dust particles, the estimated mean life of a cloud particle is about 10^4 years. Since this is much less than the age of the solar system, it is obvious that the cloud must be in a dynamic equilibrium—that is, it must be gaining new material as it loses the old. Part of the coma and tail of a comet is the result of significant quantities of dust ejected from its nucleus, and it is generally assumed that comets provide a sizeable fraction of the supply of new dust to the cloud. Since comet nuclei are believed to consist of the undifferentiated matter from which the solar system formed, much of the dust of the interplanetary cloud is most likely composed of this same low-density, fragile, primitive material. IRAS (Infrared Astronomical Satellite) data indicate that collisions of asteroids are also a significant source of dust, but it is not yet known whether comets or asteroids provide the greater input of dust to the cloud.

To an observer on Earth the most noticeable aspect of the dust cloud is meteors—larger particles of the cloud that encounter Earth at high speeds and vapourize in the upper atmosphere. In addition, sunlight scattered by the dust cloud appears as a faint (fortunately!) glow in the vicinity of the ecliptic. This glow is brightest toward the Sun, is due primarily to particles with diameters between a few micrometres and a millimetre, and is referred to as the *zodiacal light*. A slight brightening in the sky opposite the Sun, called the *Gegenschein* (German for "counterglow"), is due to a phase effect (analogous to full moon) and also, possibly, to a concentration of dust at the L3 Lagrangian point of the Earth–Sun system. The integrated visual magnitude of the dust is about −8.5, making it the brightest solar system object in the sky after the Sun and Moon. As astronomical objects the zodiacal light and the Gegenschein are unusual in that they can be seen only with the unaided eye. Because of their large angular sizes and indistinct borders, both are invisible in binoculars or a telescope.

The Zodiacal Light

Poetic references to the zodiacal light go back several centuries (e.g. see *The Observatory, 108* (1988), p. 181). The 19th-century poet Edward FitzGerald is noted for his translation of the famous poem "Rubaiyat" by the Persian Omar Khayyam. In one of the stanzas Khayyam's reference to the morning was altered by FitzGerald into haunting references to the zodiacal light: "Dreaming when Dawn's Left Hand was in the Sky" (in midnorthern latitudes the zodiacal light and the first glow of the early autumn dawn combine to produce a large, glowing, ghostly figure having an upraised left arm); and "Before the phantom of False morning died" (the zodiacal light soon vanishes in the glow of the true dawn).

When conditions are favourable, the zodiacal light is indeed a mysterious and beautiful sight. Because the zodiacal light is brightest nearest the Sun, it is best seen within half an hour following the end of evening twilight and in the half hour prior to the beginning of morning twilight (for times of twilight, see p. 167), and when the ecliptic is at a steep angle relative to the horizon. In the tropics the ecliptic is always at a steep angle to the horizon. In midnorthern latitudes the optimum geometry occurs in the evening western sky in February and March, and in the morning eastern sky in September and October. The zodiacal light appears as a huge, softly radiant pyramid of white light with its base near the horizon and its axis centred on the zodiac. In its brightest parts it exceeds the luminance of the central Milky Way.

Despite its brightness, most people have not seen the zodiacal light. As mentioned above, certain times of night and year are more favourable than others. In addition, moonlight, haze, or light pollution rule out any chance of seeing this phenomenon. Even with a dark, transparent sky the inexperienced observer may confuse the zodiacal light with twilight and thus ignore it, or may not notice it because he or she is expecting a much smaller object.

The Gegenschein

The zodiacal light extends all around the zodiac with a shallow minimum in brightness some 120° to 150° from the Sun; nevertheless, this "zodiacal band" or "light bridge" is exceedingly faint and is visible only from high-altitude sites having very dark, transparent skies. However, the slight brightening in the vicinity of the antisolar point can be seen from most dark observing sites, provided the air is transparent.

The Gegenschein is very faint. Haze, moonlight, bright nearby stars, planets, or light pollution will hide it completely. Most observers, including experienced ones, have not seen it. The Gegenschein is sufficiently faint that, except from high-altitude sites with very dark skies, a person will not notice it without making a special effort to *look* for it. It is a ghostly apparition best seen near midnight, and in midnorthern latitudes, in the autumn or winter when the antisolar point is nearest the zenith. To avoid interference from bright stars or the Milky Way, the periods late September to early November and late January to early February are best. At these times the Gegenschein is in Pisces and Cancer, respectively. It appears as a faint yet distinct, somewhat elliptical glow perhaps 10° in diameter. The luminance of the Gegenschein is about 10^{-4} cd/m^2, some 10 orders of magnitude dimmer than the brightest light the human eye can tolerate.

Don't determine the antisolar point before you look—imagination is too powerful. Find the antisolar point by locating the Gegenschein, and *then* check your star charts!

STARS

CONSTELLATIONS—NAMES AND ABBREVIATIONS

Nominative & Pronunciation	Genitive & Pronunciation	Abbr.	Meaning
Andromeda, ăn-drŏm′ē-dȧ	Andromedae, ăn-drŏm′ē-dē′	And	Daughter of Cassiopeia
Antlia, ănt′lĭ-ȧ	Antliae, ănt′lē-ē′	Ant	The Air Pump
Apus, ā′pŭs	Apodis, ăp′ă-dĭs	Aps	Bird of Paradise
Aquarius, ȧ-kwâr′ē-ŭs	Aquarii, ȧ-kwâr′ē-ī′	Aqr	The Water-bearer
Aquila, ȧ-kwĭl′ȧ	Aquilae, ȧ-kwĭl′ē	Aql	The Eagle
Ara, ā′rȧ	Arae, ā′rē	Ara	The Altar
Aries, âr′ēz	Arietis, ȧ-rī′ē-tĭs	Ari	The Ram
Auriga, ô-rī′gȧ	Aurigae, ô-rī′jē	Aur	The Charioteer
Bootes, bō-ō′tēz	Bootis, bō-ō′tĭs	Boo	The Herdsman
Caelum, sē′lŭm	Caeli, sē′lī	Cae	The Chisel
Camelopardalis kȧ-mĕl′ō-pȧr′dȧ-lĭs	Camelopardalis kȧ-mĕl′ō-pȧr′dȧ-lĭs	Cam	The Giraffe
Cancer, kăn′sĕr	Cancri, kăn′krē	Cnc	The Crab
Canes Venatici kā′nēz vē-năt′ĭ-sī	Canum Venaticorum kā′nŭm vē-năt′ĭ-kôr′ŭm	CVn	The Hunting Dogs
Canis Major, kā′nĭs mā′jĕr	Canis Majoris, kā′nĭs mā-jôr′ĭs	CMa	The Big Dog
Canis Minor, kā′nĭs mī′nĕr	Canis Minoris, kā′nĭs mī-ñôr′ĭs	CMi	The Little Dog
Capricornus, kăp′rĭ-kôr-nŭs	Capricorni, kăp′rĭ-kôr-nī	Cap	The Goat
Carina, kȧ-rī′-nȧ	Carinae, kȧ-rī′-nē	Car	The Keel
Cassiopeia, kăs′ĭ-ō-pē′yȧ	Cassiopeiae, kăs′ĭ-ō-pē′yē	Cas	The Queen
Centaurus, sĕn-tôr′ŭs	Centauri, sĕn-tôr′ī	Cen	The Centaur
Cepheus, sē′fē-ŭs	Cephei, sē′fē-ī′	Cep	The King
Cetus, sē′tŭs	Ceti, sē′tī	Cet	The Whale
Chamaeleon, kȧ-mē′lē-ŭn	Chamaeleontis, kȧ-mē′lē-ŏn′tĭs	Cha	The Chameleon
Circinus, sûr′sĭ-nŭs	Circini, sûr′sĭ-nī	Cir	The Compasses
Columba, kō-lŭm′bȧ	Columbae, kō-lŭm′bē	Col	The Dove
Coma Berenices kō′mȧ bĕr′ē-nī′sēz	Comae Berenices kō′mē bĕr′ē-nī′sēz	Com	Berenice's Hair
Corona Australis kō-rō′nȧ ôs-trā′lĭs	Coronae Australis kō-rō′nē ôs-trā′lĭs	CrA	The Southern Crown
Corona Borealis kō-rō′nȧ bôr′ē-ăl′ĭs	Coronae Borealis kō-rō′nē bôr′ē-ăl′ĭs	CrB	The Northern Crown
Corvus, kôr′vŭs	Corvi, kôr′vī	Crv	The Crow
Crater, krā′tĕr	Crateris, krā-tĕr′ĭs	Crt	The Cup
Crux, krŭks	Crucis, kro͞o′sĭs	Cru	The Cross
Cygnus, sĭg′nŭs	Cygni, sĭg′nī	Cyg	The Swan
Delphinus, dĕl-fī′nŭs	Delphini, dĕl-fī′nī	Del	The Dolphin
Dorado, dō-rȧ′dō	Doradus, dō-rȧ′dŭs	Dor	The Swordfish
Draco, drā′kō	Draconis, drā′kō′nĭs	Dra	The Dragon
Equuleus, ē-kwo͞o′lē-ŭs	Equulei, ē-kwo͞o′lē-ī′	Equ	The Little Horse
Eridanus, ē-rĭd′ȧ-nŭs	Eridani, ē-rĭd′ȧ-nī′	Eri	The River
Fornax, fôr′năks	Fornacis, fôr-năs′ĭs	For	The Furnace
Gemini, jĕm′ĭ-nī	Geminorum, jĕm′ĭ-nôr′ŭm	Gem	The Twins
Grus, grŭs	Gruis, gro͞o′ĭs	Gru	The Crane (bird)
Hercules, hûr′kū-lēz	Herculis, hûr′kū-lĭs	Her	The Son of Zeus
Horologium, hŏr′ō-lō′jĭ-ŭm	Horologii, hŏr′ō-lō′jĭ-ī	Hor	The Clock
Hydra, hī′drȧ	Hydrae, hī′drē	Hya	The Water Snake (♀)
Hydrus, hī′drŭs	Hydri, hī′drī	Hyi	The Water Snake (♂)
Indus, ĭn′dŭs	Indi, ĭn′dī	Ind	The Indian

CONSTELLATIONS—NAMES AND ABBREVIATIONS (continued)

Nominative & Pronunciation	Genitive & Pronunciation	Abbr.	Meaning
Lacerta, là-sûr′tà	Lacertae, là-sûr′tē	Lac	The Lizard
Leo, lē′ō	Leonis, lē′ō′nĭs	Leo	The Lion
Leo Minor, lē′ō mī′nẽr	Leonis Minoris lē′ō′nĭs mī-nôr′ĭs	LMi	The Little Lion
Lepus, lē′pŭs	Leporis, lĕp′ôr-ĭs	Lep	The Hare
Libra, lē′brà	Librae, lē′brē	Lib	The Balance
Lupus, lo͞o′pŭs	Lupi, lo͞o′pī	Lup	The Wolf
Lynx, lĭnks	Lyncis, lĭn′sĭs	Lyn	The Lynx
Lyra, lī′rà	Lyrae, lī′rē	Lyr	The Lyre
Mensa, mĕn′sà	Mensae, mĕn′sē	Men	The Table
Microscopium mī′krō-skō′pē-ŭm	Microscopii mī′krō-skō′pē-ī′	Mic	The Microscope
Monoceros, mō-nŏs′ẽr-ŏs	Monocerotis, mō-nŏs′ẽr-ō′tĭs	Mon	The Unicorn
Musca, mŭs′kà	Muscae, mŭs′ē	Mus	The Fly
Norma, nôr′mà	Normae, nôr′mē	Nor	The Square
Octans, ŏk′tănz	Octantis, ŏk′tăn′tĭs	Oct	The Octant
Ophiuchus, ō′fē-ū′kŭs	Ophiuchi, ō′fē-ū′kī	Oph	The Serpent-bearer
Orion, ō-rī′ŏn	Orionis, ôr′ē-ō′nĭs	Ori	The Hunter
Pavo, pā′vō	Pavonis, pà-vō′nĭs	Pav	The Peacock
Pegasus, pĕg′à-sŭs	Pegasi, pĕg′à-sī	Peg	The Winged Horse
Perseus, pûr′sē-ŭs	Persei, pûr′sē-ī′	Per	Rescuer of Andromeda
Phoenix, fē′nĭks	Phoenicis, fē-nī′cĭs	Phe	The Phoenix
Pictor, pĭk′tẽr	Pictoris, pĭk-tor′ĭs	Pic	The Painter
Pisces, pī′sēz	Piscium, pĭsh′ē-ŭm	Psc	The Fishes
Piscis Austrinus, pī′sĭs ôs-trī′nŭs	Piscis Austrini, pī′sĭs ôs-trī′nī	PsA	The Southern Fish
Puppis, pŭp′ĭs	Puppis, pŭp′ĭs	Pup	The Stern
Pyxis, pĭk′sĭs	Pyxidis, pĭk′sĭ-dĭs	Pyx	The Compass
Reticulum, rē-tĭk′-ū-lŭm	Reticuli, rē-tĭk′-ū-lī	Ret	The Reticle
Sagitta, sà-jĭt′à	Sagittae, sà-jĭt′ē	Sge	The Arrow
Sagittarius, săj′ĭ-târ′ē-ŭs	Sagittarii, săj′ĭ-târ′ē-ī′	Sgr	The Archer
Scorpius, skôr′pē-ŭs	Scorpii, skôr′pē-ī	Sco	The Scorpion
Sculptor, skŭlp′tẽr	Sculptoris, skŭlp′tôr′ĭs	Scl	The Sculptor
Scutum, skū′tŭm	Scuti, sko͞o′tī	Sct	The Shield
Serpens, sûr′pĕnz	Serpentis, sûr-pĕn′tĭs	Ser	The Serpent
Sextans, sĕks′tănz	Sextantis, sĕks-tăn′tĭs	Sex	The Sextant
Taurus, tôr′ŭs	Tauri, tôr′ī	Tau	The Bull
Telescopium tĕl′à-skō′pē-ŭm	Telescopii, tĕl′à-skō′pē-ī	Tel	The Telescope
Triangulum, trī-ăng′gū-lŭm	Trianguli, trī-ăng′gū-lī′	Tri	The Triangle
Triangulum Australe trī-ăng′gū-lŭm ôs-trā′lē	Trianguli Australis trī-ăng′gū-lī′ ôs-trā′lĭs	TrA	The Southern Triangle
Tucana, to͞o-kăn′à	Tucanae, to͞o-kăn′ē	Tuc	The Toucan
Ursa Major, ûr′să mā′jẽr	Ursae Majoris, ûr′sē mà-jôr′ĭs	UMa	The Great Bear
Ursa Minor, ûr′să mī′nẽr	Ursae Minoris, ûr′sē mī-nôr′ĭs	UMi	The Little Bear
Vela, vē′là	Velorum, vē-lôr′ŭm	Vel	The Sails
Virgo, vûr′gō	Virginis, vûr′jĭn-ĭs	Vir	The Maiden
Volans, vō′lănz	Volantis, vō-lăn′tĭs	Vol	The Flying Fish
Vulpecula, vŭl-pĕk′ū-là	Vulpeculae, vŭl-pĕk′ū-lē′	Vul	The Fox

ā dāte; ă tăp; â câre; à gàgà; ē wē; ĕ mĕt; ẽ makẽr; ī īce; ĭ bĭt; ō gō; ŏ hŏt; ô ôrb; o͞o mo͞on; ū ūnite; ŭ ŭp; û ûrn

In terms of area (based on the official IAU boundaries), of the 88 constellations the 3 largest are Hydra (1303 square degrees), Virgo (1294), and Ursa Major (1280); the 3 smallest: Sagitta (80), Equuleus (72), and Crux (68). A complete list of the areas of the constellations appears in the 1972 edition of *The Handbook of the British Astronomical Association,* and was reproduced in the June 1976 issue of *Sky & Telescope* (p. 408).

FINDING LIST OF SOME NAMED STARS

Name & Pronunciation	Con.	RA
Acamar, ā′kȧ-mȧr	θ Eri	2
Achernar, ā′kẽr-nȧr	α Eri	1
Acrux, ā′krŭks	α Cru	12
Adara, ȧ-dā′rȧ	ε CMa	6
Al Na'ir, ăl-nâr′	α Gru	22
Albireo, ăl-bĭr′ē-ō	β Cyg	19
Alcor, ăl-kôr′	80 UMa	13
Alcyone, ăl-sī′ō-nē	η Tau	3
Aldebaran, ăl-dĕb′ȧ-rȧn	α Tau	4
Alderamin, ăl-dĕr′ȧ-mĭn	α Cep	21
Algeiba, ăl-jē′bȧ	γ Leo	10
Algenib, ăl-jē′nĭb	γ Peg	0
Algol, ăl′gŏl	β Per	3
Alioth, ăl′ĭ-ŏth	ε UMa	12
Alkaid, ăl-kād′	η UMa	13
Almach, ăl′măk	γ And	2
Alnilam, ăl-nī′lăm	ε Ori	5
Alphard, ăl′fȧrd	α Hya	9
Alphecca, ăl-fĕk′ȧ	α CrB	15
Alpheratz, ăl-fē′răts	α And	0
Altair, ăl-târ′	α Aql	19
Ankaa, ăn′kȧ	α Phe	0
Antares, ăn-tā′rēs	α Sco	16
Arcturus, ark-tū′rŭs	α Boo	14
Atria, ā′trĭ-a	α TrA	16
Avior, ă-vĭ-ôr′	ε Car	8
Bellatrix, bĕ-lā′trĭks	γ Ori	5
Betelgeuse, bĕt′ĕl-jūz	α Ori	5
Canopus, kȧ-nō′pŭs	α Car	6
Capella, kȧp-pĕl′ȧ	α Aur	5
Caph, kăf	β Cas	0
Castor, kȧs′tẽr	α Gem	7
Cor Caroli, kôr kăr′ŏ-lī	α CVn	12
Deneb, dĕn′ĕb	α Cyg	20
Denebola, dĕ-nĕb′ō-la	β Leo	11
Diphda, dĭf′dȧ	β Cet	0
Dubhe, dŭb′ē	α UMa	11
Elnath, ĕl′năth	β Tau	5
Eltanin, ĕl-tā′nĭn	γ Dra	17
Enif, ĕn′ĭf	ε Peg	21
Fomalhaut, fō′măl-ôt	α PsA	22
Gacrux, gȧ′krŭks	γ Cru	12
Gemma, jĕm′ȧ	α CrB	15
Gienah, jē′nȧ	γ Crv	12
Hadar, hăd′ar	β Cen	14
Hamal, hăm′al	α Ari	2
Kaus Australis, kôs ôs-trā′lĭs	ε Sgr	18
Kochab, kō′kăb	β UMi	14
Markab, mȧr′kăb	α Peg	23
Megrez, me′grĕz	δ UMa	12
Menkar, mĕn′kȧr	α Cet	3
Menkent, mĕn′kĕnt	θ Cen	14
Merak, mē′răk	β UMa	11
Merope, mĕr′ō-pē	23 Tau	3
Miaplacidus, mī′ȧ-plăs′ĭ-dŭs	β Car	9
Mintaka, mĭn-tȧ′kȧ	δ Ori	5
Mira, mī′rȧ	o Cet	2
Mirach, mī′răk	β And	1
Mirfak, mir′făk	α Per	3
Mizar, mi′zȧr	ζ UMa	13
Nunki, nŭn′kē	σ Sgr	18
Peacock, pē′kŏk	α Pav	20
Phecda, fĕk′dȧ	γ UMa	11
Polaris, pō-lâr′ĭs	α UMi	2
Pollux, pŏl′ŭks	β Gem	7
Procyon, prō′sĭ-ŏn	α CMi	7
Pulcherrima, pŭl-kĕr′ĭ-mȧ	ε Boo	14
Rasalgethi, rȧs′ăl-jē′thē	α Her	17
Rasalhague, rȧs′ăl-hāg	α Oph	17
Regulus, rĕg′ū-lŭs	α Leo	10
Rigel, rī′gĕl	β Ori	5
Rigil Kentaurus, rī′jĭl kĕn-tô′rŭs	α Cen	14
Sabik, sā′bĭk	η Oph	17
Scheat, shē′ăt	β Peg	23
Schedar, shĕd′ȧr	α Cas	0
Shaula, shô′lȧ	λ Sco	17
Sirius, sĭr′ĭ-ŭs	α CMa	6
Spica, spī′kȧ	α Vir	13
Suhail, sŭ-hāl′	λ Vel	9
Thuban, thōō′ban	α Dra	14
Vega, vē′gȧ	α Lyr	18
Zubenelgenubi, zōō-bĕn′ĕl-jĕ-nū′bē	α Lib	14

Key to pronunciation on p. 219

THE BRIGHTEST STARS

BY ROBERT F. GARRISON AND TOOMAS KARMO

In the following table the 314 brightest stars (allowing for variability) are listed. Data for visual doubles are for the brighter component (A); the last column describes the companion(s). Where the double is too close to be resolved conveniently, data are for combined light (AB).

Apparent Visual Magnitude (V): Apparent magnitudes, with "v" appended for variables, are from HIPPARCOS. (For variables, these data are occasionally in mild conflict with published magnitude ranges.) The photoelectric system is from H.L. Johnson and W.W. Morgan, *Ap. J., 117* (1953). The (yellow) *V* filter corresponds roughly to the response of the eye. The probable error of a *V* value is at most 0.03.

Colour Index (B – V): Since *B* on this system is the brightness of a star through a blue filter, the difference *B – V,* here taken from HIPPARCOS, measures apparent colour (as possibly reddened by interstellar dust; although, in general, *B – V* and spectral type are well correlated). The probable error of a *B – V* value is at most 0.02.

Spectral Classification **(MK Type):** The "temperature type" (O, B, A, F, G, K, M) is given first, followed by a finer subtype (0–9) and a "luminosity class" (Roman numerals I–V, with "a" or "b" added occasionally to indicate slightly brighter or fainter stars within the class). O stars are hottest, M stars coolest; Ia stars are the most luminous supergiants, III stars are giants, and V stars are dwarfs. (V stars form the largest class in the cosmos, comprising the main sequence.) Other MK symbols include "e" for hydrogen emission; "f" for broad, nonhydrogen emission in hot stars; "m" for strong metallic absorption; "n" or "nn" for unusually broad absorption (a signature of rotation); "p" for peculiarities; "s" for a mixture of broad and sharp lines; and ":" for a minor uncertainty. The types are the best available from Garrison's unpublished spectrograms and the literature. Where a single star (e.g. α CMa A) is given two types (e.g. A0 and A1), with the second type flagged "m", the first is the type that best characterizes the hydrogen lines, the second the type that best characterizes the metal lines.

Parallax **(π):** Parallaxes, in milliarcseconds (mas), are from HIPPARCOS.

Absolute Visual Magnitude (M_V) and *Distance in Light-Years (D):* Absolute magnitudes and distances are determined from parallaxes, except where a colon follows the absolute magnitude; in these cases, both quantities are determined from a calibration of the spectral classification. Corrections are made for interstellar absorption, by comparing, under an unpublished intrinsic-colour calibration from Garrison, spectral classification with *B – V.*

Proper Motion **(μ)** and *Position Angle* **(PA):** Proper motion and PA are derived from D. Hoffleit and C. Jaschek, *Bright Star Catalogue,* Yale, 1982. Proper motion is the absolute value of the vector resultant from BSC individual-coordinate proper motions. PA is the direction of the proper motion, as an angle measured from north through east.

Radial Velocity **(RV):** Radial velocities are from BSC. "SB" indicates a spectroscopic binary, an unresolved system whose duplicity is revealed by periodic Doppler oscillations in its spectrum and for which an orbit is generally known. If the lines of both stars are detectable, "SB2" is used; "+" and "–" indicate, respectively, motion away from and toward the observer. "V" indicates a variable velocity in a star not observable as a spectroscopic binary. (In most "V" cases the orbit is unknown.)

Remarks: Remarks include data on variability and spectra, particulars on any companions, and traditional names. Our principal source for variability ranges is P.N. Kholopov et al., *Combined General Catalogue of Variable Stars,* 4.1 ed., 1998 (online as VizieR GCVS4). Our sources for traditional names include BSC and M.E. Bakich, *Cambridge Guide to the Constellations,* Cambridge University Press, 1995. Navigation-star names are **bold.**

TABLE OF BRIGHTEST STARS

Star Name	RA (2007.5) h m	Dec ° ′	V	B – V	MK Type	π mas	M_V	D ly	μ ″/yr	PA °	RV km/s	Remarks	
Sun	—	—	–26.75	0.63	G2 V	—	4.8	8 lm	—	—	varies		**Sun**
α And	0 08.8	+29 08	2.07	–0.04	B9p IV: (HgMn)	34	–0.5	97	0.209	139	–12 SB		Alpheratz
β Cas	0 09.6	+59 11	2.28v	0.38	F2 III	60	1.2	54	0.555	109	+11 SB	var.: 2.25–2.31, 0.10 d	Caph
γ Peg	0 13.6	+15 14	2.83v	–0.19	B2 IV	10	–2.4	300	0.008	176	+4 SB	var.: 2.78–2.89, 0.15 d	Algenib
β Hyi	0 26.1	–77 13	2.82	0.62	G1 IV	134	3.4	24	2.255	82	23		
α Phe	0 26.7	–42 16	2.40	1.08	K0 IIIb	42	–0.3	77	0.442	152	+75 SB		Ankaa
δ And A	0 39.7	+30 54	3.27	1.27	K3 III	32	0.9	101	0.161	122	–7 SB		
α Cas	0 40.9	+56 35	2.24	1.17	K0 IIIa	14	–2.5	230	0.058	117	–4 V?		Schedar
β Cet	0 44.0	–17 57	2.04	1.02	K0 III	34	–1.0	96	0.234	81	13		Diphda
η Cas A	0 49.6	+57 51	3.46	0.59	G0 V	168	4.6	19	1.218	115	+9 SB	B: 7.51, K4 Ve, 13″	Achird
γ Cas	0 57.2	+60 45	2.15v	–0.05	B0 IVnpe (shell)	5	–5.0	600	0.026	90	–7 SB	var.: 1.6–3.0; B: 8.8, 2″	Cih
β Phe AB	1 06.4	–46 41	3.32	0.88	G8 III	16	0.3:	150	0.030	279	–1	AB similar in light, spectrum, 1″	
η Cet	1 09.0	–10 09	3.46	1.16	K1.5 III CN1	28	–0.1	120	0.250	122	12		
β And	1 10.2	+35 40	2.07	1.58	M0 IIIa	16	–1.9	200	0.210	121	+3 V		Mirach
δ Cas	1 26.3	+60 16	2.66v	0.16	A5 IV	33	0.2	99	0.303	99	+7 SB	ecl.? 2.68–2.76, 759 d	Ruchbah
γ Phe	1 28.7	–43 17	3.41v	1.54	K7 IIIa	14	–1.6	230	0.204	184	+26 SB	irreg. var.: 3.39–3.49	
α Eri	1 38.0	–57 12	0.45	–0.16	B3 Vnp (shell)	23	–2.9	144	0.108	105	+16 V		**Achernar**
τ Cet	1 44.4	–15 54	3.49	0.73	G8 V	274	5.7	12	1.921	296	–16		
α Tri	1 53.5	+29 37	3.42	0.49	F6 IV	51	1.8	64	0.230	177	–13 SB		Mothallah
ε Cas	1 54.9	+63 42	3.35	–0.15	B3 IV:p (shell)	7	–2.5	400	0.036	114	–8 V		Segin
β Ari	1 55.1	+20 51	2.64	0.16	A4 V	55	1.3	60	0.145	138	–2 SB		Sheratan
α Hyi	1 59.0	–61 32	2.86	0.29	F0n III–IV	46	1.1	71	0.271	83	+1 V		
γ And A	2 04.4	+42 22	2.10	1.37	K3 IIb	9	–3.0	350	0.066	136	–12 SB	B: 5.4, B9 V, 10″; C: 6.2, A0 V; BC0.3″	Almach
α Ari	2 07.6	+23 30	2.01	1.15	K2 IIIab	49	0.5	66	0.238	127	–14 SB	calcium weak?	Hamal
β Tri	2 10.0	+35 01	3.00	0.14	A5 IV	26	0.1	120	0.153	104	+10 SB2		
ο Cet A	2 19.7	–2 57	6.47v	0.97	M5–10 IIIe	8	3.0	400	0.232	183	+64 V	LPV, 2–10; B: VZ Cet, 9.5v, Bpe, 0.5″	Mira
α UMi A	2 40.6	+89 18	1.97v	0.64	F5–8 Ib	8	–4.1	400	0.046	95	–17 SB	low-amp. Cep., 4.0 d; B: 8.2, F3 V, 19″	Polaris
γ Cet AB	2 43.7	+3 16	3.47	0.09	A2 Va	40	1.3	82	0.203	224	–5 V	A: 3.57; B: 6.23, 3″	Kaffaljidhmah
θ Eri A	2 58.5	–40 16	3.28	0.17	A5 IV	28	–0.3	100	0.065	294	+12 SB2	B: 4.35, A1 Va, 8″	Acamar
α Cet	3 02.7	+4 07	2.54	1.63	M2 III	15	–1.7	220	0.075	189	–26		Menkar
γ Per	3 05.3	+53 32	2.91	0.72	G8 III + A2 V	13	–0.8:	200	0.002	180	+3 SB	composite spectrum	
ρ Per	3 05.7	+38 52	3.32v	1.53	M4 II	10	–1.3	320	0.165	128	28	semiregular var.: 3.3–4.0	
β Per	3 08.7	+40 59	2.09v	0.00	B8 V + F:	35	–0.5	93	0.004	124	+4 SB	ecl.: 2.12–3.39, 2.9 d; composite	Algol
α Per	3 24.9	+49 53	1.79	0.48	F5 Ib	6	–4.9	600	0.033	131	–2 V	in open cluster	Mirfak
δ Per	3 43.5	+47 49	3.01	–0.12	B5 IIIn	6	–3.1	500	0.042	139	+4 SB		
δ Eri	3 43.6	–9 44	3.52	0.92	K0 IV	111	3.4	29	0.752	352	–6		Rana

TABLE OF BRIGHTEST STARS (continued)

Star Name	RA (2007.5) h m	Dec ° ′	V	$B-V$	MK Type	π mas	M_V	D ly	μ ″/yr	PA °	RV km/s	Remarks	
γ Hyi	3 47.1	−74 13	3.26	1.59	M2 III	15	−1.0	210	0.128	24	16		
η Tau	3 47.9	+24 08	2.85	−0.09	B7 IIIn	9	−1.6:	400	0.048	157	+10 V?	in Pleiades	Alcyone
ζ Per A	3 54.6	+31 54	2.84	0.27	B1 Ib	3	−6.0	1000	0.011	146	+20 SB	B: 9.16, B8 V, 13″	
ε Per A	3 58.4	+40 02	2.90	−0.20	B0.5 IV	6	−3.4	500	0.029	145	+1 SB2	B: 7.39, B9.5 V, 9″	
γ Eri	3 58.4	−13 29	2.97	1.59	M1 IIIb	15	−1.6	220	0.124	153	62	calcium, chromium weak	Zaurak
λ Tau A	4 01.1	+12 31	3.41v	−0.10	B3 V	9	−2.3	400	0.011	218	+18 SB2	ecl.: 3.37–3.91, 4.0 d; B: A4 IV	
α Ret A	4 14.5	−62 27	3.33	0.92	G8 II–III	20	−0.5	160	0.068	43	+36 SB?		
ε Tau	4 29.1	+19 12	3.53	1.01	K0 III	21	0.1	160	0.114	108	39	in Hyades	Ain
θ^2 Tau	4 29.1	+15 53	3.40	0.18	A7 III	22	0.2	150	0.105	103	+40 SB	in Hyades	
α Dor AB	4 34.2	−55 02	3.30	−0.08	A0p V: (Si)	19	0.2	180	0.051	89	26	A: 3.8; B: 4.3, B9 IV ; 0.3″; orbit 12 y	
α Tau A	4 36.4	+16 31	0.87v	1.54	K5 III	50	−0.8	65	0.200	161	+54 SB	irregular var.: 0.75–0.95	**Aldebaran**
π^3 Ori	4 50.2	+6 58	3.19	0.48	F6 V	125	3.7	26	0.463	88	+24 SB2		Tabit
ι Aur	4 57.5	+33 11	2.69v	1.49	K3 II	6	−3.6	500	0.018	167	18	var.: 2.63-2.78	Hasseleh
ε Aur A	5 02.5	+43 50	3.03v	0.54	A9 Iae + B	2	−8.0:	2000?	0.004	166	−3 SB	ecl.: 2.92–3.83, 9892 d	Almaaz
ε Lep	5 05.8	−22 22	3.19	1.46	K4 III	14	−2.0	230	0.073	166	1		
η Aur	5 07.0	+41 15	3.18	−0.15	B3 V	15	−1.2	220	0.073	157	+7 V?		Hoedus II
β Eri	5 08.2	−5 05	2.78	0.16	A3 IVn	37	0.4	89	0.128	231	−9		Cursa
μ Lep	5 13.3	−16 12	3.29v	−0.11	B9p IV: (HgMn)	18	−0.4	180	0.043	129	28	var.: 2.97–3.41, 2 d	
β Ori A	5 14.9	−8 12	0.18	−0.03	B8 Ia	4	−6.6	800	0.004	236	+21 SB	B: 7.6, B5 V, 9″; C: 7.6; BC: 0.1″	**Rigel**
α Aur AB	5 17.2	+46 00	0.08	0.80	G6:III + G2:III	77	−0.8	42	0.430	169	+30 SB	composite; A: 0.6; B: 1.1, 0.04″	**Capella**
η Ori AB	5 24.9	−2 23	3.35v	−0.24	B0.5 V + B	4	−3.9	900	0.003	288	+20 SB2	ecl.: 3.31–3.60, 8.0 d; A: 3.6; B: 5.0, 1.6″	
γ Ori	5 25.5	+6 21	1.64	−0.22	B2 III	13	−2.8	240	0.018	221	+18 SB?		Bellatrix
β Tau	5 26.8	+28 37	1.65	−0.13	B7 III	25	−1.3	130	0.178	172	+9 V		El Nath
β Lep A	5 28.6	−20 45	2.81	0.81	G5 II	20	−0.7	160	0.090	185	−14	B: 7.4, 2.6″	Nihal
δ Ori A	5 32.4	−0 18	2.25v	−0.18	O9.5 II	4	−5.4	900	0.002	252	+16 SB	ecl.: 2.14–2.26, 5.7 d	Mintaka
α Lep	5 33.1	−17 49	2.58	0.21	F0 Ib	3	−5.5	1000	0.006	279	24		Arneb
β Dor	5 33.7	−62 29	3.76v	0.64	F7–G2 Ib	3	−4.2	1000	0.007	8	+7 V	Cepheid var.: 3.46–4.08, 9.8 d	
λ Ori A	5 35.6	+9 56	3.39	−0.16	O8 IIIf	3	−4.6	1000	0.006	191	34	B: 5.61, B0 V, 4″	Meissa
ι Ori A	5 35.8	−5 54	2.75	−0.21	O9 III	2	−5.6	1000	0.005	284	+22 SB2	B: 7.3, B7 IIIp (He wk), 11″	Hatsya
ε Ori	5 36.6	−1 12	1.69	−0.18	B0 Ia	2	−6.6	1000	0.004	236	+26 SB		Alnilam
ζ Tau	5 38.1	+21 09	2.97v	−0.15	B2 IIIpe (shell)	8	−2.8	400	0.023	177	+20 SB	ecl., var.: 2.88–3.17, 133 d; B: 5.0, 0.007″	
α Col A	5 39.9	−34 04	2.65	−0.12	B7 IV	12	−1.9	270	0.026	178	+35 V?		Phakt
ζ Ori A	5 41.1	−1 56	1.74	−0.20	O9.5 Ib	4	−5.5	800	0.002	207	+18 SB	B: 4.2, B0 III, 2.4″	Alnitak
ζ Lep	5 47.3	−14 49	3.55	0.10	A2 Vann	46	1.7	70	0.023	263	+20 SB?		
κ Ori	5 48.1	−9 40	2.07	−0.17	B0.5 Ia	5	−5.0:	820	0.006	211	+21 V?		Saiph
β Col	5 51.2	−35 46	3.12	1.15	K1.5 III	38	0.2	86	0.405	7	+89 V		Wasn

TABLE OF BRIGHTEST STARS (continued)

Star Name	RA (2007.5) h m	Dec ° ′	V	$B-V$	MK Type	π mas	M_V	D ly	μ ″/yr	PA °	RV km/s	Remarks	
α Ori	5 55.6	+7 24	0.45v	1.50	M2 Iab	8	−5.0:	520	0.028	68	+21 SB	semiregular var.: 0.0–1.3	**Betelgeuse**
β Aur	6 00.1	+44 57	1.90v	0.08	A1 IV	40	−0.2	82	0.055	269	−18 SB2	ecl.: 1.89–1.98, 4.0 d (mags. equal)	Menkalinan
θ Aur AB	6 00.2	+37 13	2.65	−0.08	A0p II: (Si)	19	−1.0	170	0.097	149	+30 SB	B: 7.2, G2 V, 4″	
η Gem	6 15.3	+22 30	3.31v	1.60	M3 III	9	−1.8	300	0.068	259	+19 SB	ecl., var.: 3.2–3.9, 233 d; B: 8.8, 1.6″	Propus
ζ CMa	6 20.6	−30 04	3.02	−0.16	B2.5 V	10	−2.2	340	0.006	59	+32 SB		Furud
β CMa	6 23.0	−17 58	1.98v	−0.24	B1 II–III	7	−4.0	500	0.014	253	+34 SB	var.: 1.93–2.00, 0.25 d	Mirzam
μ Gem	6 23.4	+22 31	2.87v	1.62	M3 IIIab	14	−1.5	230	0.125	154	55	irregular var.: 2.75–3.02	Tejat Posterior
α Car	6 24.1	−52 42	−0.62	0.16	A9 Ib	10	−5.4	310	0.034	50	21		**Canopus**
ν Pup	6 38.0	−43 12	3.17	−0.10	B8 IIIn	8	−2.4	400	0.010	234	+28 SB		
γ Gem	6 38.1	+16 24	1.93	0.00	A1 IVs	31	−0.6	100	0.061	136	−13 SB		Alhena
ε Gem	6 44.4	+25 07	3.06	1.38	G8 Ib	4	−5.0	900	0.016	195	+10 SB		Mebsuta
α CMa A	6 45.5	−16 44	−1.44	0.01	A0mA1 Va	379	1.5	9	1.324	204	−8 SB	B: 8.5, WDA; 8″; orbit 50.1 y	**Sirius**
ξ Gem	6 45.7	+12 53	3.35	0.44	F5 IV	57	2.2	57	0.224	211	+25 V?		Alzirr
α Pic	6 48.3	−61 57	3.24	0.22	A6 Vn	33	0.7	100	0.275	345	21		
τ Pup	6 50.1	−50 37	2.94	1.21	K1 III	18	−1.9	180	0.079	157	+36 SB		
ε CMa A	6 58.9	−28 59	1.50	−0.21	B2 II	8	−4.1	400	0.002	27	27		**Adhara**
σ CMa	7 02.0	−27 57	3.49v	1.73	K7 Ib	3	−4.7	1000	0.008	284	22	irregular var.: 3.43–3.51	
o^2 CMa	7 03.3	−23 51	3.02	−0.08	B3 Ia	1	−6.6	3000	0.007	262	+48 SB		
δ CMa	7 08.7	−26 24	1.83	0.67	F8 Ia	2	−7.2	2000	0.008	291	+34 SB		Wezen
L_2 Pup	7 13.8	−44 39	4.42v	1.33	M5 IIIe	16	1.5	200	0.346	18	+53 V?	long-period var.: 2.6–6.2	HR2748
π Pup	7 17.4	−37 07	2.71	1.62	K3 Ib	3	−5.1	1100	0.012	284	16		
δ Gem AB	7 20.6	+21 58	3.50	0.37	F0 IV	55	2.2	59	0.029	241	+4 SB	B: 8.2, K3 V, 0.2″	Wasat
η CMa	7 24.4	−29 19	2.45	−0.08	B5 Ia	1	−7.5	3000	0.008	284	+41 V		Aludra
β CMi	7 27.6	+8 16	2.89	−0.10	B8 V	19	−0.8	170	0.065	233	+22 SB		Gomeisa
σ Pup A	7 29.5	−43 19	3.25	1.51	K5 III	18	−1.6	180	0.195	342	+88 SB	B: 8.6, G5: V, 22″	
α Gem A	7 35.1	+31 52	1.93	0.03	A1mA2 Va	63	0.6	52	0.199	239	+6 SB	[4″; orbit 445 y; max = 6.5″, in 1880;	
α Gem B	7 35.1	+31 52	2.97	0.03	A2mA5 V:	63	1.0	52	0.199	239	−1 SB	min = 1.8″, in 1965	Castor
α CMi A	7 39.7	+5 12	0.40	0.43	F5 IV–V	286	2.8	11	1.248	214	−3 SB	B: 10.3, WD ; 2″; orbit 41 y	**Procyon**
β Gem	7 45.8	+28 00	1.16	0.99	K0 IIIb	97	1.1	34	0.629	265	+3 V		**Pollux**
ξ Pup	7 49.6	−24 53	3.34	1.22	G6 Iab–Ib	2	−7.5:	3300	0.033	240	+3 SB		Asmidiske
χ Car	7 57.0	−53 00	3.46	−0.18	B3 IVp (cf. Remarks)	8	−2.0	387	0.042	306	+19 V	Si II strong	
ζ Pup	8 03.8	−40 01	2.21	−0.27	O5 Iafn	2	−6.1	1000	0.033	290	−24 V?		Naos
ρ Pup	8 07.9	−24 20	2.83v	0.46	F2mF5 II: (var)	52	1.4	63	0.100	299	+46 SB	delta Del spec.; var.: 2.68–2.87, 0.14 d	
$γ^2$ Vel	8 09.8	−47 22	1.75v	−0.14	WC8 + O9 I:	4	−5.8	800	0.007	304	+35 SB2	var.: 1.81–1.87	
β Cnc	8 16.9	+9 10	3.53	1.48	K4 III	11	−1.2	290	0.068	220	22		Tarf
ε Car	8 22.7	−59 32	1.86v	1.20	K3:III + B2:V	5	−4.8	600	0.030	301	2	ecl.?: 1.82–1.94	Avior

TABLE OF BRIGHTEST STARS (continued)

Star Name	RA (2007.5) h m	Dec ° ′	V	$B-V$	MK Type	π mas	M_V	D ly	μ ″/yr	PA °	RV km/s	Remarks	
ο UMa A	8 30.9	+60 42	3.35v?	0.86	G5 III	18	−0.3	180	0.171	230	20	var.?: 3.30?-3.36?	
δ Vel AB	8 44.9	−54 44	1.93	0.04	A1 Va	41	0.0	80	0.082	164	+ 2 V?	B: 5.0, 2″	
ε Hya ABC	8 47.2	+6 23	3.38	0.68	G5:III + A:	24	0.0	140	0.198	254	+36 SB	composite A: 3.8; B: 4.7, 0.2″; C: 7.8, 3″	
ζ Hya	8 55.8	+5 55	3.11	0.98	G9 II–III	22	−0.2	150	0.101	277	23		
ι UMa A	8 59.7	+48 01	3.12	0.22	A7 IVn	68	2.2	48	0.501	242	+9 SB	BC: 10.8, M1 V, 4″	Talitha
λ Vel	9 08.3	−43 28	2.23v	1.66	K4 Ib–IIa	6	−4.8	600	0.026	299	18	var.: 2.14–2.30	
a Car	9 11.2	−59 00	3.43v	−0.19	B2 IV–V	8	−2.2	420	0.028	283	+23 SB2	ecl.?: 3.41–3.44	HR3659
β Car	9 13.3	−69 45	1.67	0.07	A1 III	29	−1.1	111	0.183	304	−5 V?		Miaplacidus
ι Car	9 17.3	−59 18	2.21v	0.19	A7 Ib	5	−4.4	700	0.019	285	13	var.: 2.23–2.28	Tureis
α Lyn	9 21.5	+34 22	3.14	1.55	K7 IIIab	15	−1.3	220	0.223	273	38		
κ Vel	9 22.3	−55 03	2.47	−0.14	B2 IV–V	6	−3.9	500	0.012	315	+22 SB		
α Hya	9 28.0	−8 41	1.99	1.44	K3 II–III	18	−2.1	180	0.034	327	−4 V?		Alphard
N Vel	9 31.4	−57 04	3.16	1.54	K5 III	14	−1.3	240	0.034	268	−14		HR3803
θ UMa	9 33.4	+51 39	3.17	0.48	F6 IV	74	2.6	44	1.094	240	+15 SB		
ο Leo AB	9 41.6	+9 51	3.52v	0.52	F5 II + A5?	24	0.1	140	0.149	254	+27 SB	A: occ. bin. (mags. equal)	Subra
l Car	9 45.5	−62 33	3.69v	1.01	F9–G5 Ib	2	−5.8	2000	0.016	281	+4 V	Cepheid var.: 3.28–4.18, 36 d	HR3884
ε Leo	9 46.3	+23 44	2.97	0.81	G1 II	13	−1.6	250	0.048	252	+4 V?		Ras Elased Australis
υ Car AB	9 47.3	−65 06	2.92	0.29	A6 II	2	−2.5:	330	0.012	305	14	A: 3.01; B: 5.99, B7 III, 5″	
φ Vel	9 57.1	−54 36	3.52	−0.07	B5 Ib	2	−5.5	2000	0.013	293	14		
η Leo	10 07.7	+16 44	3.48	−0.03	A0 Ib	2	−5.5	2000	0.006	189	+3 V	B: 4.5, 0.1″	
α Leo A	10 08.8	+11 56	1.36	−0.09	B7 Vn	42	−0.6	78	0.248	271	+6 SB		**Regulus**
ω Car	10 13.9	−70 05	3.29	−0.07	B8 IIIn	9	−2.1	370	0.032	275	+7 V		
ζ Leo	10 17.1	+23 23	3.43	0.31	F0 IIIa	13	−1.1	260	0.023	124	−16 SB		Adhafera
q Car	10 17.3	−61 22	3.39v	1.54	K3 IIa	4	−4.2	700	0.027	276	8	irregular var.: 3.36–3.44	HR4050
λ UMa	10 17.5	+42 53	3.45	0.03	A1 IV	24	0.4	130	0.170	255	+18 V		Tania Borealis
γ Leo A	10 20.4	+19 48	2.61	1.13	K1 IIIb Fe–0.5	26	−0.7	130	0.342	116	−37 SB	4″; orbit 620 y;	
γ Leo B	10 20.4	+19 48	3.16	1.42	G7 III Fe–1	26	−1.9	130	0.358	119	−36 V	max = 5″, around 2100	Algieba
μ UMa	10 22.8	+41 28	3.06	1.60	M0 IIIp	13	−1.5	250	0.088	290	−21 SB	Ca II emission	Tania Australis
p Car	10 32.3	−61 43	3.30v	−0.09	B4 Vne	7	−2.0:	330	0.021	287	26	irregular var.: 3.27–3.37	HR4140
θ Car	10 43.2	−64 26	2.74	−0.22	B0.5 Vp	7	−3.1	400	0.022	291	+24 SB	nitrogen enhanced	
μ Vel AB	10 47.1	−49 28	2.69	1.07	G5 III + F8:V	28	−0.9	116	0.085	125	+6 SB	A: 2.72; B: 5.92, 2″	
ν Hya	10 50.0	−16 14	3.11	1.23	K2 III	24	−0.3	140	0.215	24	−1		
β UMa	11 02.3	+56 21	2.34	0.03	A0mA1 IV–V	41	0.4	79	0.087	70	−12 SB		Merak
α UMa AB	11 04.2	+61 43	1.81	1.06	K0 IIIa	26	−1.3	124	0.138	239	−9 SB	A: 1.86; B: 4.8, A8 V, <1″	Dubhe
ψ UMa	11 10.1	+44 27	3.00	1.14	K1 III	22	−0.5	147	0.075	245	−4		
δ Leo	11 14.5	+20 29	2.56	0.13	A4 IV	57	1.3	58	0.197	133	−20 V		Zosma

TABLE OF BRIGHTEST STARS (continued)

Star Name	RA (2007.5) h m	Dec ° ′	V	$B-V$	MK Type	π mas	M_V	D ly	μ ″/yr	PA °	RV km/s	Remarks	
θ Leo	11 14.6	+15 23	3.33	0.00	A2 IV (K-line var.)	18	−0.2	180	0.104	216	+8 V		Chort
ν UMa	11 18.9	+33 03	3.49	1.40	K3 III Ba0.3	8	−3.2	400	0.036	309	−9 SB	B: 9.5, 7″	Alula Borealis
ξ Hya	11 33.4	−31 54	3.54	0.95	G7 III	25	0.0	130	0.211	259	−5 V		
λ Cen	11 36.1	−63 04	3.11	−0.04	B9.5 IIn	8	−2.5	410	0.039	258	−1 V		
β Leo	11 49.4	+14 32	2.14	0.09	A3 Va	90	1.9	36	0.511	257	0 V		Denebola
γ UMa	11 54.2	+53 39	2.41	0.04	A0 Van	39	0.2	84	0.094	86	−13 SB		Phad
δ Cen	12 08.8	−50 46	2.58v	−0.13	B2 IVne	8	−3.1	400	0.034	249	+11 V	irregular var.: 2.51–2.65	
ε Crv	12 10.5	−22 40	3.02	1.33	K2 III	11	−2.3	300	0.073	278	5		Minkar
δ Cru	12 15.5	−58 47	2.79v	−0.19	B2 IV	9	−2.6	360	0.039	255	+22 V?	var.: 2.78–2.84, 0.15 d	
δ UMa	12 15.8	+56 59	3.32	0.08	A2 Van	40	1.4	81	0.102	88	−13 V		Megrez
γ Crv	12 16.2	−17 35	2.58	−0.11	B8 III	20	−0.9	160	0.163	276	−4 SB	sp. var.?	Gienah Ghurab
α Cru A	12 27.0	−63 08	1.25	−0.20	B0.5 IV	10	−4.0	320	0.030	236	−11 SB	[4″; unknown slow	**Acrux**
α Cru B	12 27.0	−63 08	1.64	−0.18	B1 Vn	10	−3.6	320	0.031	248	−1	orbit; 6″ in 1826]	**Acrux**
δ Crv A	12 30.3	−16 33	2.94	−0.01	B9.5 IVn	37	−2.0	88	0.255	236	+9 V	B: 8.26, K2 V, 24″	Algorab
γ Cru	12 31.6	−57 09	1.59v	1.60	M3.5 III	37	−0.7	88	0.269	174	21	var.: 1.60–1.67	Gacrux
β Crv	12 34.8	−23 26	2.65	0.89	G5 II	23	−0.5	140	0.059	179	−8		Kraz
α Mus	12 37.6	−69 11	2.69v	−0.18	B2 IV–V	11	−2.3	310	0.043	248	+13 V	var.: 2.68–2.73, 0.090 d	
γ Cen A	12 41.9	−49 00	2.95	−0.02	A1 IV	25	−0.1	130	0.190	268	−6 SB	[0.6″; orbit 84 y; min = 0.2″, in 1931;	
γ Cen B	12 41.9	−49 00	2.85	−0.02	A0 IV	25	−0.1	130	0.190	268	−6 SB	max = 1.7″]	
γ Vir AB	12 42.0	−1 29	2.74	0.37	F1 V + F0mF2 V	85	2.2	39	0.567	271	−20 SB	A: 3.48; B: 3.50; 0.7″ (near periastron)	Porrima
β Mus AB	12 46.7	−68 09	3.04	−0.18	B2 V + B2.5 V	10	−2.2:	420	0.041	233	+42 V	A: 3.51; B: 4.00, 1″	
β Cru	12 48.2	−59 44	1.25v	−0.24	B0.5 III	9	−4.0	350	0.042	246	+16 SB	var.: 1.23–1.31, 0.24 d	**Becrux**
ε UMa	12 54.4	+55 55	1.76v	−0.02	A0p IV: (CrEu)	40	−0.2	81	0.109	95	−9 SB?	var.: 1.76–1.78, 5.1 d	Alioth
δ Vir	12 56.0	+3 21	3.39	1.57	M3 III	16	−0.5	200	0.474	263	−18 V?		Auva
$α^2$ CVn A	12 56.4	+38 17	2.85	−0.06	A0p (SiEu)	30	0.4	110	0.242	282	−3 V	B: 5.6, F0 V, 20″	Cor Caroli
ε Vir	13 02.6	+10 55	2.85	0.93	G9 IIIab	32	0.4	100	0.274	274	−14		Vindemiatrix
γ Hya	13 19.3	−23 13	2.99	0.92	G8 IIIa	25	−0.6	130	0.081	127	−5 V?		
ι Cen	13 21.0	−36 45	2.75	0.07	A2 Va	56	1.4	59	0.351	255	0		
ζ UMa A	13 24.2	+54 53	2.23	0.06	A1 Va	42	0.3	78	0.122	102	−6 SB2	B: 3.94, A1mA7 IV–V, 14″	Mizar
α Vir	13 25.6	−11 12	0.98v	−0.24	B1 V	12	−3.6	260	0.054	232	+1 SB2	var.: 0.95–1.05, 4.0 d; mult. 3.1, 4.5, 7.5	**Spica**
ζ Vir	13 35.1	−0 38	3.38	0.11	A2 IV	45	1.6	73	0.287	277	−13		Heze
ε Cen	13 40.4	−53 30	2.29	−0.17	B1 III	9	−3.3	400	0.028	232	3		
η UMa	13 47.8	+49 17	1.85	−0.10	B3 V	32	−1.8	101	0.127	264	−11 SB?		Alkaid
ν Cen	13 50.0	−41 43	3.41	−0.22	B2 IV	7	−2.4	500	0.035	227	+9 SB		
μ Cen	13 50.1	−42 31	3.47v	−0.17	B2 IV–V pne	6	−2.8	500	0.034	220	+9 SB	variable shell: 2.92–3.47	
η Boo	13 55.0	+18 22	2.68	0.58	G0 IV	88	2.4	37	0.370	190	0 SB		Mufrid

TABLE OF BRIGHTEST STARS (continued)

Star Name	RA (2007.5) h m	Dec ° ′	V	$B-V$	MK Type	π mas	M_V	D ly	μ ″/yr	PA °	RV km/s	Remarks	
ζ Cen	13 56.0	−47 20	2.55	−0.18	B2.5 IV	8	−2.9	400	0.072	232	+7 SB2		
β Cen AB	14 04.4	−60 25	0.58v	−0.23	B1 III	6	−5.5	500	0.030	221	+6 SB	var.: 0.61–0.66, 0.16 d; B: 3.9, 1″	**Hadar**
π Hya	14 06.8	−26 43	3.25	1.09	K2 IIIb	32	0.2	101	0.049	163	27		
θ Cen	14 07.1	−36 24	2.06	1.01	K0 IIIb	54	0.1	61	0.738	225	1		Menkent
α Boo	14 16.0	+19 09	−0.05	1.24	K1.5 III Fe–0.5	89	−0.6	37	2.281	209	−5 V?	high space velocity	**Arcturus**
ι Lup	14 19.9	−46 06	3.55	−0.18	B2.5 IVn	9	−1.7	400	0.014	266	22		
γ Boo	14 32.4	+38 17	3.04	0.19	A7 IV+	38	1.0	85	0.189	322	−37 V		Seginus
η Cen	14 36.0	−42 11	2.33v	−0.16	B1.5 IV pne	11	−2.8	310	0.049	226	0 SB	variable shell: 2.30–2.41	
α Cen B	14 40.1	−60 52	1.35	0.90	K1 V	742	6.2	4	3.678	281	−21 V?	[AB 9″; orbit 80 y; min = 2″, in 1955; max 22″	
α Cen A	14 40.1	−60 52	−0.01	0.71	G2 V	742	4.2	4	3.678	281	−25 SB	[C: Proxima, 12.4, M5e, 2°	**Rigil Kentaurus**
α Lup	14 42.4	−47 25	2.30v	−0.15	B1.5 III	6	−4.1	500	0.026	220	+5 SB	var.: 2.29–2.34, 0.26 d	
α Cir	14 43.1	−65 00	3.18	0.26	A7p (Sr)	61	1.9	54	0.302	218	+7 SB?	B: 8.6, K5 V, 16″	
ε Boo AB	14 45.3	+27 03	2.35	1.34	K0 II–III+A0 V	16	−2.6	210	0.054	289	−17 V	A: 2.50; B: 4.66, 3″	Izar
β UMi	14 50.7	+74 07	2.07	1.46	K4 III	26	−1.1	126	0.036	286	+17 V		Kochab
α^2 Lib	14 51.3	−16 04	2.75	0.15	A3 III–IV	42	0.7	77	0.130	237	−23 SB		Zubenelgenubi
β Lup	14 59.0	−43 10	2.68	−0.18	B2 IV	6	−3.5	500	0.057	221	0 SB		
κ Cen	14 59.7	−42 08	3.13	−0.21	B2 V	6	−2.8	500	0.033	215	+8 SB		
β Boo	15 02.2	+40 22	3.49	0.96	G8 IIIa (cf. Remarks)	15	−0.7	220	0.056	235	−20	Ba 0.4, Fe −0.5	Nekkar
σ Lib	15 04.5	−25 19	3.25v	1.67	M2.5 III	11	−1.9	290	0.087	237	−4	semiregular var.: 3.20–3.46	Brachium
ζ Lup	15 12.8	−52 08	3.41	0.92	G8 III	28	0.1	120	0.128	237	−10		
δ Boo	15 15.8	+33 17	3.46	0.96	G8 III Fe–1	28	0.6	117	0.143	144	−12 SB		
β Lib	15 17.4	−9 25	2.61	−0.07	B8 IIIn	20	−1.0	160	0.101	275	−35 SB		Zubeneschemali
γ TrA	15 19.6	−68 42	2.87	0.01	A1 IIIn	18	−0.8	180	0.067	243	−3 V		
γ UMi	15 20.7	+71 48	3.00	0.06	A3 III	7	−0.1:	150	0.031	308	−4 V		Pherkad
δ Lup	15 21.9	−40 40	3.22	−0.23	B1.5 IVn	6	−2.8	500	0.036	207	0 V?		
ε Lup AB	15 23.2	−44 43	3.37	−0.19	B2 IV–V	6	−2.5	500	0.024	232	+8 SB2	A: 3.56; B: 5.04, <1″	
ι Dra	15 25.1	+58 56	3.29	1.17	K2 III	32	0.8	102	0.020	311	−11		Ed Asich
α CrB	15 35.0	+26 41	2.22v	0.03	A0 IV (composite)	44	0.3	75	0.151	127	+2 SB	ecl.: 2.21–2.32, 17 d	Alphecca
γ Lup AB	15 35.6	−41 11	2.80	−0.22	B2 IVn	6	−2.8	600	0.035	207	+2 V	A: 3.5; B: 3.6, <1″; similar spectra	
α Ser	15 44.6	+6 24	2.63v?	1.17	K2 IIIb CN1	45	0.9	73	0.143	72	+3 V?	var.?	Unuk al Hai
μ Ser	15 50.0	−3 27	3.54	−0.04	A0 III	21	0.3	160	0.094	253	−9 SB		
β TrA	15 55.8	−63 27	2.83	0.32	F0 IV	81	2.3	40	0.438	205	0		
π Sco A	15 59.3	−26 08	2.89	−0.18	B1 V + B2 V	7	−3.0	500	0.028	198	−3 SB2	A: occ. bin.: 3.4 + 4.5, 0.0003″ sep.	
T CrB	15 59.8	+25 54	10.08v	1.34	gM3: + Bep	0	−9.3	—	0.013	327	−29 SB	recurrent nova 1866 (mag. 3), 1946 (mag. 2)	
η Lup A	16 00.6	−38 25	3.42	−0.21	B2.5 IVn	7	−2.5	500	0.040	213	+8 V	A: 3.47; B: 7.70, 15″	
δ Sco AB	16 00.8	−22 39	2.29	−0.12	B0.3 IV	8	−4.4:	520	0.027	202	−7 SB	AB: sep. < 1″; C: 4.9, B2 IV–V, 8″	Dschubba

TABLE OF BRIGHTEST STARS (continued)

Star Name	RA (2007.5) h m	Dec ° ′	V	$B-V$	MK Type	π mas	M_V	D ly	μ ″/yr	PA °	RV km/s	Remarks	
β Sco AB	16 05.9	−19 50	2.56	−0.06	B0.5 V	6	−4.2	500	0.022	196	−1 SB	A: 2.78; B: 5.04, 1″; C: 4.93, 14″	Graffias
δ Oph	16 14.7	−3 43	2.73	1.58	M1 III	19	−0.8	170	0.153	198	−20 V		Yed Prior
ε Oph	16 18.7	−4 43	3.23	0.97	G9.5 IIIb	30	0.8	110	0.089	64	−10 V		Yed Posterior
σ Sco A	16 21.6	−25 37	2.91v	0.13	B1 III	4	−4.8:	520	0.025	201	+3 SB	var.: 2.86–2.94, 0.25 d; B: 8.3, B9 V, 20″	
η Dra A	16 24.1	+61 30	2.73	0.91	G8 IIIab	37	0.7	88	0.064	338	−14 SB?	B: 8.7, 6″	
α Sco A	16 29.9	−26 27	1.06v	1.86	M1.5 Iab	5	−5.8	600	0.024	197	−3 SB	irregular var.: 0.88–1.16; B: 5.37, 3″	**Antares**
β Her	16 30.5	+21 28	2.78	0.95	G7 IIIa	22	−0.5	150	0.100	260	−26 SB		Kornephoros
τ Sco	16 36.4	−28 14	2.82	−0.21	B0 V	8	−3.1	400	0.026	198	+2 V		
ζ Oph	16 37.6	−10 35	2.54	0.04	O9.5 Vn	7	−4.3	500	0.026	28	−15 V		
ζ Her AB	16 41.6	+31 35	2.81	0.65	G1 IV	93	2.5	35	0.614	310	−70 SB	A: 2.90; B: 5.53, G7 V, 1.1″	
η Her	16 43.2	+38 54	3.48	0.92	G7.5 IIIb Fe–1	29	0.1	112	0.089	158	+8 V?		
α TrA	16 49.5	−69 02	1.91	1.45	K2 IIb–IIIa	8	−5.0	400	0.044	141	−3		Atria
ε Sco	16 50.6	−34 18	2.29	1.14	K2 III	50	0.1	65	0.661	247	−3		
μ[1] Sco	16 52.4	−38 04	3.00v	−0.20	B1.5 IVn	4	−4.1	800	0.031	202	−25 SB2	ecl.: 2.94–3.22, 1.4 d	
κ Oph	16 58.0	+9 22	3.19	1.16	K2 III	38	1.1	86	0.293	268	−56		
ζ Ara	16 59.2	−56 00	3.12	1.55	K4 III	6	−4.5	600	0.037	200	−6		
ζ Dra	17 08.8	+65 42	3.17	−0.12	B6 III	10	−2.0	340	0.033	310	−17 V		Aldhibah
η Oph AB	17 10.8	−15 44	2.43	0.06	A2.5 Va	39	0.8	84	0.102	22	−1 SB	A: 3.0; B: 3.5, A3 V, 1″	Sabik
η Sco	17 12.7	−43 15	3.32	0.44	F2 V:p (Cr)	46	1.4	72	0.286	175	−27		
α Her AB	17 15.0	+14 23	2.78v	1.16	M5 Ib–II	9	−3.5:	1400	0.035	348	−33 V	semiregular var.: 2.7–4.0; B: 5.4, 5″	Rasalgethi
π Her	17 15.3	+36 48	3.16	1.44	K3 IIab	9	−2.2	370	0.029	276	−26		
δ Her	17 15.3	+24 50	3.12	0.08	A1 Vann	42	1.2	79	0.159	188	−40 SB	B: 8.8, 9″	Sarin
θ Oph	17 22.5	−25 00	3.27v	−0.19	B2 IV	6	−3.1	600	0.021	188	−2 SB	occ. bin.: 3.4, 5.4; var.: 3.25–3.31, 0.14 d	
β Ara	17 25.9	−55 32	2.84	1.48	K3 Ib–IIa	5	−4.1	600	0.024	182	0		
γ Ara A	17 26.0	−56 23	3.31	−0.15	B1 Ib	3	−5.7:	650	0.011	170	−3 V	broad lines for Ib; B: 10.0, 18″	
β Dra A	17 30.6	+52 18	2.79	0.95	G2 Ib–IIa	9	−2.9	360	0.026	301	−20 V	B: 11.5, 4″	Rastaban
υ Sco	17 31.3	−37 18	2.70	−0.18	B2 IV	6	−3.5	500	0.032	182	8 SB		
α Ara	17 32.4	−49 53	2.84	−0.14	B2 Vne	13	−1.8	240	0.075	199	0 SB		
λ Sco	17 34.1	−37 07	1.62v	−0.23	B1.5 IV	5	−3.6:	360	0.029	178	−3 SB2	ecl.?, var.: 1.62–1.68, 0.21 d	Shaula
α Oph	17 35.3	+12 33	2.08	0.16	A5 Vnn	70	1.3	47	0.255	157	+13 SB?		Rasalhague
θ Sco	17 37.9	−43 00	1.86	0.41	F1 III	12	−3.0	270	0.016	90	1		Sargas
ξ Ser	17 38.0	−15 24	3.54	0.26	F0 IIIb	31	0.9	110	0.076	216	−43 SB		
κ Sco	17 43.0	−39 02	2.39v	−0.17	B1.5 III	7	−3.6	500	0.030	194	−14 SB	var.: 2.41–2.42, 0.20 d	
β Oph	17 43.8	+4 34	2.76	1.17	K2 III	40	0.7	82	0.164	345	−12 V		Cebalrai
μ Her A	17 46.8	+27 43	3.42	0.75	G5 IV	119	3.6	27	0.808	202	−16 V	BC: 9.78, 33″	
ι[1] Sco	17 48.1	−40 08	2.99	0.51	F2 Ia	2	−8.0:	4000?	0.006	171	−28 SB		

TABLE OF BRIGHTEST STARS (continued)

Star Name	RA (2007.5) h m	Dec ° ′	V	$B-V$	MK Type	π mas	M_V	D ly	μ ″/yr	PA °	RV km/s	Remarks
G Sco	17 50.4	−37 03	3.19	1.19	K2 III	26	−0.6	130	0.064	58	25	HR6630
γ Dra	17 56.8	+51 29	2.24	1.52	K5 III	22	−1.1	150	0.025	213	−28	Eltanin
ν Oph	17 59.4	−9 46	3.32	0.99	G9.5 IIIa	21	0.0	150	0.118	184	13	
$γ^2$ Sgr	18 06.3	−30 25	2.98	0.98	K0 III	34	0.1	96	0.192	196	+22 SB	Nash
η Sgr A	18 18.1	−36 46	3.10v	1.50	M3.5 IIIab	22	−0.1	150	0.210	218	+1 V?	irreg. var.: 3.05–3.12; B: 8.33, G8: IV:, 4″
δ Sgr	18 21.5	−29 49	2.72	1.38	K2.5 IIIa	11	−3.3	300	0.050	127	−20	Kaus Meridionalis
η Ser	18 21.7	−2 54	3.23	0.94	K0 III–IV	53	1.4	62	0.890	218	+9 V?	
ε Sgr	18 24.7	−34 23	1.79	−0.03	A0 II:n (shell?)	23	−1.4	140	0.129	194	−15	Kaus Australis
α Tel	18 27.5	−45 58	3.49	−0.18	B3 IV	13	−1.0	250	0.048	198	0 V?	
λ Sgr	18 28.4	−25 25	2.82	1.02	K1 IIIb	42	0.4	77	0.190	193	−43	Kaus Borealis
α Lyr	18 37.2	+38 47	0.03	0.00	A0 Va	129	0.6	25	0.348	35	−14 V	**Vega**
ϕ Sgr	18 46.1	−26 59	3.17	−0.11	B8 III	14	−1.0	230	0.052	89	+22 SB	similar companion, 0.1″
β Lyr	18 50.4	+33 22	3.52v	0.00	B7 Vpe (shell)	4	−4.1	900	0.002	180	−19 SB	ecl.: 3.25–4.36, 13 d Sheliak
σ Sgr	18 55.7	−26 17	2.05	−0.13	B3 IV	15	−2.4	220	0.056	166	−11 V	Nunki
$ξ^2$ Sgr	18 58.2	−21 06	3.52	1.15	K1 III	9	0.1	400	0.035	111	−20	
γ Lyr	18 59.2	+32 42	3.25	−0.05	B9 II	5	−3.3	600	0.007	288	−21 V	Sulaphat
ζ Sgr AB	19 03.1	−29 52	2.60	0.06	A2 IV–V + A4:V:	37	1.1	90	0.014	266	+22 SB	A: 3.2; B: 3.5, <1″ Ascella
ζ Aql A	19 05.8	+13 52	2.99	0.01	A0 Vann	39	0.9	83	0.095	184	−25 SB	
λ Aql	19 06.6	−4 52	3.43	−0.10	B9 Vnp (kB7HeA0)	26	0.6	130	0.090	193	−12 V	
τ Sgr	19 07.4	−27 40	3.32	1.17	K1.5 IIIb	27	−0.4	120	0.255	192	+45 SB	
π Sgr ABC	19 10.2	−21 01	2.88	0.38	F2 II–III	7	−3.1	400	0.035	180	−10	A: 3.7; B: 3.8; C: 6.0, <1″ Albaldah
δ Dra	19 12.6	+67 40	3.07	0.99	G9 III	33	0.6	100	0.130	44	25	Nodus Secundus
δ Aql	19 25.9	+3 08	3.36	0.32	F2 IV	65	2.6	50	0.267	72	−30 SB	Deneb Okab
β Cyg A	19 31.0	+27 59	3.36	1.09	K3 II + B9.5 V	8	−2.3	390	0.002	153	−24 V	B: 5.11, 35″; C: Δm = 1.5, 0.4″ Albireo
δ Cyg AB	19 45.2	+45 09	2.86	0.00	B9.5 III	19	−0.7	170	0.069	45	−20 SB	B: 6.4, F1 V; 3″
γ Aql	19 46.6	+10 38	2.72	1.51	K3 II	7	−2.6:	330	0.016	83	−2 V	Tarazed
α Aql	19 51.1	+8 53	0.76	0.22	A7 Vnn	194	2.1	17	0.662	54	−26	**Altair**
η Aql	19 52.9	+1 02	3.87v	0.63	F6–G1 Ib	3	−4.3	1000	0.009	131	−15 SB	Cepheid var.: 3.48–4.39, 7.2 d
γ Sge	19 59.1	+19 31	3.51	1.57	M0 III	12	−0.9	270	0.070	69	−33	
θ Aql	20 11.7	−0 48	3.24	−0.07	B9.5 III	11	−1.4	290	0.037	79	−27 SB2	
β Cap A	20 21.4	−14 45	3.05	0.79	K0: II: + A5: V:n	9	−1.4	300	0.039	86	−19 SB	A: mult.: 4.0 + 4.3 + 4.8 + 6.7, <1″ Dabih
γ Cyg	20 22.5	+40 17	2.23	0.67	F8 Ib	2	−4.1:	520	0.001	27	−8	Sadr
α Pav	20 26.2	−56 43	1.94	−0.12	B2.5 V	18	−2.1	180	0.087	169	+2 SB	Peacock
α Ind	20 38.1	−47 16	3.11	1.00	K0 III CN–1	32	0.1	101	0.090	39	−1	
α Cyg	20 41.7	+45 18	1.25	0.09	A2 Ia	1	−7.5:	1500	0.005	11	−5 V	**Deneb**
η Cep	20 45.4	+61 52	3.41	0.91	K0 IV	70	2.7	47	0.827	6	−87	

TABLE OF BRIGHTEST STARS (continued)

Star Name	RA (2007.5) h m	Dec ° ′	V	$B-V$	MK Type	π mas	M_V	D ly	μ ″/yr	PA °	RV km/s	Remarks	
β Pav	20 45.6	−66 11	3.42	0.16	A6 IV	24	0.6	140	0.041	295	10		
ε Cyg	20 46.5	+34 00	2.48	1.02	K0 III	45	0.7	72	0.484	47	−11 SB		Gienah
ζ Cyg	21 13.3	+30 15	3.21	0.99	G8 IIIa Ba 0.5	22	0.2	150	0.052	181	+17 SB		
α Cep	21 18.8	+62 37	2.45	0.26	A7 Van	67	1.4	49	0.159	71	−10 V		Alderamin
β Cep	21 28.8	+70 36	3.23v	−0.20	B1 III	5	−4.0:	820	0.016	38	−8 SB	var.: 3.16–3.27, 0.19 d; B: 7.8;13″	Alfirk
β Aqr	21 32.0	−5 32	2.90	0.83	G0 Ib	5	−3.5	612	0.020	105	7		Sadalsuud
ε Peg	21 44.6	+9 55	2.38v	1.52	K2 Ib	5	−5.2	700	0.030	81	+5 V	irregular var.: 0.7–3.5 (flare in 1972)	Enif
δ Cap	21 47.5	−16 06	2.85v	0.18	A3mF2 IV:	85	2.2	39	0.394	138	−6 SB	occ. bin.: 2.81–3.05, 1.0 d, 3.2 + 5.2	
γ Gru	21 54.4	−37 20	3.00	−0.08	B8 IV–Vs	16	−1.1	200	0.104	99	−2 V?		
α Aqr	22 06.2	−0 17	2.95	0.97	G2 Ib	4	−4.3	800	0.016	104	+8 V?		Sadalmelik
α Gru	22 08.7	−46 55	1.73	−0.07	B7 Vn	32	−0.9	101	0.198	139	12		Alnair
θ Peg	22 10.6	+6 14	3.52	0.09	A2mA1 IV–V	34	1.0	97	0.277	83	−6 SB2		Baham
ζ Cep	22 11.1	+58 14	3.39	1.56	K1.5 Ib	4	−4.2	700	0.015	58	−18 SB		
α Tuc	22 19.0	−60 13	2.87	1.39	K3 III	16	−2.2	200	0.071	237	+42 SB		
δ Cep A	22 29.5	+58 27	4.07v	0.78	F5–G2 Ib	3	−4.4	1000	0.012	67	−16 SB	prototype Cepheid var.: 3.48–4.37, 5.4 d	
ζ Peg	22 41.8	+10 52	3.41	−0.09	B8.5 III	16	−0.7	210	0.080	96	+7 V?		Homam
β Gru	22 43.1	−46 51	2.07v	1.61	M5 III	19	−1.4	170	0.138	92	2	irregular var.: 2.0–2.3	
η Peg	22 43.4	+30 16	2.93	0.85	G8 II + F0 V	15	−1.2	210	0.025	148	+4 SB		Matar
ε Gru	22 49.0	−51 17	3.49	0.08	A2 Va	25	0.4	130	0.126	120	0 V		
ι Cep	22 49.9	+66 14	3.50	1.05	K0 III	28	0.6	115	0.137	209	−12		
μ Peg	22 50.4	+24 38	3.51	0.93	G8 III	28	0.8	120	0.152	104	14		Sadalbari
δ Aqr	22 55.0	−15 47	3.27	0.07	A3 IV–V (wk λ4481)	20	−0.1	160	0.047	242	+18 V		Skat
α PsA	22 58.1	−29 35	1.17	0.14	A3 Va	130	1.6	25	0.373	116	7		**Fomalhaut**
β Peg	23 04.1	+28 07	2.44v	1.66	M2 II–III	16	−1.7	200	0.236	53	+9 V	irregular var.: 2.31–2.74	Scheat
α Peg	23 05.1	+15 15	2.49	0.00	A0 III–IV	23	−0.9	140	0.073	121	−4 SB		Markab
γ Cep	23 39.7	+77 40	3.21	1.03	K1 III–IV	72	2.1	45	0.168	337	−42		Alrai

THE NEAREST STARS

BY ALAN H. BATTEN

The following changes have been made to the table that appeared last year. First, DENIS 1048-39 has been moved from its position below Altair to one much higher up, and corresponding changes have been made to the quantities dependent upon distance. Second, there are two new entries, 2MASS 1259-43 and DENIS 1845-63 (which has two components, one a brown dwarf). Although data for these objects are incomplete, I believe the parallaxes are secure. Third, the star HIP 114110 has been designated once more as BD -15 6346B; anomalies in the literature that led me to change the designation last year appear to have been resolved. Fourth, a radial velocity has been determined for GJ 169.1A, enabling me to list a space velocity for the star, although, since it is based on a single observation it should be treated with reserve. I have corrected an error of sign of the space velocity previously given for GJ 169.1B. All the usual caveats given about the uncertainties of the distances still apply. In particular, 2MASS 0253+16, LP 944-20, and GJ 754 may be farther away than indicated.

The *annual parallax* of a star is the difference between its direction as seen from Earth and the Sun. Astronomers began to look for stellar parallax as soon as they began to take seriously the idea that the Sun, and not Earth, is the centre of the planetary system. The great distances of the other stars ensured, however, that determination of parallax would be beyond the powers of early telescopes. James Bradley (1693–1762) came close to succeeding and correctly deduced that even the largest parallaxes must be less than 2″, but about another century was to elapse before success was achieved. Then, between 1838 and 1840, Bessel, Struve, and Henderson all published trustworthy parallaxes for three different stars. Two of those star systems, α Cen (Henderson) and 61 Cyg (Bessel), are indeed so close to us that they appear in this table. Struve measured the parallax of Vega, which, although a relatively close neighbour of the Sun, lies some distance beyond the limit adopted here. Progress in measuring other parallaxes remained rather slow until it became possible, toward the end of the 19th century, to apply photography to the problem.

A table like the one presented here (pp. 234–235) looks rather static, but if we think on a long enough time scale, the stars within the sphere of approximately 19-ly radius, centred on the Sun, are changing all the time—moving in and out of the sphere. Proxima Centauri has not always been our nearest neighbour nor will it always be, even though it is at present coming closer to us. Calculations by R.A.J. Matthews some time ago indicated that 32 000 years ago L 726-8 was closer to us and that in another 33 000 years Ross 248 will be closer. More recent calculations by García-Sanchez and others, based on HIPPARCOS measurements, extend the picture over some tens of millions of years. Seven million years ago, Algol would have been featured in this table; it also would have been appreciably brighter in the sky than Sirius now is. In 1.4 million years, Gliese 710 (now over 60 ly away from us) will be only 1.3 ly away and a moderately bright naked-eye star. All such calculations are approximate, of course, because there are still uncertainties in our knowledge of the distances and motions of the stars.

Massive hot stars are relatively rare. Ignoring white dwarfs, which are not massive, only Sirius, Procyon, and Altair, in this table, are hotter and more massive than the Sun, and only α Cen equals the Sun in these respects. Most of the objects listed are very faint, cool stars; five (ε Ind B and C, at 11.8 ly; LP 944-20 at 16.2 ly; and the faint companion to DENIS 1845–63B at 12.5 ly and BD −21°1377, or GJ 229 B, at 18.8 ly) are brown dwarfs—not massive enough for thermonuclear reactions to be ignited in their centres, and producing energy only by their gravitational contraction.

They are very cool, faint, and difficult to detect, "shining" mostly in the infrared. There may be other such objects within the volume of space represented in this table, but thorough searches have not yet revealed them. There is some evidence for a substellar companion to van Maanen's star, for which an approximate period of 1.6 years is proposed, but not enough is known yet to justify including it in the table. Three objects, G 208-44 B, DENIS 1048-39, and 2MASS 1835+32, are very close to the borderline between true stars and brown dwarfs.

In 2004, I extended the table from its traditional limit of about 17 ly (5 parsecs) to just over 19 ly (very nearly 6 parsecs). Almost all the objects listed here may be found in either the HIPPARCOS catalogue or the *Yale Catalogue of Trigonometric Parallaxes;* a few have either been discovered or recognized as nearby objects since the publication of those two catalogues. I have preferred HIPPARCOS parallaxes when they are available, even though a few stellar parallaxes have been measured even more accurately with the Hubble Space Telescope. I have quoted HIPPARCOS parallaxes to the nearest tenth of a milliarcsecond, and ground-based determinations of parallax are only to the nearest milliarcsecond. Exceptions to this rule are the parallaxes of 2MASS 1835+32 and DENIS 1048–39, both ground-based measurements. The convention is not entirely fair to ground-based measurements—the best modern ones are comparable in accuracy with HIPPARCOS measures—but it helps the reader appreciate the contributions made by HIPPARCOS to our knowledge of stellar distances. The full value of any parallax given to the nearest tenth of a milliarcsecond was used in computing the distance, even if the last digit does not appear in the table. That is why, occasionally, a star may appear to be out of order in the table: the parallax has been rounded up, but the distance was computed from the unrounded value. With this year's additions, the table contains 51 single stars, 16 pairs (including common-proper-motion pairs but not the possible companion to van Maanen's star), and 5 triples (α Cen A and B with Proxima; L 789-6, a pair whose brighter component is a spectroscopic binary; ε Ind A, B, and C; G 208-45 with G 208-44 A and B; and o^2 Eri A, B, and C). This total does not include planetary companions, discussed below. Some new data have been added for stars already in the old table. A few other objects are known for which there is good reason to suppose that they lie within the volume of space represented in the table, but I shall not add them until trigonometric parallaxes are determined for them.

Spectral types and magnitudes of brown dwarfs require some comment. Although some brown dwarfs have very late M spectral types, two new spectral classes, L and T, have been created. L-type brown dwarfs have effective temperatures between about 2200 K and 1500 K; T-type objects are cooler still. Often only infrared magnitudes are given for these stars. Listing such magnitudes would make these objects appear misleadingly bright. In recent years I tried to estimate a visual magnitude for LP 944-20; however, I have come to the conclusion that *any* entry in the magnitude column could be misleading, so I have not given any magnitude for the five brown dwarfs in the table. The visual magnitude given for DENIS 1048-39 is based on an observed *B* magnitude and an estimated colour index for its given spectral type; it is also uncertain.

Some nearby stars are known to have planetary companions, particularly BD +36°2147 (listed in older versions of the table as Lalande 21185) and BD –15°6290. It is possible that 61 Cyg B, ε Eri, and, as mentioned above, van Maanen's star may also have such companions. The evidence is not as strong for many other stars that were once believed to have planets, especially Barnard's star. A thorough search of the system of α Cen A and B with Proxima, our nearest neighbours, failed to provide any certain evidence of planets and has set severe limits on what sort of planets the system could contain.

Subject to these comments, the table is arranged as previously. Successive columns give the name or designation of the star, the right ascension (**RA**) and declination (**Dec**) for equinox J2000.0, the parallax (**π**) in milliarcseconds, and the distance ***(D)*** in light-years. (If you prefer the scientific unit of parsecs, just take the reciprocal of the parallax; one parsec is approximately 3.26 ly.) Subsequent columns give the spectral type (**Sp.,** in the MK system whenever possible (see p. 237)), the total proper motion (**μ**) in milliarcseconds per year, the position angle of the proper motion (**θ**) measured in degrees from north through east, the total space motion ***(W)*** in kilometres per second for those stars with known radial velocities, and the apparent and absolute visual magnitudes (***V*** and M_V, respectively). Distances of HIPPARCOS stars are given to 0.01 ly and of the others to 0.1 ly. Again, I stress that we rarely know distances that precisely. Except for stars new to the list, I have usually retained the spectral types previously used. The K and M stars were classified by R.F. Wing some years ago. Recent reclassification resulted in few significant changes. Many M-type stars are flare stars, variable in both magnitude and spectral type. The space motion is given the same sign as the radial velocity (+ for recession). This is a little misleading for the two components of BD +59°1915, whose radial velocities are small and which are travelling together, despite the difference in sign of their space motions. Several of the radial velocities are based on only one or two observations and are the least reliable data in the table. The velocities of the centres of mass of the binaries α Cen, Sirius, Procyon, and 70 Oph are, however, reasonably well known. I have taken magnitudes from HIPPARCOS whenever possible, except for 70 Oph, for which the HIPPARCOS value appears to refer to the total light of the system. Magnitudes quoted to only one decimal are not photoelectrically determined.

HIPPARCOS has determined parallaxes and proper motions separately for each component of some binary systems. The components of α Cen have the same parallax, but those of 61 Cyg are different; the components of Procyon are between them in distance, and BD +59°1915 B turns out to be closer than its brighter companion. The two components of the common-proper-motion pair CD –25°10553, included in earlier versions of this table, have been removed because further analysis makes it doubtful they are as close as previously thought. I have suppressed parallax and proper-motion entries for those components of binaries for which separate determinations were *not* made, sometimes condensing the entry to a single line. Only the B components of two BD stars are in the table: they form optical pairs with their respective brighter and more distant components.

There is no uniform nomenclature for these predominantly faint stars; some have many different names. I have used the names I thought most familiar, preferring proper names, Bayer letters or Flamsteed numbers, BD and other Durchmusterung designations. In the newer section of the table, I have often used GJ numbers. These refer to the *Catalogue of Nearby Stars,* originally compiled by Wilhelm Gliese and now maintained by Hartmut Jahreiss. I could extend the use of GJ numbers, but readers might be put off by finding, for example, Sirius called "GJ 244," and it takes some time for new discoveries (DENIS 1048-39) to be assigned a GJ number. (All stars that were in Gliese's original catalogues are given the same number in GJ lists, so, for example, Gliese 229 B and GJ 229 B are the same star.) Designations beginning with L refer to catalogues of proper-motion surveys compiled by W.J. Luyten, as do those beginning with LP (from Palomar observations). Designations beginning with G (not GJ) are from catalogues compiled by H. Giclas and colleagues at the Lowell Observatory. DENIS and 2MASS are acronyms for modern surveys in the infrared. Respectively, they are Deep-Sky Near Infrared Survey and Two-Micron All-Sky Survey.

As usual, either the compiler or the editor will be glad to be notified of errors or omissions. The extension of the table (below the line) is perhaps particularly likely to contain errors or to be incomplete. The revisions of the table were made easier by the access to the SIMBAD and HIPPARCOS catalogues provided by the Canadian Astronomy Data Centre. I also made use of the online version of the GJ catalogue and of a recent (2001) paper by Oppenheimer et al. in the *Astronomical Journal,* which lists stars within 8 parsecs north of declination −35°.

Editor's Note: For more information, see A.H. Batten, "Our Changing Views of the Solar Neighbourhood," *JRASC, 92* (1998), pp. 231–237.

TABLE OF NEAREST STARS

Name	**RA** (2000)	**Dec**	π	*D*	Sp.	μ	θ	*W*	*V*	M_V
	h m	° ′	mas	ly		mas/y	°	km/s		
Sun					G2V				−26.72	4.85
Proxima	14 30	−62 41	772.3	4.22	M5.5Ve	3 853	281	−29	11.01	15.45
α Cen A	14 40	−60 50	742.1	4.40	G2V	3 709	277	−32	−0.01	4.34
B					K1V	3 724	285	−32	1.35	5.70
Barnard's	17 58	+4 42	549.0	5.94	M5V	10 358	356	−139	9.54	13.24
Wolf 359	10 56	+7 01	419	7.79	M6.5Ve	4 702	235	+55	13.46	16.57
2MASS 0253+16	2 53	+16 53	41	7.9	M6.5V	505	138		15.40	18.6
BD +36°2147	11 03	+35 58	392.4	8.31	M2+V	4 802	187	−104	7.49	10.46
Sirius A	6 45	−16 43	379.2	8.60	A1Vm	1 339	204	−18	−1.44	1.45
B					DA2				8.44	11.33
L 726-8 A	1 39	−17 57	373	8.7	M5.5Ve	3 360	80	+52	12.56	15.42
B					M5.5Ve			+53	12.96	15.82
Ross 154	18 50	−23 50	336.5	9.69	M3.6Ve	666	107	−10	10.37	13.00
Ross 248	23 42	+44 09	316	10.3	M5.5Ve	1 588	176	−84	12.27	14.77
ε Eri	3 33	−9 27	310.8	10.50	K2V	977	271	+22	3.72	6.18
CD −36°15693	23 06	−35 51	303.9	10.73	M2V	6 896	79	+108	7.35	9.76
Ross 128	11 48	+0 48	299.6	10.89	M4+V	1 361	154	−26	11.12	13.50
L 789-6 ABC	22 39	−15 18	290	11.2	M5+Ve	3 256	47	−80	12.32	14.63
61 Cyg A	21 07	+38 45	287.1	11.36	K5V	5 281	52	−108	5.20	7.49
Procyon A	7 39	+5 13	285.9	11.41	F5IV–V	1 259	215	−21	0.40	2.68
B					DF				10.7	13.0
61 Cyg B	21 07	+38 45	285.4	11.43	K7V	5 172	53	−107	6.05	8.33
BD +59°1915 B	18 43	+59 38	284.5	11.47	M4V	2 312	323	+39	9.70	11.97
A			280.3	11.64	M3.5V	2 238	324	−38	8.94	11.18
BD +43°44 A	0 18	+44 01	280.3	11.64	M2V	2 918	82	+51	8.09	10.33
B					M4V			+54	11.10	13.34
G 51-15	8 30	+26 47	276	11.8	M6.5Ve	1 270	238	+24	14.81	17.01
2MASS 1259–43	12 59	–43 36	276	11.8	M8–9	1133	306			
ε Ind A	22 03	−56 47	275.8	11.83	K4Ve	4 705	123	−90	4.69	6.89
Ba					T1	4 697	122			
Bb					T6					
τ Cet	1 44	−15 56	274.2	11.90	G8V	1 922	296	−37	3.49	5.68
L 372-58	3 36	−44 31	273	11.9	M5.5V	828	115		13.03	15.21
L 725-32	1 12	−17 00	269.1	12.12	M5.5Ve	1 372	62	+37	11.60	13.75
BD +5°1668	7 27	+5 14	263.3	12.39	M4V	3 738	171	+70	9.84	11.94
DENIS 1845–63 A	18 45	–63 57	260	12.5	M8.5V	2558	74.8		17.4	19.5
B					T5.5					
Kapteyn's	5 12	−45 01	255.3	12.78	M1VIp	8 671	131	+294	8.86	10.89
CD −39°14192	21 17	−38 52	253.4	12.87	M0Ve	3 455	251	+69	6.69	8.71
Krüger 60 A	22 28	+57 42	249.5	13.07	M3.5V	990	242	−30	9.59	11.58
B					M4Ve	851	243	−32	10.3	12.3
DENIS 1048–39	10 48	−39 56	247.7	13.16	M8V	1 541	231	−31	(17.0)	(19.0)
Ross 614 A	6 29	−2 49	242.9	13.43	M4.0Ve	930	132	+25	11.1	13.0
B					M5.5V				14.3	16.2

TABLE OF NEAREST STARS (continued)

Name	RA (2000) h m	Dec ° ′	π mas	D ly	Sp.	μ mas/y	θ °	W km/s	V	M_V
BD −12°4523	16 30	−12 40	234.5	13.91	M4V	1 189	185	−27	10.10	11.95
CD −37°15492	0 05	−37 21	229.3	14.23	M2V	6 100	113	+128	8.56	10.36
Wolf 424 A	12 33	+9 01	228	14.3	M5+Ve	1 811	277	−38	13.10	14.89
B					M7	1 764	279		13.4	15.2
BD −13°637 B	3 22	−13 16	227.5	14.34		320	201		12.16	13.94
van Maanen's	0 49	+5 23	227.0	14.37	DG	2 978	156	+82	12.37	14.15
L 1159-16	2 00	+13 03	224	14.6	M4.5Ve	2 096	148		12.26	14.01
L 143-23	10 45	−61 12	222	14.7	M4	1 657	348		13.87	15.60
BD +68°946	17 36	+68 20	220.9	14.77	M3.5V	1 310	194	−36	9.15	10.87
LP 731-58	10 48	−11 20	221	14.8	M6.5V	1 645	158		15.60	17.32
CD −46°11540	17 29	−46 54	220.4	14.80	M3V	1 050	147	−25	9.38	11.10
G 208-45	19 54	+44 25	220	14.8	M6Ve	660	139		14.01	15.72
44 A					M6Ve	681	142		13.47	15.18
44 B					M5.5				16.76	18.47
BD −15°6346	23 07	−14 52	216.5	15.07		140	53		12.24	13.92
L 145-141	11 46	−64 50	216.4	15.07	DC:	2 688	97		11.50	13.18
G 158-27	0 07	−7 32	213	15.3	M5−5.5V	2 028	204		13.74	15.38
BD −15°6290	22 53	−14 16	212.7	15.34	M5V	1 174	125	+28	10.16	11.80
BD +44°2051 A	11 05	+43 32	206.9	15.77	M1V	4 511	282	+122	8.82	10.40
B					M5de				14.40	15.93
BD +50°1725	10 11	+49 27	205.2	15.90	K7V	1 452	250	−42	6.60	8.16
BD +20°2465	10 20	+19 52	205	15.9	M3.5Ve	491	264	+16	9.43	10.99
CD −49°13515	21 34	−49 00	202.5	16.11	M2V	819	183	+22	8.66	10.19
LP 944-20	3 40	−35 26	201	16.22	≥M9V	439	176	+14		
CD −44°11909	17 37	−44 19	198.3	16.43	M4V	1 176	217	−66	10.94	12.43
o^2 Eri A	4 15	−7 39	198.2	16.46	K1V	4 088	213	−106	4.43	5.92
B					DA	4 070	212	−100	9.52	11.01
C					M4.5Ve	4 079	213	−107	11.17	12.66
BD +43°4305 A	22 47	+44 20	198.1	16.47	M4−Ve	841	237	−20	10.29	11.77
70 Oph A	18 05	+2 30	196.6	16.59	K0V	971	173	−24	4.20	5.67
B					K4V				5.99	7.46
Altair	19 51	+8 52	194.4	16.78	A7V	661	54	−31	0.76	2.20
GJ 1116 A	8 58	+19 46	191	17.1	M8Ve	820	262		14.06	15.45
B					M5.5	820	263		14.92	16.31
GJ 3379	6 00	+2 42	186	17.5	M4	300	86	+56	11.33	12.68
GJ 445	11 48	+78 41	185.5	17.57	M3.5	885	57	−121	10.78	12.12
BD +15°2620	13 45	+14 53	184.1	17.71	M1.5	2 298	129	−61	8.46	9.79
LP 816-60	20 53	−16 58	182.2	17.89		308	174		11.41	12.71
GJ 169.1 A	4 31	+58 59	181.4	17.97	M4	2 439	147	+63	11.08	12.37
B					DC			+64	12.44	13.73
GJ 251	6 55	+33 16	181.3	17.98	M3	831	241	+42	9.89	11.18
GJ 402	10 51	+6 48	177.5	18.37	M4	1 141	224	+31	11.66	12.91
2MASS 1835+32	18 36	+33 00	176.5	18.47	M8.5	759	186		18.27	19.50
BD −3°1123	5 31	−3 41	175.7	18.55	M1.5	2 228	160	+61	7.92	9.14
GJ 754	19 21	−45 33	175.2	18.61	M4.5	3 111	165		12.23	13.44
BD −8°4352	16 55	−8 20	174.2	18.71	M3Ve	1 208	223	+38	9.04	10.24
σ Dra	19 32	+69 40	173.4	18.80	K0V	1 839	161	+57	4.70	5.89
BD −21°1377 A	6 11	−21 52	173.2	18.82	M1V	727	191	+20	8.14	9.33
B					T6.5V					
GJ 213	5 42	+12 29	172.8	18.87	M4	2 541	128	+124	11.48	12.67
BD +4°4048 A	19 16	+5 10	170.3	19.14	M2.5	1 452	203	+52	9.13	10.28
B	19 17	+5 09	170.3	19.14	M8V	1 520	203		17.30	18.46

DOUBLE AND MULTIPLE STARS

BY BRIAN D. MASON

Approximately 85% of stars are found in double or multiple systems. While the first detection of double systems dates back to the early 17th century, it was not until systematic work with large-aperture telescopes was done (notably by William Herschel) that the physical rather than the optical nature of these systems was ascertained. The larger the aperture of the telescope, the closer the stars that can be separated under good conditions. The resolving power in arcseconds can be estimated as $120/D$, where D is the diameter of the telescope objective in millimetres. Astronomers using long-baseline optical interferometry have measured double-star separations less than a milliarcsecond (0.001″).

The double stars in the table, p. 238, were selected to cover a wide variety of interests. While wide or slowly moving pairs are good for evaluating optical performance or estimating seeing, with the preponderance of inexpensive, large-aperture telescopes and the availability of interferometry for the amateur (in *Sky & Telescope* see the articles by A. Maurer, p. 91, March 1997, and H.A. McAlister, p. 34, November 1996), closer systems have been added to the list. Of the 40 listed systems, 9 have separations less than one arcsecond and 7 more between one and two arcseconds. A pair of binaries with white dwarf secondaries (α CMa and α CMi) is included to demonstrate the detection difficulty imposed by a large magnitude difference. Nine of the systems are found south of the equator. Since many of the stars selected exhibit significant motion, the predicted position angles and separations are given for both 2007.0 and 2008.0. PA (Position Angle) is the angular direction of the fainter star (B) from the brighter (A), measured counterclockwise from north (*clockwise* in an optical system having an *odd* number of reflections). Note that data for 2007.0 have been changed for some systems due to improvements in orbit calculations or more recent measurements. For systems with no orbit determination the most recently measured position is tabulated. Also included are notes on selected systems. If no 2008.0 data are provided, there is no calculation (orbit or linear) of the motion (if any) of this double. The 2007.0 data are the most recently published.

Other double stars appear in THE NEAREST STARS (pp. 231–235) and THE BRIGHTEST STARS (pp. 221–230) sections in this Handbook. Recently, an electronic journal for double-star observing was started at the University of South Alabama (see www.jdso.org). The *Journal of Double Star Observations* is a good source for free information on double and multiple stars.

Notes on some double and multiple stars in the table:

α Psc: Also known as Al Rischa, the cord (binding the fish of Pisces together). Discovered by Sir William Herschel; while the motion of the binary is certain, the characterization of the orbit (and the period) are less so.

★ **α UMi:** Polaris is a Cepheid variable and thus one of the most important stars for determining the cosmic distance scale. The parameters for AB are given in the table. The wider AC (40″) and AD (80″) pairs were discovered by Burnham in 1884 and lost until 2005, when they were recovered by amateur astronomer Jim Daley. At magnitudes 13 and 14 they are quite a challenge! The long-known astrometric companion to this bright Cepheid was finally resolved by Nancy Evans and colleagues with the Hubble Space Telescope.

α CMa: The companion to Sirius is a difficult target, usually observable only during periods of exceptional seeing, when you can use the highest magnification and move the primary off the field of view. The white dwarf secondary, predicted by Bessel and first observed by Alvan Clark, remains a challenging target for visual observers. For more information on Sirius B, see Alan MacRobert's article in the March 2001 *Sky & Telescope,* p. 24.

α CMi: Like Sirius, Procyon has a white dwarf companion. It was first detected in 1840 by the variation in the proper motion of the star but not resolved until 1896 by Shaeberle with the 36-in. refractor of Lick Observatory. For more information on doubles near Procyon, see Sissy Haas's article in the April 2001 *Sky & Telescope,* p. 102.

ψ Vel: A system that is both relatively close and fast moving, the secondary is variable with a range of about half a magnitude. The mean is given here.

ξ UMa: Many "firsts" are associated with this system. It was one of the first discovered systems (Herschel), one of the first systems whose motion led to the discovery of the physical (rather than optical) nature of double stars (Struve), and the first to have an orbit calculated for it (Savary). Always relatively wide and with an obvious position angle change of 6° per year, this is a system that will never fail to please, observing season to observing season. For more information on this system, see Roger Griffin's article in the October 1998 *Observatory*. (In the MAY ALL-SKY MAP on p. 277, ξ UMa is nearest to the letter "S" in the word "BERENICES.")

ζ UMa: This is the well-known bright multiple star Mizar (the intermediate separation pair is listed in the table). The wider pairing with Alcor is at a separation of 708″. Mizar is also the first known spectroscopic binary and was first resolved by Francis Pease using the 20-ft. beam interferometer mounted on the front end of the 100-in. at Mt. Wilson (see www.mtwilson.edu/vir/100/20fti/index.php). The 20-ft beam interferometer will be on display at the American Museum of Natural History in 2007; check for times. ζ UMa has subsequently been resolved using the Mark III Stellar Interferometer (also on Mt. Wilson) and the Navy Prototype Optical Interferometer (NPOI). A movie showing the orbital motion and recent NPOI resolutions is available at www.nofs.navy.mil/projects/npoi/science/mizarmov.gif. For a list of nearby doubles, see the article by Sissy Haas mentioned above.

α Cen: Our closest neighbour is a quick-moving double star. The brighter component is a near twin of the Sun, while the B component is cooler. The C component, Proxima, which is slightly closer to the Sun, is an extremely faint red dwarf, 2.2° away. For more information on Proxima Cen, see Alan MacRobert's article in the March 2003 *Sky & Telescope,* p. 22.

λ Oph: Also known as Marfic or Marfik, the elbow of Ophiuchus. This is a nice, easily separated binary showing slow, but good motion. The orbit is by Wulff Heintz, the recently deceased "Swarthmore Orbit Machine," who produced more orbits than any other binary star astronomer and observed more pairs than all but one.

β Cyg: Also known as Albireo. If a neophyte doubts the colour of stars, this jewel of the summer sky should change that view. Appearing as brilliant yellow and a deep blue, this wide double has shown no apparent motion. The A component has two close companions, discovered by speckle interferometry, one at a separation of about 0.4″ and the other at 0.1″. (In the JULY ALL-SKY MAP on p. 278, β Cyg lies at the south end of the stick pattern for CYGNUS.)

π Aql: Called Seat by the Dutch scholar Grotius, this slow moving system is a good test object to rate resolving power and seeing.

τ Cyg: This system was originally thought to have a close spectroscopic companion, however, that radial-velocity variation is now attributed to the 2–3 hour δ Scuti nature of the A component. The large Δm makes this system challenging.

μ Cyg: Discovered at a separation of 6″, this system closed to about 0.5″ in the 1930s and has now opened up to almost 2″. The orbit is qualified as preliminary, and more time is needed to get a true characterization.

TABLE OF DOUBLE AND MULTIPLE STARS

	RA (2000) Dec		Magnitudes			2007.0		2008.0		
						PA	Sep.	PA	Sep.	Period
Star	h m	° ′	comb.	A	B	°	″	°	″	a
ζ Psc	1 13.7	+07 35	4.8	5.2	6.2	62	22.82			
γ Ari	1 53.5	+19 18	3.8	4.5	4.6	1	7.43			
α Psc*	2 02.0	+02 46	3.9	4.3	5.2	267	1.79	266	1.78	933
γ And AB	2 03.9	+42 20	2.0	2.1	4.8	63	9.57			
γ And BC	2 03.9	+42 20	4.5	4.8	6.0	102	0.33	101	0.30	64
α UMi*	2 31.8	+89 16	2.1	2.1	9.1	233	18.56			
33 Ori	5 31.2	+03 18	5.5	5.8	6.9	26	1.85			
λ Ori	5 35.1	+09 56	3.3	3.5	5.5	44	4.33			
α CMa*	6 45.1	−16 43	−1.5	−1.5	8.5	102	7.62	98	8.04	50
α Gem	7 34.6	+31 53	1.6	2.0	2.9	59	4.42	58	4.50	445
α CMi*	7 39.3	+5 14	0.4	0.4	10.8	146	2.47	169	2.23	41
ζ Cnc AB	8 12.2	+17 39	5.0	5.6	6.0	48	1.00	44	1.03	60
ι Cnc	8 46.7	+28 46	3.9	4.0	6.6	308	30.67			
σ² UMa	9 10.4	+67 08	4.8	4.9	7.9	351	4.05	351	4.08	1 141
ψ Vel*	9 30.7	−40 28	3.6	4.0	4.8	74	0.47	87	0.61	34
γ Leo	10 20.0	+19 50	2.3	2.6	3.8	125	4.44	126	4.44	619
ξ UMa*	11 18.2	+31 32	3.8	4.3	4.8	233	1.67	226	1.64	60
α Cru	12 26.6	−63 06	0.2	0.8	1.2	114	4.00			
24 Com	12 35.1	+18 23	4.8	5.1	6.3	270	20.14			
ζ UMa*	13 23.9	+54 56	2.0	2.2	3.9	153	14.30			
α Cen*	14 39.6	−60 50	−0.3	0.0	1.3	234	9.05	237	8.09	80
ε Boo	14 45.0	+27 04	2.0	2.3	4.5	343	2.93			
η CrB	15 23.2	+30 17	5.1	5.6	6.1	138	0.50	150	0.53	42
κ Her	16 08.1	+17 03	4.8	5.1	6.2	15	27.30			
α Sco	16 29.4	−26 26	1.0	1.0	5.4	277	2.66	277	2.65	1 218
λ Oph*	16 30.9	+01 59	3.6	4.0	5.0	35	1.45	35	1.45	129
α Her	17 14.6	+14 23	3.3	3.5	5.4	104	4.65	104	4.65	3 600
τ Oph	18 03.1	−8 11	4.8	5.3	5.8	284	1.66	284	1.65	257
70 Oph	18 05.5	+02 30	3.8	4.0	6.0	135	5.25	134	5.42	88
ε Lyr AB	18 44.3	+39 40	4.7	5.0	6.1	349	2.37	348	2.35	1 804
ε Lyr CD	18 44.3	+39 40	4.6	5.2	5.5	79	2.36	79	2.36	724
β Cyg*	19 30.7	+27 58	2.9	3.1	5.1	55	34.72			
16 Cyg	19 41.8	+50 32	5.3	6.0	6.2	133	39.67	133	39.68	18 212
δ Cyg	19 45.0	+45 08	2.9	2.9	7.9	221	2.66	221	2.66	780
ε Dra	19 48.2	+70 16	3.9	4.0	6.9	19	3.16			
π Aql*	19 48.7	+11 49	5.7	6.1	6.9	106	1.40			
β Cap	20 21.0	−14 47	2.9	3.0	6.1	267	206.00			
τ Cyg*	21 14.8	+38 03	3.7	3.8	6.3	255	0.74	248	0.74	50
μ Cyg*	21 44.1	+28 45	4.4	4.7	6.1	314	1.72	315	1.70	789
ζ Aqr	22 28.8	−0 01	3.7	4.4	4.6	177	2.14	176	2.17	587
δ Cep	22 29.4	+58 25	4.0	4.1	6.3	191	40.61			

* See the preceding note.

VARIABLE STARS

BY ARNE A. HENDEN AND ELIZABETH O. WAAGEN

Variable stars reveal many stellar properties. Depending upon their type, variables can tell us their mass, radius, temperature, luminosity, internal and external structure, composition, and evolutionary history. In addition, the systematic observation of variable stars is an area in which amateur astronomers can make a valuable contribution to astronomy.

For beginning observers, charts of the fields of four different types of bright variable stars are shown below. On each chart the magnitudes (with decimal point omitted) of several suitable comparison stars are shown. A brightness estimate of the variable is made using two comparison stars, one brighter, one fainter than the variable. The magnitude, date, and time of each observation are recorded. When a number of observations have been made, a graph of magnitude versus date can be plotted. The shape of this "light curve" depends upon the type of variable. Further information about variable star observing is available from the American Association of Variable Star Observers (AAVSO), 25 Birch St, Cambridge MA 02138-1205, USA (email: aavso@aavso.org; Web site: www.aavso.org).

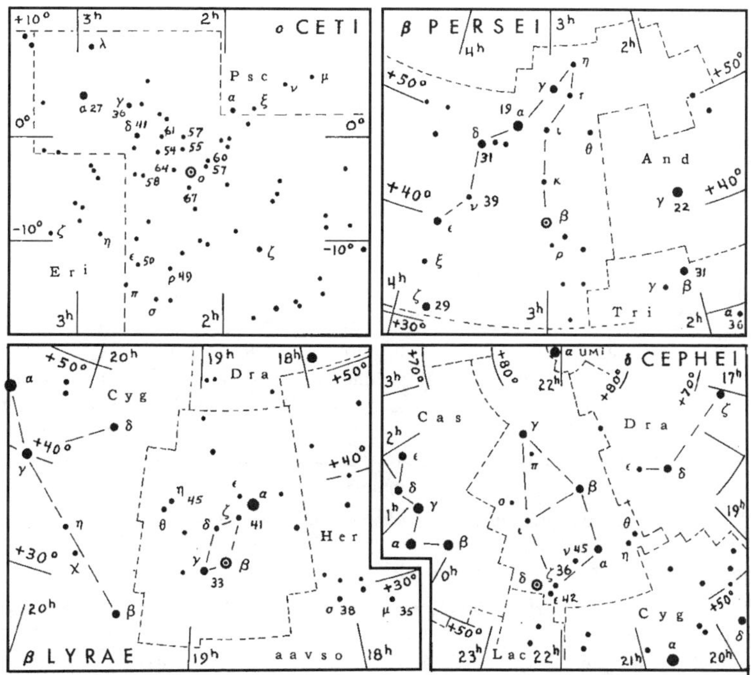

Table 1 (p. 241) is a list of long-period variables, brighter than magnitude 8.0 at maximum and north of −20°. The first column (the Harvard designation of the star) gives the position for the year 1900: the first four characters give the hours and minutes of right ascension, the next three the declination in degrees. The **Max.** column gives the mean maximum magnitude. The **Min.** column gives the mean minimum magnitude. The period **(Per.)** is in days. **Epoch** gives the predicted date of the earliest maximum occurring this year; by adding multiples of the period to this epoch, the dates of subsequent maxima can be found. These variables may reach maximum two or three weeks before or after the epoch and may remain at maximum for several weeks. This table has been prepared with AAVSO observations.

Table 2 at the right lists stars that are representative of some other types of variables. The data for the preparation of the predicted epoch of maximum for Cepheids are taken from the online edition of the *General Catalogue of Variable Stars,* at www.sai.msu.su/groups/cluster/gcvs/gcvs, the data for eclipsing binaries are from the online edition of *Rocznik Astronomiczny Obserwatorium Krakowskiego 2005,* at ftp://ftp.oa.uj.edu.pl/pub/rocznik/2005, and the data for RR Lyr are based on private communication with N.N. Samus (2005).

DESCRIPTION OF VARIABLE-STAR TYPES

Variable stars can be divided into two main classes: intrinsic variables, in which the variation is due to changes of a single star, and extrinsic variables, in which the variation is due to interaction of multiple stars or objects within a stellar system. There are many cases of overlapping variability types, such as a Mira pulsating variable as part of an eclipsing binary system. Intrinsic variables fall into three main classes: (1) pulsating stars, in which periodic expansion and contraction of the stellar surface occur; (2) eruptive variables, in which solarlike flares occur; and (3) rotating stars, in which shape distortion or star spots cause variation. Extrinsic variables consist of two main classes: (4) binary systems, in which variability is caused by orbital motion or mass transfer, and (5) cataclysmic variables, in which accretion onto a compact object can cause it to go into outburst. With modern detectors, about one percent of all stars are found to be variable. Brief and general descriptions of the major types in each class are given below.

(1) Pulsating Variables

δ Scuti stars are variables that have both radial and nonradial pulsation modes with periods from 0.01 to 0.2 days and amplitudes from barely measurable to nearly a full magnitude. They are of A-F spectral types. Typical representative: CY Aquarii.

Cepheids are variables that pulsate with periods of 1 to 70 days. They have high luminosity, and the amplitude of light variation ranges from 0.1 to 2 magnitudes. The prototypes of the group are located in open clusters and obey the well-known period–luminosity relation. They are of late F spectral class at maximum and G to K at minimum. The later (cooler) the spectral class of a Cepheid at minimum, the longer is its period. Typical representative: δ Cephei.

RR Lyrae stars are pulsating, giant variables with periods ranging from 0.2 to 1.2 days and amplitude of light variation between 0.5 and 2 magnitudes. They are usually of A spectral class. Typical representative: RR Lyrae.

RV Tauri stars are supergiant variables with a characteristic light curve of alternating deep and shallow minima. The periods, defined as the interval between two deep minima, range from 30 to 150 days. The amplitude of light variation may be as much as 3 magnitudes. Many show long-term cyclic variation of 500 to 9000 days. Generally, the spectral classes range from F-G at maximum to K-M at minimum light. Typical representative: R Scuti.

Long-period–Mira Ceti variables are giant variables that vary with visual amplitudes from 2.5 to 5 magnitudes or more. They have well-defined periodicity, ranging from 80 to 1000 days. They show characteristic emission spectra of late spectral classes M, C, and S. Typical representative: o Ceti (Mira).

(text continues on p. 242)

TABLE 1—LONG-PERIOD VARIABLE STARS NORTH OF −20°

Variable		Max. m_V	Min. m_V	Per. d	Epoch 2007
0017+55	T Cas	7.9	11.9	445	Aug. 3
0018+38	R And	6.9	14.3	409	May 11
0211+43A	W And	7.4	13.7	397	May 9
0214−03	o Cet	3.4	9.3	332	Mar. 8
0228−13	U Cet	7.5	12.6	235	Jan. 15
0231+33	R Tri	6.2	11.7	266	Jul. 2
0430+65	T Cam	8.0	13.8	374	Jun. 25
0455−14	R Lep	6.8	9.6	432	Aug. 3
0509+53	R Aur	7.7	13.3	459	—
0549+20A	U Ori	6.3	12.0	372	Jan. 26
0617−02	V Mon	7.0	13.1	335	Aug. 5
0653+55	R Lyn	7.9	13.8	379	May 31
0701+22A	R Gem	7.1	13.5	370	Dec. 22
0703+10	R CMi	8.0	11.0	338	Feb. 2
0727+08	S CMi	7.5	12.6	332	Apr. 10
0811+12	R Cnc	6.8	11.2	362	Sep. 11
0816+17	V Cnc	7.9	12.8	272	Oct. 2
0848+03	S Hya	7.8	12.7	257	Aug. 2
0850−08	T Hya	7.8	12.6	288	Sep. 20
0939+34	R LMi	7.1	12.6	372	Dec. 17
0942+11	R Leo	5.8	10.0	313	Feb. 22
1037+69	R UMa	7.5	13.0	302	Aug. 16
1214−18	R Crv	7.5	13.8	317	May 6
1220+01	SS Vir	6.8	8.9	355	Jul. 23
1231+60	T UMa	7.7	12.9	257	Aug. 18
1233+07	R Vir	6.9	11.5	146	Mar. 16
1239+61	S UMa	7.8	11.7	226	Jan. 16
1315+46	V CVn	6.8	8.8	192	May 23?
1327−06	S Vir	7.0	12.7	378	Jan. 18
1344+40	R CVn	7.7	11.9	328	Nov. 23
1425+84	R Cam	8.3	13.2	270	May 20
1425+39	V Boo	7.0	11.3	258	Jan. 7
1432+27	R Boo	7.2	12.3	223	Feb. 13
1517+31	S CrB	7.3	12.9	361	Sep. 20
1546+39	V CrB	7.5	11.0	358	Mar. 13
1546+15	R Ser	6.9	13.4	357	Oct. 27
1606+25	RU Her	8.0	13.7	484	May 1
1621+19	U Her	7.5	12.5	406	Aug. 28
1621−12	V Oph	7.5	10.2	298	Jul. 15
1632+66	R Dra	7.6	12.4	245	Feb. 2
1647+15	S Her	7.6	12.6	307	Jun. 11
1702−15	R Oph	7.6	13.3	302	Aug. 10
1717+23	RS Her	7.9	12.5	219	Feb. 6
1805+31	T Her	8.0	12.8	165	Apr. 7
1811+36	W Lyr	7.9	12.2	196	Feb. 16
1833+08	X Oph	6.8	8.8	334	Feb. 15
1901+08	R Aql	6.1	11.5	270	May 30
1910−17	T Sgr	8.0	12.6	392	May 14
1910−19	R Sgr	7.3	12.5	269	Oct. 9
1934+49	R Cyg	7.5	13.9	426	Nov. 3
1940+48	RT Cyg	7.3	11.8	190	Jun. 27
1946+32	χ Cyg	5.2	13.4	407	Sep. 27
2016+47	U Cyg	7.2	10.7	465	Aug. 12
2044−05	T Aqr	7.7	13.1	202	May 25
2108+68	T Cep	6.0	10.3	390	Dec. 15
2137+53	RU Cyg	8.0	9.4	234	Aug. 19?
2301+10	R Peg	7.8	13.2	378	—
2307+59	V Cas	7.9	12.2	228	Apr. 8
2315+08	S Peg	8.0	13.0	319	Apr. 25
2338−15	R Aqr	6.5	10.3	387	Nov. 25
2353+50	R Cas	7.0	12.6	431	Oct. 30
2357−15	W Cet	7.6	14.4	351	Aug. 9

TABLE 2—OTHER TYPES OF VARIABLE STARS

Variable		Max. m_V	Min. m_V	Type	Sp. Cl.	Period d	Epoch 2007 UT
0053+81	U Cep	6.7	9.8	Ecl.	B8 + gG2	2.493 0937	Jan. 2.09*
0258+38	ρ Per	3.3	4.0	Semi R	M4	33–55, 1100	
0301+40	β Per	2.1	3.3	Ecl.	B8 + G	2.867 321	†
0355+12	λ Tau	3.5	4.0	Ecl.	B3	3.952 952	Jan. 2.43*
0608+22	η Gem	3.1	3.9	Semi R	M3	233.4	
0619+07	T Mon	5.6	6.6	Cep	F7–K1	27.024 649	Jan. 7.53
0658+20	ζ Gem	3.6	4.2	Cep	F7–G3	10.150 73	Jan. 8.42
1544+28	R CrB	5.8	14.8	R CrB	cFpep		
1710+14	α Her	3.0	4.0	Semi R	M5	50–130, 6 y	
1842−05	R Sct	5.0	7.0	RV Tau	G0e–K0p	144	
1846+33	β Lyr	3.4	4.3	Ecl.	B8	12.940 922‡	Jan. 1.34*
1922+42	RR Lyr	6.9	8.0	RR Lyr	A2–F1	0.566 8400‡	Jan. 1.48
1947+00	η Aql	3.5	4.3	Cep	F6–G4	7.176 641	Jan. 4.70
2225+57	δ Cep	3.5	4.4	Cep	F5–G2	5.366 341	Jan. 5.85
1416+19	T Tau	9.6	10.8	INT	F8Ve–K1IV–Ve(T)		
0530−05	T Ori	9.5	12.3	INA	B8–A3EpV		
0539+09	FU Ori	8.7	9.8	FU	F2peI–II		
0749+22	U Gem	8.6	15.5	UGSS	Pec(UG) + M4.5V		
1946+35	CI Cyg	8.9	12.2	ZAND	Pec Bep + M5III		
2138+43	SS Cyg	8.0	12.5	UGSS	K5V + (Pec)UG		

* Minimum

† Algol; predictions for all minima in 2007 are given in THE SKY MONTH BY MONTH section (pp. 83–105).

‡ Changing period (period revised for 2007)

Semiregular variables are giants or supergiants showing appreciable periodicity accompanied by intervals of irregularities of light variation. The periods range from 30 to 1000 days with visual amplitudes not more than 1 to 2 magnitudes in general. Typical representative: R Ursae Minoris.

(2) Eruptive Variables

Eruptive variables are those with flares occurring in their chromospheres, along with shell mass ejections and other stellar wind phenomena. The ejected matter can cause brightness drops as well.

FU Orionis variables are young stars with accompanying cometary nebulae. Usually they have large-amplitude fluctuations that may take years to complete. Typical representative: FU Orionis.

T Tauri variables are young stars that have not yet reached the Zero Age Main Sequence. They are characterized by irregular variations of several magnitudes, often accompanied by emission lines and Algol-like fadings, probably due to dust. Typical representative: T Tauri.

UV Ceti stars are late-type dwarfs that display flare activity. The flares can range from several tenths of a magnitude to many magnitudes in size, lasting a few minutes. Typical representative: UV Ceti.

R Coronae Borealis stars are highly luminous variables that have nonperiodic drops in brightness from 1 to 9 magnitudes due to the formation of "carbon soot" in the star's atmosphere. The duration of minima varies from a few months to years. Members of this group have F to K and R spectral class. Typical representative: R Coronae Borealis.

Irregular variables are stars that at times show only a trace of periodicity or none at all. Often, poorly studied stars are placed in this category. Typical representative: RX Leporis.

(3) Rotating Variables

Rotating variables are stars with nonuniform surface brightness, caused by star spots, mass outflow, or even shape distortion.

Gamma Cassiopeiae variables are rapidly rotating B stars with mass outflow, forming equatorial rings or disks that can cause temporary fading episodes. Typical representative: γ Cassiopeiae.

RS Canum Venaticorum variables are rapidly rotating stars, usually close binary systems that undergo small amplitude changes in light that may be due to dark or bright spots on their surface. Eclipses may also be present in such systems. Typical representative: RS Canum Venaticorum.

(4) Binary Systems

Binary systems are composed of two or more stars or planets around a star, in which the orbital plane is oriented such that one object crosses the disk of another object. These are usually divided into four main classes: detached, semi-detached, contact, and transiting. The first three relate to whether two stars overfill their Roche lobes or are completely isolated from one another.

Detached systems are those in which the two stars are completely isolated from one another. Light curves usually show constant light between eclipses; eclipse depth can be quite large, depending on the relative brightness of the stellar pair. Typical representative: β Persei (Algol).

Semi-detached systems have one member (the donor) overflowing its Roche lobe, with mass accreting onto the second star. Typical representative: U Cephei.

Contact binaries have both members within a common envelope. These stars often exhibit ellipsoidal variations, with the light curves continuously varying throughout the orbit. Typical representative: β Lyrae.

Transiting systems are a new class of binary, in which a planet crosses the disk of the parent star. These variations are quite small (a few hundredths of a magnitude at best), but give a great deal of information about the host star and about the transiting planet. Typical representative: HD 209458.

(5) Cataclysmic Variables

This category contains both explosive and novalike variables. These typically show outbursts caused by thermonuclear runaway on either the star surface or on an accretion disk. They are a product of accretion from one star of a binary system onto the other star, usually a compact object such as a white dwarf or neutron star.

Novae are close binary systems that consist of a normal star and a white dwarf and increase 7 to 16 magnitudes in brightness in one to several hundred days. After the outburst the star fades slowly, returning to initial brightness in several years or decades. Near maximum brightness the spectrum is generally similar to A or F giants. Typical representative: CP Puppis (Nova 1942).

Supernovae increase in brightness by 20 or more magnitudes due to a gigantic stellar explosion. The general appearance of the light curve is similar to novae. Typical representative: CM Tauri (supernova of 1054 AD and the central star of the Crab Nebula).

U Geminorum types are dwarf novae that have long intervals of quiescence at minimum with sudden rises to maximum. Depending upon the star, the amplitude of eruptions ranges from 2 to 6 magnitudes, and the duration between outbursts tens to thousands of days. Most of these stars are spectroscopic binaries with periods of a few hours. Typical representative: SS Cygni.

Z Camelopardalis types are variables similar to U Gem stars in their physical and spectroscopic properties. They show cyclic variations interrupted by intervals of constant brightness ("stillstands") lasting for several cycles, approximately one-third of the way from maximum to minimum. Typical representative: Z Camelopardalis.

SU Ursae Majoris types are dwarf novae similar to U Gem and Z Cam stars in their physical and spectroscopic properties. They have frequent, faint, and narrow eruptions that last from one to a few days, along with infrequent, bright, and long eruptions—"superoutbursts" that last 10 to 20 days. During superoutbursts, there are small-amplitude, periodic variations—"superhumps," 2% to 3% longer than the orbital period of the system. Typical representative: SU Ursae Majoris.

VARIABLE STAR OF THE YEAR—UPDATE ON MIRA

BY ARNE A. HENDEN AND JOHN R. PERCY

Mira (o Ceti, HD 14386, spectral type M5e-M9e, V=2.0 to 10.1) is one of the most famous variable stars. At maximum, it can be seen with the unaided eye, even from urban locations. In binoculars or a small telescope, its red colour is striking—it is an extreme red-giant star. Its variability was discovered in 1596 by David Fabricius, and its 11-month period was determined in 1638 by Johann Holwarda; it was the first known periodic variable.

The name Mira—the wonderful—was bestowed on it in 1642 by Johannes Hevelius. Its finder chart is the first given on p. 239. You might think that Mira is fully understood, and that there is not much new and exciting about it. That is not the case. Its average period is 331.96 days, but this varies randomly from cycle to cycle by a few percent, for unknown reasons. Its maximum magnitude also varies, from 2 to 5, also for unknown reasons… (see Figure 1). This lack of understanding is not surprising. The outer layers of Mira are dominated by seething convection currents and convection cells, and convection is one of the most poorly understood of astrophysical processes. Astronomers like to think of stars as spherically symmetric; it makes the theory easier, but the pulsation of Mira may differ substantially from simple in-and-out motion. One of us (JRP) has done research on the long-term behaviour of Mira stars, and can vouch for the importance of systematic, long-term observations such as those made by AAVSO observers.

Mira's behaviour is further complicated by the presence of a hot, highly evolved 9th-magnitude companion, VZ Cet, about a half-arcsecond away. The two mutually orbit every 400 years, and are currently close enough so that material from Mira is pulled into a hot accretion disc around the companion. This mass stream has been imaged by the Hubble Space Telescope, and the ejected matter has also been observed by radio telescopes. Recently, the Chandra X-ray telescope has detected X-rays from both the hot accretion disc (not surprising, considering its high temperature), and from Mira itself (a bit surprising, but perhaps a result of shock waves, travelling through its atmosphere). A great image of this that includes an artist's conception of the system can be found at http://antwrp.gsfc.nasa.gov/apod/ap060722.html.

Mira stars play a crucial role in the evolution of stars like the Sun, and in the chemical evolution of galaxies. As a result of their pulsation and low gravity, matter is driven off, eventually reducing the star to a white-dwarf core. The process is somewhat like a wave machine, in which deep layers of the star expand and contract due to pulsational instability, producing waves that flow outward through the star's atmosphere. The ejected material can be seen as a beautiful planetary nebula for a few thousand years—as long as their white dwarf core is hot enough to excite it. The material eventually joins up with other interstellar material, carrying with it the products of nuclear reactions in its parent star. Some of the elements in your body were synthesized in ancient Mira stars, ejected into space by their pulsation, eventually leading to the formation of the solar system, Earth, and life.

The chart on p. 239 is suitable for observing Mira when it is near maximum. More detailed charts, showing the position of Mira, and the position and magnitudes of suitable comparison stars can be found by going to www.aavso.org/observing/charts and entering "omi Cet", and then choosing the A (brighter) or B (fainter) chart, or an R chart if you want a reversed orientation. Measure the star every few days. You can compare your measurements with those of other observers by going to the AAVSO "quick look" page www.aavso.org/data/ql and entering "omi Cet". Comparing your observations with others is fun, and very helpful when you are starting. But remember that your measurements should never be influenced by those of others, or by your expectations of what the magnitude is supposed to be! If you are a CCD observer, you might throw a really blue filter on your system and watch the flickering from VZ Cet when Mira is at minimum brightness.

If you are new to visual variable-star observing, consult the AAVSO Manual for Visual Observing of Variable Stars, at www.aavso.org/publications/manual, or the RASC's excellent variable-stars Web page at: www.rasc.ca/observing/variablestars/index.html

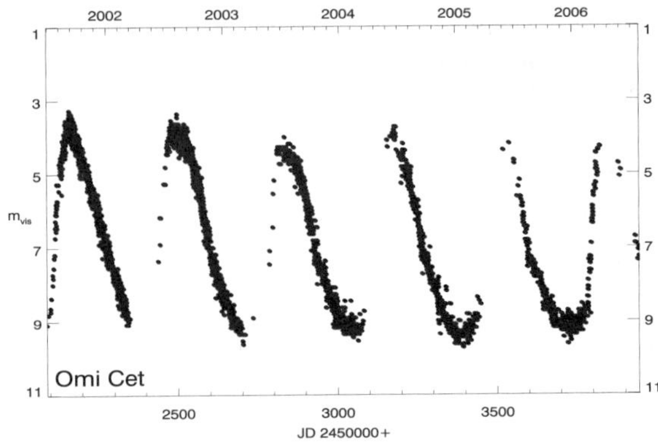

FIGURE 1 *V-band light curve of Omicron Ceti (Mira) from A. Henden and CCD/PEP observations in the AAVSO International Database.*

STAR CLUSTERS

BY ANTHONY MOFFAT AND PETER JEDICKE

The study of star clusters is crucial to the understanding of stellar structure and evolution. For most purposes, it can be assumed that the stars in a given cluster formed nearly simultaneously from the same parent cloud of gas and dust. Thus the basic factor that distinguishes one star in a cluster from another is the quantity of matter each contains. When comparing one cluster with another, it is essentially only the age and the chemical composition of their stars that differ. But what makes one cluster *appear* different from another in the sky is mainly the degree of concentration and regularity, the spread in magnitude and colour of the member stars, all of which vary mainly with age, and the total number of stars. Extremely young clusters are often irregular in shape, with clumps of newly formed stars pervaded by lanes of obscuring dust and bright nebulosity (e.g. the Orion Nebula around the Trapezium Cluster). The oldest clusters, which have not yet dissipated and have not been torn apart by external forces, tend to be symmetric in shape, with only the slower-burning, low-mass stars remaining visible; the massive stars will have spent their nuclear fuel and passed to the degenerate graveyard of white dwarfs, neutron stars, or black holes, depending upon their original mass.

The star clusters in the following tables were selected as the most conspicuous. Two types can be recognized: *open* and *globular*. Open clusters often appear as irregular aggregates of tens to thousands of stars, sometimes barely distinguishable from random fluctuations of the general field. Ranging in age from very young to very old, open clusters are concentrated toward the disk of the Milky Way and generally contain stars of chemical abundance like the Sun.

Sometimes we observe loose, extended groups of very young stars. Using precise methods of photometry, spectroscopy, and kinematics, we see that these stars often have a common, but not necessarily strictly coeval, origin. Such loose concentrations of stars are called *associations*. Dynamically, they are generally unbound over time scales of the order of ten million years, being subject to the strong tidal forces of passing clouds and the background Milky Way Galaxy. Often, they contain subconcentrations of young open clusters (e.g. the double cluster h and χ Persei of slightly different ages despite their proximity, in the association Per OB1, which stretches over some 6° of the sky), with a strong gradient in age as the star formation process rips through them from one edge to another. In view of their sparse nature, we do not consider it appropriate here to list any of the 100-plus catalogued Milky Way associations.

Globular clusters, on the other hand, are highly symmetric, extremely old and rich agglomerations of up to several million stars, distributed throughout the galactic halo but concentrated toward the centre of the Milky Way Galaxy. Compared to the Sun and other disk stars, they tend to be much less abundant in elements heavier than hydrogen and helium. For the larger and brighter globular clusters, the observer's goal is to see them well enough to distinguish a generous sprinkling of individual stars against a diffuse glowing background. Large telescope apertures and good skies will help resolve globular clusters. Higher powers are helpful for identification of smaller, more distant globular clusters.

The table on p. 262 lists all well-defined open clusters in the Milky Way Galaxy with diameters greater than 40′ and/or integrated magnitudes brighter than 5.0, as well as the richest clusters and some of special interest. The apparent integrated photographic magnitude (**m_{pg}**) is from Collinder, the angular diameter **(Diam.)** is generally from Trumpler, and the photographic magnitude of the fifth-brightest star (**m_5**) is from Shapley, except where in italics, which are new data. The distance **(Dist.)** is mainly from Becker and Fenkart (*Astr. Astrophys. Suppl. 4* (1971), p. 241). The earliest spectral type of cluster stars **(Sp)** is a measure of the age as follows: expressed in millions of years, O5 = 2, B0 = 8, B5 = 70, A0 = 400, A5 = 1000, F0 = 3000, and F5 = 10 000. Complete source lists of open clusters can be found at obswww.unige.ch/webda.

OPEN CLUSTERS

NGC/ **other†**	**RA** (2000) h m	**Dec** ° ′	**Mag.** m_{pg}	**Diam.** ′	m_5	**Dist.** 10^3 ly	**Sp**	**Remarks**
188	0 44.0	+85 21	9.3	14	14.6	5.0	F2	Oldest known
752	1 57.8	+37 41	6.6	45	9.6	1.2	A5	
869	2 19.0	+57 10	4.3	30	9.5	7.0	B1	h Per
884	2 22.4	+57 07	4.4	30	9.5	8.1	B0	χ Per, M supergiants
Perseus	3 22	+48 36	2.3	240	5	0.6	B1	Moving cl.; α Per
Pleiades	3 47.1	+24 08	1.6	120	4.2	0.41	B6	M45, best known
Hyades	4 20	+15 38	0.8	400	*3.9*	0.15	A2	Moving cl. **, in Taurus
1912	5 28.6	+35 50	7.0	18	9.7	4.6	B5	M38
1976/80	5 35.4	−5 23	2.5	50	*5.5*	1.3	O5	Trapezium, very young
2099	5 52.4	+32 32	6.2	24	9.7	4.2	B8	M37
2168	6 08.8	+24 21	5.6	29	9.0	2.8	B5	M35
2232	6 26.5	−4 45	4.1	20	*7*	1.6	B1	
2244	6 32.4	+4 52	5.2	27	*8.0*	5.3	O5	Rosette, very young
2264	6 41.0	+9 53	4.1	30	*8.0*	2.4	O8	S Mon
2287	6 47.1	−20 44	5.0	32	*8.8*	2.2	B4	M41
2362	7 18.8	−24 56	3.8	7	9.4	5.4	O9	τ CMa
2422	7 35.6	−14 30	4.3	30	9.8	1.6	B3	
2437	7 41.8	−14 49	6.6	27	10.8	5.4	B8	M46
2451	7 45.4	−37 58	3.7	37	6	1.0	B5	
2516	7 58.3	−60 54	3.3	50	10.1	1.2	B8	
2546	8 12.5	−37 39	5.0	45	7	2.7	B0	
2632	8 40.1	+20 00	3.9	90	7.5	0.59	A0	Praesepe, M44
IC 2391	8 40.3	−53 03	2.6	45	3.5	0.5	B4	
IC 2395	8 41.0	−48 11	4.6	20	10.1	2.9	B2	
2682	8 50.4	+11 50	7.4	18	10.8	2.7	F2	M67, very old
3114	10 02.6	−60 07	4.5	37	7	2.8	B5	
IC 2602	10 43.3	−64 23	1.6	65	6	0.5	B1	θ Car
Tr 16	10 45.2	−59 42	6.7	10	10	9.6	O3	η Car and Nebula
3532	11 06.4	−58 39	3.4	55	8.1	1.4	B8	
3766	11 36.1	−61 37	4.4	12	8.1	5.8	B1	
Coma	12 25.1	+26 06	2.9	300	5.5	0.3	Al	Very sparse
4755	12 53.6	−60 20	5.2	12	7	6.8	B3	κ Cru, “Jewel Box”
6067	16 13.3	−54 13	6.5	16	10.9	4.7	B3	G, K supergiants
6231	16 54.0	−41 48	3.5	16	7.5	5.8	O9	O supergiants, WR stars
Tr 24	16 57.0	−40 40	3.5	60	*7.3*	5.2	O5	
6405	17 40.1	−32 13	4.6	26	8.3	1.5	B4	M6
IC 4665	17 46.7	+5 44	5.4	50	7	1.1	B8	
6475	17 53.9	−34 48	3.3	50	7.4	0.8	B5	M7
6494	17 56.9	−19 01	5.9	27	10.2	1.4	B8	M23
6523	18 03.1	−24 23	5.2	45	*7*	5.1	O5	M8, Lagoon Nebula
6611	18 18.9	−13 47	6.6	8	10.6	5.5	O7	M16, nebula
IC 4725	18 31.7	−19 15	6.2	35	9.3	2.0	B3	M25, Cepheid U Sgr
IC 4756	18 39.3	+5 27	5.4	50	8.5	1.4	A3	
6705	18 51.1	−6 17	6.8	12.5	12	5.6	B8	M11, very rich
Mel 227	20 11.2	−79 19	5.2	60	*9*	0.8	B9	
IC 1396	21 38.9	+57 30	5.1	60	*8.5*	2.3	O6	Tr 37
7790	23 58.4	+61 13	7.1	4.5	11.7	10.3	B1	Cepheids CEa, CEb, and CF Cas

† IC = Index Catalogue, Tr = Trumpler, Mel = Melotte ** Basic for distance determination

The table below lists all the globular clusters in the Messier list and most of the globular clusters with a total apparent visual magnitude brighter than about 8.0. A table of Milky Way Galaxy globular cluster data is available on W.E. Harris's Web site: physwww.mcmaster.ca/~harris/WEHarris.html. The apparent diameter **(Diam.)** is from Cragin, Lucyk, and Rappaport (*Deep Sky Field Guide To Uranometria 2000.0,* Willmann-Bell, 1993). The concentration class **(Conc.)** is from I to XII, where I is the most compact and XII the least. The integrated spectral type **(Int. Sp. T.)** varies mainly with the abundances. An observer who can see stars down to the magnitude given in the ***V*(HB)** ("horizontal-branch" magnitude) column has a good chance of being able to resolve the globular cluster; this information is from Djorgovski and Meylan (*Structure and Dynamics of Globular Clusters,* Astronomical Society of the Pacific, 1993, p. 341).

GLOBULAR CLUSTERS

NGC	M/ other	RA (2000) h m	Dec ° ′	Mag. m_V	Diam. ′	Conc.	Int. Sp.T.	Dist. 10^3 ly	*V*(HB)
104	47 Tuc	0 24.0	−72 04	3.95	30.9	III	G4	15	14.06
362		1 03.2	−70 50	6.40	12.9	III	F9	28	15.40
1851		5 14.0	−40 02	7.14	11.0	II	F7	46	16.10
1904	79	5 24.1	−24 31	7.73	8.7	V	F5	42	16.20
2808		9 11.9	−64 51	6.20	13.8	I	F7	30	16.19
3201		10 17.6	−46 24	6.75	18.2	X	F6	17	14.75
4590	68	12 39.5	−26 44	7.84	12.0	X	F2	33	15.60
4833		12 59.5	−70 52	6.91	13.5	VIII	F3	20	15.45
5024	53	13 12.9	+18 10	7.61	12.6	V	F6	60	16.94
5139	ω Cen	13 26.8	−47 28	3.68	36.3	VIII	F5	17	14.52
5272	3	13 42.2	+28 22	6.19	16.2	VI	F6	35	15.65
5904	5	15 18.5	+2 04	5.65	17.4	V	F7	26	15.11
6093	80	16 17.0	−22 58	7.33	8.9	II	F6	33	15.86
6121	4	16 23.6	−26 31	5.63	26.3	IX	F8	14	13.35
6171	107	16 32.5	−13 03	7.93	10.0	X	G0	21	15.70
6205	13	16 41.7	+36 27	5.78	16.6	V	F6	21	14.95
6218	12	16 47.1	−1 56	6.70	14.5	IX	F8	24	14.90
6254	10	16 57.1	−4 05	6.60	15.1	VII	F3	20	14.65
6266	62	17 01.2	−30 06	6.45	14.1	IV	F9	22	15.90
6273	19	17 02.6	−26 16	6.77	13.5	VIII	F7	28	16.95
6333	9	17 19.2	−18 30	7.72	9.3	VIII	F5	27	16.10
6341	92	17 17.1	+43 08	6.44	11.2	IV	F2	26	15.05
6388		17 36.3	−44 44	6.72	8.7	III	G2	37	16.90
6397		17 40.7	−53 40	5.73	25.7	IX	F4	9	12.90
6402	14	17 37.6	−3 14	7.59	11.7	VIII	F4	29	17.50
6541		18 08.0	−43 42	6.30	13.1	III	F6	13	15.10
6626	28	18 24.5	−24 52	6.79	11.2	IV	F8	19	15.68
6637	69	18 31.4	−32 20	7.64	7.1	V	G2	28	16.20
6656	22	18 36.3	−23 54	5.10	24.0	VII	F5	10	14.15
6681	70	18 43.2	−32 17	7.87	7.8	V	F5	29	15.60
6715	54	18 55.0	−30 28	7.60	9.1	III	F7	89	17.71
6752		19 10.9	−59 58	5.40	20.4	VI	F4	17	13.85
6779	56	19 16.6	+30 11	8.27	7.1	X	F5	33	16.20
6809	55	19 40.1	−30 57	6.32	19.0	XI	F4	20	14.35
6838	71	19 53.8	+18 46	8.19	7.2	†	G1	13	14.44
6864	75	20 06.0	−21 55	8.52	6.0	I	F9	61	17.45
6981	72	20 53.5	−12 32	9.27	5.9	IX	F7	55	16.99
7078	15	21 30.1	+12 10	6.20	12.3	IV	F3	34	15.86
7089	2	21 33.5	−0 50	6.47	12.9	II	F4	40	16.05
7099	30	21 40.4	−23 10	7.19	11.0	V	F3	26	15.10

† Originally thought to be an open cluster; never assigned a concentration class

AN EXAMPLE: NGC 7419

A GALACTIC OPEN CLUSTER WITH A RECORD FIVE RED SUPERGIANTS YET NO BLUE SUPERGIANTS

Although too faint to appear in the accompanying list of open clusters, NGC 7419 is a very unusual cluster and merits discussion. At first, NGC 7419 seems like a run-of-the-mill open cluster in Cepheus, located near the plane of the Milky Way Galaxy at longitude 109.14° and latitude 1.14° (RA = 22h 54.3m, Dec = +60°50′ (equinox J2000.0)) and a distance of 6000 ly behind 6.7 magnitudes of visual interstellar extinction. With a tidal radius of 5′ it has an age of 14 million years.

NGC 7419 is unusual in that it contains five red supergiants (RSGs) (in the range V = 13–15)—a record for a cluster like this (A. Beauchamp et al., *Astrophys. J. Suppl.* (1994), pp. 93, 187)—one of which is the highly variable, molecular-line maser-emitting, very cool M7.5I star MY Cep, which owes its extremely red colour to both its intrinsic nature and the high IS extinction (see p. 237 for an explanation of the MK Type given here). Three of the other RSGs are of more modest types, M2Iab, while the fifth is M3.5I. A nearby, but unrelated, carbon star, MZ Cep, is variable and extremely red, like MY Cep.

However, what makes NGC 7419 really unusual for a cluster like this, with near solar metallicity, is that it contains no blue supergiants (BSGs), although one expects it to contain twice as many BSGs as RSGs! What could be the cause of this apparent discrepancy? Spectroscopic investigation of the brightest blue member stars of NGC 7419 (Caron et al., *Astrophys. J.* (2003), pp. 126, 1415) has revealed a high proportion of quickly rotating stars, some of which are of Be type. High stellar rotation rates shorten the BSG phase, so this likely explains why the evolved stars in NGC 7419 have become RSGs, that is, by bypassing the BSG stage. NGC 7419 is thus an exceptional case, since high stellar rotation among evolved massive stars normally tends to occur at lower metallicity (A. Maeder and G. Meynet, *ARA&A* 2000), pp. 38, 143). Presumably, NGC 7419 was formed from a giant molecular cloud with significantly higher internal motions (e.g. turbulence) than its average surroundings.

Left: A near-infrared (K-band) exposure of NGC 7419, from the 2MASS survey (see p. 249).

Right: A blue exposure of exactly the same field, from the Second Palomar Observatory Sky Survey (POSS-II).

The brightest star in the left-hand image is MY Cep; the other four RSGs and the C-star (MZ Cep, at lower left) are the other five bright stars. Note the extreme brightness of these red stars in the K-band image as compared with the blue image.

AMATEUR SUPERNOVA HUNTING
BY REV. ROBERT EVANS

The first discovery of a supernova by an amateur astronomer was by G. Romano of Italy (SN 1957B in NGC 4564); this discovery was photographic. The first visual discovery was by J. Bennett of South Africa (SN 1968L in M83). In Australia in 1980, the author began systematic visual searching using a simple 250-mm backyard telescope and made two discoveries the following year. K. Okazaki of Japan, who discovered two supernovae, one each in 1983 and 1984, was one of several Japanese amateurs to mount systematic photographic searches at that time.

By the late 1980s, most of the supernovae brighter than 15th magnitude were being found visually by amateurs. In the early 1990s, professional astronomers started using supernova studies to address major problems in cosmology; at that time, they depended largely upon amateur searches to provide them with the best and brightest supernovae in nearby galaxies. These nearby supernovae provided much of the benchmark information needed for studying supernovae at remote distances, which led to independent estimates for the expansion, age, and fate of the universe.

CCD Supernova Hunting

In the last few years, the cost of charge-coupled devices (CCDs) has fallen to the point where many amateurs can afford to use them on computer-controlled telescopes. Some of these amateurs are hunting supernovae with resounding success. There are a number of advantages to using telescopes with CCDs and computer control:

(1) You can observe in locations with some light pollution or in the presence of fairly strong moonlight.

(2) With a computer to direct the telescope to individual galaxies, it is no longer necessary to know the sky well.

(3) With appropriate computer control of the telescope, you can sit in a warm room facing the computer screen.

(4) If your equipment is good enough, it will find supernovae without your presence.

(5) Stars as faint as 18th or 19th magnitude become accessible, which includes most supernovae in nearby galaxies plus the brighter supernovae in many distant galaxies, out to about 300 million light-years.

Using a CCD brings so many thousands of galaxies within range that you will never have enough time to observe them all! However, you will need reference materials for all the galaxies on your observing list—even if you make the reference images yourself—so that you can tell when a new object appears near a galaxy.

Visual Supernova Hunting

Visual supernova hunting has a number of advantages over using a CCD:

(1) The equipment is less expensive than that needed for CCD work.

(2) An experienced visual observer usually knows the location and the normal appearance of many target galaxies and can thus work through observations of galaxies at 10 times the speed of anyone using a CCD on an amateur telescope. Professional-standard CCDs are quicker but are still much more expensive than those used by amateurs.

(3) You become very familiar with the night sky. (Personally, I think this is a great benefit of visual searching.)

(4) Amateurs who rely on computers to find galaxies are deceived by technology into being ignorant of the sky. Thus, when the technology fails (as it does from time to time), the search halts, since the observer does not know where to locate target galaxies. A visual observer who knows the sky is immune to this problem.

There are, however, special requirements:

(1) A reasonably dark observing site is needed.

(2) Your telescope needs to be easily manageable so that you can locate objects quickly, and the aperture needs to be big enough so that you can see down to about 15th magnitude. You can then observe all the nearby galaxies (out to, say, 100 million light-years). You will then be able to see most supernovae in galaxies out to about 25 million light-years and the brighter supernovae out to 100 million light-years or more. But, naturally, your chances of success decrease with the distance of the galaxy. Fainter supernovae in any given galaxy may be more numerous than the brighter ones, although the latter are the most interesting, scientifically.

(3) As in CCD searches, charts or suitable photographs of all your target galaxies are needed, so that you can tell when a new object appears.

Verification and Reporting

Verification of any suspected new discovery is vitally important. The first step is to check any suspect against all available photographs, CCD images, or charts of that galaxy. Measure carefully the offset of the new star from the nucleus of the galaxy. Watch the object for any possible movement against nearby stars. Note the time of your discovery (UT). It is necessary to have a team of other observers who can make independent observations of the new object, and who will do so immediately, if asked. These other observers must also have enough galaxy resources so that they can eliminate anything that is not a supernova, and they should be spread out over a number of locations in case bad weather puts any one observer out of action.

The Central Bureau for Astronomical Telegrams has issued instructions describing how much verification is needed about any possible new supernova, and these should be consulted (see www.cfa.harvard.edu/iau/cbat.html). CCD observers need at least five observations covering 24 hours. A visual observer should have independent observations by people who know what they are doing. And even after the Central Bureau has been notified, spectra will probably need to be obtained through one of the main observatories before the Bureau will finally announce a discovery.

When notifying the Central Bureau, provide full details of all observations of the new object: the name and location of the person making the report, the discoverer's name and location, details of the reference materials consulted, details concerning the equipment used, universal time of all observations, name and position of the galaxy, offset and brightness of the supernova, and similar details about each verifying observation. Observers who are not already known at the Bureau should be especially thorough in detailing and supporting their report. All discoveries can be emailed to the Central Bureau at cbat@cfa.harvard.edu.

★ Much helpful advice is available in the *AAVSO Supernova Search Manual,* which is available from the AAVSO, 25 Birch St, Cambridge MA 02138, USA, for the cost of postage only. It can also be viewed at www.aavso.org/observing/programs/sn/supernovasm.shtml.

Editor's Note: Robert Evans, who made his first supernova discovery in 1981, holds the record for visual discoveries of supernovae: 40. Ten of these were found using a 250-mm telescope, 8 using a 310-mm telescope, 19 with a 410-mm instrument (all "backyard" variety Newtonians), and 3 using the 1.02-m telescope at Siding Spring Observatory (Australian National University). In addition, he has discovered 4 supernovae (plus a comet) on U.K. Schmidt films taken as part of a special supernova search, all in 1996, and one on a European Southern Observatory Red Survey Schmidt film.

EXPIRED STARS

BY ROY BISHOP

Stars are where the action is, and the action is fuelled by gravitation and thermonuclear fusion. Gravitation, the midwife and undertaker, forms a star, heats it to the temperatures necessary to ignite successive stages of fusion reactions, and when nuclear fuel runs out, crushes the ashes of the star into one of three final states: white dwarf, neutron star, or black hole. Thermonuclear fusion, powered by the strong binding energy of protons and neutrons, merely delays the onset of further collapse and higher temperatures. In the case of our Sun, the first and by far the longest delay, the "hang-up" provided by hydrogen-to-helium fusion, is already half over.

White Dwarfs

Stars comparable to our Sun have insufficient gravity to reach the temperatures necessary to form nuclei heavier than carbon or oxygen. When the thermal support pressure generated by fusion wanes, gravity gradually crushes the central portion of the star. If the mass of this core is less than 1.4 solar masses (a limit discovered by a leading astrophysicist of the 20th century, Subramanyan Chandrasekhar), the collapse halts at a very hot, Earth-sized remnant known as a white dwarf. At this point, the squeeze of gravity is offset by *electron degeneracy pressure,* an intrinsic aspect of the wave–particle nature of matter and the same pressure responsible for the stability and size of an atom. However, in the case of a white dwarf, the pressure is such that the electrons are not tied to individual atomic nuclei but occupy the whole star. In this sense, the star has become a giant atom. In physics jargon: electrons are fermions (i.e. they obey Fermi–Dirac quantum statistics) and hence abide by the Pauli Exclusion Principle, which dictates that no two electrons can occupy the same quantum state. This results in an immense pressure, sufficient to prevent further collapse, provided the mass is less than the Chandrasekhar limit. White dwarf diameters are about 1% that of our Sun, which has a nearly water-like average density (1 g/cm^3). Thus a cubic centimetre of white dwarf material has a mass near 100^3 g or one tonne (like a Toyota Echo crushed into a sugar cube).

Because of their immense thermal energy and small surface area, white dwarfs cool extremely slowly. The universe is not yet old enough for any white dwarf to have cooled sufficiently to become a "black dwarf." Also, white dwarfs are intrinsically very faint; thus only those close to the solar system can be seen.

Only one white dwarf is easily observable with a small telescope: **Omicron 2 Eridani B** (also designated 40 Eridani B), located 16.5 light-years from Earth. Omicron 2 Eridani A, the bright (mag. 4.4) companion to the dim (mag. 9.5) white dwarf, is shown on the JANUARY ALL-SKY CHART on p. 275: o^2 Eri A is the eastern (left-hand) member of the close pair of stars located due west of the word "Rigel." Omicron 2 Eridani B, the white dwarf, is located only 83″ east-southeast of o^2 Eri A (position angle ≈110°). Remarkably, stars A and B are accompanied by a third star, a faint (mag. 11.2) red dwarf star, o^2 Eri C, which resides only 9″ north of B. (There is a brighter and closer white dwarf, the companion of Sirius, α CMa B, but it is usually lost in the glare of Sirius. See THE NEAREST STARS (pp. 231–236) and DOUBLE AND MULTIPLE STARS (pp. 236–238) for more information on both of these stellar systems.)

For the observer with a small telescope, o^2 Eri B is the only Earth-sized object visible in the depths of interstellar space, the only visible object with a mass density far exceeding that of ordinary matter, the only accessible star no longer powered by nuclear reactions, and the only star that has expired and can still be seen.

Neutron Stars

For a large star of about eight or more solar masses, energy-releasing reactions end in its centre with the fusion of silicon nuclei into iron. Iron has the most tightly bound nucleus (per nuclear particle) and hence is no good as a fuel for further fusion. Electron degeneracy pressure supports the inert iron core until silicon fusion in a surrounding shell supplies enough additional iron to push the inert core over the Chandrasekhar limit. Gravity then overwhelms electron degeneracy pressure, and the core collapses in less than a second, so quickly that, momentarily, the outer layers of the star stay where they were. Gravitation-induced temperatures in the core rise past 10^{10} K, sufficient to disassemble heavy nuclei synthesized over the life of the star. This absorbs energy, accelerating the collapse. Also, electrons attain sufficient energy to combine with protons to form neutrons and neutrinos, another energy-absorbing reaction that also removes electrons, further hastening the collapse.

Provided the infalling mass is less than about three solar masses, like a hammer striking an anvil, when the core reaches a diameter of about 20 km the infall is violently arrested by a combination of *neutron* degeneracy pressure and the short-range repulsive nature of the strong nuclear force, the same agents that govern the size and structure of the nuclei of atoms of ordinary matter. With a diameter 500 times smaller than that of a white dwarf, the density at this stage is 500^3 larger, 100 million tonnes per cubic centimetre (like an aircraft carrier crushed to the size of the ball of a ballpoint pen). This is the density of ordinary atomic nuclei. The star's core has effectively become a gigantic nucleus, composed primarily of neutrons.

The abrupt rebound of the nearly rigid central core reverses the infall of the adjacent layers, turning the implosion into a spectacular explosion, a Type II supernova. The explosion mechanism is complex and not yet well understood, but appears to involve interactions with the immense numbers of neutrinos generated in the neutron production, and possibly acoustic waves generated by vibrations of the core as it is pummeled by infalling material within a second of its formation. The gravitational energy released in the sudden collapse of the couple of solar masses now locked in the central neutron star is about 10^{46} J. This is far more energy than our Sun will produce in its entire 10-billion-year lifetime.

Over the next several thousand years, the remnants of the outer layers of the star form an expanding, glowing cloud of gas and dust, seeding interstellar space with the heavy chemical elements (oxygen, silicon, iron, uranium, etc.) synthesized in its outer layers both before and during the supernova explosion. The potassium ions moving in the neurons of your brain as you read these words emerged from such a conflagration some 5 billion years ago.

No neutron stars are visible in a small telescope, although one is *indirectly* visible in the **Crab Nebula,** M1. The Crab supernova was a bright, naked-eye star in the skies of Earth in the year 1054 AD, although it had taken 6000 years for the light of the explosion to reach our planet. The nebula we see today is the expanding debris cloud as it was nearly 1000 years after the initial explosion.

★ The Crab Nebula glows across the electromagnetic spectrum, from radio waves to gamma rays, powered by the rapid but decreasing spin of the neutron star at its centre. The glow of the debris cloud is like the glow of a red-hot disk brake slowing the spin of a wheel. The visible light from the cloud is *synchrotron radiation* emitted by electrons as they spiral in the tangled magnetic field of the neutron star. Nowhere else in the heavens is such an exotic light visible in a small telescope, polarized light with the brilliance of a thousand suns, emitted not by atoms but by free electrons being flung about by a spinning neutron star. The neutron star itself is known as a *pulsar* because it flashes 30 times per second, in step with its spin. However, even if the Crab pulsar were bright enough to be visible in a small telescope, the flashing would not be apparent because, as in a motion picture or cathode-ray tube monitor, the flicker is too rapid for the eye to follow.

Colour photographs of the Crab Nebula reveal a celestial gift: a package of bluish synchrotron radiation wrapped in the loops of a tattered red ribbon—fragments of the shattered star, fluorescing in hydrogen-alpha light. Unfortunately, the luminance of the fluorescence is below the threshold for vision in the red part of the spectrum. Thus all we can see is the ghostly cloud of synchrotron radiation.

The Crab Nebula is located 1° northwest of the star ζ Tau, at the tip of the east horn of Taurus. In the JANUARY ALL-SKY CHART on p. 275, the nebula is the tiny circle of dots 5 mm to the right of the cross marking the summer solstice (SS). In a telescope the nebula appears merely as a small glowing cloud, but to the knowledgeable observer, this synchrotron radiation brake of a spinning neutron star is an object for profound contemplation.

Black Holes

Stars whose masses are greater than about 20 solar masses likely retain more than 3 solar masses in their imploding cores. This is sufficient that gravitation will overwhelm not only the degeneracy pressure of electrons, but also the highly incompressible nature of nuclear matter. Within seconds spacetime itself closes around the imploding stellar core, removing all but the core's gravitational field from the observable universe. The star has become a black hole.

The earliest and best candidate for a stellar black hole is **Cygnus X-1,** one of the strongest galactic X-ray sources in the sky. Cygnus X-1 is the invisible companion of a star that can be seen in a small telescope: HDE 226868, an O9.7Iab star, a very luminous, very hot supergiant located several thousand light-years from the Sun. It orbits its nearby, unseen companion with a 5.6-day period. The mass of the companion is between 10 and 16 solar masses, far too large for it to be a white dwarf or neutron star. X-rays are generated as material from the supergiant falls toward the invisible companion. The X-rays extend to energies of 100 keV and vary on time scales as short as milliseconds, indicative of a very compact companion.

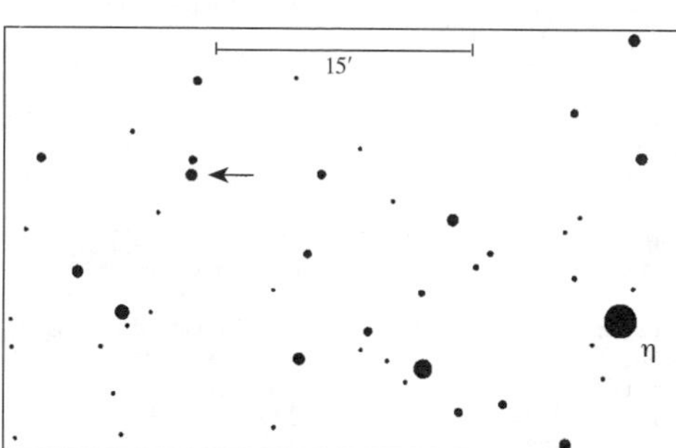

At 9th magnitude, the supergiant HDE 226868 is visible in any small telescope. It is less than half a degree from the 4th-magnitude star η Cygni, which is the star in the neck of the swan, next to the "C" in CYGNUS on the SEPTEMBER ALL-SKY CHART on p. 279. Any low magnification will more than encompass the field shown in the **finder chart** at the left. North is upward, η Cygni is at the lower right, and HDE 226868 is indicated by the small arrow. The chart magnitude limit is about 13. Although HDE 226868 is a blue supergiant, in telescopes of sufficient aperture this star appears orange because of interstellar dust between us and the star.

All that is to be seen is the hot supergiant, but the view will be worth the search if you know that at this same location in the field of your telescope lurks one of the most likely candidates for a black hole, a knot in the fabric of spacetime where a giant star has vanished. No painting, computer simulation, or Hollywood movie can match this observation.

NEBULAE AND GALAXIES

GALACTIC NEBULAE

BY WILLIAM HERBST

The following objects were selected from the brightest and largest of the various classes to illustrate the different types of interactions between stars and interstellar matter in our galaxy. *Emission regions* (HII) are excited by the strong ultraviolet flux of young, hot stars and are characterized by the lines of hydrogen in their spectra. *Reflection nebulae* (Ref) result from the diffusion of starlight by clouds of interstellar dust. At certain stages of their evolution stars become unstable and explode, shedding their outer layers into what becomes a *planetary nebula* (Pl) or a *supernova remnant* (SN). *Protostellar nebulae* (PrS) are objects still poorly understood; they are somewhat similar to the reflection nebulae, but their associated stars, often variable, are very luminous infrared stars that may be in the earliest stages of stellar evolution. Also included in the selection are three *extended complexes* (Comp) of special interest for their rich population of dark and bright nebulosities of various types. In the table *S* is the optical surface brightness in magnitude per square second of arc of representative regions of the nebula, and *m** is the magnitude of the associated star.

			RA (2000) Dec			Size	*S*		Dist.	
NGC	M	Con	h m	° ′	Type	′	mag/sq″	*m**	10^3 ly	Remarks
1435		Tau	3 47.5	+24 05	Ref	15	20	4	0.4	Merope nebula
1535		Eri	4 14.2	−12 45	Pl	0.5	17	12		
1952	1	Tau	5 34.5	+22 01	SN	5	19	16v	4	"Crab" + pulsar
1976	42	Ori	5 35.3	−5 24	HII	30	18	4	1.5	Orion Nebula
2070		Dor	5 38.6	−69 05	HII	20	—	13	200	Tarantula Nebula
ζ Ori		Ori	5 40.8	−1 56	Comp	2°			1.5	Incl. "Horsehead"
2068	78	Ori	5 46.8	+0 02	Ref	5	20		1.5	
IC 443		Gem	6 17.6	+22 36	SN	40			2	
2244		Mon	6 32.4	+4 52	HII	50	21	7	3	Rosette Nebula
2261 Neb.		Mon	6 39.1	+8 43	PrS	2		12v	4	Hubble's Variable
2392		Gem	7 29.2	+20 54	Pl	0.3	18	10	10	Clown Face Nebula
2626		Vel	8 35.6	−40 38	Ref	2	—	10	3	
3132		Vel	10 07.0	−40 25	Pl	1	17	10	—	Eight-Burst
3324		Car	10 37.5	−58 38	HII	15	—	8	9	
3372		Car	10 45.1	−59 41	HII	80	—	6v	9	Carina Nebula
3503		Car	11 01.3	−60 43	Ref	3	—	11	9	
3587	97	UMa	11 14.8	+55 01	Pl	3	21	13	12	Owl Nebula
—		Cru	12 51	−63	Dark	6°	—	—	0.5	Coal Sack
5189		Mus	13 33.5	−65 58	Pl	2.6	—	10	—	
ρ Oph		Oph	16 25.6	−23 27	Comp	4°			0.5	Bright + dark nebula
6514	20	Sgr	18 02.4	−23 02	HII	15	19		3.5	Trifid Nebula
6523	8	Sgr	18 03.6	−24 23	HII	40	18		4.5	Lagoon Nebula
6543		Dra	17 58.6	+66 37	Pl	0.4	15	11	3.5	
6618	17	Sgr	18 20.9	−16 11	HII	20	19		3	Horseshoe Nebula
6720	57	Lyr	18 53.6	+33 03	Pl	1.2	18	15	5	Ring Nebula
6726		CrA	19 01.7	−36 54	PrS	5	—	7	0.5	
6853	27	Vul	19 59.5	+22 43	Pl	7	19	13	3.5	Dumbbell Nebula
6888		Cyg	20 12.3	+38 25	HII	15				
γ Cyg		Cyg	20 22.2	+40 16	Comp	6°				HII + dark nebula
6960/95		Cyg	20 45.6	+30 42	SN	150			2.5	Cygnus loop
7000		Cyg	20 58.9	+44 19	HII	100	22		3.5	North America Nebula
7009		Aqr	21 04.1	−11 23	Pl	0.5	16	12	3	Saturn Nebula
7027		Cyg	21 07.1	+42 14	Pl	0.2	15	13		
7129		Cep	21 43.0	+65 06	Ref	3	21	10	2.5	Small cluster
7293		Aqr	22 29.6	−20 48	Pl	13	22	13		Helix Nebula

THE MESSIER CATALOGUE

BY ALAN DYER

Charles Messier's Catalogue provides a selection of the best and brightest deep-sky wonders for Northern Hemisphere viewers. Messier compiled his list in the late 1700s to aid prospective comet hunters. Some of these objects he discovered himself, some were first seen by other astronomers of the day, while a few (the Pleiades and the Beehive) were known since antiquity. The Messier numbers do not follow an ordered sequence across the sky. Rather, they are numbered in the order he discovered and catalogued them. Although he intended to, Messier never did publish a list with entries renumbered in order of right ascension.

In our version of the Messier Catalogue, we've listed the objects by season *for the evening observer,* grouping the objects within their respective constellations. The constellations are then listed roughly in order of increasing right ascension, that is constellations farther to the east and which rise later in the night are farther down the list. This is to help plan the sequence of an evening's Messier hunt.

The identity of some Messier objects is controversial. There is evidence that M91 and M102 are mistaken observations of M58 and M101, respectively. M104 and M109 were found by a colleague, Pierre Mechain, and reported to Messier for inclusion in his Catalogue. NGC 205, one of the companion galaxies to M31, the Andromeda Galaxy, was apparently found by Messier but never included in his Catalogue. Modern-day observers have dubbed this object M110. In our list, we have included 110 entries, including two objects that some have suggested as alternative candidates for M91 and M102.

Modern-day Messier hunters often wonder what telescopes Messier used. The largest were 190-mm and 200-mm reflectors. However, their speculum metal mirrors would have had the equivalent light-gathering power of a modern 80-mm to 100-mm reflector. He also used a number of 90-mm refractors. Today, a dark site and a good 80-mm refractor or 100-mm reflector should be sufficient for completing the entire list. Objects M6 and M7 are the most southerly, while M74 and M76 are often considered the faintest and most difficult. M83's low altitude and diffuse appearance make it a challenge for Canadian observers north of 50° latitude.

The columns contain the Messier number, the object's NGC (New General Catalogue) number, the constellation, the type of object, its equinox J2000.0 coordinates, visual magnitude m_V, and angular size in minutes of arc (planetary nebula sizes are given in seconds of arc (″)). Entries marked "!!" are showpiece objects. OC = open cluster; GC = globular cluster; PN = planetary nebula; EN = emission nebula; RN = reflection nebula; E/RN = combination of emission and reflection nebula; SNR = supernova remnant; G = galaxy (E = elliptical, I = irregular, SA = normal spiral, SB = barred spiral, S0 = lenticular). Data are taken from *The Deep Sky Field Guide to Uranometria 2000.0* (published by Willmann-Bell, Inc., 1993), compiled by Murray Cragin, James Lucyk, and Barry Rappaport from a variety of contemporary catalogues. Some sizes have been rounded to two significant figures. Also recommended as an excellent guide is *The Messier Objects,* by Stephen James O'Meara (Cambridge University Press, 1998).

The RASC offers observing certificates for members who observe the 110 objects in the Messier list or the 110 objects in the Finest NGC list (see pp. 259–261). For beginners or observers using binoculars the Society also offers the "Explore the Universe" Certificate. Contact your local Centre or the RASC National Office (see p. 7) for details.

NUMERICAL LISTING OF MESSIER OBJECTS

M#	Sky	Con	M#	Sky	Con	M#	Sky	Con	M#	Sky	Con	M#	Sky	Con
1	WIN	Tau	**23**	SUM	Sgr	**45**	WIN	Tau	**67**	SPR	Cnc	**89**	SPR	Vir
2	AUT	Aqr	**24**	SUM	Sgr	**46**	WIN	Pup	**68**	SPR	Hya	**90**	SPR	Vir
3	SPR	CVn	**25**	SUM	Sgr	**47**	WIN	Pup	**69**	SUM	Sgr	**91**	SPR	Com
4	SUM	Sco	**26**	SUM	Sct	**48**	WIN	Hya	**70**	SUM	Sgr	**92**	SUM	Her
5	SPR	Ser	**27**	SUM	Vul	**49**	SPR	Vir	**71**	SUM	Sge	**93**	WIN	Pup
6	SUM	Sco	**28**	SUM	Sgr	**50**	WIN	Mon	**72**	AUT	Aqr	**94**	SPR	CVn
7	SUM	Sco	**29**	SUM	Cyg	**51**	SPR	CVn	**73**	AUT	Aqr	**95**	SPR	Leo
8	SUM	Sgr	**30**	AUT	Cap	**52**	AUT	Cas	**74**	AUT	Psc	**96**	SPR	Leo
9	SUM	Oph	**31**	AUT	And	**53**	SPR	Com	**75**	SUM	Sgr	**97**	SPR	UMa
10	SUM	Oph	**32**	AUT	And	**54**	SUM	Sgr	**76**	AUT	Per	**98**	SPR	Com
11	SUM	Sct	**33**	AUT	Tri	**55**	SUM	Sgr	**77**	AUT	Cet	**99**	SPR	Com
12	SUM	Oph	**34**	AUT	Per	**56**	SUM	Lyr	**78**	WIN	Ori	**100**	SPR	Com
13	SUM	Her	**35**	WIN	Gem	**57**	SUM	Lyr	**79**	WIN	Lep	**101**	SPR	UMa
14	SUM	Oph	**36**	WIN	Aur	**58**	SPR	Vir	**80**	SUM	Sco	**102**	SPR	Dra?
15	AUT	Peg	**37**	WIN	Aur	**59**	SPR	Vir	**81**	SPR	UMa	**103**	AUT	Cas
16	SUM	Ser	**38**	WIN	Aur	**60**	SPR	Vir	**82**	SPR	UMa	**104**	SPR	Vir
17	SUM	Sgr	**39**	SUM	Cyg	**61**	SPR	Vir	**83**	SPR	Hya	**105**	SPR	Leo
18	SUM	Sgr	**40**	SPR	UMa	**62**	SUM	Oph	**84**	SPR	Vir	**106**	SPR	CVn
19	SUM	Oph	**41**	WIN	CMa	**63**	SPR	CVn	**85**	SPR	Com	**107**	SUM	Oph
20	SUM	Sgr	**42**	WIN	Ori	**64**	SPR	Com	**86**	SPR	Vir	**108**	SPR	UMa
21	SUM	Sgr	**43**	WIN	Ori	**65**	SPR	Leo	**87**	SPR	Vir	**109**	SPR	UMa
22	SUM	Sgr	**44**	SPR	Cnc	**66**	SPR	Leo	**88**	SPR	Com	**110**	AUT	And

SEASONAL LISTING OF MESSIER OBJECTS

M#	NGC	Con	Type	RA (2000) h m	Dec ° ′	m_v	Size ′	Remarks
The Winter Sky								
1	1952	Tau	SNR	5 34.5	+22 01	8.4	6 × 4	!! famous Crab Neb. supernova remnant
45	—	Tau	OC	3 47.0	+24 07	1.2	110	!! Pleiades; look for subtle nebulosity
36	1960	Aur	OC	5 36.1	+34 08	6.0	12	bright but scattered group; use low pow.
37	2099	Aur	OC	5 52.4	+32 33	5.6	20	!! finest of 3 Auriga clusters; very rich
38	1912	Aur	OC	5 28.7	+35 50	6.4	21	look for small cluster NGC 1907 0.5° S
42	1976	Ori	E/RN	5 35.4	−5 27	—	65 × 60	!! Orion Nebula; finest in northern sky
43	1982	Ori	E/RN	5 35.6	−5 16	—	20 × 15	detached part of Orion Nebula
78	2068	Ori	RN	5 46.7	+0 03	—	8 × 6	bright featureless reflection nebula
79	1904	Lep	GC	5 24.5	−24 33	7.8	8.7	200-mm telescope needed to resolve
35	2168	Gem	OC	6 08.9	+24 20	5.1	28	!! look for sm. cluster NGC 2158 0.25° S
41	2287	CMa	OC	6 47.0	−20 44	4.5	38	4° south of Sirius; bright but coarse
50	2323	Mon	OC	7 03.2	−8 20	5.9	16	between Sirius & Procyon; use low mag.
46	2437	Pup	OC	7 41.8	−14 49	6.1	27	!! contains planetary nebula NGC 2438
47	2422	Pup	OC	7 36.6	−14 30	4.4	29	coarse cluster 1.5° west of M46
93	2447	Pup	OC	7 44.6	−23 52	≈6.2	22	compact, bright cluster; fairly rich
48	2548	Hya	OC	8 13.8	−5 48	5.8	54	former "lost" Messier; large, sparse cl.

SEASONAL LISTING OF MESSIER OBJECTS (continued)

M#	NGC	Con	Type	RA (2000) h m	Dec ° ′	m_V	Size ′	Remarks
The Spring Sky								
44	2632	Cnc	OC	8 40.1	+19 59	3.1	95	!! Beehive or Praesepe; use low power
67	2682	Cnc	OC	8 50.4	+11 49	6.9	29	one of the oldest star clusters known
40	—	UMa	2 stars	12 22.4	+58 05	8.0	—	double star Winnecke 4; separation 50″
81	3031	UMa	G-SAab	9 55.6	+69 04	6.9	24 × 13	!! bright spiral visible in binoculars
82	3034	UMa	G-I0	9 55.8	+69 41	8.4	12 × 6	!! the "exploding" galaxy; M81 0.5° S
97	3587	UMa	PN	11 14.8	+55 01	9.9	194″	!! Owl Nebula; distinct grey oval
101	5457	UMa	G-SABcd	14 03.2	+54 21	7.9	26 × 26	!! Pinwheel Gal.; diffuse face-on spiral
108	3556	UMa	G-SBcd	11 11.5	+55 40	10.0	8.1 × 2.1	nearly edge-on; paired with M97 0.75° SE
109	3992	UMa	G-SBbc	11 57.6	+53 23	9.8	7.6 × 4.3	barred spiral near γ UMa
65	3623	Leo	G-SABa	11 18.9	+13 05	9.3	8.7 × 2.2	!! bright elongated spiral
66	3627	Leo	G-SABb	11 20.2	+12 59	8.9	8.2 × 3.9	!! M65 and NGC 3628 in same field
95	3351	Leo	G-SBb	10 44.0	+11 42	9.7	7.8 × 4.6	bright barred spiral
96	3368	Leo	G-SABab	10 46.8	+11 49	9.2	6.9 × 4.6	M95 in same field
105	3379	Leo	G-E1	10 47.8	+12 35	9.3	3.9 × 3.9	bright elliptical near M95 and M96
53	5024	Com	GC	13 12.9	+18 10	7.5	12.6	150-mm telescope needed to resolve
64	4826	Com	G-SAab	12 56.7	+21 41	8.5	9.2 × 4.6	!! Black Eye Gal.; eye needs big scope
85	4382	Com	G-SA0+	12 25.4	+18 11	9.1	7.5 × 5.7	bright elliptical shape
88	4501	Com	G-SAb	12 32.0	+14 25	9.6	6.1 × 2.8	bright multiple-arm spiral
91	4548	Com	G-SBb	12 35.4	+14 30	10.2	5.0 × 4.1	some lists say M91 = M58, not NGC 4548
98	4192	Com	G-SABab	12 13.8	+14 54	10.1	9.1 × 2.1	nearly edge-on spiral near star 6 Com. B.
99	4254	Com	G-SAc	12 18.8	+14 25	9.9	4.6 × 4.3	nearly face-on spiral near M98
100	4321	Com	G-SABbc	12 22.9	+15 49	9.3	6.2 × 5.3	face-on spiral with starlike nucleus
49	4472	Vir	G-E2	12 29.8	+8 00	8.4	8.1 × 7.1	very bright elliptical
58	4579	Vir	G-SABb	12 37.7	+11 49	9.7	5.5 × 4.6	bright barred spiral; M59 and M60 1° E
59	4621	Vir	G-E5	12 42.0	+11 39	9.6	4.6 × 3.6	bright elliptical paired with M60
60	4649	Vir	G-E2	12 43.7	+11 33	8.8	7.1 × 6.1	bright elliptical with M59 and NGC 4647
61	4303	Vir	G-SABbc	12 21.9	+4 28	9.7	6.0 × 5.9	face-on two-armed spiral
84	4374	Vir	G-E1	12 25.1	+12 53	9.1	5.1 × 4.1	!! w/ M86 in Markarian's Chain
86	4406	Vir	G-E3	12 26.2	+12 57	8.9	12 × 9	!! w/ many NGC galaxies in Chain
87	4486	Vir	G-E0-1	12 30.8	+12 24	8.6	7.1 × 7.1	the one with famous jet and black hole
89	4552	Vir	G-E	12 35.7	+12 33	9.8	3.4 × 3.4	elliptical; resembles M87 but smaller
90	4569	Vir	G-SABab	12 36.8	+13 10	9.5	10 × 4	bright barred spiral near M89
104	4594	Vir	G-SA	12 40.0	−11 37	8.0	7.1 × 4.4	!! Sombrero Galaxy; look for dust lane
3	5272	CVn	GC	13 42.2	+28 23	5.9	16.2	!! contains many variable stars
51	5194/5	CVn	G-SAbc	13 29.9	+47 12	8.4	8 × 7	!! Whirlpool Galaxy; superb in big scope
63	5055	CVn	G-SAbc	13 15.8	+42 02	8.6	14 × 8	!! Sunflower Galaxy; bright, elongated
94	4736	CVn	G-SAab	12 50.9	+41 07	8.2	13 × 11	very bright and comet-like
106	4258	CVn	G-SABbc	12 19.0	+47 18	8.4	20 × 8	!! superb large, bright spiral
68	4590	Hya	GC	12 39.5	−26 45	7.7	12	150-mm telescope needed to resolve
83	5236	Hya	G-SABc	13 37.0	−29 52	7.6	16 × 13	large and diffuse; superb from far south
102	5866?	Dra	G-SA0+	15 06.5	+55 46	9.9	6.6 × 3.2	or is M102 = M101? (look for 5907)
5	5904	Ser	GC	15 18.6	+2 05	5.7	17.4	!! one of the sky's finest globulars
The Summer Sky								
13	6205	Her	GC	16 41.7	+36 28	5.7	16.6	!! Hercules Cluster; NGC 6207 0.5° NE
92	6341	Her	GC	17 17.1	+43 08	6.4	11.2	9° NE of M13; fine but often overlooked
9	6333	Oph	GC	17 19.2	−18 31	7.6	9.3	smallest of Ophiuchus globulars
10	6254	Oph	GC	16 57.1	−4 06	6.6	15.1	rich globular cluster; M12 is 3° NW
12	6218	Oph	GC	16 47.2	−1 57	6.8	14.5	loose globular cluster near M10
14	6402	Oph	GC	17 37.6	−3 15	7.6	11.7	200-mm telescope needed to resolve
19	6273	Oph	GC	17 02.6	−26 16	6.7	13.5	oblate globular; M62 4° south
62	6266	Oph	GC	17 01.2	−30 07	6.7	14.1	asymmetrical; in rich field

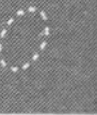

SEASONAL LISTING OF MESSIER OBJECTS (continued)

M#	NGC	Con	Type	RA (2000) h m	Dec ° ′	m_v	Size ′	Remarks
Summer Sky (cont)								
107	6171	Oph	GC	16 32.5	−13 03	8.1	10.0	small, faint globular
4	6121	Sco	GC	16 23.6	−26 32	5.8	26.3	bright globular near Antares
6	6405	Sco	OC	17 40.1	−32 13	4.2	33	!! Butterfly Cluster; best at low power
7	6475	Sco	OC	17 53.9	−34 49	3.3	80	!! excellent in binocs or rich-field scope
80	6093	Sco	GC	16 17.0	−22 59	7.3	8.9	very compressed globular
16	6611	Ser	EN + OC	18 18.6	−13 58	—	35 × 28	Eagle Neb. w/ open cl.; use neb. filter
8	6523	Sgr	EN	18 03.8	−24 23	—	45 × 30	!! Lagoon Nebula w/ open cl. NGC 6530
17	6618	Sgr	EN	18 20.8	−16 11	—	20 × 15	!! Swan or Omega Nebula; use neb. filter
18	6613	Sgr	OC	18 19.9	−17 08	6.9	10	sparse cluster; 1° south of M17
20	6514	Sgr	E/RN	18 02.3	−23 02	—	20 × 20	!! Trifid Nebula; look for dark lanes
21	6531	Sgr	OC	18 04.6	−22 30	5.9	13	0.7° NE of M20; sparse cluster
22	6656	Sgr	GC	18 36.4	−23 54	5.1	24	spectacular from southern latitude
23	6494	Sgr	OC	17 56.8	−19 01	5.5	27	bright, loose open cluster
24	—	Sgr	starcloud	18 16.5	−18 50	4.6	95 × 35	rich star cloud; best in big binoculars
25	IC 4725	Sgr	OC	18 31.6	−19 15	4.6	32	bright but sparse open cluster
28	6626	Sgr	GC	18 24.5	−24 52	6.8	11.2	compact globular near M22
54	6715	Sgr	GC	18 55.1	−30 29	7.6	9.1	not easily resolved
55	6809	Sgr	GC	19 40.0	−30 58	6.4	19.0	bright, loose globular cluster
69	6637	Sgr	GC	18 31.4	−32 21	7.6	7.1	small, poor globular cluster
70	6681	Sgr	GC	18 43.2	−32 18	8.0	7.8	small globular 2° east of M69
75	6864	Sgr	GC	20 06.1	−21 55	8.5	6	small and distant; 59 000 ly away
11	6705	Sct	OC	18 51.1	−6 16	5.8	13	!! Wild Duck Cl.; the best open cluster?
26	6694	Sct	OC	18 45.2	−9 24	8.0	14	bright, coarse cluster
56	6779	Lyr	GC	19 16.6	+30 11	8.3	7.1	within a rich starfield
57	6720	Lyr	PN	18 53.6	+33 02	8.8	>71″	!! Ring Nebula; an amazing smoke ring
71	6838	Sge	GC	19 53.8	+18 47	8.0	7.2	loose globular; looks like an open cluster
27	6853	Vul	PN	19 59.6	+22 43	7.3	>348″	!! Dumbbell Nebula; a superb object
29	6913	Cyg	OC	20 23.9	+38 32	6.6	6	small, poor open cluster 2° S of γ Cygni
39	7092	Cyg	OC	21 32.2	+48 26	4.6	31	very sparse cluster; use low power
The Autumn Sky								
2	7089	Aqr	GC	21 33.5	−0 49	6.4	12.9	200-mm telescope needed to resolve
72	6981	Aqr	GC	20 53.5	−12 32	9.3	5.9	near the Saturn Nebula, NGC 7009
73	6994	Aqr	OC	20 59.0	−12 38	8.9p	2.8	group of 4 stars only; an "asterism"
15	7078	Peg	GC	21 30.0	+12 10	6.0	12.3	rich, compact globular
30	7099	Cap	GC	21 40.4	−23 11	7.3	11	toughest in 1-night Messier marathon
52	7654	Cas	OC	23 24.2	+61 35	6.9	12	young, rich cl.; faint Bubble Neb. nearby
103	581	Cas	OC	1 33.2	+60 42	7.4	6	three NGC open clusters nearby
31	224	And	G-SAb	0 42.7	+41 16	3.4	185 × 75	!! Andromeda Gal.; look for dust lanes
32	221	And	G-E5 pec	0 42.7	+40 52	8.1	11 × 7	closest companion to M31
110	205	And	G-E3 pec	0 40.4	+41 41	8.1	20 × 12	more distant companion to M31
33	598	Tri	G-SAcd	1 33.9	+30 39	5.7	67 × 42	large, diffuse spiral; requires dark sky
74	628	Psc	G-SAc	1 36.7	+15 47	9.4	11 × 11	faint, elusive spiral; tough in small scope
77	1068	Cet	G-SABab	2 42.7	−0 01	8.9	8.2 × 7.3	a Seyfert galaxy; with starlike nucleus
34	1039	Per	OC	2 42.0	+42 47	5.2	35	best at low power
76	650/51	Per	PN	1 42.4	+51 34	10.1	>65″	Little Dumbbell; faint but distinct

THE FINEST NGC OBJECTS

BY ALAN DYER

Those looking for an observing project beyond the Messier Catalogue turn to the New General Catalogue (NGC). The NGC contains 7840 entries and forms the core database of today's computerized backyard telescopes. To match the Messier Catalogue, this list contains 110 of the finest NGC objects visible from midnorthern latitudes. The seasonal order is similar to that used in the Messier list, and there is no overlap. While the brightness of the best NGCs rivals many Messier targets, at least a 200-mm telescope is required to see all 110 objects on this list. Most are easy; a few are challenging.

The NGC was originally published by J.L.E. Dreyer in 1888, a work that expanded upon Sir John Herschel's 1864 "General Catalogue." Supplementary "Index Catalogues" were published by Dreyer in 1895 and 1908. The first IC extends the NGC with another 1529 objects discovered visually between 1888 and 1894. Most are faint, elusive targets. (To provide a flavour of this extension to the NGC, one entry from the first IC is included on this list, IC 289.) The Second Index Catalogue contains 3857 entries, most discovered photographically between 1895 and 1907.

The *Sky Atlas 2000.0,* the sets of index card charts called *AstroCards, The Night Sky Observer's Guide Vol. 1 and 2* by Kepple and Sanner, and the *Uranometria 2000.0* star atlas (the latter two published by Willmann-Bell, Inc.) are recommended finder aids. Most planetarium and deep-sky charting computer programs, as well as computerized telescopes, include all the objects on this list and many more.

Notation below is as in the Messier list. Magnitudes (m_V) are visual, with the exception of those marked "p," which are photographic, or blue, magnitudes. Most galaxies appear smaller than the sizes listed. For open clusters, the number of stars (*) is also given. Data are taken from *The Deep Sky Field Guide to Uranometria 2000.0* (see the introduction to the Messier list), with some sizes rounded to two significant figures.

SEASONAL LISTING OF FINEST NGC OBJECTS

#	NGC	Con	Type	RA (2000) h m	Dec ° ′	m_V	Size ′	Remarks
The Autumn Sky								
1	7009	Aqr	PN	21 04.2	−11 22	8.3p	>25″	!! Saturn Nebula; small bright oval
2	7293	Aqr	PN	22 29.6	−20 48	7.3	>769″	!! Helix Nebula; large, diffuse; use filter
3	7331	Peg	G-SAb	22 37.1	+34 25	9.5	10 × 4	!! large, bright spiral galaxy
4	7635	Cas	EN	23 20.7	+61 12	—	15 × 8	Bubble Neb.; very faint; 0.5° SW of M52
5	7789	Cas	OC	23 57.0	+56 44	6.7	15	!! 300*; faint but very rich cluster
6	185	Cas	G-E3	0 39.0	+48 20	9.2	14 × 12	companion to M31; small and faint
7	281	Cas	EN	0 52.8	+56 37	—	35 × 30	!! large faint nebulosity near η Cas
8	457	Cas	OC	1 19.1	+58 20	6.4	13	80*; rich; one of the best Cas. clusters
9	663	Cas	OC	1 46.0	+61 15	7.1	16	80*; look for NGCs 654 and 659 nearby
10	IC 289	Cas	PN	3 10.3	+61 19	13.3	>34″	dim oval smudge; use nebula filter!
11	7662	And	PN	23 25.9	+42 33	8.3	>12″	!! Blue Snowball; annular at high power
12	891	And	G-SAb	2 22.6	+42 21	9.9	13 × 3	!! faint, classic edge-on with dust lane
13	253	Scl	G-SABc	0 47.6	−25 17	7.6	30 × 7	!! very large and bright but at low altitude
14	772	Ari	G-SAb	1 59.3	+19 01	10.3	7.3 × 4.6	diffuse spiral galaxy
15	246	Cet	PN	0 47.0	−11 53	10.9	225″	large and faint with mottled structure
16	936	Cet	G-SB	2 27.6	−1 09	10.2	5.7 × 4.6	near M77; NGC 941 in the same field

SEASONAL LISTING OF FINEST NGC OBJECTS (continued)

#	NGC	Con	Type	RA (2000) h m	Dec ° ′	m_v	Size ′	Remarks
Autumn Sky (cont)								
17	869/884	Per	OC	2 21.0	+57 08	≈5	30/30	!! Double Cluster; 315*; use low power
18	1023	Per	G-SB0⁻	2 40.4	+39 04	9.3	8.6 × 4.2	bright lens-shaped galaxy near M34
19	1491	Per	EN	4 03.4	+51 19	—	25 × 25	visually small and faint emission nebula
20	1501	Cam	PN	4 07.0	+60 55	11.5	52″	faint; dark centre; look for NGC 1502
21	1232	Eri	G-SABc	3 09.8	−20 35	10.0	6.8 × 5.6	face-on spiral; look for NGC 1300 nearby
22	1535	Eri	PN	4 14.2	−12 44	9.6p	>18″	bright planetary with blue-grey disk
The Winter Sky								
23	1514	Tau	PN	4 09.2	+30 47	10.9	>114″	faint glow around 9.4^m central star
24	1931	Aur	E/RN	5 31.4	+34 15	—	4 × 4	haze surrounding four close stars
25	1788	Ori	RN	5 06.9	−3 21	—	5 × 3	fairly bright but diffuse reflection nebula
26	1973+	Ori	E/RN	5 35.1	−4 44	—	≈20 × 10	NGC 1973-5-7 just N. of M42 and M43
27	2022	Ori	PN	5 42.1	+9 05	11.9	>18″	small, faint & distinct with annular form
28	2024	Ori	EN	5 41.9	−1 51	—	30 × 30	bright but masked by glow from ζ Ori
29	2194	Ori	OC	6 13.8	+12 48	8.5	8	80*, fairly rich; look for 2169 nearby
30	2371/2	Gem	PN	7 25.6	+29 29	11.3	>55″	faint double-lobed planetary; use filter
31	2392	Gem	PN	7 29.2	+20 55	9.2	>15″	!! Clown Face or Eskimo Nebula
32	2237+	Mon	EN	6 32.3	+5 03	—	80 × 60	!! Rosette Neb.; very large; use filter
33	2261	Mon	E/RN	6 39.2	+8 44	var	3.5 × 1.5	Hubble's Variable Neb.; comet-shaped
34	2359	CMa	EN	7 18.6	−13 12	—	9 × 6	bright; look for 2360 & 2362 nearby
35	2440	Pup	PN	7 41.9	−18 13	9.4	>14″	almost starlike; irregular at high power
36	2539	Pup	OC	8 10.7	−12 50	6.5	21	50*; rich cluster; near M46 and M47
37	2403	Cam	G-SABc	7 36.9	+65 36	8.5	26 × 13	!! very large & bright; visible in binocs.
38	2655	Cam	G-SAB0	8 55.6	+78 13	10.1	6.0 × 5.3	bright ellipse with starlike nucleus
The Spring Sky								
39	2683	Lyn	G-SAb	8 52.7	+33 25	9.8	8.4 × 2.4	nearly edge-on spiral; very bright
40	2841	UMa	G-SAb	9 22.0	+50 58	9.2	6.8 × 3.3	!! classic elongated spiral; very bright
41	3079	UMa	G-SBc	10 02.2	+55 41	10.9	8.0 × 1.5	edge-on spiral; NGC 2950 nearby
42	3184	UMa	G-SABc	10 18.3	+41 25	9.8	7.8 × 7.2	large, diffuse face-on spiral
43	3877	UMa	G-SAc	11 46.1	+47 30	11.0	5.1 × 1.1	edge-on; same field as χ UMa
44	3941	UMa	G-SB0°	11 52.9	+36 59	10.3	3.7 × 2.6	small, bright and elliptical
45	4026	UMa	G-S0	11 59.4	+50 58	10.8	4.6 × 1.2	lens-shaped edge-on near γ UMa
46	4088	UMa	G-SABbc	12 05.6	+50 33	10.6	5.4 × 2.1	nearly edge-on; NGC 4085 in same field
47	4157	UMa	G-SABb	12 11.1	+50 29	11.3	7.1 × 1.2	a thin sliver; NGC 4026 and 4088 nearby
48	4605	UMa	G-SBcp	12 40.0	+61 37	10.3	6.4 × 2.3	bright, distinct edge-on spiral
49	3115	Sex	G-S0⁻	10 05.2	−7 43	8.9	8.1 × 2.8	Spindle Galaxy; bright and elongated
50	3242	Hya	PN	10 24.8	−18 38	7.8	>16″	!! Ghost of Jupiter; small but bright
51	3003	LMi	G-Sbc?	9 48.6	+33 25	11.9	5.2 × 1.6	faint elongated streak
52	3344	LMi	G-SABbc	10 43.5	+24 55	9.9	6.9 × 6.4	diffuse face-on barred spiral
53	3432	LMi	G-SBm	10 52.5	+36 37	11.2	6.9 × 1.9	nearly edge-on; faint flat streak
54	2903	Leo	G-SABbc	9 32.2	+21 30	9.0	12 × 6	!! very large, bright elongated spiral
55	3384	Leo	G-SB0⁻	10 48.3	+12 38	9.9	5.5 × 2.9	same field as M105 and NGC 3389
56	3521	Leo	G-SAb	11 05.8	−0 02	9.0	12 × 6	very large, bright spiral
57	3607	Leo	G-SA0°	11 16.9	+18 03	9.9	4.6 × 4.1	NGC 3605 & 3608 in same field
58	3628	Leo	G-Sb pec	11 20.3	+13 36	9.5	14 × 4	large edge-on; same field as M65 & M66
59	4111	CVn	G-SA0⁺	12 07.1	+43 04	10.7	4.4 × 0.9	bright lens-shaped edge-on spiral
60	4214	CVn	G-I AB	12 15.6	+36 20	9.8	10 × 8	large irregular galaxy
61	4244	CVn	G-SAcd	12 17.5	+37 49	10.4	17 × 2	!! large distinct edge-on spiral

SEASONAL LISTING OF FINEST NGC OBJECTS (continued)

#	NGC	Con	Type	RA (2000) h m	Dec ° ′	m_v	Size ′	Remarks
Spring Sky (cont)								
62	4449	CVn	G-I Bm	12 28.2	+44 06	9.6	5.5 × 4.1	bright with odd rectangular shape
63	4490	CVn	G-SBd p	12 30.6	+41 38	9.8	6.4 × 3.3	Cocoon Gal.; bright spiral; 4485 in field
64	4631	CVn	G-SBd	12 42.1	+32 32	9.2	16 × 3	!! large edge-on; with companion 4627
65	4656/7	CVn	G-SBm p	12 44.0	+32 10	10.5	20 × 3	!! in field with 4631; NE end curves up
66	5005	CVn	G-SABbc	13 10.9	+37 03	9.8	5.8 × 2.8	bright elongated spiral near α CVn
67	5033	CVn	G-SAc	13 13.4	+36 36	10.2	10 × 5	large bright spiral near NGC 5005
68	4274	Com	G-SBab	2 19.8	+29 37	10.4	6.7 × 2.5	NGCs 4278/83/86 in same field
69	4414	Com	G-SAc	12 26.4	+31 13	10.1	4.4 × 3.0	bright spiral with starlike nucleus
70	4494	Com	G-E1-2	12 31.4	+25 47	9.8	4.6 × 4.4	small bright elliptical
71	4559	Com	G-SABc	12 36.0	+27 58	10.0	12 × 5	large spiral with coarse structure
72	4565	Com	G-SAb	12 36.3	+25 59	9.6	14 × 2	!! superb edge-on spiral with dust lane
73	4725	Com	G-SABab	12 50.4	+25 30	9.4	10 × 8	very bright, large spiral
74	4038/9	Crv	G-SB/IB	12 01.9	−18 52	≈10.4	≈5 × 3 ea.	"Antennae" interacting galaxies
75	4361	Crv	PN	12 24.5	−18 48	10.9	>45″	small and bright; with 13^m central star
76	4216	Vir	G-SABb	12 15.9	+13 09	10.0	7.8 × 1.6	nearly edge-on; with NGC 4206 and 4222
77	4388	Vir	G-SAb	12 25.8	+12 40	11.0	5.7 × 1.6	with M84 and M86 in Markarian's Chain
78	4438	Vir	G-SA0/a	12 27.8	+13 01	10.2	8.9 × 3.6	paired w/ NGC 4435 to form the "Eyes"
79	4517	Vir	G-Scd	12 32.8	+0 07	10.4	9.9 × 1.4	faint edge-on spiral
80	4526	Vir	G-SAB0°	12 34.0	+7 42	9.7	7.1 × 2.9	between two 7th mag. stars
81	4535	Vir	G-SABc	12 34.3	+8 12	10.0	7.1 × 6.4	near M49 and 0.75° N of NGC 4526
82	4567/8	Vir	G-SAbc	12 36.5	+11 15	≈11	≈3 × 2 ea.	"Siamese Twins" interacting galaxies
83	4699	Vir	G-Sab	12 49.0	−8 40	9.5	4.4 × 3.2	small & bright; look for NGC 4697 3° N
84	4762	Vir	G-SB0°?	12 52.9	+11 14	10.3	9.1 × 2.2	flattest galaxy known; 4754 in same field
85	5746	Vir	G-SA?b	14 44.9	+1 57	10.3	6.8 × 1.0	fine edge-on near 109 Virginis
86	5466	Boo	GC	14 05.5	+28 32	9.0	11	loose class XII; like rich open cl.; faint
87	5907	Dra	G-SAc	15 15.9	+56 20	10.3	12 × 2	!! fine edge-on with dust lane; near 5866
88	6503	Dra	G-SAcd	17 49.4	+70 09	10.2	7.3 × 2.4	bright elongated spiral
89	6543	Dra	PN	17 58.6	+66 38	8.1	>18″	Cat's Eye Nebula; with 10.9^m central star
The Summer Sky								
90	6210	Her	PN	16 44.5	+23 49	8.8	>14″	blue starlike planetary
91	6369	Oph	PN	17 29.3	−23 46	11.4	>30″	"Little Ghost"; look for 6309 nearby
92	6572	Oph	PN	18 12.1	+6 51	8.1	8″	tiny bright blue oval
93	6633	Oph	OC	18 27.7	+6 34	4.6	27	sparse wide field cluster; IC 4756 nearby
94	6712	Sct	GC	18 53.1	−8 42	8.2	7.2	small globular; look for IC 1295 in field
95	6781	Aql	PN	19 18.4	+6 33	11.4	>109″	pale version of the Owl Nebula, M97
96	6819	Cyg	OC	19 41.3	+40 11	7.3	9.5	150*; faint but rich cluster in Milky Way
97	6826	Cyg	PN	19 44.8	+50 31	8.8	>25″	!! Blinking Planetary; 10.6^m central star
98	6888	Cyg	EN	20 12.0	+38 21	—	18 × 13	Crescent Nebula; faint; use nebula filter
99a	6960	Cyg	SNR	20 45.7	+30 43	—	70 × 6	!! Veil Nebula west half; use filter!
99b	6992/5	Cyg	SNR	20 56.4	+31 43	—	72 × 8	!! Veil Nebula east half; use filter!
100	7000	Cyg	EN	20 58.8	+44 20	—	120 × 100	!! North America; use filter & low power
101	7027	Cyg	PN	21 07.1	+42 14	8.5	15″	unusual protoplanetary nebula
102	6445	Sgr	PN	17 49.2	−20 01	11.2	>34″	small, bright and annular; near M23
103	6520	Sgr	OC	18 03.4	−27 54	7.6p	6	60*; small; dark nebula B86 in same field
104	6818	Sgr	PN	19 44.0	−14 09	9.3	>17″	"Little Gem"; annular; NGC 6822 0.75° S
105	6802	Vul	OC	19 30.6	+20 16	8.8	3.2	50*, at east end of Brocchi's Cluster
106	6940	Vul	OC	20 34.6	+28 18	6.3	31	60*; fairly rich cluster in Milky Way
107	6939	Cep	OC	20 31.4	+60 38	7.8	7	80*; very rich; NGC 6946 in same field
108	6946	Cep	G-SABcd	20 34.8	+60 09	8.8	13 × 13	faint, diffuse face-on spiral near 6939
109	7129	Cep	RN	21 42.8	+66 06	—	7 × 7	faint reflection neb. around sparse cluster
110	40	Cep	PN	0 13.0	+72 32	12.4	>37″	unusual red planetary; 11.6^m central star

DEEP-SKY CHALLENGE OBJECTS

BY ALAN DYER AND ALISTER LING

The beauty of the deep sky extends well past the best and brightest objects. The attraction of observing is not the sight of an object itself but our intellectual contact with what it *is*. A faint, stellar point in Virgo evokes wonder when you try to fathom the depths of this quasar billions of light-years away. The eclectic collection of objects below is designed to introduce some "fringe" catalogues while providing challenging targets for a wide range of apertures. Often more important than sheer aperture are factors such as the quality of sky, quality of the optics, use of an appropriate filter, and the observer's experience. Don't be afraid to tackle some of these with a smaller telescope.

Objects are listed in order of right ascension. Abbreviations are the same as in the Messier and NGC lists, with DN = dark nebula. Three columns have been added: **UI** and **UII** respectively list the charts where you'll find that object in the original edition and the 2001 second edition of *Uranometria 2000.0;* the last column suggests the minimum aperture, in millimetres, needed to see that object. Most data are taken from *Sky Catalogue 2000.0, Vol. 2*. Some visual magnitudes are from other sources.

#	Object	Con	Type	RA (2000) h m	Dec ° ′	m_V	Size ′	UI	UII	Min. Aper. mm
1	**NGC 7822**	Cep	E/RN	0 03.6	+68 37	—	60 × 30	15	8	300
	large, faint emission nebula; rated "eeF"; also look for E/R nebula Ced 214 (associated w/ star cluster Berkeley 59) 1° S									
2	**IC 59**	Cas	E/RN	0 56.7	+61 04	—	10 × 5	36	18	200–250
	faint emission/reflection nebula paired with IC 63 very close to γ Cas.; requires clean optics; rated as "pF"									
3	**NGC 609**	Cas	OC	1 37.2	+64 33	11.0	3.0	16	17	250–300
	faint patch at low power; high power needed to resolve this rich cluster (also look for Trumpler 1 cluster 3° S)									
4	**IC 1795**	Cas	EN	2 24.7	+61 54	—	27 × 13	17	29	200
	brightest part of a complex of nebulosity that includes IC 1805 and IC 1848; use a nebula filter									
5	**Maffei I**	Cas	G-E3	2 36.3	+59 39	≈14	5 × 3	38	29	300
	heavily reddened galaxy; very faint; requires large aperture and black skies; nearby Maffei II for extremists									
6	**NGC 1049**	For	GC	2 39.7	−34 29	11.0	0.6	354	175	250–300
	Class V globular in dwarf "Fornax System" Local Group galaxy 630 000 ly away; galaxy itself invisible?									
7	**Abell 426**	Per	Gs	3 19.8	+41 31	12–16	≈30	63	43, A4	200–400
	Perseus galaxy cluster 300 million ly away; mag. 11.6 NGC 1275 Perseus A at centre; see close-up chart A4									
8	**NGC 1432/35**	Tau	RN	3 46.1	+23 47	—	30 × 30	132	78, A12	100–150
	Pleiades nebulosity (also includes IC 349); brightest around Merope; requires transparent skies and clean optics									
9	**IC 342**	Cam	G-SBc	3 46.8	+68 06	≈12	17 × 17	18	16	200–300
	large and diffuse face-on spiral; member of UMa–Cam cloud (Kemble's Cascade of stars also on this chart)									
10	**NGC 1499**	Per	EN	4 00.7	+36 37	—	145 × 40	95	60	80–125 RFT
	California Nebula; very large and faint; use a wide-field telescope or big binoculars plus H-beta filter									
11	**IC 405**	Aur	E/RN	5 16.2	+34 16	—	30 × 19	97	59	200
	Flaming Star Nebula associated with runaway star AE Aurigae; see Burnham's Handbook p. 285 (also look for IC 410)									
12	**HH 1**	Ori	E	5 36.3	−06 45	≈14.5	8″	271	136	250
	Herbig-Haro 1; best with no filter at 250× or more; bipolar jets from forming star; not plotted; 2.5′ SW NGC 1999									
13	**IC 434 / B 33**	Ori	E/DN	5 40.9	−2 28	—	60 × 10	226	116	100–150 in dark sky!
	B 33 is the Horsehead Nebula, a dark nebula superimposed on a very faint emission nebula IC 434; use H-beta filter									
14	**Sh 2-276**	Ori	EN	5 48	+1 –	—	600 × 30!	226	116	100–150 RFT
	Barnard's Loop; SNR or interstellar bubble? difficult to detect due to size; use filter and sweep with wide field									
15	**Abell 12**	Ori	PN	6 02.4	+9 39	≈13	37″	181	96	250–300
	plotted on UII as PK 198.6–6.3; on NW edge of μ Orionis; OIII filter required									
16	**IC 443**	Gem	SNR	6 16.9	+22 47	—	50 × 40	137	76	250–300
	faint supernova remnant very close to η Gem.; use filter (also look for NGC 2174 and Sh 2–247 on this chart)									
17	**J 900**	Gem	PN	6 25.9	+17 47	12.2	8″	137	76	200
	Jonckheere 900; bright starlike planetary; plotted as PK 194.2+2.5 in UII; use OIII filter & high power									
18	**IC 2177**	Mon	E/RN	7 05.1	−10 42	—	120 × 40	273	135	200–300
	Seagull Nebula; large, faint; contains bright patches Gum 1 (−10°28′), NGC 2327 (−11°18′) & Ced 90 (−12°20′)									

DEEP-SKY CHALLENGE OBJECTS (continued)

#	Object	Con	Type	RA (2000) h m	Dec ° ′	m_V	Size ′	UI	UII	Min. Aper. mm
19	**PK 205 +14.2**	Gem	PN	7 29.0	+13 15	≈13	≈700″	184	95	200–250
	Medusa Nebula or Abell 21; larger than plotted in UI; impressive in large aperture w/ OIII filter									
20	**PK 164 +31.1**	Lyn	PN	7 57.8	+53 25	≈14	400″	43	26	250
	extremely faint with two small components; use OIII filter; sometimes confused with nearby NGC 2474–75									
21	**Leo I**	Leo	G-E3	10 08.4	+12 18	9.8	10.7 × 8.3	189	93	300
	dwarf elliptical; satellite of Milky Way; very low surface brightness; 0.3° N of Regulus! requires clean optics									
22	**Abell 1367**	Leo	Gs	11 44.0	+19 57	13–16	≈60	147	72, A11	300–400
	cluster of some 30 or more galaxies within a 1° field near 93 Leonis; Copeland's Septet nearby									
23	**NGC 3172**	UMi	G-?	11 50.2	+89 07	13.6	0.7 × 0.7	2	1	250
	"Polarissima Borealis"—closest galaxy to the north celestial pole; small, faint, and otherwise unremarkable									
24	**NGC 4236**	Dra	G-SBb	12 16.7	+69 28	9.6	18.6 × 6.9	25	13	200–250
	very large, dim barred spiral; a diffuse glow (NGC 4395 on UII chart #54 a similar large diffuse face-on)									
25	**Mrk 205**	Dra	Quasar	12 21.6	+75 18	14.5	stellar	9	5	300
	Markarian 205; a faint star on SW edge of NGC 4319; centre of redshift controversy									
26	**3C 273**	Vir	Quasar	12 29.1	+2 03	12≈13	stellar	238	111	250–300
	at 2–3 billon ly away, one of the most distant objects visible in amateur telescopes; magnitude variable									
27	**NGC 4676**	Com	Gs	12 46.2	+30 44	14.1p	2 × 1	108	53	250
	"The Mice" or VV 224—two classic interacting galaxies; very faint double nature detectable at high power									
28	**Abell 1656**	Com	Gs	13 00.1	+27 58	12–16	≈60	149	71, A8	250–300
	Coma Berenices galaxy cluster; very rich; 400 million ly away; brightest member NGC 4889; see close-up chart A8									
29	**NGC 5053**	Com	GC	13 16.4	+17 42	9.8	10.5	150	71	100–200
	faint and very loose globular 1° SE of M53; requires large aperture to resolve; difficult in hazy skies; class XI									
30	**NGC 5897**	Lib	GC	15 17.4	−21 01	8.6	12.6	334	148	150–200
	large and loose; easily hidden in hazy skies at higher latitude; brightest stars mag 13.3, main branch mag 16.3									
31	**Abell 2065**	CrB	Gs	15 22.7	+27 43	≈16	≈30	154	69	500 in superb sky!
	Corona Borealis galaxy cluster; perhaps the most difficult object for amateur telescopes; 1.5 billion ly away									
32	**NGC 6027**	Ser	Gs	15 59.2	+20 45	≈15	2 × 1	155	69	400
	Seyfert's Sextet (6027 A–F); compact group of 6 small and very faint galaxies; see Burnham's Handbook p. 1793									
33	**B 72**	Oph	DN	17 23.5	−23 38	—	30	338	146	80–125 RFT
	Barnard's dark S-Nebula or "The Snake"; opacity of 6/6; 1.5° NNE of θ Ophiuchi; area rich in dark nebulae									
34	**NGC 6791**	Lyr	OC	19 20.7	+37 51	9.5	16	118	48	200–250
	large, faint but very rich open cluster with 300 stars; a faint smear in smaller instruments; Type II 3 r									
35	**PK 64 +5.1**	Cyg	PN	19 34.8	+30 31	9.6	8″	118	48	200
	Campbell's Hydrogen Star; very bright but very starlike; also catalogued as star BD +30°3639									
36	**M 1-92**	Cyg	RN	19 36.3	+29 33	11.0	12″ × 6″	118	48	250–300
	Minkowski 1-92 or Footprint Nebula; bright, starlike reflection nebula; double at high mag.; associated star invisible									
37	**NGC 6822**	Sgr	G-Irr	19 44.9	−14 48	≈11	10.2 × 9.5	297	125	100–150
	Barnard's Galaxy; member of the Local Group; large but very low surface brightness; requires transparent skies									
38	**Palomar 11**	Aql	GC	19 45.2	−8 00	9.8	3.2	297	125	200–300
	brightest of 15 heavily reddened GCs found on Sky Survey; magnitude is misleading; 11 Terzan GCs more challenging									
39	**IC 4997**	Sge	PN	20 20.2	+16 45	10.9	2″	163	84	200
	bright but starlike planetary; the challenge is to see the disk! blink the field with and without a nebula filter									
40	**IC 1318**	Cyg	EN	20 26.2	+40 30	—	large	84	32, A2	80–150 RFT
	complex of nebulosity around γ Cygni; multitude of patches in rich starfield; use a very wide field plus filter									
41	**PK 80 −6.1**	Cyg	PN?	21 02.3	+36 42	13.5	16″	121	47	250
	the "Egg Nebula"; a very small proto-planetary nebula; can owners of large telescopes detect polarization?									
42	**IC 1396**	Cep	EN	21 39.1	+57 30	—	170 × 140	57	19	100–125 RFT
	extremely large and diffuse area of emission nebulosity; use nebula filter and very wide field optics in dark sky									
43	**IC 5146**	Cyg	E/RN	21 53.5	+47 16	—	12 × 12	86	31	200–250
	Cocoon Nebula; faint and diffuse; use H-beta filter; at the end of the long filamentary dark nebula Barnard 168									
44	**NGC 7317–20**	Peg	Gs	22 36.1	+33 57	13–14	≈1 ea.	123	46	250–300
	Stephan's Quintet; 0.5° SSW of NGC 7331; easy to pick out 3 or 4 (also look for "companions" to 7331)									
45	**Jones 1**	Peg	PN	23 35.9	+30 28	12.1	332″	124	45	250–300
	plotted as PK 104.2 −29.6 in UII; large dim glow; OIII filter required									

SOUTHERN-HEMISPHERE SPLENDOURS

BY ALAN WHITMAN

Any serious deep-sky observer yearns to experience the far-southern sky, the home of the finest emission nebula (the Eta Carinae Nebula), the most obvious dark nebula (the Coalsack), arguably the best open cluster (NGC 3532), the most impressive globular cluster (47 Tucanae), the biggest and brightest globular cluster (Omega Centauri, although it is likely the core of a small galaxy absorbed by the Milky Way), the galaxy that offers amateur telescopes hundreds of targets within it (the Large Magellanic Cloud), and the closest naked-eye star (Alpha Centauri), just to name a few. Here is a checklist of "must-see" splendours, rated with one to three exclamation marks, plus 17 other significant objects. The author has observed all of these objects under fine, dark skies. Fans of a particular class of deep-sky object will probably want to add some members of that class that are too faint or featureless to include here.

Declination −35 was chosen as the cutoff for this list. However, three slightly more northerly objects that greatly benefit from being viewed higher in the sky were included, notably M83, because it is one of the finest face-on spiral galaxies in the southern sky, but its three spiral arms are not well seen from Canada. Countries like Australia, Chile, and Namibia offer the best views of these magnificent objects. However, most objects on the list can be viewed from the southern Caribbean; many are visible from Hawaii or from the Florida Keys; and some, including Omega Centauri, Centaurus A, and the many glorious clusters in the tail of Scorpius, can be appreciated from the American Southwest. February through April are the preferred months for a southern observing run, since there are no far-southern splendours (those with exclamation marks) located between 20h and 0h of right ascension.

Data for open and globular clusters are from Archinal and Hynes's 2003 reference book *Star Clusters,* with the two noted exceptions. Data for other objects are mostly from Malin and Frew's highly recommended 1995 guidebook *Hartung's Astronomical Objects for Southern Telescopes,* 2nd ed. The dimensions of galaxies and nebulae and a few other numbers are mostly from various lists in the *Observer's Handbook* or from Sinnott's 1988 work, *NGC 2000.0.* Various sources, including private communications, have provided some difficult-to-obtain data.

Notation used below is mostly as defined on p. 255; in addition, * = star or stars, CC = concentration class of a globular cluster (see p. 247), Ast = asterism, and DN = dark nebula. Numbers without a prefix in the **NGC** column are NGC numbers.

#	NGC	Con	Type	RA (2000) h m	Dec ° ′	m_v	Size ′	Remarks
1	55	Scl	G-Sc	0 14.9	−39 11	7.9	32 × 6	! in 100-mm scope: diffuse splinter
2	104	Tuc	GC	0 24.1	−72 05	4.0	50	!!! 47 Tuc; yellow core in 370-mm scope
3	β	Tuc	Dbl*	0 31.5	−62 58	4.4, 4.5	27″	! both blue-white
4	SMC	Tuc	G-Im	0 52.6	−72 48	2.3	3.6°	!!! many NGCs included
5	300	Scl	G-Sc	0 54.9	−37 41	8.1	22 × 16	face-on spiral; low surface brightness
6	362	Tuc	GC	1 03.2	−70 51	6.8	14	! Milky Way GC beside SMC; CC III
7	p	Eri	Dbl*	1 39.8	−56 12	5.8, 5.8	12″	! both yellow-orange dwarfs
8	1097	For	G-SBb	2 46.3	−30 17	9.3	13 × 8	! in 300-mm scope: bar and tough arms
9	θ	Eri	Dbl*	2 58.3	−40 18	3.2, 4.4	8.3″	! both white
10	1313	Ret	G-SBc	3 18.3	−66 30	8.9	9 × 7	in 370-mm scope: bar, one spiral arm
11		For	Gal Cl.	3 22.7	−37 12	—	—	position is for bright 1316, Fornax A
12	1365	For	G-SBc	3 33.6	−36 08	9.5	14 × 10	!! in 300-mm scope: bar with 2 spiral arms
13	f	Eri	Dbl*	3 48.6	−37 37	4.9, 5.4	8.1″	! yellowish stars
14	1566	Dor	G-Sc	4 20.0	−54 56	9.4	13 × 9	! in 250-mm scope: 2 classic spiral arms
15	ι	Pic	Dbl*	4 50.9	−53 28	5.6, 6.5	12.5″	! very nice yellow pair
16	1851	Col	GC	5 14.1	−40 03	7.1	12	! brightest centre of any GC; CC II
17	LMC	Dor	G-SBm	5 23.6	−69 45	0.1	7.2°	!!! many nights' work for large apertures
18	2070	Dor	EN/OC	5 38.7	−69 06	5.4	20	!!! Tarantula Nebula; "spider legs" easy

SOUTHERN-HEMISPHERE SPLENDOURS (continued)

#	NGC	Con	Type	RA (2000) h m	Dec ° ′	m_v	Size ′	Remarks
19	γ	Vol	Dbl*	7 08.7	−70 30	3.9, 5.4	14.1″	! gold and light green pair
21	2451	Pup	Ast	7 45.4	−37 57	2.8	50	! not a true OC; nice contrast with 2477
21	2477	Pup	OC	7 52.2	−38 32	5.8	20	! 300*; arcs of 12th-mag.–13th-mag. stars
22	2516	Car	OC	7 58.0	−60 45	3.8	22	!! 100*; excellent in binoculars
23	γ	Vel	Dbl*	8 09.5	−47 20	1.8, 4.3	41″	! 4*; 1.8-mag. star is brightest Wolf-Rayet
24	2547	Vel	OC	8 10.2	−49 14	4.7	25	! The Heart Cluster (description by Dyer)
25	IC 2391	Vel	OC	8 40.3	−52 55	2.6	60	! o Vel Cluster; bright stars; fine in binocs
26	2808	Car	GC	9 12.0	−64 52	6.2	14	! brightest CC I; like a pile of sand
27	3114	Car	OC	10 02.7	−60 06	4.2	35	! 120*; four arcs of stars in binocs
28	3132	Vel	PN	10 07.7	−40 26	9.2	0.8	Eight-Burst Nebula; colourless
29	3199	Car	EN	10 17.1	−57 55	9.0	22	! crescent formed by Wolf-Rayet star
30	3201	Vel	GC	10 17.6	−46 25	6.9	20	star chains right through core; CC X
31	3293	Car	OC	10 35.8	−58 14	4.7	5	!! Gem Cluster; EN/RN/DN involved
32	3324	Car	EN	10 37.3	−58 38	6.7	15	two-lobed nebula
33	IC 2602	Car	OC	10 43.0	−64 24	1.6	100	! θ Car Cl, a.k.a. the Southern Pleiades
34	3372	Car	EN	10 45.1	−59 52	2.5	80	!!! Eta Carinae Nebula[A]
35	3532	Car	OC	11 05.5	−58 44	3.0	50	!!! oblate; finest OC?; needs a wide field
36	3699	Cen	PN	11 28.0	−59 57	11.3	1.1	dark rift visible in 200-mm scope
37	3766	Cen	OC	11 36.3	−61 37	5.3	15	! triangular; 60*; λ Cen Nebula nearby
38	3918	Cen	PN	11 50.3	−57 11	8.1	0.2	! the Blue Planetary; round
39	—	Mus	DN	12 25	−72	—	3° × 12′	! the Dark Doodad; near 4372 and γ Mus
40	4372	Mus	GC	12 25.8	−72 39	7.2	19	! CC XII (size is from NGC 2000.0)
41	α	Cru	Dbl*	12 26.6	−63 06	0.8, 1.2	3.9″	! blue-white pair; 3rd star 4.9 mag. at 90″
42	DY	Cru	Red*	12 47.4	−59 42	9v	—	! Ruby Crucis; 3′ W of β Cru; B−V is 5.8
43	—	Cru	DN	12 51	−63	—	6°	!!! Coalsack; forms head of the Emu DN
44	4755	Cru	OC	12 53.6	−60 21	4.2	10	! Jewel Box; sparse in small apertures
45	4833	Mus	GC	12 59.6	−70 52	6.9	14	! CC VIII (magnitude is from W.E. Harris)
46	4945	Cen	G-Sc	13 05.1	−49 28	8.4	20 × 4	! in 500-mm scope: dark lane on SW edge
47	5128	Cen	G-S0	13 25.5	−43 01	6.8	26 × 20	!! Cen A; merging spiral and elliptical[B]
48	5139	Cen	GC	13 26.8	−47 29	3.9	55	!!! Omega Cen; huge rich oval; CC VIII
49	5189	Mus	PN	13 33.5	−65 59	9.5	2.6	! the Spiral Planetary; use OIII filter
50	M83	Hya	G-SBc	13 37.0	−29 52	7.6	16 × 13	!! in 200-mm: bar, 1 arm; 370-mm: 3 arms
51	5286	Cen	GC	13 46.4	−51 22	7.4	11	! CC V; bluish PN 5307 nearby
52	5460	Cen	OC	14 07.6	−48 18	5.6	35	25 straggling*; trapezoidal asterism in S
53	α	Cen	Dbl*	14 39.6	−60 50	0.0, 1.3	9.″	!! rapidly closing yellow pair: 22″–1.7″
54	5927	Lup	GC	15 28.0	−50 40	8.0	6	CC VIII; pair with Nor GC 5946
55	B228	Lup	DN	15 45	−34	—	4° × 20′	! an unknown wonder; opacity 6
56	5986	Lup	GC	15 46.1	−37 47	7.6	10	200-mm resolves large core; CC VII
57	6025	TrA	OC	16 03.6	−60 25	5.1	15	! triangular, in three clumps
58	6067	Nor	OC	16 13.2	−54 13	5.6	15	! 100*; many pairs
59	6087	Nor	OC	16 18.9	−57 54	5.4	15	! 40*; embedded in Norma Star Cloud
60	6124	Sco	OC	16 25.3	−40 40	5.8	40	100*; many trios around circumference
61	6231	Sco	OC	16 54.2	−41 50	2.6	14	!! ζ, 6231, and Tr 24 form the False Comet
62	6242	Sco	OC	16 55.5	−39 28	6.4	9	23*; good for small scopes
63	6259	Sco	OC	17 00.7	−44 39	8.0	15	like a fainter M11; 120*
64	6281	Sco	OC	17 04.8	−37 53	5.4	8	25*; shines in modest scopes
65	6302	Sco	PN	17 13.7	−37 06	9.6	1.5 × 0.5	Bug Nebula; bright core; knots at tips
66	IC 4651	Ara	OC	17 24.7	−49 55	6.9	10	! loops and chains of 70 equal-mag. stars
67	6388	Sco	GC	17 36.3	−44 44	6.8	10	450-mm scope resolves faint stars; CC III
68	6397	Ara	GC	17 40.7	−53 40	5.3	31	!! easily resolved 10th-mag. stars; CC IX
69	6541	CrA	GC	18 08.0	−43 42	6.3	15	! huge outer halo; CC III
70	6723	Sgr	GC	18 59.6	−36 38	6.8	13	! CC VII; part of fine complex below
71	6726–7	CrA	RN	19 01.7	−36 54	—	9 × 7	! 7th-mag. stars involved[C]
72	6752	Pav	GC	19 10.9	−59 59	5.3	29	!! easily resolved 11th-mag. stars; CC VI[D]
73	7582	Gru	G-SBb	23 18.4	−42 22	10.2	4 × 1	brightest member of Grus Quartet

[A] Chevron-shaped dark lane, many other DN involved, including Keyhole Nebula; tiny orange mag. 5 (variable) Homunculus Nebula at centre; four OC involved

[B] Prominent broad dark lane; 370-mm scope reveals thin bright streak within the dark lane

[C] Part of !! complex with GC 6723, DN Bernes 157 (55′ long, opacity 6), variable RN 6729 (involved with R CrA), headlight Dbl* Brs 14 (mags. 6.6, 6.8 at 13″), and Dbl* γ CrA (both yellow-white, mags. 4.9, 5.0 at 1.3″ and widening)

[D] Curving star chains converge to a tiny central peak; very tight group of four 12th-mag. galaxies 1° SE

DARK NEBULAE

By Paul Gray

Dark nebulae, often appearing as "holes in space," are fascinating to observe. The following is a representative selection of visually observable dark nebulae. The **minimum aperture** in millimetres is what observers have found to be necessary to see each nebula; however, many may be observable with smaller apertures under excellent skies. Quality of optics, the observer's experience, and full dark adaptation are often more important than the size of the aperture. Some objects will also benefit from the use of a filter because they are superimposed upon a bright nebula.

Objects are listed in order of right ascension. The column **UI/II** lists the charts in the *Uranometria 2000.0,* editions 1 and 2, respectively, that contain the object; *italics* indicate that the object is not actually marked in the given chart. The **opacity** is based on a scale of 1 to 6, with 6 being the easiest to observe; no objects of opacity 1 or 2 are listed, since these objects are very difficult to observe visually. Two objects (L 889 and L 896) are from the *Lynds Catalogue,* one (LG 3) is from the *Le Gentil Catalogue,* and one is uncatalogued; all others are from the *Barnard Catalogue*. Showpiece objects are marked "!!." For further information, including finder charts and images, and to view or submit an observation report, visit www.rasc.ca/handbook/darkneb.

#	B	Con	RA (2000) h m	Dec ° ′	UI/II	Size ′	Opa-city	Min. Aper. mm	Remarks
1	5	Per	3 48.0	+32 54	*95*/60	22 × 9	5	200	1° NE of o Per
2	211/3	Tau	4 17.2	+27 48	*133*/78	12 × 110	3	200–250	narrow NW–SE lanes, faint bkgd starfield
3	33	Ori	5 40.9	−2 28	*226*/116	6 × 4	4	100–150	Horsehead Nebula; use H-beta filter
4	34	Aur	5 43.5	+32 39	*98*/59	20	4	200	2° W of M37; spider-like appearance
5	35	Ori	5 45.5	+9 03	181/96	20 × 10	5	150–200	near FU Ori and bright nebula Ced 59
6	37	Mon	6 33	+11	*182*/96	3°	5	150 RFT	near NGC 2245, 2247; try binoculars
7	40	Sco	16 14.7	−18 59	335/147	15	3	250	in bright nebula IC 4592; 50′ NE of ν Sco
8	44	Oph	16 40.0	−24 04	336/146	35 × 300	6	10 × 70	large dark rift; naked eye in superb sky
9	59	Oph	17 11.4	−27 29	337/146	60	6	10 × 70	3° SW of θ Oph; part of stem of Pipe Nebula
10	64	Oph	17 17.2	−18 32	337/146	20	6	150–200	30′ W of M9; causes darkening of M9
11	68	Oph	17 22.6	−23 44	338/146	3	6	200	small; near B72; region rich in dark nebulae
12	70	Oph	17 23.6	−23 58	338/146	4	4	200	small; near B72; region rich in dark nebulae
13	72	Oph	17 23.6	−23 38	338/146	30	6	80–125	!! the Snake; "S" shape; 1.5° N of θ Oph
14	78	Oph	17 33	−26	338/146	3°	6	eye	!! Pipe bowl, "Prancing Horse" hindquarters
15	84A	Sgr	17 57.5	−17 40	339/146	16	5	150–200	1.5° N of M23; try for extensions to S
16	85	Sgr	18 02.6	−23 02	339/145	5	4	100	!! dark lanes inside Trifid Nebula (M20)
17	86	Sgr	18 02.7	−27 50	339/145	4	5	200	!! Ink Spot; nice pair with NGC 6520 5′ E
18	87	Sgr	18 04.3	−32 30	377/163	12	4	200	Parrot's Head; 2° S of γ Sgr
19	88	Sgr	18 04.4	−24 07	339/145	2	4	200	on edge of M8; *not* Burnham's "Dark Comet"
20		Sgr	18 04.5	−24 14	*339/145*	2 × 1	4	200	Burnham's "Dark Comet"; use filter
21	303	Sgr	18 09.2	−24 07	339/145	1	5	200–250	inside IC 4685; use filter; challenging
22	92/3	Sgr	18 15.5	−18 11	339/145	12 × 6	6	7 × 50	!! on NW edge of Small Sgr Star Cloud, M24
23	103	Sct	18 39.2	−6 37	295/126	40 × 40	6	10 × 70	on NW side of Scutum star cloud
24	104	Sct	18 47.3	−4 32	250/105	16 × 1	5	150–200	20′ N of β Sct; a checkmark shape
25	108	Sct	18 49.6	−6 19	295/125	3	3	200	30′ W of M11; rich region
26	112	Sct	18 51.2	−6 40	295/125	20	4	200	30′ S of M11; also look for B114, B118
27	133	Aql	19 06.1	−6 50	296/125	10 × 3	6	100	on Scutum star cloud; very dark spot!
28	142/3	Aql	19 40.7	+10 57	*207*/85	80 × 50	6	10 × 50	!! Barnard's famous "E" cloud
29	145	Cyg	20 02.8	+37 40	*119*/48	6 × 35	4	200	triangular shape
30	L 889	Cyg	20 24.8	+40 10	*85*/48	100 × 20	–	7 × 50	within γ Cygni Nebula, IC 1318
31	L 896	Cyg	20 37	+42	*85*/48	6°	–	eye	"Northern Coalsack"
32	150	Cep	20 50.6	+60 18	*56*/20	60 × 3	5	250	curved filament 1.6° S of η Cep
33	353	Cyg	20 57.1	+45 32	85/32	20 × 10	5	100	in N of North America Nebula; B352 in field
34	LG 3	Cyg	21 00	+53	*85/32*	12°	–	eye	!! "Funnel Cloud Nebula"; best after Coalsack
35	361	Cyg	21 12.9	+47 22	*86*/32	20	4	100	cluster IC 1369 to N; try for 1°-tendril to W
36	365	Cep	21 34.9	+56 43	57/19	22 × 3	4	200	in IC 1396; indistinct "S" shape; use filter
37	163	Cep	21 42.2	+56 42	57/19	4	4	200	in IC 1396; use filter
38	168	Cyg	21 49.0	+47 29	86/31	100 × 20	5	7 × 50	large E–W lane; Cocoon Nebula at E end

GALAXIES: BRIGHTEST AND NEAREST

BY BARRY F. MADORE

External galaxies are generally of such low surface brightness that they often prove disappointing objects for the amateur observer. However, it must be remembered that many of these galaxies were discovered with very small telescopes and that the enjoyment of their discovery can be recaptured. In addition, the central concentration of light varies from galaxy to galaxy, making a visual classification of the types possible at the telescope. Indeed, the type of galaxy as listed in Table 1 (p. 268) is in part based on the fraction of light coming from the central bulge of the galaxy as compared to the contribution from a disk component. Disk galaxies with dominant bulges are classified as Sa; as the nuclear contribution declines, types of Sb, Sc, and Sd are assigned until the nucleus is absent at type Sm. Often the disks of these galaxies show spiral symmetry, the coherence and strength of which is denoted by Roman numerals I through V, smaller numbers indicating well-formed global spiral patterns. Those spirals with central bars are designated SB, while those with only a hint of a disk embedded in the bulge are called S0. A separate class of galaxies that possess no disk component are called ellipticals and can only be further classified numerically by their apparent flattening, with E0 being apparently round and E7 being the most flattened.

Environment appears to play an important role in determining the types of galaxies we see at the present epoch. Rich clusters of galaxies, such as the system in Coma, are dominated by ellipticals and gas-free S0 galaxies. The less dense clusters and groups tend to be dominated by the spiral, disk galaxies. Remarkably, pairs of galaxies are much more frequently of the same Hubble type than random selection would predict. Encounters between disk galaxies may in some cases result in the instabilities necessary to form the spiral structure we often see. M51 (the Whirlpool) and its companion, NGC 5195, are an often-cited example of this type of interaction. In the past, when the universe was much more densely packed, interactions and collisions may have been sufficiently frequent that entire galaxies merged to form a single large new system; it has been suggested that some elliptical galaxies formed in this way.

Table 1 lists the 40 brightest galaxies taken from the *Revised Shapley-Ames Catalog*. As well as their designations, positions, and types, the table lists the total blue magnitudes, major and minor axis lengths (to the nearest minute of arc), one modern estimate of their distances in 10^6 ly, and their radial velocities corrected for the motion of our Sun about the galactic centre. Although the universe as a whole is in expansion, there are parts that are still bound together (or at the very least, held back in their expansion) by gravity. These groups and clusters are, in essence, representative of the largest material structures in the universe. Recently, large-scale flows of material have been reported, far in excess of the velocities expected due to the perturbing presence of other galaxies and clusters of galaxies. Either there are exceedingly large concentrations of matter yet to be discovered just beyond our limited view of the world, or the universe has had a much more interesting history than our present theories indicate. The brightest and nearest galaxies in Table 1 may be moving not only as a result of the universal expansion, but also through very complex interactions with distant parts as yet only postulated but not seen.

TABLE 1—THE 40 OPTICALLY BRIGHTEST SHAPLEY-AMES GALAXIES

NGC/IC	Other	RA (2000) h m s	Dec ° ′	Type	Magnitude B_T	Size ′	Distance 10^6 ly	Rad. Vel. km/s
55		0 15 08	−39 13.2	Sc	8.22	32 × 6	10.	+115
205	M110	0 40 23	+41 41.3	S0/E5pec	8.83	22 × 11	2.4	+49
221	M32	0 42 41	+40 51.9	E2	9.01	9 × 7	2.4	+86
224	M31	0 42 45	+41 16.5	Sb I–II	4.38	190 × 60	2.4	−10
247		0 47 10	−20 45.6	Sc III–IV	9.51	21 × 7	10.	+604
253		0 47 36	−25 17.4	Sc	8.13	28 × 7	14.	+504
SMC		0 52 38	−72 48.0	Im IV–V	2.79	320 × 185	0.2	+359
300		0 54 53	−37 41.2	Sc III	8.70	22 × 16	7.8	+625
598	M33	1 33 53	+30 39.2	Sc II–III	6.26	71 × 42	2.2	+506
628	M74	1 36 42	+15 47.2	Sc I	9.77	10 × 10	55.	+507
1068	M77	2 42 41	0 00.9	Sb II	9.55	7 × 6	82.	+510
1291		3 17 19	−41 06.5	SBa	9.42	10 × 8	49.	+512
1313		3 18 16	−66 29.9	SBc III–IV	9.37	9 × 7	17.	+261
1316	Fornax A	3 22 42	−37 12.5	Sa (pec)	9.60	12 × 9	98.	+1713
LMC		5 23 36	−69 45.4	SBm III	0.63	645 × 550	0.2	+34
2403		7 36 54	+65 35.9	Sc III	8.89	22 × 12	12.	+299
2903		9 32 10	+21 29.9	Sc I–III	9.50	13 × 6	31.	+472
3031	M81	9 55 34	+69 04.1	SbI–II	7.86	27 × 14	12.	+124
3034	M82	9 55 54	+69 40.7	Amorphous	9.28	11 × 4	12.	+409
3521		11 05 49	−0 02.0	Sb II–III	9.64	11 × 5	42.	+627
3627	M66	11 20 15	+12 59.1	Sb II	9.74	9 × 4	39.	+593
4258	M106	12 18 57	+47 18.4	Sb II	8.95	19 × 7	33.	+520
4449		12 28 12	+44 05.8	Sm IV	9.85	6 × 4	16.	+250
4472	M49	12 29 47	+7 59.8	E1/S0	9.32	10 × 8	72.	+822
4486	M87	12 30 50	+12 23.6	E0	9.62	8 × 7	72.	+1136
4594	M104	12 40 00	−11 37.4	Sa/b	9.28	9 × 4	55.	+873
4631		12 42 05	+32 32.4	Sc	9.84	16 × 3	39.	+606
4649	M60	12 43 40	+11 33.1	S0	9.83	7 × 6	72.	+1142
4736	M94	12 50 54	+41 07.1	Sab	8.92	11 × 9	23.	+345
4826	M64	12 56 45	+21 41.0	Sab II	9.37	10 × 5	23.	+350
4945		13 05 26	−49 28.0	Sc	9.60	20 × 4	23.	+275
5055	M63	13 15 50	+42 01.7	Sbc II–III	9.33	13 × 7	36.	+550
5128	Cen A	13 25 29	−43 01.0	S0 (pec)	7.89	26 × 20	23.	+251
5194	M51	13 29 53	+47 11.9	Sbc I–II	8.57	11 × 7	36.	+541
5236	M83	13 37 00	−29 52.0	SBc II	8.51	13 × 12	23.	+275
5457	M101	14 03 13	+54 21.0	Sc I	8.18	29 × 27	25.	+372
6744		19 09 46	−63 51.3	Sbc II	9.24	20 × 13	42.	+663
6822		19 44 57	−14 47.7	Im IV–V	9.35	16 × 14	2.2	+15
6946		20 34 51	+60 09.4	Sc II	9.68	12 × 10	22.	+336
7793		23 57 49	−32 35.4	Sd IV	9.65	9 × 6	14.	+241

The nearest galaxies, listed in Table 2, form what is known as the Local Group of Galaxies. Many of the distances are still quite uncertain. However, in the present Hubble Space Telescope era these galaxies are prime targets for a generation of astronomers intent on accurately determining each of their distances to the best possible precision.

TABLE 2—THE NEAREST GALAXIES—OUR LOCAL GROUP

Name	RA (2000.0) h m	Dec ° ′	Magnitude B_T	Type	Distance 10^6 ly
Milky Way Galaxy	—	—	—	Sb/c	—
IC 10	0 20.4	+59 17	11.8	IBm	2.6
NGC 147	0 33.2	+48 30	10.36	dE5	2.0
And III	0 35.3	+36 31	13.5	dE	2.4
NGC 185	0 38.9	+48 20	10.13	dE3 pec	2.4
M110 = NGC 205	0 40.4	+41 41	8.83	S0/E5 pec	2.4
M31 = NGC 224	0 42.7	+41 16	4.38	Sb I–II	2.4
M32 = NGC 221	0 42.7	+40 52	9.01	E2	2.4
And I	0 45.7	+38 01	13.5	dE	2.6
SMC	0 52.7	−72 49	2.79	Im IV–V	0.2
Sculptor	1 00.2	−33 42	10.5	dE	0.3
LGS 3	1 03.8	+21 53	18.0	Irr	2.4
IC 1613	1 04.8	+2 07	10.00	Im V	2.4
And II	1 16.5	+33 26	13.5	dE	2.4
M33 = NGC 598	1 33.9	+30 39	6.26	Sc II–III	2.2
Fornax	2 39.9	−34 32	9.1	dE	0.4
LMC	5 23.7	−69 45	0.63	SBm III	0.2
Carina	6 41.6	−50 58	—	dE	0.6
Antlia	10 04.0	−27 20	16.2	dE	4.0
Leo I	10 08.5	+12 19	11.27	dE	0.8
Sextans	10 13.0	−1 36	12.0	dE	0.3
Leo II	11 13.5	+22 09	12.85	dE	0.8
Ursa Minor	15 08.8	+67 12	11.9	dE	0.2
Draco	17 20.1	+57 55	10.9	dE	0.3
Sagittarius	19 00.0	−30 30	15.5	IBm:	0.1
NGC 6822	19 45.0	−14 48	9.35	Im IV–V	1.7

Editor's Notes:

(1) Aside from those famous companions of the Milky Way Galaxy, the Large Magellanic Cloud (LMC), and the Small Magellanic Cloud (SMC), there is only one galaxy beyond our own that is easily visible to unaided human eyes: M31, the Andromeda Galaxy (730 kpc or 2.4 Mly distant). M33, the Triangulum Galaxy, can also be seen, but this is a difficult observation. To locate M31, see the NOVEMBER ALL-SKY MAP on p. 280, where the tiny cluster of six dots above the first "A" of "ANDROMEDA" indicates its location. With modest optical aid (e.g. binoculars) a dozen or more of the galaxies listed in Table 1 can be seen by experienced observers under dark skies. With a 250-mm telescope, the quasar 3C 273, at one thousand times the distance of M31, can elicit a noticeable signal in the visual cortex (see p. 263).

(2) An interesting article by G. Lake entitled "Cosmology of the Local Group" appears in *Sky & Telescope,* December 1992, p. 613.

(3) The National Aeronautics and Space Administration/Infrared Processing and Analysis Center (NASA/IPAC) Extragalactic Database (NED) is a comprehensive compilation of extragalactic data for over 7.6 million distinct extragalactic objects. The database includes most major catalogues and offers references to and abstracts of articles of extragalactic interest that have appeared in most major journals. Also online are over 21 million photometric measurements and over 2 million images. It is possible to search the main NED database for objects selected by catalogue prefix, position, type, or redshift. The database is available at:

nedwww.ipac.caltech.edu

A knowledgebase of review articles and basic information is available at:

nedwww.ipac.caltech.edu/level5

GALAXIES WITH PROPER NAMES

BY BARRY F. MADORE

Below are the catalogue designations and positions of galaxies known to have proper names which usually honour the discoverer (e.g. McLeish's Object), identify the constellation in which the galaxy is found (e.g. Andromeda Galaxy), or describe the galaxy in some easily remembered way (e.g. Whirlpool Galaxy).

Galaxy Name	Other Names / Remarks	RA (2000) h m	Dec ° ′
Ambartsumian's Knot	NGC 3561, UGC 06224, ARP 105	11 11.2	+28 42
Andromeda Galaxy	M31, NGC 224, UGC 00454	0 42.7	+41 16
Andromeda I		0 45.7	+38 01
Andromeda II		1 16.5	+33 26
Andromeda III		0 35.3	+36 31
Antennae Galaxy	Ring Tail, NGC 4038/39, ARP 244	12 01.9	−18 52
Antlia Dwarf	AM 1001-270	10 04.0	−27 20
Aquarius Dwarf	DDO 210	20 46.9	−12 51
Arp's Galaxy		11 19.6	+51 30
Atoms For Peace	NGC 7252, ARP 226	22 20.8	−24 41
Baade's Galaxies A & B	MCG+07-02-018/19	0 49.9	+42 35
Barbon's Galaxy	Markarian 328, ZWG 497.042	23 37.7	+30 08
Barnard's Galaxy	NGC 6822, IC 4895, DDO 209	19 44.9	−14 48
Bear's Paw (Claw)	NGC 2537, UGC 04274, ARP 6	8 13.2	+46 00
BL Lacertae		22 02.7	+42 17
Black Eye Galaxy	M64, NGC 4826, UGC 08062	12 56.7	+21 41
Bode's Galaxies	M81/82, NGC 3031/4, UGC 05318/22	9 55.7	+69 23
Burbidge Chain	MCG-04-03-010 to 13	0 47.5	−20 26
BW Tauri	UGC 03087, MCG+01-12-009	4 33.2	+5 21
Carafe Galaxy	Cannon's Carafe, near NGC 1595/98	4 28.0	−47 54
Carina Dwarf		6 41.6	−50 58
Cartwheel Galaxy	Zwicky's Cartwheel, MCG-06-02-022a	0 37.4	−33 44
Centaurus A	NGC 5128, ARP 153	13 25.5	−43 01
Circinus Galaxy		14 13.2	−65 20
Coddington's Nebula	IC 2574, UGC 05666, DDO 81	10 28.4	+68 25
Copeland Septet	MCG+04-28-004/05/07 to 11, UGC 06597, UGC 06602, ARP 320, NGC 3745/46/48/50/51/53/54†	11 37.8	+21 59
Cygnus A	MCG+07-41-003	19 59.4	+40 43
Draco Dwarf	UGC 10822, DDO 208	17 20.2	+57 55
Exclamation Mark Galaxy		0 39.3	−43 06
The Eyes	NGC 4435/8, UGC 07574/5, ARP 120a,b	12 27.7	+13 03
Fath 703	NGC 5892	15 13.7	−15 29
Fornax A	NGC 1316, ARP 154	3 22.7	−37 12
Fornax Dwarf	MCG-06-07-001	2 39.9	−34 32
Fourcade-Figueroa	MCG-07-28-004	13 34.8	−45 33
The Garland	S of NGC 3077 = UGC 05398	10 04.2	+68 40
Grus Quartet	NGC 7552/82/90/99	23 17.8	−42 26
GR 8 (Gibson Reaves)	UGC 08091, DDO 155	12 58.7	+14 13
Hardcastle's Galaxy	MCG-05-31-039	13 13.0	−32 41
Helix Galaxy	NGC 2685, UGC 04666, ARP 336	8 55.6	+58 44
Hercules A	MCG+01-43-006	16 51.2	+4 59
Hoag's Object		15 17.2	+21 35

† Position errors caused these to be historically marked as nonexistent in the NGC and RNGC.

GALAXIES WITH PROPER NAMES (continued)

Galaxy Name	Other Names / Remarks	RA (2000) h m	Dec ° ′
Holmberg I	UGC 05139, DDO 63	9 40.5	+71 11
Holmberg II	UGC 04305, DDO 50, ARP 268	8 19.3	+70 43
Holmberg III	UGC 04841	9 14.6	+74 14
Holmberg IV	UGC 08837, DDO 185	13 54.7	+53 54
Holmberg V	UGC 08658	13 40.6	+54 20
Holmberg VI	NGC 1325a	3 24.9	−21 20
Holmberg VII	UGC 07739, DDO 137	12 34.7	+06 17
Holmberg VIII	UGC 08303, DDO 166	13 13.3	+36 12
Holmberg IX	UGC 05336, DDO 66	9 57.6	+69 03
Horologium Dwarf	Schuster's Spiral	3 59.2	−45 52
Hydra A	MCG-02-24-007	9 18.1	−12 06
Integral Sign Galaxy	UGC 03697, MCG+12-07-028	7 11.4	+71 50
Keenan's System	NGC 5216/16a/18, UGC 08528/9, ARP 104	13 32.2	+62 43
Kowal's Object		19 29.9	−17 41
Large Magellanic Cloud	Nubecula Major	5 23.6	−69 45
Leo I	Regulus Dwarf, UGC 05470, DDO 74, Harrington-Wilson #1	10 08.5	+12 18
Leo II	Leo B, UGC 06253, DDO 93, Harrington-Wilson #2	11 13.4	+22 10
Leo III	Leo A, UGC 05364, DDO 69	9 59.3	+30 45
Lindsay-Shapley Ring	Graham A	6 42.8	−74 15
Lost Galaxy	NGC 4535, UGC 07727	12 34.3	+8 11
McLeish's Object		20 09.7	−66 13
Maffei I	UGCA 34	2 36.3	+59 39
Maffei II	UGCA 39	2 42.0	+59 37
Malin 1		12 37.0	+14 20
Mayall's Object	MCG+07-23-019, ARP 148	11 03.9	+40 50
Mice	NGC 4676a/b, UGC 07938/9, IC 819/20, ARP 242	12 46.1	+30 44
Miniature Spiral	NGC 3928, UGC 06834	11 51.8	+48 41
Minkowski's Object	ARP 133 (NE of NGC 541)	1 25.8	−01 21
Pancake	NGC 2685, UGC 04666, ARP 336	8 55.6	+58 44
Papillon	IC 708, UGC 06549	11 33.9	+49 03
Pegasus Dwarf	UGC 12613, DDO 216	23 28.5	+14 44
Perseus A	NGC 1275/6, UGC 02669	3 19.8	+41 31
Phoenix Dwarf Irr.		1 51.1	−44 26
Pinwheel Galaxy	see also Triangulum Galaxy	1 33.9	+30 39
Pinwheel Galaxy	M99, NGC 4254, UGC 07345	12 18.8	+14 25
Pinwheel Galaxy	M101, NGC 5457, UGC 08981, ARP 26	14 03.3	+54 22
Pisces Cloud	NGC 379/80/82-85, UGC 00682/3/6-9, ARP 331	1 07.5	+32 25
Pisces Dwarf	LGS 3	0 03.8	+21 54
Polarissima Australis	NGC 2573	1 42.0‡	−89 20
Polarissima Borealis	NGC 3172, ZWG 370.002	11 50.3‡	+89 07
Reinmuth 80	NGC 4517a, UGC 07685	12 32.5	+0 23
Reticulum Dwarf	Sersic 040.03	4 36.2	−58 50
Sagittarius Dwarf		19 30.0	−17 41
Sculptor Dwarf	MCG-06-03-015	1 00.2	−33 42
Sculptor Dwarf Irr.		0 08.1	−34 34

‡The high declination of these objects makes the RA particularly uncertain.

GALAXIES WITH PROPER NAMES (continued)

Galaxy Name	Other Names / Remarks	**RA** (2000) h m	**Dec** ° ′
Seashell Galaxy	Companion to NGC 5291	13 47.4	−30 23
Sextans A	UGCA 205, MCG-01-26-030, DDO 75	10 11.0	−4 41
Sextans B	UGC 05373, DDO 70	10 00.0	+5 19
Sextans C	UGC 05439	10 05.6	+00 04
Sextans Dwarf		10 13.1	−1 37
Seyfert's Sextet	Serpens Sextet, NGC 6027/6027a-e, UGC 10116	15 59.2	+20 46
Shapley-Ames 1		1 05.1	−6 13
Shapley-Ames 2	NGC 4507	12 35.1	−39 55
Shapley-Ames 3	MCG-02-33-015	12 49.4	−10 07
Shapley-Ames 4	UGC 08041	12 55.2	+0 07
Shapley-Ames 5	MCG-07-42-001	20 24.0	−44 00
Shapley-Ames 6		21 23.2	+45 46
Siamese Twins	NGC 4567/4568	12 36.5	+11 15
Silver Coin	Sculptor Galaxy, NGC 253, UGCA 13	0 47.6	−25 18
Small Magellanic Cloud	Nubecula Minor	0 52.7	−72 50
Sombrero Galaxy	M104, NGC 4594	12 39.9	−11 37
Spider	UGC 05829, DDO 84	10 42.6	+34 27
Spindle Galaxy	NGC 3115	10 05.2	−7 42
Stephan's Quintet	NGC 7317-20, UGC 12099-102, ARP 319	22 36.0	+33 58
Sunflower Galaxy	M63, NGC 5055, UGC 08334	13 15.8	+42 02
Triangulum Galaxy	Pinwheel, M33, NGC 598, UGC 01117	1 33.9	+30 39
Ursa Minor Dwarf	UGC 09749, DDO 199	15 08.8	+67 12
Virgo A	M87, NGC 4486, UGC 07654, ARP 152	12 30.8	+12 23
Whirlpool Galaxy	Rosse's Galaxy, Question Mark Galaxy, M51, NGC 5194/5, UGC 08493/4, ARP 85	13 29.9	+47 12
Wild's Triplet	MCG-01-30-032 to 34, ARP 248	11 46.8	−3 49
Wolf-Lundmark-Melotte	MCG-03-01-015, DDO 221	0 02.0	−15 28
Zwicky #2	UGC 06955, DDO 105	11 58.4	+38 03
Zwicky's Triplet	UGC 10586, ARP 103	16 49.5	+45 30

Catalogues:

AM *Catalogue of Southern Peculiar Galaxies and Associations,* by H.C. Arp and B.F. Madore, Cambridge University Press (1987).

ARP *Atlas of Peculiar Galaxies,* H. Arp, *Ap. J. Suppl. 14,* 1 (1966).

DDO *David Dunlap Observatory Publ.,* S. van den Bergh, II, No. 5, 147 (1959).

IC *Index Catalogue,* J.L.E. Dreyer, *Mem. R.A.S.* (1895–1910).

MCG *Morphological Catalogue of Galaxies,* B.A. Vorontsov-Velyaminovet al., Moscow State University, Moscow (1961–1974).

NGC *New General Catalogue of Nebulae and Clusters of Stars,* J.L.E. Dreyer, *Mem. R.A.S.* (1888).

RNGC *The Revised New General Catalogue of Nonstellar Astronomical Objects,* J.W. Sulentic and W.G. Tifft, University of Arizona Press (1973).

UGC *Uppsala General Catalogue of Galaxies,* P. Nilson, *Nova Acta Regiae Societatis Scientiarum Upsaliensis,* Ser. V: A, Vol. 1, Uppsala, Sweden (1973).

UGCA *Catalogue of Selected Non-UGC Galaxies,* P. Nilson, Uppsala Astronomical Observatory (1974).

ZWG *Catalogue of Galaxies and Clusters of Galaxies,* F. Zwicky et al., Vol. 1–6, California Institute of Technology (1961–1968).

RADIO SOURCES

BY KEN TAPPING

There are many types of cosmic radio sources, driven by a wide variety of processes. Some are thermal, that is, producing radio emissions because they have a temperature above absolute zero. Others involve the interaction of high-energy electrons with magnetic fields or complicated interactions of waves with plasmas. There are radio spectral lines from some atoms (such as the 21-cm emission from cosmic hydrogen) and an ever-increasing number of discovered molecular lines originating in cold, dense parts of the interstellar medium.

In this article we list cosmic radio sources that can be observed using small radio telescopes. Flux densities are listed for frequencies of 0.1, 0.5, 1, and 4 GHz (wavelength 3 m, 60 cm, 30 cm, and 7.5 cm respectively). The latter frequency corresponds to highly sensitive and easily available 3.7–4.2 GHz satellite TV receivers for radio astronomy. The unit of flux density used is the Jansky (Jy), where 1 Jy = 10^{-26} W·m^{-2}Hz^{-1}. In the table, m denotes visual magnitude, and z redshift.

The main solar system radio sources are the Sun, the Moon, and Jupiter. The Sun produces strong thermal emission, with enhanced emission from active regions. Flares produce intense radio bursts of seconds to minutes in duration. The flux densities for the undisturbed (quiet) Sun are 20 000, 25 0000, 450 000, and 800 000 Jy. The lunar emission is thermal and equivalent to a mean blackbody temperature of about 225 K. Flux densities are 5, 120, 480, and 8000 Jy. Wavelengths shorter than about 3 cm originate close to the lunar surface and show the temperature variations over the lunar day. Longer wavelengths come from farther down, where the temperature remains more constant. Jupiter is a bright radio source at metre wavelengths, producing strong bursts of emission.

For more information see: *Radio Astronomy,* by J.D. Kraus (Cygnus-Quasar Books, Powell, Ohio, 1986); *Astronomy, 5* (12), 50 (1977); *JRASC, 72,* L5, L22, L38,... (1978); and *Sky & Telescope, 55,* 385 and 475, and *56,* 28 and 114 (1978). Some maps of the radio sky can be found in *Sky & Telescope, 63,* 230 (1982). Some projects to try are described in *Radio Astronomy Projects,* by William Lonc (Radio-Sky Publishing, 1997). Relevant information can be found on the following Web sites: UK Amateur Radio Astronomy Network (www.ukaranet.org.uk) and the Society of Amateur Radio Astronomers (www.qsl.net/SARA).

Source	RA (2000) h m	Dec ° ′	Flux Densities Jy	Remarks
3C10	0 25.3	+64 08	180/85/56/10	remnant of Tycho's Supernova (1572)
W3	2 25.4	+62 06	—/80/150/134	IC 1795; complex, bright HII region; OH emission
3C84	3 25.4	+41 32	40/25/17/47	NGC 1725, Seyfert galaxy; m = 12.7, z = 0.018
Fornax A	3 20.4	−37 22	900/160/110/40	NGC 1316, galaxy; m = 10.1, z = 0.006
Pictor A	5 19.9	−45 47	440/140/100/50	galaxy; m = 15.8, z = 0.034
Taurus A	5 34.5	+22 01	1450/1250/1000/360	Crab Nebula; remnant of 1054 supernova
Orion A	5 35.3	−5 25	90/200/360/330	Orion Neb.; HII star-forming region; OH, IR source
3C157	6 17.6	+22 42	360/195/180/20	IC 443; supernova remnant
Puppis A	8 20.3	−42 48	650/300/100	supernova remnant
Hydra A	9 18.1	−12 05	390/110/65/25	galaxy; m =14.8, z = 0.052
3C273	12 29.1	+2 03	150/57/49/30	brightest quasar; m = 13.0, z = 0.158
Virgo A	12 30.8	+12 23	1950/450/300/170	M87, elliptical galaxy with jet
Centaurus A	13 25.4	−43 02	8500/2500/1400	NGC 5128; galaxy; m = 7.5, z = 0.002
3C295	14 11.4	+52 12	95/60/28/10	galaxy; m = 20.5, z = 0.461
Hercules A	16 51.2	+5 01	800/120/65/11	galaxy; m = 18.5, z = 0.154
Gal. Centre	17 42.0	−28 50	4400/2900/1800	strong, diffuse emission from galactic centre
Sagittarius A	17 42.5	−28 55	100/250/200/336	compact source at gal. cen.; assoc. with black hole?
Cygnus A	19 59.5	+40 44	15500/4000/2100/370	strong radio galaxy
Cygnus X	20 22.6	+40 23	400/150/30/70	complex region
Cassiopeia A	23 23.4	+58 49	25000/4500/2800/806	supernova remnant

MAPS OF THE NIGHT SKY

By Roy Bishop

The maps on pp. 275–281 cover the entire sky. Stars are shown down to a magnitude of 4.5 or 5, that is, those that are readily apparent to the unaided eye on a reasonably dark night.

The first six maps are drawn for latitude 45°N but are useful for latitudes several degrees north or south of this. They show the hemisphere of sky visible at various times of year. Because the aspect of the night sky changes continuously with both longitude and time, while time zones change discontinuously with both longitude and time of year, it is not possible to state simply when a particular observer will find that his or her sky fits exactly one of the six maps. The month indicated above each map is the time of year when the map will match the "late evening" sky. On any particular night, successive maps will represent the sky as it appears every four hours later. For example, at 2:00 or 3:00 on a March night, the May map should be used. Just after dinner on a January night, the November map will be appropriate. The centre of each map is the *zenith,* the point directly overhead; the circumference is the horizon. To identify the stars, hold the map in front of you so that the part of the horizon you are facing (west, for instance) is downward. (The four letters around the periphery of each map indicate compass directions.)

The southern sky map is centred on the south celestial pole and extends to 20°S declination at its periphery. Thus there is considerable overlap with the southern areas of the other maps. Note that the orientation of the various names is generally inverted compared to that on the first six maps. This is in recognition that most users of this Handbook will be residents of the Northern Hemisphere and will make use of the southern sky map when they make trips to the tropics. Thus in "normal" use this map will be read in an area above its centre, unlike the first six maps, which are normally read below their centres. The months indicated around the edge of the map may be used to orient it to each of the preceding six maps and have the same "late evening" significance as explained above. Tick marks around the edge of the map indicate hours of right ascension, with hours 0, 3, 6, etc., labelled. Starting at the centre of the map, the series of small crosses along 0h right ascension indicates southern declinations 90°, 80°, 70°,..., 20°. With the aid of a drawing compass, an observer in the Northern Hemisphere can quickly locate a circle, centred on the south celestial pole, which represents the southern limit of his or her sky.

On all seven maps, stars forming the usual constellation patterns are linked by straight lines, constellation names being given in uppercase letters. Three constellations (Horologium, Mensa, and Microscopium) consist of faint stars; hence no patterns are indicated and the names are placed in parentheses. Small clusters of dots indicate the positions of bright star clusters, nebulae, or galaxies. The pair of wavy dotted lines indicates roughly the borders of the Milky Way. Small asterisks locate the directions of the galactic centre (GC), the north galactic pole (NGP), and the south galactic pole (SGP). LMC, SMC, and CS signify, respectively, the Large Magellanic Cloud, the Small Magellanic Cloud, and the Coal Sack. Two dashed lines appear on each of the first six maps. The one with more dashes is the celestial equator. Tick marks along this indicate hours of right ascension, the odd hours being labelled. The line with fewer dashes is the ecliptic, the apparent annual path of the Sun across the heavens. Letters along this line indicate the approximate position of the Sun at the beginning of each month. Also located along the ecliptic are the Northern Hemisphere vernal equinox (VE), summer solstice (SS), autumnal equinox (AE), and winter solstice (WS).

JANUARY ALL-SKY MAP

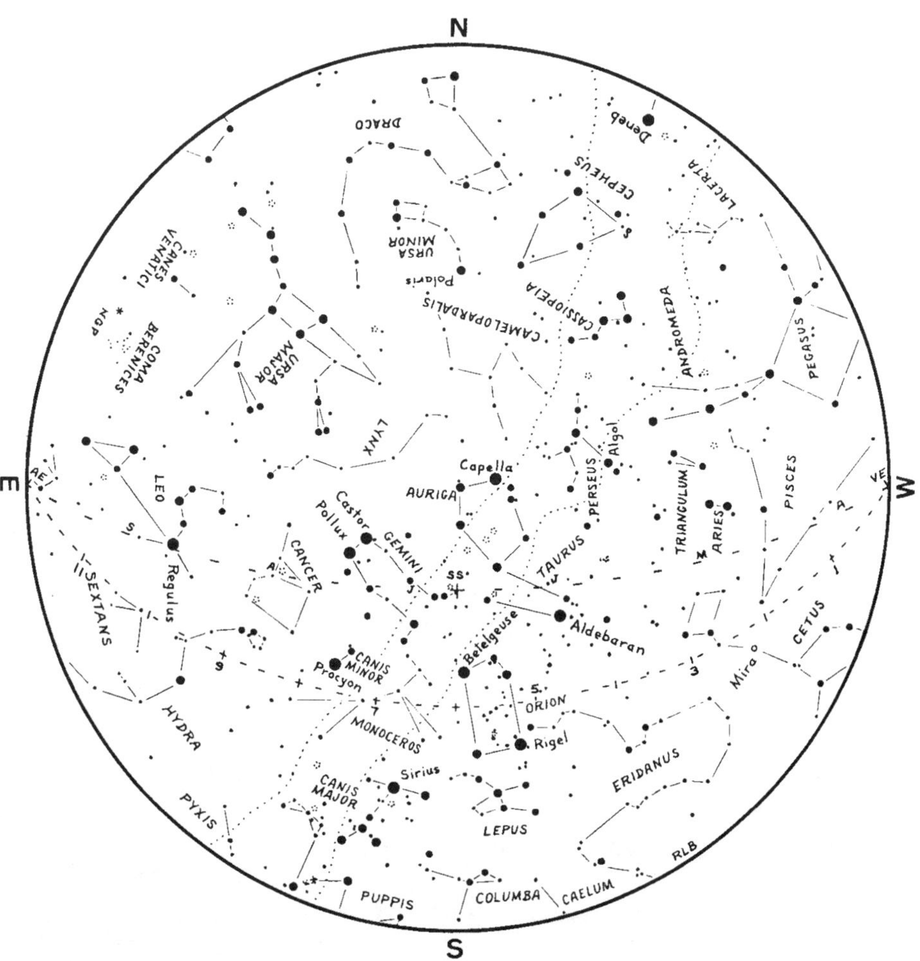

Notes:

MARCH ALL-SKY MAP

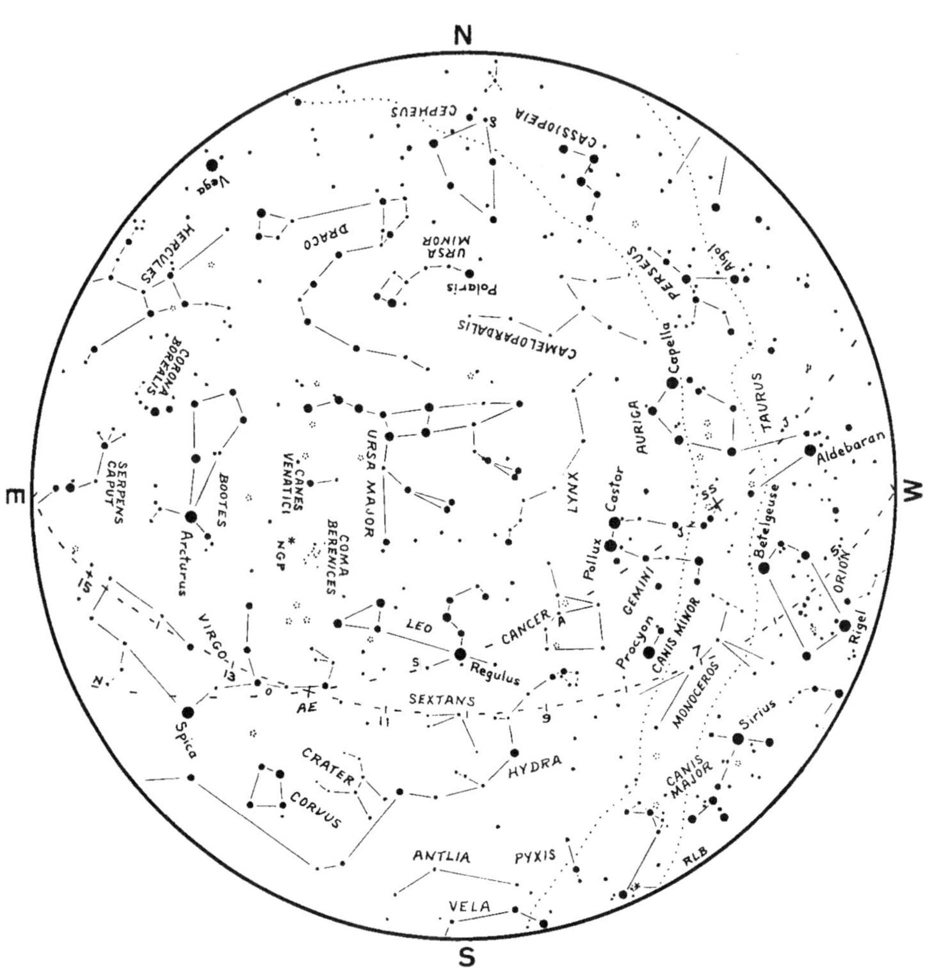

Notes:

MAY ALL-SKY MAP

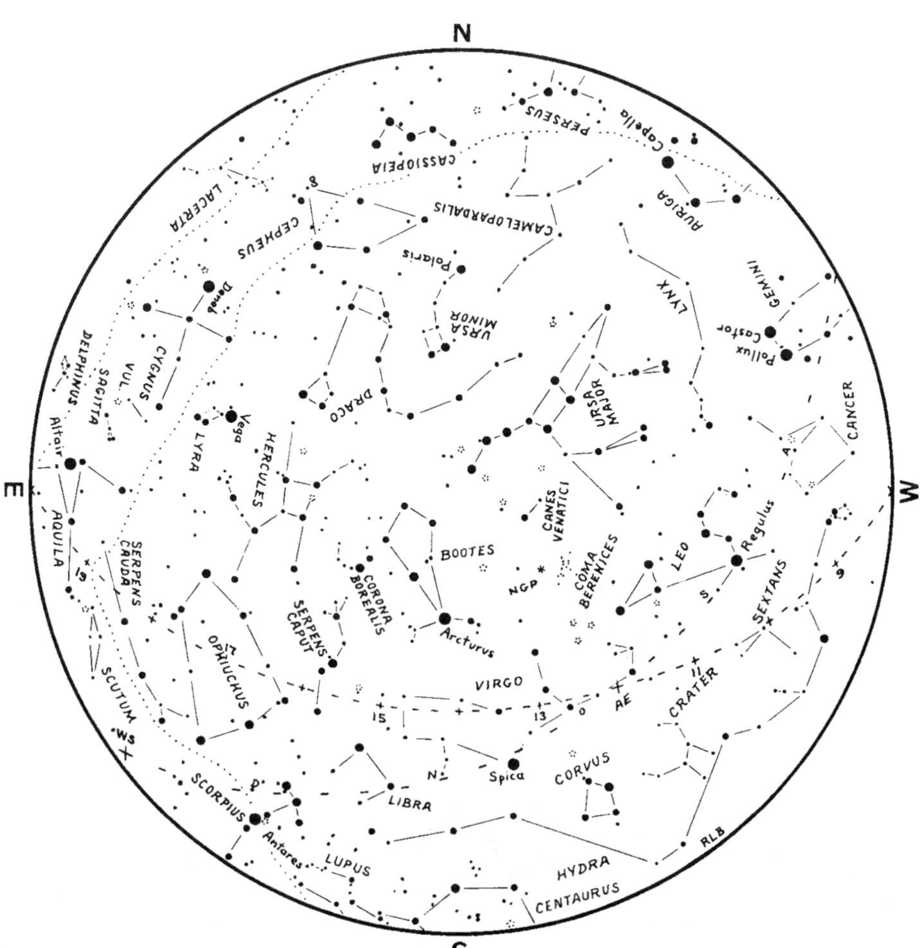

Notes:

JULY ALL-SKY MAP

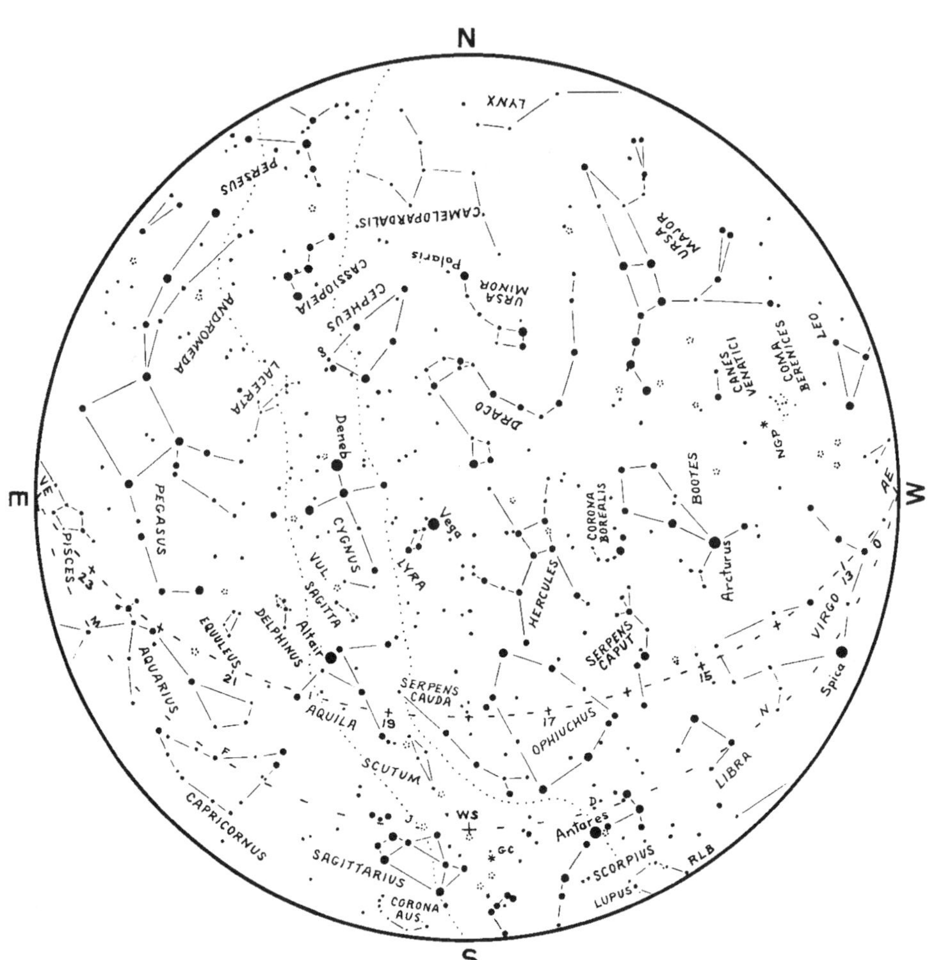

Notes:

SEPTEMBER ALL-SKY MAP

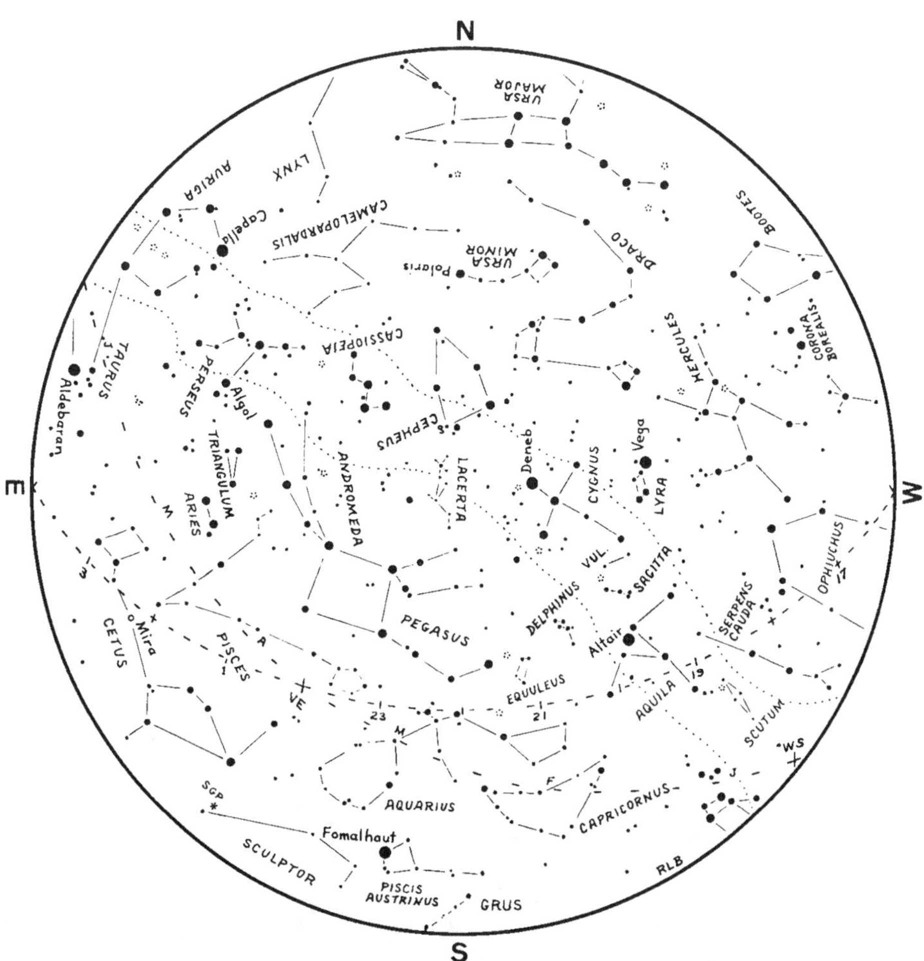

Notes:

NOVEMBER ALL-SKY MAP

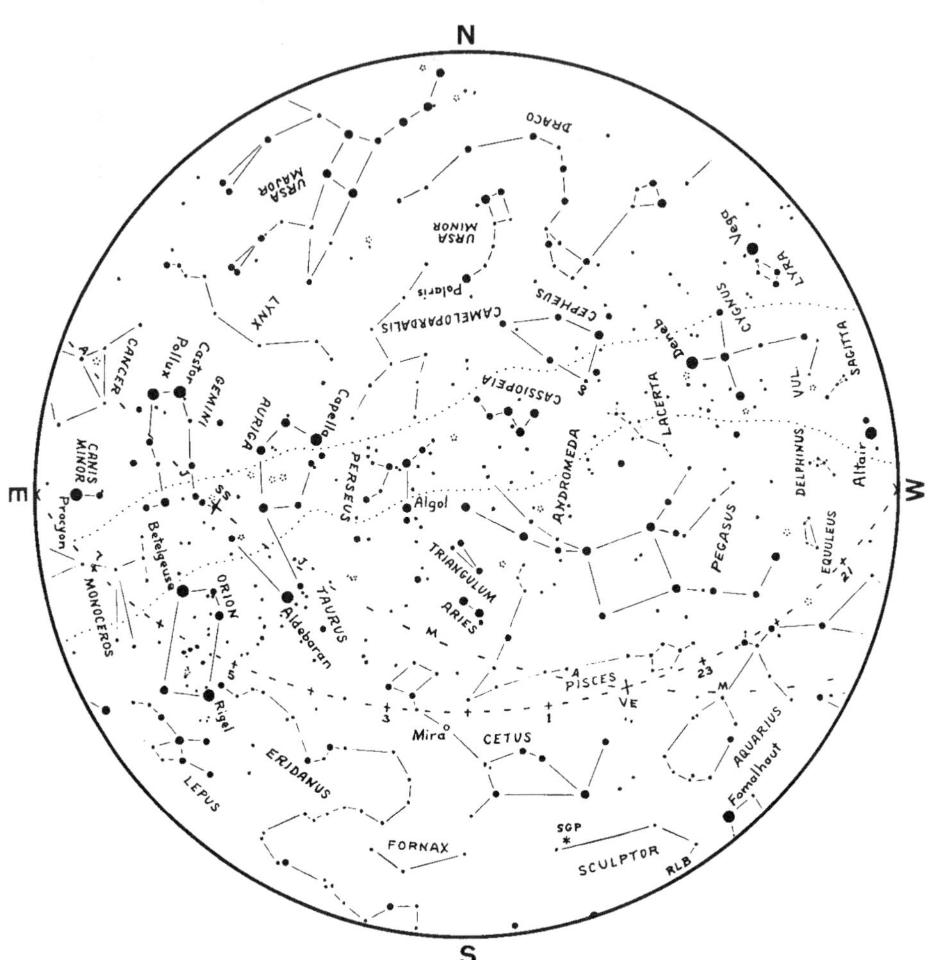

Notes:

THE SOUTHERN SKY

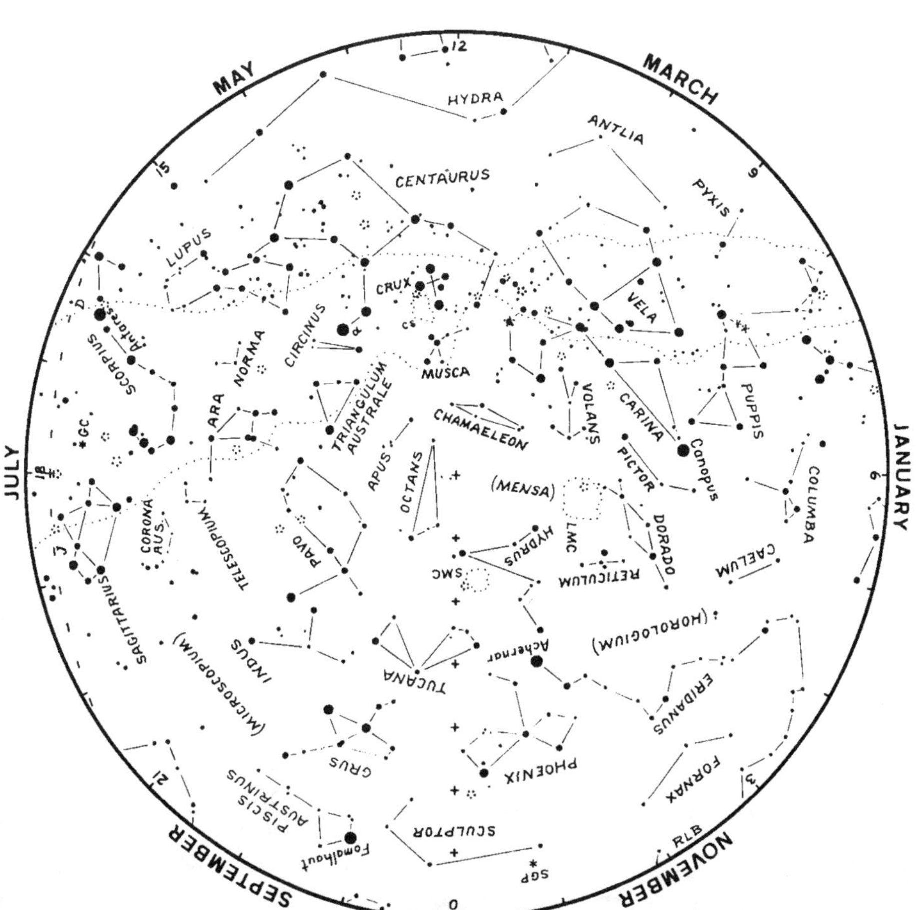

Notes:

This page intentionally left blank.

OBSERVER'S HANDBOOK 2008
ORDER FORM

(The *Observer's Handbook* for the year 2008 will be available in September 2007.)

MAIL-ORDER PRICE PER COPY FOR ORDERS OF 1–4 COPIES:

Destination	Unit Price		Shipping & Handling		GST†		Total
Canada	$25.95 Cdn.	+	$4.00 Cdn.	+	$1.80 Cdn.	=	$31.75 Cdn.
United States	$25.95 U.S.	+	$6.00 U.S.			=	$31.95 U.S.
Elsewhere	$25.95 U.S.	+	$12.00‡ U.S.			=	$37.95 U.S.

† GST registration number 119126282
‡ shipped via airmail
Bulk-order pricing is available upon request. Prices are subject to change without notice.

Please send.............. copies of the 2008 *Observer's Handbook.*

Name ....

Address ....

....

....

Payment Enclosed $ .... [ ] Cheque [ ] Money Order

[ ] Visa [ ] MasterCard [ ] Amex

Number ....

Expiry .... Signature ....

Name..

Telephone (..........) ....

Email..

Order on the Internet using your credit card at www.store.rasc.ca

or send this order form to:

Royal Astronomical Society of Canada
136 Dupont St
Toronto ON M5R 1V2
Canada

Phone: (416) 924-7973; in Canada only: (888) 924-7272
Fax: (416) 924-2911
Email: mempub@rasc.ca

To order any of the other publications of the RASC, please contact the Society or visit www.store.rasc.ca.

This page intentionally left blank.

INDEX

"MM" denotes the monthly pages of THE SKY MONTH BY MONTH on pp. 82–105.

INDEX (continued)

INDEX (continued)

"MM" denotes the monthly pages of THE SKY MONTH BY MONTH on pp. 82–105.

2007 HOLIDAYS AND SPECIAL DATES

New Year's Day	Mon.	Jan. 1			
Martin Luther King Jr. Day (U.S.)	Mon.	Jan. 15			
Islamic New Year	Fri.	Jan. 19			
Winter Star Party, Florida Keys	Mon.	Feb. 12	–	Sat.	Feb. 17
Valentine's Day	Tue.	Feb. 14			
Chinese New Year	Sun.	Feb. 18			
Presidents' Day (U.S.)	Mon.	Feb. 19			
First Day of Passover	Tue.	Apr. 3			
Good Friday	Fri.	Apr. 6			
Easter Sunday	Sun.	Apr. 8			
International Astronomy Week		Apr. 16			
International Astronomy Day	Sat.	Apr. 21			
Texas Star Party, Fort Davis, Texas	Sun.	May 13	–	Sun.	May 20
Mother's Day	Sun.	May 13			
Victoria Day (Canada)	Mon.	May 21			
Riverside Telescope Makers Conference, Calif.	Fri.	May 25	–	Mon.	May 28
Memorial Day (U.S.)	Mon.	May 28			
Father's Day	Sun.	Jun. 17			
RASC General Assembly, Calgary	Thu.	Jun. 28	–	Sun.	Jul. 3
Canada Day	Sun.	Jul. 1			
Independence Day (U.S.)	Wed.	Jul. 4			
Stellafane Convention, Springfield, Vermont	Fri.	Aug. 10	–	Sat.	Jul. 12
Civic Holiday (Most of Canada)	Mon.	Aug. 6			
Saskatchewan Star Party, Cypress Hills, Sask.	Thu.	Aug. 9	–	Sun.	Aug. 12
Starfest, Mount Forest, Ontario	Thu.	Aug. 9	–	Sat.	Aug. 12
Mount Kobau Star Party, B.C.	Sat.	Aug. 11	–	Sun.	Aug. 19
Nova East, Smileys Provincial Park, N.S.	Fri.	Aug. 17	–	Sun.	Aug. 19
Labour Day	Mon.	Sep. 3			
Alberta Star Party, Caroline, Alberta	Thu.	Sep. 6	–	Sun.	Sep. 9
Rosh Hashanah	Thu.	Sep. 13			
First day of Ramadân	Thu.	Sep. 13			
Yom Kippur	Sat.	Sep. 22			
Thanksgiving Day (Canada)	Mon.	Oct. 8			
Columbus Day (U.S.)	Mon.	Oct. 8			
Halloween	Wed.	Oct. 31			
Remembrance Day (Canada)	Sun.	Nov. 11			
Veterans Day (U.S.)	Sun.	Nov. 11			
Thanksgiving Day (U.S.)	Thu.	Nov. 22			
Christmas Day	Tue.	Dec. 25			
Boxing Day (Canada)	Wed.	Dec. 26			

See pp. 8–9 for Web sites and geographical coordinates of the listed star parties.